Advance Praise for *Cultures of the States*

"This book has a variety of uses. It presents a comprehensive overview of each state and the differences between states. It can also be used as a reference work to locate specific information on hundreds of variables about each state. The analysis of the historical events that contributed to the differences is compelling and interesting. The book will appeal to a wide group of readers, including educators, policymakers, sociologists, political scientists, and journalists.

"This book is significant due to the methodology that was used. All of the data were in the public domain. The authors mined this data and compiled it in original form. The massive amount of data, organized in this very accessible way, is a treasure trove for policymakers and researchers. Data can be extremely valuable to policymakers; however, isolated bits of data can be misleading. *Cultures of the States* should be a primer for all state legislators because it includes comprehensive data on each state in one collection. Therefore, readers can see the 'whole' picture.

"Finally, this book is significant because it reaches a compelling conclusion. The authors have a unique ability to view the world in an unorthodox way that often challenges the status quo. In this book, the phrase 'states' rights' is synonymous with 'states' abandonment of citizens' or 'states' abdication of responsibility.' Whether you agree with the authors' analysis, you can't help but view the role of state government in a new way after reading this book."—**David L. Clinefelter, chief academic officer, Kaplan College, Davenport, Iowa**

"It is nearly impossible to understand the problems and practices of a state without at the same time knowing the elements, which often appear unrelated, that make up the culture of that state. As but one example, when a state has low levels of educational achievement by the persons who live within its boundaries, then it is common to find that the citizens of the state in question also practice poor habits of health, drive their automobiles unsafely, and engage in other behaviors that cause problems that public policymakers are continuously faced with addressing.

"The authors of *Cultures of the States* have put together a vast compendium of data that should be exceedingly helpful to decision makers in understanding the complexities of the issues they face."—**Richard A. Boyd, former Mississippi state superintendent of education**

"On a personal note, I must say that the recently written book *Cultures of the States* is a handy resource for policymakers, for researchers, for those who might like to know more about the effectiveness of state governments. Differences in how we live in the various states across this country are revealed. Arrays of statistical data and clear facts provide candid pictures of the states of America.

"Not only are there differences in how we live and in the state governments that shape our lives, but significant regional differences exist as well. In an obvious way, we Americans know this, but in a more precise way, we remain uninformed. This book does it. Answers can be found on every page. And, many of these findings turn out to be complete surprises to the unprepared reader.

"We know that life in the south is different, as it is in the north, and in the far west. Until we thumb through the book, we discover how little we knew about the cultural differences that truly exist across these United States. The book accounts for much of this by taking us through significant moments in our history; a storied and dramatic history it is. Current data and facts that surprise the reader can be found on every page.

"How different is the south from the north? The answer: considerably different. Clearly, this is a book that causes you to pause and to ponder the elusive question of how we got the way we are, and how we arrived at our current condition. States differ in their support of education, in their divorce rates, in their taxation rates, and in their varying governance policies, to name a few. These differences among the states, as well as corresponding regional differences, are considerable. Can we know more about the differences? Yes. A handy reference is available. This book is a useful source of information about state governments and about the populations they serve. This recently authored book proves that it can serve as a handy reference, and as a source book for discovering the facts about the states of America."—**Charles M. Galloway, professor of educational leadership, College of Education, University of North Florida**

"*Cultures of the States* is a fascinating new book. Jack Frymier and Arliss Roaden have produced a book of merit for a broad audience. It is an insightful approach to understanding states better both internally as well as comparatively. Having lived in four states and travelled all of the rest, I found myself flipping the pages quickly, drawing comparisons, and applying my own criteria of authenticity. The volume will be of value to public officials at all levels as they pursue interest in their own states and become intrigued with the cultures of others. It is of worth, too, to businesses considering location decisions and employees in the process of determining where they would like to raise families.

"Researchers may find the methodology valuable because of its reliance on public sector data sources and the application of syntheses to summarize information from a broad range of databases. New questions arise about the relationship between patterns of public investment and the values of state leaders expressed over generations of decisions at state and local levels. The authors have been successful in delivering on their commitment to neutrality. They do not judge cultures as good or bad but provide information which provokes readers to think about states in judgmental terms if they choose to do so."—Luvern L. Cunningham, professor emeritus, Ohio State University

"Over the years most of the books I've seen ranking states or cities have not been quite satisfactory. Partly this is because most rested on pretty shaky ground. Their authors didn't always think carefully in picking measures of 'good' and measures of 'bad.' Surveys of this sort made good reading locally but produced rankings that were sometimes pretty silly. This book is different. The authors take all the indices that could find, rank these, then step back to look at the results before trying to interpret what they see. I've now given my copies to the people working most seriously on the future of Minnesota, in state government and in the private sector. My state comes out well, but Minnesota has serious challenges, too. The rankings show what we need to hold and what we need to work on."—Ted Kolderie

"This volume raises important questions and illuminates the historically neglected area of state governments. States are the linchpins of our ever-changing federal system. If we are to formulate more effective public policy in realms like education, welfare and health, citizens must have a greater understanding of the culture and governmental capacities of their states. This volume is a notable contribution to enhancing such understanding and has important implications for policymakers and citizens in every state in the nation."—Michael D. Usdan, senior fellow, Institute for Educational Leadership

"I am aware of the importance of political issues and I am also aware of the difficulties involved in attempting to find accurate collated data. I know of no resource more pertinent to the health of our nation than *Cultures of the States: A Handbook on the Effectiveness of State Governments*. Not only did I find it important as a citizen, I found it particularly important as a potential candidate for state office."—F. Karl VanDevender, M.D., The First Clinic Medical Group

Cultures of the States

A Handbook on the Effectiveness of State Governments

JACK FRYMIER
ARLISS ROADEN

The Scarecrow Press, Inc.
Lanham, Maryland, and Oxford
2003

SCARECROW PRESS, INC

Published in the United States of America
by Scarecrow Press, Inc.
A wholly owned subsidiary of The Rowman & Littlefield Publishers, Inc.
4501 Forbes Boulevard, Suite 200, Lanham, MD 20706
www.scarecrowpress.com

PO Box 317
Oxford
OX2 9RU, UK

British Library Cataloguing in Publication Information Available

Library of Congress Cataloging-in-Publication Data

Frymier, Jack Rimmel, 1925–
  Cultures of the states : a handbook on the effectiveness of state governments / Jack Frymier, Arliss Roaden.
    p. cm.
  Includes bibliographical references and index.
  ISBN 0-8108-4768-X (alk. paper)
  1. State governments—United States. 2. State governments—United States—Statistics. I. Roaden, Arliss L., 1930– II. Title
JK2408.F79 2003
320.973—dc21

2003002374

∞™ The paper used in this publication meets the minimum requirements of American National Standard for Information Sciences—Permanence of Paper for Printed Library Materials, ANSI/NISO Z39.48-1992.
Manufactured in the United States of America.

To Maxine and Mary Etta, who have endured the struggle over "power" with love and patience.

Contents

THIS BOOK HAS MANY PARTS, BUT THREE ARE ESPECIALLY important: a study of the effectiveness of the 50 state governments, a methodology, and a database. The study is reported in chapters 1 through 11. The methodology is described in Appendix B. The database includes 702 tables of numerical information (i.e., Appendix G) from reliable sources.

Governance based on law rather than personalities presumes explicit policies. The Tenth Amendment to the Constitution sets forth the framework of federalism that differentiates spheres of authority and power for those who enact, enforce, and interpret policy in the United States: "The powers not delegated to the United States by the Constitution, nor prohibited by it to the States, are reserved to the States respectively, or to the people."

To make, execute policies, and evaluate policies requires data. The purpose of this book is to make data available to policymakers, administrators, researchers, and citizens regarding areas of human activity in which policies might be considered. Data about particular topics are organized to help readers see exactly where every state stands in relation to every other state on those topics.

Education, Plato said, is for the rulers of the state. In the United States, this means that all of us must be well educated. In a sense, we are the rulers—of the United States, and of the states in which we live. We live in a republic, not a democracy. We elect representatives to govern rather than participate directly in governance processes ourselves. Ours is a democratic nation, if not a democracy. We have a lot of say and a lot of influence, but only if we use it. One purpose of this book is to encourage every citizen to understand the culture in which we live and to make intelligent decisions about our state governments, including whom we elect and how we work with others to participate in civic affairs. Decisions about whom we elect and what we believe about state government affect how we live and even how we die.

Decisions are interesting aspects of human behavior. We had a colleague once who made the point that people seldom make decisions; they come to realizations. Ideas evolve in their minds in such a way that, over time, an option seems the right thing to do. This is not the clear-cut picture of "yes" or "no" suddenly arrived at, as depicted in the voting process of legislators, or the quick answers that some administrators seem able to give under pressure. We think that "realizations" may be a better term.

In that spirit we share these pages with you. We accumulated a great deal of information—a lot of factual data—about governance and those who are governed. We have tried to place these facts in context, carefully and thoughtfully. We believe strongly in America—what it stands for, what it has accomplished, and where it is going. We know, of course, that our nation is not perfect (and never will be), but we are convinced that it can be improved. That's why we wrote this book.

Over the years some people have asked the question: Would we be better off without government or without newspapers? That is a stupid question, of course. It's cute, but it's stupid. We must have both. There is a germ of an idea inherent in the question, however, that we want to explore here. We think it has relevance for those who are interested in and concerned about governance and governors (in the larger sense of the word). Newspapers and other media tend to focus on the unusual rather than the usual. "Dog bites man" is not news. "Man bites dog" is news. In statistical terms, news media tend to seek out and inform the public about "outliers" that show up in statistical analyses—the exceptions to the pattern, the atypical, the "way out" information rather than the typical or routine. Researchers, on the other hand, focus on central tendencies (i.e., means, medians, and modes) and variance (i.e., the spread or range of differences). We think that those who govern would make better decisions if they employed the perspectives of researchers rather than the perspectives of newspapers and television media. The "way out" stuff is interesting, but it ought not be the primary source of information used by those who govern, nor of those who elect representatives to govern them. The "way out" stuff is factual, but it is also the exception and not the rule. It is not the best information for either governors or governed to use as they come to realizations (i.e., make decisions) about which course of action or which policy is most appropriate.

We cite one example, to make our point. The example is real, and we have some data to illustrate the point, but our data are limited. From our observations of policymakers and governors and those who are governed in real-life situations, however, we are convinced that the essence of this illustration is described correctly. We will use the United States Congress as the setting for our illustration, specifically the House of Representatives. Members of the U.S. House of Representatives (i.e., Congressmen and Congresswomen) pride themselves on being sensitive to their constituents. They pay attention to the people back home. They get phone calls, faxes, e-mails, and telegrams, and they talk directly with voters in their district. Congressmen and Congresswomen work hard to "stay informed" about how people think and feel about the issues of the day. When an issue emerges on the floor of the House of Representatives, policymakers begin to hear from the people back home. They hear from aides. They hear from the president. They hear from lobbyists. They hear from the media. Even when the issue is important, however, policymakers seldom get more than two or three thousand communications from constituents. Our point is simply this: that is not many communications from those who are directly affected.

The member of Congress is confronted with a critical issue (e.g., abortion, gun control, financial aid to farmers): "Which way should I vote on this issue? What should I do?" Hundreds, sometimes thousands of people make phone calls or send telegrams or e-mail, telling the Congressman or Congresswoman what he or she ought to do.

Now, consider these facts. There are 435 members of Congress. These people represent over 270 million Americans. In practical terms, that means that each member of Congress represents about 620,000 citizens since the "one man, one vote" decision by the Supreme Court in the early 1960s. (Note: About a fourth of those citizens are under the age of 18; they cannot vote. Does the Congressman or Congresswoman "represent" those citizens and take their well-being into account, as he or she comes to a realization—or makes a decision, if you prefer—about how to vote? We will ignore that question for now, but it will not go away. Back to the issue.) If the policymaker gets as many as 6,000 communications on any particular issue (and that almost never happens), the Congressperson "heard from" about one percent of his or her constituents. One percent! In most instances, though, the number of communications received is much smaller than that; one half of one percent or one fourth of one percent would be more likely. Furthermore, on any critical issue, that extremely small percentage of constituents is sharply divided on the issue.

Add to this what everybody also knows: Those who communicate their thoughts to policymakers feel strongly about the issue. They are not disinterested citizens. They are committed, "true believers" in their cause. It was those strong feelings that got them aroused in the first place; that was what got them to call or wire or write. Technically, they are probably "biased" in their beliefs, but they want action that will follow the direction of their communication.

In research terminology, the policymaker received communications from a "sample" of his or her constituents, but political science, at this level, is certainly not using generally agreed-upon rules of science. The sample of those who communicated their wishes to the policymakers would not meet any scientific definition of what constitutes an appropriate "sample" of public opinion, on that or any other issue. No member of Congress, for instance, would vote to support legislation to fund a research project in medicine, agriculture, or education that "sampled" the population that way (unless the project was in his or her district), yet the odds are overwhelming that the Congressman or Congresswoman would "pay serious attention" to that kind of information before he or she decided how to vote on the floor. Ask one. That is precisely what he or she will say.

We are not so naive as to believe that every political issue will be decided on the basis of facts (unless someone defines communications from a very small, unrepresentative, nonrandom, self-selected group of people as "factual" and "valid" just because such sentiments were expressed and received), but it seems reasonable to hope that "real facts" and "valid information" would make up at least part (if not most) of the information that policymakers use in coming to their realizations of how to vote on the floor of the Congress.

We know, of course, that many (maybe most) state policymakers are not interested in statistical information that comes from unbiased sources and pertains to issues they confront. In our part of the world, for instance, policymakers are typically more interested in who wins when Colorado plays Nebraska, but the issue is the same. Sports are important, but not as important as governance.

Governance requires good (i.e., valid) information and thoughtful consideration of that information. There are mountains of good information out there, although it is not always easy to access, to make sense of, or to compare with other related information.

We have tried to put some of that good information into usable form in this book. We are not trying to influence decisions, except to encourage both policymakers and citizens to use good data as often as possible and in every way they can. Feelings of an individual constituent are important, but factual information about an issue is equally important, if not more so. It may be that, over time, even the rulers of the state (that's all of us, remember?) will become more knowledgeable and more effective in what and how they communicate with our elected representatives. After all, it is our country and our state, too.

People love stories, but this is not a book of stories. This is a book of pictures. The pictures were taken with numbers, but they must be developed inside the reader's mind. The numbers relate to governing, and they focus on the state level, not the national level. The information here is about states, where states stand in relation to other states, and how the information "adds up" to reflect the cultures of the states. We hope you find it interesting and helpful.

Chapters 1 and 2 outline particular problems. Chapters 3 through 8 describe 120 variables that were organized into 15 logical factors for further analysis. (You may want to skip these chapters the first time through, although at some point you will probably need to study those variables to get an in-depth understanding of of all of the pieces that make up the puzzle.) Chapter 9 summarizes the data on these 120 variables for each of the 50 states, and then presents a statistical profile and narrative of each state, which positions that state in relationship to each of the other states. Chapter 10 presents an analysis of data that pertains to race and gender. Chapter 11 sets forth our findings and conclusions.

Appendix A was prepared by Ted Kolderie, a friend we asked to review our manuscript. He had just made a presentation to the Minnesota Historical Society a few days before our manuscript arrived at his home, and he sent a copy of his paper in response to receiving ours. Kolderie's paper is worthy of discussion in its own right, but it seemed particularly relevant to what we were doing, so we asked him if he would be willing to include it as an appendix in our study, and he agreed. Both the tenor and the substance of the paper are exceptional. We encourage you to read Appendix A carefully; it is a superb illustration of precisely what we are trying to understand.

Appendix B describes the methods we used to summarize the data we present in "Rankings of the States." Appendix C includes tables of analyses that pertain directly to the summary. Appendix D includes tables that pertain to race and gender. Appendix E includes tables that relate to culture, as we have used that term, and more than 100 specific findings, plus the conclusions that we reached. Appendix F is information about the Civil War. Appendix G, "Rankings of the States," comprises the data on which our analyses are based. This is the heart of the book, and includes 702 tables of statistical data, organized in rank order, by states. Appendix H is a list of references and sources.

Throughout the book we worked hard to make statistical data and statistical analyses available in appended materials rather than part of the narrative. This book includes many numbers, but you can read only the words, if that is your preference, or the numbers are close by if you'd like to refer to them. We hope this arrangement will ease your reading task but still meet whatever needs you have for numerical justification.

Some data here pertain to areas of governance in which states exercise direct control, for example, crime, punishment, education, and highway construction. Other data pertain to areas in which states exercise minimal control or none at all, such as type of employment, income, procreation, value of a house, patents issued, or cause of death. Still other data pertain to areas that may be affected indirectly but significantly by policies adopted by a state. References for every table are included at the back of the book.

Many people have reviewed these materials and helped us come this far. We want to acknowledge their critiques and their suggestions: David Clinefelter, Ronald Joekel, Jack Hough, Robert Bills, Richard Boyd, Lowell Rose, Jill Russell, Karl VanDevender, Lloyd Hunter, Larry Bowen, Cy Hawn, Carl Glickman, Michael Usdan, Ransom Whitney, Charles Kingston, Karl Openshaw, Ted Kolderie, Ted Cyphert, Mark Frymier, Philip Clark, and Charles Galloway, to name a few. Others also made comments and provided assistance. We are truly grateful for their review of the manuscript and their help. And we are deeply appreciative for what our editors at Scarecrow, Kim Tabor and Jessica McCleary, have done with an extremely complex and detailed manuscript. We are responsible, of course, for what is here.

Every piece of information was obtained from a reliable source, but that information was entered, item by item, into a database on a computer, and the database was manipulated in various ways to produce tables that show the rankings. There are undoubtedly errors, and we hope readers will communicate their concerns and their discovery of errors to us, so we can make the document more accurate and more useful. We want the information to be as accurate as possible, so suggestions or corrections will be welcomed.

We hope you find the document useful. If you have suggestions of any kind, or if you find errors, please communicate that information to Jack Frymier at 5367 Flatrock Court, Morrison, CO 80465, 303-697-0558, or jfrymier@sprynet.com. It is important that the document be accurate and useful.

Jack Frymier, Morrison, CO
Arliss Roaden, Nashville, TN

CHAPTER 1

Culture

The central conservative truth is that it is culture, not politics, that determines the success of a society. The central liberal truth is that politics can change a culture and save it from itself.

—Daniel Patrick Moynihan[1]

INTRODUCTION

PEOPLE WHO TRAVEL BY AUTOMOBILE THROUGHOUT THE United States often comment on the differences evident in various sections of the country. "East Texas is not like south Louisiana at all," some say, "even though the states are adjacent to each other," or, "Missouri is very different from Iowa, and those states are side by side." "Pennsylvania and Virginia are worlds apart," and, "South Carolina and Oregon could not be more different, even though they have about the same number of people, and both are coastal states."

States, of course, are different. They were formed by different people, for different reasons, at different times, and states have different constitutions and different laws. All states are part of the United States, but even casual observation suggests there are fundamental differences among the states in values, use of language, references to history, feelings about the future, highway design, enforcement of speed limits, use of leisure time, commitments to religion, beliefs about authority, attitudes toward minorities, availability of handguns, rivalries between colleges, editorial policies of newspapers, upkeep of businesses and homes, achievement in schools, sense of progress, and so on.

Some of these differences may be a function of climate or geography. Others may be related to physical size, natural resources, or population. Still others may have been affected by economic factors, community development, political leadership, and educational opportunities. That states differ is something about which there is little disagreement. How those differences developed and why they continue to exist is something more difficult to understand, given our common dependence on English as a language, national television as a medium, and U.S. government and history as a framework for our perceptions.

There is no doubt that an American culture exists. There is some question about whether each of the states within the United States has a culture of its own. Are the differences between states that are evident even to casual observers actually cultural differences, or are those differences more attributable to economic or geographic or

governance considerations? A primary purpose of this book was to explore that question.

WHAT IS CULTURE?

The American Heritage Dictionary defines culture as "the totality of socially transmitted behavior patterns, arts, beliefs, institutions, and all other products of human work and thought characteristic of a community or population."

Lawrence Harrison and Samuel Huntington define culture "in purely subjective terms as the values, attitudes, beliefs, orientations, and underlying assumptions prevalent among people in a society."[2] They are interested in how culture affects societal development, and the key issue is "whether political leadership can substitute for disaster in stimulating cultural change."[3]

These definitions made sense to us in terms of the way "culture" was used in this study. Given the commonalties and continuities evident throughout the United States, it may be that the word "subculture" would be more appropriately applied to states than "culture." For simplicity's sake, however, we use the word "culture" throughout this book. If others find it more convenient—even more accurate—to employ the other term, we have no quarrel with that.

Our concerns are these: Are there differences between the states? Are those differences attributable to policies or processes (i.e., are they artifact?) more than the givens of climate or geography? Is it possible to discern or infer what those policies or processes are? Would it be helpful to make suggestions regarding policies or processes that differentiate states so that people might benefit from knowing what other citizens or other state governments have done?

A WORD ABOUT THEORY

This book is a product of research and careful study, but the methods used were generally simple and straightforward. Comprehending most of the methodology should not be beyond any person who has an interest in the topic, so only a brief description of methods is included here. Additional information is provided in Appendix B.

Briefly, we collected statistical information about each of the 50 states (see Appendix G), then studied that information to see if there were patterns evident that might suggest important differences between states or among states. From this initial effort, we developed a theory of culture with which to test such differences.

1

Our notion of culture was broad, and our primary focus was the relation of culture to the concepts of federalism as set forth in the Tenth Amendment to the Constitution. And though it was not our original intention, the differences between states that became evident forced us to confront the question "Are some states 'better' than others?" We were hesitant—reluctant, in fact—to confront that question, let alone deal with it, even after it became obvious, but we thought we owed it to ourselves and our conception of science to address the question as best we could. It is a thorny issue, but an interesting one, too.

We embrace Huntington's conception of theory:

Understanding requires theory; theory requires abstraction; and abstraction requires the simplification of reality. No theory can explain all the facts, and, at times, the reader of this book may feel that its concepts and distinctions are drawn too sharply and precisely and are too far removed from reality. Obviously the real world is one of blends, irrationalities, and incongruities: actual personalities, institutions, and beliefs do not fit into neat logical categories. Yet neat logical categories are necessary if man is to think profitably about the real world in which he lives and to derive from it lessons for broader application and use. He is forced to generalize about phenomena which never quite operate according to the laws of human reason. One measure of a theory is the degree to which it encompasses and explains all the relevant facts. Another measure, and the more important one, is the degree to which it encompasses and explains those facts better than any other theory.[4]

Our theory of culture of the states begins with an assumption: *Good state government helps people live better lives.* In moral terms, "good" means honesty and transparency in government. In effectiveness terms, "good" means that government accomplishes what needs to be accomplished. In practical terms, "good state government" means that people in the state will:

(a) live longer	(i.e., lower death rates)
(b) be healthier	(i.e., lower disease rates)
(c) be more law abiding	(i.e., lower crime rates)
(d) be better educated	(i.e., higher achievement rates)
(e) be happier	(i.e., fewer mental health problems)
(f) be more productive	(i.e., higher personal income)
(g) be less frustrated	(i.e., greater sense of personal accomplishment)
(h) have more opportunities	(e.g., in education, work, family, travel, leisure)
(i) have better government	(i.e., more confidence that "government works")
(j) be treated with respect	(i.e., fewer "run-arounds")

Good government is more helpful and less coercive, more supportive and less obvious, and more practical and less ideological. Government is manifest in taxes, budgets, laws, leadership, and processes.

We define "cultures of the states" according to what happens to people within a state when the policymakers in that state, using the powers accorded the state by the Tenth Amendment to the Constitution, make policies and establish procedures designed to shape citizens' behaviors in particular ways (see next chapter). Throughout this book we infer "culture" (i.e., people's values, beliefs, and behaviors) from statistical data reflected in policymakers' decisions that affect such things as health care, cause of death, employment opportunities, crime, punishment, education, and taxes rather than from information collected in opinion polls or from direct observations.

Consider one illustration. Each state makes and executes laws related to highways and transportation. States authorize highway construction, design highways, maintain those highways, set speed limits, enforce speed limits, investigate auto accidents that occur, and provide funds to accomplish all such activities, among other things. The number of deaths from automobile accidents on highways is a statistic collected in every state. Taxes collected is another statistic collected in every state. Taxes allocated to highways and transportation are still other statistics available for every state, as are funds provided to state highway patrol officers.

With this kind of information available, death rates per population can be calculated, making comparisons among states possible of highway death rates per 10,000 population. Further, highway death rates per population in each of the states can then be compared to tax dollars provided by each state to maintain the highways (e.g., fix potholes, resurface the roads, paint white lines along the outer edges of roads), police the highways (e.g., number of highway patrol officers per 10,000 population, number of arrests made for speeding), and so on. It is possible, in other words, to look carefully and critically at state governments through the prism of statistics produced about each of the 50 states.

Following this logic, we collected statistical information on hundreds of variables (see Appendix G) from reliable sources that relate directly to what state governments do in the process of governing, and how state policies and procedures affect citizens who live in each of those states by shaping their behaviors in particular ways. After a careful study of this information, we identified 120 specific variables for further study and organized those variables into 15 general categories (e.g., crime, health care, and education) that could be analyzed in various ways to help us understand the "cultures of the states" as we defined that phrase. A detailed description of each of the 120 variables selected for careful study is presented in Chapters 3 through 8, where those variables are organized into 15 general categories (i.e., logical "factors") over which states exercise control. A detailed description of the methods used to accomplish that study is described in Appendix B, but the basic assumption underlying the whole project was that each of these 120 variables represented one thing over which states exercised control, and that control was intended to affect citizens' behavior.

Many of the concepts in this book will probably be controversial because the issues are complex and difficult to discern precisely, and because people hold different assumptions and different opinions about them all. Some of those assumptions and opinions are based on facts, but many are based on common sense or logic or historical precedent, and others are based on nothing more than gut feelings or old wives' tales. The questions implicit in the data are real, however, and those questions need to be ferreted out and made explicit, then examined by thoughtful citizens and policymakers in a multitude of creative but tough-minded ways. The old story that "no man is an island" is correct. We are all in this thing called "life" together, and we must either find or develop ways of working together that are effective and helpful for us all.

For example, will extra money spent for incarceration take criminals off the street and reduce crime rates? Will the extra taxes required to build and operate prisons provide security that will enable people to be more productive in their work and generate higher levels of income? Will more highway patrol officers reduce speeding and save lives of citizens? Will the extra taxes required to hire more officers to police the highways be economically efficient? That is, will more police protection raise the standard of living because states will spend less on ambulances and hospital services to "patch people up" after they have been involved in accidents, and more on helping people develop skills and understanding that will enable them to live a better life and make more money? Will more money for public schools and universities increase safety among drivers and productivity in the work force over time? Will higher educational achievements reduce death rates from problems such as cancer, heart disease, obesity, suicide, or homicide? These are the kinds of questions that thoughtful citizens must ask and that state policymakers must try to answer through policymaking. What we have tried to do is provide information that will help people understand the terribly complex issues involved in state governance and to help focus the thoughtful discussions that must occur if intelligent decision making is to occur.

We want to encourage people to think differently about state government than they have thought in the past, and the information in this book is designed to help them do just that. For instance, many people (i.e., citizens and policymakers) say that "low taxes are better than high taxes," but our data are clear: states that have high taxes have higher median incomes, lower crime rates, higher educational achievements, and lower death rates from all causes. States that have low taxes have the opposite. But which is cause and which is effect? The answer is not obvious. Our effort has not been to answer such questions directly, but to raise them, and to try to raise them in nonoffensive ways with an abundance of information. We do not know the answers to most such questions, but we are convinced that many common clichés and assumptions are probably incorrect, and we hope the book will evoke discussion and debate based on something other than ideology or habit or tradition. The "sound bites" allocated for presentation of such issues on television during election campaigns today are not enough to help anybody understand either the totality or the complexity of things that affect us all. Good data are important, and careful thinking is important. We have tried to provide the data. We hope that you will provide the thinking.

In the next chapter, we discuss the concept and reality of federalism in the United States, as those factors affect governance in each state and in the United States. Good government, however, cannot be characterized without attention to what might be described as the strength of government at each level and the quality of the relationship between state governments and the national government. We assume that those strengths and relationships are fairly constant in character and quality, but they also reflect tension between the two levels most of the time.

Theoretically, there are four different types of government relationships that might exist: (1) strong national/strong state; (2) strong national/weak state; (3) weak national/strong state; and (4) weak national/weak state. In numerical terms, only two of these four possibilities have many adherents: numbers one and three. Suppose we outline each of the four relationships, however, to get a better sense of what is involved, and we will do this from the perspective of the states. Leadership and tradition affect the strength of governments and the relationships.

Strong National Government/
Strong State Government
Most people in the United States want this kind of government; they want the national government to perform its functions fully (i.e., "to form a more perfect Union, establish Justice, insure domestic Tranquillity, provide for the common Defence, promote the general Welfare, and secure the Blessing of Liberty"), and they want their state government to do whatever is necessary to assure "life, liberty, and the pursuit of happiness" to them and their children by providing police protection, good schools, good roads, good hospitals, safe and healthy living conditions, and the like. Nobody wants government

at any level to intrude unnecessarily into their lives, and almost everyone wants an opportunity to make something of themselves, and for their children to have the same opportunities.

Strong National Government/Weak State Government
Alexander Hamilton argued for this kind of government in the Constitutional Convention, and James Madison leaned that way. Madison was probably less concerned that state governments be weak than that the national government be strong, and though he wavered back and forth somewhat in the years immediately after the Constitution was adopted (e.g., he authored the *Virginia Resolution*), his arguments in *The Federalist Papers* and in his own behavior over a lifetime attested to his preference for a strong national government. Some people in sparsely populated states, especially, want help from the federal government in times of disaster (e.g., drought, flooding, forest fires, economic depression), but if the times are good, they are usually willing to accept the "weak state" status and simply help their own state "make do" as best it can.

Weak National Government/Strong State Government
There are several states in which leaders at the state level (i.e., governors, legislators, news media editors) and members of the national government from those same states (viz., elected members of Congress) regularly assert a necessity to "trim the fat from the federal budget," "curtail the federal bureaucracies," and "keep government close to the people, where it belongs." This position has been prominent in America for a long time. Patrick Henry and Thomas Jefferson articulated this position more than two hundred years ago, though Jefferson acted vigorously in the other direction when the opportunity to purchase Louisiana arose. Newt Gingrich pressed this point of view. Ronald Reagan made pronouncements in support of this position, but his devolution ideas (i.e., shifting responsibility from federal government to state governments) imposed hardships on states. Certain U.S. senators and congresspeople profess this position publicly, and then work the "pork barrel" legislation route to get more from the federal government for their state or to keep defense bases in their state open when the federal government is trying to reduce spending from the federal budget by closing such bases. Their rhetoric and behavior are not always consistent.

Weak National Government/Weak State Government
Probably no one but anarchists argue for this position today, although evidence abounds that the situation which existed in America between 1777 and 1787 (i.e., under the Articles of Confederation) would have to be characterized in such terms. George Washington saw the national government that way during the Revolutionary War, and his experiences with government during those years probably explain why he accepted Hamilton's suggestions more frequently than Jefferson's during his eight years as the first president of the newly formed United States.

It may be useful to think about the national government/state government issue alongside the church/state issue. The logic is the same. History shows that the only way a nation can have strong government and strong churches is to keep the "wall of separation" between the two institutions both high and strong. When one becomes stronger than the other, we find situations in which government is strong and churches are weak, or governments are weak and churches are strong. England, for example, which formally embraced a particular religion and to this day has a government-supported church, has a strong government but weak churches. People in England are simply not "believers" in the sense that people in the United States are. England has great cathedrals everywhere, but most people do not go to church regularly. A similar situation exists in Israel, Germany, and the Scandinavian countries.

Iran, on the other hand, has a strong church but weak government. Clerics dominate the government, and the government is weak and ineffectual. The same thing exists in Afghanistan, Bosnia, and the Philippines. Only in nations in which religion and government stay (or are kept) in separate spheres do strong government and strong religion coexist. Otherwise, one will be dominant and the other subservient.

One of the great strengths of governance in the United States is the notion of federalism, which has been developed during the past two centuries by thoughtful policymakers and leaders into a creative governance tool. But this tool works most effectively when policymakers at the national level and policymakers at the state level honor the importance and integrity and purpose of those at the other level, and that has not always been the case. Some who functioned at the national level in the past deliberately sought to foster weak national government (e.g., Thomas Jefferson, John Calhoun, Jefferson Davis, Roger Taney), and some who functioned at the state level deliberately sought to strengthen state governments to the point that they were stronger than the national government (e.g., Patrick Henry, Spencer Roane).

America has always been "well governed" when the national government was strong and state governments were strong. If either level of government tries to subvert or dominate the other, problems arise and persist for the people.

State budgets and state operations are generally organized around several areas: crime and justice, highways, education, health, and human services. These areas have evolved as states devised and developed ways of governing based on the Tenth Amendment to the Constitution:

> The powers not delegated to the United States by the Constitution, nor prohibited by it to the States, are reserved to the States respectively, or to the people.

In the next chapter we examine the concept of "power" in government.

NOTES

1. Daniel Patrick Moynihan, Samuel P. Huntington quoted in "Foreword: Cultures Count," in Lawrence E. Harrison and Samuel P. Huntington (eds.), *Culture Matters: How Values Shape Human Progress* (New York: Basic Books, 2000), xiv.
2. Harrison and Huntington, *Culture Matters*, xv.
3. Harrison and Huntington, *Culture Matters*, xv.
4. Samuel P. Huntington, *The Soldier and the State: The Theory and Politics of Civil-Military Relations* (Cambridge, Mass.: The Belknap Press of Harvard University, 1958), vii.

CHAPTER 2

Power

The powers not delegated to the United States by the Constitution, nor prohibited by it to the States, are reserved to the States respectively, or to the people.

—Tenth Amendment to the Constitution

INTRODUCTION

SOVEREIGN STATES HAVE POWER. THEY ARE PARAMOUNT, supreme. A Bill of Rights would have provided protection to the people against supreme power, but there was no bill of rights in the Constitution of the United States presented to the states for ratification in 1787.

James Wilson had asked during the Constitutional Convention why, since state governments had general legislative authority, except when there were reservations to the people, and the federal government had only limited powers in the proposed constitution, enumerate powers were not granted?[1] George Mason, however, another member of the same group, remarked in the final days of the Constitutional Convention that he "wished the plan had been prefaced by a Bill of Rights," and he offered to second a motion to that effect, if one were made. Such a motion was made, but it was voted down, 10–0.[2] Later in the first Congress, the Bill of Rights was proposed by James Madison and adopted by Congress, to be submitted to the states for approval.

Discussion of "power" in relation to the Bill of Rights is important for two reasons. First, because the Tenth Amendment was included as part of the Bill of Rights, it serves, for some people, anyway, as a partial basis for what is often referred to as "states' rights." Scholars typically do not consider the Tenth Amendment as part of the Bill of Rights in which rights are seen primarily, if not exclusively, as "rights" of persons, not institutions. Leonard Levy, for example, does not even mention the Tenth Amendment in his book, *Origins of the Bill of Rights*, except as that amendment relates to the Ninth Amendment.[3]

"States' rights" is an old concept—older than the Constitution—and it has been a contentious issue for more than two-hundred years. Because the states originally agreed to join the union, one argument goes, they were free to leave it—to secede—when they were dissatisfied. Some make the case that states' rights is a legitimate concept because it has been around so long. Tradition and rhetoric bring recognition and validity.

One can also make the case that states do not have rights: states have powers and responsibilities. To argue that "states have a right to put a convicted murderer to death or to tax property" is simply to substitute the word "right" for the constitutionally specified word "power," but it is misleading to call it a "right," because that suggests that "states have rights" in the same way that "people have rights." That is not true. States have powers.

Second, and more importantly, the Tenth Amendment is an explication of federalism, as that concept was established in the Constitution and in the United States. In other words, the Tenth Amendment was an effort to separate federal powers from states' powers from people's powers. The Supreme Court, in *United States v. Sprague*, made the point this way:

> The Tenth Amendment was intended to confirm the understanding of the people at the time the Constitution was adopted, that powers not granted to the United States were reserved to the States or to the people. It added nothing to the instrument as originally ratified.[4]

Nevertheless, for approximately a century, from the death of [Chief Justice] Marshall until 1937, the Tenth Amendment was frequently invoked to curtail powers expressly granted to Congress, notably the powers to regulate commerce, to enforce the Fourteenth Amendment, and to lay and collect taxes.[5]

So we are back to the question of power.

WHAT IS POWER?

Power, authority, and influence are often described as different ways of getting some people to do what other people want them to do. A robber, for example, who confronts a person with a gun and demands, "Your money or your life!" is exercising power. A state that puts a convicted murderer to death by execution, a nation that goes to war with another nation, a store owner who fires a worker, or a parent who puts a child to bed without supper are all exercising power. Power involves doing things that relate directly to meeting people's basic needs. Power is used to assure that those basic needs will or will not be met. Power may be rooted in authority, tradition, or brute force, but power in human relations is always aimed at affecting behavior.

Authority involves efforts to affect behaviors that are rooted in socially adopted or socially approved constitutions, laws, policies, or procedures. If a police officer follows me in my car and turns on a flashing red light and sounds a siren, I stop, not because I am afraid the officer will shoot me if I do not stop (although he/she may), but because I know that the police officer has the authority of the state behind him/her (i.e., a written constitution and explicit statutes passed by the legislature and signed by the governor) to demand compliance. The flashing red light and siren are designed to capture my attention, but my behavior is affected because I recognize that the police officer is "an officer of the law"; he/she has authority.

Influence involves efforts to affect behavior based on persuasion rather than authority or power. Advertising is an example of influence, as is a letter to the editor of a newspaper or a personal suggestion made at group meetings. Influence is rooted in the ability of one person to persuade other people by logic, deception, example, or fact that a particular behavior is appropriate or inappropriate, wise or unwise, effective or ineffective, good or bad, or meets some other criterion that the person attempting to exert influence thinks is important, useful, or effective.

The Tenth Amendment to the Constitution stipulates that "the powers not delegated to the United States by the Constitution, nor prohibited by it to the States, are reserved to the States respectively, or to the people." States have power. People have power. The federal government has power. The Tenth Amendment sorts out, in a general way, which powers the states have and which powers the people have. The powers of the federal government are enumerated, and therefore finite, in the Constitution itself.

In 1871, in *Collector v. Day*, the Supreme Court held that

> . . . the States within the limits of their powers not granted, or, in the language of the Tenth Amendment, "reserved," are as independent of the general government as that government within its sphere is independent of the States.[6]

In 1939, however, *Collector v. Day* was expressly overruled in *Graves v. New York ex rel. O'Keefe*.[7] The distinctions between the powers of the federal government, the states, and the people have not always been crystal clear.

The Tenth Amendment was an attempt to draw lines and separate those powers. Because of the "necessary and proper" clause of the Constitution, however, the task of drawing the lines has never been easy or completed in any final way. Article I, Section 8, paragraph 18 of the Constitution sets forth the "necessary and proper" clause as follows:

> Section 8. The Congress shall have Power to lay and collect Taxes, Duties, Imposts and Excises, to pay the Debts and provide for the common Defence and general Welfare of the United States; but all Duties, Imposts and Excises shall be uniform throughout the United States. . . .
>
> To make all Laws which shall be necessary and proper for carrying into Execution the foregoing Powers and all other Powers vested by this Constitution in the Govern-

ment of the United States, or in any Department or Officer thereof.[8]

Article VI of the United States Constitution clarifies the point this way:

> This Constitution, and the Laws of the United States which shall be made in Pursuance thereof; and all Treaties made, or which shall be made, under the Authority of the United States, shall be the supreme Law of the Land; and the Judges in every State shall be bound thereby, any Thing in the Constitution or Laws of any state to the Contrary notwithstanding.[9]

That is power! That is sovereignty! That is supreme!

HOW IS POWER USED BY GOVERNMENTS?

The word "power" implies force, but governing is essentially a verbal endeavor. The power that governments have is almost always applied through words. People in positions of power often say "we are sending a message" as explanation of why a certain policy was adopted or action taken. The threat of force, however, is always there. Police have red lights and sirens, but they carry lethal weapons, too. Negotiators with other countries are skilled communicators, but they have armies and navies behind them.

Force, though, seldom fosters effective working relationships and cooperation with other people. It often evokes resistance and retaliation. The Boston Massacre did not bring compliance. It triggered a revolution. Few people in government, anywhere in the world, presume that force and physical confrontation are appropriate actions for government, unless there is resistance or outright refusal to acquiesce to requirements expressed in words. For these reasons, evidence of government power usually appears in the form of words. But words are often ambiguous. Consider an illustration.

Benjamin Lee Whorf was a chemical engineer who worked for an insurance company to help people prevent fires. He was also an anthropologist who studied Hopi Indians. His study of situations that led to fires and his study of the Hopi Indian language led him to develop what has come to be called the Whorf thesis. That thesis postulates that "language shapes behavior." Whorf was convinced "that linguistics is essentially the quest of meaning."[10] He wrote:

> It was in the course of my professional work for a fire insurance company in which I undertook the task of analyzing many hundreds of reports of circumstances surrounding the start of fires, and in some cases of explosions. My analysis was directed toward purely physical conditions, such as defective wiring, presence or lack of air spaces between metal flues and woodwork, etc., and the results were presented in these terms. Indeed it was undertaken with no thought that any other significances would or could be revealed. But in due course it

became evident that not only a physical situation qua physics, but the meaning of that situation to people, was sometimes a factor, through the behavior of the people, in the start of the fire. And this factor of meaning was clearest when it was a linguistic meaning, residing in the name or the linguistic description commonly applied to the situation. Thus, around a storage of what are called "gasoline drums," behavior will tend to a certain type, that is, great care will be exercised; while around a storage of what are called "empty gasoline drums," it will tend to be different—careless, with little repression of smoking or of tossing cigarette stubs about. Yet the "empty" drums are perhaps more dangerous, since they contain explosive vapor. Physically the situation is hazardous, but the linguistic analysis according to regular analogy must employ the word "empty," which inevitably suggests lack of hazard. . . . The situation is named in one pattern (2) and the name is then "acted out" or "lived up to" in another (1), this being a general formula for the linguistic conditioning of behavior into hazardous forms.[11]

Language shapes behavior. James Madison had opposed a Bill of Rights when he served as a member of the Constitutional Convention and when he authored several of *The Federalist Papers* because he thought it was unnecessary, but he realized after he returned to Virginia in late 1787 that those who opposed a strong central government intended to vote "no" on the proposed Constitution, arguing that it did not contain a Bill of Rights. Opponents of the Constitution used the lack of a Bill of Rights as the reason for the negative vote, though their major concern was with the strong central government that the proposed Constitution contained. Critics wanted states to have more power than the federal government. That had been implicit in the last paragraph of the Declaration of Independence, where Jefferson had written, "That these United Colonies are, and of Right ought to be, Free and Independent States."

Madison then changed his tactics. Patrick Henry had wedged Madison out of a seat as a Senator from Virginia in the newly formed Senate, so Madison ran for House of Representatives, won, and introduced a Bill of Rights in the first Congress to be added to the Constitution. That Bill of Rights was adopted by the Congress and then sent to the states for ratification. Madison outfoxed Patrick Henry and those who were opposed to a strong central government, got the Constitution approved, and got the people a Bill of Rights, which included the Tenth Amendment.

The language of the Tenth Amendment was designed to shape the behavior of those who governed the United States by clarifying spheres of power for the federal government, the state governments, and the people. In the years since that time, state governments have developed constitutions and written laws in language designed to shape the behavior of persons who reside within those states.

The Constitution and the Bill of Rights were means. The goal of government, expressed repeatedly in propositions and discussions leading up to the preparation and adoption of the two documents, was "protection for the lives, liberty, and property of the citizenry."[12] That goal, articulated forcefully and frequently, included language intended to shape the behavior of those who would govern and those who would be governed, both then and in the future. The preamble to the Constitution elaborated on the general goal in more explicit language:

> We the People of the United States, in Order to form a more perfect Union, establish Justice, insure domestic Tranquillity, provide for the common Defence, promote the general Welfare, and secure the Blessing of Liberty to ourselves and our Posterity, do ordain and establish this Constitution for the United States of America.[13]

THE LOGIC TODAY

To this point we have presented a brief review of events that enunciated and initiated federalism as a concept and practice into governance in the United States, and how we interpret both language and power in the overall scheme of things. In the next section we will outline a sequence of activities that seems to make government "work."

Figure 2.1 is one way to conceptualize some of the realities of governance. The cycle of activities is clockwise. The theoretical cycle that is described relates policies to behavior to consequences, pinpointing some of the functions on which we might focus to make sense of the "cultures of the states." Culture is obviously affected by policies and laws, and policies and laws influence human conduct. Human conduct is the "stuff" of culture, based on the attitudes and values undergirding the conduct; thus we need to understand each of the points of the cyclical process.

Needless to say, the diagram is a crude sketch. It does not include all of the specific activities that would be required to render a complete and more accurate picture. For example, there is no mention of "enforcing laws" or "adjudicating the laws," and those are very important functions that a more comprehensive and more detailed depicting would include. Such additional functions are certainly a part of what would be required to make a

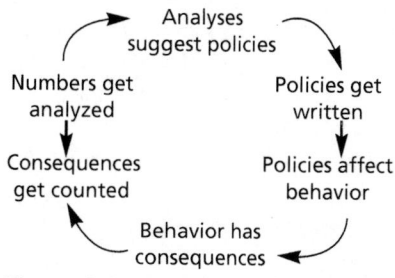

Figure 2.1. Sequence of Events in Governance

more intensive study of states than we will accomplish here, but Figure 2.1 will suffice to introduce the methods that we employed to see if there were different "cultures" evident in different states.

Suppose we "walk through" the steps outlined above to give a general picture of what we intend to present in our study of the "cultures of the states" and the use of power by governments and by the people. We will begin at the point where "policies get written."

A legislator introduces a bill in the legislature. The bill goes through various processes, including consideration by various committees and, if it is deemed worthy, is approved by one house of the legislature, then by the other house (except in Nebraska), and then goes to the governor for approval. If it is approved by a majority in each house and by the governor, it becomes law. After that, the law is promulgated; it is made known and put into effect.

The law, as passed, then begins to affect behavior. People hear about it and begin to understand that, if they do not abide by the stipulations of the law, they will be held accountable. Most people, accordingly, modify their behavior to conform to the law as passed. This process is sometimes described as "the mild coercion of the law."

However, if people do not "abide by the law," do not "do as they have been told to do," there will be consequences. They may be arrested, they may be tried in a court of law, they may be found guilty, and they may be punished, according to the law. Behavior has consequences in a society based on law: constitutional law, common law, and natural law.

Over time, those consequences get counted. If what occurred had been defined in the law as a "crime," that crime will be recorded. Each year, for example, the Federal Bureau of Investigation collects information from every county in each of the 50 states to produce what the agency calls a *Crime by Counties* report. The report totals—by municipality, by county, and by state—crimes that occurred within those jurisdictions for that year. That report is generally released in November each year for the crimes committed during the previous calendar year.

The report, sometimes described as a "Uniform Crime Report" (because the definitions and procedures used to produce the report are uniform across states) gets released by the Department of Justice and Federal Bureau of Investigation to the public, and the statistics are analyzed in both general and specific ways. For example, local news media may report that "murders are up this year," or "nonviolent crime rates are down," whereas sociologists may analyze the relationship of larceny to population density or robbery to unemployment.

Based on these analyses (some of which involve studies over time), suggestions for new polices or changes in existing policies are made, and the governance cycle begins again. Policies get written or rewritten, those policies affect behavior, that behavior has consequences, those consequences get counted, the numbers get analyzed, and those analyses suggest still further changes in the law or how the law is enforced. In this way, the power to adopt and promulgate policies shapes the behaviors of those who live within each state.

But some things that happen seem foreordained. Benjamin Franklin maintained that "in this world, nothing is certain but death and taxes." In the next seven chapters we summarize what we learned about taxes and deaths and other things in each of the states. Briefly, we collected data on more than 700 variables for each of the 50 states (see Appendix G). Then we identified 120 of those variables that seemed most appropriate to understand each state. After that, we put the data from these variables together into general factors, summarized those factors, and produced a "Problems Profile" for each state based on all of these data (see Appendix B). Following the calculations, we separated states into two groups—25 states with more problems, and 25 states with fewer problems—and compared these two groups of states on other variables. This remainder of this book describes both the processes and results of these analyses.

NOTES

1. Benjamin F. Wright (ed.), "Editor's Introduction," in Alexander Hamilton, James Madison, and John Jay, *The Federalist* (Cambridge, Mass.: Harvard University Press, 1961), 23–24.
2. Leonard W. Levy, *Origins of the Bill of Rights* (New Haven, Conn.: Yale University Press, 1999), 13.
3. Levy, *Origins*, 256.
4. Johnny H. Killian (ed.), *The Constitution of the United States of America: Analysis and Interpretation* (Washington, D.C.: U.S. Government Printing Office, 1987), 1417.
5. Killian, *The Constitution*, 1418.
6. Killian, *The Constitution*, 1418.
7. Killian, *The Constitution*, 1419.
8. Killian, *The Constitution*, 8–10.
9. Killian, *The Constitution*, 18.
10. Benjamin Lee Whorf, *Language, Thought, and Reality* (New York: Technology Press of Massachusetts Institute of Technology and John Wiley and Sons, 1956), 73.
11. Whorf, *Language*, 135.
12. Forrest McDonald, *Novus Ordo Seclorum: The Intellectual Origins of the Constitution* (Lawrence: University Press of Kansas, 1985), 3.
13. Killian, *The Constitution*, 3.

CHAPTER 3

Tax Factors

Who authorized them to speak the language of We the People, instead of We, the States? If the States be not the agents of this compact, it must be one great consolidated National government of the people of all the states.

—Patrick Henry[1]

INTRODUCTION

THE NEXT SIX CHAPTERS (PLUS APPENDIX B AND APPENDIX G) describe the "nuts and bolts" of this project. Depending upon your interest in specific details or the larger picture, you may want to skip some of these chapters and appended materials and go directly to Chapter 9, "SUMMARY Factor and Problems Profiles," or you may want to peruse with care the data and the methods we have employed. Here we take one paragraph to overview the whole process so you can decide how to proceed.

Briefly, we collected information on hundreds of variables about each of the 50 states from reliable sources (e.g., U.S. Census Bureau, Department of Justice, Bureau of Economic Analysis, National Association of State Budget Officers); organized that information into 702 tables (see Appendix G) which list every state in relation to each of the other states on that particular variable; selected 120 of those variables to describe each state numerically; placed data about every state's ranking on each of those 120 variables into one of 15 logical factors; analyzed that information statistically to produce a general SUMMARY factor; created a "Problems Profile" for each state with this summary information; then made inferences from all of these data about each state regarding the culture of that state and the effectiveness of governance in each state. Chapters 3 through 8 detail which variables were include in which factors, and Chapter 9 summarizes that information. Chapter 10 examines the relationship of gender and race to the variables and factors under study. The findings and conclusions of the study are set forth in Chapter 11. In all of these descriptions we print the names of variables or factors in all caps (e.g., SUMMARY), which refer to specific variables in our database, and the way the information on these variables is presented in Appendix G. The methods we used to create the 15 general factors and the SUMMARY factor are described in detail in Appendix B.

In this chapter we describe two general factors related to taxes and the 15 variables that comprise those two factors. One factor (i.e., GOVERNMT) relates primarily to taxes collected by the states, although some of the vari-

ables relate to taxes in general. The factor EXPEND relates strictly to expenditures by each state. These factors and the variables that make them up are described below. Where moneys come from and how those moneys are spent are major functions of government. That is what this chapter is all about.

TAXES

Taxes Paid to All Levels of Government: Proportion of income paid in taxes to federal, state, and local governments, 1999, is reported in Table G.376. This variable is labeled TAXRATE in Appendix G, and data from this variable were included in the general factor called GOVERNMT.

Per Capita State and Local Taxes: Per capita taxes paid to state and local government in 1999 is reported in Table G.378. This variable is labeled PCSTALO in Appendix G, and data from this variable were included in the general factor called GOVERNMT.

Percent of Population Working in Local Government: Percent of population working in local government, 1998, is reported in Table G.57. This variable is labeled PCLOCGOV in Appendix G, and data from this variable were included in the general factor called GOVERNMT.

Federal Funds Returned to State, per Person: Number of dollars per capita returned to each state in form of federal funds and grants, 1999, is reported in Table G.65. This variable is labeled FEDFUNPP in Appendix G, and data from this variable were included in the general factor called GOVERNMT.

Percent of Per Capita Income for All Taxes (Federal, State, and Local): Percent of per capita income paid in taxes to federal, state, and local governments, 1999, is reported in Table G.359. This variable is labeled PCTAX-ALL in Appendix G, and data from this variable were included in the general factor called GOVERNMT.

Per Capita Taxes Paid to Federal Government: Dollars paid, per capita, to the federal government in taxes, 1999, is reported in Table G.369. This variable is labeled PCFEDTAX in Appendix G, and data from this variable were included in the general factor called GOVERNMT.

Per Capita Taxes (not Including Property) Paid to Local Governments: Dollars paid, per capita, in taxes (not including taxes on property) to local governments, 1999, is reported in Table G.371. This variable is labeled PCLOCTAX in Appendix G, and data from this variable were included in the general factor called GOVERNMT.

Per Capita Taxes Paid to Federal, State, and Local Governments: Per capita taxes paid to federal, state, and local governments in 1999 is reported in Table G.372. This variable is labeled PCFSLTAX in Appendix G, and data from this variable were included in the general factor called GOVERNMT.

Information from these eight variables comprised the logical factor (i.e., not produced by factor analysis) labeled GOVERNMT. For our purposes, we call this a general factor.

EXPENDITURES

Per Capita Expenditures for Elementary and Secondary Education: Average per capita expenditures paid by states for elementary and secondary education, 1989–2000. This variable is labeled SCHOOL in Appendix G and is reported in Table G.676, and data from this variable were included in the general factor called EXPEND.

Per Capita Expenditures for Higher Education: Average per capita expenditures paid by states for higher education, 1989–2000. This variable is labeled COLLEGE in Appendix G and is reported in Table G.677, and data from this variable were included in the general factor called EXPEND.

Cash Assistance: Average per capita expenditures paid by states for cash assistance to persons in need, 1989–2000. This variable is labeled CASHHELP in Appendix G and is reported in Table G.678, and data from this variable were included in the general factor called EXPEND.

Medicaid Program: Average per capita expenditures paid by states for Medicaid, 1989–2000. This variable is labeled MEDICAID in Appendix G and is reported in Table G.679, and data from this variable were included in the general factor called EXPEND.

Corrections and Prisons: Average per capita expenditures paid by states for maintaining prisons and the costs of incarceration, 1989–2000. This variable is labeled PRISONS in Appendix G and is reported in Table G.680, and data from this variable were included in the general factor called EXPEND.

Transportation and Highways: Average per capita expenditures paid by states for highway construction and maintenance and other types of transportation expenses, 1989–2000. This variable is labeled HIGHWAYS in Appendix G and is reported in Table G.681, and data from this variable were included in the general factor called EXPEND.

All Other Expenditures: Average per capita expenditures paid by states for all other items, 1989–2000. This variable is labeled ALLOTHER in Appendix G and is reported in Table G.682, and data from this variable were included in the general factor called EXPEND.

Information from these seven variables comprised the general factor labeled EXPEND. Again, note that this was a logical rather than statistical factor; it was not created through factor analytic procedures.

NOTE

1. Patrick Henry, "A Wrong Step Now and the Republic Will Be Lost Forever," in Erik Bruun and Jay Crosby, *Our Nation's Archive: The History of the United States in Documents* (New York: Black Dog and Leventhal, 1999), 176.

CHAPTER 4

Crime and Punishment Factors

He who would do good to another must do it in Minute Particulars: General Good is the plea of the scoundrel, hypocrite, and flatterer, for Art and Science cannot exist, but in minutely organized Particulars.

—Blake[1]

INTRODUCTION

CRIME COMES UNDER THE JURISDICTION OF STATE GOVERNments in the United States, by and large. There are federal crimes—kidnapping, automobile theft, bootlegging, and harming federal officials—but most crimes are violations of state laws. Defining crimes, and then apprehending, convicting, and punishing criminals is, first and foremost, a responsibility of state and local governments. In this chapter we discuss crimes that are violations of state or local laws.

In an earlier chapter we pointed out that the Federal Bureau of Investigation (FBI) compiles information about eight different crimes from communities, counties, and states across the nation every year: murder, aggravated assault, rape, robbery, burglary, larceny, motor vehicle theft, and arson. Using definitions and procedures established by the U.S. Department of Justice, the agency produces a Uniform Crime Report each year for every community, county, and state in the nation. Occasionally a city or county does not get their report turned in to the FBI on time, so that year the report to the nation may be incomplete, but over time, reports are updated and very accurate. In this chapter we rely primarily on a compilation of data over a 39-year period by the Department of Justice, summarized in Appendix G, Tables G.259 through G.294. These data covered 39 years, 1960 to 1998. References for each table are located in Appendix H.

The FBI designates four crimes as "violent" and the others as "property" crimes. Murder, assault, rape, and robbery are violent crimes, according to the Uniform Crime Report definitions and procedures. In this study we will focus on seven crimes for which we have data over a 39-year period: murder, assault, rape, robbery, burglary, larceny, and motor vehicle theft. In addition, we included assault with a gun for 1998. Data about arson during those years was incomplete.

CRIME

Suppose we begin with murder, most heinous of crimes, and certainly a form of traumatic death. Look at Table G.267 in Appendix G, "Total Number of Murders,

1960–1998." If you sum the numbers in Table G.267 for all 50 states, you will discover that more than 688,000 people in the United States were murdered in the 39-year period from John F. Kennedy's inauguration as president to the end of 1998. And murders that occurred within the District of Columbia were not included in the tally, because the District of Columbia is not a state, therefore is not included in this study. For perspective, it may be helpful to recognize that the number of Americans who were murdered during that 1960–1998 period is more than the total number of deaths for all wars in which United States has been involved since 1898: Spanish-American War, World War I, World War II, Korean War, Vietnam War, the Gulf War, and now the wars in Afghanistan and Iraq.[2]

Perspective is important because policymakers in every state argue that life is important, murder is a heinous crime, and they are committed to reducing the murder rate, whatever it may be. The fact that murder rates are higher in America than in any other so-called civilized nation in the world, however, and that incarceration rates are second highest and execution rates fourth highest suggests that policymakers may not be as committed to reducing murder rates as they proclaim. Policymaking rhetoric and policymaking reality are not the same. The eight variables combined to make the general factor CRIME are described below.

Murder: Average murder rate per 100,000 during the period 1960–1998. This variable is labeled MURDER39 in Appendix G and is reported in Table G.268. Data from this variable were included in the general factor called CRIME.

Rape: Average rape rate per 100,000 during the period 1960–1998. This variable is labeled RAPE39 in Appendix G and is reported in Table G.272. Data from this variable were included in the general factor called CRIME.

Robbery: Average robbery rate per 100,000 during the period 1960–1998. This variable is labeled ROBBER39 in Appendix G and is reported in Table G.276. Data from this variable were included in the general factor called CRIME.

Assault: Average assault rate per 100,000 during the period 1960–1998. This variable is labeled ASSAUL39 in Appendix G and is reported in Table G.280. Data from this variable were included in the general factor called CRIME.

Burglary: Average burglary rate per 100,000 during the period 1960–1998. This variable is labeled BURGLA39 in

Appendix G and is reported in Table G.284. Data from this variable were included in the general factor called CRIME.

Larceny: Average larceny rate per 100,000 during the period 1960–1998. This variable is labeled LARCEN39 in Appendix G and is reported in Table G.288. Data from this variable were included in the general factor called CRIME.

Motor Vehicle Theft: Average motor vehicle theft rate per 100,000 during the period 1960–1998. This variable is labeled MVT39 in Appendix G and is reported in Table G.292. Data from this variable were included in the general factor called CRIME.

Assault with a Gun: Percent of all assaults that were firearm-related, 1998. This variable is labeled ASLGUN in Appendix G and is reported in Table G.407. Data from this variable were included in the general factor called CRIME.

The data in Appendix G about criminal activity from these eight variables were combined to create a general factor called CRIME. See Appendix B for further information about exactly how we did that. In the next section, we will describe the variables that we put together to create another factor, PROTECT.

POLICE PROTECTION

The U.S. Department of Justice, Bureau of Justice Statistics periodically produces the *Sourcebook of Criminal Justice Statistics,* which includes information pertaining to crime and corrections. One category provides information about the justice system of each state. The total justice system includes three components: police protection, judicial and legal, and corrections.

The term "police protection" implies that police in every state have a primary responsibility to protect the citizens of that state. Later we will point out that there seems to be little or no relationship between either the number of police officers or dollars expended for police officers with incidence of crime in a state. It may be more appropriate to say that police apprehend criminals rather than protect citizens from criminals, but we used the label PROTECT to describe the general factor created out of the five variables described below for each of the 50 states.

Percent of Total Justice System Devoted to Police Protection: Percent of total justice system full-time equivalent employment devoted to police protection in 1995. This variable is labeled POLIEMPL in Appendix G, and is reported in Table G.390. Data from this variable were included in the general factor called CRIME.

Per Capita Expenditures of Justice Costs for Police Protection: Per capita expenditures of justice system costs devoted to state and local police protection in 1996. This variable is labeled POLICE in Appendix G, and is reported in Table G.382. Data from this variable were included in the general factor called CRIME.

Percent of Justice System Payrolls Devoted to Police Protection: Percent of state and local justice system payrolls devoted to police protection costs in 1995. This variable is labeled POLICOST in Appendix G, and is reported in Table G.386. Data from this variable were included in the general factor called CRIME.

Rate per 10,000 Population of Police Protection Employees: Rate (per 10,000 population) of state and local justice system full-time equivalent employees who worked in police protection in 1995. This variable is labeled POLTOTRA in Appendix G, and is reported in Table G.394. Data from this variable were included in the general factor called CRIME.

Sworn State Police Officers per 10,000 Residents: Sworn officers per 10,000 residents of the total state population, 1997. This variable is labeled OFFPPOP in Appendix G, and is reported in Table G.401. Data from this variable were included in the general factor called CRIME.

The data in Appendix G about police protection from these five variables were combined to create a general factor called PROTECT. See Appendix B for further information about exactly how we did that. In the next section, we will describe the variables that we put together to create another general factor, PUNISH.

PUNISHMENT

Persons found guilty of criminal activity must pay a price, but society must pay taxes to impose punishments on those who are convicted. Prisoners do not pay for the prisons, society does. Prisoners do not pay for prison guards, society does. Prisoners do not pay for the food they eat, society does. Punishment costs prisoners their freedom, and sometimes their life, but society pays whatever it costs to impose punishments by imposing taxes on itself. We identified 11 variables to be included in the PUNISH factor. Each of those variables is described below.

Correction Employees: Rate (for each 10,000 population in the state) of state and local justice system full-time equivalent employees who worked in corrections in 1995 is reported in Table G.397. This variable is labeled CORRATE in Appendix G, and data from this variable were included in the general factor called PUNISH.

Persons Confined in Prisons: The number of persons incarcerated (for each 1,000 population in the state) in each state's prisons in 1996 is reported in Table G.64. This variable is labeled PRRATE96 in Appendix G, and data from this variable were included in the general factor called PUNISH.

Per Capita Cost to Maintain State Prisons: The cost per person in the state to maintain one inmate in state prisons for one year (1996) by hiring guards, purchasing food, paying for utilities, and the like is reported in Table G.71. This variable is labeled PRISCOST in Appendix G, and data from this variable were included in the general factor called PUNISH.

Percent Change in Size of Prison Population, 1992 to 1996: The number of persons incarcerated in each state's prisons in 1992 and 1996 were compared, and the difference of the two populations was recorded as percent change in Table G.73. This variable is labeled PRCH9296 in Appendix G, and data from this variable were included in the general factor called PUNISH.

Number of Convicted Persons Executed from 1950 to 1969: The number of persons executed for capital crimes by each state, per thousand total population, is reported in Table G.75. This variable is labeled EXPT5069 in Appendix G, and data from this variable were included in the general factor called PUNISH.

Number of Convicted Persons Executed from 1977 to 2000: The number of persons executed for capital crimes by each state, per thousand total population, is reported in Table G.76. This variable is labeled EXPT7700 in Appendix G, and data from this variable were included in the general factor called PUNISH.

Per Capita Expenditures of Justice System Costs Spent on Corrections: The Justice System (i.e., police protection, judicial and legal, and corrections) expenditures, per capita, that were devoted exclusively to corrections in 1996, is reported in Table G.384. This variable is labeled CORRECT in Appendix G, and data from this variable were included in the general factor called PUNISH.

Percent of Justice System Payrolls Devoted to Corrections: The percent of the Justice System (i.e., police protection, judicial and legal, and corrections) payrolls that were devoted exclusively to corrections in 1995 is reported in Table G.388. This variable is labeled CORRCOST in Appendix G, and data from this variable were included in the general factor called PUNISH.

Percent of Justice System Devoted to Corrections: The number of persons who serve as prison guards and in other roles in each state's correction system in 1995, as a percent of each state's total number of justice system employees, is reported in Table G.392. This variable is labeled

CORREMPL in Appendix G, and data from this variable were included in the general factor called PUNISH.

Cost of Food, per Inmate, per Day, in a State's Prison System: The cost to feed each incarcerated prisoner per day in 1996 is reported in Table G.70. This variable is labeled FOODPI in Appendix G, and data from this variable were included in the general factor called PUNISH. Higher expenditures were considered positive, in the sense that prisoners were being better cared for than in states with lower expenditures for this variable. It was assumed that states that spent less to provide care for prisoners were actually using prison as a place for extra punishment (i.e., lesser care) rather than separation from society as punishment.

Cost to Keep Each Inmate in a State's Prison System for a Year: The cost to keep an inmate in a state's prison system for a full year (1996) is reported in Table G.67. This variable is labeled PRISPI96 in Appendix G, and data from this variable were included in the general factor called PUNISH. Higher expenditures were considered positive, in the sense that prisoners were being better cared for than in states with lower expenditures for this variable. It was assumed that states that spent less to provide care for prisoners were actually using prison as a place for extra punishment (i.e., lesser care) rather than separation from society as punishment.

The data in Appendix G about punishment from these 11 variables were combined to create a general factor called PUNISH. See Appendix B for further information about exactly how we did that.

NOTES

1. William Blake, quoted in J. Bronowski, *Science and Human Values* (New York: Harper and Row, 1956), 85.
2. "Selected Characteristics of the Armed Forces, by War," *Historical Statistics of the United States, Colonial Times to 1970,* bicentennial edition, part 2 (Washington, D.C.: U.S. Bureau of the Census, 1975), 1140, Series Y, 856–903.

CHAPTER 5

Mortality Factors

We hold these truths to be self-evident, that all men are created equal, that they are endowed by their Creator with certain unalienable Rights, that among these are Life, Liberty, and the pursuit of Happiness.

—Declaration of Independence

INTRODUCTION

WE BEGIN THE DISCUSSION OF MORTALITY WITH AN ASSUMPtion: Life has value. Anything that protects, prolongs, or preserves life is positive. Anything that endangers, cuts short, or destroys life is negative. The Declaration of Independence enunciated the rights of life, liberty, and the pursuit of happiness, and then concluded that section of the argument with these words:

That to secure these rights, Governments are instituted among Men, deriving their just powers from the consent of the governed, That whenever any Form of Government becomes destructive of these ends, it is the Right of the People to alter or abolish it, and to institute new Government, laying its foundation on such principles and organizing its powers in such form, as to them shall seem most likely to effect their Safety and Happiness.[1]

In his book on the intellectual origins of the Constitution, Forrest McDonald makes the same point this way:

Almost to a man, Patriots were agreed that the proper ends of government were to protect people in their lives, liberty, and property and that these ends could best be obtained through a republican form.[2]

Life is important. Life is something to which state governments attend. Most state constitutions direct attention to the importance and value of life. For example, the Bill of Rights of the Constitution of the State of Ohio says this:

All men are, by nature, free and independent, and have certain inalienable rights, among which are those of enjoying and defending life and liberty, acquiring, possessing, and protecting property, and seeking and obtaining happiness and safety.[3]

The Constitution of the Commonwealth of Massachusetts addresses the significance of life in a more extended discussion in its preamble:

The end of the institution, maintenance, and administration of government, is to secure the existence of the body politic, to protect it, and to furnish the individuals who compose it with the power of enjoying in safety and tranquillity their natural rights, and the blessings of life: and whenever these great objects are not obtained, the people have a right to alter the government, and to take measures necessary for their safety, prosperity, and happiness.

The body politic is formed by a voluntary association of individuals: it is a social compact, by which the whole people covenants with each citizen, and each citizen with the whole people, that all shall be governed by certain laws for the common good. It is the duty of the people, therefore, in framing a constitution of government, to provide for an equitable mode of making laws, as well as for an impartial interpretation, and a faithful execution of them; that every man may, at all times, find his security in them.

We, therefore, the people of Massachusetts, acknowledging, with grateful hearts, the goodness of the great Legislator of the universe, in affording us, in the course of His providence, an opportunity, deliberately and peaceably, without fraud, violence or surprise, of entering into an original, explicit, and solemn compact with each other; and of forming a new constitution of civil government, for ourselves and posterity; and devoutly imploring His direction in so interesting a design, do agree upon, ordain, and establish the following Declaration of Rights, and Frame of Government, as the Constitution of the Commonwealth of Massachusetts.[4]

FROM LIFE TO DEATH

If we study the crime rate in the District of Columbia, especially the murder rate, we find that it is higher than the murder rate for any of the 50 states in the United States. If we ask ourselves, "Why is this so?" several possible explanations (i.e., hypotheses) come to mind: population of the district, proportion of the population that is minority, different governing procedures than the states, number of square miles within the district, population density of the district, proximity to the national government and public attention, and so on.

This book describes a study of the cultures of the states, and information about the District of Columbia has not been included in the study because the district is not a state. It does not have a constitution. It does not have a governor. It does not have a legislature. It does not have the same power to levy and raise taxes that states have. Governance in the District of Columbia is fundamentally different from governance in each of the 50 states.

States have powers. The District of Columbia does not have all of these same powers. The people who reside within the district have powers accorded them as people by the Tenth Amendment, but the structure and function of government within the district is markedly different from the structure and function of government in each of the 50 states. We cite this difference because we would guess that the difference in the murder rate in the District of Columbia is related more to the difference in governance structures and procedures than it is to the other possibilities cited that might account for the differences in murder rates. That guess may not be correct, but since this study is an investigation of differences among the states on factors that are directly or indirectly affected by governance and decisions within the states, it did not seem appropriate to include the District of Columbia in the comparisons.

And we intend to compare. We have not found satisfactory language yet with which to discuss the differences between states (there are important differences within states, too, though that is another aspect of the problem), but some of the differences are great, and it will be important to identify those differences and discuss them in meaningful ways. The quotation from the Declaration of Independence cited above is simply to say that we intend to organize some of our data and some of the discussion around death, the opposite of life. We assume that preservation of life and enhancement of life are major purposes of any government.

THINKING ABOUT DEATH

Life is important and life has value, but death comes to all. When death comes, and how it comes, varies. There are several types or causes of death, apart from those that occur in war: murder, suicide, accident, disease, and aging, to name a few. Certain diseases that lead to death are often brought on by the individual: lung cancer, cirrhosis, acquired immunodeficiency syndrome (AIDS), and drug-induced death, among others. Some deaths are traumatic, some are accidental, others are natural, and still others are self induced, but state governments are committed to reducing deaths within their borders, whatever the cause. "Liberty and the pursuit of happiness" are meaningless concepts without life. For the purpose of this book, we deal with murder under the heading of crime rather than death, but we created three categories of death: natural death, highway death, and traumatic death. Each of these categories included several variables that we put together mathematically, and then called factors. These factors were labeled DEATH, HIWAYDEA, and TRAUMA.

NATURAL DEATH

There are many causes of death. In Chapter 10, "Race and Gender," we report analyses of data based on 13 different causes of death (e.g., heart attacks, malignancies,

diabetes, nutritional deficiencies) in relation to race and gender. In this chapter we describe six causes of death that we combined mathematically into one general factor labeled DEATH. Each of these causes of death represents a variable in this study that is described by a table in Appendix G, and it was the data in these tables that we used to create the factor score for DEATH. The six variables are described briefly below.

Infant Mortality: Infant mortality rates in 1997 (deaths per 1,000 live births during the first 12 months of life) is reported for each state in Table G.212. This variable is labeled INFMORTT in Appendix G, and data from this variable were included in the general factor called DEATH.

Death from Heart Attack or Heart Disease: Heart attack is the most common cause of death in the United States, and information about it from 1997 is described in Table G.216. This variable is labeled DEATHART in Appendix G, and data from this variable were included in the general factor called DEATH.

Death from Malignancy: Carcinoma, or cancer, is the second major cause of death in the United States. Many types of cancer are included in this category, and information about it from 1997 is described in Table G.217. The variable is labeled DEATHCAN in Appendix G, and data from this variable were included in the general factor called DEATH.

Death from All Causes: Death from all causes in 1997 is reported in both Table G.211 as "Death Rate per 1,000 Population" and Table G.215 as "All Deaths per 100,000." We used the data from the latter variable, labeled DEATHALL, and reported in Table G.215 of Appendix G, as one source of information for the general factor called DEATH.

Death from Cerebrovascular Problems or "Stroke": Stroke is a common cause of death, especially among older people. Information about death from this cause in 1997 is depicted in Table G.218 of Appendix G under the variable name DEATHCER, and data from this variable were included in the general factor called DEATH.

Death from Diabetes: Diabetes mellitus is a major cause of death, and information about deaths from diabetes in 1997 is described in Table G.222 in Appendix G under the variable name DEATHDIA. Data from this variable were included in the general factor called DEATH.

The data in Appendix G about various causes of death from these six variables were combined to create a general factor called DEATH. See Appendix B for further information about exactly how we did that. In the next section, we will describe the variables that we put together to create a general factor that involved automobile fatalities.

HIGHWAY TRAFFIC FATALITIES

Another factor that we created from variables described in Appendix G was labeled HIWAYDEA. This factor included data from 11 variables. Each of these variables is described below. Before we proceed, however, it might be useful, again, to add perspective.

Automobiles have been used since about 1900, and there have been fatalities since the early years of that century. In general terms, deaths from highway fatalities per 100,000 total population rose steadily from about 1900 to the 1930s, then leveled off until about the 1960s. Since then, highway deaths declined slowly but steadily to a point where the rates are lower per population than they were in the 1930s. In fact, there were fewer total traffic fatalities in 2000 than there were in 1936, even though there were many more people and many more cars in 2000.

This decline in the rate of highway fatalities per 100,000 population is one of the great untold success stories of government, industry, education, media, and the general population working together to make life better. Highway fatalities represent one area of death in which states play important roles. Highways are designed, constructed, and maintained by states. White lines are painted by states along the edges of the roads. No-passing zones are identified with special paint and signs. School zones and railroad crossings are marked by states. Speed limits and rules about alcohol and seat belts are established by states. And state laws affecting all of these things are enforced by state and local police.

Good statistics, improved engineering for vehicles and highways, improved enforcement of laws, and better education of drivers by schools, insurance companies, and the media have all contributed to declining highway fatality rates in the United States. However, some states have made more progress in this area than others, as data in the "Percent Change in Traffic Fatalities over Time" variable, described below, makes clear. In other words, some states have done much more than other states in this whole matter. The 11 variables that comprise the general factor we created, HIWAYDEA, are described below.

Traffic Fatalities Involving Alcohol: Percent fatal accidents in which alcohol was involved, 1999, as described in Table G.189 in Appendix G. Data from this variable, FATALCOH, were included in the general factor called HIWAYDEA.

Traffic Fatalities per Thousand: Traffic fatalities per 1,000 total population, 1998, as described in Table G.193 in Appendix G. Data from this variable, TRAFATPT, were included in the general factor called HIWAYDEA.

Pedestrian Deaths: Pedestrian fatalities per 100,000 population, 1999, as described in Table G.339 in Appendix G. Data from this variable, PEDEATH, were included in the general factor called HIWAYDEA.

Cost of Car Insurance: Auto insurance, average expenditure per vehicle, 1998, as described in Table G.171 in Appendix G. Data from this variable, CARINSUR, were included in the general factor called HIWAYDEA.

Number of Deficient Bridges: Percent of bridges structurally deficient, 1998, as described in Table G.182 in Appendix G. Data from this variable, BRIDGDEF, were included in the general factor called HIWAYDEA.

Number of Obsolete Bridges: Percent of bridges functionally obsolete, 1998, as described in Table G.183 in Appendix G. Data from this variable, BRIDGOBS, were included in the general factor called HIWAYDEA.

Traffic Fatalities in Motor Vehicles: Death rate from motor vehicle accidents per 100,000 resident population, 1997, as described in Table G.220 in Appendix G. Data from this variable, DEATHMV, were included in the general factor called HIWAYDEA.

Traffic Fatalities Involving Any Alcohol: Percent fatal accidents in which any alcohol was involved, 1999, as described in Table G.342 in Appendix G. Data from this variable, ANYALCOH, were included in the general factor called HIWAYDEA.

Percent Change in Traffic Fatalities over Time: Percent change in traffic fatalities over time, 1975–1999, as described in Table G.345 in Appendix G. Data from this variable, PCFATCH, were included in the general factor called HIWAYDEA.

Traffic Fatalities in Which Seat Belts Were Not Used: Percent of passenger car occupants killed that were unrestrained, 1999, as described in Table G.346 in Appendix G. Data from this variable, NOBELT, were included in the general factor called HIWAYDEA.

State Tax on Gasoline: State gasoline tax rates, 1998, as described in Table G.187 in Appendix G. Data from this variable, GASTAX, were included in the general factor called HIWAYDEA.

The data in Appendix G regarding information that related to highway fatalities from these 11 variables were combined to create a general factor called HIWAYDEA. See Appendix B for further information about exactly how we did that. In the next section, we will describe the variables that we put together to create another mortality factor.

TRAUMATIC DEATHS

Death Rate from Non-auto Accidents per 100,000 Population: One form of traumatic death is death by accident. Our database includes one table with information about death rates from accidents in each state in 1997 that does not cut across gender or racial lines, under the variable name DEATHACC, which is described in Table G.219 in Appendix G. Data from this variable were included in the general factor called TRAUMA.

Suicides per 100,000 Population: A second form of traumatic death is suicide. Our database includes only one table with information about suicide rates in each state in 1997 that does not cut across gender or racial lines: Table G.224 in Appendix G, "Suicide Rate per 100,000." Data from this variable (DEATHSUI) were included in the general factor called TRAUMA.

The data in Appendix G about death from these two variables were combined to create a general factor called TRAUMA. See Appendix B for further information about exactly how we did that.

Accidental death and suicide are both deaths over which states have only some control. States can provide instruction regarding accidents and how to avoid them, and states can provide mental health services to persons who are depressed, but the nature of accidental death and suicide, as with murder, are such that the knowledge and skill of those who have accidents and the intentions of depressed persons are often difficult to discern, until it is too late. States can and do punish those who commit murder, and prosecution, adjudication, and correction efforts take big portions of every state's budget, but little effort or money is expended by states related to accidental death or suicide.

NOTES

1. Thomas Jefferson, Declaration of Independence, as reproduced in Henry Steele Commager (ed.), *Documents of American History* (New York: Appleton-Century-Crofts, 1949), 100.
2. Forrest McDonald, *Novus Ordo Seclorum: The Intellectual Origins of the Constitution* (Lawrence: University Press of Kansas, 1985), 1.
3. Ohio Constitution, Article I, Section 1.
4. Constitution of the Commonwealth of Massachusetts, Preamble.

CHAPTER 6

Health Factors

The only way to keep your health is to eat what you don't want, drink what you don't like, and do what you'd rather not.

—Mark Twain[1]

INTRODUCTION

IT HARDLY SEEMS NECESSARY TO SET FORTH A PROPOSITION that health is a reasonable area in which government could and should function legitimately. Each of us is confronted (sometimes it seems as if we are bombarded) daily with information and opportunities that relate to health, and for which we are unprepared and unable to make intelligent decisions about what to buy, what to do, or how to function.

Almost no person anywhere in the United States, for example, is in a position to know, with confidence, whether or which "natural" herbs and medicines are safe to use. This morning's news included a story about kava being dangerous to life and health; liver damage has resulted in several deaths, here and abroad. We cannot know when "natural" medicines are dangerous. To date, the Food and Drug Administration has not required that such things as kava be subjected to experimental analysis and reviewed for approval, but the agency has alerted all citizens to the possible dangers. The federal government, at least, has taken that first step.

Also in the morning news was a story about the state health department asking schools to identify children who may be seriously overweight, and to communicate information to those students' parents about the long-term consequences of being overweight. Some parents objected, suggesting that their children might be negatively perceived by peers, if such information became known. That might occur, and such a possibility needs to be taken into consideration, but it is difficult to think that, in the long run, concern for peer acceptance and approval are as important as life itself. We all know that obesity can lead to diabetes, high blood pressure, heart problems, and the like. Those are very serious health problems. Any government worthy of that label must attend to the life of its citizens, even if parents are not wise enough or concerned enough to accept a gentle admonition graciously.

Deaths from cardiovascular problems have gone down dramatically during the past 50 years. National, state, and local governments have worked in concert with private associations, universities, and agencies to collect financial contributions from individuals, allocate money from tax collections, conduct research, disseminate findings, and educate people in all walks of life about the dangers of such things as overeating, too many fats, too much cholesterol, the importance of exercise, and the like. Heart disease, more so than cancer, is a direct function of what people eat and what they do or do not do. Governments, private agencies, and individuals have worked collaboratively to "make a significant difference" in deaths from heart disease. That is a great success story and must be replicated in other areas of human endeavor.

This chapter lists 25 variables that were included in three general factors that related to health as a basis for looking at the states: health, medical insurance, and teenagers' problems.

HEALTH

Percent at Risk for Overweight: Being overweight is a major cause of health problems, and information about obesity in 1999 is described in Table G.360 in Appendix G under the variable name OBESITY. Data from this variable were included in the general factor called HEALTH.

Percent Males Who Smoke: Lung cancer is a major cause of death, and information about males who smoke is described for 1998 in Table G.241 in Appendix G under the variable name MCIGARET. Data from this variable were included in the general factor called HEALTH.

Percent Females Who Smoke: Lung cancer is a major cause of death, and information about females who smoke is described for 1998 in Table G.242 in Appendix G under the variable name FCIGARET. Data from this variable were included in the general factor called HEALTH.

AIDS Cases per 1,000 Population: Acquired immunodeficiency syndrome (AIDS) is a cause of major health problems, and information about the number of cases of AIDS per 1,000 population in 1998 is described in Table G.236 in Appendix G under the variable name AIDSPT. Data from this variable were included in the general factor called HEALTH.

Tuberculosis Cases per 1,000 Population: Tuberculosis (TB) is a serious health problem, and information about the number of cases of TB per 1,000 population in 1998 is described in Table G.240 in Appendix G under the variable name TBPT. Data from this variable were included in the general factor called HEALTH.

Percent of Children Not Immunized by Age Two: Immunization against childhood diseases is a major step in prevention of such diseases, and information about the percent of children not immunized in 1998 is described in Table G.21 in Appendix G under the variable name NOIMMUNE. Data from this variable were included in the general factor called HEALTH.

Percent of Children Born with Low Birth Weight: Children born with low birth weight are at risk of many health problems, and information about the percent of children born this way in 1998 is described in Table G.207 in Appendix G under the variable name LOWBIRWT. Data from this variable were included in the general factor called HEALTH.

Syphilis Cases per 1,000 Population: Syphilis is an illness resulting from unprotected sex and may develop into a serious problem. Information about the number of cases per 1,000 population in 1998 is described in Table G.238 in Appendix G under the variable name SYPHILPT. Data from this variable were included in the general factor called HEALTH.

The data in Appendix G regarding information that related to sickness and health in these eight variables were combined to create a general factor called HEALTH. See Appendix B for further information about exactly how we did that. In the next section, we will describe the variables that we put together to create another general factor.

MEDICAL INSURANCE

Percent Persons with No Health Insurance: Percent of people without health insurance is a major factor relating to health, and information about this problem in 1998 is described in Table G.231 in Appendix G under the variable NOCOVER. Data from this variable were included in the general factor called MEDICAL.

Percent Children with No Health Insurance: Percent of children without health insurance is a major factor relating to health, and information about this problem in 1998 is described in Table G.232 in Appendix G under the variable CHINOCOV. Data from this variable were included in the general factor called MEDICAL.

Percent of Males Age 12 to 19 Who Lack Health Insurance: Percent of young males without health insurance is a major factor relating to health, and information about this problem in 1995 is described in Table G.316 in Appendix G under the variable LACKINSM. Data from this variable were included in the general factor called MEDICAL.

Percent of Females Age 12 to 19 Who Lack Health Insurance: Percent of young females without health insurance is a major factor relating to health, and information about this problem in 1995 is described in Table G.315 in Appendix G under the variable LACKINSF. Data from this variable were included in the general factor called MEDICAL.

Dollars Paid Each Medicare Enrollee, 1999: Number of people without health insurance is a major factor relating to health, and information about this problem is described in Table G.227 Appendix G under the variable PAYENROL, which describes dollars paid each Medicare enrollee. Data from this variable were included in the general factor called MEDICAL.

Medicaid Funds Paid Each Recipient, 1998: Number of people without health insurance is a major factor relating to health, and information about this problem is described in Table G.230 in Appendix G under the variable PAYRECIP, which describes dollars paid each Medicaid enrollee. Data from this variable were included in the general factor called MEDICAL.

Physicians per 100,000 Population: Number of active physicians per 100,000 population is a factor relating to health, and information about this problem in 1998 is described in Table G.233 in Appendix G under the variable DOCTORS. Data from this variable were included in the general factor called MEDICAL.

Hospital Beds per 1,000 Population: Number of hospital beds per 1,000 population is a factor relating to health, and information about this problem in 1998 is described in Table G.256 in Appendix G under the variable HOSPBEDP. Data from this variable were included in the general factor called MEDICAL.

The data in Appendix G regarding information that related to sickness and health in these eight variables were combined to create a general factor called MEDICAL. See Appendix B for further information about exactly how we did that. In the next section, we will describe the variables that we put together to create still another general factor that affects health.

TEENAGERS WITH PROBLEMS

Percent of Births to Unmarried Teens, 1998: Percent of total children born to teenage mothers in 1998 is an indication of problems among teenagers, and information about this problem is described in Table G.208 in Appendix G under the variable TEENBRTH. Data from this variable were included in the general factor called TEENPROB.

Percent of Births to Unmarried Women: Percent of births to unmarried women in 1998 is probably an indication of problems among teenagers, and information about this problem is described in Table G.209 in Appendix G under the variable UNMARRBR. Data from this variable were included in the general factor called TEENPROB.

Gonorrhea Rates per 100,000 Females Ages 15–19: Gonorrhea among teenage females in 1996 is an indication of problems among teenagers, and information about this problem is described in Table G.319 in Appendix G under the variable GONTEEN. Data from this variable were included in the general factor called TEENPROB.

Percent Teen Births That Are Repeat Births: Percent of repeat births to teenagers in 1996 is an indication of problems among teenagers, and information about this problem is described in Table G.321 in Appendix G under the variable PCTBRB96. Data from this variable were included in the general factor called TEENPROB.

Non-Hispanic White Birth Rates per 1,000 Population: Percent of births to non-Hispanic white teenagers in 1996 is an indication of problems among teenagers, and information about this problem is described in Table G.301 in Appendix G under the variable NHWHBR. Data from this variable were included in the general factor called TEENPROB.

Percent Births to Unmarried Teenagers, 1996: Percent of births to unmarried teenagers in 1996 is an indication of problems among teenagers, and information about this problem is described in Table G.305 in Appendix G under the variable TOTPCUN. Data from this variable were included in the general factor called TEENPROB.

Percent Teen Births Involving Inadequate Prenatal Care: Percent of births to teenagers who received inadequate prenatal care in 1996 is an indication of problems among teenagers, and information about this problem is described in Table G.309 in Appendix G under the variable TOTPCINC. Data from this variable were included in the general factor called TEENPROB.

Birth Rate per 100,000 to Teens Ages 15–17: Birth rate to young teenagers in 1996 is an indication of problems among teenagers, and information about this problem is described in Table G.318 in Appendix G under the variable BRYT96. Data from this variable were included in the general factor called TEENPROB.

Percent Teen Births as Percent of All Births: Percent of births to unmarried teenagers in 1996 as a percent of all births indicates problems among teenagers, and information about this problem is described in Table G.322 in Appendix G under the variable PCTBAL96. Data from this variable were included in the general factor called TEENPROB.

The data in Appendix G regarding information about teenage problems in these nine variables were combined to create a general factor called TEENPROB. See Appendix B for further information about how we did that. In the next section, we will describe variables that we put together to create factors that relate to education.

NOTE

1. Mark Twain, quoted in Jon Winokur, *The Portable Curmudgeon* (New York: New American Library, 1987), 134.

CHAPTER 7

Education Factors

You may give them your love but not your thoughts, for they have their own thoughts. You may house their bodies but not their souls, for their souls dwell in the house of tomorrow, which you cannot visit, not even in your dreams. You may strive to be like them, but seek not to make them like you. For life goes not backward with yesterday. You are the bows from which your children as living arrows are sent forth.

—Kahlil Gibran[1]

INTRODUCTION

DAVID MCCULLOUGH DESCRIBED JOHN ADAMS' ROLE IN writing the Massachusetts Constitution as follows:

In addition, notably, there was Section II of Chapter 6 [of the Massachusetts Constitution], a paragraph headed "The Encouragement of Literature, Etc.," which was like no other declaration to be found in any constitution ever written until then, or since. It was entirely Adams' creation, his original contribution to the constitution of Massachusetts, and he rightly took great pride in it.[2]

Wisdom and knowledge, as well as virtue, diffused generally among the body of the people being necessary for the preservation of their rights and liberties; and as these depend on spreading the opportunities and advantages of education in various parts of the country, and among the different orders of the people, it shall be the duty of legislators and magistrates in all future periods of this commonwealth to cherish the interests of literature and the sciences, and all seminaries of them, especially the university at Cambridge, public schools, and grammar schools in the towns; to encourage private societies and public institutions, rewards and immunities, for the promotion of agriculture, arts, sciences, commerce, trades, manufactures, and a natural history of the country; to countenance and inculcate the principles of humanity and general benevolence, public and private charity, industry and frugality, honesty, punctuality in their dealings, sincerity, good humor, and all social affections, and generous sentiments among the people.[3]

Consider now the statement from the Ohio Constitution regarding public education:

The General Assembly shall make such provisions, by taxation, or otherwise, as with the income arising from the school trust fund, will secure a thorough and efficient system of common schools throughout the state; but no religious or other sect, or sects, shall ever have any exclusive right to, or control of, any part of the school funds of this state.[4]

It is no accident that Ohio has been plagued for decades with controversy about funding its public schools. As this is written (October 2001), the Ohio Supreme Court has ruled that the Ohio legislature must provide equitable funding for Ohio public schools, but that decision has produced a constitutional crisis: the legislature refuses to act, and the courts continue to insist. The governor seeks an arbitrated resolution of the problem.

It may be too simple to say that Ohio's problem is really one of clarifying the purposes of education for Ohio in more noble, inspiring terms than to "secure a thorough and efficient system of common schools throughout the state." We think, though, that if the constitution were modified to couch the purposes of education for Ohio in learning terms rather than economic terms, youth would be better served, and so would the state.

We created two general factors regarding education. One of these factors involved variables related to achievement (i.e., EDUCACHI), and the other factor involved variables related to support of educational efforts (i.e., EDUCSUPP). These two factors are described below.

EDUCATIONAL ACHIEVEMENT

Percent High School Graduates: Percent of persons 25 or older who reported in 1999 that they had graduated from high school is described in Table G.243 in Appendix G under the variable HSGRAD. Data from this variable were included in the general factor EDUCACHI. (Note: We are aware of the fact that these data were self-reported, but there are no other reliable estimates of high school graduation rates from the 50 states that are comparable, since each state defines high school graduation in its own terms.)

Percent College Graduates: Percent of persons 25 or older who reported in 1999 that they had graduated from college is described in Table G.244 in Appendix G under the variable COLLGRAD. Data from this variable were included in the general factor EDUCACHI. (Note: We are aware of the fact that these data were self-reported, but there are no other reliable estimates of college graduation rates from the 50 states that are comparable, since each state defines college graduation in its own terms.)

Percent Enrolled in College: Percent of total population of state enrolled in college, 1997, is described under the variable COLLEGPC in Table G.249 in Appendix G. Data from this variable were included in the general factor EDUCACHI.

Patents per 100,000 Persons: Persons granted a patent have learned—they are educational achievers—regardless of their educational credentials. The number of patents issued to residents of a state in 1998, per 100,000 persons, is described under the variable PATENTPC in Table G.174 in Appendix G. Data from this variable were included in the general factor EDUCACHI.

The data in Appendix G regarding variables that relate to educational achievement as described in these four variables were combined to create a general factor called EDUCACHI. See Appendix B for further information about exactly how we did that. In the next section, we will describe variables that we put together to create factors that relate to support for education.

SUPPORT FOR EDUCATION

We identified nine variables that provided information about how people in each of the 50 states support educational endeavors. We included this information in creating the general factor EDUCSUPP, and that process is described below.

Average Funding per Pupil: Average state and local funding per pupil in elementary and secondary schools is an index of support for education, and information about this support in 1997 is described in Table G.22 in Appendix G under the variable STALOCPP. Data from this variable were included in the general factor called EDUCSUPP.

Per Capita Expenditures for Colleges: Amount of per capita expenditures for public colleges and universities is an index of support for education, and information about this support in 1995–1996 is described in Table G.252 in Appendix G under the variable COLUNIPC. Data from this variable were included in the general factor called EDUCSUPP.

Per Capita Expenditures for Public Schools: Per capita expenditures for elementary and secondary schools in 1995–1996 is an index of support for education, and information about this support is described in Table G.258 in Appendix G under the variable ELESECPC. Data from this variable were included in the general factor called EDUCSUPP.

Support Services per Pupil: Support services per pupil in elementary and secondary schools is an index of support for education, and information about this support in 1998 is described in Table G.24 in Appendix G under the variable SUPSERV. Data from this variable were included in the general factor called EDUCSUPP.

Average Teacher Salary: Average salaries for teachers in elementary and secondary schools is an index of support for education, and information about this support in 1998 is described in Table G.26 in Appendix G under the variable AVRSALRY. Data from this variable were included in the general factor called EDUCSUPP.

Number of Students per Computer in Public Schools: Availability of computers in public elementary and secondary schools is an index of support for education, and information about this support in 1999 is described in Table G.27 in Appendix G under the variable STUMEDIA. Data from this variable were included in the general factor called EDUCSUPP.

Percent Households with Computers: Percent of households with computers is an index of support for education, and information about this support in 2000 is described in Table G.175 in Appendix G under the variable COMPUTER. Data from this variable were included in the general factor called EDUCSUPP.

Percent Households Connected to the Internet: Households connected to the Internet is an index of home support for education, and information about this support in 2000 is described in Table G.176 in Appendix G under the variable INTERNET. Data from this variable were included in the general factor called EDUCSUPP.

Per Capita Dollars for Research and Development by Universities: Per capita research and development expenditures by universities and colleges in 1998 is an index of support for education, and information about this support is described in Table G.180 in Appendix G under the variable RDUNIPC. Data from this variable were included in the general factor called EDUCSUPP.

The data in Appendix G regarding variables that relate to educational support as described in these nine variables were combined to create a general factor called EDUCSUPP. See Appendix B for further information about the way in which we did that. In the next chapter, we will describe variables that we put together to create economic factors.

NOTES

1. Kahlil Gibran, "On Children," in *The Prophet*, quoted in John Bartlett, *Familiar Quotations*, 13th and centennial edition (Boston: Little, Brown, and Company, 1955), 924.
2. David McCullough, *John Adams* (New York: Simon and Schuster, 2001), 222.
3. Constitution of the Commonwealth of Massachusetts, as quoted by McCullough, *John Adams*, 223.
4. Ohio Constitution, Part 6, Section 2, "School Funds."

CHAPTER 8

Economic Factors

Practical men, who believe themselves to be quite exempt from any intellectual influences, are usually the slaves of some defunct economist.

—John Maynard Keynes[1]

INTRODUCTION

"MONEY MAKES THE WORLD GO 'ROUND." WE DOUBT THAT God would agree with that old saying, but we would guess that God might agree that money is an important element in human existence and undertakings.

Governments have a love–hate relationship with money. Those who govern love to collect taxes (that's the way they exercise power), but they also love to profess that taxes are the bane of human existence. The harshest critics of the federal government frequently point to the increasing revenues in the federal till as an indication of federal bureaucracies out of control, not recognizing that federal income correlates precisely with increasing incomes of individuals and corporations. As personal income and corporate profits go up, dollars collected as federal taxes go up, too.

With states the situation is different since most states rely more heavily on property taxes than income taxes. But money is important to states, too, and states work hard to foster economic prosperity for the people and organizations within their borders. Those who govern states want their citizens to "live the good life"; policymakers know that increased income for individuals and corporations means more opportunities for personal and institutional development and growth, thus still more income. The cycle goes on and on, and up and up, if all goes well.

This chapter describes 17 variables identified for further analysis as we work to understand the workings of the states in economic terms. Further information about these and other variables used for analysis is described in Appendix G.

WORK

Percent of Population Who Work in Construction: People who build things—houses, factories, roads—are employed in construction industries. Information about the percent of persons in the state who worked in construction in 2000 is described in Table G.143 in Appendix G under the variable CONSTRPC. Data from this variable were included in the general factor WORK.

Percent of Population Who Work in Manufacturing: People who manufacture things—automobiles, refrigerators, computers—are employed in manufacturing industries. Information about the percent of persons in the state who worked in manufacturing in 2000 is described in Table G.144 in Appendix G under the variable MANUFAPC. Data from this variable were included in the general factor WORK.

Percent of Population Who Work in Transportation and Public Utilities: People who move things, energy, or information—boxes of produce, electricity, sewage, or talk—are employed in transportation or public utilities industries. Information about the percent of persons in the state who worked in transportation and public utilities in 2000 is described in Table G.145 in Appendix G under the variable TRANSPC. Data from this variable were included in the general factor WORK.

Percent of Population Who Work in Trade: People who sell things—clothing, groceries, or hardware—are employed in trade. Information about the percent of persons in the state who worked in trade in 2000 is described in Table G.146 in Appendix G under the variable TRADEPC. Data from this variable were included in the general factor WORK.

Percent of Population Who Work in Finance, Insurance, and Real Estate: People who deal with financial matters or housing—bankers, insurance agents, or real estate agents—are employed in finance-related businesses. Information about the percent of persons in the state who worked in these areas in 2000 is described in Table G.147 in Appendix G under the variable FINANCPC. Data from this variable were included in the general factor WORK.

Percent of Population Who Work in Service: People who provide service—waitresses, physicians, gasoline station attendants—are employed in service industries. Information about the percent of persons in the state who worked in service in 2000 is described in Table G.148 in Appendix G under the variable SERVICPC. Data from this variable were included in the general factor WORK.

Percent of Workers in a Union, 1999: Some states have laws that make it easy for workers to belong to a union. Other states have laws that make it difficult for workers to belong to a union. Information about the percent of workers in the state who were covered by a union in 1999 is described in Table G.160 in Appendix G under the variable PCUNION. Data from this variable were included in the general factor WORK.

Percent of Population Who Work for Government: People who work for any level of government—local, state, or federal—are employed in government. Information about the percent of persons in the state who worked in government in 1999 is described in Table G.142 in Appendix G under the variable GOVFSLPC. Data from this variable were included in the general factor WORK.

Unemployment Weekly Benefits: People who are unemployed are sometimes eligible for benefits of one kind or another. Information about the unemployment insurance average weekly benefits, 1998, is described in Table G.150 in Appendix G under the variable UNEMPAVR. Data from this variable were included in the general factor WORK.

Percent of Labor Force Who Are Male: Information about the percent of males in a state over the age of 16 who participated in the labor force in 1999 is described in Table G.155 in Appendix G under the variable MALABOR. Data from this variable were included in the general factor WORK.

Percent of Labor Force Who Are Female: Information about the percent of females in a state over the age of 16 who participated in the labor force in 1999 is described in Table G.156 in Appendix G under the variable FEMLABOR. Data from this variable were included in the general factor WORK.

Percent of Unemployed Who Were Insured, 1999: Information about the percent of the total population in a state over the age of 16 that participated in the civilian labor force and was unemployed in 1999 but was insured is described in Table G.158 in Appendix G under the variable INSUNEMP. Data from this variable were included in the general factor WORK.

Average Annual Pay, 1998: Information about the average pay for workers covered by state unemployment insurance laws and for federal civilian workers in 1998 is described in Table G.159 in Appendix G under the variable AVRPAY. Data from this variable were included in the general factor WORK.

Per Capita Dollars for Research and Development by Industry, 1998: Per capita research and development expenditures by industries in 1998 is an indication of commitment to improve work opportunities, and information about this support is described in Table G.179 in Appendix G under the variable RDINDPC. Data from this variable were included in the general factor called WORK.

Farm Income per Person, 1998: Per capita income from farming in 1998 is described in Table G.195 in Appendix G under the variable FARMINPP. Data from this variable were included in the general factor called WORK.

Minerals Income per Person, 1999: Per capita income from minerals and mining in 1999 is described in Table G.196 in Appendix G under the variable MINERLPP. Data from this variable were included in the general factor called WORK.

Earnings per Manufacturing Employee, 1996: Table G.198 in Appendix G describes information about the average annual wages in 1996 of manufacturing employees in each state. Data from this variable (MANPEMP) were included in the general factor called WORK.

The data in Appendix G regarding variables that relate to employment opportunities and compensation in these 17 variables were combined to create a general factor called WORK. See Appendix B for further information about how we did that.

In the next section, we describe variables that we put together to create a factor that was related to economic indices.

ECONOMIC

Percent of Population Who Live below Poverty Line, 1998: Information about percent of persons who lived below the poverty line in 1998 is described in Table G.166 in Appendix G under the variable PERBELPV. Data from this variable were included in general factor ECONOMIC.

Percent of Children Who Live below Poverty Line, 1997: Information about the percent of children who lived below the poverty line in 1997 is described in Table G.42 in Appendix G under the variable CHBELPOV. Data from this variable were included in general factor ECONOMIC.

Unemployment Rate, 2000: Information about the percent of persons in the civilian labor force who were unemployed in July 2000 is described in Table G.80 in Appendix G under the variable UNEMRATE. Data from this variable were included in the general factor ECONOMIC.

Per Capita Income, 1999: Information about per capita personal income in each of the states in 1999 is described in Table G.347 in Appendix G under the variable PCINCOME. Data from this variable were included in the general factor ECONOMIC.

Business Failures, 1998: Business failures per 1,000 population in each state is described in Table G.344 in Appendix G under the variable BUSFAIL. Data from this variable were included in the general factor ECONOMIC.

Household Median Income, 1998: Information about the median income for each household of the states in 1998 is described in Table G.165 in Appendix G under the variable MEDINC98. Data from this variable were included in the general factor ECONOMIC.

Retail Sales per Household: Information about retail sales per household in each state for 1998 is described in Table G.199 in Appendix G under the variable RETAIL. Data from this variable were included in the general factor ECONOMIC.

The data in Appendix G regarding variables that related to employment opportunities and compensation in these seven variables were combined to create a general factor called ECONOMIC. See Appendix B for further information about exactly how we did that.

In the next chapter, we summarize information generated through processes described in Chapters 3 through 8 for each of the 50 states, and present that information in three ways: a summary for each state, a "Problems Profile" of each state, and a narrative about each state. After that we will make inferences from all these data, and then describe our general conclusions.

NOTE

1. John Maynard Keynes, *The General Theory of Employment, Interest, and Money* , quoted in John Bartlett, *Familiar Quotations*, 13th and centennial edition (Boston: Little, Brown, and Company, 1955), 925.

CHAPTER 9

SUMMARY Factor and Problems Profiles

If all mankind minus one, were of one opinion, and only one person were of the contrary opinion, mankind would be no more justified in silencing that one person, than he, if he had the power, would be justified in silencing mankind.

—John Stuart Mill[1]

INTRODUCTION

THIS IS A BOOK ABOUT STATES, AND IT PROVIDES EVIDENCE related to how the states solved certain governance problems: crime, infant mortality, taxes, highway fatalities, highway construction, education, incarceration, prison construction, health services, and unemployment, for example.

All states have problems. Some states have more problems and others have fewer problems, but all states have problems. Those problems get dealt with one year, but show up again in future years—as the economy changes, the public mood changes, laws change, or elected officials change—but the reality is that some states have more problems than others. It is that "more" and "less" that we will try to describe in this chapter.

As we moved through this study of cultures of the states, we eventually produced a ranking of the 50 states, according to what each state had done over many years, to solve the governance problems it had confronted over time. Rather than talking about "good states" or "bad states," however, we elected to analyze the data in ways that would rank all states according to number and kinds of problems they faced instead of using laudatory or pejorative terminology to describe where each state stood in relation to all the other states. Critics can pick the "best movies" or the "best universities" or the "best communities in which to live," and leave those at the other end of the continuum unidentified. Researchers cannot do that. We felt compelled to describe "the whole ball of wax," so to speak, but we wanted to do it without commendation or condemnation; just according to the facts.

States exist. They are a part of our system of governance. Some states have been more effective or more creative in using their power to cope with problems over the years. Other states have been less effective or less creative. All states, however, have faced and will continue to face problems of various kinds. It is where each state stands in relation to problems confronted at the new millennium that we hope to describe.

The tragedies of September 11, 2001, are well known. Those events dramatically affected federal, state, and lo-cal governments across the United States. All data in the present project were collected before September 11, 2001; thus this information is somewhat out of date. The stability of governments, though, is a reality. The picture presented here is generally valid.

The technical details about how we produced the final ranking of states are described in Chapters 3 through 8 and Appendix B. For now it may be sufficient to know that we used data from 120 variables that were organized into 15 factors, which enabled us to generate a summation score that we labeled SUMMARY factor (i.e., we simply summed the 15 factor scores for each state to produce a SUMMARY score for each state). The data in SUMMARY factor allowed us to identify states with more problems and states with fewer problems, and the table that presents the ranking according to problems is described below.

We also present a "Problems Profile" for each of the 50 states. Each profile depicts the relationship of that state with the other 49 states on SUMMARY, and the relationship of that state with the other 49 states on each of the 15 general factors that are described in Appendix B, "Methodology: Words and Numbers." With the Problems Profile, we give a brief narrative description of that state based on some numbers included in the 15 general factors, and some numbers not included in those 15 factors.

A word or two about how to interpret the information on the pages that follow. First, Table G.702 depicts the SUMMARY values or scores for each state. The SUMMARY score is based on a summation of the 15 factor scores. The 15 factors include information on 120 variables, as described at various places in this book. Higher SUMMARY scores mean that those states have more problems; lower SUMMARY scores mean that those states have fewer problems. Note also that the SUMMARY table represents a continuum, showing exactly where each state is in relationship to the other states on the summation of the 15 factor scores.

On the pages following, there is a Problems Profile and narrative for each state which show detailed information about the 15 factor scores and the SUMMARY score for that state. Four things might be pointed out about the Problems Profile for each state.

First, the 15 factors are listed down the left-hand side of the table (i.e., Government, Expended, Crime, Protection, Punishment, and the like). Each of the 15 factors was described in detail in earlier chapters and in the

Table G.702. SUMMARY

SUMMARY Factor Based on Summation of 15 General Factor Scores

544.81	Mississippi
533.54	Arkansas
531.90	Louisiana
505.93	Tennessee
502.30	South Carolina
499.44	Oklahoma
493.89	Alabama
490.34	Texas
486.53	Florida
476.91	Arizona
467.84	Nevada
461.90	Kentucky
458.12	Georgia
449.29	New Mexico
447.44	West Virginia
441.97	North Carolina
414.37	Missouri
397.41	Idaho
396.11	Indiana
392.83	South Dakota
381.56	Montana
369.69	Michigan
369.41	California
367.02	Ohio
366.68	Delaware
366.64	Pennsylvania
358.24	Oregon
353.16	Virginia
347.27	North Dakota
345.71	Illinois
344.25	New York
343.92	Alaska
340.10	Rhode Island
336.20	Kansas
335.21	Maryland
325.31	Wyoming
325.29	Colorado
323.67	Hawaii
317.54	Utah
313.99	Washington
309.60	Maine
309.23	Nebraska
305.37	New Jersey
294.09	Iowa
279.22	Wisconsin
278.62	Connecticut
271.13	New Hampshire
257.07	Vermont
251.01	Massachusetts
245.94	Minnesota

methodology section (Appendix B), and variables were placed together in logical categories to make up each factor. The first factor, GOVERNMT (for government), included such variables as taxes paid to all levels of government, per capita state and local taxes, and federal funds per person returned to the state, among others.

Second, the actual factor scores are listed down the right-hand side of the table, opposite the factor name. Recall that factor scores are arithmetical means of all RANKed variables in that factor. For further information about these computations, see Appendix B on methodology.

Third, the continuum running from left to right across the table for each factor has 100 dots (i.e., periods, points of ink), which make a space two dots in length for each of the 50 states. The large "O" on that continuum represents where that particular state falls on that factor, compared to all of the other states.

Fourth, another continuum running from left to right across the bottom of the table describes the same information regarding SUMMARY factor (i.e., where the state portrayed in a given Problems Profile actually stands in relation to all of the other states). This continuum is the same as that represented in the listing from bottom to top in Table G.702, and it shows the same relative position of a given state to other states that Table G.702 shows, except Table G.702 has been turned on its side, so to speak.

In one sense, Table G.702 is a composite score, comparable to the Dow Jones Industrials Average, the Gross National Product, or the Inflation Index, all of which summarize diverse information into one whole number intended to be meaningful and comparable to users. Other researchers might select different variables to be included in any such composite score, but we think that we based our summation on diverse variables representing unique factors, and the fact that there are 120 variables gives both breadth and depth to the quantification, as well as stability.

One other point. To "round out" the numerical perspective, we have also prepared a narrative for each state. Some of the information in the narrative was drawn from tables in "Rankings of the States" in Appendix G that were not included in the 120 variables melded into the 15 factors, then into the SUMMARY factor that has been described. Our intention is to provide more information about each state than is subsumed in the factor scores.

The Problems Profiles were designed to display information at a glance regarding each state's position relative to other states, in terms of the kinds of problems that states grapple with in governance on a day-to-day basis.

Please see Appendix A for a detailed description of the state with the fewest problems. The paper is something of a historical review of the last half century of that state, and how political and civic leaders worked together to develop governance policies and procedures that would promote human and economic development in that state: Minnesota.

STATE OF ALABAMA PROBLEMS PROFILE

Alabama was admitted to the Union as a state in 1819, but seceded from the Union in 1861, when the Civil War began. Following that war, the legislature refused to ratify the Fourteenth Amendment to the U.S. Constitution, and the state was placed under military rule in 1867. It

Alabama Problems Profile

Factor	< Fewer Problems	More Problems >	Factor Score
Government	....O.................		30.13
Expended	....O....................		26.71
Crime	....O..................		28.44
Protection	....O...................		27.90
Punishment	....O...................		27.18
Natural Death	....O....		40.08
Highway Fatalities	....O.....		34.95
Traumatic Death	....O...................		34.25
Health	....O......		35.38
Medical Coverage	....O...........		31.88
Teen Problems	....O........		37.11
School Achievement	....O.........		36.75
Educational Support	....O.........		36.11
Work/Employment	....O...........		31.88
Economic Factor	....O..........		35.14
SUMMARY	....O...........		493.89

was readmitted to the Union in 1868. Alabama occupies an area of 51,609 square miles, and in 2000 had a population of approximately 4.4 million residents. About 86 persons per square mile live in the state, placing it mid-range among the 50 states in terms of population density. Approximately 71 percent of the residents live in a metropolitan area of the state, also placing the state about the middle of the 50 states in that respect.

More than 70 percent of the citizens of Alabama are adherents to the Christian faith, putting the state almost at the very top of other states on that variable, and 70 percent own their home, again putting the state well toward the top of all states. Only 3.14 percent of women and 1.43 percent of minorities own business firms, however, putting the state in the bottom tenth of all states on those variables. Death rates from all causes for white women, white men, and black men are in the top tenth of all states, and death rates from all causes for black women are in the top fifth of all states. Death rates for white men and black men from auto fatalities are in the top tenth of all states.

Alabama has more bankruptcies, per capita, than 46 other states, and higher infant mortality rates for whites than 48 other states. The state spends less per capita of the total budget for the state's justice system than 40 other states, and less for the judicial portion of the justice system than 39 other states, although in crimes it ranks fifth for robberies accomplished with a gun.

The state has a higher percentage of citizens who are black than 44 other states, but it has fewer minorities by actual count than 16 other states. Residents consume less alcohol, per capita, than residents of more than 40 other states, and the tax rate (i.e., the proportion of all personal income that goes for taxes) is also less than 40 other states.

Some of the data reported here were about variables in Appendix G not included in developing the Problems Profile table, where it is obvious that Alabama's profile crowds the "more problems" side of the profile.

A sign outside Montgomery, Alabama, proclaims:

Welcome to Montgomery
Birthplace of the Civil War
and Civil Rights
Come to Where It All Began

Alabama's citizens are engaged in serious debate about whether and how to revise the state constitution as this is being written (November 2001), and the debate has both focus and fury as well as facts and hyperbole. The data in this book suggest a need for changes in governance policies and procedures in Alabama.

STATE OF ALASKA PROBLEMS PROFILE

Alaska was admitted to the Union as a state in 1959, during President Eisenhower's administration. The land, originally purchased from Russia in 1867, includes 586,400 square miles of territory, making it the largest of all the 50 states. The population was slightly over half a million persons at the most recent census (2000)—619,500—and the state has the least dense population of all the states, just over one person per square mile, compared to 1,098 persons per square mile in New Jersey and 100 persons per square mile in Kentucky.

Alaska has one of the highest child abuse rates in the nation, but it is in the middle third of states in terms of average starting salary for teachers. It has the smallest proportion of people over 65 years of age (less than 1 percent), second highest proportion under 18 years of age (almost 32 percent), and a higher percentage of blacks than Arizona, Washington, West Virginia, Minnesota, New Mexico, Iowa, Oregon, and 10 other states. Alaska ranks third out of 50 states in number of persons per household, but 45th in terms of percent who own their own home. It is one of the 15 fastest growing states in the Union, and has the fourth highest median household income. Alaska ranks fourth in alcohol consumption per capita, and first in terms of the percent of a state's population in treatment

Alaska Problems Profile

Factor	< Fewer Problems ———— More Problems >	Factor Score
Government	............................O................................	24.13
Expended	O..	10.00
Crime	....O....................	34.94
Protection	..........O..	18.60
Punishment	....................O......................................	23.55
Natural Death	.O...	5.92
Highway Fatalities	..............................O............................	27.86
Traumatic Death	....................................O......	42.75
Health	.......................O..................................	30.13
Medical Coverage	...........................O..............................	29.56
Teen Problems	....................O......................................	23.17
School Achievement	..............................O............................	26.13
Educational Support	O..	6.00
Work/Employment	...........O..	22.06
Economic Factor	............O...	19.14
SUMMARY	...............O..	343.92

for drugs or alcohol abuse. In terms of tax revenues derived from sales of tobacco and alcohol, Alaska is ranked number two in the nation.

In terms of crimes per person, Alaska stands almost exactly in the center of the states, but it is in the top 10 percent in terms of incarcerated prisoners per thousand. Alaska has executed no persons for crimes since it became a state. The state is highest in terms of per capita expenditures for total state and local justice systems, and in terms of justice costs for judicial and legal charges and for corrections, although it is fourth highest in robberies with a knife and assaults with a knife. Alaska has the highest rape rate in the nation, and was 11th highest in assault rates in 1998. In terms of births to teenage mothers who smoked, Alaska was eighth in the nation. The state is sixth highest in terms of percent minority firms, and lowest in terms of bankruptcies as percent of the population. Alaska ranks fifth in terms of justice system payrolls devoted to judicial and legal costs, but 41st in terms of justice system funds devoted to police protection.

Gasoline prices in Alaska are second highest (below Hawaii) in the nation, but gasoline taxes are second lowest (only Georgia is lower). In federal Highway Trust Fund grants per capita, Alaska leads the nation. Alaska is 49th among the states in terms of adherents to the Christian faith, 30th in abortion rates per 1,000 population, and 50th in death rates from diabetes and pulmonary problems, but the state is second highest in suicide rates, just below Nevada. Alaska has few physicians per 100,000 population (i.e., 167), standing 48th out of 50 states, and is fifth highest in tuberculosis rates in the country. The state stands 16th in terms of per capita disposable income and fourth in terms of risk for being overweight.

Alaska consistently ranks toward the top of all 50 states in terms of expenditures per capita of both state and federal funds.

STATE OF ARIZONA PROBLEMS PROFILE

After the Mexican War, Arizona was ceded as part of New Mexico to the United States in 1848. The Gadsden

Arizona Problems Profile

Factor	< Fewer Problems ———— More Problems >	Factor Score
Government	.............................O...........................	29.75
Expended	....O....	35.14
Crime	....O.....	41.13
Protection	..........................O..............................	31.50
Punishment	...............................O........................	36.18
Natural Death	..............O...	15.25
Highway Fatalities	.....................................O..................	30.18
Traumatic Death	.....................................O......	43.00
Health	.....................O..................................	23.94
Medical Coverage	.....................................O....	37.88
Teen Problems	.....................................O......	39.00
School Achievement	....................O...................................	21.25
Educational Support	..............................O.........................	31.67
Work/Employment	...........................O............................	27.62
Economic Factor	............................O...........................	33.43
SUMMARY	............................O...........................	476.91

Purchase, an area south of the Gila River, was added in 1853. Arizona was admitted to the Union in 1912. In the early years of statehood, Arizona was the site of labor disputes involving copper mine owners and those who wanted to organize workers in the mines. In 1963, the Supreme Court of the United States settled a dispute between Arizona and California over use of the waters of the Colorado River, which led to cooperation among all states of the Colorado River Basin. Most of the state is either arid or semiarid. The population of Arizona in 2000 was slightly in excess of five million persons, and 88 percent of the population lives in a metropolitan area.

Arizona ranks very low (i.e., 50th) in terms of total dollars devoted to each student in public schools, and in terms of average teacher salary (i.e., 39th), but higher in terms of average starting salary for teachers (i.e., 18th). Arizona is among the highest states in terms of percent of population under 18 years of age, but in the middle range of states in terms of percent of population over 65 years of age, percent white, and number of persons per household. Almost 23 percent of its residents (i.e., ranked fourth) are of Hispanic origin, but the state ranks low (i.e., 41st) in percent minority firms. Arizona ranks second among states in terms of its increase in population and third in increasing employment opportunities, 30th in terms of median household income, but in the upper third of states in terms of percent of the population below the poverty line. Increase in median income in the state was $2,339 during the 1990s (19th in the nation). Arizona ranks third in the nation in crimes per person, and in the upper fifth in terms of prisoners per 1,000 population. Arizona stands 11th among states in terms of the average number of violent crimes between 1960 and 1998, but its rate is about half of the New York state rate for that same period. However, Arizona had the highest average number of property crimes per population of any of the 50 states during that same period.

Death rates of white women and black women from all causes are in the lowest third of states, although death rates of white men and black men from all causes are in the middle range of states. Death rates from heart disease and cancer are in the lowest quartile, although death rates from pulmonary disease, suicides, accidents, and auto fatalities are much higher. The cost of automobile insurance is among the top 10 in the nation, and 43 percent of fatal accidents involve alcohol. Dollars per Medicare enrollee and Medicaid recipient are among the lowest third of states. Arizona has half as many physicians per 100,000 as Massachusetts, and the state has the highest percentage of children with no health insurance.

Arizona is fifth in the nation in percent of births to unmarried women, and twelfth in terms of infant mortality among whites, but midrange in terms of infant mortality per 1,000 births. The state is in the lowest third of states in terms of females who smoke, in the highest tenth of states in terms of children ages 5 to 17 who are in poverty, but spending per capita for problems associated with substance abuse is low, compared to other states.

STATE OF ARKANSAS PROBLEMS PROFILE

Arkansas was admitted to the Union in 1836, and today has slightly more than 2.5 million residents. The state has 53,104 square miles, but is the smallest state west of the Mississippi, except for Hawaii. By the time Arkansas became a state, all land titles to Indian tribes had been withdrawn by Congress. Arkansas was a slave state, but did not secede from the Union until May 1861, five months after South Carolina seceded. Little Rock fell to federal troops in 1863. Arkansas was readmitted to the Union in 1868, and was severely jeopardized economically by the consequences of the war. The state was further handicapped by the collapse of state credit in 1885, and it experienced slow economic development for the next half century.

Arkansas Problems Profile

Factor	< Fewer Problems	More Problems >	Factor Score
Government	....O		39.00
Expended	...............O...		18.57
Crime	.......................O.......................................		22.13
Protection	....................................O.........................		29.30
Punishment	....................................O.........................		30.36
Natural Death	....O..		44.25
Highway Fatalities	..............................O...............................		28.09
Traumatic Death	....O.....................		42.00
Health	.....................................O....		38.50
Medical Coverage	..................................O.........		34.00
Teen Problems	....................................O....		40.22
School Achievement	....O		47.50
Educational Support	....O..		42.78
Work/Employment	.................................O.......		33.76
Economic Factor	......................................O....		43.07
SUMMARY	....O..		533.54

Arkansas is in the top fifth of the nation in terms of child abuse, and the lowest tenth (i.e., 45th) for average funding per pupil in the public schools of the nation. The state is about average in terms of the number of students per computer in the schools. More than one quarter of the population is under the age of 18, but the state is among the top ten states in terms of percent of population over 65 years of age. Sixteen percent of the population is black, and over 80 percent is white, but Arkansas is among the lowest of states (i.e., 45th) in terms of percent of minority-owned firms. There are few Hispanics in Arkansas (i.e., less than 2 percent). Almost 70 percent of the residents own their own home, but more than 17 percent live below the poverty line, and more than 25 percent of children live below the poverty line. Only two states have a smaller percentage of households with computers than Arkansas.

The state stands high (i.e., fourth) among states in terms of the number of murders per people who work in local government, and it is in the upper fourth in terms of executions since 1950. Arkansas is 44th in terms of dollars spent in operating costs to keep a prisoner in prison. The prison population in the state has increased more slowly than 42 other states in recent years.

Arkansas has the sixth highest death rate from all causes for white women and the eleventh highest death rate for black women of the 50 states, but the state is fourth highest for white women and second highest for black women for death from automobile accidents. The pattern is similar for white men and black men. The state stands low (i.e., rank of 47th) in terms of deaths from alcohol for white men, but much higher (i.e., rank of 10th) for black men.

Arkansas has the fourth highest percentage of persons working in manufacturing, but the state stands low in terms of the percentage of persons working in government, construction, trade, or finance. It also has among the lowest proportions of both males and females in the labor force. Regarding personal income per capita, Arkansas ranks 47th among the states, and 48th in terms of household median income, although the state stands seventh in terms of bankruptcies as a percent of the population. Median income decreased in Arkansas between 1990 and 1998, and the state had the fewest patents per population of any of the 50 states. Research and development funds, per capita, for both industry and universities, are among the lowest in the nation.

Arkansas is at the midpoint in the rankings of states in terms of per capita expenditures for public schools but in the upper fourth of states for such expenditures for higher education, over a 12-year period, 1989 to 2000.

STATE OF CALIFORNIA PROBLEMS PROFILE

California has the largest population of any of the 50 states; more than 33 million residents were accounted for by the 2000 census query. Ceded to the United States as part of a larger territory after Mexico signed the Treaty of Guadeloupe Hidalgo in 1848, California was admitted to the Union as a free (i.e., nonslavery) state in 1850. Statehood followed the influx of people to the state after gold was discovered in 1848, and California almost doubled in population every 10 years during the century after its acceptance into the Union. The state includes 158,693 square miles and is a major agricultural region of the United States.

California is among the top 10 states for research and development activities funded by industry, and is in the top third of states for research and development activities funded by universities. The state also leads the nation in number of marijuana plants eradicated by officials, bulk-processed marijuana seized during 1999, and number of persons arrested for possession of marijuana that year. California is midrange among states in terms of proportsion of the state's population in treatment for drug or alcohol abuse, but it has the smallest percent of clients in

California Problems Profile

Factor	< Fewer Problems More Problems >	Factor Score
Government	......O..	14.50
Expended	....................................O......................	27.29
Crime	....O......	40.88
Protection	...........................O......................	22.00
Punishment	...................................O..............	31.14
Natural Death	....O..	7.92
Highway Fatalities	........O..	22.09
Traumatic Death	......O..	8.75
Health	...........................O..........................	25.00
Medical Coverage	......................................O........	35.06
Teen Problems	...........................O....................	25.17
School Achievement	...............O....................................	19.00
Educational Support	........................O....................	28.00
Work/Employment	................................O............	26.76
Economic Factor	...................................O..............	35.86
SUMMARY	....................O..........................	369.41

treatment for alcohol abuse. California is among the top five states in terms of its violent crime rate average for the years 1960 to 1998, as it is for property crime rates for the same period. The state is seventh among states in terms of the percent of children ages 5 through 17 who live below the poverty line. It is among the 10 lowest states in terms of expenditures for pupils in public schools, and has more students per computer in public schools than any other state.

California ranks second among the 50 states for tuberculosis cases for 1,000 residents, but 41st for the percent of males who smoke and 48th for the percent of females who smoke. The state ranks 10th for AIDS cases per population, and third highest for the percent of persons who have no health insurance. California is second highest (after Texas) for total traffic fatalities among the states, but ranks 44th among states for traffic fatalities per population.

The state receives about $5,000 per person in federal funds returned to the state, ranking it in the lower third of all 50 states. California is third highest (after Hawaii and New Mexico) in percent of minorities living within the state, and it ranks sixth in terms of percent minority firms in the state. The state ranks 40th in terms of percent of population that works for government, 46th in percent that works in trade, but midrange in terms of the proportion that works in finance and service. California has a higher proportion of workers covered by a union than 35 other states, and more bankruptcies per person than 39 other states. Median income rose $1,339 in California between 1990 and 1998, and only seven states had more patents issued per 100,000 population.

In terms of retail sales per household, California ranks 41st among the 50 states, and it is second in terms of percent of residents who live in a metropolitan area. The state is among the lowest 10 states in terms of percent of the population that adheres to the Christian faith, and it ranks fourth among states in terms of abortion rates per 1,000 population. More than 40 other states rank higher than California in terms of children born with low birth weights. The state also ranks 43rd or lower in terms of infant mortality rates, adult death rates from diabetes, death rates from accidents, and death rates by suicide.

STATE OF COLORADO PROBLEMS PROFILE

Colorado was part of the Louisiana Territory, which was purchased from France in 1803. Zebulon Pike was dispatched to map and explore the territory in 1806. Gold was discovered in 1859, leading to a large influx of people to the area. Congressional legislation was passed in 1861 which provided for administrative officials to be appointed by the president, and seven governors were appointed during the next 15 years, but none ever served the full term of the appointment. Colorado was admitted to the Union in 1876.

There were slightly more than four million residents in Colorado in 2000. The state ranks sixth in the nation in terms of high school graduates, and first in terms of college graduates, but in the lowest 10 in total dollars per student spent on education. The state is in the upper third of states with percent of residents under 18 years of age, but 47th in terms of persons over 65 years of age. More than 90 percent of Colorado's residents are white, less than five percent black, but Colorado ranks seventh among states in terms of percent Hispanic. The state is among the lowest 10 states regarding percent of home owners, and 49th in terms of number of persons per household. Colorado was fifth highest in percent population change; it ranked 12th in median household income and eighth in terms of disposable income.

Colorado was midrange among the 50 states in terms of robberies, murder, burglaries, larcenies, and assaults, but eighth in the nation in terms of rape rates. The state also stands midrange in terms of percent of population in prison, cost per person in the state to fund prisons, and the percent of persons in the state who work for

Colorado Problems Profile

Factor	< Fewer Problems	More Problems >	Factor Score
Government	........O..		14.00
Expended	....O..		37.14
Crime	....O............................		33.13
Protection	....O................................		27.70
Punishment	............................O..		23.23
Natural Death	....O..		6.08
Highway Fatalities	....................O..		22.14
Traumatic Death	....O............................		31.00
Health	..............................O..		22.31
Medical Coverage	....O............................		29.13
Teen Problems	........................O..		23.06
School Achievement	O..		6.50
Educational Support	....................O..		17.67
Work/Employment	..O..		15.00
Economic Factor	....................O..		17.21
SUMMARY	....................O..		325.29

government. Colorado ranks in the upper quintile in terms of both white and black males and white females for suicides, and for alcohol-related deaths, but in the lower quintile for deaths from all causes, including malignancies and heart disease. The state stands midrange among states in terms of traffic fatalities per population and average number of automobile thefts in 1998, but seventh in property crimes per population between 1960 and 1998.

In terms of the total justice system, Colorado ranks midrange among the 50 states in percent of state and local government funds devoted to the total justice system, justice system employees, police protection employees, judicial and legal expenditures, total personnel in state law enforcement agencies, sworn state police officers, corrections costs, and prisoners per 100,000 population. Colorado ranks 10th in terms of the proportion of income paid in taxes to all levels of government.

Colorado ranks in the lowest fourth of states for percent births to unmarried teenagers, but in the top 10 states in terms of teenagers who gave birth who had inadequate prenatal care. The state ranks midrange for teenagers who had abortions, and for teenagers who gave birth and smoked in 1995. Colorado ranked sixth among the 50 states in terms of alcohol consumption per capita, but in the lowest third of states in which traffic fatalities involved any alcohol. The state ranked 49th in percent of persons at risk for being overweight.

STATE OF CONNECTICUT PROBLEMS PROFILE

The State of Connecticut was one of the 13 original English colonies in America. Although it is 48th in terms of physical size (i.e., 5,009 square miles), its 3.4 million residents make it the 29th largest state in population and fourth in population density, with 677 persons per square mile within the state. In all, 96 percent of the state's population lives in a metropolitan area; thus Connecticut is highly urban, but because it has no extremely large city, the crowded urban areas common in most other states are less in evidence than in other states. Slavery was abolished by law in 1848.

Connecticut ranks 25th among the states in terms of the number of crimes per person committed in the state. It ranks 42nd in percent of population that works in local government, but 30th in terms of persons who work for local, state, or national government. The state has executed six persons since 1950, and the number of persons in prison per population places it in the top quintile of states. Connecticut is sixth among the 50 states in terms of operating costs per inmate in prison. Almost 13 percent of all state and local government costs are devoted to total justice system expenditures (i.e., ranks 12th), but only 15 percent of those expenditures are devoted to judicial and legal costs (i.e., ranks 47th), whereas more than 31 percent (i.e., 20th) are devoted to corrections. Ten percent of all robberies in 1998 were committed with a knife.

The death rate of black males (i.e., 866 per 100,000 persons) puts Connecticut at 30th out of 50 states on that variable, but the state ranks in the lowest quartile of states for death rates of white females (i.e., 338) and black females (i.e., 497) for all deaths, including suicides. The state ranks generally low for automobile deaths for all persons (i.e., 46th). Connecticut is ranked 25th among states in terms of infant mortality rates, but fourth in terms of physicians per population. Fewer than 10 percent of the children have no health insurance. Just over 20 percent of both males and females smoke cigarettes. Connecticut ranked 43rd in birth rates for all females ages 15 through 19 in 1996, but 30th in terms of birth rates for the same age black females.

Connecticut ranks 46th in percent of workers involved in construction, but 14th in manufacturing, second in finance, and sixth in service. The state ranks ninth

Connecticut Problems Profile

Factor	< Fewer Problems	More Problems >	Factor Score
Government	..........O...		14.13
Expended	...........O..		16.43
Crime	......................O.................................		19.38
Protection	...........O..		13.80
Punishment	....O..........		29.00
Natural Death	.............................O..........................		25.42
Highway Fatalities	........................O...............................		23.00
Traumatic Death	...............O..		8.00
Health	..........................O.............................		19.19
Medical Coverage	....O...............		28.19
Teen Problems	..................O.....................................		18.56
School Achievement	...................O....................................		19.00
Educational Support	...........O..		14.78
Work/Employment	..................O.....................................		21.91
Economic Factor	O..		7.86
SUMMARY	........O...		278.62

in percent of workers who belong to a union, first in personal income per capita, seventh in household median income, and second in terms of patents issued per 100,000 population. Connecticut had the highest gasoline tax (36 cents per gallon) among the 50 states in 1998. People in the state pay the largest proportion of income in taxes to all levels of government of any of the 50 states, but have the highest per capita income after all taxes are paid.

Connecticut ranks 31st in terms of high school graduates, but fourth for expenditures per pupil in public schools. The state ranks third of the 50 states in terms of college graduates, but 40th in terms of percent enrolled in college, suggesting that the state's economy attracts college graduates from other states. Per capita expenditures for colleges, in fact, place Connecticut 48th among the 50 states. The state ranks 12th in terms of abortion rates, eighth in terms of households connected to the Internet, and 48th in terms of children who are not immunized.

STATE OF DELAWARE PROBLEMS PROFILE

Delaware was the first of the original 13 American states to ratify the Constitution of the United States. It is the second smallest state in the Union, after Rhode Island, with 2,057 square miles of territory. The state has about 750,000 residents, but ranks sixth in the nation in terms of population density, with more than 385 persons per square mile. A Southern state, Delaware did not secede from the Union when the Civil War began; its economic ties were to the North, primarily with and through Pennsylvania, although the state never voted for Lincoln.

Delaware has the fourth highest birthrate among black teenagers, 18th highest among all females ages 15 through 19, and among still younger teens (i.e., 15–17) the state ranks tenth, but is in the lowest quartile of births to teens who have inadequate prenatal care. However,

Delaware ranks second in terms of gonorrhea rates among teenagers.

In 1998, Delaware ranked eighth of the 50 states in terms of violent crime (i.e., murder, assault, rape, and robbery) and 14th in property crime (i.e., burglary, larceny, and motor vehicle theft). The state ranks second in terms of the number of crimes committed per person in government, immediately below Hawaii. In terms of murder rate for the state over a 39-year period, however, Delaware stands almost in the middle of the 50 states. It stands much higher (i.e., rank of 4th) in terms of rape rates over that same period of time. It is in the lowest third of states in arson rates.

Delaware ranks third among the 50 states in terms of alcohol consumed, per capita, but 32nd in highway fatalities, which decreased 18 percent between 1975 and 1999, even though it was sixth highest in terms of passengers killed who wore no seatbelt. The state was fifth highest in terms of percent of deaths on motorcycles in which the rider wore a helmet, although there were only seven such deaths in the state that year (i.e., 1999). Automobile insurance costs were fifth highest in the nation.

Delaware is in the top quartile of states in terms of per capita disposable income, and fifth in the nation in per capita taxes paid to state government. Delaware ranks eighth in terms of proportion of income paid in taxes to federal, state, and local governments, and 10th for per capita expenditures for police protection.

Delaware stands below the median in terms of percent of high school graduates, and at the median in terms of college graduates among its citizens, but sixth for number of patents per 100,000 population. Delaware ranks fourth among the 50 states in starting salary for teachers, and 32nd for children not immunized.

The state is 44th in terms of people under 18 years of age, but 25th among states for people over 65 years of

Delaware Problems Profile

Factor	< Fewer Problems	More Problems >	Factor Score
Government	........O.......		17.25
Expended	.......O........		20.29
Crime		.......O.......	31.50
Protection		....O.......	26.00
Punishment		........O......	32.50
Natural Death		...O........	29.83
Highway Fatalities		..O.........	25.50
Traumatic Death		..O.........	24.75
Health		......O......	31.25
Medical Coverage		....O.......	28.44
Teen Problems		...O........	33.67
School Achievement		........O......	18.88
Educational Support	...O.......		14.11
Work/Employment	....O.......		19.29
Economic Factor	...O.......		13.43
SUMMARY		....O........	366.68

age. About 78 percent of the population is white and 20 percent black, with a very small percentage of Hispanics. The state ranks 40th in terms of percent of minority-owned firms and 36th in terms of women-owned firms. More than 70 percent of Delaware residents own their own home, placing them among the top 10 states on that variable, and the state is third highest in terms of retail sales per capita.

STATE OF FLORIDA PROBLEMS PROFILE

General Andrew Jackson captured Pensacola during the War of 1812, and Florida became part of the United States in a treaty signed in 1819 and ratified in 1821. Florida was admitted to the Union in 1845 as the 27th state, following a war with the Seminole Indians, which lasted from 1835 to 1842. That war came after efforts to remove the Indians to Oklahoma and after centuries of peace with the Spanish. Florida was part of the Confederacy during the Civil War, but there was very little fighting in the state during that era. There are 58,560 square miles within the boundaries of the state.

Florida has almost 16 million residents, according to the 2000 census report, making it the fourth most populous state in the nation after California, Texas, and New York. In all, 68 percent of Florida's population is white and 32 percent of residents are minorities, about half of whom are black. Florida ranks number one among states in percentage of persons over 65, and 47th in terms of persons under 18 years of age. More than 60,000 immigrants were admitted to Florida in 1998, making it third in the nation on immigration.

Farm income per person in the state was about $150, less than one tenth the farm income per person in South Dakota, but Florida still ranked 25th in the nation on that variable. Florida ranked 19th in per capita disposable income in 1999 ($23,981), but 31st in percent of per capita income for all taxes paid: federal, state, and local. In terms of taxes paid to state government, Florida ranked

46th in the nation, paying $113.30 per person. Only Washington, Texas, Nevada, and South Dakota residents paid less.

Florida ranked second in property crimes over a 39-year period, and second in violent crimes during that same period of time. In terms of assault and burglary, Florida ranked first out of 50 states for the 1960–1998 time period in both of those crimes, and second in larceny. In terms of percent of state and local government funds devoted to total justice system, Florida ranked first in the nation; in terms of total justice system employees and corrections employees per 10,000 population in 1995, Florida ranked third in the nation.

Among teenagers, Florida ranked 28th in the nation in terms of the percent births to unmarried, non-Hispanic whites and 21st in percent births of unmarried, non-Hispanic blacks. It was 24th in ranking of teenagers who gave birth with inadequate prenatal care in 1996. It was 39th in terms of teenage mothers who gave birth and smoked in 1995, and 16th in terms of birth rates among all females, ages 15 to 19, in 1996.

Although most states have had declining traffic fatalities in the 25 years between 1975 and 1999, Florida's highway death rates have gone up 46 percent, making it fourth highest in the nation, after Mississippi, Nevada, and Arizona. More than 56 percent of passenger car occupants killed in auto accidents did not wear a seatbelt. Florida ranked fourth in the nation in terms of alcohol consumption per capita in 1998, but 33rd in traffic fatalities in which any alcohol was involved, and the state ranked second in percentage of large trucks in the United States in 1999.

STATE OF GEORGIA PROBLEMS PROFILE

Georgia is the largest state east of the Mississippi River (58,876 square miles), and the last of the 13 original English colonies that formed the United States. The colony was founded in 1732 by General James

Florida Problems Profile

Factor	< Fewer Problems	More Problems >	Factor Score
Government	.................................O................................		25.75
Expended	....O............		32.00
Crime	....O....		42.69
Protection	............................O........................		27.60
Punishment	......................................O.......		38.50
Natural Death	......................................O.......		40.00
Highway Fatalities	..................................O..........		30.50
Traumatic Death	.............................O.................		30.00
Health	..............................O................		31.63
Medical Coverage	..................................O............		32.75
Teen Problems	..............................O................		31.00
School Achievement	.................................O.............		36.75
Educational Support	..................................O...........		32.17
Work/Employment	..................................O...........		30.56
Economic Factor	.........................O.....................		24.64
SUMMARY	..................................O............		486.53

Georgia Problems Profile

Factor	< Fewer Problems More Problems >	Factor Score
Government	...............O...	20.88
Expended	....O.............	32.14
Crime	....................................O...................	36.25
Protection	....O....	37.90
Punishment	....O..	41.55
Natural Death	...........O...	16.67
Highway Fatalities	..............................O........................	28.77
Traumatic Death	...........................O..........................	28.25
Health	.................................O.....................	33.19
Medical Coverage	...............................O.......................	30.00
Teen Problems	......................................O.......	38.78
School Achievement	....O........	39.25
Educational Support	.........................O............................	28.11
Work/Employment	...............O......................................	23.32
Economic Factor	...............O......................................	23.07
SUMMARY	.....................................O.................	458.12

Oglethorpe, who hoped to provide poor people from England with a new start in life. Georgia seceded from the Union in 1861, but northern Georgia never supported secession. The state provided regiments to the Confederacy, but civil leadership in the state was divided throughout the Civil War.

Georgia is the 10th most populous state in the nation, with more than eight million residents, of whom 69 percent are white and 29 percent are black. Less than 2 percent of minorities own business firms, and less than 4 percent of business firms are owned by women. Approximately 65 percent of Georgia's citizens own their own home, with the state ranking 37th among states on that variable. About 15 percent of the residents live below the poverty line.

In 1998, Georgia ranked 12th in the nation in murders per 1,000 population, 19th in assaults, 29th in rapes, 9th in robberies, and 13th in burglaries. The state ranks 40th in terms of the money it spends to operate prisons for inmates. Those expenses to operate prisons cost each person in the state of Georgia $72 per year. There were 122 prisoners in the state who were executed between 1950 and 2000.

Approximately 200,000 Georgians are engaged in construction work, 600,000 in manufacturing, 265,000 in transportation, 200,000 in finance, more than a million in trade and a million in services, and about 8,000 in mining. In terms of farm income in 1998, Georgia ranked sixth among the 50 states. Almost 200,000 persons in the state work for foreign firms.

Georgia ranks 11th in terms of death rates from all causes for white women, and 14th for black women, and it ranks about the same for death rates for white men and black men. Georgia ranks much lower in death rates from diabetes for all persons. In terms of the number of physicians per 100,000 population, Georgia ranks 32nd in the nation. Regarding males who smoke, Georgia ranks 14th in the country, but it is 37th for females who smoke.

Fewer than 10 percent of all workers in Georgia belong to a union, making the state 39th in the nation on that variable. In terms of personal income per capita, Georgia stands 23rd in the nation. Regarding the number of bankruptcies as a percent of the population, Georgia ranks third of the 50 states. Median income in Georgia increased $2,293 between 1990 and 1998. Georgia has the lowest gasoline tax in the nation.

Georgia ranks 25th in the nation in percent of population professing to be Christian, considerably lower than many of the so-called Bible Belt states. The state ranks 15th in terms of abortion rates per thousand persons. More than a million persons in Georgia are recipients of Medicaid. Each recipient received $2,465 in 1998, putting Georgia in the 47th position among the 50 states on that factor.

STATE OF HAWAII PROBLEMS PROFILE

The State of Hawaii, a group of volcanic islands in the Pacific Ocean, was admitted to the Union in 1959 as the 50th state of the United States of America. The islands were established as a U.S. territory in 1900, and include 6,425 square miles, making the state three times as large as Delaware in physical size. With just over one million residents in 2000, the state is 41st in size in terms of population.

Thought to have been settled originally by Polynesians, Hawaii ranks first among the 50 states in terms of percent minority population (i.e., 71.30 percent) and 50th in percent described as majority population. The state also ranks 50th in terms of the percent of the population that work in local government. Only 54 percent of the population own their own home, making the state rank 49th among the 50 states on that variable. With an average of three persons living in each household, however, Hawaii ranks second, and with 185 persons per square mile, Hawaii ranks 13th out of 50 states in population density. There was a 7 percent population increase in the state between 1990 and 1999.

Hawaii Problems Profile

Factor	< Fewer Problems ——— More Problems >	Factor Score
Government	(O right of center)	31.25
Expended	(O far left)	15.00
Crime	(O center)	25.13
Protection	(O right of center)	30.40
Punishment	(O left)	14.86
Natural Death	(O left)	9.92
Highway Fatalities	(O right of center)	27.77
Traumatic Death	(O left)	13.75
Health	(O left-center)	19.25
Medical Coverage	(O far left)	10.81
Teen Problems	(O center)	21.17
School Achievement	(O right of center)	25.75
Educational Support	(O right of center)	29.28
Work/Employment	(O center)	25.62
Economic Factor	(O center)	23.71
SUMMARY	(O left-center)	323.67

In 1996, Hawaii held 3,599 persons in prisons throughout the state, but has not executed any person for any crime since becoming a state. There were 24 murders in the state in 1998, putting the state in 40th ranking among the 50 states for murder rate. It also ranked 40th in terms of assaults, 17th in arsons, 27th in robberies, 14th in burglaries, and sixth in larcenies.

Hawaii has only one school district, the whole state, which ranks 24th in total dollars expended per student in the schools. Average starting salaries for teachers in Hawaii are low, placing the state 49th among the 50 states. Average teacher salaries rank 50th. The state ranks 26th in terms of percent of students enrolled in college.

Median income per household in Hawaii was reported as $43,627 in 1997 and $40,827 in 1998, placing the state in the top third among all the states, and it ranks 30th in the percent of citizens who live below the poverty line. Hawaii had 781 business failures in 1998.

Tax revenues per capita from tobacco and alcohol place Hawaii seventh among the 50 states, and the state ranks sixth in spending per capita for substance abuse. Hawaii ranks 46th in terms of percent of citizens with no health insurance. The proportion of both males and females who smoke is very low.

Traffic fatalities in Hawaii dropped dramatically between 1975 and 1999, placing the state in 46th position among the 50 states. In terms of death from all causes and from heart, cancer, pulmonary, and diabetes problems, Hawaii is among the 10 states with the lowest rates.

Residents of Hawaii paid 12.29 percent of per capita income for all taxes—federal, state, and local—in 1999 (i.e., rank of 38th). After all taxes were paid, citizens in Hawaii had $24,150, per capita income in 1999 (i.e., rank of 18th). Hawaii received more than $8.5 billion from the federal government in 1999 (i.e., rank of 38th).

STATE OF IDAHO PROBLEMS PROFILE

Idaho was admitted to the Union in 1890 as the 43rd state. The state was part of the original Oregon Territory, ceded by Great Britain to the United States in 1846. Its

Idaho Problems Profile

Factor	< Fewer Problems ——— More Problems >	Factor Score
Government	(O right)	36.13
Expended	(O right)	33.29
Crime	(O left)	16.75
Protection	(O center)	29.10
Punishment	(O center)	26.91
Natural Death	(O left)	12.33
Highway Fatalities	(O left)	21.36
Traumatic Death	(O right)	42.25
Health	(O left)	14.50
Medical Coverage	(O right)	32.56
Teen Problems	(O left-center)	20.33
School Achievement	(O center)	25.75
Educational Support	(O center)	29.94
Work/Employment	(O center)	24.06
Economic Factor	(O right of center)	32.14
SUMMARY	(O center)	397.41

boundaries include 83,557 square miles. Physically, it is twice the size of all of the New England states together, but its population in 2000 was just over one million persons, making it the 12th least populous state in the nation. The population of Idaho increased by almost a quarter between 1990 and 2000, however, making it the third fastest growing state in the Union. Idaho has the largest supply of underground water of any state, and the federal and state governments own more than 70 percent of Idaho's land area. The state ranks 44th in terms of percent of population that lives in metropolitan areas.

Idaho ranks second in terms of the percent of children not immunized, 43rd in terms of average funding for students for public schools, and 43rd for percent of persons over 65 years of age. Idaho is 30th among states in terms of the number of children in schools per computer, but number one in patents issued per 100,000 population, 897 in 1998. The state also ranks first in terms of the percent of children referred for investigation of alleged abuse and neglect. The state ranks fifth for the proportion of persons under 18 years of age. More than 95 percent of its residents are white and less than 1 percent are black, and the state ranks seventh in terms of the average number of persons per household (i.e., 2.73). About 13 percent of its citizens live below the poverty line.

Idaho has executed four persons for murder since 1950. The murder rate per thousand population in Idaho was 34th in the nation in 1998, and the assault, burglary, robbery, rape, larceny, and arson rates were all in the lowest half of the 50 states. The state has the third highest percent of robberies committed with a knife, but the 20th lowest percent of all robberies committed with a gun.

Idaho ranks 41st in terms of the number of persons engaged in nonfarm work, and 42nd in average annual pay. The state has the least assets in insured banks of any state in the nation, and the fewest deposits in insured banks. Median income rose more than $3,000 between

1990 and 1998. The state ranks 13th in research and development funds provided by industry, but 41st in research and development funds by universities. Idaho ranks 45th in terms of per capita disposable income (i.e., what is left after taxes to all levels of government are paid).

Death rates in Idaho are among the lowest in the nation, although infant mortality rates for white children are in the highest 10 of the 50 states. Death rates from heart disease and cancer in Idaho are ranked among the 10 states with lowest rates. In terms of death from accidents, Idaho ranks much higher (i.e., 12th), as it does from death by suicide (i.e., 6th). The state has fewer physicians per 100,000 population than any of the 50 states.

Birthrates for teenage females are in the midrange of the 50 states. Idaho ranks ninth in terms of traffic fatalities per population, 36th for traffic fatalities that involved speeding, and 31st for traffic fatalities that involved any use of alcohol.

STATE OF ILLINOIS PROBLEMS PROFILE

Illinois was admitted to the Union in 1818 as the 21st state in the United States of America. The state has always been sharply divided, socially and politically, into a northern portion around Chicago that now includes about two-thirds of the state's population, and a "downstate" portion consisting of 75 percent of the physical part of the state and about one-third of the population. Population of the state in the 2000 census was approximately 12.5 million residents; density per square mile is 218 persons, making the state 11th out of 50 in that respect.

About 12 percent of the Illinois population is over 65 years of age, and 26 percent is under the age of 18. The population increased about 6 percent in the last decade of the century. In terms of racial or ethnic background, 71 percent of the population is white non-Hispanic, 10

Illinois Problems Profile

Factor	< Fewer Problems	More Problems >	Factor Score
Government	...............O..		18.50
Expended	....O..................		31.29
Crime	....O......................		35.50
Protection	......O...		10.80
Punishment	..............................O..		20.50
Natural Death	....O........................		26.42
Highway Fatalities	............O..		19.23
Traumatic Death	........O..		5.25
Health	....O................		33.25
Medical Coverage	...................................O..		24.13
Teen Problems	....O................		35.17
School Achievement	................O..		17.63
Educational Support	..........................O..		22.78
Work/Employment	............O..		20.15
Economic Factor	..............................O..		25.14
SUMMARY	..............................O..		345.71

percent Hispanic, and 15 percent black. About 64 percent of the residents own their own homes, which average 2.66 persons per household. More than 25 percent of the population of the state is classified as "minority," but less than 2 percent of business firms are owned by minorities.

Approximately 11 percent of the population lives below the poverty line. Retail sales per capita were $8,992 in 1997, and the median household income in 1997 was more than $41,000. Illinois received more than $55 billion from the federal government in 1999, making the state seventh in terms of funds received from that source. Almost half a million persons are employed by local governments within the state.

Illinois ranks 24th among the states in terms of percent of high school graduates, but it is fourth in total number of patents issued in 1998 (i.e., 15th in number of patents per population). The state is seventh out of 50 states in total funds for research and development provided by industry (i.e., 17th per capita), and fifth in total funds provided for research and development by universities (i.e., 28th per capita).

Illinois ranked 17th out of 50 states in murder rate per 100,000 persons between 1960 and 1998, but it ranked third in robbery, eighth in assault, and ninth in automobile thefts during that same time period. Illinois executed 23 persons between 1950 and 2000, but recent actions by the governor have frozen further executions until the entire judicial process is reviewed.

In terms of black women's deaths, Illinois ranks third among the 50 states in deaths from all causes, fourth from malignancies, seventh from cardiovascular problems, fifth from pneumonia, third from falls, third from homicides, seventh from drugs, and thirteenth from accidents. For black men, the state ranks first among the 50 states in deaths from all causes, fifth from malignancies, sixth from cardiovascular problems, first from pneumonia, 11th from accidents, second from falls, and second from homicides. The rankings are lower for deaths among whites in Illinois.

Illinois ranks 14th in terms of percent of births to unmarried women, and ninth in abortion rates. In terms of infant mortality rates per 1,000 births, Illinois ranks 11th.

STATE OF INDIANA PROBLEMS PROFILE

Indiana was admitted to the Union in 1816. It was part of the Northwest Territory that was ceded to the United States by the Treaty of Paris, which ended the Revolutionary War in 1783. The Northwest Ordinance of 1787 prohibited slavery, but did not abolish slavery already in existence. The revised Indiana Constitution of 1851 prohibited entrance of Negroes into the state, but that provision was struck down by the United States Supreme Court in 1866.

Just over six million persons reside in Indiana, according to the 2000 census, which means that there are approximately 166 persons, on average, within each square mile. Approximately 72 percent of the population lives within a metropolitan area, putting Indiana in the middle of the 50 states on that variable. Ninety percent of the state's population is white and 8 percent is black. Indiana has a very small Hispanic population.

More than 70 percent of Hoosiers own their own homes, putting them eighth in the nation on a ranking with that variable, and fewer than 10 percent of the residents fall below the poverty line (i.e., rank of 41). Three million persons are employed in Indiana in nonfarm work. Indiana ranks 20th in terms of percent of workers who belong to a union, and the state ranks eighth in terms of bankruptcies as a percent of the state's population. Median income assessed at different times puts Indiana in the midrange of all 50 states, but the state ranks 45th in the nation in terms of tax on gasoline, at 15 cents per gallon.

Indiana ranks fourth in terms of death from all causes for black women, eighth from malignancies, 11th from

Indiana Problems Profile

Factor	< Fewer Problems	More Problems >	Factor Score
Government	...............O...............		20.63
Expended		...............O...........	33.57
Crime	...............O...............		23.50
Protection		...........O...........	28.30
Punishment	..........O..........		21.59
Natural Death		.........O.........	32.67
Highway Fatalities	..........O..........		22.64
Traumatic Death	...........O...........		24.00
Health		.........O.........	31.81
Medical Coverage		.........O.........	29.25
Teen Problems		.........O.........	32.22
School Achievement		...........O...........	34.25
Educational Support	.......O.......		17.39
Work/Employment	.............O.............		25.44
Economic Factor	........O........		18.86
SUMMARY		.........O.........	396.11

diabetes, first from nutritional deficiencies, 16th from cardiovascular problems, 20th from pneumonia, 17th from accidents, first from suicides, first from homicides, 10th from drugs, and fifth from alcohol. Deaths of white women rank lower on almost every causal variable except cardiovascular problems. Deaths for black men and white men do not follow the same pattern, but generally hover around a ranking between 15th and 20th for both groups, except for homicides for black males, where Indiana ranks first in the nation, with 89.4 deaths of black males by homicide per 100,000 population. In terms of traffic fatalities per 1,000 population, Indiana ranks 25th, and the state ranks 40th in the nation in number of physicians per 100,000 population.

Indiana ranked sixth in murder rate per population in 1998, and the state ranked first in black men's homicides in 1996, but over a 39-year period, the state ranked 24th in the nation. In most other categories of crime, Indiana almost always ranked in the middle of the distribution. The state ranks low (i.e., rank of 39th) in child abuse, and fairly high in average teacher salary (i.e., rank of seventh), but 47th in percent of college graduates and 33rd in percent of high school graduates. Indiana ranked ninth in births to black teenagers in 1996, and on the percent change in birthrate among teenagers, Indiana ranked sixth (i.e., high, meaning "little change"). On most other variables, Indiana ranks close to the middle of the 50 state distribution.

Personal income tax payments to the state brought in more than $4.5 billion for Indiana in 1999. That money, plus the other taxes paid to state and local governments, meant that total state taxes in Indiana amounted to $1,008, per capita, in 1999.

STATE OF IOWA PROBLEMS PROFILE

The State of Iowa includes 56,290 square miles, 95 percent of which is tillable—more than any other state—making it one of the major "breadbaskets" of the nation.

Iowa is second only to California in combined agricultural output, and a large part of the industry in Iowa is directly related to farming. The state was part of the Louisiana Purchase from France in 1803, and it became the 29th state in the Union in 1846.

Iowa had just under three million residents in the 2000 census, putting the state 30th among the 50 states in population. More than 96 percent of the residents are white (rank of fifth), 2 percent are black, and 2 percent Hispanic. One-quarter of the residents of Iowa are under the age of 18, and 15 percent are over the age of 65. The state ranks fifth in the nation in terms of proportion of older persons as residents, and Iowa ranks 47th in terms of number of persons in the household (i.e., 2.51). Seventy percent of the state's residents own their own home, putting the state in the upper quintile on that variable. In all, 8.48 percent of the population of Iowa works for government at some level (i.e., federal, state, or local), putting the state 11th out of 50 states in that category.

Iowa ranks low in crime: 44th in average of total crime between 1960 and 1998. The state ranked 49th in both murder and rape rates during that time period. The state has executed three persons for murder since 1950. Iowa spent $5.08 for food per day in 1996 for each incarcerated inmate, which placed the state fourth among the 50 states on that variable. More than half of the states spent $3.00 or less per day.

In terms of traffic fatalities per 100,000 population, Iowa stands exactly in the middle of the 50 states in rate of deaths from that cause. In terms of white women's deaths from all causes, Iowa ranks 45th in the nation; for white men the ranking on the same variable is 39th. Iowa ranked second in terms of fatal automobile accidents involving large trucks.

Iowa's gross state product was $80.5 billion in 1997, putting the state 27th among the 50 states on that variable. Percent unemployed was 2.5 in 1999, the lowest in the nation. Iowa ranks 10th among the 50 states in terms

Iowa Problems Profile

Factor	< Fewer Problems	More Problems >	Factor Score
Government		O	28.75
Expended		O	19.57
Crime	O		7.88
Protection		O	29.20
Punishment	O		11.86
Natural Death		O	34.00
Highway Fatalities	O		14.82
Traumatic Death		O	24.00
Health		O	21.00
Medical Coverage	O		14.75
Teen Problems	O		14.33
School Achievement	O		18.50
Educational Support		O	20.83
Work/Employment	O		19.74
Economic Factor	O		14.86
SUMMARY	O		294.09

of females in the labor force (i.e., 66.1 percent). Industry put more than $1 billion into research and development money in 1998, while universities spent $358 million for that same purpose that year. Median income in Iowa rose $1,592 between 1990 through 1998, putting per capita income for the state at $25,727 in 1999 (i.e., rank of 30), which meant that citizens in the state had $22,373 per capita left, after all taxes were paid that year. Farm income per person in the state was $793.54 in 1998, making the state fourth in the nation in that area.

Iowa averaged $584.51 per capita on expenditures for elementary and secondary schools in the state 1989 to 2000, making the state 22nd of the 50 states for expenditures on public schools. Iowa ranks seventh of the 50 states in terms of high school graduates (i.e., 89.7 percent) and 25th in average teacher salary (i.e., $37,169), and the state is in the lowest third (i.e., fewer students on each computer) of all states in terms of number of students per computer in schools.

STATE OF KANSAS PROBLEMS PROFILE

The State of Kansas was part of the Louisiana Purchase, which was obtained by the United States in 1803 from France. Before it became a state, the territory was used by the rest of the country as a place to relocate Indians. Kansas joined the Union as a free state in 1861, following violent clashes between settlers who were slavery oriented and those who were opposed to the idea of slavery. The state embraces 82,264 square miles within its borders, which includes the exact center of the 48 coterminous states. There were 2.7 million residents of the state who responded to the 2000 census, making it larger than 17 less populous states in the nation.

Citizens of the state had a per capita disposable income of $23,143 in 1999, which placed the state in almost the exact center of the distribution of 50 states on that variable. The rate of unemployment in 1999 was 3 percent, making the state 32nd out of 50 on unemployment rate. Kansas ranked ninth in the nation in percent of males in the labor force, and eighth in percent of females in the labor force.

Kansas ranked 33rd in the nation in terms of per capita expenditures for total state and local justice system costs, and it was 36th for funds expended for corrections, even though it ranked 19th in the rate of corrections employees per 10,000 population. The state had a lower robbery rate than 32 other states, but it ranked sixth in the nation in percent of robberies with a gun in 1998. Kansas had 27 bank robberies in 1998. For the 39-year period from 1960 to 1998, Kansas average murder rate placed it 32nd in the nation.

Kansas ranked about 30th in the nation in rate of deaths for white males from all causes, including malignancies, diabetes, cardiovascular problems, pneumonia, suicides, homicides, drugs, and alcohol. The same pattern existed for white females for deaths from all causes, malignancies, cardiovascular problems, pneumonia, suicides, and homicides, although the rate was slightly higher for deaths from falls, automobile accidents, accidents, diabetes, and nutritional deficiencies. Some states with "wide-open spaces" (e.g., Wyoming and Montana) have very high rates of death from automobile accidents, but Kansas ranked 22nd on that variable.

Kansas ranked 49th in the nation for child abuse, 34th for average starting salary for teachers (i.e., $24,944), and 42nd in the nation in terms of number of students in school per computer used for instructional purposes.

More than 86 percent of the residents of Kansas are white non-Hispanic, about 6 percent are Hispanic, and fewer than 6 percent are black. Almost 68 percent own their own home, and the average household has 2.53 persons, making Kansas 43rd in nation on that variable. About 11 percent live below the poverty line. Kansas increased in population during the past decade more than 7 percent, making it the 29th fastest growing state in the nation. With an average of 32 persons per square mile,

Kansas Problems Profile

Factor	< Fewer Problems	More Problems >	Factor Score
Government	.....................................O...................................		22.63
Expended	....O...............................		26.29
Crime	....O...............................		24.81
Protection	..............................O.......................................		23.20
Punishment	...................................O..................................		22.36
Natural Death	....O.......................		26.58
Highway Fatalities	..................................O...................................		23.45
Traumatic Death	....O........................		26.50
Health	............O...		15.63
Medical Coverage	............O...		17.69
Teen Problems	...................................O..................................		22.61
School Achievement	..............O...		17.75
Educational Support	...................O..		19.56
Work/Employment	........O..		19.65
Economic Factor	....O.........................		27.50
SUMMARY	.......................O...		336.20

Kansas ranks 40th in terms of population density among all 50 states, in which the median value is about 100 persons per square mile. The state ranked fourth in terms of percent of citizens who work in local government.

STATE OF KENTUCKY PROBLEMS PROFILE

The Commonwealth of Kentucky became the 15th state by joining the Union in 1792. Originally a judicial district of Virginia, it was the first region west of the Appalachian Mountains to become a state. In 1800 a second constitution was developed. The processes leading up to the adoption of that constitution revealed internal tensions among the state's residents regarding economics, transportation rights on major rivers, slavery, Spain, and federal legislation labeled the Alien and Sedition Acts. Henry Clay became influential as a political leader during that era, then served at the national level as the "great compromiser" for the next half century. During the Civil War about 90,000 men fought for the Union, and 40,000 men fought for the Confederacy, though after the war sentiment became strongly pro-South.

Kentucky had slightly more than four million residents in the 2000 census, putting the state in the middle of the 50 states of the Union in terms of size of population. For white women's deaths from all causes, Kentucky ranked fourth in the nation, for malignancies the state ranked eighth, for diabetes it was ninth, for cardiovascular problems fourth, for pneumonia 12th, for accidents tenth, and for auto deaths 13th. Death rates for white women are high in Kentucky. For white men the problem is the same. Death rates for white men from all causes show Kentucky ranks second in the nation; for malignancies it ranks first; for diabetes 12th; for cardiovascular problems fourth; for death from pneumonia it ranks eighth; for death from accidents it ranks 10th; and for deaths from auto accidents it ranks eighth. Death rates for white men are high in Kentucky, too. A similar pattern exists for death rates for black women and black

men, although in some instances there were not enough cases to determine rankings.

Kentucky spends less than 35 other states to fund prisons in the state. Crime rates for various types of crime generally show Kentucky in the lowest half of the 50 states. For traffic fatalities in which any alcohol was involved, Kentucky ranked 36th out of 50 states. For traffic fatalities in which occupants who wore no seatbelts were killed, Kentucky ranked ninth. The state ranked 14th for traffic fatalities per 100,000 population.

Kentucky ranks second out of 50 states for males who smoke and first for females. Abortion rates for teenagers are in the lowest third of all 50 states, but birthrates for teenaged females 15 to 17 in 1996 were ranked 16th in the nation.

The state ranks 47th in terms of high school graduates, 45th for college graduates, and 44th for percent enrolled in college. In terms of dollars spent per pupil in average daily attendance in public schools, Kentucky ranks slightly above the median of the 50 states. Per capita expenditures for colleges places the state slightly below the median. In terms of infant mortality per 1,000 births, Kentucky is at the median.

Research and development funds provided by industry and universities in Kentucky were below the median in terms of both total dollars provided and per capita expenditures. In terms of personal income per capita and median household income, Kentucky generally ranks 30th or below. For per capita disposable income after taxes, Kentucky ranks 44th in the nation.

STATE OF LOUISIANA PROBLEMS PROFILE

The area that became Louisiana was a French colony in the early 1700s, but in 1762 was ceded to Spain. In 1800, the region was re-ceded to France, and in 1803 it was part of a much larger area purchased by the United States from France, the Louisiana Purchase. After that, the territory was divided into two parts: the Territory of

Kentucky Problems Profile

Factor	< Fewer Problems	More Problems >	Factor Score
Government	...............................O............................		25.63
Expended	..........O..		16.43
Crime	...............O..		17.19
Protection	....O..............		42.40
Punishment	...............................O........................		28.50
Natural Death	...................................O....................		36.08
Highway Fatalities	...............................O........................		29.05
Traumatic Death	...............................O........................		36.25
Health	....O................		33.31
Medical Coverage	..........................O............................		27.38
Teen Problems	.........................O.............................		25.28
School Achievement	....O....		45.38
Educational Support	....O...............		34.83
Work/Employment	....O.........		32.21
Economic Factor	...............................O.......................		32.00
SUMMARY	...............................O.......................		461.90

Louisiana Problems Profile

Factor	< Fewer Problems	More Problems >	Factor Score
Government		O	35.25
Expended	O		24.29
Crime		O	38.13
Protection	O		24.50
Punishment		O	37.36
Natural Death		O	34.08
Highway Fatalities		O..	35.91
Traumatic Death		O	29.50
Health		O	42.94
Medical Coverage		O	33.75
Teen Problems		O..	41.22
School Achievement		O	39.25
Educational Support		O....	41.50
Work/Employment		O.....	34.94
Economic Factor		O	39.29
SUMMARY		O.....	531.90

Orleans, which consisted essentially of what is currently the state of Louisiana, and the rest of the purchased area, which was called Louisiana at that time. The State of Louisiana became a part of the Union in 1812. In 1861, the state seceded from the Union and became a part of the Confederacy, and in 1862 New Orleans was occupied. The state was readmitted to the Union in 1868.

Louisiana had almost four and a half million residents in 2000, making it the 21st largest state. More than 36 percent of the residents are members of some minority group. Population density per square mile is 100 persons, putting the state in the midrange of states on that variable. Louisiana ranks 12th in the nation in percent of the population that works in local government. The state had the ninth lowest increase (i.e., 3.6 percent) in population between 1990 and 1999, but the sixth highest number of persons per household in the nation. Louisiana ranks seventh in percent of persons under 18 years of age, and 39th in persons over 65 years old. The state ranks fifth in percent of the population that adheres to the Christian faith.

In retail sales per capita, Louisiana ranks 46th in the nation. The state ranks second highest of the 50 states in persons below poverty and children below poverty. Median household income (i.e., $30,466) placed the state 45th of 50 states. Federal grants for improving transportation in the state (i.e., HTF, per capita) put the state at 48th in the nation. Foreign investors invested $25 billion in Louisiana in 1997.

In the area of crimes per person in the state, Louisiana ranks fourth in the nation. In the area of violent crimes (i.e., murder, assault, rape, and robbery), Louisiana ranks seventh in the nation for the 39-year period from 1960 to 1998. It ranked number one in murder rate in 1998, fourth in assault rate, 20th in rape rate, and sixth in robbery rate. Expenditures for food per incarcerated inmate put Louisiana 49th in the nation. For total operating costs per inmate, the state ranks 45th of 50 states, and for utilities per inmate per

day, Louisiana ranks 50th. In all, 53 persons have been executed by the state since 1950.

Louisiana ranked 46th in average funding per pupil in public schools, and 42nd in average teacher salary. In terms of children not immunized, Louisiana stands midrange in the nation. Research and development funding by industry puts Louisiana at a rank of 47th for the nation. Research and development funding by universities ranks Louisiana 32nd in the nation.

Death rates of white women are high in Louisiana: ninth for all deaths of white women; 12th for malignancies; second for diabetes; seventh for deaths from poor nutrition; 11th for cardiovascular problems; 14th for accidents; seventh for suicides; and 13th for homicides. The pattern is almost identical for black women in Louisiana. Likewise, the pattern is almost identical for white men and black men in Louisiana, too. Death rates are high in the state. Infant mortality rates put Louisiana fifth highest in the nation.

STATE OF MAINE PROBLEMS PROFILE

Maine is the largest of the six New England states, with 33,215 square miles of land mass. The state was admitted to the Union in 1820 as a free state, under the Missouri Compromise. It had a population of 1.25 million residents in the 2000 census, with a population density of 41 persons per square mile, making it 37th in the nation on that point.

Maine has 23 percent of its residents who are under the age of 18, putting the state in 49th position, and 14 percent are over the age of 65, ranking the state sixth on that variable. The state is very much like Florida, Pennsylvania, and West Virginia in those respects. More than 98 percent of its residents are white, and almost 71 percent own their own home, making Maine rank sixth among the 50 states on home ownership. The state also ranks sixth in percent of business firms owned by women.

Maine, along with Massachusetts and Connecticut, ranks lowest of all states in percent of children not immunized. Maine ranked 48th in birthrate for females ages

Maine Problems Profile

Factor	< Fewer Problems More Problems >	Factor Score
Government	......................................O.....................	26.25
Expended	................O...	18.00
Crime	......O...	6.63
Protection	..............O...	22.00
Punishment	........O...	12.64
Natural Death	............................O.............................	29.17
Highway Fatalities	......O...	17.55
Traumatic Death	..............O...	15.25
Health	....O...	10.38
Medical Coverage	......................O...................................	22.38
Teen Problems	....O...	10.61
School Achievement	....O.............	32.25
Educational Support	....O..............	30.22
Work/Employment	....O...........	31.15
Economic Factor	.........................O...............................	25.14
SUMMARY	................O..	309.60

15 through 19 in 1996, but 18th in births to unmarried teens in that same year. The state ranked third for teenage mothers who smoked in 1995. The birthrate for teenage mothers between 1991 and 1996 placed Maine in 49th position, having declined 28 percent during that period. Gonorrhea rates among female teenagers put the state at a ranking of 47th. In terms of teenagers who give birth with inadequate prenatal care, Maine ranks 47th, also.

In percent of per capita income paid for all taxes—federal, state, and local—Maine ranked 21st in the nation. It ranked 38th in average annual pay and 40th in bankruptcies, as a percent of the state's population.

Maine ranks 38th in suicide rate per 100,000, 13th in deaths from all causes, sixth in deaths from cancer, 32nd in deaths from automobile accidents, 17th in deaths from heart problems, 34th in deaths from accidents, and 23rd in deaths from diabetes. It ranks 49th in infant mortality. Maine had no syphilis cases reported, and it ranked 47th in AIDS cases per 1,000 population. It was 48th in tuberculosis cases per 1,000, and 47th for percent of males who smoke. For females who smoke, however, the state ranks ninth out of the 50 states.

The state of Maine ranked 10th in percent of high school graduates, but 33rd for college graduates. The state ranked 26th in average per capita expenditures for elementary and secondary schools from 1989 to 2000, but 48th in terms of expenditures for higher education during that same period.

The state ranks 44th or lower in murder, assault, rape, auto theft, and robbery rates. Crime is a less serious problem than in most of the other states in the Union.

Maine ranks 30th in terms of traffic fatalities per 100,000 population, 45th for traffic fatalities involving any alcohol, 38th for traffic fatalities in which speeding was a factor, and 45th for fatalities in which occupants did not wear a seatbelt.

STATE OF MARYLAND PROBLEMS PROFILE

Maryland was one of the original 13 states of the United States, having been an English colony named in honor of the wife of King Charles I by Lord Baltimore, who was

Maryland Problems Profile

Factor	< Fewer Problems More Problems >	Factor Score
Government	..O...	8.75
Expended	..........................O...............................	27.00
Crime	.....................................O...................	38.56
Protection	..........O...	16.60
Punishment	..................................O.......................	32.50
Natural Death	....................O.....................................	23.92
Highway Fatalities	..........O...	19.91
Traumatic Death	........O...	6.00
Health	..........................O...............................	30.38
Medical Coverage	..........................O...............................	29.00
Teen Problems	.........................O...............................	27.22
School Achievement	..................O.......................................	20.25
Educational Support	...............O..	17.94
Work/Employment	................O...	22.68
Economic Factor	........O...	14.50
SUMMARY	................O..	335.21

granted a charter in 1632 for a place in which Catholics might avoid restrictions placed on them in England. The Maryland Toleration Act, adopted in 1649, stipulated "That whatsoever person or persons within this province . . . shall from henceforth blaspheme God . . . or shall deny our Saviour Jesus Christ to bee the sonne of God, or shall deny the holy Trinity the father sonne and holy ghost, or the Godhead . . . shall be punished with death and confiscation or forfeiture of all his or her lands. . . ," setting forth a new definition of "tolerance," although history has it that the harsh provisions were never enforced.

The state has 10,577 square miles of territory; with approximately 5.3 million residents, that puts Maryland near the top of the 50 states (i.e., fifth) in terms of population density per square mile (i.e., 529 persons), just behind New Jersey, Rhode Island, Massachusetts, and Connecticut. Persons from Maryland were very much involved in the Revolutionary War and the War of 1812, but loyalties of the residents were divided during the Civil War. A new constitution in 1864 abolished slavery and removed power from the rural aristocracy. A third constitution adopted in 1867 remains in effect today, though it has been drastically amended.

One quarter of the population is under the age of 18, and slightly more than 11 percent of residents are over 65 years of age; 68 percent are white and 28 percent are black, putting Maryland fifth out of 50 states in proportion of blacks in the state's population. In all, 65 percent of residents own their own home, making the state rank 35th on that variable, while 9.5 percent live below the poverty line, putting the state at a rank of 45th in terms of poverty. The state ranks eighth in percent of minority-owned firms, and 23rd in firms owned by women. Maryland has the third highest median household income in the nation and the eighth largest increase in income in the nation during the 1990–1998 period.

Maryland ranks in the upper third of states in terms of prisoners per population; 10 persons have been executed since 1950. The murder rate in 1998 placed Maryland fourth highest in the nation, and highest in robberies. Reported cases of abuse place the state in mid-range of the 50 states.

Average teacher salaries place Maryland in the upper third of all states; the state ranks fourth highest in terms of the number of students per computer in schools, and 29th in high school graduation rates. Maryland has the second largest percent of college graduates of all 50 states, and the state ranks first in research and development funds provided by universities.

In federal funds per person returned to the states, Maryland stands third in the country. In spending per capita related to substance abuse, Maryland is in the middle of the 50 states, as it is in terms of expenditures for colleges.

Maryland stands 39th among the 50 states in traffic fatalities per 1,000 population, seventh in infant mortality rates, 35th in deaths from heart problems, and 34th from cancer.

STATE OF MASSACHUSETTS PROBLEMS PROFILE

The State of Massachusetts was one of the original 13 English colonies established in the New World in the 17th century. The borders of the state enclose 8,257 square miles, making it the 45th state in terms of physical size, but its population of almost 6.5 million residents makes it 13th in population size and third in population density (i.e., 788 persons per square mile).

More than 84 percent of the residents of Massachusetts are white non-Hispanic, less than 7 percent are black, and about the same proportion are Hispanic. Less than 60 percent of the residents own their own home, putting the state at 45th among the 50 states on that variable. The population increased less than 3 percent during the past decade, making it one of the slowest-growing states in the Union.

Massachusetts Problems Profile

Factor	< Fewer Problems More Problems >	Factor Score
Government	.....O..	12.75
Expended	...........................O..	20.71
Crime	....O...	24.38
Protection	O...	7.80
Punishment	.....................O...	16.68
Natural Death	...................................O...	21.17
Highway Fatalities	....O....................................	25.68
Traumatic Death	....O..	3.50
Health	...............O...	18.00
Medical Coverage	..............O..	18.50
Teen Problems	.........O..	13.94
School Achievement	.........O..	9.75
Educational Support	..........................O..	22.67
Work/Employment	..............O...	20.91
Economic Factor	............O...	14.57
SUMMARY	..O...	251.01

Median household income in Massachusetts was $43,015 (i.e., rank of sixth) in 1997. The state ranks fourth in percent of workers involved in finance, second in service, 12th in trade, 26th in manufacturing, 43rd in government at any level, and 40th in construction. Less than 3.5 percent of its residents work in local government, putting the state in the lowest third of the 50 states on that variable.

Massachusetts ranks 38th in death rate from all causes for white women, and 38th in death rates from all causes for black women. Massachusetts ranked 50th in death rates caused by automobile accidents for both white women and black women, with an almost identical pattern for white and black men's deaths from that cause. The state ranks 48th in infant mortality rates per 1,000 births and 45th in suicide death rate.

Massachusetts ranked 25th in percent of residents who are only high school graduates, and sixth in percent of residents who are college graduates. The state ranks third out of 50 in terms of the number of patents per 100,000 residents (i.e., 3,735 in 1998). Research and development funds expended by industry amounted to $2,167, per capita, in 1998 (i.e., rank of second). Research and development expenditures by universities was $217, per capita (i.e., rank of second).

The state was 19th in terms of syphilis cases and 13th in AIDS cases per 1,000 population. The state ranks 43rd for persons without health insurance, 45th for children without health insurance, and first among 50 states for the number of physicians per population. Massachusetts ranked third in percent of births to unmarried teenagers in 1996, but 49th in terms of teen births as a percent of all births in the state.

Massachusetts ranked eighth in per capita expenditures of justice system costs for police protection in 1996, and 37th in percent of total justice system expenditures devoted to corrections. The state ranked 43rd in percent of all robberies committed with a gun in 1998, but first in all robberies committed with a knife. It ranked 47th in terms of all assaults that were gun related. Massachusetts had 154 bank robberies in 1998, making the state 16th among the 50 states on that variable. The state ranked sixth in percent of state population in treatment for drugs or alcohol in 1997.

STATE OF MICHIGAN PROBLEMS PROFILE

Michigan was admitted to the Union as the 26th state in 1837, and all of its 83 counties were settled before 1900. The territory was awarded to the United States in 1783, following the Revolutionary War, but the British refused to leave Detroit until 1796. Michigan was made a part of Northwest Territory in 1787. The state had almost 10 million residents in the 2000 census, making it the eighth largest state. With its territory encompassing 58,216 square miles, that meant that it had 174 people per square mile, making it 14th in population density. In all, 83 percent of its residents live in a metropolitan area. Almost half (i.e., 49.2 percent) of its residents profess to adhere to the Christian faith, meaning that the state ranks 30th on that variable.

In 1999, 86 percent of its residents over 25 years of age reported that they had graduated from high school, putting Michigan 23rd out of 50, and 21 percent of its residents had completed college. The state ranked 9th in per capita expenditures for college. Michigan ranks 27th for children ages 5 through 17 who live below the poverty line. Industry put more than $13 billion into research and development efforts in 1998, and the state ranked eighth in per capita expenditures in that category; it ranked 26th for research and development by universities that same year. Average annual pay was $34,542 in 1998, placing the state sixth among the 50 states on that variable. The state ranked 46th out of 50 for federal funds per person returned to states.

The death rate for white women from all causes was 363 per 100,000 persons (rank 22nd), and the death rate

Michigan Problems Profile

Factor	< Fewer Problems	More Problems >	Factor Score
Government	....O..		20.75
Expended	....O.....................		27.29
Crime	....O........		40.88
Protection	....O.............		33.30
Punishment	....O....................		26.27
Natural Death	....O..		25.83
Highway Fatalities	....O..		25.32
Traumatic Death	........................O...		11.00
Health	....O...................		33.06
Medical Coverage	........................O...		18.81
Teen Problems	....O......................................		27.22
School Achievement	....O..		23.50
Educational Support	..O..		12.72
Work/Employment	....O..		23.74
Economic Factor	...................................O..		20.00
SUMMARY	....O......................................		369.69

for black women from all causes was 573 per 100,000 (rank 15th). The death rate for white men from all causes was 571 for the same population (rank 28th), and 980 per 100,000 for black men (rank 13th). Michigan ranked 37th for white men's homicides, but fifth for black men's homicides; it ranked 42nd for white men's suicide rate and fourth for black men's suicide rate. Traffic fatalities in the state declined 22 percent between 1975 and 1999, making the state 36th in percent change in traffic fatalities during that time period. The state was 13th in infant mortality rates.

Michigan ranked ninth in the nation for percent at risk for being overweight in 1999. Birthrates for all females ages 15 through 19 placed Michigan 26th in the nation in 1996. The state ranked 20th for children not immunized. Michigan paid $3,188 for each Medicaid recipient. Almost 25 percent of females in Michigan smoke cigarettes, placing the state fourth in ranking on that variable; more than 30 percent of males smoke cigarettes, putting the state fifth in that category.

Michigan ranked 18th in murder rate over a 39-year period, 1960 to 1998, second in rape rate, seventh for robberies, seventh for motor vehicle thefts, and 12th for assaults. The state has had no executions since 1950, but ranked 14th for number of incarcerated prisoners per 1,000 persons in the state.

The state of Michigan ranked 43rd out of 50 in percent of minority-owned business firms, and 37th in percent of women-owned business firms. The state is 26th of the 50 states in terms of physicians per population.

STATE OF MINNESOTA PROBLEMS PROFILE

Minnesota became a territory in 1849 and a state in 1858. The state has 84,068 square miles within its borders and a population just under five million, which makes its population density per square mile (i.e., 60 persons) 31st in the nation. Many homesteaders were recruited from Germany, Sweden, and Norway in the 1880s, and the Mesabi Range was discovered at Iron Mountain in 1890.

Median household income was $41,591 in 1997, and the state received more than $21 billion from the federal government, ranking 25th on that variable. Just under 200,000 Minnesotans work in local government, putting the state 18th out of 50 on that factor. More than 91 percent of the state's residents are classified "majority" (i.e., rank of seventh), with less than 3 percent black residents and 2 percent Hispanic residents. In all, 72 percent own their own home (i.e., rank of second) and less than 9 percent live below the poverty line (i.e., rank of 47th). Almost 27th percent of the state's residents are under the age of 18, and 12 percent are over 65 years of age.

Minnesota spent $312 per capita for total state and local justice systems in 1996, putting the state 30th in the nation in that respect; $140 went for police protection, $98 for corrections, and $74 for judicial and legal costs. The number of sworn state police officers put Minnesota 49th out of 50 states in 1997. Thirty persons were arrested for marijuana in 1999, and 30,000 marijuana plants were eradicated. Minnesota had 165 assaults per 100,000 population (rank of 42nd) and 81 bank robberies. The average murder rate between 1960 and 1998 was 2.35 per 100,000, putting the state at a rank of 44th out of 50 states. For rape the state ranked 26th; it was 31st for robbery, 42nd for assault, 33rd for burglary, and 26th for larceny.

Minnesota ranked in the lowest third of states in terms of students per computer in the schools, 14th out of 50 states for average teacher salary, and 14th for average funding per pupil. The high school graduation rate is more than 91 percent, putting the state third out of 50 on that variable, and Minnesota ranks fourth in terms of percent of college graduates.

Minnesota ranks among the lowest 20 percent of states for syphilis cases for 1,000 population, 40th for

Minnesota Problems Profile

Factor	< Fewer Problems	More Problems >	Factor Score
Government	.............O...		15.25
Expended	......O...		15.43
Crime	.............................O............................		19.81
Protection	....O..		38.70
Punishment	................O..		17.18
Natural Death	....................O....................................		14.83
Highway Fatalities	....O..		17.23
Traumatic Death	...................O.....................................		13.75
Health	O..		9.38
Medical Coverage	........O..		15.81
Teen Problems	................O..		17.17
School Achievement	..O..		7.00
Educational Support	................O..		17.00
Work/Employment	O..		12.12
Economic Factor	................O..		15.29
SUMMARY	O..		245.94

AIDS cases, 32nd for tuberculosis, 31st for gonorrhea rates for teenage females, 40th for female teenagers who lack health insurance, and 49th for male teenagers who lack health insurance. The state ranks 35th for percent of teen births that are repeat births, and 45th for teen births as a percent of all births in 1996. Minnesota's rate of deaths per 100,000 white women made it 47th out of 50, the same place it ranked for deaths for white men. Infant mortality rates were in the lowest quintile. Medicaid payments for each recipient were $5,435 in 1998 in Minnesota.

In 1999, per capita disposable income (i.e., after all taxes) was $26,063, putting the state 10th in the nation on that variable. Residents paid $1,045 per capita in taxes to the state in 1999, making the state ninth out of 50 on that variable, and it was 13th in per capita taxes paid to the federal government. Minnesota ranked eighth in terms of percent of workers who belong to a union. Retail sales per household were in excess of $27,000 in 1998 (see also Appendix A).

STATE OF MISSISSIPPI PROBLEMS PROFILE

Mississippi became the 20th state when it was admitted to the Union in 1817. It had 2.8 million residents in the 2000 census. The state includes 47,716 square miles within its borders, for a population density of 59 persons per square mile. Slightly more than 36 percent of the population lives in a metropolitan area, putting the state in 44th position among the 50 states on that variable; only Vermont, Wyoming, Montana, South Dakota, and Maine have smaller proportions of their population living in metropolitan areas. More than 70 percent of residents adhere to the Christian faith, and the state ranks sixth on that variable; almost 72 percent own their own home. Less than 0.1 percent of the population is Jewish. Mississippi has the largest percentage of blacks (i.e., 36.5 percent) of any of the 50 states, and less than 1 percent

Hispanic; 62 percent are white non-Hispanic. With an average of 2.75 persons per household, Mississippi ranks fifth in the nation on that factor. Slightly more than 18 percent of the residents live below the poverty line, but almost a quarter of the children in the state live below the poverty line (i.e., rank of seventh).

Median household income in Mississippi was $28,527 in 1997, putting the state in 48th place. A total of 8.64 percent of citizens work for government at some level, putting the state 10th on that variable. Less than 2 percent are employed in construction, about 9 percent in manufacturing, 2 percent in transportation, 9 percent in trade (i.e., rank of 50th), less than 2 percent in finance (i.e., rank of 50th), and 10 percent in service (i.e., rank of 50th). The state provides next to the lowest unemployment weekly benefits, although the state ranks 22nd in percent of the unemployed who are insured.

Mississippi ranks number one in infant mortality, with a rate of 10.6 deaths per 1,000 births. The state ranks eighth in death rate for the total population, second for deaths from heart problems, 19th for deaths from cancer, first for deaths from automobile accidents, and first for deaths from accidents in general. The state ranks 49th in terms of physicians per 100,000 population (i.e., 163), and it has the highest syphilis rate (i.e., first of all 50 states). Among males, 27 percent are smokers (i.e., rank 23rd); among females, 22 percent are smokers (rank 20th).

In high school graduation rates, Mississippi ranks 49th (i.e., 78 percent) among the states, and it is 46th in percent of residents who are college graduates (i.e., 19 percent). In terms of expenditures per pupil in average daily attendance, Mississippi ranks 49th (i.e., $4,658), although the state ranks 29th in terms of average per capita expenditure for elementary and secondary schools over a 12-year period. In terms of average per capita expenditures for higher education, Mississippi ranks 19th (i.e., $367) for the same period of time.

Mississippi Problems Profile

Factor	< Fewer Problems	More Problems >	Factor Score
Government		O	37.63
Expended		O	27.14
Crime		O	22.38
Protection		O	25.60
Punishment		O	32.14
Natural Death		O	37.83
Highway Fatalities		O	36.45
Traumatic Death		O	39.50
Health		O	38.88
Medical Coverage		O	35.31
Teen Problems		O	42.22
School Achievement		O	45.75
Educational Support		O	43.61
Work/Employment		O	38.94
Economic Factor		O	41.43
SUMMARY		O	544.81

In crime rates between 1960 and 1998, Mississippi ranked fifth for murder, 29th for rape, 37th for robbery, 27th for assault, and 36th for burglary. The state has executed 50 persons since 1950, and spends almost 40 percent more (i.e., $53.76) per citizen per year in the state than Minnesota (i.e., $38.95) to maintain its prison system. The total prison population increased 47 percent between 1992 and 1996.

STATE OF MISSOURI PROBLEMS PROFILE

Missouri was admitted to the Union as a slave state in 1821. The state includes 69,686 square miles of territory, and with 5.5 million residents in 2000, that means that the state has a population density of just under 80 persons per square mile, placing it 27th among the 50 states. Missouri has 14 percent minority population, including 11 percent black. Almost 26 percent of the residents are under the age of 18, and 14 percent are over 65, putting the state in the midrange of states on both of those variables.

The death rate from all causes for white women is 383 per 100,000, making the state rank 12th out of 50 states on that variable, and it is ninth out of 50 in terms of death rate (i.e., 587) for all causes for black women. The state ranks 12th and ninth for deaths from all causes for white males and black males, also.

In terms of deaths from automobile accidents, Missouri ranks 11th in the nation; it was ninth in the nation for fatalities involving large trucks in 1999. The state was 27th in alcohol consumption per capita in 1998, and 20th in traffic fatalities in which any alcohol was involved. Traffic fatalities in Missouri have increased 5 percent since 1975, putting the state in the top quarter of states with such increases; most states declined in traffic deaths during that period.

Gonorrhea rates for teenage females in Missouri place the state 13th among 50 on that variable, and it was 18th in percent of teen births that were repeat births in 1996.

Missouri ranked 20th for being at risk for obesity in the nation in 1999.

Missouri was 18th in the nation for violent crime rates in 1998 and 15th for property crime rates. The state ranked 20th for murder, 21st for rape, ninth for robbery, 18th for assault, 17th for burglary, and 23rd for larceny between 1960 and 1998. There were 113 bank robberies in Missouri in 1998. About 26 percent of all assaults were gun related in 1998, 18 percent were knife related, and 21 percent were fist related. More than 32,000 marijuana plants were eradicated (i.e., ranked 14th) by police in 1999, and the state ranked seventh in bulk-processed marijuana seized. In all, 94 weapons were seized during marijuana arrests in 1999.

Residents of Missouri paid 13 percent of per capita income (i.e., $3,535) for taxes to all levels of government, making the state 27th in the nation on that variable. Residents of Missouri paid less than a thousand dollars per capita in state and local taxes in 1999, putting the state almost exactly in the center of the distribution of all 50 states on that matter. The state ranked 36th in per capita expenditures (i.e., $262.50) for total state and local justice system in 1996, of which $134 went for police protection, $42 for judicial and legal costs, and $86 for corrections. As a percent of justice system payrolls devoted to police protection, Missouri ranked first among the 50 states, with almost 62 percent devoted to that purpose.

Eighty-five percent of persons over the age of 25 in Missouri report that they completed high school, putting the state at 26th position on that variable; 23 percent report that they have finished college. Average funding per pupil (i.e., $4,779) puts the state 33rd in the nation. Average starting salary for teachers is almost $27,000.

STATE OF MONTANA PROBLEMS PROFILE

Montana is the fourth largest state in the Union, with 147,138 square miles, but the state has only 902,000 citi-

Missouri Problems Profile

Factor	< Fewer Problems	More Problems >	Factor Score
Government	...............................O...		22.88
Expended	....O............		33.14
Crime	....O...................		34.50
Protection	............O...		15.20
Punishment	...............................O...................................		23.68
Natural Death	....O................		37.58
Highway Fatalities	....O........		32.32
Traumatic Death	....O...................		35.25
Health	......................................O...........................		30.00
Medical Coverage	.............O...		18.94
Teen Problems	..............................O...................................		29.11
School Achievement	..............................O...................................		26.75
Educational Support	..............................O...................................		30.11
Work/Employment	..................O...		22.76
Economic Factor	...................O..		22.14
SUMMARY	....O...................		414.37

Montana Problems Profile

Factor	< Fewer Problems	More Problems >	Factor Score
Government		O	34.38
Expended	O		23.29
Crime	O		16.50
Protection	O		22.90
Punishment	O		18.45
Natural Death	O		20.33
Highway Fatalities		O	26.45
Traumatic Death		O	46.50
Health	O		15.31
Medical Coverage		O	25.44
Teen Problems	O		13.56
School Achievement		O	25.13
Educational Support		O	28.56
Work/Employment		O	26.06
Economic Factor		O	38.71
SUMMARY		O	381.56

zens. That makes the state rank 48th out of 50, with 6.1 persons per square mile within the state. Wyoming and Alaska have lower population density. The state received $6 billion back from the federal government for various projects, putting the state at a rank of seventh in the nation in that respect.

The state of Montana ranks 47th in median household income, but 13th in percent of persons below poverty. Just over 13 percent of the residents are over the age of 65 (i.e., rank 20th), and 25 percent are under the age of 18 (i.e., rank 27th).

Montana ranks 38th in number of students per computer in the schools, but 47th in average salary for beginning teachers and 45th for average teacher salary. The state ranks 11th in terms of children not immunized and second in child abuse rate in the nation. Montana ranks 33rd out of 50 states in percent of households with a computer, and 40th in percent of households on the Internet. The state is 11th in percent of residents over 25 years of age who report that they have finished high school, and 25th in percent of college graduates. Just under 5 percent of the state's residents are enrolled in college.

Montana ranks fifth in traffic fatalities per 100,000 population, and first in percent of occupants killed in car crashes who wore no seatbelt. Regarding percent of traffic fatalities involving any amount of alcohol, Montana ranks fourth, although highway deaths have declined 24 percent since 1975. Less than one person per 100,000 was killed as a pedestrian on the highways, and Montana ranks 46th in that area. Residents consumed 2.46 gallons of alcohol per capita in 1998, putting the state 10th in that area.

Montana was 22nd in females age 12 to 19 who lacked health insurance in 1995, but 44th in males that age who lacked health insurance. Nine percent of teenage females who gave birth in 1996 lacked adequate prenatal care, while Montana ranked 50th in teenage females who had gonorrhea. The state ranked 46th for percent males who smoke, but 23rd for females.

In terms of death rates from various causes, Montana ranked 30th in infant mortality, 32nd in death attributable to heart problems, 30th in death from cancer, 24th in death rates from strokes, 39th in death from diabetes, second in death rates from pulmonary problems, and sixth from general accidents.

Montana has one of the highest state taxes on gasoline, 27 cents per gallon, and the state ranked fourth in per capita for Highway Trust Fund grants.

The state averaged $63.21 per person in the state spent for corrections, 1989 to 2000. That put Montana 37th in the nation, in that expenditure area. Montana was 46th out of 50 states in violent crime rate in 1998, and 34th in property crime rate. The state ranked 37th in murder rate between 1960 and 1998.

STATE OF NEBRASKA PROBLEMS PROFILE

Nebraska was admitted to the Union in 1867 as the 37th state. Its boundaries include 77,227 square miles of territory. With 1.7 million residents in the 2000 census, Nebraska has 21.7 persons per square mile, placing it 42nd among the 50 states in population density. Most of the residents live close to the Missouri or Platte Rivers, so much of the state is sparsely populated. The state received more than $8 billion in federal funds returned to states in 1999. The state's population increased 5.6 percent during the 1990s, putting the state 36th in population change for that period.

Median household income in Nebraska was $35,337 in 1997, with 9.6 percent living below the poverty line. Median income increased $1,076 between 1990 and 1998, with the state ranking 36th in increase. The state had $9,981 in retail sales per capita in 1997, making it 14th of the 50 states on that variable. There were 75,377

Nebraska Problems Profile

Factor	< Fewer Problems .... More Problems >	Factor Score
Government	................................O................................	24.25
Expended	....................................O....................	27.86
Crime	..........O....................................	12.50
Protection	..........O....................................	21.90
Punishment	............O..................................	18.09
Natural Death	........................O......................	26.33
Highway Fatalities	..................O............................	22.86
Traumatic Death	..................O............................	21.00
Health	............O..................................	18.00
Medical Coverage	....O...	11.81
Teen Problems	............O..................................	17.50
School Achievement	....................O..........................	23.13
Educational Support	..................O............................	21.22
Work/Employment	..........O....................................	21.71
Economic Factor	..............O................................	21.07
SUMMARY	..........O....................................	309.23

persons employed in local government in 1997 in Nebraska, putting the state third out of 50 states (i.e., 4.52 percent) in that respect.

Almost 90 percent of the residents are white, non-Hispanic origin, 4 percent are black, and 5 percent are Hispanic. In all, 66.5 percent of the residents own their own home, placing Nebraska 29th among the 50 states on that variable. About 27 percent (rank of 13th) of Nebraska residents are under the age of 18, and 13.7 percent (rank of 12th) are over 65 years of age. More than 63 percent of the state's residents (i.e., rank of 13th) adhere to the Christian faith.

Nebraska has only 7.1 students per computer in the public schools, putting the state 48th on that factor, and it spent $5,171 in average funding per pupil in public schools in 1997. The state ranked 29th in percent child abuse and 21st in children not immunized. Average teacher salary in 1998 was $35,470, and there were 233 patents issued to residents in 1998. Nebraska ranked 13th in per capita expenditures (i.e., $111.64) for research and development by universities in 1998.

The state of Nebraska ranked 35th in the nation in average number of violent crimes per 100,000 persons between 1960 and 1998. The state ranked 40th in murder rate, 40th in rape rate, 40th in robbery rate, 36th in assault rate, and 47th in burglary rate during that same period. The state incarcerated 1.83 prisoners per 1,000 residents in 1996, putting the state 43rd on that variable. Nebraska has executed five persons since 1950, and the state spent $41.94 per resident per year to fund state prisons.

The infant mortality rate in Nebraska is 7.4 per 1,000 births, making the state 22nd out of 50 states on that factor. White women's death rate from all causes (i.e., 334.5 per 100,000) put Nebraska at a rank of 43rd, while the black women's death rate from all causes (i.e., 623.1 per 100,000) put the state first in the nation on that variable. Black women's death rate from cardiovascular problems (243.7) was third in the nation; white women's death rate (i.e., 113.3) was 32nd for the same cause. The state ranked 20th in the nation in traffic fatalities per 1,000 population. There were 218 physicians per 100,000 population (rank 29th) in the state in 1998, and only 5.5 percent of children had no health insurance (rank 50th).

STATE OF NEVADA PROBLEMS PROFILE

Nevada joined the Union as the 36th state in 1864. Its population was almost exactly two million persons in 2000, or about 16.5 persons per square mile; the state ranked 43rd among the 50 states in population density that year. Nevada has grown rapidly in population in recent years. The state includes 110,540 square miles of territory.

Almost 11 percent of Nevada's population lives below the poverty line; more than 15 percent of its children live in poverty. Median household income was 39,280 in 1997. Retail sales were $10,874, putting the state fourth in that category among the 50 states. A total of 677 businesses in the state failed in 1998 (rank 26th). Citizens of Nevada paid 13.48 percent of per capita income for taxes to all levels of government in 1999. The state ranked 46th in per capita taxes paid to state and local governments in 1999. The state did not provide information about gaming taxes collected in 1996.

Less than 12 percent of the population is over 65 years of age, but more than 27 percent is under 18 years of age. Thirty percent of its residents are classified as "minority," and 70 percent are non-Hispanic whites. Fewer than 30 percent of residents adhere to the Christian faith, putting Nevada 50th in that area; 3.4 percent adhere to the Jewish faith. Nevada ranks 44th in percent of citizens who work for local government, and 41st in percent of women who own business firms.

Nevada has the highest abortion rate in the country, 44.6 per 1,000 population. Births to women who are unmarried was at 35 percent (rank of eighth) in 1998. The state ranks 36th in infant mortality. Death rates from all

Nevada Problems Profile

Factor	< Fewer Problems More Problems >	Factor Score
Government	....O...........................	27.50
Expended	....O..............	32.14
Crime	....O..	41.88
Protection	..............................O..............................	27.20
Punishment	....O.......	38.91
Natural Death	..........O..	11.42
Highway Fatalities	....O..........	32.32
Traumatic Death	....O.................	38.50
Health	....O.............	34.19
Medical Coverage	....O..	39.50
Teen Problems	....O...............	35.17
School Achievement	....O...............	35.50
Educational Support	.................................O....................	31.78
Work/Employment	....................O................................	22.21
Economic Factor	....................O..................................	19.64
SUMMARY	....O..............	467.84

causes (797.7 per 100,000) put Nevada at 38th in the nation, while the state ranks 13th in traffic fatalities, eighth in death from pulmonary problems, 48th in death from diabetes, and first in death by suicide.

Nevada ranks third in the nation for percent of males who smoke, and second for percent of females who smoke. Birthrates per 1,000 population for females ages 15 through 19 were sixth in the nation in 1996. The state ranked fifth for percent of teens that gave birth that year and had inadequate prenatal care.

Just over 86 percent of residents over 25 reported that they had graduated from high school (rank of 19th), and 20 percent reported they had graduated from college (rank of 44th), but only four percent are currently enrolled in college (rank of 49th). Average teacher salary was $40,816.

In terms of violent crime rates in 1998, Nevada ranked 11th in the nation; it was 13th in property crime rates that same year. Over a 39-year period, Nevada ranked sixth in murder rates, third in rape, fifth in robbery, 14th

in assault, second in burglary, fourth in larceny, and fourth in auto theft rates per population. The state spent $67.41 per person in the state to fund prisons for one year, which included $2.39 per day to feed each inmate. Nevada ranked 12th in the nation in terms of prisoners per 1,000 population in the state for 1996.

STATE OF NEW HAMPSHIRE PROBLEMS PROFILE

New Hampshire was one of the 13 English colonies, and it became one of the 13 original states in 1787. In the mid-1600s, the region was governed by Massachusetts, but it became a separate colony in 1679. The state has 9,304 square miles within its borders, and had 1.25 million residents in 2000. The population increased 8.3 percent in the past decade. With 134 persons per square mile, New Hampshire ranks 19th in population density. Its towns are governed by town meetings.

New Hampshire expended $265.98 per capita for total state and local justice system (rank of 35th) in 1996, of which $125.78 went for police protection (rank of 34th),

New Hampshire Problems Profile

Factor	< Fewer Problems More Problems >	Factor Score
Government	....O.....................	34.13
Expended	....O..............	30.29
Crime	....O..	6.00
Protection	..............O..	16.80
Punishment	O..	10.64
Natural Death	....................O................................	16.92
Highway Fatalities	.....................................O................	26.18
Traumatic Death	................O.....................................	11.75
Health	......O..	10.75
Medical Coverage	...................O..................................	21.63
Teen Problems	O..	8.39
School Achievement	.............O..	14.50
Educational Support	.....................................O................	25.83
Work/Employment	....O..........	26.26
Economic Factor	..O..	11.07
SUMMARY	......O...	271.13

$64.39 for judicial and legal expenses (rank of 29th), and $75.81 for corrections (rank of 44th). The state's average murder rate over 39 years, 1960 to 1998, was 46th in the nation. The rape rate was 42nd, robbery rate 47th, assault rate 48th, burglary rate 45th, larceny rate 44th, and automobile theft rate 40th during that 39-year period. The state has not put any prisoner to death for more than the half century for which we have records.

Retail sales per capita were $13,477 in 1997, putting the state in second place in the nation on that variable. New Hampshire has the lowest percent of total population below the poverty line (i.e., 7.5 percent), and it has the lowest percent of children below poverty (i.e., 10 percent) of any of the 50 states. There were 322 business failures in New Hampshire in 1998. Per capita income in the state was $31,325 in 1999, putting the state seventh in the nation.

New Hampshire ranks 48th in percent of residents at risk for being overweight. It ranked 43rd in gonorrhea rate per 100,000 females ages 15 through 19, 50th in percent of teen births that were repeat births in 1996, and 50th in teen births as percent of all births in 1996. In New Hampshire 25.7 percent of males smoke (rank of 25th), and 21 percent of females smoke (rank of 26th). For tuberculosis cases per 1,000, New Hampshire ranks 26th, for syphilis cases per 1,000 population the state ranks 44th, and for AIDS cases per 1,000 it ranks 42nd. The state ranked 43rd in gonorrhea rate per 100,000 in 1996. In terms of percent of population without health insurance, New Hampshire ranks 39th. Medicaid payments to each recipient in the state were $6,447, putting New Hampshire second in the nation.

In expenditures for pupils in public schools, New Hampshire ranked 19th in the nation with $6,839 per pupil. In all, 86.5 percent of residents (rank of 18th) reported that they graduated from high school, and 27.2 percent of residents (rank of 11th) reported that they graduated from college.

Death rates from all causes per 100,000 population (i.e., 807) put New Hampshire 36th out of 50 states. The state ranked 33rd for death rate from heart problems, 28th for deaths from cancer, 27th for death from diabetes, 46th for deaths from accidents, and 45th for deaths from automobile accidents. Pedestrian deaths per 100,000 population in 1999 were 50th in the nation. Alcohol consumption per capita in gallons in New Hampshire ranked first out of 50 states, and the state was fifth in the nation in traffic fatalities in which any alcohol was involved.

STATE OF NEW JERSEY PROBLEMS PROFILE

New Jersey is the fifth smallest state in the Union, with 7,836 square miles, but the most densely populated (i.e., 1,098 persons per square mile). It was one of the original 13 colonies, and the third to ratify the Constitution. Historically, the people of the state have favored home rule rather than strong state government, and the state is a mix of rural and urban and poor and wealthy people. More than $40 billion was returned to the state by the federal government in 1999, putting the state in 11th position out of 50 in the nation on that variable.

New Jersey had 2,555 sworn state police officers (rank of fifth) in 1997, out of 3,521 total personnel in state law enforcement agencies. Per capita expenditures in the state for state and local justice system costs was $488.20 in 1996 (i.e., rank of fifth), of which $225.00 went for police protection (i.e., rank of fourth), $122.19 went for judicial and legal expenses (i.e., rank of third), and $141.01 went for corrections (i.e., rank of 14th). Traffic fatalities in New Jersey dropped 30 percent between 1975 and 1999, putting the state in 45th position on that variable. The state ranked 30th in murder rates over a 39-year period, 32nd in rape rates, 8th in robberies, 25th in assaults, 24th in burglaries, 33rd in larcenies, and sixth in auto thefts. Car insurance costs were higher in New Jersey in 1998 (i.e., $1,138) than in any other state. Taxes on gaso-

New Jersey Problems Profile

Factor	< Fewer Problems	More Problems >	Factor Score
Government	...............O..		15.88
Expended	....O................................		25.57
Crime	....O......................		26.13
Protection	..O..		9.40
Punishment	....O..................................		22.36
Natural Death	....O......................		28.83
Highway Fatalities	....O......................		27.18
Traumatic Death	......O..		4.75
Health	....O............................		25.06
Medical Coverage	....O................		29.31
Teen Problems	....O..................................		22.28
School Achievement	...................................O......................................		20.00
Educational Support	....O..		13.00
Work/Employment	...............................O..		22.62
Economic Factor	......O..		13.00
SUMMARY	...............O..		305.37

line (i.e., 10.5 cents per gallon) were less than in 47 other states in 1998.

The state had 2,024 business failures in 1998. Per capita income in 1999 was $35,612, or second in the nation. New Jersey ranked 18th in state and local taxes paid, per capita, in 1999, but fourth in proportion of income paid to federal, state, and local governments that same year. In all, 212,000 persons in New Jersey worked for foreign firms in 1997, and more than 35,000 immigrants were admitted in 1998.

Industries in New Jersey put $1,395.98 per capita into research and development efforts in 1998 (rank of seventh), and universities expended $59.56 per capita for research and development in that same year (rank of 41st). The state ranked ninth (i.e., 31.3 percent) in households connected to the Internet, and ninth (i.e., 48.1 percent) of households with a computer. New Jersey was also ninth in patents per 100,000 population that were issued in 1998.

New Jersey ranked 50th in percent of workers in construction, 33rd in manufacturing, fifth in transportation, 28th in trade, 10th in finance, and 12th in service occupations.

Death rates from all causes for white women (i.e., 358.4 per 100,000 population) put New Jersey in a rank of 29th out of 50 states, but it was tenth in the nation for death rates from all causes for black women (i.e., 586.7 per 100,000 population). Death rates from malignancies for white women (i.e., 117.8) were slightly lower than for black women (i.e., 139.4), while death rates for white women from cardiovascular problems (i.e., 118.4) were lower than death rates for black women (i.e., 179.7) from that cause. Death rates for white men from all causes (i.e., 564.2) were considerably lower than death rates for black men from all causes (i.e., 963.0). Death rates for white men from auto deaths (i.e., 13.6 per 100,000) were comparable to death rates for black men from auto deaths (i.e., 17.9 per 100,000). The same thing was true for sui-cides for white men (i.e., 11.5 per 100,000) and black men (i.e., 8.7 per 100,000).

STATE OF NEW MEXICO PROBLEMS PROFILE

New Mexico is a southern state, in that it borders Mexico, Texas, and Arizona, but it is almost always thought of as part of the "Old West" of cattle drives and cowboys. It was admitted to the Union as the 47th state in 1912, and has 121,666 square miles within its borders. The state had 1.8 million residents in 2000 and a population density of 14.3 persons per square mile, placing the state 45th out of 50 on that variable.

In terms of crimes per person in the state, New Mexico ranked second in the country in 1998, immediately beneath Florida and above Arizona and Louisiana. Over a 39-year period (i.e., 1960 to 1998), New Mexico ranked 13th in the nation in murder rate, sixth in rape, 22nd in robbery, third in assault, sixth in burglary, and tenth in larceny. There were no arrests for marijuana in 1999. The state and federal authorities held 256 prisoners per 100,000 population, putting the state 37th out of 50 in that respect.

New Mexico had 424 traffic fatalities in 1998, and 45 percent of the fatal accidents involved alcohol. Traffic fatalities declined 17 percent between 1975 and 1999, putting the state midrange among the 50 states, although traffic fatalities per population (i.e., 26.44 per 100,000) in 1999 placed New Mexico fourth in the nation on that score. It ranked 26th out of 50 states in percent of passenger car occupants killed in a car crash who did not wear a seatbelt.

New Mexico had 585 business failures in 1998. Per capita income in 1999 was $21,836, meaning that the state ranked 48th out of 50 on that variable. In terms of proportion of income paid in taxes to federal, state, and local governments, New Mexico was 44th out of 50 states.

In percent of births to unmarried non-Hispanic white teens in 1996, New Mexico stood 34th in the nation. In

New Mexico Problems Profile

Factor	< Fewer Problems	More Problems >	Factor Score
Government		O	32.75
Expended	O		14.86
Crime		O	39.31
Protection		O	29.20
Punishment		O	28.09
Natural Death	O		8.92
Highway Fatalities		O	31.59
Traumatic Death		O	47.25
Health		O	24.00
Medical Coverage		O	33.50
Teen Problems		O	36.22
School Achievement		O	23.63
Educational Support		O	25.06
Work/Employment		O	31.21
Economic Factor		O	43.71
SUMMARY		O	449.29

percent of births to unmarried Hispanic teens in 1996, the state ranked ninth. New Mexico was second in percent of teen births in which inadequate prenatal care was available in that same year. The state ranked fifth in percent of residents without health insurance, 28th in percent of males who smoke, and 36th in percent of females who smoke.

New Mexico had a death rate from all causes (i.e., 731.5 per 100,000) which put the state at 45th in the nation. It was 45th in deaths from cancer, 46th in deaths from heart disease, 45th in deaths from cerebral problems, 27th in deaths from pulmonary diseases, 28th in deaths from diabetes, and fifth from suicides. Each Medicaid recipient received $2,620, putting the state 46th out of 50 in terms of Medicaid. There were 212 physicians per 100,000 population (rank of 31st) in the state. The state had few cases of syphilis or tuberculosis in 1998, although New Mexico ranked 21st in AIDS cases per 1,000 residents.

New Mexico had 81 percent of residents who reported that they had graduated from high school (i.e., rank of 38th), and 24.5 percent who graduated from college (i.e., rank of 22nd). The state ranked 43rd for expenditures per pupil in average daily attendance, but had 7.5 students per computer (rank of 45th) in the schools. The average teacher salary in New Mexico was $31,441 in 1998.

STATE OF NEW YORK PROBLEMS PROFILE

For decades, New York had the largest population of any state in the Union. In 2000 there were almost 19 million residents in the state, putting it third in the nation on that variable. The state includes 49,576 square miles within its boundaries, and averages 385 persons per square mile, making it seventh in the nation in population density.

Median household income in New York was $36,369 in 1997, putting the state 25th out of 50 in that regard. Almost a quarter of its children live below the poverty line (i.e., rank of fifth). In all, 65 percent of its residents are non-Hispanic white, 15 percent are Hispanic, and 18 percent are black. Just over 13 percent are more than 65 years of age (rank of 17th), and 24 percent are under 18 (rank of 38th). The state ranks 28th in terms of percent of children not immunized, and 14th for percent of children abused.

The state ranks 28th in the number of persons in mining, and it ranks fourth in the number in construction, seventh in manufacturing, third in transportation, fourth in trade, second in finance, and second in service. New York ranked fourth in per capita disposable income in 1999 (i.e., $28,031), and was first in per capita state and local taxes in 1999 (i.e., $1,701). The state ranked third in proportion of income paid in taxes to federal, state, and local governments.

New York ranked 21st in death rate (i.e., 363.4 per 100,000) from all causes for white women, 35th (i.e., 490.8) for black women, 20th (i.e., 592.8) for white men, and 33rd (i.e., 842.4) for black men. For white women's death rate from diabetes (i.e., 8.6) the state ranked 40th; it was 37th for black women (i.e., 20.3), 43rd for white men (i.e., 11.0), and 34th for black men (i.e., 21.9) from that cause. New York was 30th for deaths of white women from homicides (i.e., 2.2 per 100,000), 24th for deaths of black women (i.e., 6.9), 16th for white men (i.e., 7.5), and 25th for black men (i.e., 40.4) from that same cause.

The murder rate for New York state was 23rd in the nation in 1998, but over a 39-year period covering 1960 to 1998 the murder rate was ninth, and it was 23rd in rapes, first in robberies, seventh in assaults, eighth in burglaries, 20th in larcenies, and fourth in auto thefts over that same time period. The state executed 62 persons between 1950 and 1969, but none after 1977. New York state held fewer prisoners per 1,000 population than 20 other states in 1996, and it spent more for operating costs per inmate in 1996 than 39 other states.

New York Problems Profile

Factor	< Fewer Problems More Problems >	Factor Score
Government	O	5.38
Expended	.....O	24.00
Crime	..........O	36.31
Protection	..O	12.90
Punishment	........O	31.05
Natural Death	.....O	21.50
Highway Fatalities	..O	17.73
Traumatic Death	.O	3.75
Health	............O	34.94
Medical Coverage	..........O	30.13
Teen Problems	......O	26.83
School Achievement	...O	19.75
Educational Support	...O	20.89
Work/Employment	.......O	25.68
Economic Factor	.........O	33.43
SUMMARY	.....O	344.25

New York state spent $7,412 average funding per pupil in public schools in 1997, and the average teacher salary was $44,405, putting the state third out of 50 states on that variable. It was 18th in terms of number of students per computer in the public schools, 36th in high school graduation rate (i.e., 81.9 percent), and 13th in percent of residents who are college graduates (i.e., 26.9 percent).

Traffic fatalities in New York state decreased 35 percent between 1975 and 1999, making the state 48th in the nation on that factor, and the state ranked 48th in terms of traffic fatalities per 100,000 population in 1999. It ranked 40th in percent of car occupants killed who did not wear a seatbelt.

STATE OF NORTH CAROLINA PROBLEMS PROFILE

North Carolina was one of the 13 original states that formed the Union. It has 52,586 square miles of area, and eight million residents were counted in the 2000 census. In terms of population density, 157 residents live in each square mile of the state, on average, giving the state a rank of 17th out of 50 on that variable. About 22 percent of residents are black, 73 percent are white non-Hispanic, and 2.3 percent Hispanic. There are slightly more than 2.5 persons per household in a state in which 68 percent of the residents own their own home. Approximately 12.5 percent of those residents are over the age of 65 (rank of 27th), and 25.4 percent are under 18 years of age (rank of 26th). Almost 75 percent of eligible males are in the labor force (rank of 29th), and slightly more than 60 percent of females are in the labor force (rank of 33rd).

Personal income in North Carolina totaled more than $200 billion in 1999, which came to $26,220 per person in the state (rank of 28th in the nation). Only 3.9 percent of workers in the state belong to a union, putting the state 49th out of 50 on that variable. Fourteen percent of citizens lived below the poverty line in 1998 in a state which

had a gross state product of $219 billion. Median income increased $518 between 1990 and 1998, putting the state in the lowest quartile of states on that factor. Banks in North Carolina held more than $936 billion in insured assets (rank of second) and $604 billion in insured deposits (rank of second), next only to New York.

There were 1,840 patents issued to North Carolina citizens in 1998, making the state rank 27th on that variable. Average funding per pupil in public schools was $4,392 in 1997, and average salary for teachers was $31,307 in 1998, putting North Carolina 47th out of 50 states.

Infant mortality rates were 9.2 per 1,000 births, with the state ranking sixth out of 50 on that variable in 1997. Death rates from all causes were 889.2 per 100,000 (rank of 26th) in 1997, death rates from heart problems were 260.0 (rank of 30th), deaths from cancer were 204.3 (rank of 28th), deaths from stroke were 70.4 (rank of 10th), deaths from accidents were 41.2 (rank of 18th), and deaths from automobile accidents were 21.0 (rank of 16th). Death rates of black women (562.4 per 100,000) from all causes were higher than death rates of white women (364.1) from all causes. The same pattern held for black men (1,028.8) and white men (623.9) for deaths from all causes in the state.

North Carolina ranked 11th in average murder rate over 39 years (i.e., 1960 to 1998), 36th in rape rate, 29th in robbery rate, ninth in assault rate, 21st in burglary, 38th in larcenies, and 39th in automobile thefts. The state ranked 19th in number of incarcerated prisoners per 1,000 population in 1996, and it has executed 35 persons for murder since 1950. A total of 47 percent of all robberies in the state were accomplished with a gun, 7.9 percent with a knife, and 34.6 percent were fist related.

North Carolina ranked 19th in percent of residents (i.e., 59.6) who adhere to the Christian faith. Abortion rates (20.2 per 1,000 residents) in North Carolina put the state at 19th out of 50 states. State and local taxes came to $1,071.56 per capita in 1999.

North Carolina Problems Profile

Factor	< Fewer Problems	More Problems >	Factor Score
Government	....O..		24.50
Expended	....O..		28.71
Crime	....O..		27.94
Protection	....O...		26.60
Punishment	....O................................		35.55
Natural Death	....O..		30.83
Highway Fatalities	....O...		24.14
Traumatic Death	....O..		29.25
Health	....O...................................		33.06
Medical Coverage	....O...		27.44
Teen Problems	....O......................................		33.11
School Achievement	....O......................................		32.63
Educational Support	....O.........		36.89
Work/Employment	....O..		26.32
Economic Factor	....O..		25.00
SUMMARY	....O..		441.97

North Dakota Problems Profile

Factor	< Fewer Problems More Problems >	Factor Score
Government	....O........	37.63
Expended	......................O..................................	21.00
Crime	O..	1.75
Protection	....O.........	34.60
Punishment	......O..	12.14
Natural Death	...............................O...................	32.42
Highway Fatalities	.................O................................	22.23
Traumatic Death	............................O.................	28.25
Health	..O..	10.25
Medical Coverage	......................O.....................	21.38
Teen Problems	......O..	11.56
School Achievement	.............................O..............	28.38
Educational Support	................................O.........	31.83
Work/Employment	..............................O...............	26.24
Economic Factor	..............................O..............	27.64
SUMMARY	...........................O.....................	347.27

STATE OF NORTH DAKOTA PROBLEMS PROFILE

North Dakota is one of seven west north-central states. Its boundaries include 70,665 square miles, and it had a population of 642,000 residents in the 2000 census. It is one of the least densely populated (i.e., 9.2 persons per square mile) of the 50 states (i.e., rank of 47th). About 94 percent of the state's population is white, and less than 1 percent is black. The state ranks sixth in the nation in percent of persons (i.e., 14.6 percent) over 65 years of age, and it ranks 31st in percent (i.e., 25.3 percent) under 18 years of age. North Dakota received $4.5 billion in federal funds (i.e., rank of 47th) in 1999, and the state has declined in population 1 percent since 1990.

Median household income was $31,764 in 1997, and 16.8 percent of the children in North Dakota lived below the poverty line (i.e., rank of 26th) in 1997. Retail sales per capita were $10,457 in 1997, ranking North Dakota sixth in the nation on that variable. In all, 144 businesses failed (i.e., rank of 48th) in the state in 1998.

The state spent $4,704 per pupil in average daily attendance in 1999, which placed North Dakota at a rank of 48th out of 50. In all, 6.15 percent of the residents (i.e., rank of 10th) were enrolled in college in 1997, and 84.9 percent (rank of 27th) reported that they had graduated from high school. Over 40 percent of the households (i.e., rank of 36th) have a computer, and 20.6 percent (rank of 44th) were connected to the Internet. Research and development funds expended by universities were $89.95 per capita (rank of 25th).

North Dakota ranked 17th in percent of births to unmarried teenagers who were non-Hispanic whites in 1996. Ten percent of teen births (i.e., rank of 17th) involved inadequate prenatal care that year. In 1995, 30 percent (rank of seventh) of teens in the state who gave birth smoked cigarettes. Eleven percent (rank of 42nd) of females age 12 to 19 lacked health insurance in 1995, and 12 percent (rank of 41st) of males the same age lacked health insurance. The state ranked 48th in teenage females per 100,000 population who had gonorrhea in 1996. About 36 percent of the residents (i.e., rank of 12th) were at risk for being overweight in 1999.

North Dakota had the smallest number of total murders of any state from the years 1960 to 1998 (i.e., 293 murders), and the state ranked 50th in the average murder rate per 100,000 during that same period. It had the lowest rape rate, robbery rate, assault rate, and burglary rate during that 39-year period, also. In larcenies it ranked 45th, and in auto thefts it was 49th between 1960 and 1998. The state ranked 50th in number of prisoners per 1,000 population in 1992 and 1996. No prisoner in North Dakota has been executed for crimes since 1950.

Residents of North Dakota paid 10.88 percent of per capita income for taxes to all levels of government—federal, state, and local—in 1999, putting the state at a rank of 48th on that variable. In terms of per capita in state and local taxes paid in that year (i.e., $496.76), North Dakota ranked 40th in the nation.

Death rates from all causes in North Dakota were 9.3 per 1,000 population (i.e., rank of 15th), and the state ranked 29th in deaths from automobile accidents.

STATE OF OHIO PROBLEMS PROFILE

Ohio was the first part of the Northwest Territory to become a state. It joined the Union in 1803 as the 17th state. The state has 41,222 square miles (excluding 3,457 square miles in Lake Erie) within its borders, and a population of 11.33 million residents (rank of seventh), so Ohio has 275 persons per square mile in the state, making it ninth out of 50 in population density. Slightly more than 13 percent of the population in Ohio is over 65 years of age (i.e., rank of 20th), and 25.3 percent is under the age of 18 (i.e., rank of 28th).

Just under 86 percent of Ohio's population is "majority" (i.e., rank of 22nd), and 14 percent is classified as "minority" (i.e., rank of 29th) population. In all, 2.09 percent of business firms are owned by minorities (i.e.,

Ohio Problems Profile

Factor	< Fewer Problems	More Problems >	Factor Score
Government	...............O..		18.63
Expended	....O......................		29.86
Crime	....O...............................		25.69
Protection	....O...........................		32.40
Punishment	......................................O....................................		26.18
Natural Death	....O...........................		36.67
Highway Fatalities	..O...		16.50
Traumatic Death	..........O...		8.75
Health	......................................O....................................		28.81
Medical Coverage	..................O...		20.19
Teen Problems	....O............................		28.56
School Achievement	...............................O...		24.75
Educational Support	...................................O......................................		21.22
Work/Employment	...............................O..		24.68
Economic Factor	...............................O..		24.14
SUMMARY	...............................O..		367.02

rank of 23rd), and 3.86 percent are owned by women (i.e., rank of 35th).

Ohio ranks 15th in average funding per pupil (i.e., $5,584) and 11th in average teacher salary (i.e., $40,856), but has experienced several court cases in recent years regarding equity in funding schools that have not been resolved as this is being written (i.e., April 2002). The state ranks 47th in terms of number of students per computer in the schools (i.e., 7.4 students), and 12th in percent of children not immunized.

In terms of employment, 2.11 percent of Ohio workers (i.e., rank of 38th) are in construction, 9.60 percent are in manufacturing (i.e., rank of 6th), 2.21 percent are in transportation (i.e., rank of 40th), 11.89 percent are in trade (i.e., rank of 16th), 2.77 percent are in finance (i.e., rank of 19th), and 13.99 percent are in service (i.e., rank of 26th). Personal income per capita in Ohio was $27,081 in 1999 (i.e., rank of 25th), and 11.2 percent of the state's residents lived below the poverty line (i.e., rank of 25th).

The murder rate in Ohio in 1998 put the state at 25th in the nation, exactly where it was from 1960 to 1998. The state executed 39 persons for murder between 1950 and 1969, and one person between 1977 and 2000. There was a 16 percent increase in prison population in Ohio between 1992 and 1996, putting the state 40th out of the 50 states in terms of that change. Ohio spent $90.16 per person in the state (i.e., rank of 11th) to keep a person in prison for one year in 1996. There were 2,198 (rank of 13th) adults on probation (state and federal jurisdiction) in 1999.

Death rates for white women from all causes (i.e., 383.2 per 100,000) put the state at a rank of 13th in the nation on that variable, and the death rate for black women from all causes (i.e., 553.6 per 100,000) put the state at a rank of 21st. Death rates for white men from all causes (i.e., 610.9) and death rates for black men from all causes (i.e., 931.9) were higher. The infant mortality rate

was 7.8 per 1,000 births (i.e., rank of 14th), and the death rate from automobile accidents (i.e., 12.9 per 100,000) put the state 39th out of 50 states on that variable. Ohio had 329 bank robberies in 1998, and the state made 71 arrests for marijuana in 1999, including 68 arrests in which weapons were seized. In all, 40,726 marijuana plants were eradicated in 1999.

STATE OF OKLAHOMA PROBLEMS PROFILE

Oklahoma had 3.45 million residents in 2000, which meant that approximately 49 persons per square mile (i.e., rank of 35th) live within the 69,919 square miles that are enclosed by the state's borders. Eighty percent of the residents are white non-Hispanic, 4 percent are Hispanic, and 8 percent are black. More than 26 percent of the citizens of Oklahoma are under the age of 18 years (rank of 16th), and about 13 percent (i.e., rank of 15th) are over 65 years of age. Slightly more than 68 percent own their own home (i.e., rank of 19th). Almost 67 percent of the residents of Oklahoma adhere to the Christian faith (i.e., rank of eighth), and slightly more than 60 percent live in a metropolitan area of the state (i.e., rank of 33rd).

Abortion rates in Oklahoma were 11.8 percent in 1996 (rank of 36th), and 33.2 percent of all births in the state were to unmarried women (i.e., rank of 19th) in 1998. Infant mortality rates were 7.5 per 1,000 births (i.e., rank of 20th). Birthrates among non-Hispanic white teenagers were 55 per 1,000 (i.e., rank of third), and among black teenagers the rate was 93 per 1,000 (i.e., rank of 22nd) in 1996. Nine percent of white non-Hispanic teenagers who gave birth in 1996 had inadequate prenatal care (i.e., rank of sixth). Twenty percent of teens who gave birth in 1995 smoked.

Oklahoma had 739 traffic fatalities in 1999, 276 of which involved speeding, and 33 percent of which involved alcohol. In terms of traffic fatalities per 100,000 population, Oklahoma ranked 10th in the nation; 56.8 percent of car

Oklahoma Problems Profile

Factor	< Fewer Problems More Problems >	Factor Score
Government	....O....................	32.00
Expended	......................................O.....................	28.57
Crime	....................................O.......................	28.38
Protection	...........................O..............................	24.20
Punishment	....O.............	36.45
Natural Death	....O..........	40.50
Highway Fatalities	....................................O.......................	28.36
Traumatic Death	....O.............	42.00
Health	...................................O........................	32.88
Medical Coverage	....O.............	33.88
Teen Problems	...................................O........................	33.50
School Achievement	.................................O..........................	30.50
Educational Support	....O.............	36.44
Work/Employment	....O...........	35.00
Economic Factor	....O.............	36.79
SUMMARY	....O.............	499.44

occupants killed wore no seatbelt. Oklahoma's traffic fatalities declined 2 percent between 1975 and 1999.

Per capita income in Oklahoma was $22,958 in 1999, putting the state 43rd out of 50 in the nation on that factor. Average annual pay was $25,122 in 1998 (i.e., rank of 43rd). Residents of Oklahoma paid more than $6.5 billion to the federal government in taxes in 1999, and slightly more than $2.5 billion to the state government that same year. Per capita taxes to federal, state, and local governments in 1999 were $2,851 (rank of 40th). Per capita expenditures for total state and local justice system were $261.42 in 1996 (i.e., rank of 36th), which included $121.66 for police protection (i.e., rank of 36th), $46.09 for judicial and legal costs (i.e., rank of 44th), and $93.67 for corrections (i.e., rank of 33rd).

Average funding per pupil in public schools in 1997 was $3,907 (rank of 44th). Almost 38 percent of households in Oklahoma have a computer (i.e., rank of 39th). Research and development expenditures by industry was $152.77 per capita (rank of 44th), and research and development expenditures by universities was $62.24 per capita (rank of 40th). Almost 84 percent of residents over the age of 25 reported that they had graduated from high school (rank of 32nd), and 24 percent reported they had graduated from college (rank of 29th).

Oklahoma's death rate from all causes was 1,023 per 100,000 in 1997 (i.e., rank of 5th), death rate from heart problems was 340 (i.e., rank of sixth), death rate from cancer was 218 (i.e., rank of 17th), death rate from stroke was 72 (i.e., rank of eighth), death rate from accidents was 48 (i.e., rank of seventh), death rate from pulmonary problems was 52 (i.e., rank of seventh), and death rate from diabetes was 28 per 100,000 (i.e., rank of seventh). Death rates are high in Oklahoma.

STATE OF OREGON PROBLEMS PROFILE

Oregon was admitted to the Union in 1859 as the 33rd state. The state includes 96,981 square miles and had a population in the 2000 census of 3.42 million persons. Slightly more than 34 residents per square mile puts Ore-

Oregon Problems Profile

Factor	< Fewer Problems More Problems >	Factor Score
Government	.................O..	21.63
Expended	...........................O..............................	27.86
Crime	...........................O..............................	31.00
Protection	.....................O....................................	26.40
Punishment	...................O......................................	22.23
Natural Death	.....................O....................................	25.50
Highway Fatalities	............O...	20.27
Traumatic Death	...............................O.........................	36.25
Health	.........O..	18.25
Medical Coverage	...................O......................................	23.13
Teen Problems	.................O..	20.72
School Achievement	............O...	18.13
Educational Support	..........O...	16.17
Work/Employment	............O...	22.00
Economic Factor	.............................O...........................	28.71
SUMMARY	......................O...................................	358.24

gon's rank at 39th out of 50 states in population density. The state received more than 15.5 billion dollars in federal funds in 1999, and employed 117,999 persons in local government in 1997. Almost 88 percent of its citizens are white non-Hispanic, 6.4 percent are Hispanic, and 1.9 percent are black. In all, 13.1 percent (i.e., rank of 23rd) are over the age of 65, and 25 percent (i.e., rank of 34th) are under 18 years of age. Oregon had 2.51 persons per household, on average (i.e., rank of 48th).

Oregon had a teenage abortion rate of 30 per 1,000 females ages 15 to 19 (i.e., rank of 6th), and 28 percent of teens who gave birth in 1995 smoked (i.e., rank of 11th). Seventeen percent of females ages 12 to 19 lacked health insurance in 1995 (i.e., rank of 20th), and 15 percent of males of that age lacked health insurance in 1995 (i.e., rank of 27th). The birthrate for females age 15 to 19 dropped 7 percent between 1991 and 1996, less than the decline in 42 other states during that same period.

Oregon had 32.8 percent of its citizens who were at risk for being overweight in 1999 (i.e., rank of 32nd), 14.3 percent with no health insurance (i.e., rank of 28th), and 225 physicians per 100,000 population (i.e., rank of 25th). The state received 24.43 percent of taxes for the money it spent on substance abuse. Each Medicaid recipient got $2,697 (i.e., rank of 45th).

Death rates from diabetes per 100,000 in 1997 were 25.0 (i.e., rank of 18th), death rates from pulmonary problems were 50.5 (i.e., rank of ninth), death rates from stroke were 79.2 (i.e., rank of second), death rates from cancer were 208.7 (i.e., rank of 23rd), death rates from heart disease were 231.8 (i.e., rank of 38th), and death rates from automobile accidents per 100,000 were 16.9 (i.e., rank of 27th). In 1999, the death rate from traffic fatalities per 100,000 was 12.48 (i.e., rank of 38th). Infant mortality rates per 1,000 births were 5.8 (i.e., rank of 44th).

Oregon citizens paid $1,287 per capita in state and local taxes in 1999, and they had $23,044 left, per capita, af-

ter they paid taxes to federal, state, and local governments (i.e., rank of 27th). Median household income in 1998 was $39,067 (i.e., rank of 23rd). The gasoline tax in Oregon was 24 cents per gallon in 1998 (i.e., rank of 11th).

The state ranked 20th in high school graduation rate and 14th in percent of college graduates. Teacher salaries averaged $42,556 in 1998 (i.e., rank of eighth). More than 50 percent of households had a computer (i.e., rank of sixth), and 47 patents per 100,000 citizens in the state were granted in 1998 (i.e., rank of 11th).

Oregon ranked 34th in murder rate average from 1960 to 1998, 11th in rape rate, 20th in robbery rate, 23rd in assault rate, 12th in burglary rate, seventh in larceny rate, and 19th in auto theft rate. Oregon had 12.2 judicial and legal employees per 10,000 population in 1995 (i.e., rank of 20th), 17.8 corrections employees per 10,000 population (i.e., rank of 32nd), and 16.9 police protection employees per 10,000 population (i.e., rank of 41st).

STATE OF PENNSYLVANIA PROBLEMS PROFILE

Pennsylvania was one of the original 13 colonies. It is the sixth most populous state in the Union, with more than 12 million residents and a population density of 268 persons per square mile (i.e., rank of eighth). The state was founded in 1681 by William Penn, one of the world's greatest advocates of religious tolerance. More than 86 percent of the state's population is white non-Hispanic, 10 percent is black, and almost 3 percent Hispanic. The state's population grew less than 1 percent during the past decade. Pennsylvania stands fifth in terms of home ownership (i.e., 70.6 percent). Almost 16 percent (i.e., rank of second) of its citizens are over 65 years of age, and 23.8 percent (i.e., rank of 45th) are under the age of 18.

Pennsylvania spent $1,041 per capita (i.e., rank of 24th) for public schools in 1995–1996, and $6,319 per pupil (i.e., rank of eighth) in 1997. The average salary for teachers in 1998 was $45,542 (rank of second). There

Pennsylvania Problems Profile

Factor	< Fewer Problems	More Problems >	Factor Score
Government	...............O...............		19.75
Expended	...............O...............		24.71
Crime	...............O...............		18.88
Protection	...............O...............		22.40
Punishment	...............O...............		25.09
Natural Death		...............O....	43.92
Highway Fatalities	...............O...............		23.45
Traumatic Death	...............O...............		24.50
Health	...............O...............		26.69
Medical Coverage	......O...............		15.94
Teen Problems	...............O...............		23.28
School Achievement	...............O...............		26.00
Educational Support	...............O...............		21.22
Work/Employment	...............O...............		25.38
Economic Factor	...............O...............		25.43
SUMMARY	...............O...............		366.64

were more than two million school-age children in Pennsylvania in 1999 (rank of sixth). The state had a high school graduation rate of 86.1 percent (i.e., rank of 21st) in 1999, college graduation rate of 23.9 percent (i.e., rank of 27th), and 4.9 percent of its citizens were enrolled in college in 1997 (i.e., rank of 34th). Eighteen percent of children ages 5 to 17 in Pennsylvania live below the poverty line (i.e., rank of 18th).

Median income in the state in 1997 was $37,267, and household median income in 1998 was $39,015 (i.e., rank of 24th). Per capita taxes paid to the federal government were $3,086 (i.e., rank of 19th), and per capita taxes paid to state government were $643 (i.e., rank of 32nd). Over 18 percent of Pennsylvania workers belonged to a union.

The gonorrhea rate per 100,000 females ages 15 through 19 was 600 in 1996 (i.e., rank of 22nd), and teen births as percent of all births in the state in 1996 were 10 percent (i.e., rank in lowest quartile). Less than 10 percent of both females and males in Pennsylvania lacked health insurance in 1995 (i.e., rank of 46th).

There were 24,253 murders in Pennsylvania between 1960 and 1998, and the state had an average murder rate of 5.24 per 100,000 over that 39-year period (i.e., rank of 29th). The average rape rate during that same period was 18.97 per 100,000 (i.e., rank of 38th), the average robbery rate was 132.41 (i.e., rank of 16th), average assault rate was 143.23 (i.e., rank of 38th), average burglary rate was 670.07 (i.e., rank of 43rd), and average larceny rate was 1,442.09 (i.e., rank of 48th). There were 371 arrests for marijuana in 1999, 184 where weapons were seized. Pennsylvania ranked 29th in average number of violent crimes committed during 1960–1998.

Pennsylvania ranked 38th in traffic fatalities in 1998 and 18th in infant mortality in 1997. In death rate from all causes per 100,000 persons, Pennsylvania ranked third (i.e., 1,064). In death rate from heart problems it ranked third, it was third in death rate from cancer, 11th from stroke, 22nd in death rate from pulmonary problems, and fourth in death rate from diabetes. In terms of Medicaid payments to each recipient, Pennsylvania provided $3,992 (i.e., rank of 20th). Just over 10 percent of the state's citizens had no health insurance in 1998. There were 291 physicians per 100,000 population in the state.

STATE OF RHODE ISLAND PROBLEMS PROFILE

Rhode Island is the smallest state in the union, approximately 48 miles long and 37 miles wide, with an area of 1,214 square miles. The area was first settled in 1636 by Roger Williams and followers, who had been banished from Massachusetts Bay Colony for advocating freedom of conscience in religion. In 1772 a British vessel ran aground, and it was burned that night by a group of men from Providence, the first act of violence in what became the war for independence.

There were just over one million residents in Rhode Island in 2000, making it the second highest state in terms of population density (i.e., 948 persons per square mile). The state includes 7 percent Hispanic, almost 87 percent white non-Hispanic, and 5 percent black citizens. Almost 16 percent of the population is over 65 years of age (i.e., rank of 3rd), and 24 percent is under the age of 18 (i.e., rank of 42nd).

The state confined 2,775 persons in prisons in 1992 and 3,041 persons in 1996. No person has been executed in Rhode Island since 1950. Food costs per inmate were $4.42 per day (i.e., rank of sixth) in 1996, while operating costs per inmate per year were $35,739 (i.e., rank of second). The murder rate in Rhode Island over a 39-year period was 2.98 per 100,000 persons in the state (i.e., rank of 41st), the rape rate was 15.75 (i.e., rank of 45th), robbery rate was 81.82 (i.e., rank of 33rd), assault rate was 179.28 (i.e., rank of 29th), burglary rate was 1,081 (i.e., rank of 18th), and larceny rate was 2,288 (i.e., rank of 27th).

Expenditures per pupil in average daily attendance at public schools were $8,239 in 1999 (i.e., rank of sixth),

Rhode Island Problems Profile

Factor	< Fewer Problems	More Problems >	Factor Score
Government		O	27.50
Expended	O		20.86
Crime	O		21.75
Protection	O		22.80
Punishment	O		17.50
Natural Death		O	39.08
Highway Fatalities		O	28.32
Traumatic Death	O		1.75
Health	O		23.38
Medical Coverage	O		22.63
Teen Problems	O		21.11
School Achievement	O		17.25
Educational Support	O		22.94
Work/Employment		O	27.09
Economic Factor		O	26.14
SUMMARY	O		340.10

and the average teacher salary was $41,324 in 1998 (i.e., rank of 10th). Almost 81 percent of the residents over the age of 25 graduated from high school (i.e., rank of 38th), and 27 percent graduated from college (i.e., rank of 15th). More than 7 percent were enrolled in college in 1997 (i.e., rank of second). Research and development funds expended by universities were $113.04 per capita in 1998 (i.e., rank of 11th), and research and development funds expended by industry were $1,692.54 per capita in 1998 (i.e., rank of fourth).

Tax revenue from tobacco and alcohol for the state, per capita, was $72.80. Residents paid $955.52 in state and local taxes in 1999 (i.e., rank of 21st), but had $25,400 income, per capita, after all taxes were paid to federal, state, and local governments (i.e., rank of 12th).

Just over 6 percent of all citizens in Rhode Island work for government (i.e., rank of 49th), less than 2 percent are in construction (i.e., rank of 45th), 7.55 percent are in manufacturing (i.e., rank of 22nd), 1.62 percent are in transportation (i.e., rank of 50th), 10.92 percent are in trade (i.e., rank of 38th), 3 percent are in finance (i.e., rank of 14th), and 16.35 percent are in service (i.e., rank of seventh).

Average annual pay in Rhode Island in 1998 was $30,148 in 1998 (i.e., rank of 20th), and 19 percent of workers belonged to a union (i.e., rank of 13th). Household median income in 1998 was $40,686 (i.e., rank of 18th). Median income increased $3,987 between 1990 and 1998. In all, 11.6 percent of residents were below the poverty line in 1998 (i.e., rank of 22nd).

STATE OF SOUTH CAROLINA PROBLEMS PROFILE

South Carolina was one of the original 13 states of the United States. Its boundaries include 31,055 square miles of territory, and the census of 2000 recorded just over four million residents. South Carolina has 129 persons per square mile. The population increased more than 11 percent (i.e., rank of 16th) over the last decade. Less than

70 percent of the state's residents are white (i.e., rank of 45th), and 30 percent are black (i.e., rank of 3rd). Fifteen percent of the population lives below the poverty line, and 23 percent of children live below the poverty line.

Median household income in 1997 was $33,325, and average annual pay in 1998 was $26,151. Personal income exceeded $91 billion in 1999 (i.e., rank of 27th), and personal income per capita was $23,538 in 1999 (i.e., rank of 38th). In terms of percent of per capita income for all taxes—federal, state, and local—South Carolina ranked 37th in 1999. That amounted to $693.86 to state and local governments and $2,214.41 to the federal government.

Traffic fatalities were 27.41 per 100,000 population in 1999 (i.e., rank of third). Pedestrian fatality rate was 2.9 per 100,000 (i.e., rank of fifth). In terms of total traffic fatalities in which speeding was involved, South Carolina ranked sixth (i.e., 502 deaths), the state ranked 41st in percent of total traffic fatalities in which any alcohol was involved, but it ranked 10th in percent of passenger car occupants killed who wore no seatbelt (i.e., 61.6 percent).

White women died from all causes at a rate of 382.1 per 100,000 (i.e., rank of 15th) and black women died from all causes at a rate of 592.9 per 100,000 (i.e., rank of sixth). White men died from all causes in South Carolina at a rate of 653.1 (i.e., rank of 10th), and black men died from all causes at a rate of 1,045.3 (i.e., rank of sixth). White men died from homicide at a rate of 7.7 per 100,000 (i.e., rank of 14th), and black men died from homicide at a rate of 31.9 (i.e., rank of 36th). Infant mortality for whites was 6.4 per 1,000 births (i.e., rank of 19th) and 15.4 per 1,000 births for blacks (i.e., rank of 15th).

South Carolina had 37.3 percent of residents at risk for obesity in 1999. The state ranked 10th for syphilis cases per 1,000 persons and it ranked 13th for tuberculosis cases. Thirty percent of the males smoke and 20 percent of females smoke. Almost 10 percent of children

South Carolina Problems Profile

Factor	< Fewer Problems	More Problems >	Factor Score
Government		O	34.88
Expended		O	30.86
Crime		O	34.25
Protection	O		27.40
Punishment		O	39.27
Natural Death		O	34.42
Highway Fatalities		O	30.05
Traumatic Death	O		28.50
Health		O	37.13
Medical Coverage		O	31.44
Teen Problems		O	37.22
School Achievement		O	39.75
Educational Support		O	32.61
Work/Employment		O	31.47
Economic Factor		O	33.07
SUMMARY		O	502.30

were born with low birth weight in 1998, and 39 percent of births in the state were to unmarried women (i.e., rank of fourth). Each recipient of Medicaid got $3,393 (i.e., rank of 32nd), and there were more than half a million persons who received Medicaid in 1998. South Carolina has 207 physicians per 100,000 population (i.e., rank of 34th); 15.4 percent of residents have no health insurance (i.e., rank of 21st)

South Carolina ranked 45th in percent of residents who had graduated from high school (i.e., 78.6 percent) and 40th in percent who had graduated from college (i.e., 20.9 percent). Less than 5 percent were enrolled in college (i.e., rank of 41st). The state spent $4,068 per pupil in public schools (i.e., rank of 36th).

South Carolina ranked seventh in murder rates over a 39-year period, 13th in rape rate, 25th in robbery rate, second in assault rate, and 14th in burglary rate.

STATE OF SOUTH DAKOTA PROBLEMS PROFILE

South Dakota became the 40th state to enter the Union when it received congressional approval in 1889. There had been consideration of the possibility of one state—Dakota—to be created which would include what is now North Dakota, but dual statehood based on a division below the 46th parallel was decided. The Homestake Mine in South Dakota is the largest producer of gold in the western hemisphere, but the economy of the state is closely tied to agriculture and industry. South Dakota encompasses 77,047 square miles and has 728,000 inhabitants, according to the 2000 census, making its population density 9.7 persons per square mile (i.e., rank of 46th).

South Dakota received almost $6 billion in federal funds in 1996 (i.e., rank of 46th). Research and development expenditures by industry were $81.84 per capita (i.e., rank of 50th) and research and development expenditures by universities were $34.10 per capita (i.e., rank of 49th) in 1998. In all, 41.6 percent of households have a computer

(i.e., rank of 29th), and 23.9 percent of households are connected to the Internet (i.e., rank of 33rd). Average starting salary for teachers was $23,860 in 1998 (i.e., rank of 42nd), and average teacher salary was $30,967 (i.e., rank of 48th). Almost 89 percent of persons over 25 have graduated from high school (i.e., rank of 12th), and 25.6 percent have graduated from college (i.e., 18th).

Retail sales in South Dakota were $30,507, per capita, in 1998, and median income was $32,786 that same year, with 10.8 percent of citizens below the poverty line (i.e., rank of 28th). Residents of South Dakota paid 9.2 percent of per capita income for taxes—federal, state, and local—and ranked 50th on that variable. Per capita state and local taxes were $145.86 for 1999 (i.e., rank of 50th). Per capita income after all taxes were paid was $22,558 (rank of 32nd).

Regarding health, 36.1 percent of residents were at risk for being overweight (i.e., rank of 14th), and 11 percent of females (i.e., rank of 39th) and 13 percent of males (i.e., rank of 36th) lacked health insurance in 1995. Birthrate per 1,000 females ages 15 through 19 declined 17 percent between 1991 and 1996 (i.e., rank of 43rd). The state has six hospital beds per 1,000 persons in the state (rank of second), and 184 physicians per 100,000 residents (i.e., rank of 43rd). The state ranks number one in percent of males who smoke, but 44th for females who smoke.

South Dakota had the lowest murder rate in the nation in 1998, and it ranked 48th over the 39 years between 1960 and 1998. In violent crimes (i.e., murder, rape, assault, and robbery) during that period, the state ranked 46th; in property crimes it ranked 47th. South Dakota spent $251.94 per capita for total state and local justice systems in 1996 (i.e., rank of 39), of which $109.57 went for police protection (i.e., rank of 42nd), $61.73 for judicial and legal costs (i.e., rank of 30th), and $80.64 went for corrections (i.e., rank of 41st).

South Dakota Problems Profile

Factor	< Fewer Problems	More Problems >	Factor Score
Government		O..	38.38
Expended		O	27.71
Crime	..O		5.88
Protection		O	30.80
Punishment	..O		13.50
Natural Death		O	36.33
Highway Fatalities		O	26.68
Traumatic Death		O	39.00
Health	..O		18.50
Medical Coverage	O		21.31
Teen Problems	O		19.94
School Achievement		O	25.38
Educational Support		O	36.39
Work/Employment		O	26.18
Economic Factor		O	26.86
SUMMARY		O	392.83

South Dakota had 150 traffic fatalities in 1999, which put the state 15th in the nation in fatalities per 100,000. The state ranked 17th in infant mortality rate, and 16th in death rate per 1,000 persons from all causes (i.e., 930 per 100,000 persons). Death rates from stroke put the state third in the nation, but for most other causes the state was in the upper half of the 50 states.

STATE OF TENNESSEE PROBLEMS PROFILE

Tennessee entered the Union in 1796 as the 16th state. It had more than 5.5 million residents in 2000 within its 42,244 square miles. The state is 432 miles long and 112 miles wide, and has a population density of 133 persons per square mile (i.e., rank of 20th). In all, 68 percent of its residents live in a metropolitan area of the state (i.e., rank of 31st). Just under 61 percent of Tennessee's citizens adhere to the Christian faith, and the state ranks 15th on that variable among the 50 states. Eighty-two percent of Tennessee's residents are white (i.e., rank of 35th), and almost 17 percent are black (i.e., rank of 11th). Less that 2 percent of its minorities own business firms (i.e., rank of 34th), and just under 4 percent of its females own business firms (i.e., rank of 45th).

There were 1,731 personnel in state law enforcement agencies in 1997, including 913 sworn state police officers. The state had 1.67 sworn state police officers per 10,000 residents in 1997 (i.e., rank of 38th). Tennessee ranked 11th in robberies per 100,000 population in 1998, and fourth in percent of robberies with a gun. It was 12th in the nation in average rate of murders over a 39-year period, 1960 to 1998, 15th in rapes, 15th in robberies, 20th in assaults, 23rd in burglaries, and 43rd in larcenies. There were 977 arrests for marijuana in 1999 (i.e., rank of 4th), 107 of which involved weapons that were seized. Ten prisoners have been executed since 1950. The state spent $22,904 in operating costs to keep a prisoner confined for one year (i.e., rank of 20th) in 1996, and the

prison population increased 28.66 percent between 1992 and 1996 (i.e., rank of 16th).

Tennessee received almost $31 billion in federal funds in 1999 (i.e., rank of 17th). Tennessee has 2.7 million persons involved in nonfarm work, including over 4,000 persons in mining, 129,000 in construction, 507,000 in manufacturing, 173,000 in transportation, 638,000 in trade, 131,000 in finance, and 734,000 in services. More than $17 billion was invested in Tennessee by persons from foreign nations in 1997 (i.e., rank of 16th), and more than 149,000 persons work for foreign firms. Retail sales per household in 1998 were $26,982 (i.e., rank of 26th). Median household income in 1998 was $34,091 (i.e., rank of 40th). In all, 13.4 percent of residents live below the poverty line (i.e., rank of 19th).

Tennessee ranks 10th in traffic fatalities per 1,000 residents, fourth in syphilis cases per 1,000 population, and 10th in tuberculosis cases. More than 30 percent of the males smoke (i.e., rank of 4th), and 22.4 percent of females smoke. Medicaid recipients received $1,717 each in 1998 (i.e., rank of 49th). Death rates for white women from all causes were 398 per 100,000 population (i.e., rank of seventh), and death rates for black women from all causes were 621 per 100,000 population (i.e., rank of second). Death rates for white men from all causes were 685.7 (i.e., rank of fifth), and death rates for black men from all causes were 1,096 (i.e., rank of second).

Residents of Tennessee paid just over one billion dollars in state and local taxes in 1999 (i.e., $187.64 per capita, rank of 47th), and had $22,739 per capita income after all taxes—federal, state, and local—were paid that year (i.e., rank of 31st).

STATE OF TEXAS PROBLEMS PROFILE

Texas is the nation's second largest state geographically, and the second largest state in population (i.e., almost 21 million persons) in 2000. Texas has, within its borders,

Tennessee Problems Profile

Factor	< Fewer Problems	More Problems >	Factor Score
Government		O	37.63
Expended		O	34.14
Crime		O	31.81
Protection		O	34.20
Punishment		O	26.05
Natural Death		O	38.50
Highway Fatalities		O	29.95
Traumatic Death		O	38.50
Health		O	37.63
Medical Coverage	O		20.94
Teen Problems		O	34.94
School Achievement		O	42.00
Educational Support		O	39.00
Work/Employment		O	29.35
Economic Factor		O	31.29
SUMMARY		O	505.93

Texas Problems Profile

Factor	< Fewer Problems ———————— More Problems >	Factor Score
Government	···O····················	31.88
Expended	···O········	42.00
Crime	···O·············	40.38
Protection	··O···········	34.60
Punishment	···O·······	46.32
Natural Death	··········O··	13.92
Highway Fatalities	··O················	30.91
Traumatic Death	·················O··	17.75
Health	·······································O···················	32.44
Medical Coverage	···O···········	40.50
Teen Problems	··O·················	36.06
School Achievement	·····································O····················	32.63
Educational Support	····························O·······························	28.67
Work/Employment	·······················O···································	25.88
Economic Factor	···O·············	36.43
SUMMARY	···O··················	490.34

267,338 square miles. The state has 76.5 persons per square mile in population density, putting it almost in the middle (i.e., rank of 27th) of the 50 states on that variable. In all, 30 percent of the residents are Hispanic (rank of third), 50 percent are white non-Hispanic (i.e., rank of 47th), and 12 percent are black (i.e., rank of 17th).

When the United States purchased the Louisiana Territory in 1803, it claimed title to lands as far west as the Rio Grande. By 1819, however, the United States had accepted the Sabine River as the western boundary of the territory. Stephen Fuller Austin secured permission of the Spanish government to establish a colony on a grant of 200,000 acres. When Mexico became independent in 1821, the grant was continued. Mexican General Antonio Lopez de Santa Anna later accomplished a coup in Mexico, and Texas then formed a provisional government and issued a declaration of independence in 1836. The siege of the Alamo followed, and the Republic of Texas was established. A treaty of annexation by the United States was approved by Texas and the United States in 1845, and Texas became a state in 1846. Fifteen years later it seceded and joined the Confederacy.

In 1999 Texas collected state and local taxes of $181.02 (i.e., rank of 49th), and Texans had left $23,619, per capita, after taxes were paid for federal, state, and local governments. Citizens paid 11.98 percent of per capita income for all taxes (i.e., rank of 40th). Retail sales, per capita, were $9,430 in 1997.

Average murder rates were 11.64 per 100,000 persons in Texas between 1960 and 1998 (i.e., rank of fourth), robbery rates were 154.65 (i.e., rank of 11th), assault rates were 267.88 (i.e., rank of 15th), rape rates were 33.80 (i.e., rank of 10th), burglary rates were 1,353.05 (i.e., rank of 5th), larceny rates were 2,854.95 (i.e., rank of 12th), and motor vehicle theft rates were 483.11 (i.e., rank of 13th).

Texas has executed 321 prisoners since 1950, and the state had an increase in prison population of 109.45 percent between 1992 and 1996. The state pays $12,215 in operating costs to keep an inmate in prison for one year (i.e., rank of 47th), which costs each person in the state $85.51 per year (i.e., rank of 13th).

Death rates from all causes were 734.5 per 100,000 (i.e., rank of 44th), death rates from heart problems were 224.4 (i.e., rank of 39th), death rates from cancer were 165.6 (i.e., rank of 43rd), and death rates from automobile accidents were 19.3 (i.e., rank of 21st). Each Medicaid recipient in Texas received $3,071 in 1998 (i.e., rank of 39th).

In all, 78.2 percent of Texas residents over 25 reported that they had graduated from high school (i.e., rank of 48th), 24.4 percent reported that they had graduated from college (i.e., rank of 23rd), and 4.83 percent were currently enrolled in college (i.e., rank of 37th). Texas spent $1,052, per capita, to support public schools in the state. A total of $537.51 was spent by industry on research and development, per capita, in 1998; $84.71 was spent by universities.

STATE OF UTAH PROBLEMS PROFILE

Utah became the 45th state in the Union in 1896, after decades of failure to attain statehood. Utah has a population of approximately 2.25 million residents, more than doubling its population in the past 30 years. The state has 84,916 square miles of territory, giving it a population density of 25.9 persons per square mile, but more than three-quarters of the state's population lives in a metropolitan area. Eighty percent of its population adheres to the Christian faith (i.e., ranked first); Salt Lake City is the world headquarters of the Church of Jesus Christ of the Latter-day Saints (i.e., Mormons). Utah's population is 95 percent white and 1 percent black. Less than 9 percent of its residents are over 65 years of age (i.e., rank of 49th), and 33 percent are under the age of 18 (i.e., rank of first), reflecting the same age discrepancy pattern as is evident

Utah Problems Profile

Factor	< Fewer Problems	More Problems >	Factor Score
Government	....O............		36.00
Expended	....O................		31.00
Crime	......................O..		20.31
Protection	....O..............		30.60
Punishment	............................O..		20.64
Natural Death	O..		5.17
Highway Fatalities	....................O..		21.32
Traumatic Death	.................................O..................................		26.00
Health	..............O..		15.88
Medical Coverage	...............................O....................................		21.69
Teen Problems	..............O..		17.11
School Achievement	......O..		8.75
Educational Support	...............................O....................................		25.28
Work/Employment	............................O..		23.09
Economic Factor	...................O...		14.71
SUMMARY	...................O...		317.54

in Alaska. There are 3.15 persons per household in Utah (i.e., rank of first), and 68 percent own their own home (i.e., rank of 18th).

More than 90 percent of Utah residents report that they graduated from high school (i.e., rank of fourth), 28 percent graduated from college (i.e., rank of 10th), and 7.42 percent are enrolled in college (i.e., rank of first). Expenditures per pupil in average daily attendance were $4,059 in 1999 (i.e., rank of 50th).

Citizens in Utah paid $815.62 per capita in taxes to the state government in 1999 (i.e., rank of 21st), and $2,047.88 per capita in taxes to the federal government (i.e., rank of 42nd). The state expended $324.28 per capita for total state and local justice systems in 1996, of which $132.27 went for police protection (i.e., rank of 32nd), $81.91 went for judicial and legal costs (i.e., rank of 14th), and $110.10 for corrections (i.e., rank of 26th).

Utah ranks 50th for percent of both males and females who smoke, 36th for syphilis cases per 1,000 population, 36th for tuberculosis cases, and 33rd for AIDS cases. Each Medicaid recipient in the state received $2,866 in 1998, and the state has 200 physicians per 100,000 population (i.e., rank of 38th); 13.9 percent of the population had no health insurance in 1998 (i.e., rank of 32nd).

The murder rate average over the 39 years 1960 to 1998 was 2.93 per 100,000 persons, (i.e., 42nd). The rape rate average was 23.83 (i.e., rank of 27th), robbery rate average was 55.82 (i.e., rank of 39th), assault rate average was 134.92 (i.e., rank of 39th), burglary rate average was 878.51 (i.e., rank of 32nd), larceny rate average was 3,294.62 (i.e., rank of 6th), and the motor vehicle theft rate average was 274.89 (i.e., rank of 30th). Utah has executed 13 persons since 1950, and its prison population increased 28 percent between 1992 and 1996.

Just over one million persons are employed in non-farm work, 8,000 in mining, 78,000 in construction, 133,000 in manufacturing, 61,000 in transportation, 254,000 in trade, 57,000 in finance, and 305,000 in services. More than 4 percent of business firms are owned by women (i.e., rank of 25th).

Utah has very low death rates per 1,000 population (i.e., rank of 49th), reflecting its high percentage of persons under the age of 18. Traffic fatalities are moderate (i.e., rank of 26th).

STATE OF VERMONT PROBLEMS PROFILE

Vermont was a territory disputed by New Hampshire and New York. Vermonters created an independent republic in 1777, which remained independent until it joined the Union as the 14th state in 1791. Its borders enclose 9,609 square miles. The state had 609,000 residents in 2000, making it the second smallest state, in terms of population, but with 64 persons per square mile, it ranks 30th in population density. Vermont's population is 98.4 percent white (i.e., rank of first), and 0.5 percent black (i.e., rank of 48th). Only Maine is as homogenous racially. Just over 12 percent of the citizens are over 65 years of age (i.e., rank of 33rd), and 23.5 percent are under the age of 18 (i.e., rank of 48th). The state ranks 15th in terms of home ownership (i.e., 69 percent).

Personal income per capita was $25,892 in 1999 (i.e., rank of 32nd), but median household income was $39,372 in 1998 (i.e., rank of 22nd). Median income increased $4,162 between 1990 and 1998. Depositors have just over six billion dollars in insured banks. State and local taxes in 1999, per capita, were $862.94 (i.e., rank of 29th), and after taxes were paid to all levels of government—federal, state, and local—per capita income was $22,386 in 1999.

In all, 48.7 percent of households had a computer (i.e., rank of eighth), and 31.8 percent were connected to the Internet (i.e., rank of seventh). Universities in the state spent $97.69 per capita on research and development (i.e., rank of 20th), and 343 residents of Vermont obtained patents in 1998, putting the state sixth in the nation in patents, per capita. Teacher average salary was

Vermont Problems Profile

Factor	< Fewer Problems .... More Problems >	Factor Score
Government	....O..............	34.50
Expended	....................O...	21.71
Crime	..........O...	8.88
Protection	.....................O..	23.60
Punishment	..O...	11.77
Natural Death	......................O..	21.00
Highway Fatalities	..............O..	20.23
Traumatic Death	.......................O...	21.50
Health	.........O...	10.94
Medical Coverage	O...	7.50
Teen Problems	..O...	9.83
School Achievement	....O...	8.63
Educational Support	.............O...	15.11
Work/Employment	........................O...	24.09
Economic Factor	..................O..	17.79
SUMMARY	....O...	257.07

$37,078 in 1998 (i.e., rank of 27th). More than 89 percent of Vermont residents over 25 years of age reported that they had graduated from high school (i.e., rank of eighth), and 28.3 percent had graduated from college (i.e., rank of ninth).

The average murder rate in Vermont over the years 1960 to 1998 was 2.11 per 100,000 population (i.e., rank of 47th). The average rape rate was 18.72 (i.e., rank of 39th), average robbery rate was 13.9 (i.e., rank of 49th), average assault rate was 62.53 (i.e., rank of 48th), average burglary rate was 8,438.95 (i.e., rank of 35th), average larceny rate was 1,883.40 (i.e., rank of 41st), and average auto theft rate was 162.19 per 100,000 (i.e., rank of 46th). The state has executed two prisoners since 1950. Vermont spent $56.43 per person in the state to fund prisons (i.e., rank of 33rd). The state spent $3.93 per inmate for food each day (i.e., rank of 13th).

There were 30 births in Vermont in 1996 per 1,000 to all females ages 15 through 19 (i.e., rank of 49th), and among teens who gave birth in 1995, 38 percent smoked

(i.e., rank of first). Of Vermont residents, 40.4 percent adhere to the Christian faith (i.e., rank of 40th).

Vermont had 15.15 traffic fatalities per 100,000 population in 1999 (i.e., rank of 28th). In all, 53.1 percent of car occupants killed wore no seatbelt (i.e., rank of 29th). Death rate of white women from all causes per 100,000 was 360.4 (i.e., rank of 25th), and death rate of white men from all causes was 572.6 (i.e., rank of 27th). Death rate of white women from diabetes was 12.7 (i.e., rank of 8th), and death rate of white men from diabetes was 16.7, rank of sixth). Vermont has 305 physicians per 100,000 population (i.e., rank of sixth), and only 6.3 percent of children have no health insurance (i.e., rank of 49th).

STATE OF VIRGINIA PROBLEMS PROFILE

Virginia, the "Old Dominion," was one of the 13 original colonies. Early settlement dates back to Jamestown in 1607, and its charter granted most of the unexplored lands west of the Atlantic to the Mississippi River. Its statesmen were leaders in the American Revolution and

Virginia Problems Profile

Factor	< Fewer Problems .... More Problems >	Factor Score
Government	......O...	13.38
Expended	....O........	33.71
Crime	.............O...	20.00
Protection	....O............	33.50
Punishment	....O....	40.27
Natural Death	..............O...	18.42
Highway Fatalities	..................O...	22.73
Traumatic Death	...............O...	16.00
Health	.................................O...............................	31.63
Medical Coverage	.............O...	20.13
Teen Problems	...................O..	22.72
School Achievement	..............O...	19.75
Educational Support	.......................O..	23.17
Work/Employment	........................O...	26.12
Economic Factor	......O...	11.64
SUMMARY	...................O..	353.16

in the first Continental Congress, and four of the first five presidents were from Virginia. The state had abolished the slave trade in 1778, but slavery was allowed to continue. There were just over seven million residents of Virginia in the 2000 census. With 173 persons per square mile, the population density of Virginia ranked 15th in the nation. In all, 24.2 percent of the population is below the age of 18 years (i.e., rank of 43rd), and 11.3 percent is over the age of 65 (i.e., rank of 44th). Seventeen percent of the children in the state live below the poverty line (i.e., rank of 24th). More than 78 percent of the population lives in a metropolitan area (i.e., rank of 19th).

Almost 76 percent of Virginia's population is white (i.e., rank of 41st) and 20 percent is black (i.e., rank of eighth). In all, 66.3 percent own their own home (i.e., rank of 30th). Nine percent of the state's adults work for government at one level or another (i.e., rank of eighth). Three percent work in construction (i.e., rank of 12th), 5.71 percent in manufacturing (i.e., rank of 33rd), 2.69 percent in transportation (i.e., rank of 18th), 10.93 percent in trade (i.e., rank of 37th), 2.72 percent in finance (i.e., rank of 22nd), and 16.20 percent in service (i.e., rank of ninth).

Personal income totaled more than $204 billion in 1999 (i.e., rank of 12th), resulting in $25,247 per capita income that same year (i.e., rank of 15th). Residents of the state paid $1,184.73 per capita in state and local taxes that year (i.e., rank of 10th). Per capita expenditures for total state and local justice systems were $338.02 in 1996 (i.e., rank of 25th), of which $136.40 was for police protection (i.e., rank of 28th), $52.23 was for judicial and legal costs (i.e., rank of 36th), and $149.39 was for corrections (i.e., rank of 10th). Retail sales per capita were $9,293 in 1997 (i.e., rank of 32nd). Virginia received $8,416 in federal funds per person in the state in 1999. Women owned 3.94 percent of all business firms in 1992 (i.e., rank of 32nd), and minorities owned 2.46 percent of all business firms that same year (i.e., rank of 28th).

Virginia had a violent crime rate average of 299.57 per 100,000 population over a 39-year period (i.e., rank of 30th), a property crime rate average of 3,295.44 over that same 39-year period (i.e., rank of 33rd), and a murder rate average of 8.66 (i.e., rank of 19th). The state has executed 105 persons for crimes since 1950, and its prison population increased 30.86 percent between 1992 and 1996 (i.e., rank of 10th). The state spends $69.36 per person in the state to operate the state's prison system, which includes $2.96 for food for each inmate ever day (i.e., rank of 27th).

Over 87 percent of Virginia residents report that they graduated from high school (i.e., rank of 16th), and 31.6 percent report that they graduated from college (i.e., rank of fifth). Just over 5 percent are currently enrolled in college (i.e., rank of 24th). State expenditures per pupil in average daily attendance were $6,550 in 1999 (i.e., rank of 26th). Average starting salary for teachers was $26,179 in 1998 (i.e., rank of 23rd), and average teacher salary was $38,091 (i.e., rank of 23rd).

STATE OF WASHINGTON PROBLEMS PROFILE

Washington was admitted to the Union in 1889 as the 42nd state. Its borders contain 68,192 square miles of territory, divided roughly by the Cascade Range. Washington has just under six million residents, putting the state in the middle range of the 50 states in terms of population density (i.e., 86.5 per square mile). Almost 83 percent of its residents are white non-Hispanic (i.e., rank of 24th), 6.5 percent are Hispanic (i.e., rank of 16th), and 3.5 percent are black (i.e., rank of 35th). Just over 11 percent are over the age of 65 (i.e., rank of 42nd), and 25.8 percent are under 18 years of age (i.e., rank of 22nd). Just over 32 percent of residents adhere to the Christian faith (i.e., rank of 47th).

More than 8 percent of those employed work for government at some level (i.e., rank of 13th), 2.85 percent work in construction (i.e., rank of 13th), 6.09 percent

Washington Problems Profile

Factor	< Fewer Problems	More Problems >	Factor Score
Government		O	23.38
Expended		O	20.14
Crime		O	32.13
Protection		O	35.60
Punishment		O	20.36
Natural Death	O		10.58
Highway Fatalities		O	22.27
Traumatic Death		O	24.00
Health	O		16.38
Medical Coverage	O		19.81
Teen Problems	O		19.33
School Achievement	O		12.25
Educational Support	O		17.17
Work/Employment	O		16.74
Economic Factor		O	23.86
SUMMARY	O		313.99

work in manufacturing (i.e., rank of 31st), 2.46 percent work in transportation (i.e., rank of 24th), 11.33 percent work in trade (i.e., rank of 29th), 2.43 percent work in finance (i.e., rank of 32nd), and 13.28 percent work in service (i.e., rank of 36th). Average annual pay was $33,076 in 1998 (i.e., rank of 10th). Median household income in 1998 was $47,241 (i.e., rank of fifth). Nine percent of residents in Washington lived below the poverty line in 1998 (i.e., rank of 45th).

More than 91 percent of the state's residents over 25 years of age reported that they had graduated from high school (i.e., rank of second), 28.6 percent had graduated from college (i.e., rank of eighth), and 5.47 percent were currently enrolled in college (i.e., rank of 21st). Washington spent $5,446 per pupil in public schools in 1997, and the average teacher salary in the state was $37,408 in 1998. Over 56 percent of households in Washington have a computer (i.e., rank of third), and 36.6 percent are connected to the Internet (i.e., rank of third). Research and development funds expended by industry averaged $1,470.72 per capita (i.e., rank of sixth), and research and development funds spent by universities averaged $92.77 per capita (i.e., rank of 24th).

There were 6,905 murders in Washington state between 1960 and 1998, putting the state at a rank of 35th in that category of crime. Rapes were reported 65,992 times during that 39-year period, putting the state average in rape over those years at 37.78 per 100,000 population (i.e., rank of fifth). Robberies averaged 103.81 per 100,000 population (i.e., rank of 24th), and assaults averaged 192.63 (i.e., rank of 26th). Burglaries averaged 1,304.52 per 100,000 population (i.e., rank of seventh). Almost 19 percent of all assaults in 1998 were gun related (i.e., rank of 24th). In all, $362.51 were devoted to state and local funds for total justice system costs in 1996 (i.e., rank of 18th), of which $145.70 was provided for police protection (i.e., rank of 23rd),

$79.34 was provided for judicial and legal costs, and $137.47 was expended on corrections. There were 200 adults on parole in 1999 under state and federal jurisdiction (i.e., rank of 48th).

Death rate from all causes in 1997 was 739 per 100,000 population (i.e., rank of 43rd). Death rates from auto accidents were 13.6 per 100,000 (i.e., rank of 37th). Each recipient of Medicaid in Washington state got $1,447 (i.e., rank of 50th). There are 235 physicians per 100,000 (i.e., rank of 19th). Washington had 141 cases of syphilis reported in 1998, and 265 cases of tuberculosis (i.e., .05 cases per 1,000 population, for a rank of 25th).

STATE OF WEST VIRGINIA PROBLEMS PROFILE

West Virginia was originally a part of the state of Virginia, but when secession was proposed in 1861, a majority of the western delegates of the state were opposed. Two meetings were then held in Wheeling, and the second Wheeling convention pronounced the Richmond government void. Congress consented to West Virginia's admission to the Union on June 20, 1863. The population of West Virginia was about 1.8 million persons in the 2000 census, and with 75 persons per square mile, the state ranks 29th in population density. Just over 40 percent of the state's population lives in a metropolitan area. In terms of religion, 41.3 percent of the residents adhere to the Christian faith (i.e., rank of 38th), and one tenth of one percent are Jewish (i.e., rank of 50th).

More than 21,000 workers in West Virginia are engaged in mining (i.e., rank of 5th), 32,700 thousand are engaged in construction, 82,100 work in manufacturing, 37,700 are in transportation, 164,100 work in trade, 29,700 work in finance, and 220,600 are employed in services. In addition, 142,000 work for government at some level. Median household income was $27,432 in 1997 (i.e., rank of 50th), and 16.8 percent of the population lives below the poverty line (i.e., rank of fifth). More than

West Virginia Problems Profile

Factor	< Fewer Problems	More Problems >	Factor Score
Government		..........O..........	37.00
Expended	........O..........		15.86
Crime	..........O..........		9.50
Protection	..........O..........		23.40
Punishment	..........O..........		15.36
Natural Death		....................O	47.25
Highway Fatalities		.............O..........	29.95
Traumatic Death		.............O..........	38.00
Health		.........O..........	27.50
Medical Coverage		.........O..........	25.88
Teen Problems	..............O..........		20.06
School Achievement		.................O......	43.75
Educational Support		..............O..........	32.44
Work/Employment		...................O..	37.71
Economic Factor		....................O	43.79
SUMMARY		.............O..........	447.44

24 percent of children live in poverty (i.e., rank of fourth). Median income in West Virginia decreased $728 between 1990 and 1998 (i.e., rank of 48th).

West Virginia's death rate from all causes is 1,150 per 100,000 (i.e., rank of first). Death rate from heart problems is 381.3 per 100,000 (i.e., rank of first), and the rate from cancer is 262 (i.e., rate of first). Death rate from pulmonary problems is 62.7 per 100,000 population (i.e., rank of first), and the rate from diabetes is 37.6 (i.e., rank of second). The infant mortality rate is 9.6 per 1,000 births (i.e., rank of second). There are 215 physicians per 100,000 population in West Virginia (i.e., rank of 30th), and 17.2 percent of the population has no health insurance (i.e., rank of 16th).

Three-fourths of adults over 25 in West Virginia reported that they had graduated from high school (i.e., rank of 50th), and 17.9 percent said they had graduated from college (i.e., rank of 48th). West Virginia has 28.3 percent of households which have a computer (i.e., rank of 49th), and 17.6 percent of households are connected to the Internet.

More than 29 percent of West Virginia males smoke (i.e., rank of ninth), and 26 percent of females smoke (i.e., rank of third). Births to unmarried women were 32.4 percent (i.e., rank of 25th), and abortion rates were 6.6 per 1,000 (i.e., rank of 47th). Eight percent of children are born with low birth weights in West Virginia (i.e., rank of 17th).

For the 39-year period from 1960 to 1998, average murder rates in West Virginia were 5.40 per 100,000 population. Average rape rates were 13.02 (i.e., rank of 47th), average robbery rates were 34.18 (i.e., rank of 42nd), average assault rates were 94.94 (i.e., rank of 43rd), average burglary rates were 511.85 (i.e., rank of 48th), average larceny rates were 1,102 (i.e., rank of 50th), and average automobile theft rates were 138.74 per 100,000 (i.e., rank of 48th). It costs each person in the state $25.98 to incarcerate a prisoner for a year (i.e., rank of 49th).

STATE OF WISCONSIN PROBLEMS PROFILE

Wisconsin was admitted to the Union in 1830 as the 30th state. The state includes 56,154 square miles of territory, and with 5.36 million people in 2000, the population density is 96.7 persons per square mile. Almost 92 percent of the population is white (i.e., rank of 17th) and 5.6 percent is black (i.e., rank of 28th); 13.2 percent is over the age of 65 (i.e., rank of 22nd), and 25.7 percent is under the age of 18 (i.e., rank of 24th). Wisconsin has 2,295 licensed child care centers, and 67.2 percent of females are in the labor force (i.e., rank of 3rd). Median income increased $1,527 (i.e., rank of 30th) between 1990 and 1998 to $41,327 (i.e., rank of 15th). Just under 9 percent of the population was below the poverty line in 1998 (i.e., rank of 47th).

Infant mortality rates in Wisconsin were 6.5 per 1,000 births (i.e., rank of 34th) in 1997. Abortion rates were 12.3 per 1,000 in 1996 (i.e., rank of 35th), and 6.5 percent of children born were of low birth weight in 1998 (i.e., rank of 38th). Death rates from all causes were 868.4 for 100,000 population (i.e., rank of 30th) in 1997. Death rates from heart problems were 264.9 (i.e., rank of 28th), death rates from cancer were 204.6 (i.e., rank of 28th), death rates from stroke were 71.2 (i.e., rank of 9th), death rates from pulmonary problems were 39.0 (i.e., rank of 34th), and death rates from diabetes were 22.7 (i.e., rank of 30th). There were 227 physicians per 100,000 population in 1998 (i.e., rank of 24th), and 11.8 percent of the population had no health insurance (i.e., rank of 38th). Almost 34 percent of all residents are at risk for overweight (i.e., rank of 26th).

The percent of all robberies with a gun was 55.7 percent in 1998 (i.e., rank of third), but the average rate of robberies between 1960 and 1998 was 59.96 per 100,000

Wisconsin Problems Profile

Factor	< Fewer Problems	More Problems >	Factor Score
Government	....................................O...		20.38
Expended	................O...		17.14
Crime	................O...		16.44
Protection	....................................O...		22.80
Punishment	................O...		17.45
Natural Death	....O...		24.42
Highway Fatalities	..........O...		18.64
Traumatic Death	....................O...		16.50
Health	........................O...		19.56
Medical Coverage	..........O...		17.06
Teen Problems	........................O...		20.00
School Achievement	..........................O...		19.75
Educational Support	......O...		13.94
Work/Employment	..........O...		19.85
Economic Factor	................O...		15.29
SUMMARY	..........O...		279.22

(i.e., rank of 38th), and the average rate of assaults was 83.57 per 100,000 population (i.e., rank of 46th). There were 5,392 murders committed in Wisconsin from 1960 to 1998, and the average murder rate per 100,000 persons was 2.93 per 100,000 (i.e., rank of 43rd) during that period. The rape rate during that time period was 13.67 (i.e., rank of 47th), the assault rate was 83.57 (i.e., rank of 46th), and the burglary rate was 655.80 per 100,000 population (i.e., rank of 44th). The state spends $27,771 to incarcerate a prisoner for one year.

More than 86 percent of all persons over 25 years of age responded that they had graduated from high school (i.e., rank of 17th), and 23.6 percent said they had graduated from college (i.e., rank of 29th). Wisconsin expended $489 per capita in the state to support colleges and universities.

In all, 63.9 percent of Wisconsin residents are Christian (i.e., rank of 10th), 19 percent of workers belong to a union, and the state received $4,305 in funds per person in the state from the federal government in 1999. Wisconsin residents paid 15 percent of income to all levels of government in taxes—federal, state, and local—in 1999. In Wisconsin, that meant that citizens sent $2,932.04 to Washington, DC and $1,193.41 to state and local governments; $366.21 sent to Wisconsin were accounted for as per capita expenditures for total state and local justice system costs in 1996 (i.e., rank of 17th). Of that amount, $169.28 went for police protection, $123.90 for corrections, and the rest for judicial and legal costs.

STATE OF WYOMING PROBLEMS PROFILE

Wyoming is the last state, alphabetically, and the smallest state in population, just under half a million residents. The state includes 97,914 square miles, and has 4.9 persons per square mile, and thus is the second least populated state (next to Alaska) in the Union. Wyoming was created as a territory in 1868, and became a state in 1890.

The first territorial legislature in 1869 granted women the right to vote. That right was included in the constitution prepared in 1889, and Wyoming elected the first woman governor in 1925. More than 26 percent of its residents are under the age of 18 (i.e., rank of 15th), and 11.6 percent are over the age of 65 (i.e., rank of 37th). More than 96 percent of the residents are white.

More than 10 percent of Wyoming's residents work for some level of government—local, state, or federal—putting the state third among the 50 states in that respect. Average funding per pupil in the public schools of the state was $5,294 in 1997 (i.e., rank of 20th), and the average teacher salary was $32,642 (i.e., rank of 43rd). Support services per pupil were $2,429 (i.e., rank of seventh). Wyoming has fewer students per computer (i.e., 6.9) than any state in the nation, and 46 percent of households have a computer (i.e., rank of 14th).

Wyoming has had 808 murders since 1960, averaging 5.03 murders per 100,000 population between 1960 and 1998 (i.e., rank of 31st). It had 20.81 rape rate average per 100,000 during that period (i.e., rank of 33rd), 25.75 robbery rate average (i.e., rank of 44th), 163.67 assault rate average (i.e., rank of 33rd), 638.14 burglary rate average (i.e., rank of 46th), 2,542.45 larceny rate average (i.e., rank of 17th), and 184.64 auto theft rate average (i.e., rank of 41st). There were four bank robberies in 1998, and four persons were arrested for marijuana in 1999. The state had 2.90 prisoners per 1,000 population in 1996 (i.e., rank of 28th), a 30.67 percent increase in the prison population since 1992 (i.e., rank of 11th). The prison system cost each person in the state $60.52 to operate for a year (i.e., rank of 30th).

Household median income in Wyoming was $35,250 in 1998 (i.e., rank of 38th), and 10.6 percent of residents lived below the poverty line (i.e., rank of 31st). Median income increased $2,053 between 1990 and 1998 (i.e., rank of 21st). Per capita income in 1999 was $26,363 (i.e.,

Wyoming Problems Profile

Factor	< Fewer Problems	More Problems >	Factor Score
Government	...................O................		19.25
Expended	..........O..............		17.00
Crime	...........O...............		15.00
Protection	....O.................		9.40
Punishment	.....................O........		23.05
Natural Death	........O..............		8.00
Highway Fatalities	....O......		32.91
Traumatic Death	....O..		46.50
Health	...................O...............		19.63
Medical Coverage	..........................O..........		26.94
Teen Problems	...........O..............		16.44
School Achievement	...................O...............		22.63
Educational Support	...........O..............		16.39
Work/Employment	.........................O...........		25.82
Economic Factor	.........................O...........		26.36
SUMMARY	................O................		325.31

rank of 30th). Per capita taxes paid to state and local governments were $290.51 in 1999 (i.e., rank of 43rd). After taxes were paid to all levels of government—federal, state, and local—citizens had $22,782 per capita remaining (i.e., rank of 29th).

Wyoming had 5.8 infant mortality per 1,000 births in 1997 (i.e., rank of 45th). The death rate from all causes per 100,000 population was 780.6 in 1997 (i.e., rank of 40th). Death rate from automobile accidents was 25 per 100,000 (i.e., rank of sixth). More than 68 percent of passenger car occupants killed wore no seatbelt (i.e., rank of fourth). Each Medicaid recipient re-

ceived $4,174 (i.e., rank of 16th). There are 171 physicians per 100,000 population in Wyoming (i.e., rank of 46th). There were six cases of AIDS reported in the state in 1998, two syphilis cases, and four tuberculosis cases. Males who smoke comprise 23.9 percent of the population (i.e., rank of 34th), and 21.7 percent of females smoke (i.e., rank of 21st).

NOTE

1. John Stuart Mill, *On the Liberty of Thought and Discussion,* in Howard Mumford Jones (ed.), *Primer of Intellectual Freedom* (Cambridge: Harvard University Press, 1949), 111.

CHAPTER 10

Race and Gender

In answer to the question as to what shall be done with the Negro, I have sometimes replied, "Do nothing with him, give him fair play, and let him alone." They willingly accepted my idea of letting the Negro alone, but not so my idea of giving the Negro fair play. . . . When we consider the long years of slavery, the years of injustice, of cruel strife and degradation to which the Negro was doomed, the duty of the nation is not, and cannot be, performed by simply letting him alone.

—Frederick Douglass[1]

INTRODUCTION

THOSE WHO ARE SKILLED WITH "SMALL TALK" OFTEN MAINTAIN that the rules for good conversation are these: never talk about politics, never talk about religion, never talk about race, and never talk about sex. What is generally meant by that advice is "don't talk about politics, religion, or race in ways that get people to expose their basic beliefs and values; that will start an argument." The admonition not to talk about sex is aimed at males in the group: "Don't tell any dirty stories."

There are no variables in this study that relate directly to attitudes or beliefs, but the whole effort was based on the supposition that elected officials would be better public servants if they were knowledgeable about facts that relate to proposed policies before they act in policy-making roles. Citizens would be better citizens, if they were knowledgeable, too.

The first section of this chapter will focus on death rates of white women, black women, white men, and black men for 13 different causes of death. The second section will examine death rates of these same four groups by comparing death rates of people who lived in states confronted with more problems with death rates of people who lived in states confronted with fewer problems. A final section will be devoted to comparisons of states with more problems and states with fewer problems on variables not included in any of the factors created especially to make up the SUMMARY factor, which summarizes much of the data reported in Chapter 9. These final analyses will not be related to race and gender. All statistical tables for this chapter are included in Appendix D.

CAUSES OF DEATH, BY GENDER AND RACE

The information about death that relates to gender and race in Appendix G came from the National Center for Health Statistics (see Tables G.89 through G.140). These data were not included in any of the 15 factors that made up the SUMMARY factor, because many states did not have enough minorities as residents to get accurate estimates of death rates by cause of death as related to race. Information from the 52 tables cited above was not included in any of the three death factors that we created (i.e., DEATH, HIWAYDEA, and TRAUMA); thus these variables were not included in the final SUMMARY factor (see Appendix B for a list of the 120 variables that were included in the 15 factors). We did analyze the data in those 52 tables, however, and the analyses are summarized in this chapter for states for which we had information about death as related to gender, sex, and place of residence.

If you study Tables G.89 through G.140 in Appendix G, you will note that there are four sets of tables: one for white women, one for black women, one for white men, and one for black men. In each of those four sets of tables, 13 causes of death are described, with data about deaths per 100,000 reported where there were enough cases in a state to make accurate estimates of death rates by race and gender. This is interesting and important information about causes of death, but it is not available for every state, for the reasons described above.

We begin by summarizing Tables D.1 through D.13, which are included in Appendix D. As said above, each of the 13 tables includes information about death rates of four categories of persons (i.e., white women, black women, white men, and black men), as compared with each of the other categories, on one cause of death (e.g., malignancy, cardiovascular disease, suicide, or death from all causes). We used paired t-test analysis to make these comparisons. For each of the 13 causes of death for which we had data about death rates per 100,000 persons over a three-year period (1994–1996), we determined the statistical significance of the difference of mean scores by computing the "t" statistic with a paired t-test, which compared mean scores for those states for which we had data. The following six comparisons for each of the 13 causes of death are described in Tables D.1 through D.13 in Appendix D, according to the cause of death, as reported to the National Center for Health Statistics:

white women	and	black women
white women	and	white men
white women	and	black men
black women	and	white men
black women	and	black men
white men	and	black men

In almost every comparison made, women lived longer than men and whites lived longer than blacks, and almost every difference was statistically significant at the .01 level or beyond. Most of these differences were very large (e.g., black men tended to have death rates about twice those of white women), suggesting something about the cultures of the states that affects people where it really hurts: life itself.

States differed dramatically on reported death rates, especially for blacks. Note the standard deviations reported in Table D.1 in Appendix D, for instance, which were 30.42 for white women on all deaths and 178.42 for black men on all deaths. These numbers suggest that death rates for black men were extremely high in some states and markedly lower in other states. A careful study of Table G.116 in Appendix G indicates that states with high death rates for black males have rates almost triple those of states with low death rates for black males.

Illinois has the highest death rate from all causes for black males of any of the 50 states. Mississippi has the highest percentage of blacks of any state, but Illinois has more blacks than Mississippi, by almost a two-to-one ratio. Illinois has a rate of 1,105 deaths per 100,000 black males, while Mississippi has a rate of 1,050 deaths for the same number of black males, but the rate for black females in Illinois is 615, just over half the rate for black males. Both states have problems, when compared to Massachusetts (death rates for black males of 777 and 460 for black females per 100,000) or Maine (death rates for black males of 577 and 364 for black females per 100,000). These figures suggest that something related to race and gender affects death rates differently across the country.

If you study Table G.89 in Appendix G, it immediately becomes apparent that most of the states with highest death rates for white women are in the South, whereas most of the states with lowest death rates for white women are in the North. If you study Table G.90 in Appendix G, however, which presents information about black women's death rates, most of the states with low death rates are in the North or West. States with high death rates for black women are primarily in the South, as was true for white women, but Nebraska, Illinois, and Indiana are also among the states with high death rates for black women. The picture for black females is mixed in terms of death rate as related to geography.

The data we have been discussing pertains to death from all causes. If we turn our attention to death from malignancies or cardiovascular diseases (i.e., Table D.2 and Table D.4 in Appendix D), we note that death from cancer is almost twice as high among black males as white females. Listing death rates from cancer in rank order, high to low, we note this sequence—black males, white

males, black females, and white females—and the statistical significance of the difference of mean scores among these groups is very high. These differences are real; they did not occur by chance.

Black males and black females have much higher death rates from diabetes than white males or white females. Black males and white males die at much higher rates than black females or white females from both general accidents and motor vehicle accidents, and the same thing is true for death from pneumonia, suicide, and homicide. Differences in motor vehicle deaths and homicides among blacks and whites, females and males, are also great. The death rates of black males from homicide are astronomical; more than seven times as high as death rates of white males.

We encourage you to study the tables in Appendix G. See where your state stands. There are powerful forces at work affecting death rates, and it is not immediately obvious just what those forces are. States may have little or no effect on the death rates we have been describing, or they may have a lot of effect in some cases and less in others.

COMPARISON OF DEATH RATES BY STATES, RANKED ACCORDING TO PROBLEMS

In the previous chapter, we described how we developed a Problems Profile for each state by adding 15 factor scores and creating a SUMMARY factor that summarized information from 120 selected variables into this one variable. We then listed all 50 states in rank order, according to the SUMMARY score. For the analyses reported here, we divided that SUMMARY list into two groups: a top half and a bottom half (i.e., 25 states above the median and 25 states below the median). Those in the top half were described as states with more problems. Those in the bottom half were described as states with fewer problems.

In this section we compare death rates of persons categorized by gender and race—white females, black females, white males, and black males—according to whether those persons lived in states with more problems or fewer problems. Tables D.14 through D.17 describe the results of these comparisons, which were accomplished by computing the "t" statistic for each of the 52 analyses involved (i.e., 4 categories of people and 13 causes of death: $4 \times 13 = 52$). The "t" statistic estimates the statistical significance of the difference of mean scores for two groups.

Among white males, there was a difference in rate of death caused by malignancies for persons who lived in states with more problems, when compared with persons who lived in states with fewer problems. The death rate was significantly lower for those who lived in states with fewer problems.

Among all groups—white females, black females, white males, and black males—there were significant differences in the rates of death from cardiovascular causes. In every comparison, death rates were significantly lower for persons who lived in states with fewer problems.

Among both groups of males—white and black—death rates from homicide were lower for those who lived in states with fewer problems than they were for those who lived in states with more problems.

Finally, in 20 of the 52 comparisons made, persons who lived in states with fewer problems died at significantly lower rates than persons who lived in states with more problems. In two comparisons—black females and black males—death rates for drug-induced death were higher for persons who lived in states with fewer problems than for those who lived in states with more problems. In the other 30 comparisons, none of the differences were significant statistically.

FURTHER COMPARISONS
Most of this chapter has been devoted to looking at individual states in terms of their relationship to the other 49 states on special factors developed from 120 variables to create the general SUMMARY factor. The SUMMARY factor summarizes information in ways that enabled us to rank states according to the number of problems each state faces, as described in Chapter 9.

In this section we repeat one of the processes described already (i.e., we separated states into a "more problems" half and a "fewer problems" half), but this time we compared those two groups of states on variables that were not included in any factor that went to make up the SUMMARY factor. These comparisons, however, were made without regard to race or gender. We were looking for clues about how these two sets of states might differ on variables that had not been used to create new factors (although we occasionally made exceptions to this rule to demonstrate a particular point). We begin the discussion with one of the exceptions. All information about these comparisons is reported in Appendix D, beginning with Table D.18. In this section we report differences between states with more problems and states with fewer problems only when differences occurred at a level that was significant statistically.

In developing the factor EDUCSUPP (i.e., support for public education), we included AVRSALRY (average salary of public school teachers), as shown in Table G.26 of Appendix G in calculating values for EDUC-SUPP, but we did not include information about the average starting salary of public school teachers (AVRSTART), shown in Table G.25 of Appendix G. In the comparison being described here, there were significant differences in the starting salaries of school teachers in states that had more problems (i.e., the top half of the SUMMARY factor; see Table G.702 in Ap-

pendix G), when compared with starting salaries of teachers in states that had fewer problems. Beginning teachers from states with more problems were paid about $1,500 more per year, on average, than beginning teachers from states with fewer problems. There were no significant differences in average salaries paid to all teachers for the same two groups, however.

We had noted earlier that starting teacher salaries in Alabama were $32,467, whereas starting teacher salaries in Massachusetts were only $24,565, while average teacher salaries in Alabama were $36,688, and average salaries in Massachusetts were $38,949. That same differential (i.e., high starting teacher salary, low average teacher salary for a state with more problems, but low starting teacher salary and high average teacher salary for a state with fewer problems) did not hold up across the board, however. States with more problems are making an effort to help children in those states learn by paying, on average, higher starting teacher salaries and comparable average teacher salaries.

The percentage of blacks who lived in states with more problems is more than twice as high as the percentage of blacks who lived in states with fewer problems. Likewise, the percentage of people who owned their own homes was higher in states with more problems than in states with fewer problems. In another comparison, though, states with fewer problems had significantly more minority firms, per capita, than states with more problems.

States with more problems had automobile death rates more than twice as high as states with fewer problems, and we used a different statistic for comparison purposes than the one entered into the HIWAYDEA factor. Infant mortality rates for whites were higher in states with more problems than in states with fewer problems. States with more problems also had a greater proportion of large trucks than states with fewer problems, but states with fewer problems had higher per capita disposable income.

SUMMARY
This chapter examined death rates in terms of race and gender in the 50 states. With few exceptions, women live longer than men, whites live longer than blacks, and persons who reside in states with fewer problems live longer than persons who reside in states with more problems. These differences in death rates warrant further study. Blacks, especially, are dying at earlier ages than whites. If life is important, higher death rates for blacks cry out for explanation. Black Americans are not getting their share of "life, liberty, and the pursuit of happiness," if we read these data accurately.

Further, areas in which states with more problems differed from states with fewer problems that fell outside the scope of the various factors and SUMMARY factor included these: states with more problems had higher starting salaries for teachers, higher proportion of blacks in the population, fewer per capita minority firms, less disposable personal income, higher home ownership, more large trucks, and less money per capita for substance abuse treatment than states with fewer problems.

In the next chapter, we will review the important findings that have been identified in this study, then draw conclusions that relate to understanding culture as that concept applies to states.

NOTE

1. Frederick Douglass, "Giving the Negro Fair Play," in Erik Bruun and Jay Crosby (eds.), *Our Nation's Archive: The History of the United States in Documents* (New York: Black Dog and Leventhal, 1999), 433.

CHAPTER 11

Cultures of the States: Conclusions

The central conservative truth is that it is culture, not politics, that determines the success of a society. The central liberal truth is that politics can change a culture and save it from itself.

—Daniel Patrick Moynihan[1]

INTRODUCTION

WE REPEAT THE STATEMENT BY FORMER SENATOR MOYNIHAN that we started with in Chapter 1, because those two sentences say it all: culture determines the success of a society, and politics can change a culture and save it from itself. In Chapter 1 we outlined our theoretical perspective in the following terms:

Our theory of culture of the states begins with an assumption: *Good state government helps people live better lives.* In moral terms, "good" means honesty and transparency in government. In effectiveness terms, "good" means that government accomplishes what needs to be accomplished. In practical terms, "good state government" means that people in the state will:

(a) live longer	(i.e., lower death rates)
(b) be healthier	(i.e., lower disease rates)
(c) be more law abiding	(i.e., lower crime rates)
(d) be better educated	(i.e., higher achievement rates)
(e) be happier	(i.e., fewer mental health problems)
(f) be more productive	(i.e., higher personal income)
(g) be less frustrated	(i.e., greater sense of personal accomplishment)
(h) have more opportunities	(e.g., in education, work, family, travel, leisure)
(i) have better government	(i.e., more confidence that "government works")
(j) be treated with respect	(i.e., fewer "run-arounds")

Good government is more helpful and less coercive, more supportive and less obvious, and more practical and less ideological. Government is manifest in taxes, budgets, laws, leadership, and processes.

In this chapter we relate what we have learned in a study of the states to our theory of culture. We followed a three-step process in reaching general conclusions.

First, we explicated the findings of this study with reference to variables by describing each finding in one sentence. These findings are all listed in Appendix E. Note the table in Appendix G from which the information for a finding based on a particular variable was based (e.g., "(G.231)" means "Table G.231 in Appendix G"). Second, we drew conclusions from the findings, then described the conclusions in terms of "acculturation." Finally, we related conclusions to the theoretical propositions set forth earlier in this book, and restated earlier in this chapter.

FINDINGS

To introduce the idea of findings (all listed in Appendix E), we begin with something that may have made sense to you before you began to read this book: differences between regions of the country seem more pronounced than differences between states. Sharp differences between states are evident on many of the variables for which we collected information, but what seemed to "jump out" at us as we studied the tables carefully was how often the numerical values for certain contiguous states clustered together in the rankings of all 50 states on many variables.

The statistical logic used in Chapter 9 forced a linear perspective on the data reported as SUMMARY in Table G.702, and this linear perspective does not lend itself to studying the unique cultural phenomena of each state. Suppose we pair states at extremes on the continuum, however, for a different perspective. Listed below, in the left-hand column, are the 10 states with the lowest factor scores on SUMMARY (i.e., states with fewer problems), and listed in the right-hand column are the 10 states with the highest factor scores on SUMMARY (i.e., states with more problems).

What we did here was pair the state with the lowest score (i.e., Minnesota) with the state with the highest score (i.e., Mississippi), then the state with the next lowest score (i.e., Massachusetts) with the state with the next highest score (i.e., Arkansas), and so forth, moving toward the center of the distribution in the ranking. We list here only those states that comprise the upper and lower quintiles of the total distribution.

Fewer Problems	*More Problems*
Minnesota	Mississippi
Massachusetts	Arkansas
Vermont	Louisiana
New Hampshire	Tennessee
Connecticut	South Carolina
Wisconsin	Oklahoma
Iowa	Alabama
New Jersey	Texas
Nebraska	Florida
Maine	Arizona

What is immediately obvious is that the ten states included in the top quintile in terms of problems would have to be considered Southern states, even though Oklahoma and Arizona were admitted to the Union after the Civil War. Likewise, the ten states included in the bottom quintile in terms of problems would be considered Northern states, although Nebraska was also admitted to the Union after the Civil War.

How do we explain the differences reflected in these pairs of states, and in the general ranking of all 50 states on the SUMMARY factor described in Chapter 9? The most reasonable explanation seems to be the notion of "acculturation."

ACCULTURATION

The American Heritage Dictionary defines "acculturation" two ways. The first definition says that acculturation is the modification of a culture as a result of contact with another culture. The second definition says that acculturation is the process by which the culture of a particular society is instilled in a human being from infancy. We use the second definition, which means that we are really talking about learning, and that is an area in which we feel very much at home.

We are educators. We have spent our entire adult lives working in and with and for institutions—teaching, administering, research, service—that were devoted to helping people learn. When we started working on this project, it was not immediately apparent to us that learning would be an important theoretical construct in a study of governance and governing and culture. Maybe it should have been, but it was not. We were thinking about laws, enforcement, judicial decisions, taxes, and the like, but it is obvious now that "acculturation" is a term that must be used to describe how those who govern and those who are governed learn to function in their immediate environment; how those persons create and perpetuate the culture in which they live.

We go back to the definition: Acculturation is the process by which the culture of a particular society is instilled in a human being from infancy. Culture is instilled. Acculturation is the process by which that occurs. Several things about both culture and acculturation might be pointed out.

Acculturation as a process is both intentional and incidental. It involves positive and negative ends, as well as positive and negative means. People who influence or direct the acculturation processes (e.g., parents, teachers, policymakers, governors, judiciary, and the media), almost always mean well, but the results of acculturation may affect those who are the targets of the efforts in negative as well as positive ways. Further, it may affect some negatively and others positively, as intended, or it may affect some people negatively and others positively, but in the opposite way from that which was intended. Finally, acculturation may be effective and enduring over time and lead to the betterment of all concerned, or it may be effective and enduring over time, but lead to the detriment and degradation of all concerned. That is, it may be something positive that enables people to live longer, richer, healthier, happier lives, or it may be something negative that grates on people in negative but perpetuating ways, causing people to lead shorter, poorer, unhealthy, unhappy lives. Acculturation is real, it does occur, and some people live wonderful lives as the result, while other people live uncomfortable or even degrading lives as a consequence of what is instilled at an early age.

We see clear evidence of acculturation in our data. Some of this evidence demonstrates that people who live in certain states live longer, lead richer lives, make more money, make more positive contributions to society, engage in fewer criminal activities and social disruptions, and have more positive feelings about themselves and their fellow human beings than those who live in different states and lead shorter, more barren lives, make less money, make more negative contributions to society, engage in more criminal activities and social disruptions, and have more negative feelings about themselves and their fellow human beings. States are different.

Acculturation is conceptualized here as a "bundled" concept: a series of discrete but related phenomena that might be thought of as bundled together, much like a rope is a series of separate strands, bundled together, to make a unified but linear whole. In the description that follows, we outline some of the specifics or various "strands" of the total concept, but the important point to keep in mind is that it is the totality—the overall gestalt—that comprises acculturation.

Table 11.1 outlines our conception of how people in states with fewer problems and more problems might be characterized. Note that the descriptions pertain to beliefs and behaviors of individuals; they are not characteristics of institutions or society. Acculturation manifests itself in what people have learned, how people perceive, how people cope, what motivates people, and how people relate to other people and the world around them. Most of the terms we use come from psychology, but our inferences to identify the behaviors came from data in the statistical tables about death and taxes and all of the other factors that are appended to this report.

Before we proceed, however, it may be appropriate to consider an aspect of statistics that is not always well understood. Imagine a hypothetical research project in medicine which demonstrated that, when an experimental group was treated in a new way, the death rate was 2 percent, while for a control group treated in the conventional way the death rate was 8 percent. One report of this research might say "the experimental treatment was four times as effective as the conventional procedure" (i.e., eight deaths per 100 are four times as many as two deaths per 100). Another report might say that "more than 90

Table 11.1. Characteristics of People in States with More or Fewer Problems

Behaviors in "Fewer Problems" States	Behaviors in "More Problems" States
accepting behaviors	rejecting behaviors
positive concept of others	negative concept of others
positive concept of self	negative concept of self
open to experience	closed to experience
accurate perceptions of reality	distorted perceptions of reality
perceives more of the world	perceives less of the world
open-minded	closed-minded
attracted to complexity	repelled by complexity
tolerant of ambiguity	intolerant of ambiguity
realistic awareness of time	unrealistic awareness of time
internalized locus of control	externalized locus of control
assigns responsibility internal to self	assigns responsibility ßexternal to self
locus of attention external to self	locus of attention internal to self
attracted to ideas	distracted by ideas
pragmatic	ideological
more knowledgeable	less knowledgeable
more educated	less educated
motivated toward learning	motivated away from learning
reasonable perception of authority	defiant of authority
life-oriented values	death-oriented values
healhy	unhealthy
supportive	vengeful
helpful	hurtful
forgiving	holds a grudge
cooperative	competitive
considerate	inconsiderate
careful	careless
honest	devious
shares	possessive
democratic	authoritarian
flexible	inflexible
independent	dependent
egalitarian	dominating or submissive

percent of all patients treated survived, whichever procedure was used." Obviously, both reports would be correct. Comparing the 98/2 ratio with the 92/8 ratio may be statistically significant, depending on how large the samples were, but in such a comparison it would also be accurate to say that an overwhelming majority of all patients survived, no matter which medical procedure was employed.

This same phenomenon is implicit in Table 11.1. It is probably true (we do not actually know) that most people in all 50 states could be described by terms under the heading "Behaviors in 'Fewer Problems' States," but our analyses indicate that proportionately more people in states with more problems must be described by terms under the heading "Behaviors in 'More Problems' States," and such differences are significant statistically.

Note that what is described in Table 11.1 are personal behaviors—what people do, not what governments or institutions do—and note also that those behaviors listed down the left-hand side of the table are positive, while those listed down the right-hand side of the table are neg-

ative. To avoid misunderstanding, note again what we said:

It is probably true (we do not actually know) that most people in all 50 states could be described by terms under the heading "Behaviors in 'Fewer Problems' States," but our analyses indicate that proportionately more people in states with more problems must be described by terms under the heading "Behaviors in 'More Problems' States," and such differences are significant statistically.

These behaviors are related in such a way that, for any given person, there is a tendency toward the left-hand side of the table, a tendency toward the right-hand side of the table, or a tendency toward something in between. In other words, the pattern of behaviors for any individual would generally be in the direction of behaviors in "fewer problems" states, in the direction of behaviors in "more problems" states, or somewhere in the middle of each continuum.

Human behavior is generally "of a piece," integrated and theoretically consistent. Few people would display "accepting behaviors," on the one hand, and "negative concept of self" on the other hand. Neither would they be "less knowledgeable" and "motivated toward learning." In the same way, people would generally not be "tolerant of ambiguity," "honest," "cooperative," and "open-minded," but "defiant of authority," "ideological," and "hold a grudge."

We developed Table 11.1 by reviewing all of the tables in Appendix G several times, looking for patterns in those data, then making inferences about specific behaviors that might lie behind those patterns. This was an inferential process, and some may question the inferences we made, but we are confident that the behavioral patterns outlined in Table 11.1 are implicit in the hundreds of tables in Appendix G.

Consider a specific illustration. Table G.340 in Appendix G includes 10 of the 11 "Old South" (i.e., those states that seceded and formed the Confederacy) states in the top half of "Total Traffic Fatalities" reported in 1999, and one Old South state in the bottom half (i.e., Arkansas is ranked 27th out of the 50 states, just below the midpoint of the distribution). Further, most of those Southern states are not the most highly populated states in the Union. Next, if you study Table G.343, "Traffic Fatalities per 100,000 Population," you can note again that 10 Southern states are in the top half of that distribution, and one state (i.e., Virginia) falls in the bottom half, when automobile fatality rate per population is considered. The pattern is clear: states in the South have both more traffic fatalities and higher traffic fatality rates than states in other parts of the country.

How might one explain these high death rates from automobile accidents in states in the South? High auto deaths could be explained in any one of several different ways: drivers are careless, less educated, death-oriented, defiant of authority, less knowledgeable, inconsiderate, competitive (i.e., safe drivers cooperate), they assign responsibility external to self (i.e., someone else is to blame), they have a negative concept of self or a negative concept of others, or all of those things. Or, such terms might apply to policymakers who made policy decisions about highway design, highway maintenance, automobile inspections, and the like. Few would argue that the people who died in auto accidents or persons who made policies in those states functioned in ways opposite to the behaviors cited here.

Consider another illustration. Table G.238, "Syphilis Cases per 1,000 Population," shows that 11 states in the Old South are in the top half of the distribution. What contributes to behaviors that lead to high syphilis rates in those 11 states? We would guess that the following might help account for such rates: closed-minded, careless, less educated, locus of attention internal to self, assigns responsibility external to self, distorted perceptions of reality, dominating or submissive, and maybe defiant of authority.

One more example. Study Tables G.391 and G.392 carefully, "Percent of Total Justice System Devoted to Judicial and Legal" operations, and "Percent of Total Justice System Devoted to Corrections." Note that 10 of the 11 states from the Old South are in the bottom half of the "justice and legal" costs to the states, whereas 9 of the same 11 states are in the top half of the "corrections" distribution. These data seem to suggest that states in the South allocate less money for the judicial and legal aspects of the justice system (i.e. prosecution, evidence, etc.), and more money to corrections (i.e., incarceration). The exceptionally high incarceration rates in Southern states require more prisons and more guards (see Table G.64, "Prisoners per 1,000 Population"), but the low expenditures for food for each inmate (see Table G.70, "Food Costs per Inmate") suggests that the higher proportion of the population that is incarcerated may not be as well cared for as in most other states. Such patterns suggest rejecting, negative concept of others, vengefulness, hurtful, holds a grudge, dominating, and authoritarian behaviors. The opposite behaviors are not implicit in the data in those tables to which we have referred.

What we did in developing the logic and specifics of Table 11.1 was based on careful study of hundreds of tables in Appendix G. We recognize that other people might study those same tables and come to other conclusions; we doubt that they would reach conclusions diametrically opposed to ours in terms of the positive or negative ends of the continuums. Table 11.1 is based in part on speculation and in part on direct inference, but we share the outline with you because we are reasonably certain that the general pattern set forth is substantiated by the data presented in the hundreds of tables in Appendix G.

If you study carefully, for example, Table G.702, "SUMMARY Factor Based on Summation of 15 General Factor Scores," it is immediately obvious that 10 of the 11 states from the Old South are in the top half of the distribution (9 of those 10 states are actually in the top 12 states listed). Those 9 states have more problems than 38 other states, as reflected in the 15 general factor scores that make up the SUMMARY factor, suggesting that states in the South have more problems in several areas of life that other states tend not to have.

What might possibly explain why those 11 states in the South evidence so many more problems than most of the other states in the United States?

ONE POSSIBLE EXPLANATION

Since the most obvious differences discerned thus far relate to persons who live in different sections of the country, with special attention to the 11 states in what is often called the Old South, how can we account for the differences between people who live now in states that were involved in a war almost 150 years ago from people in other parts of the United States on variables such as those listed in Table 11.1? Different perspectives might be used to answer that question: income, economics, employment possibilities, immigrants' racial or ethnic or geographic background, migration routes, religion, geography, or history, to mention a few. We have relied primarily on history. Other perspectives might prove as useful, or maybe more useful, to other persons, but we were persuaded that Civil War history affected how and why people who grow up and live in the South now have been acculturated in different ways from those who grew up elsewhere.

A short review of 12 months of history may be especially helpful. November 1860 to April 1861, and November 1864 to April 1865—the period immediately before the Civil War began, and the period immediately before the Civil War ended—set in motion the events and activities that ran from 1865 to 1875: Reconstruction. We think that that period has profoundly affected people in the South for more than 100 years. The 1865 to 1875 period affected people in the North, too, but the effects dissipated when those who were primary participants died or left the scene.

Events which occurred from 1865 to 1875 may help us understand why acculturation proceeded along different paths in the South and other regions of the country. Many things outside the two 6-month periods mentioned above and the 10 years that followed were extremely important in the lives of the people involved, of course, but we want to focus attention on those three time periods. At the very least, what is described below is an interesting hypothesis.

First, we will give an overview of our understanding of the two six-month periods in just a few sentences here. Then we will take additional space and document those few sentences with detail in Appendix F. Recall also that we have included in Appendix E 135 specific findings from our study of the statistical data, which are important to our conclusions. Here is our overview:

Policymakers in the South took a series of actions that precipitated the Civil War. At the end of the war, and after Lincoln's assassination, many policymakers in the North became very upset and angry and worked hard to punish the South to avenge Lincoln's death and to atone for slavery. People in the South reacted by developing activities and a "movement" which guaranteed that slavery was seen as just and the "glory of the South" would be remembered forever. People in the North forgot their anger, shifted their attention to the future, and moved on with their lives.

In the next section, we extrapolate from the statistical findings (see Appendix E) and the review of history (see Appendix F), and try to understand all that we now know regarding the differences that are so pronounced between states in the Old South and other states, as reflected in the problems that currently exist in the South and show up in hundreds of our statistical tables.

WHAT MAY HAVE LED TO "MORE PROBLEMS" IN SOME STATES TODAY

The discussion that follows is partly conjecture and partly fact. We have leaned heavily on four things: the findings outlined earlier in this chapter and presented in Appendix E; historical analogies; historical analyses; plus myths that were initiated, nurtured, developed over time, and still persist today. In addition, five books helped shape our interpretation: *Race and Reunion*, by David Blight; *The Myth of the Lost Cause and Civil War History*, edited by Gary Gallagher and Alan Nolan; *Founding Brothers: The Revolutionary Generation*, by Joseph Ellis; *What Kind of Nation*, by James Simon; and *Reconstruction: America's Unfinished Revolution*, by Eric Foner.

Just as the "hot head" policymakers in the South fired on Fort Sumter, seceded from the Union, and moved to establish a new government and an army to assure their separation from the Union before Lincoln was even inaugurated, so too did the "hot head" policymakers in the North, after Lincoln's assassination, take steps to humiliate and humble the South and impose punishment on the people in the South for what the Northerners perceived as a dastardly act (i.e., killing the president), for which they held the whole South, not just John Wilkes Booth, accountable.

The war, once begun, was generally fought as "fairly and squarely" as wars are ever fought. Men on both sides were courageous, valiant, and hard-fighting. But just as extremists in the South precipitated armed conflict in 1861, so did extremists in the North precipitate hatred and revenge after Lincoln was killed. Reconstruction (circa 1865 to 1875) developed out of that hatred and confusion, and remembrances known as the "Lost Cause" grew out of grievances and reactions to the hatred expressed by policymakers in the North.

Andrew Johnson, who succeeded Lincoln as president, was lenient and partial toward the South. Radical Republicans in the Congress and radicals outside the Congress were bent on punishment and revenge against the South. The shrill language of Charles Sumner, Thaddeus Stevens, Ralph Waldo Emerson, Ebon Ingersoll, James Garfield, and many others about how to deal with the defeated South drove many Southerners away from any real possibility of reunion and back to perpetuation of the society they had known and loved before the war.

Reconstruction tore the reconstituted union apart again: socially, politically, morally, economically, racially, and psychologically. Southerners who retreated into their recollections, supported by Lost Cause efforts to assure remembrances in the decades that followed, never forgot. Northerners who criticized Southerners harshly after Lincoln's death drove those same Southerners into psychological shells. Then the Northerners died off and the whole North forgot.

Southerners moved back toward the past in time. Northerners moved forward, into the future. People in both sections of the country moved away from the issues involved.

> During Reconstruction, many Americans increasingly realized that remembering the war, even the hatreds and deaths on a hundred battlefields—facing all those graves on Memorial Day—became, with time, easier than struggling over the enduring ideas for which those battles had been fought.[2]

TWO HISTORICAL ANALOGIES

To this point we have set forth the idea that policymakers in the South started the Civil War, and the North won that war after four years of horrendous conflict, but Northern policymakers were angered that a Southerner assassinated President Lincoln and that Southerners had supported slavery, so they imposed severe demands on Southern states that were both intended and perceived as punishments for wrongs done. Reconstruction became a decade-long series of humiliations and criticisms that spawned the Lost Cause ideology of remembrance and a revival of states' rights rhetoric and actions.

Before we proceed to look at these two factors—Lost Cause and states' rights—we pause to review two examples of the consequences of nations imposing harsh punishments on other nations which had been defeated in war: what happened in Germany after World War I, and what happened in Germany after World War II.

After four years of conflict that cost more lives than any other war in history, Germany and its allies were defeated in 1918.

> "My Fellow Countrymen: The armistice was signed this morning. Everything for which America fought has been accomplished. The war thus comes to an end."
>
> Speaking to the Congress and the people of the United States, President Wilson made this declaration on November 11, 1918. A few hours before he made this statement, Germany, the empire of blood and iron, had agreed to an armistice, terms of which were the hardest and most humiliating ever imposed upon a nation of the first class.[3]

The Treaty of Versailles imposed harsh demands on belligerents of Germany, Turkey, and Austria. The agreement with Germany included 35 specific requirements (e.g., cessation of all operations, immediate evacuation of invaded countries, repatriation within 15 days, surrender of all military equipment, evacuation of the left bank of the Rhine, evacuation of all territory held by the Germans, no destruction of any kind, five thousand locomotives, revealing all mines and delayed action fuses on territory within 48 hours, immediate repatriation of all prisoners of war, evacuation of German troops to begin at once, renunciation of the treaties of Bucharest and Brest-Litovsk, immediate cessation of all hostilities, prisoners of war to be returned immediately without reciprocity, surrender of all submarines and their armaments, all surface warships to be disarmed, freedom of access to and from the Baltic, abandonment of all ships, tugs, lighters, cranes, and other apparatus in Belgium, all Black Sea ports to be evacuated, no destruction of ships or materials, no transfer of German shipping of any description to any neutral flag), and the following financial conditions:

> Reparation for damage done. While such armistice lasts no public securities shall be removed by the enemy which can serve as a pledge to the Allies for the recovery or repatriation of the cash deposit, in the National Bank of Belgium, and in general immediate return of all documents, specie, stocks, shares, [and] paper money together with plant for the issue thereof, touching public or private interests in the invaded countries. Restitution of the Russian and Roumanian gold yielded to Germany or taken by that Power. This gold to be delivered in trust to the Allies until the signature of peace.[4]

These conditions created havoc and political instability in Germany during the next few years. The imposition of a "democratic" government (i.e., the Weimar Republic) on the German people, economic chaos, and social unrest allowed Adolf Hitler to achieve political power through political means. Bullock's classic study, *Hitler: A Study in Tyranny*, documents how shrewdly Hitler cultivated and exploited the anger of German citizens at the existing German government, and what he called the humiliation of Versailles. Hitler's rise to power was based on hundreds of speeches such as the following:

> We are now met by the question: Do we wish to restore Germany to freedom and power? If "yes," then the first thing to do is rescue it from the Jew who is ruining our country. . . . We want to stir up a storm. Men must not sleep: They ought to know that a thunderstorm is coming up. We want to prevent our Germany from suffering, as Another did, the death upon the Cross.[5]

Without discussing the Treaty of Versailles in more detail, the point is simple: harsh demands on a defeated enemy reaped negative rewards without end.

Move now to the mid-1940s. A similar situation, but this time America took a different tack. Admittedly, the United States was apprehensive about what Russia might do, but President Harry Truman and Secretary of State George Marshall decided that the United States had to help Germany get back on its feet.

George Kennan (the man who conceptualized and implemented the "containment" policy that neutralized Russian influence for almost 50 years until, as he predicted, the collapse of Russian Communism) was asked by Secretary Marshall in May 1947 to prepare a policy proposal that would stabilize and then energize European economic development. He and his associates had less than three weeks to prepare the plan, which included the following:

> It is necessary to distinguish clearly between a program for the economic revitalization of Europe on the one hand, and a program of American support for such revitalization on the other. . . .
>
> It would be neither fitting nor efficacious for this government to undertake to draw up unilaterally and to promulgate formally on its own initiative a program designed to place Western Europe on its feet economically. That is the business of the Europeans. The formal initiative must come from Europe; and Europeans must bear the basic responsibility for it. The role of this country should consist of friendly aid in the drafting of a European program and of the later support for such a program, by financial and other means, at European request.[6]

Again, we know what happened. Whereas harsh demands on the Germans in 1918 led to upheaval and a second great war, cooperation, assistance, latitude, and support after the Second World War (i.e., the Marshall Plan was announced in 1947) led to phenomenal economic development and growth, and peaceful and harmonious relationships with other countries.

The rules imposed by the victors after the First World War led to economic stagnation, political upheaval, and belligerent resurgence that culminated in another war. The rules imposed by the victors after the Second World War led to economic prosperity, social and political development, and peaceful relations with almost all parties involved.

There may be important lessons here. Admittedly, these lessons come late. The United States government (i.e., the North) took the wrong road after Lincoln's assassination in 1865, and the vanquished moved to prove to themselves that they deserved a better fate than the one imposed on them by policymakers from Northern states; they developed the Lost Cause. But the Lost Cause was built out of thin air. States' rights were also revived as a kind of clarion call, and that call has been sounding ever since, although it is clearly a siren's call.

THE LOST CAUSE

In December 1865, the *Richmond Dispatch* resumed publication following the cessation of hostilities. Blight says of its first issue after the war ended, in an article on "Past and Present,"

> one finds virtually all the ingredients (except organizations and rituals) that would form the Lost Cause: a public memory, a cult of the fallen soldier, a righteous political cause defeated only by superior industrial might, a heritage community awaiting its exodus, and a people forming a collective identity as victims and survivors. Nowhere in the paper's reflection on the "Past and Present" was there a single mention of slavery or black freedom.[7]

Edward Pollard warned that "what the South had lost on battlefields, it would carry on in a war of ideas."[8]

Only two years later . . . Pollard wrote a campaign tract, *The Lost Cause Regained* (1868), in which he counseled reconciliation with conservative Northerners on Southern terms. Those terms coalesced in a central idea. "To the extent of securing the supremacy of the white man," wrote Pollard, "and the traditional liberties of the country . . . she (the South) really triumphs. . . ."[9]

Blight gives a careful and exhaustive review of Lost Cause ideology and activities, including names of those who were active in fomenting the ideas and instilling into the minds of youth the remembrances that they hoped would serve the cause for decades to come.[10]

In the introduction to *The Myth of the Lost Cause and Civil War History*, Gallagher and Nolan present a similar review:

> White Southerners emerged from the Civil War thoroughly beaten but largely unrepentant. Four years of brutal struggle had ravaged their military-age population, vastly altered their physical landscape and economic infrastructure, and destroyed their slave-based social system. They grimly acknowledged the superior might of the United States military forces and understood the futility of further armed resistance. Yet the majority of ex-Confederates, who had remained hopeful of establishing a new slaveholding republic until late in the conflict, did not believe they had fought for an unworthy cause. During the decades following the surrender at Appomattox, they nurtured a public memory of the Confederacy that placed their wartime sacrifice and shattering defeat in the best possible light. This interpretation addressed the nature of antebellum Southern society and the institution of slavery, the constitutionality of secession, the causes of the Civil War, the characteristics of their wartime society, and the reasons for their defeat. Widely known then and now as the Lost Cause explanation of the Confederate experience, it drew strength from the pages of participants' memoirs, from speeches at veterans' reunions, from ceremonies at the graves and other commemorative events, and from artwork with Confederate themes.
>
> The architects of the Lost Cause acted from various motives. They collectively sought to justify their own actions and allow themselves and other former Confederates to find something positive in all-encompassing failure. They also wanted to provide their children and future generations of white Southerners with a "correct" narrative of the war.[11]

The Lost Cause was not an organization, it was a movement, inspired by Pollard but taken up in the last third of the nineteenth century by former Confederate officers and women's groups dedicated to Southern causes. These unofficial leaders worked to establish organizations that would accumulate and disseminate information about what they called "a true picture" of the peacefulness and harmony of the antebellum South, to persuade others that the Civil War was fought for noble purposes, and that white supremacy was a worthy social goal.

That books such as *The South Was Right* are published today demonstrates that Lost Cause ideas are still alive and well in the South, more than 140 years later. The following quotes from *The South Was Right* epitomize Lost Cause ideology and methodology:

> In 1889, when the Sons of Confederate Veterans was formed, Gen. Stephen D. Lee gave as part of the commission to the Sons, "It is your duty to see that the true history of the South is presented to future generations."[12]
>
> Southerners did not desire secession; it was forced upon them.[13]
>
> In the history of the Northern states there is a long record of those states nullifying acts of Congress, parts of the Constitution, and decrees of the federal Supreme Court.[14]
>
> When the Southern states seceded, the North saw its "milch cow" escaping and waged aggressive war against the South to maintain its commercial empire.[15]
>
> It is the task of Southern Nationalists and all true conservatives to use the most efficient political methods possible to return this country to its original form of government—a constitutional federal republic of sovereign states.[16]
>
> The Northern people from the very beginning of this nation were told that Southerners were illiterate, lazy, barbaric slave masters.[17]

Unfortunately, such writing does not enable or encourage either citizens or policymakers to solve problems or to make things better. These are words of hate and retribution. The kinds of words that Northern policymakers used in 1865 are still with us today, but they come now from those who have not moved into the future because they are blinded and tortured by the past.

Gallagher and his associates describe the Lost Cause as a myth. Compared with history, it is a false palliative, but nurtured over the years, it has become an enduring, if false, perspective on the Civil War. In that sense, it may have become an impediment to progress and development in the South, accounting for many of the "problems" which characterize Southern states more frequently than other states. But another issue, essentially Southern in perspective, is also very much at work: states' rights.

STATES' RIGHTS
We see the crux of "more problems" among Southern states today as a misinterpretation of constitutional law that has existed, in one form or another, for more than 200 years: the "states' rights" issue. This was a real issue in the 1780s,[18] and again in the 1820s, when nullification

first reared its ugly head,[19] and it was an issue that precipitated out of political disagreements that led to war in 1861. It is not an issue today, except in some people's remembrances—not of reality, but of what never was and never can be—the glory of the antebellum South.

The father of states' rights, for all practical purposes, was Thomas Jefferson. If not the first, he was the prime mover for half a century of an idea whose time had come and gone. From 1776 to 1826, when he died, Jefferson was continuously talking about, writing about, advocating, and manipulating information, people, events, and circumstances to accord states more power and more authority and more importance than the national government.

Jefferson's chief opponent to these ideas during most of those years was John Marshall, albeit Alexander Hamilton is usually accorded that honor. Hamilton had a powerful mind, but Marshall imposed his ideas through judicial interpretations of constitutional law. Simon describes this fundamental disagreement as "the epic struggle to create a United States."[20]

Marshall won that struggle. Jefferson never gave up and he never gave in, and though subsequent chief justices such as Roger Taney put some of Marshall's judicial rulings on hold, later Supreme Courts went back to Marshall's basic theses and reinstated the dominance of federal over states' powers. States have rights, but not the right to overrule decisions by either Congress or the Supreme Court, for which Jefferson had argued. Sovereignty reigns at the federal level. States' rights, as advocated by Jefferson, is dead. It is a regressive ideology that fosters disagreement, costs human lives (study the data), and holds people back.

Southerners still lean on Jefferson's charisma and his remarkable facility with words, but Jefferson was naive to argue that a state's legislature had the right to ignore the Constitution or overrule the Supreme Court of the United States. Marshall's logic was overpowering in *Marbury v. Madison*:

> That the people have an original right to establish for their future government such principles as, in their opinion, shall most conduce to their own happiness, is the basis on which the whole American fabric has been erected. The exercise of this original right is a very great exertion, nor can it nor ought it to be frequently repeated. The principles therefore so established are deemed fundamental. And as the authority from which they proceed is supreme and can seldom act, they are designed to be permanent. . . .
>
> The powers of the legislature are defined and limited; and that those limits may not be mistaken or forgotten, the constitution is written. To what purpose are powers limited, and to what purpose is that limitation committed to writing, if these limits may, at any time, be passed by those intended to be restrained? The distinction between a government with limited and unlimited powers

is abolished if those limits do not confine the persons on whom they are imposed and if acts prohibited and acts allowed are of equal obligation. It is a proposition too plain to be contested, that the constitution controls any legislative act repugnant to it; or, that the legislature may alter the constitution by an ordinary act.

Between these alternatives there is no middle ground. The constitution is either a superior paramount law, unchangeable by ordinary means, or it is on a level with ordinary legislative acts, and, like other acts, is alterable when the legislature shall please to alter it.

If the former part of the alternative be true, then a legislative act contrary to the constitution is not law; if the latter part be true, then written constitutions are absurd attempts, on the part of the people, to limit a power in its own nature illimitable. . . .

If, then, the courts are to regard the constitution, and the constitution is superior to any ordinary act of the legislature, the constitution, and not such ordinary act, must govern the case to which they both apply.

Those, then, who controvert the principle that the constitution is to be considered in court as a paramount law, are reduced to the necessity of maintaining that courts must close their eyes on the constitution and see only the law.

This doctrine would subvert the very foundation of all written constitutions. It would declare that an act which, according to the principles and theory of our government, is entirely void, is yet, in practice, completely obligatory. It would declare that, if the legislature shall do what is expressly forbidden, such act, not withstanding the express prohibition, is in reality effectual. It would be giving to the legislature a practical and real omnipotence with the same breath which professes to restrict their powers within narrow limits. It is prescribing limits and declaring that those limits may be passed at pleasure.

That it thus reduces to nothing what we have deemed the greatest improvement on political institutions, a written constitution, would of itself be sufficient, in America, where written constitutions have been viewed with so much reverence, for rejecting the construction.

The judicial power of the United States is extended to all cases arising under the constitution.

Could it be the intention of those who gave this power to say that in using it the constitution should not be looked into? That a case arising under the constitution should be decided without examining the instrument under which it arises?

This is too extravagant to be maintained. . . .

Thus, the particular phraseology of the constitution of the United States confirms and strengthens the principle, supposed to be essential to all written constitutions, that a law repugnant to the constitution is void, and that courts, as well as other departments, are bound by that instrument.[21]

Marshall's reasoning presents a logical and compelling response to those who advocate states' rights today. His reasoning was appropriate and valid in 1803. It is appropriate and valid today. No legislature, state or national, can override the Constitution. No executive, state or national, can override the Constitution.

The Supreme Court can make interpretations of the Constitution, and such interpretations may cause discomfort for a time, as did the *Plessy v. Ferguson* decision in 1896. Those who argue that "the Court should interpret the Constitution and not make law from the bench" should recognize that, if the Court "made law" one way in 1954 in *Brown v. Board of Education*, it "made law" in the opposite direction in 1896 when the justices decided the *Plessy v. Ferguson* case. In other words, our system is not perfect, but things tend to become clearer and more just over time. Judicial decisions are an important part of how acculturation takes place.

POSTSCRIPT

One question that remains relates to economics: Do poor economic conditions cause states to develop more problems, or do more problems cause states to develop poor economic conditions? This is not a history book; it is an attempt to make sense of information about people in all 50 states at the turn of the millennium. The book documents and illuminates the point that some states in the United States have more problems, while other states have fewer problems. And speaking generally, states with more problems are most frequently in the South. Our assumption is that problems are direct consequences of how policymakers think and what policymakers do.

Consider two illustrations; both involve driving automobiles. Both of us lived for a time in Alabama. We both have driven the full length of Alabama many times. When we drive the full length of the state, we set our cruise control on the speed limit, then count the number of cars that we pass as we drive, and the number of cars that pass us. Driving completely across the state, the count typically is more than 20 cars that pass us for every car that we pass; in urban areas the count is more like 50 to 1. Our observations on these trips leads us to the conclusion that many people who drive in Alabama defy authority: the authority of the law, the authority of experience, and the authority of expertise.

We have also driven the full width of New York State many times. Driving across that state, about five cars pass us for every car we pass. Furthermore, most of the cars that pass us seem to move "out of view" more slowly than the cars in Alabama, which disappear almost immediately. Most people who drive in New York State seem to accept the authority of the state, the authority of experience, and the authority of expertise. That is, people in New York State seem more willing to accept and more understanding of authority, in relation to driving on the highway, than people in Alabama.

Theoretically, of course, driving in New York is more demanding and more complex than driving in Alabama.

There are more people, more cars, more traffic, and worse driving conditions in winter, all of which would suggest more accidents and more deaths than driving in Alabama. And those things do occur (e.g., see Table G.190 in Appendix G regarding number of traffic fatalities in the 50 states), but even though New York had 1,498 deaths from traffic fatalities in 1998 and Alabama had 1,071, New York state also has over 18 million residents, while Alabama has about 4.5 million residents. The death rate from automobile accidents in Alabama, per 100,000 population (see Table G.343 in Appendix G), was three times as high (i.e., fifth in the nation) as the death rate in New York state (i.e., 48th in the nation). And if one reads down the list of states in Table G.343, starting with high traffic fatalities at the top of the table, every Southern state but one (viz., Virginia) is in the top half of the distribution (i.e., higher fatalities).

What affects traffic fatality rates? Highway construction, highway markings, highway maintenance, tires, speed limits, enforcement of speed limits, automobile inspections, automobile design, headlights, taillights, brakes, drivers' knowledge, drivers' skills, drivers' attitudes, drivers' experience, and on and on. Most of these factors are affected by state policymakers' decisions.

We cite this illustration only to suggest that statistics about highway fatalities are simply indicators; they do not provide solid information about why the death rate on the highway is three times as high in Alabama as it is in New York. But there are clues. Some of these clues relate to culture.

New York requires annual inspections of automobiles. New York may enforce speed limit laws more effectively than Alabama (we do not know). Police in New York state may issue more tickets for speeding or driving under the influence of alcohol (again, we were unable to get such information). Or, the people in New York may be more intelligent and better trained to drive than people in Alabama. We do not know what accounts for the difference, but the difference in death rates is not minuscule; it is dramatic. Highway construction and highway traffic is a function of state law.

Table G.395 in Appendix G indicates that New York had 36.5 sworn employees in police protection in 1995 per 10,000 population (ranked first in the nation), whereas Alabama had 19.7 such employees per 10,000 population (ranked 30th in the nation). If Alabama had as many people living within its borders as New York has, and if the death rate in the state of Alabama from deaths on the highways stayed about where it is now, almost 4,500 persons would die in car crashes in Alabama every year. Such a total number of deaths would be unconscionable. Or, if we reverse the logic and assume that Alabama could get its highway fatality rate down to the rate in New York State, Alabama would have about 350 fatalities each year instead of a thousand.

Our thesis is simple. The number of traffic deaths in Alabama is as large as it is because something is causing drivers in Alabama to drive in ways that might be characterized as careless, inexperienced, unintelligent, uneducated, defiant of authority, death-oriented, inconsiderate, assigning responsibility external to self, or all of these things. And these kinds of things are directly related to educational opportunities and enforcement of laws, as well as values and behaviors evidenced by policymakers and others.

For example, if people are taught to defy the authority of federal government, those same people will defy the authority of state government. If people are taught that public officials cannot be trusted, those same people will learn that no one can be trusted. If people are taught that courage counts more than competence, those same people will press policymakers to "dumb down" political proposals to meaningless slogans such as "No more taxes!" Every American deserves better than that.

There are significant differences among states on many dimensions, but states in the South press toward the "more problems" end of the Problems Profile, while most other states spread across the board or press toward the "less problems" end. We are convinced that the culture of many states in the South is holding those states back. Some states in the South have made great progress in the past half century, but an old quip still seems to apply: "The faster I go, the behinder I get." The world moves forward and the world moves on.

The past is a terrible burden to carry into the future, especially if that past includes what was detrimental or degrading to people involved (i.e., slavery), or if it is false. Life is too sacred. Work is too meaningful. Learning is too important. Improvement and progress are too significant. False rhetoric and false remembrances are terrible burdens to carry. Neither the Lost Cause nor states' rights help people. Such ideas hold people back.

> States can develop ways of celebrating history without condemning themselves and others to a narrow interpretation of what is, without doubt, a "make believe" past. People can center their attention on the future. They can deal with problems, but focus on possibilities. They can commit themselves and their children to the preservation and enhancement of life for all people, not just a few. They can emphasize the power of learning; they can create a newer, better culture for themselves and for their own.

Now consider a second illustration. While this was being written (February 2002), the Indiana legislature considered a proposal by the governor to raise the gasoline tax one penny per gallon. The state tax on gasoline in Indiana now is 15 cents per gallon, sixth lowest in the nation (see Table G.187 in Appendix G). Assuming that a typical driver drives about 15,000 miles each year, and further assuming that an automobile gets at least 15 miles per gallon, that would mean that the one cent increase in tax on gasoline would cost an average driver in Indiana about 10 dollars a year (i.e., 1,000 gallons of gasoline would raise additional taxes of $10 per year, at one cent per gallon), or three cents a day.

The Indiana legislature refused to impose the one cent tax increase on gasoline. Told that it would only cost about $10 per year per automobile, legislators who voted against the tax increase said: "We know, but it's the principle of the thing." That is defiance of authority. That is uneducated, ideological behavior. That represents closed-mindedness and distorted perceptions of reality.

Gasoline taxes are used to repair and maintain the state's highways. Potholes from lack of road repair cause tires to blow or front wheels to get out of alignment, and even accidents. One cannot get a tire repaired for as little as 10 dollars, but drivers do not pay the money to the state of Indiana; they pay it to a tire repair shop, and the pothole remains.

Who pays for repairs on an automobile, if the roads are in poor shape? Automobile owners do, of course, and automobile owners are taxpayers. Taxpayers pay for everything that gets done, by government and by other agencies. There is no money except that which comes from taxpayers, whether the funds go to governments, grocery stores, dress shops, churches, restaurants, theaters, ball games, or whatever. Money for anything comes from taxpayers. Fewer taxes means that tire repair shops and wheel alignment shops will make more money, in this example, but Indiana will not have solved the problem. Maybe the state legislature wants to support private enterprise.

Shoddy politics, distorted promises, and faulty logic bind too many policymakers and too many citizens to a mired existence instead of releasing them to a hopeful future. Study the data in this book. Does your state have problems? Does your state solve problems with intelligence or with ideology? Is your state moving toward the future or toward the past?

We think that faith in people is more important than faith in the sea coast or farmlands or mountains. States with fewer problems value human life more than money or things. States with fewer problems develop supportive and corrective approaches to crime and education rather than coercive and punitive approaches. States with fewer problems demand more of elected officials. The people in states with fewer problems view government as a positive means to positive ends. They accept the fact that progress and improvement cost money, but not as much as regress and stalemate. Life is good for those people, but they have learned to make it better.

"We the people" are the rulers of the states. "We the people" can make a difference. "We the people" can solve our problems and move forward, but we need leadership and information and opportunities and support. States do not deserve the best. Outstanding states provide the best: highways, health care, education, police protection, environmental protection, judicial systems, safety provisions, working conditions, and opportunities. It is the culture of the state that makes the difference.

NOTES

1. Daniel Patrick Moynihan, as cited in Samuel P. Huntington, "Foreword: Cultures Count," in Lawrence E. Harrison and Samuel P. Huntington (eds.), *Culture Matters: How Values Shape Human Progress* (New York: Basic Books, 2000), xiv.
2. David Blight, *Race and Reunion: The Civil War in American Memory* (Cambridge, Mass.: Belknap Press of Harvard University, 2001), 31. See also Eric Foner, *Reconstruction: America's Unfinished Revolution, 1863–1877* (New York: Harper and Row, 1988), Chapter 6.
3. Francis A. March and Richard J. Beamish, *History of the World War* (Philadelphia: United Publishers of the United States and Canada, 1919), 19.
4. March and Beamish, *History*, 648–659.
5. Adolf Hilter, quoted in Alan Bullock, *Hitler: A Study in Tyranny* (New York: Harper Torchbooks, 1962), 96.
6. George F. Kennan, *Memoirs: 1925–1950* (New York: Pantheon Books, 1967), 336.
7. Blight, *Race and Reunion*, 38.
8. Adolf Hilter, quoted in Blight, *Race and Reunion*, 260.
9. Blight, *Race and Reunion*, 260.
10. Blight, *Race and Reunion*, Chapter 8.
11. Gary W. Gallagher and Alan T. Nolan (eds.), *The Myth of the Lost Cause and Civil War History* (Bloomington: Indiana University Press, 2000), 1.
12. James Ronald Kennedy and Walter Donald Kennedy, *The South Was Right* (Gretna, La.: Pelican, 1994), 17.
13. Kennedy and Kennedy, *The South*, 212.
14. Kennedy and Kennedy, *The South*, 213.
15. Kennedy and Kennedy, *The South*, 234.
16. Kennedy and Kennedy, *The South*, 235.
17. Kennedy and Kennedy, *The South*, 271.
18. Joseph E. Ellis, *Founding Brothers: The Revolutionary Generation* (New York: Alfred A. Knopf, 2001), Chapter 3.
19. William W. Freehling, *Prelude to Civil War: The Nullification Controversy in South Carolina, 1816–1836* (Oxford: Oxford University Press, 1966).
20. James F. Simon, *What Kind of Nation: Thomas Jefferson, John Marshall, and the Epic Struggle to Create a United States* (New York: Simon and Schuster, 2002).
21. C. J. Marshall, "*Marbury v. Madison*," in Henry Steele Commager (ed.), *Documents of American History*, vol. I (New York: Appleton-Century-Crofts, 1949), 191–195.

Minnesota: Cold Sunbelt, by Ted Kolderie[1]

Ted Kolderie was kind enough to review our manuscript and to send to us a copy of this paper, which he had presented to the Minnesota Historical Society. The paper is a scholarly treatise on the culture of one state (Minnesota). Many of the state characteristics that are included in this paper exemplify with such clarity characteristics that we were identifying in our research, we asked for and received permission to include it. We urge the reader to review carefully this exceptionally fine paper.

INTRODUCTION

MINNESOTA HAS BEEN TRYING TO DO WHAT MIGHT SEEM not possible: to run a high-tech, high-service, high-tax economy from a cold, remote location up against the Canadian border in the middle of the continent. Sunny, actually, but definitely cold. Our January weather map looks exactly like college students' ideas of where not to live.

Astonishingly, we have done this quite successfully. Minneapolis and Saint Paul began providing processing, trade, transportation, and financial services to this agricultural region: the central Northwest, the upper Midwest. When Al Godward wrote his remarkable 50-year projection for the *Minneapolis Star* in September 1929, that was still our function. But by 1950 we were on our way to a new economy built on high-value manufacturing and business services. Population grew by half from 1940 to 1960; then has doubled since. In the '90s we grew faster than even some areas in the warm Sunbelt.

People attribute our success largely to the "quality of life." But most of this is not God-given. With all due respect, our water bodies—Red and Leech and Winnibigoshish—are not quite Long Island Sound and San Francisco Bay and the west coast of Florida. Hard as we try, it is not easy to persuade people it is fun to ski on flat land.

Rather, the "livability" of this place is *made*. It is the quality of public facilities and housekeeping . . . the high level of education—in 1950 most adults in Minnesota had not been to high school; by 1990 most adults had some college . . . the range and quality of our sports and cultural activities . . . a health care system able to care for—and to insure—the people better than most. Some of it is intangible: the entrepreneurial drive, the openness, our more than ordinary clean government, a decent ethical climate. As my wife observed when we moved here: an optimal combination of big city and small town. And, underlying all this, what Dan Elazar called "moralistic" politics, in which there is a felt obligation to deal with public problems rather than to enrich one's clan. This has given us an unusual ability to generate leadership and to raise and resolve issues . . . to capture opportunities and deal with problems. This comparative advantage in collective action is one of this state's priceless assets. "Social capital," as Robert Putnam wrote in *Bowling Alone*.

All this is made and sustained by Minnesotans' determination to have here private institutions and governmental institutions of national and world class; to count in this country for more than the 2 percent we represent of its population.

This theme goes back to the beginning of Minnesota's history. This small frontier community realized from the start the importance of deliberately massing resources. "Divide your resources for elementary and secondary education," Folwell advised; "concentrate your resources for higher education. Found but one university." Minnesota was the only state to combine the state and land-grant university and to put it initially into the population center of the state. Minnesota put almost everything into one major "city": the university, the Capitol, the Fair, the prison, and in time the headquarters of almost every major business and nonprofit institution.

But we did not always have the reputation we have today. The 1917 plan for Minneapolis was put on the shelf. In the '20s, aldermen were facing prosecution. In the '30s, there was an overspill of racketeering from Chicago: far too many people were being shot in bars in the middle of the night. When Gurney Breckenfeld came here in the 1970s to write about our urban success, he brought along *Fortune*'s famous April 1936 article on the decline of the Northwest. The timber was gone, the flour mills were moving out, the truck strikes had ended the ability to exploit labor, and, "if tomorrow Saint Paul should slide off its banks and disappear into the Mississippi River, it would scarcely create a ripple in the economic life of the United States of America." A little later Carey McWilliams, in *The Nation*, tagged Minneapolis as "the most anti-Semitic city in America."

BUILDING

Then about 1938 Minnesota began a remarkable revival of its public life. What was built in the generation that followed gave us the community we have today; gave us the national reputation we have today. Let me sketch in a few major pieces of this.

NEW LEADERSHIP

The Cowles came up from Iowa in the '30s and put together the ownership of the Minneapolis newspapers; willing to challenge old attitudes about isolationism, about political life, and about newspapering. In Minneapolis, younger people replaced the little group of bearded men who used to walk to work from their mansions near Washburn Fair Oaks. Coming out of the war communities all across Minnesota had a remarkable drive for civic improvement. Humphrey appeared in Minneapolis: ran for mayor in 1943; successfully in 1945. In business the Dayton brothers took over the store.

THE POLITICAL PARTIES

Politics revived, on the Republican side first, around Harold Stassen as governor, then again in the 1960s with what Betty Wilson loved to call "the young Turks" in Hennepin County. On the Democratic side, the old party was merged into the '40s with the remains of the Farmer-Labor Party to create the modern DFL. Pre-primary endorsement and the central financing of candidates produced a generation of public officials only recently retired; including two vice presidents and two nominees for the presidency, not to mention members of the cabinet and Supreme Court.

THE REBUILDING OF THE CITIES

The cities began to fix themselves up. Minneapolis under Humphrey cleaned up its police department, and then its reputation for anti-Semitism, the foundation for Humphrey's later work on civil rights. The first effort to fix Minneapolis' governmental structure, in 1948, was cut off when Humphrey left for the Senate. The Citizens League was formed in 1952 to carry on that work. The Downtown Council appeared in 1954. City planning was revived, in Minneapolis and in Saint Paul, with Dave Loeks, partly anticipating the coming of the freeways. CLIC was established, to give Minneapolis some orderly capital budgeting. Mechanisms for urban renewal were created. Minnesota passed its law for housing and redevelopment authorities in 1949, five years before the federal government began to provide big financial support. Through the '50s we were a big importer of urban know-how; business people and public officials flying elsewhere to get ideas; often on the *Star* and *Tribune* plane.

THE PROBLEMS OF SUBURBAN AND METROPOLITAN GROWTH

In the late '40s, Orville Peterson, secretary of the league of municipalities, saw the coming postwar growth and persuaded the legislature to provide a method by which suburban villages could convert to a manager form. This got competent government into place just before the big wave of development. In 1959, after two unsuccessful runs for Congress, Joe Robbie got the legislature to assert the interest of the state in the expansion of municipal boundaries. We owe it to his Municipal Commission that the Twin Cities area today is not a crazy-quilt like suburban Chicago.

By the 1950s fundamental questions were appearing about governmental arrangements in the metropolitan area. In Hennepin County a county administrator began to emerge, and in the reapportionment after the 1960 census, the legislature was persuaded not to build-in the conflict then growing between Minneapolis and its suburbs, but to create a majority of districts overlapping the city/suburban boundary. Freed from that conflict, the county—and, after Hennepin, other counties—began their remarkable expansion into parks, libraries, the courts, health care, and social services.

The metropolitan institutions began to appear initially as joint efforts of the two cities: the sanitary district in the mid-1930s; the Airports Commission in 1943—the work of the Jaycees, of all things—putting an end to any thought of scheduled airline service between Minneapolis and Saint Paul. In 1957 Senator Elmer Anderson got the legislature to create the Metropolitan Planning Commission. Two years later the lady in New Hope called the health department and said, "I turn on my tap and the water has a head on it, like beer," touching off a debate about sewage disposal than ran for a decade; resolved only in 1969 after a long and searching public discussion had persuaded the legislature first to create a policymaking body, the Metropolitan Council, to develop the regional consensus required for the state to act.

Over time, more and more non-governmental institutions have taken a fully regional form; most recently the United Way.

STATE GOVERNMENT

The Department of Administration and Civil Service Reform appeared in Stassen's time. The state structure was strengthened again under Governor Freeman. In the '60s, Senator Rosenmeier gave the governors a planning agency. In Wendell Anderson's time the Department of Finance emerged. A legislature that up to about 1960 did not print bills as a public service was reconstructed: the "flexible" session appeared in 1971: 120 days divided between two years. Legislative staffing grew rapidly, and professionalized.

SOCIAL INSTITUTIONS AND SOCIAL POLICY

Let me take just one area of social policy: health care. As science and medicine writer for the *Minneapolis Tribune* in the 1960s, Victor Cohn began to educate this community about the coming problem of cost-control and the idea of pre-paid medical groups like Kaiser-Permanente. Hospital planning mechanisms developed here early. Paul Ellwood moved from the Kenny Institute to start ARF—and then, with Walter McClure, InterStudy—to work on the strategy for change and improvement. Both as a strategy and as a business, the HMO developed here.

The overuse of hospitals stimulated by third-party payment came down dramatically. In response, with the help of the Metropolitan Health Board and a new Hospital Trustees Council, and as the hospitals merged into larger groups, the hospital plant was brought down to appropriate size. In the '80s and '90s, the business Health Care Action Group was formed to carry on the effort to improve costs and quality.

THE FOUNDATIONS

Saint Paul had Hill and Wilder and its community foundation for years before organized philanthropy appeared in Minneapolis, when Russ Ewald moved into the Syndicate building about 1967 to set up the Equal Opportunities Fund. Soon after, Minneapolis' Community Foundation evolved out of the trust department of the Northwestern Bank. Two of the 3M fortunes generated new, large foundations: McKnight and—thanks partly to Elmer Andersen and Doug Head—Bush. Later a Council on Foundations appeared.

New mechanisms were created for research, discussion, and action as new questions appeared. The Urban Coalition appeared, and lasted, as it did not in many cities. Cameron Thompson started the Upper Midwest Research and Development Council to claim for Minnesota a place in the space-and-defense industry. The University of Minnesota geographers added an urban study through which John Borchert became invaluable as an educator of the business community. The Business Partnership followed, in 1977. Spring Hill Center appeared in the 1970s. NSP started the Itasca Seminar. The University upgraded its school of public affairs into the Humphrey Institute. Minnesota Public Radio became a phenomenon, and educational television was transformed into "public television."

EROSION

In the 1970s, the rest of the country began to pay attention to Minnesota. The Twin Cities area became an exporter of know-how. Magazine writers, newspaper reporters, graduate students, Neil Pierce doing research for his book on the states. The governor was on the cover of *Time*. Foundations like Kettering showed up, asking initially about what we'd done here. Quickly they became curious about *how* it was done; about our process of policy development. "I could have had this meeting in my city," I remember someone saying in that period. "But on the average, the people would have been 10 to 15 years older." After a discussion on health-care issues, a visitor from New York said: "If we'd had this discussion where I live, people would have been at each others' throats in five minutes."

Minnesota basked comfortably in this approval. About 1980, in a conference at Spring Hill, Bob Holland from the Committee for Economic Development was asking what people saw as the next challenges coming. He was astonished not to get a response. I remember

Harlan Cleveland, then newly arrived as dean of the Humphrey Institute, saying in the parking lot afterward: "Any community that thinks all it has to do is sit on its accomplishments is not in business in the last quarter of the 20th century."

That was prophetic. In the '80s, some powerful forces began to erode our institutional structure of policy development. Let me touch on two that seem to be especially significant.

THE GROWTH OF SCALE

First has been the sheer growth of scale, affecting especially the role of the business firms in civic and public affairs.

Into the 1960s, many of the major firms here not only were headquartered here, but they also did most of their business here. At the core were what Wayne Thompson used to call the "can't run" businesses: the newspaper, the department store, the electric and telephone utilities, the banks. Some may in truth have been owned by the trust departments of the New York banks, but they felt like—more important, behaved like—local businesses.

Don Dayton brought Wayne here about 1965 from city management, and made him responsible "for everything outside the walls of the business." Quickly other CEOs, especially in Minneapolis, moved to this unusual pattern of corporate public affairs. It made a difference for this function to be directly under the CEO and to be staffed by persons with background in government, who functioned as much to represent the community to the company as the company to the community.

But about the same time, business and its public affairs was becoming much more national. Disliking the increasingly aggressive policy actions of state governments, business looked to Washington for decision making. Public affairs officers asked each other: "Which would you rather fight: 50 chimps or one gorilla?" and the correct answer was "one gorilla." I remember in the '70s calling on the public-affairs vice president of Honeywell. He was happy to renew their contribution. But he said to me: "My problem is Congress." By 1980 we heard an executive of the Saint Paul companies say: "The insurance industry is the last major industry in America still to believe in a framework of state regulation as a matter of principle. And you can't imagine the pressure we're under to change that."

In the '80s and '90s the corporate public-affairs function changed. Giving, government relations, civic affairs consolidated under a single officer. Budgets tightened. Increasingly, public affairs had to justify itself to—had to serve—the line units of the company. Inevitably this meant general community problems had a smaller claim on scarce resource and time. The public-affairs officer was no longer the CEO's private staff. And as the firms grew larger, the headquarters city became a smaller part of their total concern. Perhaps the Twin Cities is not quite in the national pattern. There has always been an effort here to socialize new CEOs into the civic culture. The concern today is that this might put them at risk for their own career in their own organization.

Al Sorensen was a friend of my father in Omaha. Al grew up poor; had a lot of life experiences early; quit school early. When his local electric-supply business was going well in the 1950s, Al got into civic affairs; first with the Chamber. He got AAA baseball for Omaha, got a new city charter adopted, became president of the new City Council, then mayor. "Our biggest companies," Al said to me, "are the poorest citizens we have." This was hard for a Minnesotan to understand at the time.

THE MEDIA: "THINGS HAVE CHANGED"

Into the 1970s, people from the radio-TV stations would come around to civic organizations each year, doing the assessment of public needs required by the FCC; reflecting the original notion that the air waves were public, and that licensees had an obligation to serve the public interest. Even then it was an empty procedure, a dead routine.

It was always the newspapers—not licensed, but out of their civic responsibility, their curiosity, perhaps their desire to be influential—that sent reporters really into the institutions of public life to find out what was going on, and to tell the community about it. Through this period, the press was an important part of the policy process. John Cowles' concept of the newspaper as an educational institution . . . of the reporter as the equivalent of a college professor . . . was something you heard about when you joined the *Star* and *Tribune* in the late '50s; not from management, but from other reporters. In the 1960s, when the papers let their beat reporters follow their stories into the legislature—traditionally covered for the political story and the tax story—it changed what the legislature did; affected what could and could not pass.

Then three things happened.

Television happened, radically altering the newspaper, first as a business, and then as an institution; in a process still continuing.

The postwar prosperity broke down what Daniel Yankelovich describes as the old "ethic of self-denial." Rapidly a new "ethic of self-fulfillment" spread from college students to other young people; then to their parents. By the mid-1970s, the newspapers were moving to serve this new interest in "You": your life, your health, your career, your home, your family.

And in the '60s, public confidence in institutions—including government—massively declined. This powerfully reinforced the press' interest in private affairs over public affairs, offering a plausible explanation for not doing what they could no longer afford to do anyway. It also changed the perspective of their reporting of public affairs: away from the traditional coverage of government that the last editor of the *Minneapolis Star* loved to deride as "inside baseball" (surely ironic, given the way the pa-

pers now cover sports) toward a new emphasis on how what "they" are doing affects *you*.

Coverage changed, editors changed, management changed, ownership changed. I remember calling an editor about a story on a decision about an issue I did not recall the newspaper ever having reported under discussion. I said, "It's as if the reporter comes back and the editor asks, 'What did they do?' and the reporter said 'they just talked about it.' Then the editor said, 'Let me know when something happens.'" "Yes," she said, "we say that to reporters a lot."

Public affairs is the discussion before the vote is taken. When the discussion itself is no longer something to be followed and reported closely, something significant has changed in our policy process.

Changes like these affecting institutions as important as the business community and the newspapers are bound to affect civic life in major ways: changing contributions, changing the pattern of individual involvement. Some civic organizations and programs have disappeared. Spring Hill is gone. The Minneapolis Foundation has dropped the Itasca Seminar. Some organizations have declined or shifted their focus. State Planning has been reduced to an "office." The Metro Council, built for policy leadership, is preoccupied now with growth management and with its sewer and transit operations. In his first year as administrator, Jim Solem said he was spending a third of his time settling bus drivers' grievances. The legislature does less talking and thinking now in the interim between sessions. The head of the policy shop at the University said recently that its contacts with the state have almost disappeared, and that this is true across the University.

CONSEQUENCES

Change is inevitable. There is a life cycle to organizations. The question is: Are we replacing what we lose? Are we keeping up, overall, the institutions of public life? Or, are we coasting now . . . drawing down and not replacing the social capital built up in that remarkable generation of institutional development that began about 1940 and ran into the mid-1970s?

Somehow, Minnesota needs to retain the ability to understand and to deal with the causes of problems. Other states are as good at building projects and setting up programs. This state has had an unusual ability to see why things happen, and to change the systems that determine why organizations behave the way they do. Without this ability to think in system terms, we will be an easy mark for those—always around—who want to persuade us that the answers lie in conventional responses: listening to the people who run the operating organizations (or, alternatively, changing the people who run them), or investing in more professional service or in some kind of big machine.

Minnesota has been really good at what Walt McClure calls "large-system architecture." People understood why a health-care system could not last when—as Somers said—reimbursement is guaranteed for costs that are neither controlled by competition nor regulated by public authority, and in which no incentive for economy can be discerned. They understood that land use and transportation is a system; understood why we cannot travel like Europeans if we want to live like Americans.

It is important to be able to shape the issues correctly; to understand that issues are not topics. Issues are choices, about methods. A discussion simply about goals, however passionately advocated, will not be very productive. Nothing happens without methods. So:

"Health care" is not an issue. Whether to provide health care through a single-payer system rationing care, or to have the payers identify the quality providers and send them patients, that is an issue.

"Housing" is not an issue. Whether to build single-family houses for low-income families, or to build smaller units for the single persons and couples now under-occupying existing single-family issues, that is an issue.

THE ISSUES IN K–12 EDUCATION

Nothing is now testing the ability to raise and resolve issues like the problem of public education. "Half the kids in high school are on a treadmill to nowhere," to quote Judy Codding of the National Center on Restructuring Education.

All the good efforts and all the altruism of the people who work in it do not overcome the reality that public education is a deeply inequitable institution. Lacking both exit and voice, the kids in poor families are the least well served. Far too many learn little and leave early; uninterested in a schooling responsive mainly to the districts important constituency of better-educated and more-aspiring families; disadvantaged by an institution that sends the least experienced teachers to the most educationally needy kids. Not enough people are angry about this, as Gary Sudduty was angry before he died. Too many of us think the schools are fine because we did well and our kids did well. Joe Graba likes to say: "Everybody wants the schools to be better, but hardly anyone wants them to be different." Yet if they are not different, they will not interest, and therefore will not work for, the half of the kids now not doing well.

We are having a hard time understanding why this institution—so full of good people, who mean well—cannot deal with this challenge well enough, fast enough. Too many people still think it makes a critical difference who is superintendent or is on the board, or whether the legislature and the taxpayers provide enough money. Endlessly in meetings, people talk about the bad things that ought to be stopped and the good things that ought to be done. Nobody disagrees, and everybody has heard it all before. Surely something must be blocking improvement. Yet rather than trying to find what it is, and change that, we keep on exhorting our schools and districts to do good things and not to do bad things. We are not thinking our

way very well to the heart of the problem. It is not very practical to exhort organizations to do things they have no incentive to do, and not to do things they have reasons and opportunities—and incentives—to do.

We should see that districts and schools behave as they do because state law has assured them that nothing, really, depends on whether the students learn: not their clientele, not their revenues, not their jobs, not their existence. It has been a system that, as Albert Shanker said at the Itasca Seminar in 1988, "can take its customers for granted." It is not smart to arrange a system in ways that assure the organizations their success, whether the mission they have been given to perform is accomplished or not.

So if half the kids are not learning acceptably well, it is not really the fault of the districts or the people in the schools, or of the teachers and their unions. It is a failure in the design of the system. The structure and incentives exist in law; its defects can be changed only by changing state law.

Legislators do understand the problem, and to their credit are well started on a reconstruction of the institution. They are making it possible for people to start new schools that can try new approaches. It is possible that the job that needs to be done with urban and low-income kids cannot be done by the organizations we have; that the districts simply cannot change their schools enough, quickly enough; or cannot politically generate new schools as different as may be required to interest the kids, who today simply quit. But legislators are slowed by a resistance that remains intense.

It would be easier for legislators to move as fast as they should, if the leaders in public education would say in public what they know—and say in private—about the districts' own difficulty with change. It would help if the media would be as candid about the reasons for the resistance to change as they are about the power of private interests in other systems, and would not accept quite at face value the assertions that everything would be all right if districts just had loyal support and adequate financing. It would help if business executives could understand that the problem in education is not a problem in the management of the organization but is, fundamentally, a problem in the structuring of the "industry."

PROSPECTS

We should talk about all this, over the next year or so. Perhaps there is a problem. But I am not the only one raising essentially these concerns. If there is a problem, perhaps we can do something about it. It's pretty clear what generally would need to be done.

> There'll need to be a continuing effort to develop leadership among those committed to this place; using the talents of people not previously involved.
> The foundations are clearly a major hope, if they will give the design and development of our policy process and its institutions something like the priority they now

give to human-service programs and to the improvement of the physical environment. TrendWatch, now fully regional, is a hopeful start, but at this point has one, new, staff person, and is probably not connected yet with the policy mechanisms that will have to think about the implications.

Clearly we will need to take care of our governmental institutions for issue-raising and issue-resolving. The legislature remains the critical builder of public systems. In a state that is opportunity-driven, that relies on getting at problems before they become crises, it is critical to have people in public office who can move at times with "state capitol policy initiatives." No groundswell of public opinion supported Rudy Perpich and Connie Levi when they moved in 1985 for open enrollment and the post-secondary option. The public support came afterward.

We will need to find new discussion mechanisms for turning "problems" into "issues" and for generating proposals for action. Perhaps web sites and e-mail will provide new and low-cost forums for the reporting and discussion of public issues; filling in the gap left by the change in the commercial media. Read Jason Epstein's Book Business for a little hope. Just when everyone had decided that quality publishing and independent bookselling had been destroyed, along come new technologies that make it possible to publish books on the web and print on demand.

The reasons to be hopeful go back to what I said at the beginning: Go back to the fundamentals.

The desire runs very deep in this state to be successful . . . to count for something . . . to be "major league" as we said in the '60s. But it is no way ordained that the 15th largest metropolitan area in America is bound to be located where the Minnesota flows into the Mississippi River. If we are to succeed in this cold-sunbelt location, we will have to keep up all those elements of 'livability' that attract people to come here and to stay here. And to do that, we will have to maintain our historic comparative advantage in collective action. This is created by the community institutions that can see ahead, that know how to get to the causes of things, that can explain to the public the choices it faces, and that can act with vision and with courage.

Those institutions are, simply, necessary. People talk a lot in politics about what is possible; about what is realistic. What can be more realistic than to do what is necessary? Anybody can do . . . it is no real challenge to do . . . what is merely possible. And things that are necessary do tend to happen, even in public life.

I came across a remark not long ago that I hadn't heard before: "Politics is not the art of the possible. Politics is the art of making possible what is necessary." That's a nice line. And probably a good one to end on.

NOTE

1. Ted Kolderie lives in Saint Paul, Minnesota. This paper was presented at the Stans Lecture, Minnesota Historical Society, October 18, 2001.

Methodology: Words and Numbers

INTRODUCTION

WE COLLECTED STATISTICAL INFORMATION ABOUT EACH OF the states from various sources, then entered those data into a spreadsheetlike database in the SPSS computer program (i.e., Statistical Package Social Sciences). States were listed down the side. Variables were listed across the top. Information came from reliable sources (e.g., Centers for Disease Control, Bureau of the Census, Bureau of Economic Analysis, Department of Justice). In all, we collected or created (e.g., per capita from total) information on more than 700 variables for each of the 50 states.

We tried to collect data that would be comparable across states (e.g., per capita or percent information). When such information was not available, we calculated per capita or percent values from the information that was available. If we knew the total number of murders in a given state reported to the Federal Bureau of Investigation in 1998, for example, we divided that number by the population of the state and produced a number which would be the "murder rate" for each state that year. The resultant value became a new variable that was added to the database, and which would enable us to compare "murder rates" of each of the other states.

Using this process, we prepared more than 700 tables (one for each variable) in which all 50 states were listed in order, according to the numerical value for each state on each variable. States with larger values were always at the top of the list. We call this detailed statistical information "Rankings of the States," which is Appendix G in this book, along with all references and sources in Appendix H. "Rankings" was the major source of information for this study of cultures of the states.

We used the "Rankings of the States" database in various ways, especially to create new data from calculations based on the "Rankings" data. In the process of accomplishing these calculations, however, we came face to face with a problem that must be described to be understood. It was a problem inherent in the fact that we were using both words and numbers to describe the realities within each state. Suppose we start with an example outside the field.

Every year, toward the end of the football season, media pundits and the general public begin to ask the question: "Which team is number 1?" By definition, the "number 1" team in football is "top of the heap," "best there is," or "national champion." Being "number 1" in football is viewed in positive ways.

But consider another example. Every year, also toward the end of the football season, the Federal Bureau of Investigation releases an annual report, *Crime by Counties*, in which data on various categories of crime (e.g., murder, aggravated assault, rape, robbery, burglary, larceny, and auto theft) are released. Every municipality, every county, and every state notes whether the murder rate is up or down from the previous year. If a state ranks "number 1" in murder, however, that is viewed in negative ways.

A "number 1" ranking in football is different from a "number 1" ranking in murder. One notion is positive, the other notion is negative, but both rankings are "number 1." In studying statistical information about the states, personal income and graduation from high school are positive concepts; larceny and death from diabetes or malignancy are negative concepts. These examples highlight part of the problem that we had to solve.

Arithmetically, the problem was solved easily: we simply reversed the logic of the number line implicit in some ordered rankings, then created a "ranked order" for those variables that began at the opposite end of that number line. Understanding how we did that, however, is more complex.

When we created a table for a variable (i.e., every table in Appendix G), we always listed the arithmetical values for that variable from high to low. The tables in Appendix G present information in rank order, in other words, but there is generally no rank value assigned to each state according to that state's specific position in the overall ranking (e.g., a rank of 1 or 27). The numerical value of the variable is described (e.g., dollars, population, or deaths). Please note that tables G.327, G. 328, G.329, G. 330, G. 331, G.332, and G.333 are exceptions to the rule stated above. These tables were produced by a RANK command.

Later we determined the precise rank order of each state on 120 selected variables. That is, we ran the RANK command in SPSS for the 120 selected variables after we had produced the original tables for "Rankings of the States." The RANK command produced a list of the 50 states, ranked from highest to lowest or lowest to highest, depending on whether we had assigned a positive or negative valence to the variable. In other words, the RANK command in SPSS assigned a rank-ordered number (i.e., a number from 1 to 50 for each of the 50 states), according to the arithmetical values that had been entered into the database for each state for the variable involved.

When we ran the RANK command on the computer and ordered variables that had been assigned a positive valence (e.g., personal income) in the opposite way from variables that had negative valence (e.g., murder), we created information that was manipulable arithmetically, as well as useful and defensible in dealing with variables that were "positive" and "negative" in nature.

Suppose we take a moment to illustrate these ideas. The variable selected (i.e., Table G.268 in Appendix G, "Average Murder Rate per 100,000") is negative in nature. Louisiana, with a murder rate of 13.20 per 100,000, is at the top of the table; in other words, Louisiana was "number 1" on murder rate. However, for the purposes of this project, we reversed the logic and created a table in which Louisiana was ranked number 50 instead of number 1. We did this, not to deceive anybody, but to be able to add and subtract unlike values (e.g., murder rate and personal income) to get a valid picture of where each state stood on a host of different factors. The sequence of states along a number line is identical in both tables, but the larger numbers, which represent "real" murder rate values, are listed at the top of the table on the left, whereas the larger numbers, which represent RANKed values on the same variable, are listed at the bottom of the table on the right. This illustrates what we mean by keeping the relationship of states with other states identical, but inverting the sequence. Because murder is a negative concept, larger values for states with higher murder rates reflects a logic that shows the negative nature of murder in a direction consistent with other negative concepts.

Ranking and RANK are different processes, though closely related. Ranking is shown in every table in Appendix G (except those seven that have been RANKed by the computer, and where the label at the top of the table always begins with an "R," as in RMURDER). Those tables list all 50 states, with a numerical value for a variable, alongside each state's name. Ranking always involves numbers (it may be in dollars, percent, per capita, or some other value), and these arithmetical values are always listed from highest to lowest, whether the variable is negative (e.g., murder) or positive (e.g., personal income) in Appendix G, but RANK always assigns a value from 1 to 50 to each state listed. Running the RANK process made it possible to sum RANKed scores of all variables in a given factor for every state. This process produced a mean score for every state on every factor, and those scores were comparable. Unless you are experienced with RANK as a statistical procedure, the language we are using may not be crystal clear, but we hope the illustration will make things more understandable, anyway.

RANK as a computer command produced a listing of the states in the same order as Ranking, but this time the numerical values produced by the computer ran from 1 to 50 instead of the original numerical values that were included in the Ranking tables, as said above.

In other words, the sequence of states is identical in both tables, but the table on the left lists what might be called "real" values and the table on the right lists RANKed values. Because the valence of the illustrated variable (i.e., murder rate) is negative, however, the

Table G.268		Example of Table G.268 (RANKed)	
Average Murder Rate per 100,000 over 39 Years, 1960–1998		Average Murder Rate per 100,000 over 39 Years, 1960–1998	
13.20	Louisiana	1.00	North Dakota
12.29	Georgia	2.00	Iowa
11.68	Alabama	3.00	South Dakota
11.64	Texas	4.00	Vermont
11.63	Mississippi	5.00	New Hampshire
11.34	Nevada	6.00	Maine
11.17	South Carolina	7.00	Minnesota
10.79	Florida	8.50	Wisconsin
10.04	Alaska	8.50	Utah
10.04	New York	10.00	Rhode Island
9.90	North Carolina	11.00	Nebraska
9.54	Tennessee	12.00	Massachusetts
9.41	Maryland	13.00	Idaho
9.41	New Mexico	14.00	Montana
9.15	California	15.00	Connecticut
9.03	Arkansas	16.00	Washington
8.94	Illinois	17.00	Oregon
8.87	Michigan	18.00	Hawaii
8.66	Virginia	19.00	Kansas
8.55	Missouri	20.00	Wyoming
7.83	Kentucky	21.00	New Jersey
7.77	Arizona	22.00	Pennsylvania
7.29	Oklahoma	23.00	West Virginia
6.12	Indiana	24.00	Colorado
5.85	Ohio	25.00	Delaware
5.75	Delaware	26.00	Ohio
5.70	Colorado	27.00	Indiana
5.40	West Virginia	28.00	Oklahoma
5.24	Pennsylvania	29.00	Arizona
5.06	New Jersey	30.00	Kentucky
5.03	Wyoming	31.00	Missouri
4.88	Kansas	32.00	Virginia
4.41	Hawaii	33.00	Michigan
4.24	Oregon	34.00	Illinois
4.21	Washington	35.00	Arkansas
3.82	Connecticut	36.00	California
3.67	Montana	37.50	New Mexico
3.44	Idaho	37.50	Maryland
3.25	Massachusetts	39.00	Tennessee
3.00	Nebraska	40.00	North Carolina
2.98	Rhode Island	41.50	New York
2.93	Utah	41.50	Alaska
2.93	Wisconsin	43.00	Florida
2.35	Minnesota	44.00	South Carolina
2.23	Maine	45.00	Nevada
2.15	New Hampshire	46.00	Mississippi
2.11	Vermont	47.00	Texas
2.09	South Dakota	48.00	Alabama
1.85	Iowa	49.00	Georgia
1.16	North Dakota	50.00	Louisiana
	MURDER39		RMURDER3

table on the left has high values at the top, while the RANKed list on the right has been inverted and has high numbers at the bottom. When negative values were ranked, in other words, states that had high arithmetical values on a variable as described in Appendix G were listed at the bottom instead of at the top, and the one with the highest numerical value was assigned a rank of 50 not 1.

We are confident that the calculations were done appropriately (if not, others will discover where we erred). We attempted to overcome any difficulties associated with understanding these ideas with thorough, but probably redundant, discussion in the narrative of the report, but these were the processes that we used. Now the specific steps that we followed.

STEPS FOLLOWED

Described below are the six steps we followed to collect and create the numerical information that served as a basis for this study: (1) created a database that included close to 700 variables; (2) developed 15 factors that included 120 of those variables; (3) rank-ordered each variable that was in any factor from high to low (with "number 50" reflecting negative valence and "number 1" reflecting positive valence); (4) created a SUMMARY table based on a summation of mean scores for each state on the 15 factors; (5) developed a "Problems Profile" for each state; and (6) studied the SUMMARY table to make inferences about cultures in the states. After we had accomplished these six steps, we added a short narrative about each state that was based primarily on variables that had not been included in any of the calculations.

Step One: Created a Database Comprised of Variables
We collected statistical information about each of the states from various sources, then entered those data into a spreadsheet-like database, with variables listed horizontally across the top and states listed vertically along the side. All information was loaded into SPSS software for calculation purposes. With these data we then created, where necessary, per capita or percent information that would enable us to make comparisons between states. Those data are all reported in the more than 700 tables in Appendix G, "Rankings of the States," included with this book. All tables list high values at the top and low values at the bottom, whether the variable is positive or negative in nature. Source information and definitions for each variable are described in "References and Sources," Appendix H.

Step Two: Conceptualized 15 Factors, Each of Which Included Several Variables
Over a period of several months we collected information on each of more than 700 variables and entered

those data into the software program, as described above. During this time we "played with the data" in various ways—correlation analyses, regression analyses, cluster analyses, comparison of mean scores analyses, and summation analyses—trying to get a "feel" for what we had. It quickly became apparent that relationships among certain variables existed, regardless of which statistical techniques we employed.

Following our sense of the statistical relationships that began to emerge, we put together combinations of variables and formed "logical factors." The factors were logical in that the decisions to include or exclude variables in a factor were made on the basis of logic rather than on the basis of factor analysis by the computer. We thought we had too few cases (i.e., 50 states) and too many variables (i.e., close to 700) to do a regular factor analysis, although that decision may reflect more about our lack of statistical sophistication than anything else. At any rate, that is what we did.

The 15 factors that we created are described below. Four kinds of information are included in this description: (1) the name of each factor; (2) the abbreviation of each variable included in a factor, which is also printed in ALL CAPS at the top of each table in Appendix G; (3) the valence (+) or (−) attributed to each variable; and (4) a brief description of each variable included in every factor. The name we assigned to each factor is listed at the top of the list of variables that make up that factor, and the factor name is printed in ALL CAPS and underlined. Descriptions of all variables are included at the right.

The decision to classify a variable as positive (+) or negative (−) was arbitrary but thoughtful, although readers may quarrel with some of our designations. We realize, for example, that some people equate "good government" with "low taxes," but we thought that a statement attributed to Justice Oliver Wendell Holmes Jr., "I like to pay taxes; that's the way I buy civilization," was indicative of "good government," and we assigned a positive valence to taxes. States may misuse or waste tax dollars, but that is another problem; it is not inherent in the idea of taxes for public services at all. Collecting taxes on gasoline, for example, is a reasonable way to maintain highways: no taxes, no maintenance. Other examples of positive variables might be cited (e.g., more doctors per 100,000 population, high personal income, high graduation rate from high school, more police per 10,000 population, and the like). If a variable represented something helpful or good for people, we classified it as positive (+). If a variable represented something that was harmful or bad for people directly affected, we classified it as negative (−).

Listed on the next few pages are the 15 general factors that we created by placing variables in a category. The factors are listed in the same order as they were described and discussed in Chapters 3 through 8 earlier.

GOVERNMT		Description of Variables
TAXRATE	(+)	Taxes paid to all levels of government, 1999
PCSTALO	(+)	Per capita state and local taxes, 1999
PCLOCGOV	(+)	Percent of population working in local government, 1998
FEDFUNPP	(+)	Federal funds returned to states, per person, 1999
PCTAXALL	(+)	Percent of per capita income for all taxes (federal, state, local), 1999
PCFEDTAX	(+)	Per capita taxes paid to federal government, 1999
PCLOCTAX	(+)	Per capita taxes (not including property) paid to local government, 1999
PCFSLTAX	(+)	Per capita taxes paid to federal, state, and local government, 1999

EXPEND		Description of Variables
SCHOOL	(+)	Average expenditures for public schools, per capita, 1989–2000
COLLEGE	(+)	Average expenditures for higher education, per capita, 1989–2000
CASHHELP	(+)	Average expenditures for cash assistance, per capita, 1989–2000
MEDICAID	(+)	Average expenditures for Medicaid, per capita, 1989–2000
PRISONS	(−)	Average expenditures for corrections, per capita, 1989–2000
HIGHWAYS	(+)	Average expenditures for transportation and highways, per capita, 1989–2000
ALLOTHER	(+)	Average expenditures for all other items, per capita, 1989–2000

CRIME		Description of Variables
MURDER39	(−)	Average murder rate per 100,000 over 39 years, 1960–1998
RAPE39	(−)	Average rape rate per 100,000 over 39 years, 1960–1998
ROBBER39	(−)	Average robbery rate per 100,000 over 39 years, 1960–1998
ASSAUL39	(−)	Average assault rate per 100,000 over 39 years, 1960–1998
BURGLA39	(−)	Average burglary rate per 100,000 over 39 years, 1960–1998
LARCEN39	(−)	Average larceny rate per 100,000 over 39 years, 1960–1998
MVT39	(−)	Average auto theft rate per 100,000 over 39 years, 1960–1998
ASLGUN	(−)	Percent of all assaults that were gun-related, 1998

PROTECT		Description of Variables
POLIEMPL	(+)	Percent of total justice system devoted to police protection, 1995
POLICE	(+)	Per capita expenditures of justice costs for police protection, 1996
POLICOST	(+)	Percent of justice system payrolls devoted to police protection, 1995
POLTOTRA	(+)	Rate of police protection employees per 10,000 population, 1995
OFFPPOP	(+)	Sworn state police officers per 10,000 residents, 1997

PUNISH		Description of Variables
CORRATE	(−)	Number of corrections employees (e.g., guards) per 10,000 citizens, 1995
PRRATE96	(−)	Number of persons in state prisons for each 1,000 population, 1996
PRISCOST	(−)	Costs per person in the state to maintain the state prison system, 1996
PRCH9296	(−)	Percent change in prison population between 1992 and 1996
EXPT5069	(−)	Number of persons executed per person, as in G.75, 1950–1969
EXPT7700	(−)	Number of persons executed per per person, as in G.76, 1977–2000
CORRECT	(−)	Per capita expenditures for total justice system costs, 1999
CORRCOST	(−)	Percent of justice system payrolls devoted to corrections, 1999
CORREMPL	(−)	Percent of justice system personnel devoted to corrections, 1995
FOODPI	(+)	Cost of food, per inmate, per day, 1996
PRISPI96	(+)	Cost to keep a person in state prison system for one year, 1996

DEATH		Description of Variables
INFMORT	(−)	Infant mortality per 1,000 births, 1997
DEATHART	(−)	Death from heart attack per 100,000 population, 1997
DEATHCAN	(−)	Death from cancer per 100,000 population, 1997
DEATHALL	(−)	Death from all causes per 100,000 population, 1997
DEATHCER	(−)	Death from stroke per 100,000 population, 1997
DEATHDIA	(−)	Death from diabetes per 100,000 population, 1997

HIWAYDEA		Description of Variables
FATALCOH	(−)	Percent fatal accidents in which alcohol was involved, 1998
TRAFATPT	(−)	Traffic fatalities per 1,000 population, 1998
PEDEATH	(−)	Pedestrian fatalities per 100,000 population, 1999
CARINSUR	(−)	Average cost of car insurance, 1998
BRIDGDEF	(−)	Percent of state highway bridges that were deficient, 1998
BRIDGOBS	(−)	Percent of state highway bridges that were obsolete, 1999
DEATHMV	(−)	Automobile death rates per 100,000 population, 1997
ANYALCOH	(−)	Percent of traffic fatalities in which alcohol was involved, 1999
PCFATCH	(−)	Percent change in traffic fatalities between 1975 and 1999

| NOBELT | (−) | Percent passenger car occupants killed, seat belt not used, 1999 |
| GASTAX | (+) | State gasoline tax, per gallon, 1998 |

TRAUMA — Description of Variables

| DEATHACC | (−) | Death rate from accidents, per 100,000 population, 1997 |
| DEATHSUI | (−) | Death rate from suicides, per 100,000 population, 1997 |

HEALTH — Description of Variables

OBESITY	(−)	Percent of persons at risk for being overweight, 1999
MCIGARET	(−)	Percent of males who smoke, 1998
FCIGARET	(−)	Percent of females who smoke, 1998
AIDSPT	(−)	Number of AIDS cases per 1,000 population, 1998
TBPT	(−)	Number of tuberculosis cases per 1,000 population, 1998
NOIMMUNE	(−)	Percent of children under three not immunized, 1998
LOWBIRWT	(−)	Percent of children born with low birth weight, 1998
SYPHILPT	(−)	Number of syphilis cases per 1,000 population, 1998

MEDICAL — Description of Variables

NOCOVER	(−)	Percent of persons without health insurance, 1998
CHINOCOV	(−)	Percent of children without health insurance, 1998
LACKINSM	(−)	Percent of young males without health insurance, 1995
LACKINSF	(−)	Percent of young females without health insurance, 1995
PAYENROL	(+)	Dollars paid to each Medicare enrollee, 1999
PAYRECIP	(+)	Dollars paid to each Medicaid enrollee, 1999
DOCTORS	(+)	Number of active physicians per 100,000 population, 1998
HOSPBEDP	(+)	Number of hospital beds per 1,000 population, 1998

TEENPROB — Description of Variables

TEENBRTH	(−)	Percent of total children born to teenage mothers, 1998
UNMARRBR	(−)	Percent of births to unmarried women, 1998
GONTEEN	(−)	Gonorrhea rates per 100,000 females ages 15 to 19, 1996
PCTBRB96	(−)	Percent of repeat births to teenagers, 1996
NHWHBR	(−)	Percent of births to non-Hispanic white teenagers, 1996
TOTPCUN	(−)	Percent of births to unmarried teenagers, 1996
TOTPCINC	(−)	Percent of births to teenagers who received inadequate care, 1996
BRYT96	(−)	Birth rate per 100,000 to teenagers ages 15 to 17, 1996
PCTBAL	(−)	Percent of births to unmarried teenagers as percent of all births, 1996

EDUCACHI — Description of Variables

HSGRAD	(+)	Percent of persons 25 or older who graduated from high school, 1999
COLLGRAD	(+)	Percent of persons 25 or older who graduated from college, 1999
COLLEGPC	(+)	Percent of total population enrolled in college, 1997
PATENTPC	(+)	Number of patents issued per 100,000 population, 1998

EDUCSUPP — Description of Variables

STALOCPP	(+)	Average state and local funding for public schools, 1997
COLUNIPC	(+)	Per capita expenditures for public colleges and universities, 1995–1996
ELESECPC	(+)	Per capita expenditures for elementary and secondary schools, 1995–1996
SUPSERV	(+)	Average funding for support services for public schools, 1998
AVRSALRY	(+)	Average salaries for teachers in public schools, 1998
STUMEDIA	(−)	Number of students per computer in public schools, 1999
COMPUTER	(+)	Percent of households with computers
INTERNET	(+)	Percent of households connected to the Internet
RDUNIPC	(+)	Per capita research and development expenditures by universities, 1998

WORK — Description of Variables

CONSTRPC	(+)	Percent of population that works in construction, 2000
MANUFAPC	(+)	Percent of population that works in manufacturing, 2000
TRANSPC	(+)	Percent of population that works in transportation and public utilities, 2000
TRADEPC	(+)	Percent of population that works in trade, 2000
FINANCPC	(+)	Percent of population that works in finance, insurance, real estate, 2000
SERVICPC	(+)	Percent of population that works in service, 2000
PCUNION	(+)	Percent of workers covered by a union, 1999
GOVFSLPC	(+)	Percent of workers who work for government: federal, state, local, 2000
UNEMPAVR	(+)	Unemployment insurance average weekly benefits, 1998
MALABOR	(+)	Percent of males over 16 who were in labor force, 1999
FEMLABOR	(+)	Percent of females over 16 who were in labor force, 1999

INSUNEMP	(+)	Percent of unemployed covered by unemployment insurance, 1999
AVRPAY	(+)	Average pay for workers covered by state unemployment laws, 1998
RDINDPC	(+)	Per capita research and development expenditures by industries, 1998
FARMINPP	(+)	Per capita income from farming, 1998
MINERLPP	(+)	Per capita income from minerals and mining, 1998
MANPEMP	(+)	Average annual wages for manufacturing employees, 1996
ECONOMIC		**Description of Variables**
PERBELPV	(−)	Percent of all persons living below poverty line, 1998
CHBELPOV	(−)	Percent of children living below poverty line, 1997
BUSFAIL	(−)	Per capita business failures, 1998
UNEMRATE	(−)	Percent of civilian labor force unemployed, July 2000
PCINCOME	(+)	Per capita personal income, 1999
MEDINC98	(+)	Median income per household, 1998
RETAIL	(+)	Retail sales per household, 1998

Step Three: Ranked Each Variable Assigned to Any Factor from High to Low

After we placed variables in categories called factors, we ran the RANK command in SPSS software for each variable in that factor. This process created a new variable for each of the 120 variables listed above, and that new variable listed the states in rank order from 1 to 50. For those variables that were negative (e.g., murder), 1 was assigned to the state which had the lowest rate on that variable, and 50 was assigned to the state with the highest rate on that variable. For variables with a positive valence (e.g., personal income), 1 was assigned to the state which had the largest arithmetical value and 50 was assigned to the state which had the smallest arithmetical value. This logic created a process that produced high scores for states that had more problems and low scores for states that had fewer problems. More about that in Chapter 9.

After we RANKed each state on each variable, we summed the values for each state on all the variables included in a given factor, divided that sum by the number of variables included in the factor, and got a mean or average score for RANK of each state on each factor. The process of RANK assigned every state a value from 1 to 50 on any particular variable, thus making it possible to "add apples and oranges," so to speak. It is inappropriate to sum 2.67 percent of the population in construction work and $28,907 per capita in average pay, for example, but RANK creates values that can be summed, then averaged, and thus compared.

Rank-ordering every state on every variable in a factor made it possible for us to generate a mean score for each state on each factor. It is a complicated process and difficult to describe in simple terms, but the process works. Those scores could be compared statistically; i.e., we could test hypotheses derived from the theory outlined in Chapter 1.

Step Four: Summed 15 Factor Scores for Each State and Created a SUMMARY Score

After we determined an average (i.e., arithmetical mean) score for each state on each factor, we summed those scores to produce a SUMMARY value for each state, including a

table depicting the rank-ordering of states according to those SUMMARY scores. The SUMMARY scores ranged from a low of 245.94 for Minnesota to a high of 544.81 for Mississippi. This score showed where each state stood in relation to every other state on the 15 factors. Hypothetically, with 15 factors including data for 50 states, the smallest value possible would have been 15 if the same state had RANKed number 1 on all 15 factors (i.e., $15 \times 1 = 15$). The largest value possible, hypothetically, would have been 750, if the same state had RANKed 50 on all 15 factors (i.e., $15 \times 50 = 750$). Such rankings did not occur, of course, but the SUMMARY values generated show exactly where each state stood in the overall ranking.

Recall that larger numbers represent negative values and smaller numbers represent positive values. With these calculations, we were finally in a position to make inferences from the mass of data regarding the cultures of the states. Chapters 3 through 8 describe data used to summarize information on the 15 factors created. That summary is reported in Chapter 9.

Step Five: Developed a "Problems Profile" for Each of the States

Finally, we put all of the information we had generated into a half-page summary that we labeled "Problems Profile" for each of the 50 states. Recall that each factor score was actually an arithmetical average of the RANKed scores of several variables which comprised a given factor. Higher scores indicated more problems. Lower scores indicated fewer problems. The Problems Profile displayed all of the information about where each state stood on each of the factors and on the SUMMARY factor, visually and arithmetically.

The name of the state is listed at the top of the profile. Brief descriptions of factors are listed down the left-hand side of the table, and factor scores are listed down the right-hand side of the table. In between the label and the score for each factor is a continuum, with the position of that state indicated on that continuum. At the bottom of the table is a separate continuum for the SUMMARY factor, and the position of the state on that continuum is also shown. States with fewer problems on a given factor are depicted toward the left end of each continuum. States with more problems on a given factor are depicted toward the right end of each continuum.

Since each continuum consists of 100 dots on a line (a dot is a periods or "."), there is a precise position for each of the 50 states in relation to all of the remaining states at one point on each continuum, so a chart results which shows where each state stands on each of the various factors, both numerically and visually. We call this the "Problems Profile." It might be thought of as a diagnostic tool, but it is basically a marking mechanism which enables readers to see exactly where each state stands in relation to all of the other states on each of 15 factors. Appendix G shows where each state stands in relation to all of the other states on each of the 702 variables and factors.

A narrative about each state is printed along with that state's Problems Profile. The brief narrative adds perspective to the numerical information about each state, and is based primarily on data from variables not included in any of the factors.

Step Six: Studied the SUMMARY Table for Inferences about Culture

If you even look at the tables in Appendix G, you may ask yourself: "What do all those numbers mean?" That was a question we asked ourselves, in fact. How can we make sense out of all that information?

Some may think that it is not possible to study culture by examining the kinds of data that we have collected. We disagree. People who commit murder, rape, or robbery obviously have different values and different beliefs than people who are law abiding. People who neglect their health—or consciously engage in behaviors that are unhealthy, such as smoking, unprotected sex, or overeating—have different values and different attitudes than people who do not take care of themselves.

Likewise, policymakers who refuse to raise taxes to provide needed hospital or road repairs are shaping behavior in ways that reflect certain attitudes and values. And policymakers who are more concerned with providing public schools that are economically efficient than schools that are educationally effective are doing the same thing. We think that studying numerical data in the array of tables included in Appendix G is an appropriate way to study culture. The SUMMARY table summarizes information on 120 variables that were subsumed into 15 factors for each of the 50 states, and represents a one-number score for each state, showing the precise relationship of that state to each of the other states.

Tables on Factors That Comprise SUMMARY

Table C.1. Comparison on 14 Factor Scores for States with High GOVERNMT Rates (upper half) and Low GOVERNMT Rates (lower half)

Compared on	Table	Upper Half Mean	Lower Half Mean	Upper SD	Lower SD	t
EXPEND	G.688	25.62	25.38	7.32	6.77	.12
CRIME	G.689	23.00	28.00	13.19	8.36	−1.60
PROTECT	G.690	28.07	22.93	5.24	9.30	2.40*
PUNISH	G.691	25.26	25.74	10.94	6.87	−.18
DEATH	G.692	27.97	23.03	12.92	10.10	1.50
HIWAYDEA	G.693	27.65	23.35	5.46	4.25	3.10*
TRAUMA	G.694	31.00	20.00	12.04	12.64	3.15*
HEALTH	G.695	25.62	25.38	10.48	7.18	.09
MEDICAL	G.696	27.23	23.78	8.69	6.09	1.63
TEENPROB	G.697	26.29	24.71	11.37	6.41	.60
EDUCACHI	G.698	30.03	20.98	11.33	7.68	3.31*
EDUCSUPP	G.699	31.40	19.60	6.79	6.46	6.29*
WORK	G.700	28.89	22.11	4.91	3.65	5.54*
ECONOMIC	G.701	30.10	20.90	9.55	6.88	3.91*

*Significant beyond .05 level of confidence.

Table C.2. Comparison on 14 Factor Scores for States with High EXPEND Rates (upper half) and Low EXPEND Rates (lower half)

Compared on	Table	Upper Half Mean	Lower Half Mean	Upper SD	Lower SD	t
GOVERNMT	G.687	25.80	25.20	8.70	8.93	.24
CRIME	G.689	29.29	21.72	11.01	10.28	2.51*
PROTECT	G.690	26.89	24.11	6.67	8.90	1.25
PUNISH	G.691	29.13	21.87	9.32	7.25	3.08*
DEATH	G.692	24.70	26.30	11.55	12.11	−.48
HIWAYDEA	G.693	25.73	25.27	5.04	5.65	.30
TRAUMA	G.694	26.30	24.70	12.54	14.47	.42
HEALTH	G.695	27.88	23.12	7.91	9.33	1.95
MEDICAL	G.696	27.46	23.55	7.49	7.40	1.86
TEENPROB	G.697	28.62	22.38	8.33	9.05	2.53*
EDUCACHI	G.698	26.56	24.44	10.18	11.14	.70
EDUCSUPP	G.699	27.47	23.53	7.91	9.47	1.60
WORK	G.700	25.65	25.35	4.84	6.16	.19
ECONOMIC	G.701	25.15	25.85	8.34	10.62	−.26

*Significant beyond .05 level of confidence.

Table C.3. Comparison on 14 Factor Scores for States with High CRIME Rates (upper half) and Low CRIME Rates (lower half)

Compared on	Table	Upper Half Mean	Lower Half Mean	Upper SD	Lower SD	t
GOVERNMT	G.687	23.54	27.46	8.37	8.60	−1.61
EXPEND	G.688	28.10	22.90	6.85	6.21	2.81*
PROTECT	G.690	25.59	25.41	7.85	8.13	.08
PUNISH	G.691	30.68	20.32	7.33	7.56	4.92*
DEATH	G.692	24.45	26.55	11.86	11.78	−.63
HIWAYDEA	G.693	26.64	24.36	5.45	5.00	1.54
TRAUMA	G.694	25.96	25.04	13.84	13.27	.24
HEALTH	G.695	30.29	20.71	6.16	8.71	4.49*
MEDICAL	G.696	29.16	21.84	6.29	7.16	3.84*
TEENPROB	G.697	30.99	20.01	6.32	8.30	5.27*
EDUCACHI	G.698	26.54	24.47	9.50	11.73	.69
EDUCSUPP	G.699	25.51	25.49	9.51	11.73	.01
WORK	G.700	25.36	25.64	5.23	5.83	−.18
ECONOMIC	G.701	26.88	24.12	8.58	10.24	−1.04

*Significant beyond .05 level of confidence.

Table C.4. Comparison on 14 Factor Scores for States with High PROTECT Rates (upper half) and Low PROTECT Rates (lower half)

Compared on	Table	Upper Half Mean	Lower Half Mean	Upper SD	Lower SD	t
GOVERNMT	G.687	27.78	23.23	7.93	9.05	1.89
EXPEND	G.688	27.54	23.46	7.73	5.59	2.14*
CRIME	G.689	27.05	23.95	11.65	10.78	.98
PUNISH	G.691	27.66	23.34	9.90	7.69	1.72
DEATH	G.692	24.22	26.78	12.78	10.72	−.77
HIWAYDEA	G.693	25.74	25.26	5.30	5.42	.32
TRAUMA	G.694	28.61	22.39	10.83	15.18	1.67
HEALTH	G.695	26.69	24.32	8.92	8.88	.94
MEDICAL	G.696	26.51	24.49	8.03	7.22	.94
TEENPROB	G.697	27.95	23.05	8.75	9.08	1.95
EDUCACHI	G.698	27.74	23.26	11.59	9.23	1.51
EDUCSUPP	G.699	27.98	23.02	7.95	9.18	2.04*
WORK	G.700	25.38	25.62	5.38	5.69	−.15
ECONOMIC	G.701	26.06	24.94	8.68	10.32	.41

*Significant beyond .05 level of confidence.

Table C.5. Comparison on 14 Factor Scores for States with High PUNISH Rates (upper half) and Low PUNISH Rates (lower half)

Compared on	Table	Upper Half Mean	Lower Half Mean	Upper SD	Lower SD	t
GOVERNMT	G.687	25.35	25.65	9.63	7.92	−.12
EXPEND	G.688	27.50	23.50	6.57	6.93	2.10*
CRIME	G.689	31.24	19.76	8.86	10.47	4.19*
PROTECT	G.690	27.68	23.32	6.91	8.37	2.01*
DEATH	G.692	27.54	23.46	11.79	11.57	1.24
HIWAYDEA	G.693	27.15	23.85	5.44	4.72	2.30*
TRAUMA	G.694	27.13	23.87	13.56	13.36	.86
HEALTH	G.695	31.38	19.62	6.39	6.97	6.22*
MEDICAL	G.696	29.94	21.06	6.49	5.95	5.04*
TEENPROB	G.697	31.78	19.22	6.83	6.54	6.65*
EDUCACHI	G.698	30.61	20.40	9.62	9.12	3.85*
EDUCSUPP	G.699	29.01	21.99	9.01	7.31	3.02*
WORK	G.700	27.80	23.20	4.91	5.13	3.24*
ECONOMIC	G.701	28.66	22.34	10.06	7.78	2.48*

*Significant beyond .05 level of confidence.

Table C.6. Comparison on 14 Factor Scores for States with High DEATH Rates (upper half) and Low DEATH Rates (lower half)

Compared on	Table	Upper Half Mean	Lower Half Mean	Upper SD	Lower SD	t
GOVERNMT	G.687	27.93	23.07	7.55	9.29	2.03*
EXPEND	G.688	25.72	25.28	5.56	8.28	.22
CRIME	G.689	23.19	27.81	10.94	11.22	−1.48
PROTECT	G.690	25.68	25.32	7.09	8.80	.16
PUNISH	G.691	25.07	25.93	8.67	9.55	−.33
HIWAYDEA	G.693	26.41	24.59	5.78	4.73	1.21
TRAUMA	G.694	26.83	24.17	11.86	14.95	.70
HEALTH	G.695	28.51	22.49	8.84	8.03	2.52*
MEDICAL	G.696	25.31	25.69	6.71	8.58	−.17
TEENPROB	G.697	27.91	23.09	9.24	8.61	1.91
EDUCACHI	G.698	30.84	20.16	9.91	8.52	4.08*
EDUCSUPP	G.699	29.25	21.75	9.10	6.95	3.28*
WORK	G.700	27.77	23.23	5.82	4.10	3.19*
ECONOMIC	G.701	27.87	23.13	8.67	9.78	1.82

*Significant beyond .05 level of confidence.

Table C.7. Comparison on 14 Factor Scores for States with High HIWAYDEA Rates (upper half) and Low HIWAYDEA Rates (lower half)

Compared on	Table	Upper Half Mean	Lower Half Mean	Upper SD	Lower SD	t
GOVERNMT	G.687	29.53	21.48	7.20	8.36	3.65*
EXPEND	G.688	25.38	25.62	7.93	6.06	−.12
CRIME	G.689	27.36	23.64	11.24	11.10	1.18
PROTECT	G.690	25.24	25.76	8.69	7.22	−.23
PUNISH	G.691	27.46	23.54	9.98	7.70	1.56
DEATH	G.692	27.33	23.67	13.35	9.82	1.10
TRAUMA	G.694	31.15	19.85	14.12	10.11	3.25*
HEALTH	G.695	28.54	22.46	8.40	8.47	2.55*
MEDICAL	G.696	28.55	22.45	7.27	6.82	3.05*
TEENPROB	G.697	28.68	22.32	10.01	7.10	2.60*
EDUCACHI	G.698	30.92	20.08	10.55	7.59	4.17*
EDUCSUPP	G.699	29.92	21.08	8.97	6.25	4.04*
WORK	G.700	28.46	22.54	5.11	4.13	4.50*
ECONOMIC	G.701	29.54	21.46	9.80	7.25	3.32*

*Significant beyond .05 level of confidence.

Table C.8. Comparison on 14 Factor Scores for States with High TRAUMA Rates (upper half) and Low TRAUMA Rates (lower half)

Compared on	Table	Upper Half Mean	Lower Half Mean	Upper SD	Lower SD	t
GOVERNMT	G.687	29.65	21.35	7.16	8.27	3.79*
EXPEND	G.688	26.17	24.83	7.31	6.73	.68
CRIME	G.689	27.03	23.98	11.50	10.93	.96
PROTECT	G.690	27.07	23.93	6.76	8.77	1.42
PUNISH	G.691	28.02	22.98	8.45	9.06	2.04*
DEATH	G.692	27.49	23.51	13.27	9.87	1.20
HIWAYDEA	G.693	28.64	22.36	4.48	4.11	5.16*
HEALTH	G.695	27.95	23.05	9.08	8.16	2.00*
MEDICAL	G.696	28.86	22.14	5.92	7.76	3.45*
TEENPROB	G.697	29.02	21.98	9.30	7.70	2.92 *
EDUCACHI	G.698	31.29	19.72	10.38	7.26	4.57*
EDUCSUPP	G.699	30.34	20.70	9.18	5.29	4.54*
WORK	G.700	27.85	23.15	5.89	3.89	3.33*
ECONOMIC	G.701	30.87	20.13	7.95	7.70	4.86*

*Significant beyond .05 level of confidence.

Table C.9. Comparison on 14 Factor Scores for States with High HEALTH Rates (upper half) and Low HEALTH Rates (lower half)

Compared on	Table	Upper Half Mean	Lower Half Mean	Upper SD	Lower SD	t
GOVERNMT	G.687	25.19	25.81	9.14	8.48	−.25
EXPEND	G.688	27.38	23.62	7.03	6.54	1.96
CRIME	G.689	30.46	20.54	8.75	11.35	3.46*
PROTECT	G.690	26.51	24.49	7.66	8.18	.90
PUNISH	G.691	31.07	19.93	7.62	6.65	5.51*
DEATH	G.692	30.74	20.26	11.08	10.08	3.50*
HIWAYDEA	G.693	27.30	23.70	5.48	4.54	2.53*
TRAUMA	G.694	26.97	24.03	12.48	14.41	.77
MEDICAL	G.696	28.37	22.63	6.49	7.71	2.84*
TEENPROB	G.697	31.80	19.20	6.22	7.09	6.68*
EDUCACHI	G.698	32.20	18.80	9.39	6.95	5.74*
EDUCSUPP	G.699	28.18	22.82	10.05	6.66	2.22*
WORK	G.700	27.66	23.34	5.54	4.58	3.01*
ECONOMIC	G.701	27.70	23.30	9.42	9.15	1.68

*Significant beyond .05 level of confidence.

Table C.10. Comparison on 14 Factor Scores for States with High MEDICAL Rates (upper half) and Low MEDICAL Rates (lower half)

Compared on	Table	Upper Half Mean	Lower Half Mean	Upper SD	Lower SD	t
GOVERNMT	G.687	24.70	26.30	9.63	8.16	−.64
EXPEND	G.688	26.45	24.55	7.81	6.07	.96
CRIME	G.689	31.06	19.94	8.77	10.74	4.01*
PROTECT	G.690	25.19	25.81	8.12	7.85	−.28
PUNISH	G.691	31.73	19.27	6.57	6.54	6.72*
DEATH	G.692	24.27	26.73	12.66	10.87	−.74
HIWAYDEA	G.693	27.74	23.26	5.09	4.59	3.27*
TRAUMA	G.694	29.14	21.86	13.84	12.19	1.97*
HEALTH	G.695	30.23	20.78	6.88	8.22	4.41*
TEENPROB	G.697	31.00	20.00	7.60	7.13	5.28*
EDUCACHI	G.698	29.55	21.45	10.46	9.30	2.89*
EDUCSUPP	G.699	27.13	23.87	10.31	6.96	1.31
WORK	G.700	27.07	23.93	5.63	4.96	2.09*
ECONOMIC	G.701	27.94	23.06	10.37	7.90	1.87

*Significant beyond .05 level of confidence.

Table C.11. Comparison on 14 Factor Scores for States with High TEENPROB Rates (upper half) and Low TEENPROB Rates (lower half)

Compared on	Table	Upper Half Mean	Lower Half Mean	Upper SD	Lower SD	t
GOVERNMT	G.687	25.29	25.71	8.94	8.70	−.17
EXPEND	G.688	28.09	22.91	6.18	6.89	2.79*
CRIME	G.689	32.74	18.26	7.75	9.36	5.96*
PROTECT	G.690	26.80	24.20	7.47	8.27	1.17
PUNISH	G.691	31.72	19.28	6.55	6.59	6.69*
DEATH	G.692	29.16	21.84	11.33	11.20	2.30*
HIWAYDEA	G.693	27.44	23.56	5.58	4.31	2.75*
TRAUMA	G.694	27.06	23.94	13.31	13.63	.82
HEALTH	G.695	32.57	18.43	4.63	5.99	9.34*
MEDICAL	G.696	29.60	21.40	6.64	6.29	4.48*
EDUCACHI	G.698	31.17	19.83	9.42	8.61	4.44*
EDUCSUPP	G.699	29.10	21.90	8.87	7.39	3.12*
WORK	G.700	27.65	23.35	5.07	5.11	2.99*
ECONOMIC	G.701	29.24	21.76	8.75	8.77	3.02*

*Significant beyond .05 level of confidence.

Table C.12. Comparison on 14 Factor Scores for States with High EDUCACHI Rates (upper half) and Low EDUCACHI Rates (lower half)

Compared on	Table	Upper Half Mean	Lower Half Mean	Upper SD	Lower SD	t
GOVERNMT	G.687	29.99	21.01	6.78	8.31	4.21*
EXPEND	G.688	26.37	24.63	7.57	6.38	.88
CRIME	G.689	25.26	25.74	11.59	11.06	−.15
PROTECT	G.690	27.98	23.02	6.02	8.87	2.31*
PUNISH	G.691	27.68	23.32	9.85	7.73	1.74
DEATH	G.692	30.52	20.48	12.13	9.04	3.32*
HIWAYDEA	G.693	27.77	23.23	5.14	4.51	3.32*
TRAUMA	G.694	31.70	19.30	10.05	13.67	3.65*
HEALTH	G.695	28.97	22.03	9.12	7.30	2.97*
MEDICAL	G.696	27.70	23.30	7.32	7.41	2.11*
TEENPROB	G.697	28.78	22.22	9.38	7.83	2.68*
EDUCSUPP	G.699	31.16	19.84	8.27	5.01	5.86*
WORK	G.700	28.53	22.47	4.92	4.25	4.65*
ECONOMIC	G.701	29.94	21.06	7.73	9.04	3.74*

*Significant beyond .05 level of confidence.

Table C.13. Comparison on 14 Factor Scores for States with High EDUCSUPP Rates (upper half) and Low EDUCSUPP Rates (lower half)

Compared on	Table	Upper Half Mean	Lower Half Mean	Upper SD	Lower SD	t
GOVERNMT	G.687	31.23	19.77	6.36	6.83	6.15*
EXPEND	G.688	27.39	23.61	6.86	6.71	1.97*
CRIME	G.689	25.47	25.54	12.87	9.54	−.02
PROTECT	G.690	27.95	23.05	6.16	8.79	2.28*
PUNISH	G.691	27.77	23.23	10.59	6.63	1.82
DEATH	G.692	27.57	23.43	13.01	10.18	1.25
HIWAYDEA	G.693	28.14	22.86	4.75	4.52	4.03*
TRAUMA	G.694	31.28	19.72	10.69	13.56	3.35*
HEALTH	G.695	27.30	23.71	10.11	7.24	1.44
MEDICAL	G.696	28.55	22.45	7.36	6.77	3.06*
TEENPROB	G.697	28.07	22.93	10.60	6.75	2.05*
EDUCACHI	G.698	32.01	18.99	10.03	6.42	5.47*
WORK	G.700	28.77	22.23	4.76	4.06	5.24*
ECONOMIC	G.701	30.24	20.76	8.59	7.86	4.07*

*Significant beyond .05 level of confidence.

Table C.14. Comparison on 14 Factor Scores for States with High WORK Rates (upper half) and Low WORK Rates (lower half)

Compared on	Table	Upper Half Mean	Lower Half Mean	Upper SD	Lower SD	t
GOVERNMT	G.687	29.43	21.57	8.65	6.97	3.53*
EXPEND	G.688	25.34	25.66	7.24	6.86	−.16
CRIME	G.689	24.78	26.22	12.68	9.74	−.45
PROTECT	G.690	26.66	24.34	7.15	8.59	1.04
PUNISH	G.691	27.30	23.70	10.41	7.20	1.42
DEATH	G.692	28.08	22.92	12.62	10.41	1.58
HIWAYDEA	G.693	28.03	22.97	4.94	4.45	3.81*
TRAUMA	G.694	29.08	21.92	14.07	11.98	1.94
HEALTH	G.695	27.53	23.47	9.64	7.38	1.64
MEDICAL	G.696	28.17	22.83	6.93	7.47	2.62*
TEENPROB	G.697	27.39	23.61	10.45	7.42	1.47
EDUCACHI	G.698	30.69	20.31	9.95	8.66	3.94*
EDUCSUPP	G.699	31.49	19.51	6.88	6.18	6.48*
ECONOMIC	G.701	31.43	19.57	8.74	5.74	5.67*

*Significant beyond .05 level of confidence.

Table C.15.   Comparison on 14 Factor Scores for States with High ECONOMIC Rates (upper half) and Low ECONOMIC Rates (lower half)

Compared on	Table	Upper Half Mean	Lower Half Mean	Upper SD	Lower SD	t
GOVERNMT	G.687	29.02	21.98	8.75	7.30	3.09*
EXPEND	G.688	25.49	25.51	6.79	7.31	−.01
CRIME	G.689	24.99	26.01	11.91	10.69	−.32
PROTECT	G.690	25.74	25.26	7.46	8.49	.21
PUNISH	G.691	26.39	24.61	8.86	9.31	.70
DEATH	G.692	28.82	22.18	12.29	10.38	2.07*
HIWAYDEA	G.693	27.09	23.91	5.53	4.65	2.20*
TRAUMA	G.694	30.44	20.56	14.16	10.79	2.77*
HEALTH	G.695	26.81	24.19	9.65	8.05	1.04
MEDICAL	G.696	28.20	22.80	6.60	7.75	2.65*
TEENPROB	G.697	27.62	23.38	9.88	8.04	1.66
EDUCACHI	G.698	29.73	21.27	10.10	9.53	3.04*
EDUCSUPP	G.699	30.25	20.35	7.87	6.84	4.73*
WORK	G.700	28.65	22.35	5.07	3.88	4.93*

*Significant beyond .05 level of confidence.

Table C.16. Correlations among SUMMARY Factors

Factors	GOVERNMT	EXPEND	CRIME	PROTECT	PUNISH
GOVERNMT	1.000	.028	−.253	.347*	−.115
EXPEND	.028	1.000	.362*	.198	.412*
CRIME	−.253	.362*	1.000	.068	.688*
PROTECT	.347*	.198	.068	1.000	.178
PUNISH	−.115	.412*	.688*	.178	1.000
DEATH	.278	.001	−.184	−.017	.037
HIWAYDEA	.421*	.083	.312*	.050	.436*
TRAUMA	.572*	.063	.020	.257	.222
HEALTH	.030	.269	.569*	.103	.718*
MEDICAL	.165	.263	.543*	.012	.711*
TEENPROB	.087	.373*	.720*	.227	.792*
EDUCACHI	.493*	.099	.127	.244	.442*
EDUCSUPP	.674*	.255	.027	.284*	.296*
WORK	.590*	.029	−.007	.141	.289*
ECONOMIC	.538*	−.019	.151	.160	.256

Factors	DEATH	HIWAYDEA	TRAUMA	HEALTH	MEDICAL
GOVERNMT	.278	.421*	.572*	.030	.165
EXPEND	.001	.083	.063	.269	.263
CRIME	−.184	.312*	.020	.569*	.543*
PROTECT	−.017	.050	.257	.103	.012
PUNISH	.037	.436*	.222	.718*	.711*
DEATH	1.000	.220	.065	.403*	−.023
HIWAYDEA	.220	1.000	.543*	.496*	.495*
TRAUMA	.065	.543*	1.000	.159	.387*
HEALTH	.403*	.496*	.159	1.000	.548*
MEDICAL	−.023	.495*	.387*	.548*	1.000
TEENPROB	.274	.530*	.279*	.866*	.658*
EDUCACHI	.507*	.606*	.496*	.626*	.462*
EDUCSUPP	.441*	.525*	.449*	.398*	.396*
WORK	.455*	.553*	.374*	.417*	.465*
ECONOMIC	.305*	.440*	.536*	.325*	.477*

Factors	TEENPROB	EDUCACHI	EDUCSUPP	WORK	ECONOMIC
GOVERNMT	.087	.493*	.668*	.590*	.538*
EXPEND	.373*	.099	.214	.029	−.019
CRIME	.720*	.127	−.048	−.007	.151
PROTECT	.227	.244	.306*	.141	.160
PUNISH	.792*	.442*	.262	.289*	.256
DEATH	.274	.507*	.498*	.455*	.305*
HIWAYDEA	.530*	.606*	.541*	.553*	.440*
TRAUMA	.279*	.496*	.544*	.374*	.536*
HEALTH	.866*	.626*	.364*	.417*	.325*
MEDICAL	.658*	.462*	.329*	.465*	.477*
TEENPROB	1.000	.564*	.404*	.367*	.422*
EDUCACHI	.564*	1.000	.743*	.681*	.553*
EDUCSUPP	.417*	.697*	1.000	.771*	.630*
WORK	.367*	.681*	.702*	1.000	.692*
ECONOMIC	.422*	.553*	.664*	.692*	1.000

*Significant beyond .05 level of confidence.

Tables on Race, Gender, and Death

Table D.1. Comparison of Death Rates in the United States for All Deaths, by Gender and Race

Variable Appendix G	Table	Number of States	Mean	SD	t
WWALLDEA	G.89	44	364.06	30.42	−15.04*
WBALLDEA	G.90	44	526.54	83.21	
WWALLDEA	G.89	50	360.46	31.25	−51.15*
MWALLDEA	G.115	50	590.84	58.50	
WWALLDEA	G.89	48	361.64	30.80	−21.39*
MBALLDEA	G.116	48	864.90	178.42	
WBALLDEA	G.90	44	526.54	83.21	−6.47*
MWALLDEA	G.115	44	596.58	59.96	
WBALLDEA	G.90	44	526.54	83.21	−25.91*
MBALLDEA	G.116	44	889.18	162.74	
MWALLDEA	G.115	48	592.77	58.83	−12.44*
MBALLDEA	G.116	48	864.90	178.42	

*t-value significant beyond .01 level of confidence
WW = White women
WB = Black women
MW = White men
MB = Black men

Table D.2. Comparison of Death Rates in the United States for Malignancies, by Gender and Race

Variable Appendix G	Table	Number of States	Mean	SD	t
WWMALIG	G.91	41	107.13	8.09	−10.37*
WBMALIG	G.92	41	130.39	15.13	
WWMALIG	G.91	50	106.29	9.15	−28.71*
MWMALIG	G.117	50	148.67	15.92	
WWMALIG	G.91	42	106.54	8.88	−19.28*
MBMALIG	G.118	42	210.43	37.73	
WBMALIG	G.92	41	130.39	15.13	−8.27*
MWMALIG	G.117	41	150.34	15.44	
WBMALIG	G.92	41	130.39	15.13	−21.28*
MBMALIG	G.118	41	213.17	33.68	
MWMALIG	G.117	42	149.39	16.44	−13.76*
MBMALIG	G.118	42	210.43	37.73	

*t-value significant beyond .01 level of confidence
WW = White women
WB = Black women
MW = White men
MB = Black men

Table D.3. Comparison of Death Rates in the United States for Diabetes, by Gender and Race

Variable Appendix G	Table	Number of States	Mean	SD	t
WWDIABET	G.93	38	10.57	2.17	−23.89*
WBDIABET	G.94	38	29.87	5.94	
WWDIABET	G.93	50	10.60	2.33	−14.82*
MWDIABET	G.119	50	13.20	2.41	
WWDIABET	G.93	37	10.56	2.20	−17.02*
MBDIABET	G.120	37	30.29	8.16	
WBDIABET	G.94	38	29.87	5.94	20.16*
MWDIABET	G.119	38	13.16	2.23	
WBDIABET	G.94	37	29.82	6.02	−.42
MBDIABETG	G.120	37	30.29	8.16	
MWDIABET	G.119	37	13.16	2.26	−15.23*
MBDIABET	G.120	37	30.29	8.16	

*t-value significant beyond .01 of confidence
WW = White women
WB = Black women
MW = White men
MB = Black men

Table D.4. Comparison of Death Rates in the United States for Cardiovascular Disease, by Gender and Race

Variable Appendix G	Table	Number of States	Mean	SD	t
WWCARDIO	G.97	42	122.34	15.96	−17.50*
WBCARDIO	G.98	42	192.16	35.41	
WWCARDIO	G.97	50	120.36	15.53	−44.70*
MWCARDIO	G.123	50	209.97	28.00	
WWCARDIO	G.97	43	122.21	15.79	−21.18*
MBCARDIO	G.124	43	287.36	62.93	
WBCARDIO	G.98	42	192.16	35.41	−6.09*
MWCARDIO	G.123	42	212.58	29.45	
WBCARDIO	G.98	42	192.16	35.41	−20.27*
MBCARDIO	G.124	42	289.33	62.33	
MWCARDIO	G.123	43	212.34	29.14	−12.19*
MBCARDIO	G.124	43	287.36	62.93	

*t-value significant beyond .01 level of confidence
WW = White women
WB = Black women
MW = White men
MB = Black men

Table D.5. Comparison of Death Rates in the United States, Other than Motor Vehicle Accidents, by Gender and Race

Variable Appendix G	Table	Number of States	Mean	SD	t
WWACCID	G.101	33	18.99	4.75	−2.95
WBACCID	G.102	33	20.78	4.77	
WWACCID	G.101	50	18.72	4.79	−26.80*
MWACCID	G.127	50	45.22	11.32	
WWACCID	G.101	37	19.00	4.49	−19.99*
MBACCID	G.128	37	55.57	13.79	
WBACCID	G.102	33	20.78	4.77	−17.86*
MWACCID	G.127	33	45.10	10.66	
WBACCID	G.102	33	20.78	4.77	−19.12*
MBACCID	G.128	33	55.71	13.87	
MWACCID	G.127	37	45.17	10.20	−6.56*
MBACCID	G.128	37	55.57	13.79	

*t-value significant beyond .01 level of confidence
WW = White women
WB = Black women
MW = White men
MB = Black men

Table D.6. Comparison of Death Rates in the United States for Pneumonia, by Gender and Race

Variable Appendix G	Table	Number of States	Mean	SD	t
WWPNEUMO	G.99	35	10.28	1.51	−5.55*
WBPNEUMO	G.100	35	12.60	2.45	
WWPNEUMO	G.99	50	9.80	1.66	−29.63*
MWPNEUMO	G.125	50	15.04	2.55	
WWPNEUMO	G.99	33	10.40	1.46	−16.95*
MBPNEUMO	G.126	33	22.80	4.30	
WBPNEUMO	G.100	35	12.60	2.45	−6.92*
MWPNEUMO	G.125	35	15.93	2.18	
WBPNEUMO	G.100	33	12.45	2.43	−13.91*
MBPNEUMO	G.126	33	22.80	4.30	
MWPNEUMO	G.125	33	16.10	2.11	−9.44*
MBPNEUMO	G.126	33	22.80	4.30	

*t-value significant beyond .01 level of confidence
WW = White women
WB = Black women
MW = White men
MB = Black men

Table D.7. Comparison of Death Rates in the United States for Suicide, by Gender and Race

Variable Appendix G	Table	Number of States	Mean	SD	t
WWSUICID	G.107	18	4.61	1.05	8.92*
WBSUICID	G.108	18	2.01	.47	
WWSUICID	G.107	50	4.74	1.28	−28.47*
MWSUICID	G.133	50	20.98	5.01	
WWSUICID	G.107	30	4.75	1.37	−17.04*
MBSUICID	G.134	30	12.99	3.23	
WBSUICID	G.108	18	2.01	.47	−24.36*
MWSUICID	G.133	18	19.39	2.98	
WBSUICID	G.108	18	2.01	.47	−27.98*
MBSUICID	G.134	18	12.17	1.68	
MWSUICID	G.133	30	20.32	5.01	11.67*
MBSUICID	G.134	30	12.99	3.23	

*t-value significant beyond .01 level of confidence
WW = White women
WB = Black women
MW = White men
MB = Black men

Table D.8. Comparison of Death Rates in the United States for Motor Vehicle Accidents, by Gender and Race

Variable Appendix G	Table	Number of States	Mean	SD	t
WWMOTVEH	G.103	24	11.89	4.09	4.93*
WBMOTVEH	G.104	24	10.26	3.81	
WWMOTVEH	G.103	50	11.27	3.70	−23.58*
MWMOTVEH	G.129	50	23.65	7.16	
WWMOTVEH	G.103	32	11.58	3.82	−12.14*
MBMOTVEH	G.130	32	25.20	9.34	
WBMOTVEH	G.104	24	10.26	3.81	−14.03*
MWMOTVEH	G.129	24	25.37	8.25	
WBMOTVEH	G.104	24	10.26	3.81	−12.57*
MBMOTVEH	G.130	24	27.07	9.71	
MWMOTVEH	G.129	32	24.44	7.72	−.90
MBMOTVEH	G.130	32	25.20	9.34	

*t-value significant beyond .01 level of confidence
WW = White women
WB = Black women
MW = White men
MB = Black men

Table D.9. Comparison of Death Rates in the United States for Falls, by Gender and Race

Variable Appendix G	Table	Number of States	Mean	SD	t
WWFALLS	G.105	19	1.83	.27	8.83*
WBFALLS	G.106	19	1.18	.29	
WWFALLS	G.105	49	1.96	.41	−31.47*
MWFALLS	G.131	49	3.96	.70	
WWFALLS	G.105	19	1.83	.27	−9.31*
MBFALLS	G.132	19	3.64	.84	
WBFALLS	G.106	19	1.18	.29	−29.97*
MWFALLS	G.131	19	3.71	.44	
WBFALLS	G.106	19	1.18	.29	−17.40*
MBFALLS	G.132	19	3.64	.84	
MWFALLS	G.131	19	3.71	.44	.40
MBFALLS	G.132	19	3.64	.84	

*t-value significant beyond .01 level of confidence
WW = White women
WB = Black women
MW = White men
MB = Black men

Table D.10. Comparison of Death Rates in the United States for Homicide, by Gender and Race

Variable Appendix G	Table	Number of States	Mean	SD	t
WWHOMICI	G.109	26	2.67	.94	−13.82*
WBHOMICI	G.110	26	10.54	2.95	
WWHOMICI	G.109	42	2.66	.92	−9.04*
MWHOMICI	G.135	42	6.82	3.64	
WWHOMICI	G.109	37	2.73	.94	−17.72*
MBHOMICI	G.136	37	53.18	17.19	
WBHOMICI	G.110	26	10.54	2.95	4.64*
MWHOMICI	G.135	26	6.85	2.93	
WBHOMICI	G.110	26	10.54	2.95	−14.37*
MBHOMICI	G.136	26	54.62	18.15	
MWHOMICI	G.135	37	7.20	3.69	−15.79*
MBHOMICI	G.136	37	53.18	17.19	

*t-value significant beyond .01 level of confidence
WW = White women
WB = Black women
MW = White men
MB = Black men

Table D.11. Comparison of Death Rates in the United States Induced by Drugs, by Gender and Race

Variable Appendix G	Table	Number of States	Mean	SD	t
WWDRUGIN	G.111	21	2.97	.77	−3.17*
WBDRUGIN	G.112	21	4.59	2.65	
WWDRUGIN	G.111	48	3.04	1.23	−8.49*
MWDRUGIN	G.137	48	6.69	4.01	
WWDRUGIN	G.111	31	3.10	1.01	−7.43*
MBDRUGIN	G.138	31	13.67	8.32	
WBDRUGIN	G.112	21	4.59	2.65	−4.09*
MWDRUGIN	G.137	21	6.58	3.25	
WBDRUGIN	G.112	21	4.59	2.65	−6.58*
MBDRUGIN	G.138	21	13.16	8.13	
MWDRUGIN	G.137	31	6.92	3.55	−5.89*
MBDRUGIN	G.138	31	13.67	8.32	

*t-value significant beyond .01 level of confidence
WW = White women
WB = Black women
MW = White men
MB = Black men

Table D.12. Comparison of Death Rates in the United States Attributed to Alcohol, by Gender and Race

Variable Appendix A	Table	Number of States	Mean	SD	t
WWALCOHO	G.113	18	.89	.31	−6.41*
WBALCOHO	G.114	18	2.11	.88	
WWALCOHO	G.113	39	1.03	.46	−22.04*
MWALCOHO	G.139	39	4.06	1.24	
WWALCOHO	G.113	28	.90	.35	−12.27*
MBALCOHO	G.140	28	10.25	4.14	
WBALCOHO	G.114	18	2.11	.88	−9.22*
MWALCOHO	G.139	18	3.76	.83	
WBALCOHO	G.114	18	2.11	.88	−11.17*
MBALCOHO	G.140	18	10.83	4.11	
MWALCOHO	G.139	28	3.72	.88	−9.12*
MBALCOHO	G.140	28	10.25	4.14	

*t-value significant beyond .01 level of confidence
  WW = White women
  WB = Black women
  MW = White men
  MB = Black men

Table D.13. Comparison of Death Rates in the United States for Inadequate Nutrition, by Gender and Race

Variable Appendix A	Table	Number of States	Mean	SD	t
WWNUTRI	G.95	16	.61	.14	−5.72*
WBNUTRI	G.96	16	.93	.29	
WWNUTRI	G.95	38	.57	.19	2.11
MWNUTRI	G.121	38	.53	.17	
WWNUTRI	G.95	12	.59	.15	−6.38*
MBNUTRI	G.122	12	1.32	.42	
WBNUTRI	G.96	15	.94	.29	6.35*
MWNUTRI	G.121	15	.58	.14	
WBNUATRI	G.96	12	.84	.25	−4.48*
MBNUTRI	G.122	12	1.32	.42	
MWNUTRI	G.121	11	.56	.13	−6.60*
MBNUTRI	G.122	11	1.27	.41	

*t-value significant beyond .01 level of confidence
  WW = White women
  WB = Black women
  MW = White men
  MB = Black men

Table D.14. Comparison of Death Rates in 13 Areas for White Females from States with High SUMMARY Scores (upper half) and Low Summary Scores (lower half)**

Compared on	Table	Upper N	Lower N	Upper Half Mean	Lower Half Mean	Upper SD	Lower SD	t
All Deaths	G.89	25	25	377.14	343.79	29.72	23.04	4.44*
Malignancies	G.91	25	25	106.97	105.60	7.21	10.86	.52
Diabetes	G.93	25	25	10.03	10.17	2.39	2.23	1.32
Cardiovascular	G.97	25	25	128.58	112.13	15.52	10.52	4.39*
Accidents	G.101	25	25	21.45	15.99	3.81	4.10	4.88*
Pneumonia	G.99	25	25	10.24	9.18	1.69	1.41	2.84*
Suicide	G.107	25	25	5.21	4.28	1.26	1.15	2.72*
Motor Vehicles	G.103	25	25	13.46	9.08	2.92	3.06	5.19*
Falls	G.105	25	24	1.94	1.98	.34	.49	−.36
Homicide	G.109	24	18	3.18	1.96	.83	.47	5.58*
Drug Induced	G.111	25	23	3.10	2.98	1.29	1.19	.34
Alcohol	G.113	21	18	1.03	1.02	.53	.38	.11
Nutrition	G.95	25	22	.60	.53	.14	.23	1.39

*Significant beyond .05 level of confidence.
**SUMMARY was modified by subtracting DEATH, HIWAYDEA, TRAUMA

Table D.15. Comparison of Death Rates in 13 Areas for Black Females from States with High SUMMARY Scores (upper half) and Low Summary Scores (lower half)**

Compared on	Table	Upper N	Lower N	Upper Half Mean	Lower Half Mean	Upper SD	Lower SD	t
All Deaths	G.90	23	21	557.35	495.73	51.39	97.71	2.62*
Malignancies	G.92	23	18	131.87	128.68	15.74	14.62	.67
Diabetes	G.94	22	16	30.81	28.72	6.34	5.37	1.08
Cardiovascular	G.98	23	19	208.41	174.28	24.91	37.11	3.53*
Accidents	G.102	21	12	22.59	18.00	4.29	4.20	3.03*
Pneumonia	G.100	22	13	12.40	12.89	2.48	2.46	−.58
Suicide	G.108	15	3	2.09	1.80	.49	.37	1.19
Motor Vehicles	G.104	19	5	11.68	6.833	.48	2.00	3.43*
Falls	G.106	15	4	1.17	1.20	.28	.36	−.21
Homicide	G.110	19	7	11.11	9.462	.82	3.06	1.39
Drug Induced	G.112	15	6	3.49	6.382	.20	2.43	−2.81*
Alcohol	G.114	15	3	2.23	1.78	.98	.47	.97
Nutrition	G.96	14	2	.99	.67	.26	.31	1.93

*Significant beyond .05 level of confidence.
**SUMMARY was modified by subtracting DEATH, HIWAYDEA, TRAUMA

Table D.16. Comparison of Death Rates in 13 Areas for White Males from States with High SUMMARY Scores (upper half) and Low Summary Scores (lower half) **

Compared on	Table	Upper N	Lower N	Upper Half Mean	Lower Half Mean	Upper SD	Lower SD	t
All Deaths	G.115	25	25	629.99	552.98	53.65	33.16	6.03*
Malignancies	G.117	25	25	154.84	142.50	14.54	15.05	2.95*
Diabetes	G.119	25	25	13.33	13.07	2.30	2.55	.39
Cardiovascular	G.123	25	25	226.61	195.33	27.62	19.80	4.31*
Accidents	G.127	25	25	50.51	38.92	9.32	9.79	4.70*
Pneumonia	G.125	25	25	16.07	14.01	2.38	2.32	3.10*
Suicide	G.133	25	25	22.98	18.97	4.66	4.60	3.06*
Motor Vehicles	G.129	25	25	28.40	18.89	5.85	4.82	6.28*
Falls	G.131	25	24	3.91	4.02	.61	.78	−.54
Homicide	G.135	24	23	8.54	4.58	3.82	1.63	4.59*
Drug Induced	G.137	25	24	6.08	7.18	4.00	4.00	−.97
Alcohol	G.139	25	25	4.164	3.92	1.31	1.18	.63
Nutrition	G.121	22	16	.59	.46	.16	.17	2.43*

*Significant beyond .05 level of confidence.
**SUMMARY was modified by subtracting DEATH, HIWAYDEA, TRAUMA

Table D.17. Comparison of Death Rates in 13 Areas for Black Males from States with High SUMMARY Scores (upper half) and Low Summary Scores (lower half)**

Compared on	Table	Upper N	Lower N	Upper Half Mean	Lower Half Mean	Upper SD	Lower SD	t
All Deaths	G.116	25	23	907.06	819.07	169.18	180.47	1.74
Malignancies	G.118	23	19	219.51	200.44	36.06	37.86	1.67
Diabetes	G.120	22	15	30.42	30.13	8.48	7.98	.11
Cardiovascular	G.124	23	20	319.48	253.70	47.58	60.12	3.99*
Accidents	G.128	22	15	59.71	50.33	13.52	12.53	2.20*
Pneumonia	G.126	22	11	23.23	22.04	4.11	4.70	.76
Suicide	G.134	21	9	13.46	12.18	3.26	3.15	1.05
Motor Vehicles	G.130	21	11	29.40	18.20	9.13	4.08	4.00*
Falls	G.132	15	4	3.52	3.90	.79	.96	−.93
Homicide	G.136	23	14	52.71	53.87	17.60	17.16	−.20
Drug Induced	G.138	19	12	9.14	19.92	4.87	8.14	−4.61*
Alcohol	G.140	19	9	10.61	9.68	4.36	3.90	.57
Nutrition	G.122	10	2	1.42	1.00	.44	.10	1.60

*Significant beyond .05 level of confidence.
**SUMMARY was modified by subtracting DEATH, HIWAYDEA, TRAUMA

Tables for Other Comparisons

Table E.1. Comparison on 13 Variables for States with High SUMMARY Values (upper half) and Low SUMMARY Values (lower half)

Compared on	Table	Upper Half Mean	Lower Half Mean	Upper SD	Lower SD	t
AVRSTART	G.25	26,541	25,342	2,532	2,286	1.76
PCBLACK	G.34	13.71	6.72	10.56	7.18	2.74*
PCHISP	G.35	8.02	5.77	11.43	4.06	.93
PCHOME	G.37	67.25	64.70	4.50	5.15	1.86
PERHOUSE	G.38	2.62	2.63	.09	.15	−.30
PCEMPCHG	G.43	24.27	12.18	9.97	25.90	2.18*
POPDENSE	G.49	112.94	238.86	95.68	317.59	−1.90
PCMINOR	G.51	24.92	18.32	13.30	14.88	1.65
PCMINFRM	G.55	2.03	2.53	.58	.95	−2.24*
PCWOMFRM	G.56	3.99	4.88	.67	.86	−4.80*
MURPLOGV	G.58	.0017	.0012	.0007	.0006	3.39*
CRIMLOGV	G.66	1.24	1.21	.40	.81	.15
GOVTFSL	G.74	475.84	342.41	505.42	320.01	1.12

*Significant beyond .05 level of confidence.

Table E.2. Comparison of Percent of All Expenditures on Higher Education for States with High SUMMARY Values (upper half) and Low SUMMARY Values (lower half)

Compared on	Table	Upper Half Mean	Lower Half Mean	Upper SD	Lower SD	t*
HIGHED89	G.509	13.64	12.99	4.31	5.64	.46
HIGHED90	G.516	13.34	12.91	4.21	5.81	.30
HIGHED91	G.523	13.60	12.25	4.53	5.96	.91
HIGHED92	G.530	12.94	12.19	4.57	6.56	.47
HIGHED93	G.537	12.40	11.35	4.53	5.99	.70
HIGHED94	G.544	12.30	11.11	5.15	5.81	.77
HIGHED95	G.551	12.30	10.95	5.43	5.50	.87
HIGHED96	G.558	13.08	11.16	5.17	5.47	1.28
HIGHED97	G.565	13.01	10.82	4.92	5.46	1.49
HIGHED98	G.572	12.94	11.34	4.85	5.52	1.09
HIGHED99	G.579	12.04	10.79	4.28	5.29	.92
HIGHED00	G.586	13.14	10.84	4.80	5.46	1.59

*None significant beyond .05 level of confidence.

Table E.3. Comparison of Percent of All Expenditures on Public Elementary and Secondary Education for States with High SUMMARY Values (upper half) and Low SUMMARY Values (lower half)

Compared on	Table	Upper Half Mean	Lower Half Mean	Upper SD	Lower SD	t
ELESEC89	G.508	24.97	19.34	4.70	5.10	4.06*
ELESEC90	G.515	24.03	19.23	4.00	5.29	3.62*
ELESEC91	G.522	24.37	19.36	4.14	4.55	4.07*
ELESEC92	G.529	22.84	19.28	3.87	5.19	2.75*
ELESEC93	G.536	22.46	18.95	3.44	5.34	2.76*
ELESEC94	G.543	21.99	18.67	3.72	5.69	2.44*
ELESEC95	G.550	22.23	18.78	4.71	5.31	2.43*
ELESEC96	G.557	23.09	19.10	4.57	5.24	2.87*
ELESEC97	G.564	23.07	19.43	4.34	5.59	2.57*
ELESEC98	G.571	23.15	19.84	4.44	4.53	2.61*
ELESEC99	G.578	22.55	20.50	4.59	5.36	1.45
ELESEC00	G.585	22.69	20.65	4.47	4.44	1.62

*Significant beyond .05 level of confidence.

Table E.4. Comparison of Percent of All Expenditures on Medicaid for States with High SUMMARY Values (upper half) and Low SUMMARY Values (lower half)

Compared on	Table	Upper Half Mean	Lower Half Mean	Upper SD	Lower SD	t*
MEDIC89	G.511	9.81	10.20	3.17	3.55	−.41
MEDIC90	G.518	11.88	10.56	2.75	3.77	1.42
MEDIC91	G.525	13.30	12.17	2.94	4.10	1.11
MEDIC92	G.532	16.14	15.49	4.08	6.83	.41
MEDIC93	G.539	18.41	16.53	4.49	6.91	1.14
MEDIC94	G.546	18.59	16.78	4.59	7.20	1.06
MEDIC95	G.553	17.40	17.07	4.22	6.42	.21
MEDIC96	G.560	18.39	18.68	3.91	7.12	−.18
MEDIC97	G.567	18.38	17.97	3.67	6.80	.26
MEDIC98	G.574	18.12	17.79	3.48	6.94	.21
MEDIC99	G.581	17.87	18.42	4.26	6.91	−.34
MEDIC00	G.588	18.03	18.42	4.01	6.73	−.25

*None significant beyond .05 level of confidence.

Table E.5. Comparison of Percent of All Expenditures on Corrections for States with High SUMMARY Values (upper half) and Low SUMMARY Values (lower half)

Compared on	Table	Upper Half Mean	Lower Half Mean	Upper SD	Lower SD	t*
CORREC89	G.512	2.98	2.73	1.38	1.38	.65
CORREC90	G.519	3.03	2.77	1.19	1.22	.70
CORREC91	G.526	3.09	2.96	1.09	1.11	.42
CORREC92	G.533	3.10	2.77	1.19	1.00	1.07
CORREC93	G.540	2.99	2.61	1.08	.86	1.38
CORREC94	G.547	2.98	2.52	1.26	.92	1.46
CORREC95	G.554	3.35	2.74	1.68	1.11	1.52
CORREC96	G.561	3.32	2.86	1.22	1.07	1.40
CORREC97	G.568	3.40	3.04	1.16	1.04	1.17
CORREC98	G.575	3.55	3.01	1.39	.93	1.85
CORREC99	G.582	3.38	3.05	1.06	1.01	1.14
CORREC00	G.589	3.48	3.42	1.05	1.24	.17

*None significant beyond .05 level of confidence.

Table E.6. Comparison of Percent of All Expenditures on Highways for States with High SUMMARY Values (upper half) and Low SUMMARY Values (lower half)

Compared on	Table	Upper Half Mean	Lower Half Mean	Upper SD	Lower SD	t
TRANS89	G.513	11.93	12.46	3.55	3.60	−.52
TRANS90	G.520	11.24	12.60	3.49	4.25	−1.24
TRANS91	G.527	10.84	12.56	2.62	4.30	−1.71
TRANS92	G.534	10.30	11.90	2.56	4.05	−1.68
TRANS93	G.541	9.96	11.01	2.35	3.49	−1.25
TRANS94	G.548	9.77	10.74	2.80	2.99	−1.18
TRANS95	G.555	9.06	10.98	2.56	3.11	−2.38*
TRANS96	G.562	9.60	10.71	2.73	2.73	−1.44
TRANS97	G.569	9.52	10.99	2.92	3.00	−1.76
TRANS98	G.576	9.78	10.71	2.73	3.53	−1.04
TRANS99	G.583	9.45	10.96	3.37	3.54	−1.46
TRANS00	G.590	9.58	10.53	3.22	3.88	−.95

*Significant beyond .05 level of confidence.

Table E.7

Finding	See Table
1. States with the highest murder rates were almost all in the South	(G.12)
2. States with the highest assault rates were almost all in the South	(G.13)
3. Half of the states with highest rates of child abuse were in the West half in the South	(G.20)
4. Most of the states with highest rates of children not immunized were in the West	(G.21)
5. Most of the states with lowest average funding per pupil in schools were in the South and West	(G.22)
6. Most of the states with lowest average salary for teachers were in the West	(G.26)
7. States with the most children under the age of 18 were in the South and West	(G.31)
8. States with highest percent black residents (except for New York) were in the South	(G.34)
9. New York has more black residents than any state in the South	(calculated G.34 and G.435)
10. California has more Hispanics than any of the other 49 states	(calculated G.35 and G.435)
11. Most of the states with the highest increase in population are in the West	(G.40)
12. Most of the states with the highest percent of people below the poverty line are in the South	(G.41)
13. Most of the states with highest percent of children below the poverty line are in the South	(G.42)
14. Every state (except Ohio) with highest density per square mile is on the east coast	(G.49)
15. Almost all of the states with highest crimes per person rate in 1998 were in the South or West	(G.50)
16. Texas executed more persons than 44 other states combined	(G.60)
17. Texas had more prisoners per 1,000 population than 48 other states in 1996	(G.64)
18. All states (except three) that received highest federal funds per person were in West	(G.65)
19. No state that had higher operating costs per inmate in prison was in the South	(G.67)
20. No state that had higher medical care costs per inmate in prison was in the South	(G.69)
21. No state that had higher food costs per inmate in prison was in the South	(G.70)
22. Almost every state that had lower operating costs per inmate was in the South	(G.67)
23. Almost every state that had lower medical care costs per inmate was in the South	(G.69)
24. Almost every state that had lower food costs per inmate was in the South	(G.70)
25. States with highest overall death rates for white women were usually in the South	(G.89)
26. States with highest cancer death rates for women were usually in the North or Midwest	(G.91, G.92)
27. States with highest heart death rates for women were usually in the South	(G.97, G.98)
28. States with highest auto death rates for women were usually in the South	(G.103, G.104)
29. States with highest suicide rates for women were usually in the South or West	(G.107, G.108)
30. States with highest death rates for white women from drugs were in the West	(G.111)
31. States with highest death rates for black women from drugs were almost all in the East or Midwest	(G.112)
32. States with highest overall death rates for white men were all in the South	(G.115)
33. States with highest overall death rates for black men were usually in the South	(G.116)
34. States with highest cancer death rates for men were almost all in the South	(G.117, G.118)
35. States with highest heart death rates for men were almost all in the South	(G.123, G.124)
36. States with highest pneumonia death rates for men were almost all in South	(G.125, G.126)
37. States with highest nonauto accident death rate for men were usually in the South	(G.127, G.128)
38. States with highest auto death rates for men were almost all in the South	(G.129, G.130)
39. States with highest suicide rates for white men were almost all in the West	(G.133)
40. States with highest murder rates for white men were all in the South or West	(G.135)
41. States with highest murder rates for black men were usually in the Midwest or North	(G.136)
42. Most of the states with highest drug deaths for white men were in the West and North	(G.137)
43. Most of the states with highest drug deaths for black men were in the North and West	(G.138)
44. Most of the states with highest alcohol deaths for white men were in the West	(G.139)
45. Death rates from alcohol were more than twice as high for black men as white men	(G.139, G.140)
46. Most of the states with lowest percent working for government were in the North	(G.142)
47. Most of the states with highest eligible for unemployment insurance were in the North	(G.149)
48. All of the states with highest eligible for unemployment benefits were in the North or West	(G.150)
49. Almost all of the states with lowest percent females in labor force were in the South	(G.156)
50. Almost all of the states with highest annual pay were in the North or West	(G.159)
51. All of the states with highest percent workers in a union were in the North or West	(G.160)
52. Almost all of the states with highest per capita personal income were in the North	(G.162)
53. Almost all states with highest bankruptcies as percent of population were in the South	(G.164)
54. Almost all states with highest household income were in the North or West	(G.165)
55. Almost all states with highest gasoline prices at refinery were in the West	(G.167)
56. All of the states with highest number of patents per capita were in the North or West	(G.174)
57. Almost all states with lowest percent households with computers were in the South	(G.175)
58. Almost all states with lowest percent households on the Internet were in the South	(G.176)
59. States with highest percent bridges deficient are from all sections of country except Southwest	(G.182)
60. No state in the Midwest is among states with highest percent bridges obsolete	(G.183)
61. All states with highest traffic fatalities per 1,000 population are in the South or West	(G.193)
62. Almost all states with highest earnings in manufacturing are in the North or West	(G.198)

(continued)

Finding	See Table
63. All states with highest minerals income per person are in the West	(G.196)
64. Three states with highest percent believers in Christianity are in the Deep South and the West	(G.205)
65. No state with highest percent believers in Judaism has even 10 percent believers	(G.206)
66. Almost all the states with highest percent low birth weight children are in the South	(G.207)
67. Almost all states with highest percent births to unmarried women are in the South	(G.209)
68. Most of the states with the highest abortion rates are in the Northeast or West	(G.210)
69. Almost all of the states with highest infant mortality rates are in the South	(G.212)
70. All of the states with the highest suicide rates are in the West	(G.224)
71. All of the states with the highest Medicaid payments to recipients are in the North	(G.230)
72. Almost all of the states with highest percent without health insurance are in the South or West	(G.231)
73. Almost all states with highest ratio of physicians per population are in the North	(G.233)
74. Almost all of the states with highest syphilis rates are in the Southeast	(G.238)
75. States with the highest rates of tuberculosis are spread across the country	(G.240)
76. Almost all states with the lowest percent of high school graduates are in the South	(G.243)
77. Most of the states with the lowest percent enrolled in college are in the South	(G.249)
78. Almost all states with lowest per capita expenditures for schools are in South	(G.258)
79. Most of the states with highest murder rates over 39-year period are in the South	(G.268)
80. Most of the states with highest rape rates over 39-year period are in the West	(G.272)
81. States with the highest robbery rates over 39-year period are all across the country	(G.276)
82. States with the highest assault rates over 39-year period are mostly in the West	(G.280)
83. States with highest burglary rates over 39-year period are all across the country	(G.284)
84. Most of the states with highest birth rates for females 15 to 19 are in the South	(G.300)
85. States with the highest larceny rates over 39-year period are mostly in the West	(G.288)
86. States with highest auto theft rates over 39-year period are in the North and West	(G.292)
87. Most states with highest percent births to teens who smoked are in the North	(G.314)
88. Most of the states with highest birth rates for young teens are in the South	(G.318)
89. States with the highest alcohol consumption per capita are all across the country	(G.337)
90. States with the lowest alcohol consumption per capita are all across the country	(G.337)
91. States with the highest percent pedestrian fatality rates are in the West and South	(G.339)
92. Most states with highest increase in traffic fatalities over 25 years are in the West and South	(G.345)
93. Most states with highest traffic fatalities, no seat belt, are in the West and South	(G.346)
94. Most of the states with highest per capita disposable income are in the Northeast	(G.348)
95. Most of the states with highest percent at risk for obesity are in the South	(G.360)
96. Most of the states with highest taxes paid to all levels government are in the Northeast	(G.372)
97. Most of the states with highest per capita income after taxes are in the Northeast	(G.375)
98. States with highest percent justice system payrolls for corrections are in the South	(G.388)
99. Most of the states with highest correction employees rates are in the South	(G.397)
100. Most of the states with highest percent of robberies with a gun are in the South	(G.403)
101. Most of the states with highest percent of robberies with a knife are in the North	(G.404)
102. Most of the states with highest percent of assaults with a gun are in the South	(G.407)
103. States eradicated marijuana plants in extremely uneven numbers across the country	(G.411)
104. Arrests for marijuana were made in extremely uneven numbers across the country	(G.413)
105. Most of the states with highest number of prisoners per population are in the South	(G.416)
106. Most of the states with the highest population are in the North	(G.435)
107. Most states with lowest per capita expenditures for college are in the Midwest or East	(G.677)
108. Most states with lowest per capita expenditures for assistance are in the South	(G.678)
109. Most states with highest per capita expenditures for Medicaid are in the North	(G.679)
110. Most states with highest collection of gaming taxes are in the South	(G.686)

(Note: The following findings were drawn from tables in Appendices C and D.)

111. Correlation between crime and punishment is positive	(C.16)
112. Correlation between expenditures and punishment is positive	(C.16)
113. Correlation between highway fatalities and punishment is positive	(C.16)
114. Correlation between highway fatalities and traumatic deaths is positive	(C.16)
115. Correlation between medical costs and crime is positive	(C.16)
116. Correlation between medical costs and punishment is positive	(C.16)
117. Correlation between teenage problems and crime is positive	(C.16)
118. Correlation between work and government collecting taxes is positive	(C.16)
119. Correlation between work and health factors is positive	(C.16)
120. Correlation between economic factors and highway deaths is positive	(C.16)
121. Correlation between economic factors and medical costs is positive	(C.16)
122. Correlation between medical costs and health factors is positive	(C.16)
123. Correlation between educational achievement and teenage problems is positive	(C.16)
124. Correlation between educational achievement and education support is positive	(C.16)

Factual Information about the Civil War[1]

NOVEMBER 1860 THROUGH APRIL 1861

ABRAHAM LINCOLN WAS ELECTED PRESIDENT OF THE UNITED States in November 1860. South Carolina seceded from the Union in December 1860, with the following resolution:

We, the people of the State of South Carolina, in Convention assembled, do declare and ordain, and it is hereby declared and ordained, that the Ordinance adopted by us in Convention of the twenty-third day of May, in the year of our Lord one thousand seven hundred and eighty-eight, whereby the Constitution of the United States was ratified, and also all Acts and parts of Acts, of the General Assembly of this State, ratifying amendments of the said Constitution, are hereby repealed; and that the union now subsisting between South Carolina and other States, under the name of "The United States of America," is hereby dissolved.[2]

There was no debate. The motion carried, 169 to 0.[3]

Mississippi seceded in January 1861. The steamer *Star of the West* was fired on by South Carolina on January 9, 1861. Florida seceded on January 10, 1861. Alabama seceded on January 11, 1861. Georgia seceded on January 18, 1861.[4] Jefferson Davis made a farewell speech in the U.S. Senate and pleaded for peace on January 21, 1861.

In January 1861, the governor of Louisiana seized federal forts on the Mississippi River and the U.S. arsenal at Baton Rouge.[5]

William T. Sherman, superintendent of a military college in Alexandria, Louisiana, was asked by the governor of Louisiana to receive at the school and store several thousand muskets that had been taken from the arsenal at Baton Rouge. Sherman wrote the governor of Louisiana, as follows:

Louisiana State Seminary of Learning and Military Academy, January 18, 1861

Governor Thomas O. Moore, Baton Rouge, La.

Sir: As I occupy a quasi-military position under the laws of the State, I deem it proper to acquaint you that I accepted such a position when Louisiana was a State in the Union, and when the motto of this seminary was inserted in marble over the main door: "By the liberality of the General Government of the United States. The Union—*Esto Perpetua.*"

Recent events foreshadow a great change and it becomes all men to choose. If Louisiana withdraws from the Federal Union, I prefer to maintain my allegiance to the Constitution as long as a fragment of it survives, and my longer stay here would be wrong in every sense of the word.

In that event, I beg you will send or appoint some authorized agent to take charge of the arms and munitions of war belonging to the State, or advise me what disposition to make of them.

And furthermore, as President of the Board of Supervisors, I beg of you to take immediate steps to relieve me as Superintendent, the moment the State determines to secede, for on no earthly account will I do any act or think any thought hostile to or in defiance of the old Government of the United States.

With Great respect, I am your obedient servant,

W. T. Sherman, Superintendent[6]

Louisiana seceded from the Union on January 26, 1861.[7]

Texas seceded from the Union of February 1, 1861, by a vote of 166 to 7.[8]

Lieutenant Colonel Robert E. Lee, U.S. Army, stationed in Texas, was ordered by the War Department in February 1861, to report in person to the general in chief in Washington by April 1, 1861.[9]

On February 3, 1861, President Buchanan presented his final annual message to Congress by denouncing Northern abolitionists, urging them to let the sovereign states of the South manage their own domestic institutions.[10] Buchanan said:

Our Union rests upon public opinion and can never be cemented by the blood of its citizens shed in a civil war. If it cannot live in the affections of its people it must one day perish. Congress possesses many means of preserving it by conciliation, but the sword was not placed in their hands to preserve it by force.[11]

On February 18, 1861, Jefferson Davis and Alexander Stephens were inaugurated as president and vice president of the Confederate States of America.[12]

On March 4, 1861, Abraham Lincoln was inaugurated as president of the United States of America. At his inauguration, Lincoln took the following oath, specified in the Constitution, before he entered into the execution of his office:

I do solemnly swear that I will faithfully execute the Office of President of the United States, and will to the best of my Ability, preserve, protect, and defend the Constitution of the United States.[13]

Abraham Lincoln then made his first inaugural address, which included the following:

Apprehension seems to exist among the people of the Southern States that by the accession of a Republican administration, their property and their peace and personal security are to be endangered. There has never been any reasonable cause for such apprehension. Indeed, the most ample evidence to the contrary has all the while existed and been open to their inspection. It is found in nearly all the public speeches of him who now addresses you. I do but quote from one of those speeches when I declare that "I have no purpose, directly or indirectly, to interfere with the institution of slavery in the States where it exists. I believe I have no lawful right to do so, and I have no inclination to do so . . ."

I hold that, in contemplation of universal law and of the Constitution, the Union of these States is perpetual. Perpetuity is implied, if not expressed, in the fundamental law of all national governments. It is safe to assert that no government proper ever had a provision for its own termination. Continue to execute all the express provisions of our national Constitution, and the Union will endure forever—it being impossible to destroy it except by some action not provided for in the instrument itself.

Again, if the United States be not a government proper, but an association of States in the nature of contract merely, can it as a contract be peaceably unmade by less than all the parties who made it? One party to a contract may violate it—break it, so to speak; but does it not require all to lawfully rescind it?

Descending from these general principles, we find the proposition that in legal contemplation the Union is perpetual confirmed by the history of the Union itself. The Union is much older than the Constitution. It was formed, in fact, by the Articles of Association in 1774. It was matured and continued by the Declaration of Independence in 1776. It was further matured, and the faith of all the then thirteen States expressly plighted and engaged that it should be perpetual, by the Articles of Confederation in 1778. And finally, in 1787 one of the declared objects for ordaining and establishing the Constitution was "to form a more perfect Union."

But if the destruction of the Union by one or by a part only of the States be lawfully possible, the Union is less perfect than before the Constitution, having lost the vital element of perpetuity.

It follows from these views that no State upon its own mere motion can lawfully get out of the Union; that resolves and ordinances to that effect are legally void; and that acts of violence within any State or States, against the authority of the United States, are insurrectionary or revolutionary, according to circumstances.

I therefore consider that, in view of the Constitution and the laws, the Union is unbroken; and to the extent of my ability I shall take care, as the Constitution itself expressly enjoins upon me, that the laws of the Union be faithfully executed in all the States. . . .

In doing this there needs to be no bloodshed or violence; and there shall be none, unless it be forced upon the national authority. The power confided to me will be used to hold, occupy, and possess the property and places belonging to the Government, and to collect the duties and imposts; but beyond what may be necessary for these objects, there will be no invasion, no using of force against or among the people anywhere. . . .

Shall fugitives from labor be surrendered by national or by State authority? The Constitution does not expressly say. May Congress prohibit slavery in the Territories? The Constitution does not expressly say. Must Congress protect slavery in the Territories? The Constitution does not expressly say.

From questions of this class spring all our constitutional controversies, and we divide upon them into majorities and minorities. If the minority will not acquiesce, the majority must, or the government must cease. There is no other alternative; for continuing the Government is acquiescence on one side or the other. . . .

One section of our country believes slavery is right, and ought to be extended, while the other believes it is wrong, and ought not to be extended. That is the only substantial dispute. . . . Physically speaking, we cannot separate. We cannot remove our respective sections from each other, nor build an impassable wall between them. A husband and wife may be divorced and go out of the presence and beyond the reach of each other; but the different parts of the country cannot do this. They cannot but remain face to face, and intercourse, either amicable or hostile, must continue between them. Is it possible, then, to make that intercourse more advantageous or more satisfactory after separation than before? Can aliens make treaties easier than friends? Suppose you go to war, you cannot fight always and when, after much loss on both sides, and no gain on either, you cease fighting, the identical old questions as to terms of intercourse are again upon you.

This country, with its institutions, belongs to the people who inhabit it. Whenever they shall grow weary of the existing government, they can exercise their constitutional right of amending it, or their revolutionary right to dismember or overthrow it. . . I understand a proposed amendment to the Constitution—which amendment, however, I have not seen—has passed Congress, to the effect that the Federal Government shall never interfere with the domestic institutions of the States, including that of persons held to service. . . I have no objection to its being made express and irrevocable. . . .

I am loath to close. We are not enemies, but friends. We must not be enemies. Though passion may be strained, it must not break our bonds of affection. The mystic chords of memory, stretching from every battlefield and patriot grave to every living heart and hearthstone all over this broad land, will yet swell the chorus of the Union when again touched, as surely they will be, by the better angels of our nature.[14]

The Constitution of the Confederate States of America was adopted March 11, 1861, in Montgomery, Alabama, by seven states: South Carolina, Georgia, Florida, Alabama, Mississippi, Louisiana, and Texas.[15] That constitution, as adopted, stipulated:

Section 9. (1) The importation of negroes of the African race, from any foreign country, other than the slaveholding States or Territories of the United States of America, is hereby forbidden; and Congress is required to pass such laws as shall effectually prevent the same. . . .

(3) No slave or other person held to service or labor in any State or Territory of the Confederate States, under the laws thereof, escaping or unlawfully carried into another, shall, in consequence of any law or regulation therein, be discharged from such service or labor; but shall be delivered up on claim of the party to whom such slave belongs, or to whom such service or labor may be due. . . .

Section 3. (3) The Confederate States may acquire new territory; and Congress shall have power to legislate and provide governments for the inhabitants of all territory belonging to the Confederate States, lying without the limits of the several States, and may permit them, at such times and in such manner as it may by law provide, to form such States to be admitted into the Confederacy. In all such territory, the institution of negro slavery, as it now exists in the Confederate States, shall be recognized and protected by Congress and by the territorial government; and the inhabitants of the several Confederate States and Territories shall have the right to take to such territory any slaves lawfully held by them in any of the States or Territories of the Confederate States.[16]

Robert E. Lee was promoted to colonel on March 28, 1861, and his commission, which he accepted, was signed by Abraham Lincoln.[17]

Fort Sumter was bombarded by the state of South Carolina on April 12, 1861.[18] Virginia, North Carolina, Arkansas, and Tennessee immediately adopted secession ordinances and joined the other Southern states in the Confederacy.[19]

On the morning of April 18 Lee rode up to the Blair son's house on Pennsylvania Avenue. Francis Blair promptly explained his reason for asking Lee to call. A large army, he said, was soon to be called into the field to enforce the Federal law; the President had authorized him to ask Lee if he would accept the command. . . . He said, "If the Union is dissolved and the government disrupted, I shall return to my native state and share the miseries of my people and save in defence will draw my sword on none."[20]

Bidding farewell to Blair, Lee went to [General Winfield] Scott's office. He sensed Scott's deep interest in his action, and as soon as he arrived he told him what Blair had offered and what he had answered. "Lee," said Scott, deeply moved, "you have made the greatest mistake of your life, but I feared it would be so."[21]

NOVEMBER 1864 THROUGH APRIL 1865

Abraham Lincoln was reelected president of the United States on November 8, 1864. Lincoln had defeated the Democratic candidate, General George McClellan, who immediately resigned his army commission and sailed for Europe.

McClellan had been removed as commander of the Army of the Potomac by Lincoln for failure to pursue Lee and the Confederates following battle victories, and he was known to have sympathies for the South. Even though he was a staunch Unionist, he believed in states' rights. Because he opposed Lincoln in the presidential election, and because of his stated willingness to end the war in ways that would have allowed the South to go its own way and continue slavery, Lincoln was fearful that the Union would not be preserved and that all that had been fought for would be lost, if McClellan was elected.[22]

Sherman's Army had left Chattanooga in early May 1864 and captured Atlanta in the first week of September.[23] From Atlanta, he started what came to be called Sherman's "March to the Sea" on November 16, 1864.[24] When he began, Sherman intended to reach the sea, and he informed Grant that, if he was unable to reach the East Coast, he would move toward Mobile on the Gulf Coast.[25] There was no communication after November 16 between Sherman and Grant for almost two months, but Sherman had advised Grant to follow his progress by checking reports in Southern newspapers.[26]

Sherman began his trek southeast out of Atlanta with 60,000 able-bodied men, rations for 20 days, forage for animals for 5 days, 2,500 wagons, 600 ambulances, and a good supply of beef on the hoof. The first field order from Sherman ran as follows:

The General commanding deems it proper to inform the men of the Fourteenth, Fifteenth, Seventeenth and Twentieth corps, that he has organized them into an army for a special purpose, well known to the War Department and to General Grant. It is sufficient for you to know that it involves a departure from our present base, and a long and difficult march to a new one. All the chances of war have been considered and provided for as far has human sagacity can. All he asks of you is to maintain that discipline, patience, and courage which have characterized you in the past; and he hopes, through you, to strike a blow at our enemy that will have a material effect in producing what we all so much desire—his complete overthrow. Of all things, the most important is that the men during the marches and in camp keep their places, and do not scatter about as stragglers or foragers, to be picked up by hostile people in detail. It is also of the utmost importance that our wagons should not be loaded with anything but rations and ammunition.[27]

The second field order specified the details of conduct and management. It ran:

1. For purposes of military operations this army is divided into two wings, viz: Right wing, General O. O. Howard, commanding, composed of Fifteenth and Seventeenth corps; left wing, General H. W. Slocum commanding, composed of Fourteenth and Twentieth corps.

2. The habitual order of march will be, whenever practicable, by four roads, as nearly parallel as possible, converging at points hereafter to be indicated in orders. . . .

3. There will be no general train of supplies, but each corps will have its ammunition and provision train, distributed habitually as follows: behind each regiment should follow one wagon and one ambulance; behind each brigade should follow a due proportion of ambulances, ammunition, and provision wagons. In case of danger, each corps commander should change this order of march, by having his advance and rear brigades unencumbered by wheels. The separate columns will start habitually at 7 A.M. and make about fifteen miles a day, unless otherwise fixed in orders.

4. The army will forage liberally on the country during the march. To this end each brigade commander will organize a good and sufficient foraging party, under the command of one or more discreet officers, who will gather near the route traveled, corn or forage of any kind, meat of any kind, vegetables, corn meal or whatever is needed by the command, aiming at all times to keep in the wagons at least ten days' provisions for his command, and three days' forage. Soldiers must not enter the dwellings of the inhabitants, or commit any trespass; but during a halt or camp, they may be permitted to gather turnips, potatoes or other vegetables, and to drive in stock in sight of camp. To regular foraging parties must be entrusted the gathering of provisions and forage, at any distance from the road traveled.

5. To corps commanders alone is entrusted the power to destroy mills, houses, cotton gins, etc., and for them this general principle is laid down, in districts and neighborhoods where the army is immolested, no destruction of such property should be permitted; but should guerrillas or bushwhackers molest our march, or should the inhabitants burn bridges, obstruct roads, or otherwise manifest local hostility, then army commanders should order and enforce devastation more or less relentless, according to the measure of such hostility.[28]

On December 13, 1864, Fort McAllister at Savannah was captured. There was very little armed conflict along the whole route from Atlanta. Casualties during the march were 103 killed, 428 wounded, and 278 missing.[29] In all, 200 miles of railroad had been destroyed; not one wagon was lost.[30]

Sherman's dispatch to President Lincoln on December 24, 1864, said simply:

I beg to present you as a Christmas gift the city of Savannah, with one hundred and fifty heavy guns and plenty of ammunition, also about twenty-five thousand bales of cotton.[31]

Sherman later said:

I only regarded the march from Atlanta to Savannah as a shift of base, as the transfer of a strong army which had no opponent and had finished its then work, from the interior to a point on the sea coast, from which it could achieve other important results. I considered this march as a means to an end, and not as an essential act of war.[32]

On January 2, 1865, before he left Savannah, Sherman received a lengthy communication from Grant, summarizing developments in all theaters of operations. The letter from Grant concluded with the following:

I have thought that Hood being so completely wiped out for the present, I might bring A. J. Smith here with fourteen to fifteen thousand men. With this increase I could hold my lines and move out with a greater force against Lee. It would compel Lee to retain all his present force in defence of Richmond, or abandon them entirely. This latter contingency is probably the only danger to the success of your expedition. In the event you should meet Lee's army, you would be compelled to beat it or find the sea-coast, of course. I shall not let Lee's army escape, if I can help it, and will not let it go without following to the best of my ability.

Without waiting further direction then, you may make your preparations to start on your northern expedition without delay. Break up the railroads in North and South Carolina, and join the armies now operating against Richmond as soon as you can. . . .[33]

On January 19, 1865, Sherman gave final orders to move northward into the Carolinas. This movement eventually became known as his "March through the Carolinas." Columbia, South Carolina, was captured on February 17.[34] Robert E. Lee sent the following dispatch to his government about this time:

The accounts received from South and North Carolina are unfavorable. Beauregard reports from Charlotte that four corps of the enemy are advancing on that place, another tearing up railroads, and they will probably reach that place before he can concentrate his troops there. He states Sherman will doubtless unite with Schofield at Raleigh or Weldon. Bragg reports that Schofield is preparing to advance from Newbern to Goldsboro. He says no assistance can be expected from the State of North Carolina. Sherman seems to have everything his own way, which is calculated to cause apprehension. Beauregard does not say what he proposes to do or what he can do. I do not know where his troops are or on what line they are moving. . . . It is necessary to bring out all our strength and, I fear, to unite our armies, as, separately, they do not seem to make head against the enemy. Everything should be destroyed that cannot be moved out of the way of Sherman and Schofield. Provisions must be accumulated in Virginia, and every man in all the States must be brought out. I fear it may be necessary to abandon all our cities, and preparations should be made for this contingency.[35]

On March 4, 1865, Abraham Lincoln was inaugurated for a second term, and made his second inaugural address. Portions of that address are included below:

On the occasion corresponding to this four years ago, all thoughts were anxiously directed to an impending civil war. All dreaded it—all sought to avert it. While the inaugural address was being delivered from this place, devoted altogether to saving the Union without war, insurgent agents were in the city seeking to destroy it without war—seeking to dissolve the Union, and divide effects, by negotiation. Both parties deprecated war; but one of them would make war rather than let the nation survive; and the other would accept war rather than let it perish. And the war came.

Neither party expected for the war the magnitude, or the duration, which it has already attained. Neither anticipated that the cause of the conflict might cease with, or even before, the conflict itself should cease. Each looked for an easier triumph and a result less fundamental and outstanding. Both read the same Bible, and pray to the same God; and each invokes His aid against the other. It may seem strange that any men should dare to ask a fair God's assistance in wringing their bread from the sweat of other men's faces; but let us judge not that we be not judged. The prayers of both could not be answered; that of neither has been answered fully. The Almighty has his own purposes. . . .

With malice toward none; with charity for all; with firmness in the right, as God gives us to see the right, let us strive on to finish the work we are in; to bind up the nation's wounds; to care for him who shall have borne the battle, and for his widow, and his orphan—to do all which may achieve and cherish a just, and a lasting peace, among ourselves, and with all nations.[36]

On March 27, 1865, Sherman went to City Point, Virginia, to communicate directly with General Grant.[37] President Lincoln was present. General Sheridan also came to the meeting. On March 28 Sherman returned to his army. Lincoln was still at the front.[38]

Grant finally broke the siege at Petersburg on April 3, 1865. Lee's army moved westward in an attempt to escape, but Grant's armies caught up and surrounded his forces at Appomattox. On April 7, Grant sent a letter through the lines and offered to discuss terms of surrender with Lee, who responded that he would meet with Grant to discuss such terms.[39]

On April 9, 1865, Lee agreed to Grant's terms for surrender, as set forth below:

Appomattox Court House, Va., April 9, 1865

General: In accordance with the substance of my letter to you of the 8th instant, I propose to receive the surrender of the army of Northern Virginia on the following terms, to wit: Rolls of all the officers and men to be made in duplicate, one copy to be given to an officer to be designated by me, the other to be retained by such officer or officers as you may designate. The officers to give their

individual paroles not to take up arms against the government of the United States until properly exchanged; and each company or regimental commander to sign a like parole for the men of their commands. The arms, artillery, and public property to be parked and stacked, and turned over to the officers appointed by me to receive them. This will not embrace the side-arms of the officers nor their private horses or baggage. This done, each officer and man will be allowed to return to his home, not to be disturbed by United States authority so long as they observe their paroles and the laws in force where they may reside.

U. S. Grant, Lieutenant-General
[to] General R. E. Lee[40]

Lee then explained that the horses of his cavalry and artillery were the property of his soldiers, and asked if these men could be permitted to keep their animals. Grant replied that the terms of the surrender would not allow this, but added:

I believe the war is now over, and that the surrender of this army will be followed soon by that of all the others; I know that the men, and indeed the whole South, are impoverished. I will not change the terms of the surrender, General Lee, but I will instruct my officers who receive the paroles to allow the cavalry and artillery men to retain their horses and take them home to work their little farms.[41]

Lee then wrote out his letter of surrender in these words:

Head-quarters, Army of Northern Virginia
April 9, 1865

General: I have received your letter of this date containing the terms of the surrender of the Army of Northern Virginia, as proposed by you. As they are substantially the same as those expressed in your letter of the 8th instant, they are accepted. I will proceed to designate the proper officers to carry the stipulations into effect.

R. E. Lee, General
[to] Lieutenant-General U. S. Grant.[42]

Lincoln made an address from a window in the White House on April 11 to a crowd on the White House lawn. Afterward, John Wilkes Booth, who had listened to the speech as he stood amongst the crowd, turned to his companion at the time and said, "Now, by God, I'll put him through."[43] Lincoln went to Ford Theater on the evening of April 14, 1865, and was assassinated by John Wilkes Booth as he sat in his box at the theater, watching a play.[44]

On April 15, 1865, General Sherman entered Raleigh, North Carolina. He had received a communication from General Joseph Johnston on the 14th, said to have been dictated by Jefferson Davis, then a refugee, living in a boxcar at Greensboro.[45] The message was dated April 13, 1865:

The results of the recent campaign in Virginia have changed the relative military condition of the belligerents. I am, therefore, induced to address you in this form the inquiry whether to stop the further effusion of blood and devastation of property, you are willing to make a temporary suspension of active operations, and to communicate to Lieutenant-General Grant, commanding the armies of the United States, the request that he will take like action in regard to other armies, the object being to permit the civil authorities to enter into the needful arrangements to terminate the existing war.[46]

Sherman replied to this communication as follows:

General J. E. Johnston,
commanding the Confederate Army.

General: I have this moment received your communication of this date. I am fully empowered to arrange with you any terms for the suspension of further hostilities between the armies commanded by you and those commanded by myself, and will be willing to confer with you to that end. I will limit the advance of my main column, tomorrow, to Morrisville, and the cavalry to the University, and expect that you will also maintain the present position of your forces until each has a notice of failure to agree.

That a basis of action may be had, I undertake to abide by the same terms and conditions as were made by Generals Grant and Lee at Appomattox Court House, on the 9th instant, relative to our two armies; and, furthermore, to obtain from General Grant an order to suspend the movements of any troops from the direction of Virginia. General Stoneman is in my command, and my order will suspend any devastation or destruction contemplated by him. I will add that I really desire to save the people of North Carolina the damage they would sustain by the march of this army through the central or western part of the state.

I am, with respect, your obedient servant,
W. T. Sherman, Major-General[47]

As Sherman was leaving to meet with Johnston on April 17, he received the news of Lincoln's assassination. When they met, Sherman told Johnston of Lincoln's death, before they began to discuss terms of the surrender. Johnston thought that was a calamity for the South.[48]

Sherman took the ground that since Lee had surrendered, Johnston could do the same with honor and propriety. He, however, refused to accept any terms addressed to the government of the United States by those who claimed to represent the civil power of the Confederacy. The matter resolved itself, therefore, into such agreement as the two generals, representing the respective armies, might conclude.

On the next day, April 18, after consulting fully with his generals, and agreeing that some terms of surrender ought to be concluded, he started for his second interview with Johnston, at the place of the former one. Johnston, meanwhile, had summoned Breckinridge, Confederate secretary of war, and Reagan, postmaster general, and they had prepared terms which they thought would be satisfactory to the authorities they represented. When they presented them, Sherman objected to dealing with a member of the civic side of the Confederacy, but on Johnston's representation that Breckinridge was also a major-general, and disposed to sink his office of secretary of war in his military title, Sherman consented to hear his views. After discussion was exhausted Sherman sat down and wrote his views, which he said he would present to President Johnson for approval, provided both armies would maintain the status quo till a reply could be received. Both Johnston and Breckinridge assented to Sherman's views and to the extensions of the truce. The truce did not effect Sherman's railroad building in his rear, and he took advantage of the time to complete his connections back to Raleigh. Here is his announcement to Grant or Halleck, of his agreement with Johnston, together with a memorandum of its terms:[49]

Headquarters, Military Division
of the Mississippi, in the Field
Raleigh, N.C., April 18, 1865

Lieutenant-General U. S. Grant, or Major-General Halleck, Washington, D.C.: General: I enclose herewith a copy of an agreement made this day between General Joseph E. Johnston and myself, which, if approved by the President of the United States, will produce peace from the Potomac to the Rio Grande. Mr. Breckinridge was present at our conference, in the capacity of major-general, and satisfied me of the ability of General Johnston to carry out to their full extent the terms of this agreement; and if you will get the President to simply endorse the copy; and commission me to carry out the terms, I will follow them to the conclusion.

You will observe that it is an absolute submission of the enemy to the lawful authority of the United States, and disperses his armies absolutely; and the point to which I attach most importance is that the dispersion and disbandment of these armies is done in such a manner as to prevent their breaking up into guerrilla bands. On the other hand, we can retain just as much of an army as we please. I agreed to the mode and manner of the surrender of arms set forth, as it gives the States the means of suppressing guerrillas, which we could not expected them to do if we stripped them of all arms.

Both Generals Johnston and Breckenridge admitted that slavery was dead, and I could not insist on embracing it in such a paper, because it can be made with the States in detail. I know that all the men of substance [in the] South sincerely want peace, and I do not believe they will resort to war again during this century. I have no doubt that they will in future be perfectly subordinate to the laws of the United States. The moment my action in this matter is approved, I can spare five corps, and will ask for orders to leave Gen. Schofield here with the tenth corps, and to march myself with the Fourteenth, Fifteenth, Seventeenth, Twentieth and Twenty-third corps via Burkesville and Gordonsville to Frederick or Hagerstown, Maryland, there to be paid and mustered out. . . .

I am, with great respect, your obedient servant,
W. T. Sherman, Major-General commanding[50]

Memorandum, or Basis of Agreement, made this 18th day of April, A.D., near Durham Station, in the State of North Carolina, by and between General Joseph E. Johnston, commanding the Confederate Army, and Major-General William T. Sherman, commanding the Army of the United States in North Carolina, both present:

1. The contending armies now in the field to maintain the status quo until notice is given by the commanding general of any one to its opponent, and reasonable time, say forty-eight hours, allowed.
2. The Confederate armies now in existence to be disbanded and conducted to their several State capitals, there to deposit their arms and public property in the State arsenal; and each officer and man to execute and file an agreement to cease from acts of war, and to abide the action of the State and federal authority; the number of arms and munitions of war to be reported to the chief of ordnance at Washington city, subject to the future action of the Congress of the United States, and, in the meantime, to be used solely to maintain peace and order within the borders of the States respectively.
3. The recognition, by the Executive of the United States, of the several State governments, on their officers and legislatures taking the oath prescribed by the Constitution of the United States, and, where conflicting State governments have resulted from the war, the legitimacy of all shall be submitted to the Supreme Court of the United States.
4. The re-establishment of all the Federal courts in the several States, with powers as defined by the Constitution of the United States and of the states respectively.
5. The people and inhabitants of all the States to be guaranteed, so far as the Executive can, their political rights and franchises, as well as their rights of person and property, as defined by the Constitution of the United States and of the States respectively.
6. The executive authority of the government of the United States not to disturb any of the people by reason of the late war, so long as they live in peace and quiet, and obey the laws in existence at the place of their residence.
7. In general terms, the war to cease; a general amnesty, as far as the Executive of the United States can command, on condition of the disbandment of the Confederate armies, the distribution of arms, and the resumption of peaceful pursuits by the officers and men hitherto composing said armies.

Not being fully empowered by our respective principals to fulfill these terms, we individually and officially pledge ourselves to promptly obtain the necessary authority, and to carry out the above programme.

W. T. Sherman, Major-General
Commanding Army of the
United States in North Carolina.

J. E. Johnston, General,
Commanding Confederate States Army
in North Carolina[51]

Grant submitted Sherman's letter and memorandum of agreement with Johnston to the president, and immediately received the following from the secretary of war:

War Department, Washington City, April 21, 1865

Lieutenant-General Grant:

General: The memorandum or basis agreed upon between General Sherman and General Johnston having been submitted to the President, they are disapproved. You will give notice of the disapproval to General Sherman, and direct him to resume hostilities at the earliest moment.

The instructions given to you by the late President, Abraham Lincoln, on the 3rd of March, by my telegraph of that date, addressed to you, express substantially the views of President Andrew Johnson, and will be observed by General Sherman. A copy is herewith appended.

The President desires that you proceed immediately to the head-quarters of General Sherman, and direct operations against the enemy. Yours truly,

Edwin M. Stanton, Secretary of War[52]

On the same date, Grant sent the response of the secretary of war to Sherman, accompanied by the following letter:

Headquarters, Armies of the United States
Washington, D.C., April 21, 1865

Major-General W. T. Sherman,
Commanding Military Division of the Mississippi:

General: The basis of agreement entered into between yourself and General J. E. Johnston, for the disbandment of the Southern army, and the extension of the authority of the general government over all the territory belonging to it, is received.

I read it carefully myself before submitting it to the President and Secretary of War, and felt satisfied that it could not possibly be approved. My reason for these views I will give you at another time, in a more extended letter.

Your agreement touches upon questions of such vital importance that, as soon as read, I addressed a note to the Secretary of War, notifying him of their receipt, and the importance of immediate action by the President; and suggested, in view of their importance, that the entire cabinet be called together, that all might give an expression of their opinions on the matter. The result was a disapproval by the President of the basis laid down; a disapproval of the negotiations altogether—except for the surrender of the army commanded by General Johnston, and directions to me to notify you of this decision. I cannot do so better than by sending you the enclosed copy of a dispatch (penned by the late President, though signed by the Secretary of War) in answer to me, on sending a letter received from General Lee, proposing to meet me for the purpose of submitting the question of a peace to a convention of officers.

Please notify General Johnston immediately on receipt of this and resume hostilities against his army at the earliest moment you can, acting in good faith.

Very respectfully, your obedient servant
U. S. Grant, Lieutenant-General[53]

The following is President Lincoln's dispatch to Grant, which became the basis of the terms upon which Lee surrendered:

Washington, March 3, 1865, 12 P.M.

Lieutenant-General Grant:

The President directs me to say to you that he wishes you to have no conference with General Lee, unless it be for the capitulation of General Lee's army, or on some minor or purely military matter. He instructs me to say that you are not to decide, discuss, or confer upon any political questions. Such questions the President holds in his own hands, and will submit them to no military conferences or conventions.

Meantime, you are to press to the utmost your military advantages.

Edward M. Stanton
Secretary of War[54]

On April 20, Robert E. Lee, at home in Richmond with his ailing wife, and separated completely from his army, sat at his desk and wrote a letter to Jefferson Davis.

This, his last letter to the Confederate president, though cloaked in the guise of military analysis, was a supremely political act, even if he would have denied it as such. And an act of humanity. Lee took dead aim at Davis's proposed "new phase" of warfare. "A partisan war may be continued," he wrote, and "the hostilities protracted, causing individual suffering and the devastation of the country." But, he continued, "I see no prospect by that means of achieving independence." Knowing that Davis was calling for guerrilla war if all else failed, he in effect told Davis to think long and hard about his actions. "To save useless effusion of blood, I would recommend measures be taken for the suspension of hostilities and the restoration of peace."[55]

Sherman communicated the following to General Johnston:

General Johnston, commanding
Confederate Army, Greensboro:

You will take notice that the truce or suspension of hostilities agreed to between us will cease in forty-eight hours after this is received at your lines, under the first articles of agreement.

W. T. Sherman, Major-General[56]

Sherman also enclosed another message, as follows:

I have replies from Washington to my communication of April 18th. I am instructed to limit my operations to your immediate command, and not to attempt civil negotiations. I therefore demand the surrender of your army on the same terms as were given to General Lee at Appomattox, April 9th instant, purely and simply.[57]

The next day General Sherman sent this communication to the secretary of war:

Headquarters, Military Division
of the Mississippi, in the Field
Raleigh, N.C., April 25, 1865

Hon. E. M. Stanton, Secretary of War, Washington:

Dear Sir: I have been furnished a copy of your letter of April 21st to General Grant, signifying your disapproval of the terms on which General Johnston proposed to disarm and disperse the insurgents, on condition of amnesty, etc. I admit my folly in embracing in a military convention any civil matters; but, unfortunately, such is the nature of our situation that they seem inextricably united, and I understood from you at Savannah that the financial state of the country demanded military success, and would warrant a little bending to policy.

When I had my conference with General Johnston, I had the public examples before me of General Grant's terms to Lee's army, and General Weitzel's invitation to the Virginia legislature to assemble at Richmond.

I still believe the general government of the United States has made a mistake; but that is none of my business—mine is a different task; and I had flattered myself that, by four years of patient, unremitting, and successful labor, I deserved no reminder such as is contained in the last paragraph of your letter to General Grant.

You may assure the President that I heed his suggestion. I am, truly, etc.,

W. T. Sherman
Major-General Commanding[58]

On the same day, Sherman received a communication from Johnston that he would meet him at Bennett's house the next day (i.e., April 26, 1865). Johnston was willing to sign an agreement to the same terms as Lee had signed.[59] The following represents the agreement that was then drawn up and agreed to by both commanders:

Terms of a Military Convention, entered into this 26th day of April, 1865, at Bennet's House, near Durham's Station, North Carolina, between General Joseph E. Johnston, Commanding the Confederate Army, and Major-General W. T. Sherman, Commanding the United States Army, in North Carolina.

1. All acts of war on the part of the troops under General Johnston's command shall cease.

2. All arms and public property to be deposited at Greensboro and delivered to an ordnance officer of the United States army.

3. Rolls of all the officers and men to be made in duplicate; one copy to be retained by the commander of the troops, and the other to be given to an officer to be designated by General Sherman. Each officer and man to give his individual obligation in writing not to take up arms against the government of the United States, until properly released from his obligation.

4. The side-arms of all officers, and their private horses and baggage, to be retained by them.

5. This being done, all the officers and men will be permitted to return to their homes, not to be disturbed by the United States authorities so long as they observe their obligation and the laws in force where they may reside.

W. T. Sherman, Major-General,
Commanding United States Forces
in North Carolina

J. E. Johnston, General,
Commanding Confederate Forces in North Carolina

Approved: U. S. Grant, Lieutenant-General[60]

NOTES

1. This information is presented without interpretation to encourage readers to make their own inferences about what these facts mean.

2. Bruce Catton, *The Coming Fury* (Garden City, N.Y.: Doubleday, 1961), 133.

3. Catton, *Fury*, 133.

4. Douglas Southall Freeman, *Lee*, as abridged in one volume by Richard Harwell (New York: Collier Books, 1991), 106.

5. James P. Boyd, *The Life of General William T. Sherman* (Publishers' Union, 1891), 44.

6. Boyd, *The Life*, 45.

7. Boyd, *The Life*, 46.

8. Freeman, *Lee*, 107.

9. Freeman, *Lee*, 107.

10. Catton, *Fury*, 128.

11. Catton, *Fury*, 128.

12. Catton, *Fury*, Chapter 4, "Two Presidents," 212. See also Boyd, *The Life*, 46.

13. Johnny H. Killian (ed.), *The Constitution of the United States of America: Analysis and Interpretation* (Washington, D.C.: U.S. Government Printing Office, 1987), 13.

14. Henry Steele Commager, *Documents of American History*, 5th edition (New York: Appleton-Century-Crofts, 1949), 385.

15. Commager, *Documents*, 376.

16. "Constitution of the Confederate States of America," in Erik Bruun and Jay Crosby, *Our Nation's Archive: The History of the United States in Documents* (New York: Black Dog and Leventhal, 1999), 343.

17. Freeman, *Lee*, 109.

18. Freeman, *Lee*, 109. See also Boyd, *The Life*, 49.

19. Boyd, *The Life*, 49.

20. Freeman, *Lee*, 110.

21. Freeman, *Lee*, 110.

22. David H. Donald, *Lincoln*, (New York: Tombstone, Simon and Schuster, 1996), 369–390; see also Boyd, *The Life*, 309.

23. Boyd, *The Life*, Chapter 11, 261–310.

24. Boyd, *The Life*, 345.

25. Boyd, *The Life*, 358.

26. Boyd, *The Life*, 348.

27. Boyd, *The Life*, 353.

28. Boyd, *The Life*, 354.

29. Boyd, *The Life*, 373.

30. Boyd, *The Life*, 373.

31. Boyd, *The Life*, 386.

32. Boyd, *The Life*, 373.

33. Boyd, *The Life*, 391.

34. Boyd, *The Life*, 404.

35. Boyd, *The Life*, 408.

36. Abraham Lincoln, "With Malice toward None," in Erik Bruun and Jay Crosby, *Our Nation's Archive: The History of the United States in Documents* (New York: Black Dog and Leventhal, 1999), 376.

37. Boyd, *The Life*, 424.

38. Boyd, *The Life*, 424.

39. Freeman, *Lee*, 478–481.

40. Freeman, *Lee*, 490.

41. Boyd, *The Life*, 439.

42. Freeman, *Lee*, 493.

43. Philip B. Kunhardt Jr., Philip B. Kunhardt III, and Peter W. Kunhardt, *Lincoln* (New York: Alfred A. Knopf, 1992), 268.

44. Donald, *Lincoln*, 597.

45. Boyd, *The Life*, 443.

46. Boyd, *The Life*, 443.

47. Boyd, *The Life*, 443.

48. Boyd, *The Life*, 444.

49. Boyd, *The Life*, 444.

50. Boyd, *The Life*, 447.

51. Boyd, *The Life*, 448.

52. Boyd, *The Life*, 450.

53. Boyd, *The Life*, 450.

54. Boyd, *The Life*, 454.

55. Jay Wink, *April 1865: The Month That Saved America* (New York: HarperCollins, 2001), 317.

56. Boyd, *The Life*, 459.

57. Boyd, *The Life*, 459.

58. Boyd, *The Life*, 460.

59. Boyd, *The Life*, 461.

60. Boyd, *The Life*, 461.

Rankings of the States

Table G.1. POP

Population (in 1,000s) 1998

32,651.387	California
19,731.597	Texas
18,099.279	New York
14,862.298	Florida
12,045.000	Illinois
11,420.882	Pennsylvania
9,361.449	Michigan
8,115.001	New Jersey
8,020.599	Ohio
7,467.667	North Carolina
7,455.374	Georgia
6,679.152	Virginia
5,911.454	Massachusetts
5,610.295	Washington
5,224.000	Wisconsin
5,131.641	Maryland
4,785.431	Tennessee
4,725.001	Minnesota
4,712.303	Missouri
4,515.182	Arizona
4,283.774	Indiana
4,232.665	Alabama
4,186.539	Louisiana
3,936.000	Kentucky
3,829.103	South Carolina
3,685.729	Colorado
3,343.162	Oklahoma
3,276.431	Oregon
2,812.720	Connecticut
2,629.000	Kansas
2,578.425	Iowa
2,533.761	Arkansas
1,987.323	Utah
1,810.231	West Virginia
1,747.001	Nevada
1,649.459	Nebraska
1,552.431	Mississippi
1,456.119	New Mexico
1,242.115	Maine
1,220.792	Idaho
1,193.001	Hawaii
988.001	Rhode Island
744.001	Delaware
591.791	North Dakota
559.392	Vermont
542.124	Alaska
509.373	South Dakota
495.254	Montana
477.241	Wyoming
423.765	New Hampshire

Table G.2. MODINDEX

Total Number of Crimes 1998

1,445,773	California
1,027,580	Florida
1,017,083	Texas
615,174	New York
455,362	Michigan
403,224	Georgia
398,943	North Carolina
368,286	Pennsylvania
351,912	Ohio
324,639	Washington
299,807	Arizona
298,678	New Jersey
276,846	Maryland
254,155	Louisiana
247,405	Missouri
246,374	Virginia
245,496	Tennessee
224,071	South Carolina
197,052	Indiana
196,586	Massachusetts
191,745	Alabama
191,494	Minnesota
185,327	Oregon
168,560	Oklahoma
167,297	Colorado
124,693	Connecticut
110,632	Utah
108,751	Arkansas
99,919	New Mexico
92,906	Nevada
87,778	Iowa
84,255	Mississippi
71,878	Nebraska
63,997	Hawaii
46,265	West Virginia
45,640	Idaho
39,869	Delaware
37,900	Maine
35,148	Rhode Island
24,313	Alaska
18,163	Montana
18,146	Wyoming
17,490	Vermont
16,168	North Dakota
15,181	South Dakota
12,741	New Hampshire
*	Illinois
*	Kansas
*	Kentucky
*	Wisconsin

Table G.3. MURD

Total Number of Murders 1998

2,170	California
1,346	Texas
1,008	Illinois
966	Florida
893	New York
725	Michigan
607	North Carolina
605	Georgia
605	Pennsylvania
541	Louisiana
513	Maryland
421	Tennessee
409	Virginia
385	Indiana
372	Missouri
365	Arizona
358	Ohio
344	Alabama
321	New Jersey
311	South Carolina
216	Washington
204	Oklahoma
201	Arkansas
190	Wisconsin
187	Mississippi
182	Kentucky
172	Colorado
170	Nevada
154	Kansas
149	New Mexico
135	Connecticut
125	Minnesota
122	Oregon
121	Massachusetts
78	West Virginia
62	Utah
51	Nebraska
49	Iowa
36	Alaska
36	Idaho
26	Maine
24	Hawaii
24	Rhode Island
23	Delaware
14	Wyoming
8	New Hampshire
8	Vermont
7	Montana
7	North Dakota
6	South Dakota

*Incomplete data

Table G.4. RAPES

Total Number of Rapes 1998

9,777	California
7,913	Texas
7,393	Florida
5,142	Michigan
4,095	Illinois
3,730	New York
3,443	Ohio
3,017	Pennsylvania
2,780	Washington
2,334	Minnesota
2,295	Tennessee
2,288	North Carolina
2,234	Georgia
1,814	South Carolina
1,785	Virginia
1,770	Colorado
1,698	Maryland
1,624	New Jersey
1,597	Massachusetts
1,594	Indiana
1,540	Louisiana
1,512	Oklahoma
1,405	Arizona
1,395	Alabama
1,343	Missouri
1,301	Oregon
1,153	Kentucky
1,119	Kansas
1,037	Wisconsin
911	Nevada
890	Arkansas
842	Utah
777	New Mexico
728	Connecticut
707	Mississippi
660	Iowa
416	Nebraska
396	Idaho
373	Alaska
352	Hawaii
346	Rhode Island
337	West Virginia
225	Maine
204	South Dakota
197	New Hampshire
194	North Dakota
158	Vermont
132	Wyoming
112	Montana
0	Delaware

Table G.5. ROB

Total Number of Robberies 1998

99,509	Illinois
68,752	California
48,107	New York
36,119	Florida
28,665	Texas
19,013	Pennsylvania
15,294	Maryland
15,120	Michigan
15,110	New Jersey
14,009	Georgia
12,018	North Carolina
11,773	Ohio
9,205	Tennessee
8,384	Louisiana
7,978	Missouri
7,544	Arizona
7,099	Virginia
6,438	Washington
5,995	Indiana
5,993	South Carolina
5,629	Massachusetts
5,553	Alabama
4,474	Wisconsin
4,453	Nevada
4,378	Connecticut
4,366	Minnesota
3,443	Oregon
3,083	Colorado
3,076	Oklahoma
2,966	Kentucky
2,633	Mississippi
2,525	New Mexico
2,436	Arkansas
2,283	Kansas
1,486	Delaware
1,391	Utah
1,286	Nebraska
1,225	Hawaii
1,077	Iowa
674	West Virginia
657	Rhode Island
470	Alaska
262	Idaho
262	Maine
174	New Hampshire
137	South Dakota
123	Montana
77	Wyoming
60	North Dakota
54	Vermont

Table G.6. ASLT

Total Number of Assaults 1998

149,055	California
95,123	Florida
73,530	Texas
62,261	Illinois
60,308	New York
39,689	Michigan
28,347	North Carolina
28,057	Massachusetts
26,834	South Carolina
25,220	Georgia
24,894	Pennsylvania
23,234	Maryland
23,155	Tennessee
21,695	Louisiana
18,662	New Jersey
18,361	Missouri
16,903	Arizona
15,591	Ohio
14,412	Washington
14,095	Alabama
13,243	Oklahoma
12,679	Indiana
12,485	Virginia
10,109	New Mexico
9,269	Colorado
8,872	Arkansas
8,794	Oregon
7,777	Minnesota
7,308	Wisconsin
6,882	Kansas
6,877	Kentucky
6,750	Connecticut
5,727	Iowa
5,710	Nevada
5,616	Nebraska
4,117	Utah
3,948	Mississippi
3,794	Delaware
3,322	West Virginia
2,775	Idaho
2,377	Alaska
2,032	Rhode Island
1,345	Hawaii
1,047	Maine
935	Wyoming
641	Montana
593	South Dakota
377	Vermont
273	North Dakota
269	New Hampshire

Table G.7. LARC

Total Number of Larcenies 1998

723,707	California
606,141	Texas
577,953	Florida
337,191	Illinois
336,774	New York
249,536	Michigan
245,705	Georgia
230,170	North Carolina
216,971	Ohio
215,509	Pennsylvania
205,636	Washington
178,050	Arizona
171,189	New Jersey
167,191	Virginia
158,213	Maryland
150,867	Missouri
149,039	Louisiana
132,502	Tennessee
128,134	Wisconsin
127,922	Minnesota
127,046	South Carolina
122,727	Oregon
120,119	Indiana
115,976	Alabama
107,210	Colorado
102,068	Massachusetts
97,455	Oklahoma
87,845	Kansas
80,026	Utah
77,473	Connecticut
68,884	Kentucky
65,164	Arkansas
58,119	Iowa
55,905	New Mexico
48,721	Mississippi
48,107	Nebraska
47,367	Nevada
43,914	Hawaii
31,184	Idaho
27,065	West Virginia
26,353	Maine
24,629	Delaware
21,276	Rhode Island
15,154	Alaska
13,564	Wyoming
13,490	Montana
12,349	Vermont
12,318	North Dakota
11,032	South Dakota
9,181	New Hampshire

Table G.8. BURG

Total Number of Burglaries 1998

268,820	California
202,440	Florida
194,492	Texas
99,509	Illinois
98,766	North Carolina
98,605	New York
83,390	Michigan
72,861	Georgia
66,982	Ohio
59,427	Pennsylvania
58,513	Washington
54,734	Arizona
54,461	New Jersey
51,142	Tennessee
48,623	Louisiana
47,182	Maryland
44,855	South Carolina
43,072	Missouri
39,228	Alabama
38,223	Oklahoma
37,457	Virginia
37,347	Indiana
34,636	Massachusetts
32,336	Minnesota
30,345	Oregon
29,240	Wisconsin
29,188	Colorado
25,088	Kentucky
23,466	Kansas
23,461	Arkansas
21,802	Connecticut
20,640	New Mexico
20,460	Mississippi
19,873	Nevada
16,728	Iowa
16,245	Utah
11,169	Hawaii
11,086	West Virginia
10,229	Nebraska
8,445	Idaho
8,278	Maine
6,465	Delaware
6,422	Rhode Island
3,679	Vermont
3,525	Alaska
2,653	Wyoming
2,575	Montana
2,553	South Dakota
2,113	North Dakota
1,857	New Hampshire

Table G.9. THEFT

Total Number of Auto Thefts 1998

195,406	California
104,004	Florida
96,555	Texas
64,499	New York
57,474	Michigan
52,932	Illinois
41,316	Georgia
40,490	Pennsylvania
39,574	Arizona
35,185	New Jersey
34,544	Washington
33,402	Ohio
28,123	Maryland
25,444	Tennessee
24,383	North Carolina
24,051	Massachusetts
23,415	Missouri
23,010	Louisiana
18,102	Virginia
17,682	Indiana
17,186	Oregon
16,267	South Carolina
15,302	Minnesota
15,188	Colorado
14,499	Alabama
14,210	Wisconsin
13,766	Nevada
13,551	Oklahoma
12,705	Connecticut
9,492	New Mexico
8,573	Kentucky
7,503	Utah
7,329	Mississippi
7,161	Arkansas
5,988	Kansas
5,742	Nebraska
5,594	Hawaii
4,794	Iowa
3,816	Rhode Island
3,373	West Virginia
3,316	Delaware
2,239	Idaho
2,201	Alaska
1,506	Maine
1,132	Montana
1,122	North Dakota
985	New Hampshire
820	Vermont
661	Wyoming
585	South Dakota

Table G.10. ARSN

Total Number of Arsons 1998

28,086	California
8,441	Texas
5,331	Pennsylvania
4,286	Michigan
3,582	Florida
3,392	Ohio
2,589	Maryland
2,364	North Carolina
2,258	New York
2,126	New Jersey
2,100	Washington
1,997	Missouri
1,846	Virginia
1,417	Colorado
1,409	Oregon
1,332	Tennessee
1,332	Minnesota
1,323	Louisiana
1,296	Oklahoma
1,274	Georgia
1,251	Indiana
1,232	Arizona
951	South Carolina
722	Connecticut
656	Nevada
655	Alabama
624	Iowa
575	Rhode Island
566	Arkansas
446	Utah
431	Nebraska
427	Massachusetts
374	Hawaii
330	West Virginia
322	New Mexico
303	Idaho
270	Mississippi
203	Maine
177	Alaska
156	Delaware
110	Wyoming
83	Montana
81	North Dakota
71	South Dakota
70	New Hampshire
45	Vermont
*	Illinois
*	Kansas
*	Kentucky
*	Wisconsin

*Incomplete data

Table G.11. TOTINDEX

Total Number of Crimes 1998

1,445,773	California
1,027,580	Florida
1,017,083	Texas
615,174	New York
455,362	Michigan
403,224	Georgia
398,943	North Carolina
368,286	Pennsylvania
351,912	Ohio
324,639	Washington
299,807	Arizona
298,678	New Jersey
276,846	Maryland
254,155	Louisiana
247,405	Missouri
246,374	Virginia
245,496	Tennessee
224,071	South Carolina
197,052	Indiana
196,586	Massachusetts
191,745	Alabama
191,494	Minnesota
185,327	Oregon
168,560	Oklahoma
167,297	Colorado
124,693	Connecticut
110,632	Utah
108,751	Arkansas
99,919	New Mexico
92,906	Nevada
87,778	Iowa
84,255	Mississippi
71,878	Nebraska
63,997	Hawaii
46,265	West Virginia
45,640	Idaho
39,869	Delaware
37,900	Maine
35,148	Rhode Island
24,313	Alaska
18,163	Montana
18,146	Wyoming
17,490	Vermont
16,168	North Dakota
15,181	South Dakota
12,741	New Hampshire
*	Illinois
*	Kansas
*	Kentucky
*	Wisconsin

*Incomplete data

Table G.12. MURDER

Murder Rate per 1,000 1998

.1292	Louisiana
.1205	Mississippi
.1023	New Mexico
.1000	Maryland
.0973	Nevada
.0899	Indiana
.0880	Tennessee
.0837	Illinois
.0813	North Carolina
.0813	Alabama
.0812	South Carolina
.0811	Georgia
.0808	Arizona
.0793	Arkansas
.0789	Missouri
.0774	Michigan
.0682	Texas
.0665	California
.0664	Alaska
.0650	Florida
.0612	Virginia
.0610	Oklahoma
.0586	Kansas
.0530	Pennsylvania
.0493	New York
.0480	Connecticut
.0467	Colorado
.0462	Kentucky
.0446	Ohio
.0431	West Virginia
.0396	New Jersey
.0385	Washington
.0372	Oregon
.0364	Wisconsin
.0312	Utah
.0309	Nebraska
.0309	Delaware
.0295	Idaho
.0293	Wyoming
.0265	Minnesota
.0243	Rhode Island
.0209	Maine
.0205	Massachusetts
.0201	Hawaii
.0190	Iowa
.0189	New Hampshire
.0143	Vermont
.0141	Montana
.0118	North Dakota
.0118	South Dakota

Table G.13. ASSAULT

Assault Rate per 1,000 1998

7.0079	South Carolina
6.9424	New Mexico
6.4003	Florida
5.1821	Louisiana
5.1690	Illinois
5.0995	Delaware
4.8386	Tennessee
4.7462	Massachusetts
4.5650	California
4.5276	Maryland
4.3846	Alaska
4.2396	Michigan
3.9612	Oklahoma
3.8964	Missouri
3.7960	North Carolina
3.7436	Arizona
3.7265	Texas
3.5015	Arkansas
3.4048	Nebraska
3.3828	Georgia
3.3321	New York
3.3301	Alabama
3.2685	Nevada
2.9598	Indiana
2.6840	Oregon
2.6177	Kansas
2.5688	Washington
2.5431	Mississippi
2.5148	Colorado
2.3998	Connecticut
2.2997	New Jersey
2.2731	Idaho
2.2211	Iowa
2.1797	Pennsylvania
2.0716	Utah
2.0567	Rhode Island
1.9592	Wyoming
1.9439	Ohio
1.8692	Virginia
1.8351	West Virginia
1.7472	Kentucky
1.6459	Minnesota
1.3989	Wisconsin
1.2943	Montana
1.1642	South Dakota
1.1274	Hawaii
.8429	Maine
.6739	Vermont
.6348	New Hampshire
.4613	North Dakota

Table G.14. RAPE

Rape Rate per 1,000 1998

.6880	Alaska
.5493	Michigan
.5336	New Mexico
.5215	Nevada
.4974	Florida
.4955	Washington
.4940	Minnesota
.4802	Colorado
.4796	Tennessee
.4737	South Carolina
.4649	New Hampshire
.4554	Mississippi
.4523	Oklahoma
.4293	Ohio
.4256	Kansas
.4237	Utah
.4010	Texas
.4005	South Dakota
.3971	Oregon
.3721	Indiana
.3678	Louisiana
.3513	Arkansas
.3502	Rhode Island
.3400	Illinois
.3309	Maryland
.3296	Alabama
.3278	North Dakota
.3244	Idaho
.3112	Arizona
.3064	North Carolina
.2996	Georgia
.2994	California
.2929	Kentucky
.2951	Hawaii
.2850	Missouri
.2824	Vermont
.2766	Wyoming
.2702	Massachusetts
.2672	Virginia
.2642	Pennsylvania
.2588	Connecticut
.2560	Iowa
.2522	Nebraska
.2261	Montana
.2061	New York
.2001	New Jersey
.1985	Wisconsin
.1862	West Virginia
.1811	Maine
.0000	Delaware

Table G.15. ROBBERY

Robbery Rate per 1,000 1998

2.9803	Maryland
2.6580	New York
2.5489	Nevada
2.4846	Illinois
2.4302	Florida
2.1056	California
2.0026	Louisiana
1.9973	Delaware
1.9235	Tennessee
1.8790	Georgia
1.8620	New Jersey
1.7341	New Mexico
1.6960	Mississippi
1.6930	Missouri
1.6708	Arizona
1.6648	Pennsylvania
1.6151	Michigan
1.6093	North Carolina
1.5651	South Carolina
1.5565	Connecticut
1.4678	Ohio
1.4527	Texas
1.3995	Indiana
1.3119	Alabama
1.1475	Washington
1.0629	Virginia
1.0508	Oregon
1.0268	Hawaii
.9614	Arkansas
.9522	Massachusetts
.9240	Minnesota
.9201	Oklahoma
.8684	Kansas
.8670	Alaska
.8564	Wisconsin
.8365	Colorado
.7796	Nebraska
.7536	Kentucky
.6999	Utah
.6650	Rhode Island
.4177	Iowa
.4106	New Hampshire
.3723	West Virginia
.2690	South Dakota
.2484	Montana
.2146	Idaho
.2109	Maine
.1613	Wyoming
.1014	North Dakota
.0965	Vermont

Table G.16. ARSON

Arson Rate per 1,000 1998

.8602	California
.5820	Rhode Island
.5045	Maryland
.4668	Pennsylvania
.4578	Michigan
.4300	Oregon
.4278	Texas
.4238	Missouri
.4229	Ohio
.3877	Oklahoma
.3845	Colorado
.3755	Nevada
.3743	Washington
.3265	Alaska
.3166	North Carolina
.3160	Louisiana
.3135	Hawaii
.2920	Indiana
.2819	Minnesota
.2783	Tennessee
.2764	Virginia
.2729	Arizona
.2620	New Jersey
.2613	Nebraska
.2567	Connecticut
.2484	South Carolina
.2482	Idaho
.2420	Iowa
.2410	Florida
.2305	Wyoming
.2244	Utah
.2234	Arkansas
.2211	New Mexico
.2097	Delaware
.1823	West Virginia
.1739	Mississippi
.1709	Georgia
.1676	Montana
.1652	New Hampshire
.1634	Maine
.1547	Alabama
.1394	South Dakota
.1369	North Dakota
.1248	New York
.0804	Vermont
.0722	Massachusetts
*	Illinois
*	Kansas
*	Kentucky
*	Wisconsin

*Incomplete data

Table G.17. BURGLARY

Burglary Rate per 1,000 1998

14.1747	New Mexico
13.6210	Florida
13.2258	North Carolina
13.1793	Mississippi
12.1222	Arizona
11.7142	South Carolina
11.6141	Louisiana
11.4332	Oklahoma
11.3755	Nevada
10.6870	Tennessee
10.4296	Washington
9.8569	Texas
9.7730	Georgia
9.3621	Hawaii
9.2679	Alabama
9.2616	Oregon
9.2594	Arkansas
9.1943	Maryland
9.1403	Missouri
8.9258	Kansas
8.9078	Michigan
8.7182	Indiana
8.6895	Delaware
8.3512	Ohio
8.2614	Illinois
8.2330	California
8.1743	Utah
7.9192	Colorado
7.7512	Connecticut
6.9176	Idaho
6.8436	Minnesota
6.7112	New Jersey
6.6644	Maine
6.5768	Vermont
6.5022	Alaska
6.5000	Rhode Island
6.4877	Iowa
6.3740	Kentucky
6.2014	Nebraska
6.1241	West Virginia
5.8591	Massachusetts
5.6930	Wisconsin
5.6080	Virginia
5.5590	Wyoming
5.4480	New York
5.2034	Pennsylvania
5.1994	Montana
5.0120	South Dakota
4.3821	New Hampshire
3.5705	North Dakota

Table G.18. LARCENY

Larceny Rate per 1,000 1998

40.2682	Utah
39.4336	Arizona
38.8872	Florida
38.3932	New Mexico
37.4575	Oregon
36.8097	Hawaii
36.6533	Washington
35.5996	Louisiana
33.4138	Kansas
33.1791	South Carolina
33.1035	Delaware
32.9568	Georgia
32.0156	Missouri
31.3837	Mississippi
30.8309	Maryland
30.8222	North Carolina
30.7193	Texas
29.1653	Nebraska
29.1505	Oklahoma
29.0879	Colorado
28.4217	Wyoming
28.0405	Indiana
27.9943	Illinois
27.9530	Alaska
27.6886	Tennessee
27.5438	Connecticut
27.4002	Alabama
27.2385	Montana
27.1133	Nevada
27.0734	Minnesota
27.0517	Ohio
26.6557	Michigan
25.7183	Arkansas
25.5441	Idaho
25.0318	Virginia
24.5279	Wisconsin
22.5405	Iowa
22.1647	California
22.0758	Vermont
21.6653	New Hampshire
21.6580	South Dakota
21.5344	Rhode Island
21.2162	Maine
21.0954	New Jersey
20.8148	North Dakota
18.8697	Pennsylvania
18.6070	New York
17.5010	Kentucky
17.2661	Massachusetts
14.9511	West Virginia

Table G.19. CARTHEFT

Auto Thefts per 1,000 1998

8.7647	Arizona
7.8798	Nevada
6.9978	Florida
6.5187	New Mexico
6.1573	Washington
6.1394	Michigan
5.9846	California
5.5418	Georgia
5.4962	Louisiana
5.4803	Maryland
5.3170	Tennessee
5.2453	Oregon
4.9689	Missouri
4.8934	Texas
4.7210	Mississippi
4.6890	Hawaii
4.5170	Connecticut
4.4570	Delaware
4.3945	Illinois
4.3358	New Jersey
4.2483	South Carolina
4.1645	Ohio
4.1277	Indiana
4.1208	Colorado
4.0685	Massachusetts
4.0600	Alaska
4.0533	Oklahoma
3.8623	Rhode Island
3.7754	Utah
3.5636	New York
3.5453	Pennsylvania
3.4811	Nebraska
3.4255	Alabama
3.2651	North Carolina
3.2385	Minnesota
2.8262	Arkansas
2.7201	Wisconsin
2.7102	Virginia
2.3244	New Hampshire
2.2857	Montana
2.2777	Kansas
2.1781	Kentucky
1.8959	North Dakota
1.8633	West Virginia
1.8593	Iowa
1.8341	Idaho
1.4659	Vermont
1.3850	Wyoming
1.2124	Maine
1.1485	South Dakota

Table G.20. ABUSE

Child Abuse, Percent Population 1998

.0265	Idaho
.0245	Montana
.0189	Alaska
.0172	Arizona
.0152	Oklahoma
.0150	Michigan
.0147	California
.0147	Missouri
.0146	West Virginia
.0143	Arkansas
.0139	North Carolina
.0130	Delaware
.0130	Utah
.0130	New York
.0130	Wyoming
.0125	Nevada
.0125	Florida
.0115	Iowa
.0114	Kentucky
.0111	Ohio
.0107	North Dakota
.0106	Louisiana
.0106	Mississippi
.0104	Georgia
.0104	Connecticut
.0104	Massachusetts
.0103	South Carolina
.0103	Rhode Island
.0100	Nebraska
.0096	Illinois
.0095	Maryland
.0087	Alabama
.0086	New Mexico
.0086	New Jersey
.0084	Oregon
.0083	Wisconsin
.0082	Texas
.0081	Maine
.0080	Indiana
.0080	Virginia
.0076	New Hampshire
.0067	Washington
.0066	South Dakota
.0060	Tennessee
.0056	Minnesota
.0048	Colorado
.0040	Vermont
.0035	Hawaii
.0030	Kansas
.0019	Pennsylvania

Table G.21. NOIMMUNE

Percent Children Not Immunized 1998

29	Utah
28	Idaho
28	Oklahoma
27	Nevada
27	Oregon
27	Virginia
26	Arizona
26	Colorado
26	Indiana
26	Wyoming
25	Montana
25	Ohio
25	Texas
24	California
24	Illinois
24	Iowa
23	Alaska
23	Arkansas
23	Louisiana
23	Michigan
23	Nebraska
23	New Mexico
22	Missouri
22	New Jersey
22	South Dakota
22	Tennessee
21	Florida
21	New York
20	South Carolina
20	Washington
20	Wisconsin
19	Delaware
19	Georgia
19	Hawaii
19	Kentucky
19	Minnesota
19	Mississippi
19	North Carolina
18	Kansas
18	Maryland
18	Pennsylvania
18	West Virginia
17	North Dakota
16	Rhode Island
15	New Hampshire
14	Alabama
14	Vermont
13	Connecticut
13	Maine
13	Massachusetts

Table G.22. STALOCPP

Average Funding per Pupil 1997

9,675	New Jersey
7,412	New York
7,383	Connecticut
7,372	Vermont
6,488	Michigan
6,342	Alaska
6,335	Indiana
6,319	Pennsylvania
6,256	Delaware
6,152	Wisconsin
6,139	Massachusetts
5,952	Rhode Island
5,906	Maryland
5,864	Minnesota
5,584	Ohio
5,574	New Hampshire
5,534	Maine
5,446	Washington
5,368	Illinois
5,294	Wyoming
5,290	Kentucky
5,248	Hawaii
5,238	Kansas
5,228	Virginia
5,171	Nebraska
5,117	Iowa
5,014	Colorado
4,982	Nevada
4,953	West Virginia
4,899	Florida
4,850	Oregon
4,831	Georgia
4,779	Missouri
4,775	California
4,658	Texas
4,608	South Carolina
4,392	North Carolina
4,371	Montana
4,265	Arizona
4,204	South Dakota
4,083	North Dakota
4,017	Alabama
3,935	Idaho
3,907	Oklahoma
3,891	Arkansas
3,732	Louisiana
3,723	Tennessee
3,689	Utah
3,656	New Mexico
3,176	Mississippi

Table G.23. TOTINST

Total Dollars per Student 1998

5,365	New York
5,062	New Jersey
4,920	Connecticut
4,826	Rhode Island
4,704	Wisconsin
4,638	Vermont
4,622	Maine
4,488	Delaware
4,482	Pennsylvania
4,404	Massachusetts
4,377	West Virginia
4,318	Maryland
4,230	Nebraska
4,225	Indiana
4,168	Iowa
4,122	Wyoming
4,091	Minnesota
4,074	Michigan
3,963	Oregon
3,938	Montana
3,834	New Hampshire
3,817	Virginia
3,771	Georgia
3,760	Hawaii
3,719	Alaska
3,699	Ohio
3,690	Kansas
3,671	Illinois
3,631	North Dakota
3,595	Missouri
3,591	North Carolina
3,566	Kentucky
3,547	Texas
3,518	Tennessee
3,497	South Carolina
3,479	Louisiana
3,426	Arkansas
3,421	Washington
3,416	Florida
3,363	South Dakota
3,343	Nevada
3,320	Alabama
3,318	Colorado
3,309	Oklahoma
3,191	Idaho
3,092	California
3,081	New Mexico
3,018	Mississippi
2,744	Utah
2,678	Arizona

Table G.24. SUPSERV

Support Services per Pupil 1998

3,053	New Jersey
2,663	Michigan
2,588	Alaska
2,515	Wisconsin
2,450	Oregon
2,441	Connecticut
2,429	Wyoming
2,408	Delaware
2,392	Kansas
2,337	Ohio
2,309	New York
2,302	Iowa
2,298	Vermont
2,291	Pennsylvania
2,263	West Virginia
2,243	Maryland
2,235	Indiana
2,212	Colorado
2,169	Rhode Island
2,169	Illinois
2,156	Minnesota
2,124	Washington
2,113	Virginia
2,103	Montana
2,098	Florida
2,042	New Mexico
2,037	Nevada
2,015	South Carolina
2,014	Massachusetts
2,014	Missouri
2,003	Maine
1,995	Nebraska
1,944	Georgia
1,931	Oklahoma
1,927	Kentucky
1,922	Texas
1,843	Louisiana
1,835	New Hampshire
1,818	North Dakota
1,799	South Dakota
1,778	North Carolina
1,761	California
1,735	Hawaii
1,731	Alabama
1,714	Idaho
1,671	Arizona
1,617	Tennessee
1,599	Arkansas
1,551	Mississippi
1,175	Utah

Table G.25. AVRSTART

Average Starting Teacher Salary 1998

32,467	Alabama
30,151	Pennsylvania
29,872	Georgia
29,642	Delaware
29,564	Michigan
29,044	Texas
28,987	Illinois
28,676	Oklahoma
28,322	Oregon
28,267	Indiana
28,168	New York
27,593	Nevada
27,564	North Carolina
27,409	Kentucky
26,937	Missouri
26,522	Connecticut
26,513	Iowa
26,349	Arizona
26,307	Alaska
26,304	Wisconsin
26,283	West Virginia
26,179	Virginia
26,172	Maryland
26,132	South Carolina
25,864	Vermont
25,848	Louisiana
25,759	Florida
25,751	Maine
25,607	New Jersey
25,484	New Mexico
25,378	Minnesota
25,321	California
25,068	Tennessee
24,944	Kansas
24,781	Nebraska
24,672	Colorado
24,631	Rhode Island
24,565	Massachusetts
24,200	Arkansas
24,200	Mississippi
23,908	Ohio
23,860	South Dakota
23,724	Utah
23,050	New Hampshire
22,768	Wyoming
22,601	Washington
22,419	Montana
21,665	Idaho
21,289	Hawaii
20,322	North Dakota

Table G.26. AVRSALRY

Average Teacher Salary 1998

51,067	Michigan
47,542	Pennsylvania
44,405	New York
43,663	Illinois
43,541	Connecticut
43,461	New Jersey
43,162	Indiana
42,556	Oregon
41,771	Delaware
41,324	Rhode Island
40,856	Ohio
40,816	Nevada
40,487	Wisconsin
40,438	Minnesota
40,315	Georgia
38,949	Massachusetts
38,877	Maryland
38,842	Kentucky
38,635	California
38,620	Alaska
38,469	Tennessee
38,091	Virginia
37,693	West Virginia
37,408	Washington
37,305	Texas
37,169	Iowa
37,078	Vermont
37,013	South Carolina
36,791	Florida
36,688	Alabama
36,582	Arkansas
36,580	Kansas
36,438	Colorado
36,210	Missouri
35,470	Nebraska
35,302	Maine
35,159	Oklahoma
34,653	New Hampshire
34,277	Arizona
34,238	Idaho
34,213	Utah
33,175	Louisiana
32,642	Wyoming
32,566	Mississippi
32,060	Montana
31,441	New Mexico
31,307	North Carolina
30,967	South Dakota
30,161	North Dakota
28,152	Hawaii

Table G.27. STUMEDIA

Students per Computer 1999

14.8	California
14.1	Utah
13.5	Rhode Island
13.1	Maryland
12.4	North Carolina
12.3	New Hampshire
12.3	Louisiana
12.2	Nevada
11.9	Hawaii
11.7	Arizona
11.5	Alabama
11.4	Vermont
11.4	Mississippi
11.3	Oregon
11.3	Kentucky
10.7	Connecticut
10.7	Washington
10.6	New York
10.5	Massachusetts
10.5	Tennessee
10.4	Maine
10.2	Arkansas
9.7	Pennsylvania
9.7	Illinois
9.7	Colorado
9.6	Oklahoma
9.5	Georgia
9.5	Florida
9.1	Michigan
9.1	Idaho
9.0	Virginia
8.9	Texas
8.8	West Virginia
8.7	South Carolina
8.6	Minnesota
8.5	Iowa
8.4	Indiana
8.4	Montana
8.3	Wisconsin
8.3	Missouri
8.2	North Dakota
8.0	Kansas
7.9	New Jersey
7.7	Alaska
7.5	New Mexico
7.5	South Dakota
7.4	Ohio
7.1	Nebraska
6.9	Delaware
6.9	Wyoming

Table G.28. POPEST99

Population Estimate (1,000s) 1999

33,145.121	California
20,044.141	Texas
18,196.601	New York
15,111.244	Florida
12,128.370	Illinois
11,994.016	Pennsylvania
11,256.654	Ohio
9,863.775	Michigan
8,143.412	New Jersey
7,788.240	Georgia
7,650.789	North Carolina
6,872.912	Virginia
6,175.169	Massachusetts
5,942.901	Indiana
5,756.361	Washington
5,483.535	Tennessee
5,468.338	Missouri
5,250.446	Wisconsin
5,171.634	Maryland
4,778.332	Arizona
4,775.508	Minnesota
4,372.035	Louisiana
4,369.862	Alabama
4,056.133	Colorado
3,960.825	Kentucky
3,885.736	South Carolina
3,358.044	Oklahoma
3,316.154	Oregon
3,282.031	Connecticut
2,869.413	Iowa
2,768.619	Mississippi
2,654.052	Kansas
2,551.373	Arkansas
2,129.836	Utah
1,809.253	Nevada
1,806.928	West Virginia
1,739.844	New Mexico
1,666.028	Nebraska
1,253.040	Maine
1,251.700	Idaho
1,201.134	New Hampshire
1,185.497	Hawaii
990.819	Rhode Island
882.779	Montana
753.538	Delaware
733.133	South Dakota
633.666	North Dakota
619.500	Alaska
593.740	Vermont
479.602	Wyoming

Table G.29. MALEPOP

Male Population (1,000s) 1999

16,579.707	California
9,887.415	Texas
8,770.974	New York
7,330.099	Florida
5,916.083	Illinois
5,765.533	Pennsylvania
5,441.233	Ohio
4,799.912	Michigan
3,946.443	New Jersey
3,791.130	Georgia
3,710.119	North Carolina
3,358.569	Virginia
2,977.965	Massachusetts
2,891.620	Indiana
2,862.019	Washington
2,649.479	Missouri
2,646.694	Tennessee
2,580.153	Wisconsin
2,513.133	Maryland
2,364.468	Arizona
2,353.020	Minnesota
2,103.825	Louisiana
2,097.319	Alabama
2,010.784	Colorado
1,923.606	Kentucky
1,875.030	South Carolina
1,639.559	Oklahoma
1,637.721	Oregon
1,592.801	Connecticut
1,397.208	Iowa
1,326.704	Mississippi
1,305.408	Kansas
1,232.955	Arkansas
1,058.639	Utah
921.070	Nevada
870.356	West Virginia
856.048	New Mexico
814.663	Nebraska
624.504	Idaho
611.437	Maine
592.037	Hawaii
590.941	New Hampshire
476.331	Rhode Island
438.758	Montana
366.275	Delaware
360.485	South Dakota
325.077	Alaska
315.167	North Dakota
292.120	Vermont
240.943	Wyoming

Table G.30. FEMALPOP

Female Population (1,000s) 1999

16,565.414	California
10,156.726	Texas
9,425.627	New York
7,781.145	Florida
6,228.483	Pennsylvania
6,212.287	Illinois
5,815.421	Ohio
5,063.863	Michigan
4,196.969	New Jersey
3,997.110	Georgia
3,940.670	North Carolina
3,514.343	Virginia
3,197.204	Massachusetts
3,051.281	Indiana
2,894.342	Washington
2,836.841	Tennessee
2,818.859	Missouri
2,670.293	Wisconsin
2,658.501	Maryland
2,422.488	Minnesota
2,413.864	Arizona
2,272.543	Alabama
2,268.210	Louisiana
2,045.349	Colorado
2,037.219	Kentucky
2,010.706	South Carolina
1,718.485	Oklahoma
1,689.230	Connecticut
1,678.433	Oregon
1,472.205	Iowa
1,441.915	Mississippi
1,348.644	Kansas
1,318.418	Arkansas
1,071.197	Utah
936.572	West Virginia
888.183	Nevada
883.796	New Mexico
851.365	Nebraska
641.603	Maine
627.196	Idaho
610.193	New Hampshire
593.460	Hawaii
514.488	Rhode Island
444.021	Montana
387.263	Delaware
372.648	South Dakota
318.499	North Dakota
301.620	Vermont
294.423	Alaska
238.659	Wyoming

Table G.31. PCUND18

Percent under 18 1999

33.2	Utah
31.8	Alaska
28.5	Texas
28.5	New Mexico
28.0	Idaho
27.9	Arizona
27.2	Louisiana
27.2	Mississippi
27.2	Nevada
27.0	South Dakota
26.9	California
26.6	Minnesota
26.6	Nebraska
26.4	Georgia
26.4	Wyoming
26.3	Colorado
26.3	Oklahoma
26.3	Kansas
26.2	Illinois
26.0	Michigan
25.9	Arkansas
25.8	Washington
25.7	Indiana
25.7	Wisconsin
25.6	Missouri
25.4	North Carolina
25.4	Montana
25.3	Ohio
25.3	Maryland
25.3	New Hampshire
25.3	North Dakota
25.2	Connecticut
25.1	Iowa
25.0	Oregon
24.6	New Jersey
24.6	South Carolina
24.5	Tennessee
24.4	New York
24.4	Alabama
24.4	Kentucky
24.4	Hawaii
24.3	Rhode Island
24.2	Virginia
24.2	Delaware
23.8	Pennsylvania
23.8	Massachusetts
23.6	Florida
23.5	Vermont
23.2	Maine
22.3	West Virginia

Table G.32. PCOVER65

Percent over 65 1999

18.1	Florida
15.8	Pennsylvania
15.6	Rhode Island
15.1	West Virginia
14.9	Iowa
14.6	North Dakota
14.4	South Dakota
14.3	Connecticut
14.2	Arkansas
14.0	Maine
13.9	Massachusetts
13.7	Nebraska
13.7	Hawaii
13.6	Missouri
13.6	New Jersey
13.4	Oklahoma
13.4	New York
13.3	Kansas
13.2	Montana
13.2	Ohio
13.2	Arizona
13.2	Wisconsin
13.1	Oregon
13.0	Alabama
13.0	Delaware
12.5	Indiana
12.5	North Carolina
12.5	Kentucky
12.4	Michigan
12.4	Tennessee
12.3	Minnesota
12.3	Illinois
12.3	Vermont
12.2	South Carolina
12.1	Mississippi
12.0	New Hampshire
11.6	Wyoming
11.5	New Mexico
11.5	Louisiana
11.5	Nevada
11.5	Maryland
11.4	Washington
11.3	Idaho
11.3	Virginia
11.0	California
10.1	Texas
10.1	Colorado
9.8	Georgia
8.7	Utah
.6	Alaska

Table G.33. PCWHITE

Percent Population White 1999

98.4	Vermont
98.3	Maine
97.8	New Hampshire
96.9	Idaho
96.4	Iowa
96.3	West Virginia
96.0	Wyoming
95.1	Utah
93.7	North Dakota
93.6	Nebraska
93.4	Oregon
92.9	Minnesota
92.5	Montana
92.3	Colorado
92.1	Rhode Island
91.9	Kentucky
91.9	Wisconsin
91.4	Kansas
90.4	Indiana
90.4	South Dakota
89.4	Massachusetts
88.7	Arizona
88.7	Washington
88.4	Pennsylvania
87.8	Connecticut
87.2	Missouri
87.0	Ohio
86.3	New Mexico
85.6	Nevada
84.3	Texas
83.4	Michigan
83.0	Oklahoma
82.6	Arkansas
82.3	Florida
82.1	Tennessee
81.1	Illinois
79.4	California
79.3	New Jersey
77.7	Delaware
76.2	New York
75.8	Virginia
75.3	North Carolina
75.2	Alaska
73.0	Alabama
69.1	South Carolina
69.0	Georgia
67.5	Maryland
65.9	Louisiana
62.4	Mississippi
33.0	Hawaii

Table G.34. PCBLACK

Percent Population Black 1999

36.5	Mississippi
32.4	Louisiana
29.8	South Carolina
28.7	Georgia
28.1	Maryland
26.1	Alabama
22.0	North Carolina
20.1	Virginia
19.8	Delaware
17.7	New York
16.6	Tennessee
16.1	Arkansas
15.4	Florida
15.3	Illinois
14.7	New Jersey
14.3	Michigan
12.3	Texas
11.6	Ohio
11.3	Missouri
9.8	Pennsylvania
9.4	Connecticut
8.4	Indiana
7.8	Oklahoma
7.7	Nevada
7.5	California
7.3	Kentucky
6.6	Massachusetts
5.9	Kansas
5.6	Wisconsin
5.1	Rhode Island
4.3	Colorado
4.1	Nebraska
3.9	Alaska
3.7	Arizona
3.5	Washington
3.1	West Virginia
3.1	Minnesota
2.8	Hawaii
2.6	New Mexico
2.0	Iowa
1.9	Oregon
.9	Wyoming
.9	Utah
.8	New Hampshire
.7	South Dakota
.6	Idaho
.6	North Dakota
.5	Vermont
.5	Maine
.4	Montana

Table G.35. PCHISP

Percent Hispanic 1999

40.7	New Mexico
31.6	California
30.2	Texas
22.7	Arizona
16.8	Nevada
15.4	Florida
14.9	Colorado
14.6	New York
12.6	New Jersey
10.5	Illinois
8.5	Connecticut
8.1	Hawaii
7.4	Idaho
7.1	Utah
6.9	Rhode Island
6.5	Washington
6.4	Oregon
6.3	Massachusetts
6.1	Wyoming
5.6	Kansas
4.6	Nebraska
4.1	Oklahoma
4.0	Alaska
3.9	Maryland
3.9	Virginia
3.7	Delaware
3.1	Georgia
2.8	Michigan
2.7	Louisiana
2.7	Pennsylvania
2.7	Wisconsin
2.6	Indiana
2.3	North Carolina
2.1	Arkansas
2.1	Iowa
1.9	Minnesota
1.8	Montana
1.7	Missouri
1.6	Ohio
1.6	New Hampshire
1.4	South Carolina
1.2	Tennessee
1.2	South Dakota
1.1	North Dakota
1.0	Alabama
.9	Mississippi
.9	Kentucky
.9	Vermont
.7	Maine
.6	West Virginia

Table G.36. PCWNHISP

Percent White Non-Hispanic 1999

97.6	Vermont
97.6	Maine
96.3	New Hampshire
95.8	West Virginia
94.4	Iowa
92.7	North Dakota
91.2	Minnesota
91.1	Kentucky
91.0	Montana
90.4	Wyoming
90.0	Idaho
89.5	Wisconsin
89.4	Nebraska
89.1	South Dakota
88.6	Utah
88.0	Indiana
87.6	Oregon
86.5	Rhode Island
86.3	Kansas
86.1	Pennsylvania
85.7	Missouri
85.6	Ohio
84.4	Massachusetts
82.8	Washington
81.1	Tennessee
80.9	Michigan
80.7	Arkansas
80.2	Connecticut
79.6	Oklahoma
78.3	Colorado
74.6	Delaware
73.3	North Carolina
72.4	Virginia
72.1	Alabama
71.9	Alaska
71.2	Illinois
70.3	Nevada
68.4	New Jersey
68.0	Florida
67.9	South Carolina
67.6	Arizona
66.3	Georgia
65.1	New York
64.3	Maryland
63.6	Louisiana
61.7	Mississippi
55.3	Texas
49.9	California
47.5	New Mexico
28.7	Hawaii

Table G.37. PCHOME

Percent Own Home 1999

74.1	West Virginia
71.8	Minnesota
71.5	Mississippi
71.0	Michigan
70.6	Pennsylvania
70.5	Maine
70.5	Alabama
70.2	Indiana
70.2	Delaware
70.1	Idaho
70.0	Iowa
69.8	South Carolina
69.6	Kentucky
69.6	Arkansas
69.0	Vermont
68.8	Missouri
68.2	New Hampshire
68.1	Utah
68.1	Oklahoma
68.0	Tennessee
68.0	North Carolina
67.9	Kansas
67.8	Wyoming
67.5	Ohio
67.4	New Mexico
67.3	Montana
67.2	Florida
66.7	Wisconsin
66.5	Nebraska
66.3	Virginia
66.1	South Dakota
65.9	Louisiana
65.6	North Dakota
65.6	Connecticut
65.0	Maryland
64.9	New Jersey
64.9	Georgia
64.2	Illinois
64.2	Arizona
63.1	Oregon
62.6	Washington
62.2	Colorado
60.9	Texas
59.5	Rhode Island
59.3	Massachusetts
56.1	Alaska
55.6	California
54.8	Nevada
53.9	Hawaii
52.2	New York

Table G.38. PERHOUSE

Persons per Household 1999

3.15	Utah
3.00	Hawaii
2.79	Alaska
2.79	California
2.75	Mississippi
2.74	Louisiana
2.73	Idaho
2.73	New Mexico
2.73	Texas
2.71	New Jersey
2.68	South Carolina
2.67	Maryland
2.66	Georgia
2.66	Illinois
2.65	Michigan
2.63	New York
2.62	Alabama
2.62	New Hampshire
2.62	Wyoming
2.61	Indiana
2.61	Delaware
2.61	Wisconsin
2.61	Virginia
2.61	Arizona
2.60	Kentucky
2.59	Ohio
2.59	Connecticut
2.58	Minnesota
2.58	South Dakota
2.58	Massachusetts
2.57	Pennsylvania
2.57	Arkansas
2.57	Vermont
2.56	Maine
2.56	Tennessee
2.56	Rhode Island
2.55	West Virginia
2.54	Missouri
2.54	North Carolina
2.54	Nebraska
2.54	North Dakota
2.53	Oklahoma
2.53	Kansas
2.53	Montana
2.53	Washington
2.52	Nevada
2.51	Iowa
2.51	Oregon
2.50	Colorado
2.46	Florida

Table G.39. MEDINCOM

Median Household Income 1997

47,903	New Jersey
46,648	Connecticut
45,289	Maryland
43,657	Alaska
43,627	Hawaii
43,015	Massachusetts
42,023	New Hampshire
41,715	Washington
41,591	Minnesota
41,315	Delaware
41,179	Illinois
40,853	Colorado
40,209	Virginia
39,800	Wisconsin
39,595	California
39,280	Nevada
38,884	Utah
38,883	Michigan
37,909	Indiana
37,284	Oregon
37,267	Pennsylvania
36,699	Rhode Island
36,488	Kansas
36,372	Georgia
36,369	New York
36,029	Ohio
35,427	Iowa
35,337	Nebraska
35,320	North Carolina
35,210	Vermont
34,751	Arizona
34,502	Missouri
34,478	Texas
33,612	Idaho
33,325	South Carolina
33,197	Wyoming
33,140	Maine
32,877	Florida
32,047	Tennessee
31,764	North Dakota
31,730	Kentucky
31,354	South Dakota
30,836	New Mexico
30,790	Alabama
30,466	Louisiana
30,002	Oklahoma
29,672	Montana
28,527	Mississippi
27,875	Arkansas
27,432	West Virginia

Table G.40. PCCHANGE

Percent Change Population 1990–1999

50.6	Nevada
30.4	Arizona
24.3	Idaho
23.6	Utah
23.1	Colorado
20.2	Georgia
18.3	Washington
18.0	Texas
16.8	Florida
16.7	Oregon
15.4	North Carolina
14.8	New Mexico
13.1	Delaware
12.6	Alaska
12.4	Tennessee
11.5	South Carolina
11.2	California
11.0	Virginia
10.5	Montana
9.1	Minnesota
8.5	Arkansas
8.3	New Hampshire
8.2	Maryland
8.2	Alabama
7.5	Mississippi
7.4	Kentucky
7.3	Wisconsin
7.2	Indiana
7.1	Kansas
7.0	Hawaii
6.9	Missouri
6.8	Oklahoma
6.1	Illinois
6.1	Michigan
5.7	Wyoming
5.6	Nebraska
5.5	Vermont
5.3	South Dakota
5.1	New Jersey
3.8	Ohio
3.6	Louisiana
3.3	Iowa
2.6	Massachusetts
2.0	Maine
1.1	New York
.9	Pennsylvania
.7	West Virginia
−.2	Connecticut
−.8	North Dakota
−1.3	Rhode Island

Table G.41. PCBELPOV

Percent below Poverty 1997

19.3	New Mexico
18.4	Louisiana
18.1	Mississippi
17.5	Arkansas
16.8	West Virginia
16.7	Texas
16.3	Oklahoma
16.2	Alabama
16.0	California
16.0	Kentucky
15.6	New York
15.5	Arizona
15.5	Montana
14.9	South Carolina
14.7	Georgia
14.4	Florida
14.0	South Dakota
13.6	Tennessee
13.0	Idaho
12.6	North Carolina
12.5	North Dakota
12.2	Missouri
12.0	Wyoming
11.6	Oregon
11.6	Virginia
11.5	Michigan
11.3	Illinois
11.2	Alaska
11.2	Rhode Island
11.1	Hawaii
11.0	Ohio
10.9	Kansas
10.9	Pennsylvania
10.7	Nevada
10.7	Maine
10.7	Massachusetts
10.2	Colorado
10.2	Washington
10.0	Utah
10.0	Delaware
9.9	Indiana
9.9	Iowa
9.7	Vermont
9.6	Nebraska
9.5	Maryland
9.3	New Jersey
9.2	Wisconsin
8.9	Minnesota
8.9	Connecticut
7.5	New Hampshire

Table G.42. CHBELPOV

Percent Children below Poverty 1997

27.5	New Mexico
26.0	Louisiana
25.0	Arkansas
24.7	West Virginia
24.7	New York
24.6	California
24.5	Mississippi
23.8	Alabama
23.7	Oklahoma
23.6	Texas
23.2	Arizona
23.1	Kentucky
23.0	South Carolina
22.8	Georgia
21.8	Florida
21.3	Montana
19.0	South Dakota
18.9	Tennessee
18.6	North Carolina
18.0	Michigan
17.7	Missouri
17.5	Illinois
17.3	Idaho
17.3	Rhode Island
17.0	Virginia
17.0	Massachusetts
16.8	North Dakota
16.6	Pennsylvania
16.3	Oregon
16.2	Alaska
16.2	Hawaii
16.0	Ohio
15.4	Kansas
15.4	Nevada
15.4	Delaware
15.3	Wyoming
15.2	Washington
14.9	Maine
14.9	Maryland
14.8	Indiana
14.8	New Jersey
14.7	Connecticut
14.6	Colorado
14.3	Wisconsin
13.7	Iowa
13.1	Minnesota
12.7	Vermont
12.6	Nebraska
12.5	Utah
10.0	New Hampshire

Table G.43. PCEMPCHG

Percent Employment Change 1990–1998

51.7	Utah
49.2	Nevada
42.6	Arizona
41.1	Idaho
40.8	Colorado
34.5	South Dakota
29.6	Mississippi
29.2	New Mexico
29.1	Texas
28.9	Oregon
28.0	Georgia
26.8	North Dakota
25.8	Arkansas
24.9	Florida
24.9	Montana
24.3	Alaska
24.1	Louisiana
24.1	Oklahoma
24.0	Wyoming
24.0	Minnesota
23.0	Tennessee
22.7	Nebraska
21.7	Kentucky
21.1	Washington
21.0	Kansas
20.5	South Carolina
20.4	Iowa
20.3	North Carolina
19.4	Alabama
19.0	Wisconsin
18.2	Indiana
17.9	New Hampshire
16.3	Virginia
14.9	Michigan
14.7	Missouri
14.0	Delaware
13.4	West Virginia
13.2	Ohio
11.1	Vermont
7.7	Maine
7.1	Maryland
6.7	Pennsylvania
6.3	California
5.5	Massachusetts
4.6	New Jersey
2.3	Rhode Island
.8	Connecticut
−1.2	New York
−3.7	Hawaii
−95.2	Illinois

Table G.44. RETAILPC

Retail Sales, per Capita 1997

16,018	South Dakota
13,477	New Hampshire
11,206	Delaware
10,874	Nevada
10,690	Connecticut
10,457	North Dakota
10,417	Colorado
10,297	Oregon
10,297	Florida
10,268	Alaska
10,260	Minnesota
10,229	Maine
10,020	Vermont
9,981	Nebraska
9,922	New Jersey
9,748	Indiana
9,740	North Carolina
9,715	Wisconsin
9,666	Utah
9,657	Arizona
9,646	Georgia
9,623	Idaho
9,579	Massachusetts
9,576	Michigan
9,516	Hawaii
9,482	Missouri
9,448	Tennessee
9,438	Wyoming
9,430	Texas
9,363	Washington
9,362	Iowa
9,293	Virginia
9,181	Ohio
9,150	Pennsylvania
9,116	Maryland
8,992	Illinois
8,874	South Carolina
8,853	Montana
8,697	New Mexico
8,627	Kansas
8,575	Arkansas
8,530	Kentucky
8,477	Alabama
8,229	Louisiana
8,167	California
8,166	Oklahoma
7,743	West Virginia
7,678	New York
7,605	Mississippi
7,605	Rhode Island

Table G.45. MINFIRMS

Minority-Owned Firms 1992

541,414	California
241,334	Texas
173,287	Florida
160,751	New York
67,603	Illinois
64,074	New Jersey
55,587	Maryland
52,131	Georgia
46,666	Virginia
41,111	Hawaii
37,670	North Carolina
33,844	Ohio
32,712	Pennsylvania
31,740	Michigan
29,784	Louisiana
26,729	New Mexico
26,185	Arizona
25,935	Washington
23,463	Colorado
21,127	South Carolina
20,749	Massachusetts
19,382	Tennessee
17,432	Alabama
16,386	Mississippi
15,437	Missouri
13,865	Indiana
13,435	Connecticut
12,865	Oklahoma
10,160	Oregon
8,223	Nevada
7,619	Wisconsin
7,594	Arkansas
7,449	Minnesota
7,421	Kentucky
7,244	Kansas
5,382	Alaska
4,352	Utah
3,301	Delaware
3,138	Nebraska
3,047	Rhode Island
2,939	Iowa
2,747	Idaho
2,070	West Virginia
1,498	Montana
1,463	New Hampshire
1,195	Wyoming
1,099	Maine
891	South Dakota
747	Vermont
613	North Dakota

Table G.46. WOMFIRMS

Women-Owned Firms 1992

801,487	California
414,179	Texas
395,944	New York
352,048	Florida
250,613	Illinois
227,500	Pennsylvania
224,693	Ohio
193,820	Michigan
164,798	New Jersey
147,572	Massachusetts
143,045	Georgia
142,516	North Carolina
138,494	Virginia
136,337	Washington
125,411	Indiana
124,143	Minnesota
121,777	Maryland
121,659	Colorado
117,885	Missouri
101,134	Tennessee
99,357	Wisconsin
93,300	Arizona
87,970	Oregon
82,894	Oklahoma
79,931	Connecticut
76,849	Louisiana
74,280	Kentucky
71,466	Alabama
71,040	Iowa
66,429	Kansas
64,812	South Carolina
50,440	Arkansas
45,626	Utah
43,637	Nebraska
40,879	Mississippi
40,636	New Mexico
35,260	Maine
32,430	Nevada
31,492	New Hampshire
30,644	West Virginia
29,946	Idaho
29,743	Hawaii
25,310	Montana
21,353	Rhode Island
21,033	Vermont
19,380	Alaska
18,215	South Dakota
15,355	North Dakota
14,904	Delaware
14,617	Wyoming

Table G.47. FEDFUNDS

Federal Funds (1,000s) 1999

166,049,702	California
101,808,595	New York
97,987,610	Texas
87,214,874	Florida
69,448,043	Pennsylvania
57,842,231	Virginia
55,835,957	Illinois
53,262,164	Ohio
43,871,642	Michigan
41,990,244	Maryland
40,397,603	New Jersey
39,214,971	Georgia
37,803,043	Massachusetts
37,227,647	North Carolina
33,231,030	Missouri
31,993,053	Washington
30,866,836	Tennessee
26,959,312	Arizona
26,828,144	Indiana
26,775,609	Alabama
24,384,277	Louisiana
22,603,768	Wisconsin
22,198,101	Kentucky
21,755,430	Colorado
21,665,794	Minnesota
20,833,188	South Carolina
19,240,532	Connecticut
19,188,706	Oklahoma
16,487,905	Mississippi
15,601,525	Iowa
15,592,250	Oregon
14,447,020	Kansas
13,630,842	Arkansas
13,580,214	New Mexico
11,028,115	West Virginia
9,238,662	Utah
8,793,324	Nebraska
8,568,210	Hawaii
7,941,909	Nevada
7,281,484	Maine
6,225,015	Montana
6,164,663	Idaho
6,036,064	Rhode Island
5,301,370	New Hampshire
5,278,716	Alaska
4,909,016	South Dakota
4,535,216	North Dakota
3,765,733	Delaware
3,114,291	Vermont
2,916,241	Wyoming

Table G.48. LOCGOV

Local Government Employment 1997

1,194,169	California
860,168	New York
850,380	Texas
543,525	Florida
459,893	Illinois
421,092	Ohio
365,556	Pennsylvania
332,671	Michigan
324,480	Georgia
298,363	New Jersey
293,505	North Carolina
253,219	Virginia
220,747	Indiana
213,917	Massachusetts
201,633	Wisconsin
201,609	Missouri
194,274	Tennessee
188,845	Minnesota
185,152	Washington
175,369	Alabama
171,635	Maryland
169,976	Louisiana
165,331	Arizona
153,146	Colorado
143,952	South Carolina
134,740	Kentucky
129,462	Oklahoma
122,256	Mississippi
118,302	Kansas
117,999	Oregon
112,667	Iowa
104,338	Connecticut
90,806	Arkansas
75,377	Nebraska
69,941	New Mexico
63,884	Utah
59,926	West Virginia
56,607	Nevada
46,260	Maine
46,035	Idaho
38,830	New Hampshire
32,676	Montana
29,102	Rhode Island
27,423	Wyoming
26,567	South Dakota
23,132	Alaska
21,221	North Dakota
18,865	Delaware
17,841	Vermont
14,319	Hawaii

Table G.49. POPDENSE

Population Density per Square Mile 1999

1,097.7	New Jersey
948.2	Rhode Island
787.9	Massachusetts
677.3	Connecticut
529.1	Maryland
385.5	Delaware
385.3	New York
280.2	Florida
274.9	Ohio
267.6	Pennsylvania
218.2	Illinois
212.5	California
184.6	Hawaii
173.6	Michigan
173.6	Virginia
165.7	Indiana
157.0	North Carolina
134.5	Georgia
133.9	New Hampshire
133.0	Tennessee
129.0	South Carolina
100.4	Louisiana
99.7	Kentucky
96.7	Wisconsin
86.5	Washington
86.1	Alabama
79.4	Missouri
76.5	Texas
75.0	West Virginia
64.2	Vermont
60.0	Minnesota
59.0	Mississippi
51.4	Iowa
49.0	Arkansas
48.9	Oklahoma
42.0	Arizona
40.6	Maine
39.1	Colorado
34.5	Oregon
32.4	Kansas
25.9	Utah
21.7	Nebraska
16.5	Nevada
15.1	Idaho
14.3	New Mexico
9.7	South Dakota
9.2	North Dakota
6.1	Montana
4.9	Wyoming
1.1	Alaska

Table G.50. CRIMESPP

Crimes per Person 1998

.0691	Florida
.0686	New Mexico
.0664	Arizona
.0607	Louisiana
.0585	South Carolina
.0579	Washington
.0566	Oregon
.0557	Utah
.0543	Mississippi
.0541	Georgia
.0539	Maryland
.0536	Hawaii
.0536	Delaware
.0534	North Carolina
.0532	Nevada
.0525	Missouri
.0515	Texas
.0513	Tennessee
.0504	Oklahoma
.0486	Michigan
.0460	Indiana
.0454	Colorado
.0453	Alabama
.0448	Alaska
.0443	Connecticut
.0443	California
.0439	Ohio
.0436	Nebraska
.0429	Arkansas
.0405	Minnesota
.0380	Wyoming
.0374	Idaho
.0369	Virginia
.0368	New Jersey
.0367	Montana
.0356	Rhode Island
.0340	Iowa
.0340	New York
.0333	Massachusetts
.0322	Pennsylvania
.0313	Vermont
.0305	Maine
.0301	New Hampshire
.0298	South Dakota
.0273	North Dakota
.0256	West Virginia
*	Illinois
*	Kentucky
*	Wisconsin
*	Kansas

*Incomplete data

Table G.51. PCMINOR

Percent Minority 1999

71.30	Hawaii
52.50	New Mexico
50.10	California
44.70	Texas
38.30	Mississippi
36.40	Louisiana
35.70	Maryland
34.90	New York
33.70	Georgia
32.40	Arizona
32.10	South Carolina
32.00	Florida
31.60	New Jersey
29.70	Nevada
28.80	Illinois
28.10	Alaska
27.90	Alabama
27.60	Virginia
26.70	North Carolina
25.40	Delaware
21.70	Colorado
20.40	Oklahoma
19.80	Connecticut
19.30	Arkansas
19.10	Michigan
18.90	Tennessee
17.20	Washington
15.60	Massachusetts
14.40	Ohio
14.30	Missouri
13.90	Pennsylvania
13.70	Kansas
13.50	Rhode Island
12.40	Oregon
12.00	Indiana
11.40	Utah
10.60	Nebraska
10.60	South Dakota
10.50	Wisconsin
10.00	Idaho
9.60	Wyoming
9.00	Montana
8.90	Kentucky
8.80	Minnesota
7.30	North Dakota
5.60	Iowa
4.20	West Virginia
3.70	New Hampshire
2.40	Vermont
2.40	Maine

Table G.52. PCMAJOR

Percent Majority 1999

97.60	Vermont
97.60	Maine
96.30	New Hampshire
95.80	West Virginia
94.40	Iowa
92.70	North Dakota
91.20	Minnesota
91.10	Kentucky
91.00	Montana
90.40	Wyoming
90.00	Idaho
89.50	Wisconsin
89.40	Nebraska
89.40	South Dakota
88.60	Utah
88.00	Indiana
87.60	Oregon
86.50	Rhode Island
86.30	Kansas
86.10	Pennsylvania
85.70	Missouri
85.60	Ohio
84.40	Massachusetts
82.80	Washington
81.10	Tennessee
80.90	Michigan
80.70	Arkansas
80.20	Connecticut
79.60	Oklahoma
78.30	Colorado
74.60	Delaware
73.30	North Carolina
72.40	Virginia
72.10	Alabama
71.90	Alaska
71.20	Illinois
70.30	Nevada
68.40	New Jersey
68.00	Florida
67.90	South Carolina
67.60	Arizona
66.30	Georgia
65.10	New York
64.30	Maryland
63.60	Louisiana
61.70	Mississippi
55.30	Texas
49.90	California
47.50	New Mexico
28.70	Hawaii

Table G.53. MAJORPOP

Majority Population (1,000s) 1999

16,539.415	California
11,845.987	New York
11,084.410	Texas
10,326.848	Pennsylvania
10,275.646	Florida
9,635.696	Ohio
8,635.399	Illinois
7,979.794	Michigan
5,608.028	North Carolina
5,570.094	New Jersey
5,229.753	Indiana
5,211.843	Massachusetts
5,163.603	Georgia
4,975.988	Virginia
4,766.267	Washington
4,699.149	Wisconsin
4,686.366	Missouri
4,447.147	Tennessee
4,355.263	Minnesota
3,608.312	Kentucky
3,325.361	Maryland
3,230.152	Arizona
3,175.952	Colorado
3,150.671	Alabama
2,904.951	Oregon
2,780.614	Louisiana
2,708.726	Iowa
2,673.003	Oklahoma
2,638.415	South Carolina
2,632.189	Connecticut
2,290.447	Kansas
2,058.958	Arkansas
1,887.035	Utah
1,731.037	West Virginia
1,708.238	Mississippi
1,489.429	Nebraska
1,271.905	Nevada
1,222.967	Maine
1,156.692	New Hampshire
1,126.530	Idaho
857.058	Rhode Island
826.426	New Mexico
803.329	Montana
655.421	South Dakota
587.408	North Dakota
579.490	Vermont
562.139	Delaware
445.421	Alaska
433.560	Wyoming
340.238	Hawaii

Table G.54. MINORPOP

Minority Population (1,000s) 1999

16,605.706	California
8,959.731	Texas
6,350.614	New York
4,835.598	Florida
3,492.971	Illinois
2,624.637	Georgia
2,573.318	New Jersey
2,042.761	North Carolina
1,896.924	Virginia
1,883.981	Michigan
1,846.273	Maryland
1,667.168	Pennsylvania
1,620.958	Ohio
1,591.421	Louisiana
1,548.180	Arizona
1,247.321	South Carolina
1,219.191	Alabama
1,060.381	Mississippi
1,036.388	Tennessee
990.094	Washington
963.326	Massachusetts
913.418	New Mexico
880.181	Colorado
845.259	Hawaii
781.972	Missouri
713.148	Indiana
685.041	Oklahoma
649.842	Connecticut
551.297	Wisconsin
537.348	Nevada
492.415	Arkansas
420.245	Minnesota
411.203	Oregon
363.605	Kansas
352.513	Kentucky
242.801	Utah
191.399	Delaware
176.599	Nebraska
174.079	Alaska
160.687	Iowa
133.761	Rhode Island
125.170	Idaho
79.450	Montana
77.712	South Dakota
75.891	West Virginia
46.258	North Dakota
46.042	Wyoming
44.442	New Hampshire
30.073	Maine
14.250	Vermont

Table G.55. PCMINFRM

Percent Minority Firms per Minority Population 1992

5.24	Vermont
4.86	Hawaii
3.65	Maine
3.58	Florida
3.29	New Hampshire
3.26	California
3.09	Alaska
3.01	Maryland
2.93	New Mexico
2.73	West Virginia
2.69	Texas
2.67	Colorado
2.62	Washington
2.60	Wyoming
2.53	New York
2.49	New Jersey
2.47	Oregon
2.46	Virginia
2.28	Rhode Island
2.19	Idaho
2.15	Massachusetts
2.11	Kentucky
2.09	Ohio
2.07	Connecticut
1.99	Kansas
1.99	Georgia
1.97	Missouri
1.96	Pennsylvania
1.94	Indiana
1.94	Illinois
1.89	Montana
1.88	Oklahoma
1.87	Louisiana
1.87	Tennessee
1.84	North Carolina
1.83	Iowa
1.79	Utah
1.78	Nebraska
1.77	Minnesota
1.72	Delaware
1.69	South Carolina
1.69	Arizona
1.68	Michigan
1.55	Mississippi
1.54	Arkansas
1.53	Nevada
1.43	Alabama
1.38	Wisconsin
1.33	North Dakota
1.15	South Dakota

Table G.56. PCWOMFRM

Percent Women Firms per Female Population 1992

6.97	Vermont
6.58	Alaska
6.12	Wyoming
5.95	Colorado
5.70	Montana
5.50	Maine
5.24	Oregon
5.16	New Hampshire
5.13	Nebraska
5.12	Minnesota
5.01	Hawaii
4.93	Kansas
4.89	South Dakota
4.84	California
4.83	Iowa
4.82	Oklahoma
4.82	North Dakota
4.77	Idaho
4.73	Connecticut
4.71	Washington
4.62	Massachusetts
4.60	New Mexico
4.58	Maryland
4.52	Florida
4.26	Utah
4.20	New York
4.18	Missouri
4.15	Rhode Island
4.11	Indiana
4.08	Texas
4.03	Illinois
3.94	Virginia
3.93	New Jersey
3.87	Arizona
3.86	Ohio
3.85	Delaware
3.83	Michigan
3.83	Arkansas
3.72	Wisconsin
3.65	Pennsylvania
3.65	Nevada
3.65	Kentucky
3.62	North Carolina
3.58	Georgia
3.57	Tennessee
3.39	Louisiana
3.27	West Virginia
3.22	South Carolina
3.14	Alabama
2.84	Mississippi

Table G.57. PCLOCGOV

Percent in Local Government 1998

5.72	Wyoming
4.73	New York
4.52	Nebraska
4.46	Kansas
4.42	Mississippi
4.24	Texas
4.17	Georgia
4.02	New Mexico
4.01	Alabama
3.95	Minnesota
3.93	Iowa
3.89	Louisiana
3.86	Oklahoma
3.84	Wisconsin
3.84	North Carolina
3.79	Illinois
3.78	Colorado
3.74	Ohio
3.73	Alaska
3.71	Indiana
3.70	South Carolina
3.70	Montana
3.69	Maine
3.69	Missouri
3.68	Virginia
3.68	Idaho
3.66	New Jersey
3.62	South Dakota
3.60	California
3.60	Florida
3.56	Arkansas
3.56	Oregon
3.54	Tennessee
3.46	Massachusetts
3.46	Arizona
3.40	Kentucky
3.37	Michigan
3.35	North Dakota
3.32	Maryland
3.32	West Virginia
3.23	New Hampshire
3.22	Washington
3.18	Connecticut
3.13	Nevada
3.05	Pennsylvania
3.00	Vermont
3.00	Utah
2.94	Rhode Island
2.50	Delaware
1.21	Hawaii

Table G.58. MURPLOGV

Murders per Local Government 1998

.00318	Louisiana
.00300	Nevada
.00299	Maryland
.00221	Arkansas
.00221	Arizona
.00219	Illinois
.00218	Michigan
.00217	Tennessee
.00216	South Carolina
.00213	New Mexico
.00207	North Carolina
.00196	Alabama
.00186	Georgia
.00185	Missouri
.00182	California
.00178	Florida
.00174	Indiana
.00168	Hawaii
.00166	Pennsylvania
.00162	Virginia
.00158	Texas
.00158	Oklahoma
.00156	Alaska
.00153	Mississippi
.00135	Kentucky
.00130	West Virginia
.00130	Kansas
.00129	Connecticut
.00122	Delaware
.00117	Washington
.00112	Colorado
.00108	New Jersey
.00104	New York
.00103	Oregon
.00097	Utah
.00094	Wisconsin
.00085	Ohio
.00082	Rhode Island
.00078	Idaho
.00068	Nebraska
.00066	Minnesota
.00057	Massachusetts
.00056	Maine
.00051	Wyoming
.00045	Vermont
.00043	Iowa
.00033	North Dakota
.00023	South Dakota
.00021	Montana
.00021	New Hampshire

Table G.59. EXEC5069

Executions 1950–1969

104	California
103	Texas
99	Georgia
62	New York
61	Florida
46	Mississippi
39	Ohio
34	South Carolina
34	Pennsylvania
29	Virginia
28	Louisiana
27	Arkansas
25	Alabama
23	Minnesota
20	North Carolina
20	New Jersey
17	Kentucky
13	Oklahoma
12	Arizona
11	Nevada
11	Missouri
11	Illinois
10	Kansas
9	Tennessee
9	West Virginia
9	Colorado
8	Washington
7	Maryland
7	Utah
6	Connecticut
5	Oregon
4	New Mexico
3	Indiana
3	Idaho
3	Iowa
2	Nebraska
2	Vermont
1	Wyoming
0	Michigan
0	Hawaii
0	Alaska
0	Delaware
0	Rhode Island
0	Massachusetts
0	Maine
0	North Dakota
0	South Dakota
0	Montana
0	New Hampshire
0	Wisconsin

Table G.60. EXEC7700

Executions 1977–2000

218	Texas
76	Virginia
46	Florida
42	Missouri
26	Oklahoma
25	Louisiana
24	South Carolina
23	Georgia
22	Arkansas
22	Alabama
21	Arizona
15	North Carolina
12	Illinois
10	Delaware
8	California
8	Nevada
7	Indiana
6	Utah
4	Mississippi
3	Pennsylvania
3	Washington
3	Maryland
3	Nebraska
2	Kentucky
2	Oregon
2	Montana
1	Ohio
1	Tennessee
1	Colorado
1	Idaho
1	Wyoming
0	New York
0	Minnesota
0	New Jersey
0	Kansas
0	West Virginia
0	Connecticut
0	New Mexico
0	Iowa
0	Vermont
0	Michigan
0	Hawaii
0	Alaska
0	Rhode Island
0	Massachusetts
0	Maine
0	North Dakota
0	South Dakota
0	New Hampshire
0	Wisconsin

Table G.61. PRISON92

Persons in Prison 1992

109,496	California
61,736	New York
61,178	Texas
48,302	Florida
39,113	Michigan
38,378	Ohio
31,640	Illinois
25,290	Georgia
24,974	Pennsylvania
22,653	New Jersey
21,199	Virginia
20,896	Louisiana
20,454	North Carolina
19,977	Maryland
18,643	South Carolina
17,453	Alabama
16,477	Arizona
16,189	Missouri
14,821	Oklahoma
13,945	Indiana
11,849	Tennessee
11,403	Connecticut
10,364	Kentucky
10,053	Massachusetts
9,959	Washington
8,997	Colorado
8,912	Wisconsin
8,780	Mississippi
8,285	Arkansas
6,583	Oregon
6,049	Nevada
6,028	Kansas
4,518	Iowa
4,051	Delaware
3,822	Minnesota
3,271	New Mexico
2,926	Hawaii
2,865	Alaska
2,775	Rhode Island
2,699	Utah
2,514	Nebraska
2,256	Idaho
1,777	New Hampshire
1,674	West Virginia
1,519	Maine
1,498	Montana
1,487	South Dakota
1,254	Vermont
1,063	Wyoming
477	North Dakota

Table G.62. PRISON96

Persons in Prison 1996

136,492	California
128,140	Texas
68,556	New York
63,521	Florida
44,540	Ohio
41,371	Michigan
37,870	Illinois
34,363	Georgia
32,151	Pennsylvania
28,999	North Carolina
27,742	Virginia
26,878	New Jersey
25,476	Louisiana
21,616	Maryland
21,433	Arizona
20,753	Alabama
19,880	South Carolina
19,437	Missouri
18,260	Oklahoma
16,133	Indiana
15,245	Tennessee
14,896	Connecticut
12,900	Mississippi
12,180	Kentucky
11,710	Massachusetts
11,669	Washington
11,284	Wisconsin
11,156	Colorado
9,333	Arkansas
7,960	Oregon
7,744	Nevada
7,124	Kansas
5,920	Iowa
4,874	Minnesota
4,851	Delaware
4,201	New Mexico
3,599	Hawaii
3,466	Alaska
3,455	Utah
3,380	Idaho
3,049	Nebraska
3,041	Rhode Island
2,535	West Virginia
2,036	New Hampshire
2,015	Montana
1,888	South Dakota
1,430	Maine
1,389	Wyoming
1,075	Vermont
617	North Dakota

Table G.63. PRRATE92

Prisoners per 1,000 Population 1999

5.87	Delaware
5.18	South Carolina
4.89	Louisiana
4.88	Alaska
4.63	Oklahoma
4.54	Nevada
4.26	Arizona
4.22	Alabama
4.13	Michigan
4.07	Maryland
3.74	Georgia
3.58	Florida
3.55	California
3.49	Ohio
3.48	Connecticut
3.47	Texas
3.46	Arkansas
3.41	New York
3.36	Mississippi
3.32	Virginia
3.12	Missouri
2.99	North Carolina
2.89	New Jersey
2.77	Rhode Island
2.76	Kentucky
2.72	Illinois
2.60	Colorado
2.54	Hawaii
2.47	Indiana
2.39	Kansas
2.36	Tennessee
2.30	Wyoming
2.21	Oregon
2.20	Vermont
2.12	Idaho
2.10	South Dakota
2.08	Pennsylvania
2.07	New Mexico
1.94	Washington
1.82	Montana
1.78	Wisconsin
1.68	Massachusetts
1.61	Iowa
1.60	New Hampshire
1.57	Nebraska
1.48	Utah
1.23	Maine
.93	West Virginia
.85	Minnesota
.75	North Dakota

Table G.64.   PRRATE96

Prisoners per 1,000 Population 1999

6.74	Texas
6.67	Delaware
5.87	Louisiana
5.73	Alaska
5.55	Oklahoma
5.32	South Carolina
4.85	Nevada
4.84	Alabama
4.84	Arizona
4.76	Mississippi
4.69	Georgia
4.56	Connecticut
4.40	Florida
4.29	California
4.27	Maryland
4.25	Michigan
4.16	Virginia
3.98	Ohio
3.97	North Carolina
3.78	New York
3.73	Arkansas
3.62	Missouri
3.36	New Jersey
3.17	Illinois
3.14	Kentucky
3.08	Rhode Island
3.04	Hawaii
2.93	Colorado
2.89	Wyoming
2.87	Tennessee
2.85	Idaho
2.76	Indiana
2.74	Kansas
2.67	Pennsylvania
2.58	South Dakota
2.49	Oregon
2.46	New Mexico
2.30	Montana
2.18	Wisconsin
2.12	Washington
2.08	Iowa
1.92	Massachusetts
1.85	Nebraska
1.83	Vermont
1.75	New Hampshire
1.71	Utah
1.39	West Virginia
1.15	Maine
1.05	Minnesota
.96	North Dakota

Table G.65.   FEDFUNPP

Federal Funds per Person Returned to State 1999

8,521	Alaska
8,416	Virginia
8,119	Maryland
7,805	New Mexico
7,228	Hawaii
7,157	North Dakota
7,052	Montana
6,696	South Dakota
6,127	Alabama
6,122	Massachusetts
6,103	West Virginia
6,092	Rhode Island
6,081	Wyoming
6,077	Missouri
5,955	Mississippi
5,862	Connecticut
5,811	Maine
5,790	Pennsylvania
5,772	Florida
5,714	Oklahoma
5,642	Arizona
5,629	Tennessee
5,604	Kentucky
5,595	New York
5,577	Louisiana
5,558	Washington
5,443	Kansas
5,437	Iowa
5,364	Colorado
5,361	South Carolina
5,343	Arkansas
5,278	Nebraska
5,245	Vermont
5,035	Georgia
5,010	California
4,997	Delaware
4,961	New Jersey
4,925	Idaho
4,889	Texas
4,866	North Carolina
4,732	Ohio
4,702	Oregon
4,604	Illinois
4,537	Minnesota
4,514	Indiana
4,448	Michigan
4,414	New Hampshire
4,390	Nevada
4,338	Utah
4,305	Wisconsin

Table G.66.   CRIMLOGV

Crime Rate per Person in Local Government 1998

4.47	Hawaii
2.11	Delaware
1.89	Florida
1.81	Arizona
1.75	Washington
1.73	Utah
1.64	Nevada
1.61	Maryland
1.57	Oregon
1.56	South Carolina
1.50	Louisiana
1.43	New Mexico
1.37	Michigan
1.36	North Carolina
1.30	Oklahoma
1.26	Tennessee
1.24	Georgia
1.23	Missouri
1.21	California
1.21	Rhode Island
1.20	Arkansas
1.20	Texas
1.20	Connecticut
1.09	Alabama
1.09	Colorado
1.05	Alaska
1.01	Minnesota
1.01	Pennsylvania
1.00	New Jersey
.99	Idaho
.98	Vermont
.97	Virginia
.95	Nebraska
.92	Massachusetts
.89	Indiana
.84	Ohio
.82	Maine
.78	Iowa
.77	West Virginia
.76	North Dakota
.72	New York
.69	Mississippi
.66	Wyoming
.57	South Dakota
.56	Montana
.33	New Hampshire
*	Kentucky
*	Kansas
*	Illinois
*	Wisconsin

*Incomplete data

Table G.67. PRISPI96

Operating Costs per Inmate per Year 1996

37,825	Minnesota
35,739	Rhode Island
33,711	Maine
32,415	Alaska
32,361	Utah
31,912	Connecticut
31,837	Oregon
31,094	Vermont
30,773	New Jersey
29,491	New Mexico
28,426	New York
28,067	Michigan
28,063	Pennsylvania
27,771	Wisconsin
26,662	Washington
26,002	Massachusetts
25,303	North Carolina
24,286	Iowa
23,318	Hawaii
22,904	Tennessee
22,271	Nebraska
22,247	Maryland
22,242	Kansas
21,385	California
21,020	Colorado
20,839	New Hampshire
20,782	Montana
20,188	Indiana
19,613	Ohio
19,456	Wyoming
19,351	Illinois
19,091	Arizona
17,987	Delaware
17,787	South Dakota
17,327	Florida
17,245	West Virginia
17,154	North Dakota
16,320	Kentucky
16,306	Virginia
16,277	Idaho
15,933	Georgia
15,370	Nevada
13,977	South Carolina
13,341	Arkansas
12,832	Missouri
12,304	Louisiana
12,215	Texas
11,156	Mississippi
10,601	Oklahoma
7,987	Alabama

Table G.68. TOTPRISN

Total for Prisons ($1,000s) 1996

3,031,047	California
2,220,586	New York
1,713,935	Texas
1,224,933	Florida
1,167,610	Michigan
1,014,917	Ohio
978,769	Pennsylvania
839,308	New Jersey
756,829	North Carolina
740,423	Illinois
560,358	Georgia
520,263	Maryland
497,838	Connecticut
476,715	Virginia
418,094	Arizona
360,439	Wisconsin
357,862	Washington
350,575	Tennessee
338,195	Indiana
316,245	Louisiana
315,539	South Carolina
309,674	Massachusetts
262,787	Missouri
254,330	Oregon
249,833	Colorado
208,706	Kentucky
198,290	Oklahoma
185,983	Minnesota
170,848	Kansas
168,989	Alabama
148,852	Mississippi
146,069	Iowa
133,729	Arkansas
125,602	New Mexico
121,960	Nevada
116,664	Alaska
113,394	Utah
109,596	Rhode Island
87,961	Delaware
87,417	Hawaii
69,867	Nebraska
56,957	Idaho
51,713	Maine
46,949	West Virginia
42,970	New Hampshire
42,448	Montana
34,152	South Dakota
33,505	Vermont
29,025	Wyoming
10,749	North Dakota

Table G.69. MEDICPI

Medical Care per Inmate 1996

12.57	Michigan
11.31	Wyoming
11.20	New Hampshire
11.12	Alaska
10.18	Pennsylvania
10.13	Washington
9.32	Massachusetts
9.32	Vermont
8.71	Nevada
8.62	Utah
8.39	Florida
8.27	Connecticut
7.59	California
7.48	Rhode Island
7.24	North Carolina
6.69	New Mexico
6.62	Georgia
6.53	New York
6.47	Maine
6.40	Kansas
6.30	New Jersey
6.22	South Dakota
6.18	Hawaii
5.92	Texas
5.80	West Virginia
5.78	Idaho
5.48	Montana
5.45	Colorado
5.28	Arkansas
5.27	Tennessee
5.08	Arizona
4.98	Oregon
4.86	Ohio
4.74	Maryland
4.66	Delaware
4.48	Wisconsin
4.09	Iowa
3.61	Kentucky
3.50	Missouri
3.49	Illinois
3.22	Mississippi
3.21	Nebraska
2.84	Alabama
2.80	South Carolina
2.76	North Dakota
2.25	Oklahoma
*	Virginia
*	Indiana
*	Louisiana
*	Minnesota

*Incomplete data

Table G.70. FOODPI

Food Costs per Inmate per Day 1996

5.60	Pennsylvania
5.54	Hawaii
5.32	Washington
5.08	Iowa
4.67	South Dakota
4.42	Rhode Island
4.32	Michigan
4.32	New Mexico
4.29	Ohio
4.22	Connecticut
4.18	Tennessee
4.05	Alaska
3.93	Vermont
3.82	Wisconsin
3.75	Kansas
3.72	Delaware
3.59	Oregon
3.57	California
3.53	Florida
3.49	Colorado
3.46	West Virginia
3.30	Utah
3.17	New Hampshire
3.11	Georgia
3.04	Arizona
3.03	Illinois
2.96	Virginia
2.93	North Dakota
2.86	Montana
2.85	Idaho
2.83	Indiana
2.80	New York
2.77	Nebraska
2.75	Maine
2.69	Wyoming
2.66	North Carolina
2.54	New Jersey
2.39	Nevada
2.23	Maryland
2.20	Massachusetts
2.12	Arkansas
2.10	Missouri
1.80	Mississippi
1.61	Kentucky
1.41	Texas
1.26	South Carolina
1.18	Oklahoma
1.12	Louisiana
.84	Alabama
*	Minnesota

*Incomplete data

Table G.71. PRISCOST

Prison Costs per Inmate per Day per Person in State 1996

188.32	Alaska
151.69	Connecticut
122.03	New York
118.37	Michigan
116.73	Delaware
110.61	Rhode Island
103.07	New Jersey
100.60	Maryland
98.92	North Carolina
91.45	California
90.16	Ohio
87.50	Arizona
85.51	Texas
81.60	Pennsylvania
81.20	South Carolina
81.06	Florida
76.69	Oregon
73.74	Hawaii
72.33	Louisiana
72.19	New Mexico
71.95	Georgia
69.36	Virginia
68.65	Wisconsin
67.41	Nevada
64.37	Kansas
63.93	Tennessee
62.17	Washington
61.59	Colorado
61.05	Illinois
60.52	Wyoming
59.05	Oklahoma
56.91	Indiana
56.43	Vermont
53.76	Mississippi
53.24	Utah
52.69	Kentucky
52.41	Arkansas
50.91	Iowa
50.15	Massachusetts
48.08	Montana
48.06	Missouri
46.58	South Dakota
45.50	Idaho
41.94	Nebraska
41.27	Maine
38.95	Minnesota
38.67	Alabama
35.77	New Hampshire
25.98	West Virginia
16.96	North Dakota

Table G.72. UTILPIPD

Utilities per Inmate per Day 1996

4.59	Maine
3.18	Minnesota
3.09	Connecticut
3.06	New Hampshire
3.05	Alaska
2.90	Tennessee
2.71	New Jersey
2.62	New Mexico
2.61	Pennsylvania
2.60	West Virginia
2.56	New York
2.51	Hawaii
2.50	Rhode Island
2.47	Wisconsin
2.45	Washington
2.43	Maryland
2.33	Utah
2.29	Iowa
2.23	Delaware
2.17	North Carolina
2.15	Oregon
2.15	North Dakota
2.12	South Carolina
2.03	Vermont
1.98	Massachusetts
1.96	Georgia
1.91	Michigan
1.90	Illinois
1.88	Nevada
1.84	Kansas
1.65	Nebraska
1.63	Missouri
1.62	Ohio
1.61	Florida
1.61	Colorado
1.58	California
1.56	Indiana
1.56	Alabama
1.54	Arizona
1.49	Wyoming
1.45	Virginia
1.38	Kentucky
1.31	South Dakota
1.18	Idaho
1.16	Texas
1.10	Mississippi
1.10	Montana
1.07	Arkansas
.97	Oklahoma
.85	Louisiana

Table G.73. PRCH9296

Prison Population Change 1992–1996

109.45	Texas
51.43	West Virginia
49.82	Idaho
46.92	Mississippi
41.78	North Carolina
35.88	Georgia
34.51	Montana
31.51	Florida
31.03	Iowa
30.86	Virginia
30.67	Wyoming
30.63	Connecticut
30.08	Arizona
29.35	North Dakota
28.74	Pennsylvania
28.66	Tennessee
28.43	New Mexico
28.02	Nevada
28.01	Utah
27.52	Minnesota
26.97	South Dakota
26.62	Wisconsin
24.65	California
24.00	Colorado
23.20	Oklahoma
23.00	Hawaii
21.92	Louisiana
21.28	Nebraska
20.98	Alaska
20.92	Oregon
20.06	Missouri
19.75	Delaware
19.69	Illinois
18.91	Alabama
18.65	New Jersey
18.18	Kansas
17.52	Kentucky
17.17	Washington
16.48	Massachusetts
16.06	Ohio
15.69	Indiana
14.58	New Hampshire
12.65	Arkansas
11.05	New York
9.59	Rhode Island
8.20	Maryland
6.64	South Carolina
5.77	Michigan
−5.86	Maine
−14.27	Vermont

Table G.74. GOVTFSL

Persons in Government (1,000s) 2000

2,317.7	California
1,498.7	Texas
1,446.1	New York
991.2	Florida
840.1	Illinois
784.1	Ohio
721.6	Pennsylvania
682.4	Michigan
631.3	North Carolina
622.6	Virginia
600.5	Georgia
573.0	New Jersey
478.3	Washington
427.8	Massachusetts
423.3	Maryland
418.7	Indiana
406.8	Tennessee
405.2	Wisconsin
402.7	Missouri
393.2	Minnesota
370.6	Arizona
361.0	Louisiana
353.0	Alabama
322.8	Colorado
319.5	South Carolina
313.0	Kentucky
273.3	Oklahoma
268.4	Oregon
243.2	Iowa
240.4	Connecticut
239.2	Mississippi
224.4	Kansas
178.0	Arkansas
177.0	New Mexico
169.8	Utah
153.8	Nebraska
142.5	West Virginia
122.2	Nevada
114.3	Hawaii
108.6	Idaho
98.1	Maine
83.0	New Hampshire
74.8	Alaska
73.0	South Dakota
72.9	Montana
71.3	North Dakota
63.3	Rhode Island
58.0	Delaware
52.3	Wyoming
49.1	Vermont

Table G.75. EXPT5069

Executions per 1,000 Persons 1950–1969

.016615	Mississippi
.012711	Georgia
.010583	Arkansas
.008750	South Carolina
.006404	Louisiana
.006080	Nevada
.005721	Alabama
.005139	Texas
.004981	West Virginia
.004816	Minnesota
.004292	Kentucky
.004219	Virginia
.004037	Florida
.003871	Oklahoma
.003768	Kansas
.003465	Ohio
.003407	New York
.003368	Vermont
.003287	Utah
.003138	California
.002835	Pennsylvania
.002614	North Carolina
.002511	Arizona
.002456	New Jersey
.002397	Idaho
.002299	New Mexico
.002219	Colorado
.002085	Wyoming
.002012	Missouri
.001828	Connecticut
.001641	Tennessee
.001508	Oregon
.001390	Washington
.001354	Maryland
.001200	Nebraska
.001046	Iowa
.000907	Illinois
.000505	Indiana
.000000	Michigan
.000000	Massachusetts
.000000	Wisconsin
.000000	Hawaii
.000000	Maine
.000000	New Hampshire
.000000	Alaska
.000000	South Dakota
.000000	Montana
.000000	North Dakota
.000000	Rhode Island
.000000	Delaware

Table G.76. EXPT7700

Executions per 1,000 Persons 1977–2000

.013271	Delaware
.011058	Virginia
.010876	Texas
.008623	Arkansas
.007743	Oklahoma
.007681	Missouri
.006176	South Carolina
.005718	Louisiana
.005034	Alabama
.004422	Nevada
.004395	Arizona
.003044	Florida
.002953	Georgia
.002817	Utah
.002266	Montana
.002085	Wyoming
.001961	North Carolina
.001801	Nebraska
.001445	Mississippi
.001178	Indiana
.000989	Illinois
.000799	Idaho
.000603	Oregon
.000580	Maryland
.000521	Washington
.000505	Kentucky
.000250	Pennsylvania
.000247	Colorado
.000241	California
.000182	Tennessee
.000089	Ohio
.000000	West Virginia
.000000	Minnesota
.000000	Kansas
.000000	New York
.000000	Vermont
.000000	New Jersey
.000000	New Mexico
.000000	Connecticut
.000000	Iowa
.000000	Michigan
.000000	Massachusetts
.000000	Wisconsin
.000000	Hawaii
.000000	Maine
.000000	New Hampshire
.000000	Alaska
.000000	South Dakota
.000000	North Dakota
.000000	Rhode Island

Table G.77. CIVILABOR

Labor Force (in 1,000s) 2000

16,966.9	California
10,491.0	Texas
8,959.6	New York
7,593.9	Florida
6,430.0	Illinois
5,957.1	Pennsylvania
5,878.5	Ohio
5,159.7	Michigan
4,224.6	New Jersey
4,177.3	Georgia
3,921.3	North Carolina
3,641.6	Virginia
3,294.7	Massachusetts
3,123.8	Indiana
3,080.4	Washington
3,027.4	Wisconsin
2,973.8	Missouri
2,845.4	Tennessee
2,817.0	Maryland
2,762.5	Minnesota
2,394.5	Arizona
2,354.4	Colorado
2,187.6	Alabama
2,079.8	Louisiana
2,007.1	South Carolina
1,989.9	Kentucky
1,815.7	Oregon
1,703.3	Connecticut
1,675.5	Oklahoma
1,576.2	Iowa
1,477.8	Kansas
1,326.0	Mississippi
1,285.5	Arkansas
1,127.5	Utah
985.5	Nevada
940.6	Nebraska
846.1	New Mexico
806.5	West Virginia
691.0	Maine
686.4	New Hampshire
671.4	Idaho
597.6	Hawaii
509.0	Rhode Island
493.4	Montana
408.3	Delaware
401.8	South Dakota
341.5	Vermont
338.0	North Dakota
318.8	Alaska
270.4	Wyoming

Table G.78. EMPLOYED

Persons Employed (in 1,000s) 2000

16,096.5	California
10,022.0	Texas
8,579.6	New York
7,311.2	Florida
6,151.1	Illinois
5,718.1	Pennsylvania
5,633.6	Ohio
4,973.7	Michigan
4,067.4	New Jersey
4,039.0	Georgia
3,794.7	North Carolina
3,549.4	Virginia
3,198.5	Massachusetts
3,010.1	Indiana
2,930.5	Washington
2,916.7	Wisconsin
2,891.3	Missouri
2,742.0	Tennessee
2,725.6	Maryland
2,693.3	Minnesota
2,305.7	Arizona
2,290.5	Colorado
2,097.7	Alabama
1,972.0	Louisiana
1,927.3	South Carolina
1,913.1	Kentucky
1,725.6	Oregon
1,662.0	Connecticut
1,626.2	Oklahoma
1,543.0	Iowa
1,429.5	Kansas
1,251.4	Mississippi
1,227.3	Arkansas
1,091.7	Utah
950.9	Nevada
914.5	Nebraska
797.3	New Mexico
763.0	West Virginia
667.1	Maine
665.4	New Hampshire
641.6	Idaho
573.5	Hawaii
488.8	Rhode Island
471.0	Montana
392.8	Delaware
392.6	South Dakota
332.3	Vermont
329.2	North Dakota
301.4	Alaska
261.0	Wyoming

Table G.79. UNEMPLOY

Unemployed (in 1,000s) July 2000

870.4	California
469.0	Texas
379.9	New York
282.8	Florida
279.0	Illinois
244.9	Ohio
239.1	Pennsylvania
186.0	Michigan
157.2	New Jersey
149.9	Washington
138.3	Georgia
126.5	North Carolina
113.7	Indiana
110.7	Wisconsin
107.7	Louisiana
103.4	Tennessee
96.1	Massachusetts
92.2	Virginia
91.4	Maryland
90.1	Oregon
89.9	Alabama
88.8	Arizona
82.5	Missouri
79.8	South Carolina
76.8	Kentucky
74.6	Mississippi
69.2	Minnesota
63.9	Colorado
58.3	Arkansas
49.3	Oklahoma
48.8	New Mexico
48.3	Kansas
43.5	West Virginia
41.3	Connecticut
35.8	Utah
34.6	Nevada
33.3	Iowa
29.9	Idaho
26.1	Nebraska
24.1	Hawaii
23.9	Maine
22.4	Montana
21.0	New Hampshire
20.1	Rhode Island
17.4	Alaska
15.4	Delaware
9.4	Wyoming
9.2	South Dakota
9.2	Vermont
8.8	North Dakota

Table G.80. UNEMRATE

Unemployment Rate, Percent July 2000

5.8	New Mexico
5.6	Mississippi
5.5	Alaska
5.4	West Virginia
5.2	Louisiana
5.1	California
5.0	Oregon
4.9	Washington
4.5	Texas
4.5	Arkansas
4.5	Idaho
4.5	Montana
4.3	Illinois
4.2	New York
4.2	Ohio
4.1	Alabama
4.0	Pennsylvania
4.0	South Carolina
4.0	Hawaii
4.0	Rhode Island
3.9	Kentucky
3.8	Delaware
3.7	Florida
3.7	New Jersey
3.7	Wisconsin
3.7	Arizona
3.6	Michigan
3.6	Indiana
3.6	Tennessee
3.5	Nevada
3.5	Maine
3.5	Wyoming
3.3	Georgia
3.3	Kansas
3.2	North Carolina
3.2	Maryland
3.2	Utah
3.1	New Hampshire
2.9	Massachusetts
2.9	Oklahoma
2.8	Missouri
2.8	Nebraska
2.7	Colorado
2.7	Vermont
2.6	North Dakota
2.5	Virginia
2.5	Minnesota
2.4	Connecticut
2.3	South Dakota
2.1	Iowa

Table G.81. NONFARMT

Number (1,000s) Nonfarm Work 2000

14,436.2	California
9,364.7	Texas
8,615.0	New York
7,171.0	Florida
6,018.3	Illinois
5,609.0	Pennsylvania
5,588.7	Ohio
4,620.9	Michigan
4,003.5	Georgia
3,934.9	North Carolina
3,920.4	New Jersey
3,465.2	Virginia
3,299.8	Massachusetts
3,005.6	Indiana
2,820.2	Wisconsin
2,737.9	Missouri
2,724.4	Tennessee
2,693.9	Washington
2,650.3	Minnesota
2,418.6	Maryland
2,268.1	Arizona
2,203.1	Colorado
1,947.2	Alabama
1,900.2	Louisiana
1,872.9	South Carolina
1,837.6	Kentucky
1,696.2	Connecticut
1,600.3	Oregon
1,492.7	Iowa
1,480.8	Oklahoma
1,340.0	Kansas
1,161.4	Arkansas
1,155.0	Mississippi
1,066.1	Utah
1,031.0	Nevada
890.7	Nebraska
742.0	New Mexico
730.8	West Virginia
610.2	New Hampshire
599.8	Maine
561.0	Idaho
545.0	Hawaii
473.3	Rhode Island
424.8	Delaware
393.7	Montana
377.3	South Dakota
324.2	North Dakota
296.5	Vermont
282.8	Alaska
244.0	Wyoming

Table G.82.   MINING

Number (1,000s) in Mining 2000

144.5	Texas
46.8	Louisiana
28.0	Oklahoma
23.0	California
21.4	West Virginia
20.9	Kentucky
18.8	Pennsylvania
16.2	Wyoming
14.1	New Mexico
13.0	Colorado
12.4	Ohio
11.0	Nevada
10.6	Illinois
10.0	Arizona
9.8	Virginia
9.7	Alaska
9.4	Alabama
8.2	Utah
7.8	Georgia
7.1	Minnesota
7.0	Michigan
6.6	Kansas
6.4	Florida
6.2	Mississippi
6.1	Indiana
5.3	Missouri
4.8	Montana
4.5	New York
4.2	Tennessee
4.0	North Carolina
3.5	North Dakota
3.3	Washington
3.2	Arkansas
2.5	Idaho
2.4	Wisconsin
2.2	Iowa
2.0	New Jersey
1.8	South Carolina
1.8	Oregon
1.4	Massachusetts
1.4	Maryland
1.2	Nebraska
1.2	South Dakota
.8	Connecticut
.6	Vermont
.5	New Hampshire
.3	Rhode Island
.1	Maine
.1	Delaware
.0	Hawaii

Table G.83.   CONSTRUC

Number (1,000s) in Construction 2000

740.4	California
564.0	Texas
380.0	Florida
331.4	New York
254.7	Illinois
237.8	Ohio
237.4	Pennsylvania
231.0	North Carolina
204.2	Virginia
199.6	Georgia
195.7	Michigan
171.8	Colorado
163.8	Washington
158.2	Maryland
156.9	Arizona
147.8	Missouri
147.5	Indiana
145.1	New Jersey
131.4	Louisiana
129.1	Tennessee
126.6	Massachusetts
123.2	Wisconsin
120.4	South Carolina
113.7	Minnesota
109.9	Alabama
91.6	Nevada
88.6	Kentucky
88.4	Oregon
78.5	Utah
74.0	Kansas
68.9	Iowa
62.1	Oklahoma
61.8	Connecticut
56.0	Arkansas
52.5	Mississippi
45.7	New Mexico
43.4	Nebraska
38.3	Idaho
32.7	West Virginia
30.2	Maine
26.2	New Hampshire
25.0	Delaware
23.8	Hawaii
22.8	Montana
19.3	Wyoming
18.7	Rhode Island
16.7	South Dakota
16.0	North Dakota
14.7	Vermont
14.0	Alaska

Table G.84.   MANUFACT

Number (1,000s) in Manufacturing 2000

1,920.7	California
1,086.4	Texas
1,080.1	Ohio
977.2	Michigan
955.0	Illinois
934.3	Pennsylvania
882.1	New York
781.6	North Carolina
693.0	Indiana
614.0	Wisconsin
604.7	Georgia
507.4	Tennessee
490.3	Florida
460.4	New Jersey
438.5	Minnesota
429.7	Massachusetts
399.6	Missouri
392.3	Virginia
365.3	Alabama
350.3	Washington
341.8	South Carolina
319.1	Kentucky
266.7	Connecticut
262.6	Iowa
253.9	Arkansas
240.9	Mississippi
240.8	Oregon
216.2	Arizona
212.7	Kansas
204.8	Colorado
186.4	Louisiana
184.8	Oklahoma
177.2	Maryland
132.8	Utah
117.2	Nebraska
106.0	New Hampshire
85.6	Maine
82.1	West Virginia
77.2	Idaho
74.8	Rhode Island
58.8	Delaware
48.9	South Dakota
47.9	Vermont
44.0	Nevada
42.9	New Mexico
25.0	Montana
24.6	North Dakota
16.8	Hawaii
13.9	Alaska
11.1	Wyoming

Table G.85. TRANSPU

Number (1,000s) in Transport and Public Utilities 2000

746.1	California
584.8	Texas
424.8	New York
359.9	Florida
352.3	Illinois
298.1	Pennsylvania
265.3	Georgia
262.0	New Jersey
249.3	Ohio
184.6	Virginia
181.1	North Carolina
178.8	Michigan
173.1	Tennessee
168.1	Missouri
145.9	Indiana
142.1	Colorado
141.6	Washington
141.2	Massachusetts
133.2	Wisconsin
132.2	Minnesota
115.4	Maryland
114.2	Louisiana
109.8	Arizona
107.6	Kentucky
96.2	Alabama
90.0	South Carolina
82.2	Oklahoma
79.9	Kansas
79.2	Oregon
78.4	Connecticut
73.8	Iowa
71.4	Arkansas
60.8	Utah
57.9	Mississippi
57.9	Nebraska
54.5	Nevada
37.7	West Virginia
35.2	New Mexico
27.5	Idaho
26.8	Alaska
24.8	Maine
22.6	Montana
20.9	New Hampshire
18.8	North Dakota
17.9	Delaware
16.8	South Dakota
16.1	Rhode Island
14.5	Wyoming
12.5	Vermont
.0	Hawaii

Table G.86. TRADE

Number (1,000s) in Trade 2000

3,280.3	California
2,252.3	Texas
1,768.5	Florida
1,745.8	New York
1,354.1	Illinois
1,338.0	Ohio
1,253.9	Pennsylvania
1,083.7	Michigan
1,016.0	Georgia
924.5	New Jersey
879.1	North Carolina
751.4	Virginia
744.7	Massachusetts
704.5	Indiana
652.3	Washington
649.3	Missouri
643.0	Wisconsin
638.4	Tennessee
632.0	Minnesota
560.8	Maryland
529.6	Arizona
524.9	Colorado
452.2	Alabama
451.3	South Carolina
440.8	Louisiana
435.7	Kentucky
393.4	Oregon
363.3	Connecticut
361.4	Iowa
343.5	Oklahoma
323.3	Kansas
270.3	Arkansas
254.2	Utah
247.9	Mississippi
213.4	Nevada
212.8	Nebraska
175.9	New Mexico
164.1	West Virginia
160.9	New Hampshire
149.6	Maine
140.1	Idaho
135.9	Hawaii
108.2	Rhode Island
105.9	Montana
92.6	South Dakota
92.5	Delaware
80.8	North Dakota
68.4	Vermont
57.8	Alaska
56.8	Wyoming

Table G.87. FINANCE

Number (1,000s) in Finance, Insurance, and Real Estate 2000

832.9	California
753.2	New York
539.2	Texas
462.5	Florida
407.8	Illinois
322.6	Pennsylvania
312.1	Ohio
261.3	New Jersey
229.8	Massachusetts
206.2	Georgia
205.6	Michigan
190.0	North Carolina
186.9	Virginia
169.6	Missouri
160.5	Minnesota
150.7	Wisconsin
146.5	Arizona
142.4	Indiana
141.7	Connecticut
140.9	Maryland
140.7	Colorado
139.9	Washington
130.8	Tennessee
95.4	Oregon
92.8	Alabama
86.1	Iowa
85.0	Louisiana
83.5	South Carolina
75.3	Oklahoma
71.8	Kentucky
64.5	Kansas
61.2	Nebraska
57.0	Utah
51.3	Delaware
47.5	Arkansas
44.6	Nevada
41.9	Mississippi
34.5	Hawaii
33.5	New Mexico
32.9	New Hampshire
30.6	Maine
29.9	Rhode Island
29.7	West Virginia
25.8	South Dakota
23.5	Idaho
18.2	Montana
16.4	North Dakota
12.7	Alaska
12.4	Vermont
8.3	Wyoming

Table G.88. SERVICES	Table G.89. WWALLDEA	Table G.90. WBALLDEA
Number (1,000s) in Services 2000	Women White All Deaths (per 100,000) 1994–1996	*Women Black All Deaths (per 100,000) 1994–1996*

4,575.1	California	425.4	West Virginia	623.1	Nebraska
3,027.1	New York	415.3	Nevada	620.6	Tennessee
2,712.2	Florida	415.0	Oklahoma	614.6	Illinois
2,694.8	Texas	405.8	Kentucky	598.8	Indiana
1,843.7	Illinois	400.8	Mississippi	594.4	Delaware
1,822.3	Pennsylvania	399.7	Arkansas	592.9	South Carolina
1,574.9	Ohio	398.0	Tennessee	588.9	Mississippi
1,292.1	New Jersey	397.5	Alabama	587.7	Louisiana
1,290.5	Michigan	396.4	Louisiana	587.2	Missouri
1,198.6	Massachusetts	387.7	Indiana	586.7	New Jersey
1,113.4	Virginia	386.8	Georgia	586.6	Arkansas
1,103.4	Georgia	383.3	Missouri	586.5	Pennsylvania
1,036.8	North Carolina	383.2	Ohio	579.5	Kentucky
841.4	Maryland	383.2	Delaware	575.8	Georgia
795.5	Missouri	382.1	South Carolina	573.1	Michigan
773.1	Minnesota	371.7	Maine	564.1	Alabama
764.4	Washington	367.8	Pennsylvania	562.4	North Carolina
748.5	Wisconsin	365.7	Texas	560.6	Oklahoma
747.5	Indiana	365.6	Oregon	554.8	Florida
734.6	Tennessee	364.1	North Carolina	554.2	Maryland
728.5	Arizona	363.4	New York	554.2	Kansas
683.0	Colorado	362.9	Michigan	553.6	Ohio
543.1	Connecticut	361.6	Illinois	552.5	Wisconsin
534.6	Louisiana	361.6	Maryland	550.9	Virginia
480.9	Kentucky	361.2	Virginia	549.8	Rhode Island
468.4	Alabama	360.4	Vermont	546.4	Texas
464.6	South Carolina	359.1	Wyoming	541.3	California
449.7	Nevada	359.0	New Hampshire	525.0	West Virginia
432.9	Oregon	358.4	New Jersey	516.8	Minnesota
431.6	Oklahoma	355.7	New Mexico	516.7	Iowa
394.5	Iowa	352.2	California	500.6	Nevada
354.6	Kansas	351.8	Arizona	497.3	Connecticut
304.8	Utah	346.6	Kansas	493.2	Arizona
281.1	Arkansas	346.3	Washington	491.1	Washington
268.5	Mississippi	343.3	Montana	490.8	New York
243.2	Nebraska	342.1	Alaska	473.6	Oregon
220.6	West Virginia	341.9	Rhode Island	469.3	Colorado
217.7	New Mexico	341.2	Massachusetts	459.8	Massachusetts
180.8	Maine	338.1	Connecticut	454.7	Utah
179.8	New Hampshire	336.7	Colorado	453.1	Wyoming
178.1	Hawaii	336.0	Idaho	374.3	New Mexico
162.0	Rhode Island	334.6	Florida	363.5	Maine
143.3	Idaho	334.3	Nebraska	358.3	Alaska
121.5	Montana	331.7	Wisconsin	188.6	Hawaii
121.2	Delaware	331.1	Iowa	*	Vermont
102.3	South Dakota	325.8	Utah	*	New Hampshire
92.8	North Dakota	314.5	Minnesota	*	Montana
90.9	Vermont	304.1	North Dakota	*	Idaho
73.1	Alaska	302.0	South Dakota	*	North Dakota
65.5	Wyoming	270.5	Hawaii	*	South Dakota

*Incomplete data

Table G.91. WWMALIG

Women White Death Malignancies (per 100,000) 1994–1996

119.9	New Hampshire
119.8	Maine
118.5	West Virginia
118.4	Nevada
117.8	Delaware
117.8	New Jersey
117.8	Rhode Island
116.7	Kentucky
113.8	Massachusetts
113.7	Ohio
113.5	Maryland
113.2	Louisiana
112.7	Indiana
112.7	New York
110.7	Illinois
110.7	Oklahoma
110.4	Vermont
110.1	Missouri
110.1	Pennsylvania
109.8	Oregon
108.7	Washington
108.3	Tennessee
108.1	Connecticut
107.8	Arkansas
107.5	Michigan
107.4	Virginia
106.7	Wyoming
106.6	California
106.1	Alabama
106.0	Florida
104.2	Mississippi
103.9	Alaska
103.8	Georgia
102.9	South Carolina
102.3	Wisconsin
102.2	North Carolina
101.9	Minnesota
101.7	Texas
101.4	Iowa
101.1	Kansas
101.1	Montana
99.7	Arizona
97.8	New Mexico
97.3	Nebraska
95.2	North Dakota
94.7	Idaho
92.1	South Dakota
91.0	Colorado
82.0	Hawaii
76.8	Utah

Table G.92. WBMALIG

Women Black Deaths Malignancies (per 100,000) 1994–1996

167.5	Delaware
155.8	Kentucky
153.4	Rhode Island
149.3	Illinois
147.7	Pennsylvania
146.9	Missouri
146.6	Tennessee
144.7	Indiana
142.8	Ohio
140.9	Louisiana
139.4	New Jersey
138.3	Wisconsin
136.4	Arkansas
136.1	Virginia
135.4	Maryland
135.1	Minnesota
133.6	Texas
133.5	Michigan
133.3	Utah
132.5	California
131.5	South Carolina
131.5	North Carolina
130.7	Kansas
126.8	Mississippi
126.5	Nebraska
126.2	Iowa
125.8	Oklahoma
125.4	Washington
123.0	Massachusetts
121.5	Alabama
121.1	Georgia
119.2	West Virginia
118.5	Florida
116.4	Nevada
114.3	New York
113.2	Connecticut
110.3	Arizona
108.7	Alaska
105.9	Colorado
103.1	Oregon
97.3	New Mexico
*	New Hampshire
*	Maine
*	Vermont
*	Wyoming
*	Montana
*	North Dakota
*	Idaho
*	South Dakota
*	Hawaii

*Incomplete data

Table G.93. WWDIABET

Women White Deaths Diabetes (per 100,000) 1994–1996

16.5	West Virginia
15.6	Louisiana
14.9	Texas
14.7	Utah
14.1	Ohio
13.5	Alaska
12.9	New Mexico
12.7	Vermont
12.5	Kentucky
12.5	New Jersey
12.4	Delaware
12.2	Maryland
11.8	Pennsylvania
11.8	Indiana
11.7	Maine
11.5	Michigan
11.3	Tennessee
11.0	Missouri
11.0	Washington
11.0	New Hampshire
11.0	Idaho
10.9	Kansas
10.9	Oregon
10.6	Wyoming
10.5	South Carolina
10.5	Alabama
10.4	Illinois
10.1	Wisconsin
10.0	Arkansas
9.9	Arizona
9.8	California
9.8	Oklahoma
9.6	Montana
9.5	North Carolina
9.4	Rhode Island
9.4	Iowa
9.1	Minnesota
9.0	Massachusetts
8.7	Virginia
8.6	New York
8.4	South Dakota
8.3	Florida
8.3	Colorado
8.2	Nevada
8.1	Connecticut
8.0	Georgia
7.9	North Dakota
7.7	Mississippi
7.5	Nebraska
4.2	Hawaii

Table G.94. WBDIABET

Women Black Deaths Diabetes (per 100,000) 1994–1996

45.9	Louisiana
39.2	South Carolina
36.6	Minnesota
36.4	Delaware
35.8	Washington
35.5	West Virginia
35.1	Kansas
34.3	New Jersey
34.2	Texas
34.2	Arizona
33.8	Indiana
33.3	Alabama
33.1	Wisconsin
32.8	North Carolina
32.1	Kentucky
31.9	Maryland
31.9	Tennessee
31.8	Oregon
31.3	Florida
30.9	Nebraska
30.6	Oklahoma
30.2	Ohio
28.8	Rhode Island
27.5	Iowa
27.0	Arkansas
26.1	California
25.6	Pennsylvania
24.4	Virginia
24.3	Illinois
23.9	Missouri
23.9	Georgia
23.6	Michigan
23.2	Massachusetts
23.1	Mississippi
22.9	Connecticut
21.7	Colorado
20.3	New York
18.0	Nevada
*	Utah
*	Alaska
*	New Mexico
*	Vermont
*	Maine
*	New Hampshire
*	Idaho
*	Wyoming
*	Montana
*	South Dakota
*	North Dakota
*	Hawaii

*Incomplete data

Table G.95. WWNUTRI

Women White Deaths Nutrition (per 100,000) 1994–1996

1.1	New Hampshire
.9	Georgia
.8	Missouri
.8	Colorado
.8	Utah
.8	Wyoming
.7	Louisiana
.7	Delaware
.7	Kansas
.7	Arizona
.7	Alabama
.7	Wisconsin
.7	Oklahoma
.7	Ohio
.7	Michigan
.7	Maine
.6	South Carolina
.6	Minnesota
.6	West Virginia
.6	Texas
.6	Indiana
.6	Tennessee
.6	Arkansas
.6	Virginia
.6	Nevada
.6	New Mexico
.6	Idaho
.6	Montana
.5	Washington
.5	North Carolina
.5	Kentucky
.5	Pennsylvania
.5	Illinois
.5	Mississippi
.5	South Dakota
.5	North Dakota
.4	New Jersey
.4	Maryland
.4	Oregon
.3	Florida
.3	Nebraska
.3	Iowa
.3	Massachusetts
.3	Connecticut
.2	Rhode Island
.2	California
.2	New York
*	Alaska
*	Vermont
*	Hawaii

*Incomplete data

Table G.96. WBNUTRI

Women Black Deaths Nutrition (per 100,000) 1994–1996

1.4	Indiana
1.3	Mississippi
1.2	Georgia
1.2	Louisiana
1.2	Tennessee
1.0	Ohio
1.0	Virginia
.9	Michigan
.9	South Carolina
.9	Texas
.9	North Carolina
.8	Mississippi
.7	Alabama
.6	Pennsylvania
.5	Florida
.4	Illinois
*	New Hampshire
*	Colorado
*	Utah
*	Wyoming
*	Delaware
*	Kansas
*	Arizona
*	Wisconsin
*	Oklahoma
*	Maine
*	Minnesota
*	West Virginia
*	Arkansas
*	Nevada
*	New Mexico
*	Idaho
*	Montana
*	Washington
*	Kentucky
*	South Dakota
*	North Dakota
*	New Jersey
*	Maryland
*	Oregon
*	Nebraska
*	Iowa
*	Massachusetts
*	Connecticut
*	Rhode Island
*	California
*	New York
*	Alaska
*	Vermont
*	Hawaii

*Incomplete data

Table G.97. WWCARDIO

Women White Deaths Cardiovascular (per 100,000) 1994–1996

154.8	West Virginia
150.3	Mississippi
149.5	Oklahoma
144.8	Kentucky
142.1	Tennessee
137.3	Arkansas
137.0	Alabama
136.4	Georgia
136.0	Indiana
135.9	Missouri
134.0	Louisiana
134.0	New York
133.9	Ohio
133.4	Nevada
133.3	South Carolina
130.8	Pennsylvania
129.6	Michigan
125.8	Delaware
125.1	Texas
124.8	Illinois
123.7	North Carolina
121.9	Virginia
118.9	Maine
118.6	Vermont
118.4	New Jersey
117.1	New Hampshire
116.9	California
116.0	Maryland
115.3	Iowa
115.1	Rhode Island
113.5	Kansas
113.3	Nebraska
113.0	Connecticut
111.3	Wisconsin
109.8	Oregon
108.7	Arizona
107.8	Idaho
107.3	Wyoming
107.1	Massachusetts
106.3	New Mexico
106.0	Washington
105.1	Florida
103.5	South Dakota
103.4	Montana
103.2	North Dakota
102.7	Alaska
101.3	Colorado
101.0	Utah
95.0	Minnesota
87.9	Hawaii

Table G.98. WBCARDIO

Women Black Deaths Cardiovascular (per 100,000) 1994–1996

255.2	Mississippi
244.9	Tennessee
243.7	Nebraska
228.9	South Carolina
227.1	Arkansas
225.6	Georgia
223.1	Illinois
221.6	Missouri
216.9	Oklahoma
216.4	Michigan
212.8	Kentucky
212.8	Texas
212.1	Louisiana
209.8	Alabama
209.7	Indiana
207.3	California
205.0	North Carolina
202.6	Virginia
202.0	Ohio
200.8	West Virginia
198.0	Florida
197.9	Iowa
193.0	Pennsylvania
191.1	Delaware
190.8	Kansas
188.9	Wisconsin
184.3	Oregon
183.7	Connecticut
182.8	Nevada
182.7	Rhode Island
179.7	New Jersey
179.6	Maryland
179.4	New York
168.8	Arizona
163.0	Washington
160.9	Utah
160.1	Colorado
153.2	Minnesota
137.8	Massachusetts
135.4	New Mexico
98.9	Alaska
82.3	Hawaii
*	Maine
*	Vermont
*	New Hampshire
*	Idaho
*	Wyoming
*	South Dakota
*	Montana
*	North Dakota

*Incomplete data

Table G.99. WWPNEUMO

Women White Deaths Pneumonia and Influenza (per 100,000) 1994–1996

14.0	California
12.8	Oklahoma
12.6	Mississippi
12.3	Tennessee
12.0	Arkansas
12.0	Georgia
12.0	Missouri
11.7	Utah
11.5	Massachusetts
11.4	North Carolina
11.2	Nevada
10.9	Kentucky
10.8	New York
10.5	Virginia
10.3	Alabama
10.2	Indiana
10.2	Washington
10.2	Wyoming
10.0	Colorado
9.9	Idaho
9.8	Illinois
9.8	Michigan
9.8	Delaware
9.7	South Carolina
9.7	West Virginia
9.7	Iowa
9.7	Maryland
9.6	Ohio
9.6	Arizona
9.4	Kansas
9.3	Louisiana
9.3	Connecticut
9.2	Nebraska
9.2	Texas
9.2	Montana
9.1	Pennsylvania
9.1	New Jersey
9.1	Hawaii
9.0	Wisconsin
8.8	Oregon
8.6	New Mexico
8.5	Vermont
8.4	Maine
8.3	North Dakota
8.1	South Dakota
7.6	Rhode Island
7.5	Minnesota
6.4	Florida
6.1	New Hampshire
5.9	Alaska

Table G.100. WBPNEUMO

Women Black Deaths Pneumonia and Influenza (per 100,000) 1994–1996

16.9	Tennessee
16.6	Nevada
16.2	Nebraska
16.1	California
15.4	Illinois
15.2	New York
14.8	Colorado
14.7	Michigan
14.5	Kentucky
14.2	Georgia
13.8	Pennsylvania
13.8	Minnesota
13.6	Maryland
13.4	New Jersey
13.2	Connecticut
13.0	Missouri
12.9	Oklahoma
12.5	Mississippi
12.3	Virginia
12.1	Indiana
11.9	Massachusetts
11.8	North Carolina
11.5	Florida
11.4	Delaware
11.4	Texas
11.2	Alabama
11.1	Arkansas
11.1	South Carolina
10.7	Arizona
10.4	Ohio
10.1	Kansas
10.0	Louisiana
8.8	Wisconsin
8.0	Washington
6.3	West Virginia
*	Utah
*	Wyoming
*	Idaho
*	Iowa
*	Montana
*	Hawaii
*	Oregon
*	New Mexico
*	Vermont
*	Maine
*	North Dakota
*	South Dakota
*	Rhode Island
*	New Hampshire
*	Alaska

*Incomplete data

Table G.101. WWACCID

Women White Deaths Accidents (per 100,000) 1994–1996

29.4	Mississippi
27.1	Alabama
26.9	Wyoming
26.5	Arkansas
26.4	New Mexico
25.8	Oklahoma
24.4	Idaho
24.0	Tennessee
23.7	South Carolina
22.4	Kentucky
22.4	Georgia
22.0	Missouri
21.8	Nevada
21.6	Louisiana
20.9	Oregon
20.8	Alaska
20.6	Colorado
20.6	Montana
20.4	North Carolina
20.0	Arizona
19.9	Kansas
19.5	Texas
19.1	West Virginia
18.5	Nebraska
18.4	Indiana
18.3	Florida
18.3	Utah
18.2	Delaware
18.0	Iowa
17.3	South Dakota
17.2	Wisconsin
17.0	Washington
16.8	Michigan
16.2	Minnesota
15.8	Pennsylvania
15.8	Vermont
15.8	Maine
15.7	Virginia
15.2	California
15.0	Ohio
14.3	Illinois
14.3	Connecticut
14.1	Maryland
14.1	North Dakota
12.5	New Hampshire
12.3	New York
12.2	New Jersey
10.8	Hawaii
9.3	Rhode Island
8.4	Massachusetts

Table G.102. WBACCID

Women Black Deaths Accidents (per 100,000) 1994–1996

32.3	Mississippi
28.2	Arkansas
26.7	Arizona
25.8	Oklahoma
25.5	Tennessee
24.8	Georgia
24.5	Alabama
24.4	South Carolina
24.2	Delaware
24.2	Washington
23.3	North Carolina
23.1	Missouri
22.9	Illinois
22.6	Pennsylvania
20.9	Michigan
20.7	Virginia
20.5	Indiana
20.4	Texas
19.8	Louisiana
19.5	Kentucky
19.4	California
19.0	Minnesota
18.9	Wisconsin
18.8	Florida
18.5	New Jersey
17.9	Colorado
16.4	Maryland
15.5	Kansas
15.0	Connecticut
14.9	Ohio
14.8	Nevada
13.3	New York
9.1	Massachusetts
*	Wyoming
*	New Mexico
*	Idaho
*	Oregon
*	Alaska
*	Montana
*	West Virginia
*	Nebraska
*	Utah
*	Iowa
*	South Dakota
*	Vermont
*	Maine
*	North Dakota
*	New Hampshire
*	Hawaii
*	Rhode Island

*Incomplete data

Table G.103. WWMOTVEH

Women White Auto Deaths (per 100,000) 1994–1996

21.3	Mississippi
18.4	Wyoming
17.8	Alabama
17.3	Arkansas
16.7	Oklahoma
15.3	South Carolina
15.3	Idaho
14.7	Tennessee
14.6	New Mexico
14.3	Georgia
13.8	Missouri
13.8	Nevada
13.6	Kentucky
13.5	Louisiana
13.3	Montana
12.8	North Carolina
12.8	Kansas
12.4	Texas
12.2	Colorado
12.2	West Virginia
12.2	Nebraska
11.7	Florida
11.7	Oregon
11.6	Delaware
11.6	Utah
11.3	Arizona
11.3	Iowa
11.3	South Dakota
10.8	Michigan
10.7	Indiana
10.1	Wisconsin
9.6	Alaska
9.3	Maine
9.0	Washington
8.8	Minnesota
8.6	Vermont
8.3	Illinois
8.3	California
8.3	Maryland
8.2	Virginia
8.2	Ohio
8.0	North Dakota
7.9	Pennsylvania
7.2	Connecticut
6.5	New Hampshire
6.2	New York
6.1	New Jersey
5.1	Rhode Island
5.0	Hawaii
4.5	Massachusetts

Table G.104. WBMOTVEH

Women Black Auto Deaths (per 100,000) 1994–1996

18.4	Mississippi
16.4	Arkansas
16.1	Oklahoma
13.9	South Carolina
13.7	North Carolina
12.9	Tennessee
12.8	Georgia
12.6	Alabama
10.9	Florida
10.8	Louisiana
10.8	Texas
10.1	Missouri
9.8	Michigan
9.4	Virginia
9.1	Kentucky
8.2	Illinois
8.0	Indiana
7.9	Maryland
7.4	California
6.8	Pennsylvania
6.5	New Jersey
5.8	Connecticut
4.8	Ohio
3.2	New York
*	Wyoming
*	Idaho
*	New Mexico
*	Nevada
*	Montana
*	Kansas
*	Colorado
*	West Virginia
*	Nebraska
*	Oregon
*	Delaware
*	Utah
*	Arizona
*	Iowa
*	South Dakota
*	Wisconsin
*	Alaska
*	Maine
*	Washington
*	Minnesota
*	Vermont
*	North Dakota
*	New Hampshire
*	Rhode Island
*	Hawaii
*	Massachusetts

*Incomplete data

Table G.105. WWFALLS

Women White Death from Falls (per 100,000) 1994–1996

3.1	Minnesota
2.6	New Mexico
2.6	Montana
2.6	Wisconsin
2.5	Wyoming
2.5	Colorado
2.4	Idaho
2.4	Oregon
2.4	Utah
2.4	Vermont
2.3	North Carolina
2.2	Virginia
2.2	Kentucky
2.2	Nebraska
2.2	South Dakota
2.1	Mississippi
2.1	Georgia
2.1	Kansas
2.1	Arizona
2.1	Washington
2.0	Missouri
2.0	Tennessee
2.0	Louisiana
2.0	Delaware
2.0	Iowa
2.0	North Dakota
1.9	Pennsylvania
1.9	South Carolina
1.9	Ohio
1.8	Maryland
1.8	Alabama
1.7	Michigan
1.7	Texas
1.7	Arkansas
1.7	Oklahoma
1.7	Indiana
1.7	Connecticut
1.7	Maine
1.6	New York
1.6	New Hampshire
1.5	Illinois
1.5	Florida
1.5	West Virginia
1.4	New Jersey
1.4	California
1.4	Massachusetts
1.3	Nevada
1.3	Rhode Island
1.1	Hawaii
*	Alaska

*Incomplete data

Table G.106. WBFALLS

Women Black Death from Falls (per 100,000) 1994–1996

1.7	Pennsylvania
1.6	Missouri
1.6	Illinois
1.4	Mississippi
1.4	Georgia
1.4	Michigan
1.3	North Carolina
1.3	Tennessee
1.2	South Carolina
1.2	Ohio
1.1	Maryland
1.1	Texas
1.0	Louisiana
1.0	New York
.9	Virginia
.9	New Jersey
.8	Florida
.8	California
.7	Alabama
*	Minnesota
*	New Mexico
*	Montana
*	Wisconsin
*	Wyoming
*	Colorado
*	Idaho
*	Oregon
*	Utah
*	Vermont
*	Kentucky
*	Nebraska
*	South Dakota
*	Kansas
*	Arizona
*	Washington
*	Delaware
*	Iowa
*	North Dakota
*	Arkansas
*	Oklahoma
*	Indiana
*	Connecticut
*	Maine
*	New Hampshire
*	West Virginia
*	Massachusetts
*	Nevada
*	Rhode Island
*	Hawaii
*	Alaska

*Incomplete data

Table G.107. WWSUICID

Women White Suicides (per 100,000) 1994–1996

9.0	Nevada
7.0	Hawaii
6.7	New Mexico
6.4	Montana
6.3	Colorado
6.3	Arizona
6.2	Louisiana
6.2	Oklahoma
6.0	South Carolina
6.0	Florida
6.0	Alaska
5.9	Utah
5.7	Mississippi
5.7	Oregon
5.5	North Carolina
5.4	Arkansas
5.0	Tennessee
5.0	Virginia
4.9	Georgia
4.9	Alabama
4.9	Wyoming
4.9	Idaho
4.8	California
4.8	Washington
4.8	New Hampshire
4.7	Missouri
4.7	Texas
4.4	West Virginia
4.2	Nebraska
4.2	South Dakota
4.1	Kansas
4.1	Delaware
3.9	North Dakota
3.9	Indiana
3.8	Pennsylvania
3.8	Maryland
3.8	Wisconsin
3.8	Maine
3.7	Vermont
3.6	Kentucky
3.5	Michigan
3.5	Minnesota
3.4	Iowa
3.3	Illinois
3.3	Connecticut
3.2	Ohio
3.1	New Jersey
3.1	Massachusetts
3.0	Rhode Island
2.8	New York

Table G.108. WBSUICID

Women Black Suicides (per 100,000) 1994–1996

3.2	Indiana
2.9	California
2.4	Pennsylvania
2.3	Michigan
2.3	Ohio
2.1	Texas
2.0	South Carolina
2.0	Tennessee
1.9	Louisiana
1.9	Florida
1.9	Alabama
1.9	Maryland
1.6	Mississippi
1.6	North Carolina
1.6	Virginia
1.6	Illinois
1.5	Georgia
1.5	New York
*	Nevada
*	Hawaii
*	New Mexico
*	Montana
*	Colorado
*	Arizona
*	Oklahoma
*	Alaska
*	Utah
*	Oregon
*	Arkansas
*	Wyoming
*	Idaho
*	Washington
*	New Hampshire
*	Missouri
*	West Virginia
*	Nebraska
*	South Dakota
*	Kansas
*	Delaware
*	North Dakota
*	Wisconsin
*	Maine
*	Vermont
*	Kentucky
*	Minnesota
*	Iowa
*	Connecticut
*	New Jersey
*	Massachusetts
*	Rhode Island

*Incomplete data

Table G.109. WWHOMICI

Women White Homicides (per 100,000) 1994–1996

5.4	Oklahoma
4.7	Nevada
4.2	Mississippi
3.9	Arkansas
3.7	New Mexico
3.5	Arizona
3.4	Florida
3.4	West Virginia
3.3	Alabama
3.3	Delaware
3.2	Texas
3.2	Tennessee
3.1	Louisiana
3.0	Kentucky
2.9	South Carolina
2.9	North Carolina
2.8	California
2.8	Montana
2.7	Oregon
2.7	Washington
2.6	Indiana
2.6	Georgia
2.5	Virginia
2.5	Colorado
2.5	Missouri
2.3	Maryland
2.3	Illinois
2.3	Idaho
2.2	New York
2.2	Kansas
2.0	Utah
1.9	Michigan
1.7	Pennsylvania
1.7	Iowa
1.6	Ohio
1.6	Wisconsin
1.6	Maine
1.5	Nebraska
1.5	Minnesota
1.5	New Jersey
1.4	Connecticut
1.4	Massachusetts
*	Hawaii
*	Alaska
*	Wyoming
*	New Hampshire
*	South Dakota
*	North Dakota
*	Vermont
*	Rhode Island

*Incomplete data

Table G.110. WBHOMIC

Women Black Homicides (per 100,000) 1994–1996

17.7	Indiana
15.4	Michigan
15.1	Illinois
14.4	Missouri
12.9	Louisiana
12.8	Wisconsin
12.7	Arkansas
12.6	Oklahoma
11.2	Mississippi
11.2	California
10.9	Alabama
10.5	Pennsylvania
9.8	Virginia
9.5	Tennessee
9.5	Maryland
9.2	Georgia
8.8	North Carolina
8.8	Ohio
8.6	Texas
8.4	Florida
8.3	Kentucky
8.3	South Carolina
8.2	Connecticut
6.9	New York
6.8	New Jersey
5.5	Massachusetts
*	Nevada
*	New Mexico
*	Arizona
*	West Virginia
*	Delaware
*	Montana
*	Oregon
*	Washington
*	Colorado
*	Idaho
*	Kansas
*	Utah
*	Iowa
*	Maine
*	Nebraska
*	Minnesota
*	Hawaii
*	Alaska
*	Wyoming
*	New Hampshire
*	South Dakota
*	North Dakota
*	Vermont
*	Rhode Island

*Incomplete data

Table G.111. WWDRUGIN

Women White Drug Deaths (per 100,000) 1994–1996

7.0	New Mexico
6.0	Nevada
5.3	Hawaii
4.9	Utah
4.6	California
4.5	Arizona
4.5	Oregon
4.3	Washington
4.2	Alaska
4.0	Colorado
3.8	New Jersey
3.7	Oklahoma
3.5	Pennsylvania
3.5	Massachusetts
3.5	Delaware
3.4	Maryland
3.4	Florida
3.3	South Carolina
3.2	Tennessee
3.2	Texas
3.1	Rhode Island
3.0	Louisiana
3.0	Connecticut
2.9	Idaho
2.8	Georgia
2.7	Michigan
2.6	North Carolina
2.5	Missouri
2.5	Arkansas
2.5	Kentucky
2.5	New York
2.3	Alabama
2.3	Montana
2.3	New Hampshire
2.2	Wisconsin
2.2	Virginia
2.1	Indiana
2.1	Nebraska
1.8	Illinois
1.8	Mississippi
1.7	Ohio
1.7	West Virginia
1.7	Iowa
1.7	South Dakota
1.6	Maine
1.6	Minnesota
1.6	Vermont
1.4	Kansas
*	Wyoming
*	North Dakota

*Incomplete data

Table G.112. WBDRUGIN

Women Black Drug Deaths (per 100,000) 1994–1996

10.3	Washington
8.6	New Jersey
8.5	California
7.9	Michigan
6.8	Pennsylvania
6.5	Maryland
6.3	Illinois
5.5	New York
4.8	Massachusetts
3.8	Indiana
3.3	Texas
3.2	Missouri
3.1	Ohio
3.0	Georgia
2.6	Louisiana
2.4	Tennessee
2.3	Florida
2.2	North Carolina
2.2	Virginia
1.8	Alabama
1.3	South Carolina
*	New Mexico
*	Nevada
*	Hawaii
*	Utah
*	Arizona
*	Oregon
*	Alaska
*	Colorado
*	Oklahoma
*	Delaware
*	Rhode Island
*	Connecticut
*	Idaho
*	Arkansas
*	Kentucky
*	Montana
*	New Hampshire
*	Wisconsin
*	Nebraska
*	Mississippi
*	West Virginia
*	Iowa
*	South Dakota
*	Maine
*	Minnesota
*	Vermont
*	Kansas
*	Wyoming
*	North Dakota

*Incomplete data

Table G.113. WWALCOHO

Women White Alcohol Deaths (per 100,000) 1994–1996

2.6	New Mexico
2.1	Nevada
1.8	Colorado
1.6	Utah
1.6	Oregon
1.5	California
1.5	South Carolina
1.4	Florida
1.3	Wisconsin
1.2	Maine
1.2	Minnesota
1.1	Washington
1.1	Georgia
1.1	Arizona
1.1	New Hampshire
1.0	Missouri
1.0	North Carolina
.9	New Jersey
.9	Michigan
.9	New York
.9	Massachusetts
.9	Oklahoma
.9	Iowa
.8	Illinois
.8	Louisiana
.8	West Virginia
.7	Texas
.7	Virginia
.7	Kentucky
.7	Mississippi
.7	Kansas
.6	Maryland
.6	Indiana
.6	Tennessee
.6	Alabama
.6	Connecticut
.6	Arkansas
.5	Ohio
.4	Pennsylvania
*	Hawaii
*	Alaska
*	Delaware
*	Rhode Island
*	Idaho
*	Montana
*	Nebraska
*	South Dakota
*	Vermont
*	Wyoming
*	North Dakota

*Incomplete data

Table G.114. WBALCOHO

Women Black Alcohol Deaths (per 100,000) 1994–1996

3.9	North Carolina
3.4	Georgia
3.3	South Carolina
2.9	Missouri
2.9	Indiana
2.6	New York
2.1	California
2.1	Alabama
2.0	Florida
1.7	Maryland
1.7	Tennessee
1.6	New Jersey
1.6	Ohio
1.5	Michigan
1.5	Illinois
1.5	Virginia
.9	Louisiana
.7	Texas
*	New Mexico
*	Nevada
*	Colorado
*	Utah
*	Oregon
*	Wisconsin
*	Maine
*	Minnesota
*	Washington
*	Arizona
*	New Hampshire
*	Massachusetts
*	Oklahoma
*	Iowa
*	West Virginia
*	Kentucky
*	Mississippi
*	Kansas
*	Connecticut
*	Arkansas
*	Pennsylvania
*	Hawaii
*	Alaska
*	Delaware
*	Rhode Island
*	Idaho
*	Montana
*	Nebraska
*	South Dakota
*	Vermont
*	Wyoming
*	North Dakota

*Incomplete data

Table G.115. MWALLDEA

Men White All Deaths (per 100,000) 1994–1996

709.9	Mississippi
700.3	Kentucky
699.6	West Virginia
687.4	Arkansas
685.7	Tennessee
684.6	Alabama
683.7	Oklahoma
675.5	Nevada
668.2	Louisiana
653.1	South Carolina
644.0	Georgia
633.0	Missouri
623.9	North Carolina
621.6	Indiana
611.8	Texas
610.9	Ohio
605.5	Pennsylvania
597.3	Delaware
595.3	Maine
592.8	New York
589.0	Arizona
588.4	Illinois
588.2	New Mexico
580.9	Florida
580.2	Virginia
577.0	Wyoming
572.6	Vermont
571.1	Michigan
569.1	Rhode Island
568.7	Kansas
568.5	Oregon
566.0	Maryland
564.2	New Jersey
561.9	Montana
560.8	California
559.3	New Hampshire
553.0	Massachusetts
550.5	Nebraska
545.8	Iowa
544.9	Wisconsin
541.9	South Dakota
540.4	Idaho
536.1	Washington
533.0	Connecticut
530.8	Colorado
530.2	Alaska
523.7	North Dakota
514.2	Minnesota
494.5	Utah
460.2	Hawaii

Table G.116. MBALLDEA

Men Black All Deaths (per 100,000) 1994–1996

1,105.0	Illinois
1,096.2	Tennessee
1,084.1	Pennsylvania
1,062.0	Arkansas
1,050.1	Mississippi
1,045.3	South Carolina
1,042.6	Louisiana
1,039.6	Alabama
1,030.0	Missouri
1,028.8	North Carolina
1,023.0	Georgia
990.2	Maryland
980.4	Michigan
979.7	West Virginia
971.5	Nebraska
966.3	Indiana
963.0	New Jersey
953.0	Kentucky
941.3	Wisconsin
941.0	Delaware
936.6	Virginia
936.5	Iowa
931.9	Ohio
922.5	Kansas
913.4	Florida
899.8	Texas
890.5	Oklahoma
879.4	Oregon
865.7	Connecticut
864.8	California
849.2	Minnesota
842.4	New York
838.7	Rhode Island
820.1	Nevada
787.0	Utah
782.9	Arizona
776.6	Massachusetts
754.8	Montana
742.4	Washington
680.7	Colorado
609.7	New Hampshire
594.7	Alaska
577.0	Maine
572.5	South Dakota
553.7	New Mexico
540.1	Wyoming
454.2	Idaho
404.4	Hawaii
*	Vermont
*	North Dakota

*Incomplete data

Table G.117. MWMALIG

Men White Death Malignancies (per 100,000) 1994–1996

183.1	Kentucky
171.2	Arkansas
170.4	Tennessee
170.2	West Virginia
169.3	Louisiana
167.8	Mississippi
166.3	Alabama
165.4	Maine
163.7	Delaware
162.4	Rhode Island
160.8	Oklahoma
159.8	Indiana
158.8	New Hampshire
157.5	Ohio
157.4	Missouri
156.6	Georgia
156.4	North Carolina
156.3	South Carolina
155.8	Massachusetts
155.8	Vermont
155.6	Pennsylvania
154.8	Nevada
151.8	Illinois
151.7	Maryland
151.2	New Jersey
150.3	Florida
150.1	Virginia
148.0	Texas
147.5	Michigan
146.9	New York
143.0	Oregon
142.4	Wisconsin
142.1	Kansas
141.2	South Dakota
140.7	Iowa
139.0	Connecticut
138.7	Nebraska
137.6	Washington
137.6	Wyoming
137.1	Arizona
136.6	Minnesota
134.9	North Dakota
133.7	Montana
133.3	California
131.7	Idaho
129.4	Alaska
126.7	New Mexico
122.4	Colorado
110.5	Hawaii
102.1	Utah

Table G.118. MBMALIG

Men Black Death Malignancies (per 100,000) 1994–1996

256.2	Tennessee
253.6	Delaware
250.8	Kentucky
250.4	Louisiana
249.1	Illinois
248.1	Pennsylvania
243.9	Wisconsin
241.2	Arkansas
240.7	Mississippi
240.4	North Carolina
239.9	South Carolina
235.5	Virginia
234.4	Alabama
234.3	Missouri
232.6	West Virginia
229.8	Maryland
229.8	Texas
229.4	Georgia
229.4	Minnesota
229.0	Ohio
217.3	New Jersey
217.1	Kansas
216.6	Indiana
209.9	Nebraska
208.8	Michigan
207.9	Iowa
202.9	Oklahoma
201.3	Florida
198.8	Connecticut
197.3	Massachusetts
196.1	Utah
191.4	Oregon
189.9	California
189.0	Rhode Island
182.4	Arizona
175.3	New York
173.4	Washington
164.0	Nevada
153.6	Alaska
147.9	Colorado
100.7	New Mexico
97.9	Hawaii
*	Maine
*	New Hampshire
*	Vermont
*	South Dakota
*	Wyoming
*	North Dakota
*	Montana
*	Idaho

*Incomplete data

Table G.119. MWDIABET

Men White Deaths Diabetes (per 100,000) 1994–1996

18.1	Louisiana
17.8	West Virginia
17.2	Texas
17.2	Ohio
17.1	New Hampshire
16.7	Vermont
16.6	New Jersey
16.3	Utah
15.8	Maryland
15.4	Rhode Island
15.4	New Mexico
14.7	Kentucky
14.7	Pennsylvania
14.5	Indiana
14.5	Maine
14.3	Michigan
14.1	Alaska
13.6	Massachusetts
13.5	Illinois
13.3	Washington
13.2	North Carolina
13.2	Minnesota
13.1	Delaware
13.0	South Carolina
13.0	Oregon
13.0	North Dakota
12.9	Tennessee
12.8	Missouri
12.6	Florida
12.5	Wisconsin
12.5	Idaho
12.4	Oklahoma
12.3	Alabama
12.1	Kansas
12.1	California
11.8	South Dakota
11.5	Arkansas
11.4	Arizona
11.3	Nevada
11.1	Iowa
11.1	Wyoming
11.0	Georgia
11.0	New York
10.8	Virginia
10.8	Montana
10.6	Connecticut
10.1	Nebraska
9.9	Colorado
9.4	Mississippi
6.7	Hawaii

Table G.120. MBDIABET

Men Black Deaths Diabetes (per 100,000) 1994–1996

59.0	West Virginia
46.2	Rhode Island
43.0	Louisiana
41.5	Iowa
38.5	New Jersey
37.8	Minnesota
37.1	Indiana
34.5	Kentucky
34.1	Maryland
33.6	Delaware
33.2	Ohio
32.4	North Carolina
31.9	South Carolina
31.1	Nebraska
30.7	Washington
30.3	Arkansas
29.6	Pennsylvania
29.2	Texas
28.8	Alabama
28.6	Illinois
28.4	Wisconsin
27.1	Florida
26.4	Arizona
26.2	California
25.9	Virginia
25.7	Missouri
25.1	Michigan
25.1	Massachusetts
24.8	Tennessee
24.6	Oklahoma
23.7	Kansas
23.7	Connecticut
22.7	Georgia
21.9	New York
21.7	Nevada
21.5	Mississippi
15.2	Colorado
*	New Hampshire
*	Vermont
*	Utah
*	New Mexico
*	Maine
*	Alaska
*	Oregon
*	North Dakota
*	Idaho
*	South Dakota
*	Wyoming
*	Montana
*	Hawaii

*Incomplete data

Table G.121. MWNUTRI

Men White Deaths Nutrition (per 100,000) 1994–1996

.9	New Hampshire
.8	Missouri
.7	Arizona
.7	Colorado
.7	Louisiana
.7	Ohio
.7	Oklahoma
.7	South Carolina
.7	Tennessee
.7	West Virginia
.6	Alabama
.6	Arkansas
.6	Georgia
.6	Indiana
.6	Kansas
.6	Kentucky
.6	Nevada
.6	North Carolina
.6	Texas
.6	Utah
.5	Nebraska
.5	New Mexico
.5	Pennsylvania
.5	Virginia
.5	Wisconsin
.4	Illinois
.4	Maryland
.4	Massachusetts
.4	Michigan
.4	Minnesota
.4	New Jersey
.4	Oregon
.3	Connecticut
.3	Florida
.3	Iowa
.3	Washington
.2	New York
.1	California
*	Alaska
*	Delaware
*	Hawaii
*	Idaho
*	Maine
*	Mississippi
*	Montana
*	North Dakota
*	Rhode Island
*	South Dakota
*	Vermont
*	Wyoming

*Incomplete data

Table G.122. MBNUTRI

Men Black Deaths Nutrition (per 100,000) 1994–1996

2.2	Louisiana
1.8	South Carolina
1.8	Mississippi
1.6	Georgia
1.2	Alabama
1.2	Texas
1.1	Pennsylvania
1.0	Ohio
1.0	North Carolina
1.0	Illinois
1.0	Florida
.9	Virginia
*	New Hampshire
*	Missouri
*	Arizona
*	Colorado
*	Oklahoma
*	Tennessee
*	West Virginia
*	Arkansas
*	Indiana
*	Kansas
*	Kentucky
*	Nevada
*	Utah
*	Nebraska
*	New Mexico
*	Wisconsin
*	Maryland
*	Massachusetts
*	Michigan
*	Minnesota
*	New Jersey
*	Oregon
*	Connecticut
*	Iowa
*	Washington
*	New York
*	California
*	Alaska
*	Delaware
*	Hawaii
*	Idaho
*	Maine
*	Montana
*	North Dakota
*	Rhode Island
*	South Dakota
*	Vermont
*	Wyoming

*Incomplete data

Table G.123. MWCARDIO

Men White Deaths Cardiovascular (per 100,000) 1994–1996

272.3	Mississippi
258.2	West Virginia
256.5	Oklahoma
256.4	Kentucky
251.1	Tennessee
245.5	South Carolina
244.9	Alabama
243.3	Arkansas
236.4	Louisiana
234.3	Georgia
234.0	Missouri
232.8	Nevada
231.6	Indiana
230.1	Ohio
227.6	North Carolina
226.8	New York
225.6	Pennsylvania
219.8	Illinois
218.5	Michigan
215.6	Texas
212.3	Delaware
210.3	Maine
209.4	Virginia
207.6	Rhode Island
206.7	Iowa
206.2	New Jersey
205.9	North Dakota
204.4	Wisconsin
204.3	South Dakota
202.3	Vermont
202.1	New Hampshire
202.1	Nebraska
199.9	Kansas
198.8	Maryland
195.3	Florida
194.6	Connecticut
192.0	California
189.8	Massachusetts
188.4	Arizona
185.6	Oregon
184.0	Wyoming
183.0	Montana
181.4	Washington
179.5	Minnesota
178.3	Idaho
172.6	New Mexico
163.8	Alaska
163.6	Colorado
158.7	Utah
154.4	Hawaii

Table G.124. MBCARDIO

Men Black Deaths Cardiovascular (per 100,000) 1994–1996

400.1	Mississippi
388.0	Tennessee
365.0	Arkansas
363.4	South Carolina
351.2	Alabama
348.3	Illinois
345.1	Georgia
343.6	North Carolina
339.6	Missouri
338.3	Oklahoma
332.5	Michigan
331.0	Iowa
329.4	Nebraska
328.2	Kentucky
323.3	Louisiana
321.1	Texas
319.8	Pennsylvania
316.1	Virginia
311.3	Ohio
309.2	West Virginia
308.8	Indiana
292.8	California
291.2	Kansas
288.8	Wisconsin
282.8	Delaware
282.0	Nevada
280.0	Maryland
279.0	Florida
266.1	New York
262.6	New Jersey
262.6	Oregon
257.4	Connecticut
251.6	Rhode Island
227.9	Washington
226.4	Arizona
218.2	Massachusetts
209.4	Minnesota
204.4	New Hampshire
201.3	Colorado
196.9	New Mexico
175.7	Utah
146.3	Alaska
139.6	Hawaii
*	Maine
*	North Dakota
*	South Dakota
*	Vermont
*	Wyoming
*	Montana
*	Idaho

*Incomplete data

Table G.125. MWPNEUMO

Men White Deaths Pneumonia and Influenza (per 100,000) 1994–1996

19.9	Mississippi
19.4	California
19.1	Oklahoma
18.6	Massachusetts
18.5	Arkansas
18.4	Georgia
18.3	North Carolina
18.3	Kentucky
18.0	Tennessee
17.4	Missouri
17.3	Nevada
16.9	New York
16.8	Virginia
16.6	South Carolina
16.5	West Virginia
16.2	Alabama
16.1	Illinois
15.7	Iowa
15.7	Utah
15.6	Michigan
15.4	Indiana
15.1	Maryland
15.0	Connecticut
14.9	Pennsylvania
14.9	Delaware
14.7	Ohio
14.7	Wisconsin
14.6	South Dakota
14.5	Kansas
14.4	Arizona
14.2	Colorado
14.2	New Mexico
14.1	Washington
14.0	New Jersey
14.0	Vermont
13.9	Nebraska
13.8	Louisiana
13.5	Rhode Island
13.5	Montana
13.4	Wyoming
13.2	Texas
13.2	Idaho
13.0	Maine
12.4	Oregon
12.4	Hawaii
12.4	North Dakota
12.3	Minnesota
10.4	Florida
9.3	New Hampshire
7.4	Alaska

Table G.126. MBPNEUMO

Men Black Deaths Pneumonia and Influenza (per 100,000) 1994–1996

31.9	Illinois
30.9	Tennessee
29.7	Georgia
27.9	North Carolina
27.9	Michigan
26.8	Missouri
25.4	New York
25.2	Mississippi
25.1	Maryland
24.6	Delaware
24.4	West Virginia
24.1	Arizona
23.8	South Carolina
23.8	Pennsylvania
23.7	California
23.4	Oklahoma
23.3	New Jersey
22.6	Connecticut
22.0	Alabama
21.8	Florida
21.7	Virginia
21.4	Massachusetts
21.4	Kentucky
21.4	Wisconsin
20.1	Arkansas
19.8	Texas
19.5	Ohio
18.7	Louisiana
18.1	Indiana
17.6	Kansas
16.6	Washington
14.1	Nevada
13.7	Colorado
*	Iowa
*	Utah
*	South Dakota
*	New Mexico
*	Vermont
*	Nebraska
*	Rhode Island
*	Montana
*	Wyoming
*	Idaho
*	Maine
*	Oregon
*	Hawaii
*	North Dakota
*	Minnesota
*	New Hampshire
*	Alaska

*Incomplete data

Table G.127. MWACCID

Men White Deaths Accidents (per 100,000) 1994–1996

70.0	New Mexico
67.2	Mississippi
65.5	Alabama
64.8	Alaska
63.5	Wyoming
60.3	Arkansas
60.1	Tennessee
57.4	Oklahoma
55.7	Idaho
55.4	Kentucky
55.4	Louisiana
53.7	Arizona
52.9	Montana
52.2	West Virginia
51.7	South Carolina
51.6	Missouri
49.9	Georgia
49.2	Nevada
49.1	Oregon
47.9	Texas
46.9	North Carolina
46.6	Florida
46.3	Colorado
44.4	Kansas
42.8	Delaware
42.8	Indiana
42.8	South Dakota
41.3	Pennsylvania
41.1	Iowa
40.9	Washington
40.8	Utah
40.3	Nebraska
39.4	California
38.5	Vermont
38.1	Virginia
38.1	Wisconsin
36.4	North Dakota
36.3	Minnesota
36.1	Illinois
36.0	Maine
35.6	Michigan
35.0	Connecticut
34.8	Hawaii
34.7	Ohio
32.9	New York
32.8	New Jersey
30.6	Maryland
29.4	New Hampshire
24.1	Rhode Island
21.5	Massachusetts

Table G.128. MBACCID

Men Black Deaths Accident (per 100,000) 1994–1996

91.6	Mississippi
81.1	South Carolina
80.6	Arkansas
77.8	Alabama
68.5	Pennsylvania
68.2	North Carolina
68.1	Oregon
66.4	Tennessee
65.0	Louisiana
63.8	Iowa
63.3	Illinois
62.4	Georgia
56.3	Connecticut
56.2	Missouri
55.7	Kentucky
55.7	Virginia
55.6	Arizona
54.2	Florida
53.6	New Jersey
51.9	Oklahoma
50.8	West Virginia
50.8	Michigan
50.6	Indiana
50.4	Delaware
48.6	Texas
48.6	California
48.5	Wisconsin
48.3	Kansas
48.3	Washington
48.1	Nevada
47.1	Minnesota
43.5	Colorado
40.3	New York
39.2	Ohio
39.0	Maryland
34.7	Nebraska
23.1	Massachusetts
*	New Mexico
*	Alaska
*	Wyoming
*	Idaho
*	Montana
*	South Dakota
*	Utah
*	Vermont
*	North Dakota
*	Maine
*	Hawaii
*	New Hampshire
*	Rhode Island

*Incomplete data

Table G.129. MWMOTVEH

Men White Auto Deaths (per 100,000) 1994–1996

41.4	Mississippi
39.9	Alabama
37.0	Arkansas
34.9	Tennessee
32.9	Wyoming
32.3	Oklahoma
31.9	New Mexico
30.0	South Carolina
29.9	Kentucky
29.8	Louisiana
29.6	Missouri
29.1	Georgia
28.8	West Virginia
28.5	Montana
27.5	Idaho
27.2	Nevada
27.0	Texas
26.8	Florida
26.1	North Carolina
25.7	Arizona
25.7	Kansas
23.6	South Dakota
23.5	Iowa
23.4	Indiana
23.2	Oregon
23.1	Colorado
22.6	Delaware
22.5	Nebraska
21.9	Utah
20.6	Michigan
20.3	Vermont
20.0	Alaska
19.8	Wisconsin
19.0	Maine
18.6	Pennsylvania
18.5	Illinois
18.4	California
18.1	Virginia
18.1	Washington
18.1	Ohio
17.9	North Dakota
17.4	Minnesota
17.3	Maryland
16.2	New Hampshire
14.3	New York
14.2	Connecticut
13.6	New Jersey
13.5	Hawaii
11.7	Rhode Island
10.9	Massachusetts

Table G.130. MBMOTVEH

Men Black Auto Deaths (per 100,000) 1994–1996

53.2	Mississippi
41.5	South Carolina
40.2	Arkansas
40.1	Alabama
35.3	North Carolina
32.9	Georgia
32.5	Louisiana
30.9	Tennessee
28.4	Florida
27.6	Nevada
25.4	Kentucky
25.4	Michigan
25.3	Texas
25.1	Oklahoma
24.1	Arizona
23.6	Kansas
23.5	Virginia
23.3	Missouri
22.8	Illinois
22.1	Indiana
20.5	Delaware
20.4	Maryland
19.2	Connecticut
19.1	California
18.9	Colorado
18.3	Pennsylvania
17.9	New Jersey
15.4	Wisconsin
15.1	Ohio
14.1	Washington
12.5	Massachusetts
11.8	New York
*	Wyoming
*	New Mexico
*	West Virginia
*	Montana
*	Idaho
*	South Dakota
*	Iowa
*	Oregon
*	Nebraska
*	Utah
*	Vermont
*	Alaska
*	Maine
*	North Dakota
*	Minnesota
*	New Hampshire
*	Hawaii
*	Rhode Island

*Incomplete data

Table G.131. MWFALLS

Men White Death from Falls (per 100,000) 1994–1996

5.7	Minnesota
5.3	Wyoming
5.2	New Mexico
5.1	Colorado
5.0	Wisconsin
5.0	Montana
4.7	Iowa
4.6	Nebraska
4.6	Utah
4.5	Idaho
4.5	South Dakota
4.4	Mississippi
4.4	Georgia
4.4	Missouri
4.4	West Virginia
4.2	Tennessee
4.1	Oklahoma
4.1	Vermont
4.0	Kansas
4.0	Virginia
4.0	Oregon
4.0	Maine
3.9	North Carolina
3.9	Louisiana
3.9	Kentucky
3.9	Arizona
3.9	Washington
3.8	Pennsylvania
3.7	Nevada
3.7	Illinois
3.7	Connecticut
3.7	North Dakota
3.7	Rhode Island
3.6	Alabama
3.6	Texas
3.6	New York
3.5	South Carolina
3.5	Arkansas
3.5	Indiana
3.5	Maryland
3.4	Michigan
3.4	Ohio
3.3	New Hampshire
3.2	Florida
3.2	Massachusetts
3.1	California
2.9	New Jersey
2.5	Delaware
2.3	Hawaii
*	Alaska

*Incomplete data

Table G.132. MBFALLS

Black Death from Falls (per 100,000) 1994–1996

5.0	Pennsylvania
5.0	Illinois
4.8	Missouri
4.7	Michigan
4.3	North Carolina
4.0	New York
3.8	Mississippi
3.8	Georgia
3.7	Tennessee
3.6	Louisiana
3.6	South Carolina
3.5	New Jersey
3.3	Maryland
2.8	Ohio
2.7	Alabama
2.7	Florida
2.7	California
2.6	Virginia
2.5	Texas
*	Minnesota
*	Wyoming
*	New Mexico
*	Colorado
*	Wisconsin
*	Montana
*	Iowa
*	Nebraska
*	Utah
*	Idaho
*	South Dakota
*	West Virginia
*	Oklahoma
*	Vermont
*	Kansas
*	Oregon
*	Maine
*	Kentucky
*	Arizona
*	Washington
*	Nevada
*	Connecticut
*	North Dakota
*	Rhode Island
*	Arkansas
*	Indiana
*	New Hampshire
*	Massachusetts
*	Delaware
*	Hawaii
*	Alaska

*Incomplete data

Table G.133. MWSUICID

Men White Suicides (per 100,000) 1994–1996

36.3	Nevada
33.4	Montana
29.6	Wyoming
29.5	New Mexico
27.2	Colorado
26.8	Arizona
25.7	Idaho
24.9	Oklahoma
24.9	Alaska
24.4	Utah
24.4	Oregon
24.0	Arkansas
23.6	West Virginia
23.4	Mississippi
22.9	Florida
22.4	Missouri
22.4	South Dakota
22.3	Louisiana
21.6	Tennessee
21.4	South Carolina
21.4	Washington
21.1	Georgia
20.9	Alabama
20.8	North Carolina
20.5	Kentucky
20.3	Indiana
20.2	Virginia
20.2	Delaware
20.0	North Dakota
19.9	Kansas
19.6	Texas
19.4	Pennsylvania
19.3	Maine
18.9	Vermont
18.8	Iowa
18.6	Wisconsin
18.5	Hawaii
18.3	New Hampshire
17.8	Maryland
17.7	California
17.6	Nebraska
17.2	Michigan
16.8	Minnesota
15.6	Ohio
14.1	Illinois
14.1	Connecticut
13.1	Rhode Island
12.8	New York
12.7	Massachusetts
11.5	New Jersey

Table G.134. MBSUICID

Men Black Suicides (per 100,000) 1994–1996

24.8	Nevada
19.1	Washington
17.3	Arizona
15.3	Missouri
15.0	Colorado
14.6	Tennessee
14.5	Pennsylvania
14.0	Michigan
13.9	Arkansas
13.8	Indiana
13.2	Ohio
12.9	Louisiana
12.9	Alabama
12.6	Illinois
12.4	Georgia
12.3	South Carolina
12.3	Wisconsin
12.2	North Carolina
12.1	Kentucky
11.6	Virginia
11.4	California
11.3	Oklahoma
11.3	Connecticut
11.2	Maryland
10.8	Florida
10.4	Mississippi
10.2	Texas
9.7	Massachusetts
8.7	New Jersey
8.0	New York
*	Montana
*	Wyoming
*	New Mexico
*	Idaho
*	Alaska
*	Utah
*	Oregon
*	West Virginia
*	South Dakota
*	Delaware
*	North Dakota
*	Kansas
*	Maine
*	Vermont
*	Iowa
*	Hawaii
*	New Hampshire
*	Nebraska
*	Minnesota
*	Rhode Island

*Incomplete data

Table G.135. MWHOMICI

Men White Homicides (per 100,000) 1994–1996

16.7	Arizona
15.6	New Mexico
15.0	Nevada
14.7	California
11.3	Oklahoma
10.7	Mississippi
10.7	Texas
8.9	Arkansas
8.7	Tennessee
8.5	Florida
8.3	Louisiana
8.1	Alabama
7.8	Alaska
7.7	South Carolina
7.6	North Carolina
7.5	New York
7.0	Illinois
6.8	Colorado
6.8	West Virginia
6.7	Kentucky
6.4	Georgia
5.7	Montana
5.7	Hawaii
5.6	Missouri
5.6	Oregon
5.5	Washington
5.4	Kansas
5.2	Idaho
5.0	Virginia
4.7	Wyoming
4.6	Indiana
4.5	Maryland
4.5	Delaware
4.4	Utah
4.3	Pennsylvania
4.3	Connecticut
4.0	Michigan
3.8	New Jersey
3.6	Nebraska
3.3	Rhode Island
3.1	Ohio
3.1	Massachusetts
3.0	Wisconsin
2.8	Minnesota
2.5	Iowa
2.4	Maine
2.4	New Hampshire
*	South Dakota
*	North Dakota
*	Vermont

*Incomplete data

Table G.136. MBHOMICI

Men Black Homicides (per 100,000)
1994–1996

89.4	Indiana
83.8	Illinois
82.3	Missouri
77.7	Louisiana
77.6	Michigan
75.1	Pennsylvania
73.2	Kansas
69.0	Wisconsin
67.7	Minnesota
65.3	Maryland
63.9	Arkansas
62.4	Tennessee
61.4	California
59.4	Nevada
56.1	Nebraska
55.8	Alabama
53.2	New Mexico
51.6	Arizona
51.2	Oregon
50.2	Oklahoma
46.5	Mississippi
45.0	Connecticut
42.6	Florida
40.9	Kentucky
40.4	New York
40.3	Ohio
39.7	Virginia
39.5	North Carolina
37.3	Georgia
36.9	Colorado
36.9	Washington
36.5	West Virginia
35.5	Texas
33.9	New Jersey
33.8	Massachusetts
31.9	South Carolina
23.6	Delaware
*	Alaska
*	Montana
*	Hawaii
*	Idaho
*	Wyoming
*	Utah
*	Rhode Island
*	Iowa
*	Maine
*	New Hampshire
*	South Dakota
*	North Dakota
*	Vermont

*Incomplete data

Table G.137. MWDRUGIN

Men White Drug Deaths (per 100,000)
1994–1996

18.7	New Mexico
16.0	Hawaii
12.9	Nevada
12.8	Arizona
12.6	New Jersey
11.4	California
11.2	Pennsylvania
11.2	Utah
11.0	Maryland
11.0	Oregon
10.4	Washington
10.0	Delaware
9.9	Massachusetts
9.8	Connecticut
8.7	New York
8.6	Rhode Island
7.5	Alaska
7.2	Florida
7.2	Colorado
6.6	Texas
5.4	New Hampshire
5.3	Louisiana
5.2	Oklahoma
4.9	Tennessee
4.8	Michigan
4.7	Idaho
4.6	Missouri
4.3	Illinois
4.3	Virginia
4.3	South Carolina
4.2	Kentucky
4.2	Maine
3.9	Arkansas
3.9	West Virginia
3.9	Montana
3.9	Vermont
3.8	North Carolina
3.7	Mississippi
3.5	Ohio
3.5	Georgia
3.3	Wyoming
3.1	Indiana
2.8	Wisconsin
2.7	Kansas
2.7	Alabama
2.3	Iowa
2.3	South Dakota
2.2	Minnesota
1.9	Nebraska
*	North Dakota

*Incomplete data

Table G.138. MBDRUGIN

Men Black Drug Deaths (per 100,000)
1994–1996

36.2	Oregon
28.2	Pennsylvania
27.9	New Jersey
27.4	Maryland
21.8	Washington
19.5	California
19.4	Connecticut
19.1	Illinois
17.9	New York
16.7	Nevada
16.3	Michigan
14.3	Minnesota
13.6	Massachusetts
13.5	Arizona
13.4	Wisconsin
13.0	Delaware
13.0	Colorado
11.2	Missouri
9.4	Ohio
8.9	Indiana
8.7	Tennessee
6.8	Virginia
6.6	Texas
6.3	Florida
6.1	Louisiana
5.8	North Carolina
5.7	Georgia
5.3	Arkansas
4.6	South Carolina
4.6	Alabama
2.4	Mississippi
*	New Mexico
*	Hawaii
*	Utah
*	Rhode Island
*	Alaska
*	New Hampshire
*	Oklahoma
*	Idaho
*	Kentucky
*	Maine
*	West Virginia
*	Montana
*	Vermont
*	Wyoming
*	Kansas
*	Iowa
*	South Dakota
*	Nebraska
*	North Dakota

*Incomplete data

Table G.139. MWALCOHO

Men White Alcohol Deaths (per 100,000) 1994–1996

8.6	New Mexico
6.9	Alaska
6.3	Nevada
5.8	Oregon
5.8	Wyoming
5.4	California
5.4	Arizona
5.3	Colorado
5.3	North Carolina
5.0	Maine
4.8	Utah
4.6	Minnesota
4.6	West Virginia
4.5	South Carolina
4.4	Wisconsin
4.4	Tennessee
4.4	Georgia
4.3	Washington
4.3	New York
4.3	Florida
4.0	Kentucky
3.8	Oklahoma
3.8	Idaho
3.7	Massachusetts
3.7	Missouri
3.7	Rhode Island
3.7	Montana
3.6	South Dakota
3.5	Michigan
3.5	North Dakota
3.4	Illinois
3.3	New Jersey
3.3	Delaware
3.3	Indiana
3.3	New Hampshire
3.2	Louisiana
3.2	Mississippi
3.2	Kansas
3.1	Virginia
3.1	Texas
3.1	Hawaii
3.0	Maryland
3.0	Vermont
3.0	Iowa
2.9	Connecticut
2.9	Alabama
2.7	Arkansas
2.6	Nebraska
2.5	Ohio
1.9	Pennsylvania

Table G.140. MBALCOHO

Men Black Alcohol Deaths (per 100,000) 1994–1996

19.0	North Carolina
17.9	Minnesota
17.4	Georgia
16.5	Missouri
15.1	South Carolina
14.4	Indiana
13.3	Wisconsin
11.7	New York
11.6	Alabama
10.7	Colorado
10.6	Arkansas
10.3	Tennessee
10.3	Virginia
9.7	Mississippi
9.4	Illinois
9.4	New Jersey
8.4	Maryland
7.9	Oklahoma
7.9	Ohio
7.7	California
7.3	Michigan
7.2	Florida
7.2	Louisiana
6.5	Kentucky
6.2	Connecticut
4.8	Massachusetts
4.4	Pennsylvania
4.1	Texas
*	New Mexico
*	Alaska
*	Nevada
*	Oregon
*	Wyoming
*	Arizona
*	Maine
*	Utah
*	West Virginia
*	Washington
*	Idaho
*	Rhode Island
*	Montana
*	South Dakota
*	North Dakota
*	Delaware
*	New Hampshire
*	Kansas
*	Hawaii
*	Vermont
*	Iowa
*	Nebraska

*Incomplete data

Table G.141. BURDENPR

Cost per Person to Fund Prisons 1996–1999

188.32	Alaska
151.69	Connecticut
122.03	New York
118.37	Michigan
116.73	Delaware
110.61	Rhode Island
103.07	New Jersey
100.60	Maryland
98.92	North Carolina
91.45	California
90.16	Ohio
87.50	Arizona
85.51	Texas
81.60	Pennsylvania
81.20	South Carolina
81.06	Florida
76.69	Oregon
73.74	Hawaii
72.33	Louisiana
72.19	New Mexico
71.95	Georgia
69.36	Virginia
68.65	Wisconsin
67.41	Nevada
64.37	Kansas
63.93	Tennessee
62.17	Washington
61.59	Colorado
61.05	Illinois
60.52	Wyoming
59.05	Oklahoma
56.91	Indiana
56.43	Vermont
53.76	Mississippi
53.24	Utah
52.69	Kentucky
52.41	Arkansas
50.91	Iowa
50.15	Massachusetts
48.08	Montana
48.06	Missouri
46.58	South Dakota
45.50	Idaho
41.94	Nebraska
41.27	Maine
38.95	Minnesota
38.67	Alabama
35.77	New Hampshire
25.98	West Virginia
16.96	North Dakota

Table G.142. GOVFSLPC

Percent Work for Government 2000

12.07	Alaska
11.25	North Dakota
10.90	Wyoming
10.17	New Mexico
9.96	South Dakota
9.64	Hawaii
9.23	Nebraska
9.06	Virginia
8.68	Idaho
8.64	Mississippi
8.48	Iowa
8.45	Kansas
8.31	Washington
8.27	Vermont
8.26	Montana
8.26	Louisiana
8.25	North Carolina
8.23	Minnesota
8.22	South Carolina
8.19	Maryland
8.14	Oklahoma
8.09	Oregon
8.08	Alabama
7.97	Utah
7.96	Colorado
7.95	New York
7.90	Kentucky
7.89	West Virginia
7.83	Maine
7.76	Arizona
7.72	Wisconsin
7.71	Georgia
7.70	Delaware
7.48	Texas
7.42	Tennessee
7.36	Missouri
7.32	Connecticut
7.05	Indiana
7.04	New Jersey
6.99	California
6.98	Arkansas
6.97	Ohio
6.93	Massachusetts
6.93	Illinois
6.92	Michigan
6.91	New Hampshire
6.75	Nevada
6.56	Florida
6.39	Rhode Island
6.02	Pennsylvania

Table G.143. CONSTRPC

Percent in Construction 2000

5.06	Nevada
4.24	Colorado
4.02	Wyoming
3.69	Utah
3.32	Delaware
3.28	Arizona
3.10	South Carolina
3.06	Idaho
3.06	Maryland
3.02	North Carolina
3.01	Louisiana
2.97	Virginia
2.85	Washington
2.81	Texas
2.79	Kansas
2.70	Missouri
2.67	Oregon
2.63	New Mexico
2.60	Nebraska
2.58	Montana
2.56	Georgia
2.52	North Dakota
2.51	Alabama
2.51	Florida
2.48	Indiana
2.48	Vermont
2.41	Maine
2.40	Iowa
2.38	Minnesota
2.35	Tennessee
2.35	Wisconsin
2.28	South Dakota
2.26	Alaska
2.24	Kentucky
2.23	California
2.19	Arkansas
2.18	New Hampshire
2.11	Ohio
2.10	Illinois
2.05	Massachusetts
2.01	Hawaii
1.98	Michigan
1.98	Pennsylvania
1.90	Mississippi
1.89	Rhode Island
1.88	Connecticut
1.85	Oklahoma
1.82	New York
1.81	West Virginia
1.78	New Jersey

Table G.144. MANUFACPC

Percent in Manufacturing 2000

11.69	Wisconsin
11.66	Indiana
10.22	North Carolina
9.95	Arkansas
9.91	Michigan
9.60	Ohio
9.25	Tennessee
9.18	Minnesota
9.15	Iowa
8.82	New Hampshire
8.80	South Carolina
8.70	Mississippi
8.36	Alabama
8.13	Connecticut
8.07	Vermont
8.06	Kentucky
8.01	Kansas
7.87	Illinois
7.80	Delaware
7.79	Pennsylvania
7.76	Georgia
7.55	Rhode Island
7.31	Missouri
7.26	Oregon
7.03	Nebraska
6.96	Massachusetts
6.83	Maine
6.67	South Dakota
6.24	Utah
6.17	Idaho
6.09	Washington
5.79	California
5.71	Virginia
5.65	New Jersey
5.50	Oklahoma
5.42	Texas
5.05	Colorado
4.85	New York
4.54	West Virginia
4.52	Arizona
4.26	Louisiana
3.88	North Dakota
3.43	Maryland
3.24	Florida
2.83	Montana
2.47	New Mexico
2.43	Nevada
2.31	Wyoming
2.24	Alaska
1.42	Hawaii

Table G.145. TRANSPC

Percent in Transportation and Public Utilities 2000

4.33	Alaska
3.50	Colorado
3.48	Nebraska
3.41	Georgia
3.22	New Jersey
3.16	Tennessee
3.07	Missouri
3.02	Wyoming
3.01	Nevada
3.01	Kansas
2.97	North Dakota
2.92	Texas
2.90	Illinois
2.85	Utah
2.80	Arkansas
2.77	Minnesota
2.72	Kentucky
2.69	Virginia
2.61	Louisiana
2.57	Iowa
2.56	Montana
2.54	Wisconsin
2.49	Pennsylvania
2.46	Washington
2.46	Indiana
2.45	Oklahoma
2.39	Connecticut
2.39	Oregon
2.38	Florida
2.38	Delaware
2.37	North Carolina
2.33	New York
2.32	South Carolina
2.30	Arizona
2.29	South Dakota
2.29	Massachusetts
2.25	California
2.23	Maryland
2.21	Ohio
2.20	Alabama
2.20	Idaho
2.11	Vermont
2.09	Mississippi
2.09	West Virginia
2.02	New Mexico
1.98	Maine
1.81	Michigan
1.74	New Hampshire
1.62	Rhode Island
*	Hawaii

*Incomplete data

Table G.146. TRADEPC

Percent in Trade, Insurance, and Real Estate 2000

13.40	New Hampshire
13.23	Minnesota
13.05	Georgia
12.94	Colorado
12.77	Nebraska
12.75	North Dakota
12.63	South Dakota
12.59	Iowa
12.28	Delaware
12.25	Wisconsin
12.18	Kansas
12.06	Massachusetts
12.00	Montana
11.94	Maine
11.94	Utah
11.89	Ohio
11.87	Missouri
11.86	Oregon
11.85	Indiana
11.84	Wyoming
11.79	Nevada
11.70	Florida
11.64	Tennessee
11.61	South Carolina
11.52	Vermont
11.49	North Carolina
11.46	Hawaii
11.35	New Jersey
11.33	Washington
11.24	Texas
11.19	Idaho
11.16	Illinois
11.08	Arizona
11.07	Connecticut
11.00	Kentucky
10.99	Michigan
10.93	Virginia
10.92	Rhode Island
10.84	Maryland
10.59	Arkansas
10.45	Pennsylvania
10.35	Alabama
10.23	Oklahoma
10.11	New Mexico
10.08	Louisiana
9.90	California
9.59	New York
9.33	Alaska
9.08	West Virginia
8.95	Mississippi

Table G.147. FINANCPC

Percent in Finance 2000

6.81	Delaware
4.32	Connecticut
4.14	New York
3.72	Massachusetts
3.67	Nebraska
3.52	South Dakota
3.47	Colorado
3.36	Illinois
3.36	Minnesota
3.21	New Jersey
3.10	Missouri
3.07	Arizona
3.06	Florida
3.02	Rhode Island
3.00	Iowa
2.91	Hawaii
2.88	Oregon
2.87	Wisconsin
2.77	Ohio
2.74	New Hampshire
2.72	Maryland
2.72	Virginia
2.69	Texas
2.69	Pennsylvania
2.68	Utah
2.65	Georgia
2.59	North Dakota
2.51	California
2.48	North Carolina
2.47	Nevada
2.44	Maine
2.43	Washington
2.43	Kansas
2.40	Indiana
2.39	Tennessee
2.24	Oklahoma
2.15	South Carolina
2.12	Alabama
2.09	Vermont
2.08	Michigan
2.06	Montana
2.05	Alaska
1.94	Louisiana
1.93	New Mexico
1.88	Idaho
1.86	Arkansas
1.81	Kentucky
1.73	Wyoming
1.64	West Virginia
1.51	Mississippi

Table G.148. SERVICPC

Percent in Service 1998

24.86	Nevada
19.41	Massachusetts
17.95	Florida
16.84	Colorado
16.64	New York
16.55	Connecticut
16.35	Rhode Island
16.27	Maryland
16.20	Virginia
16.19	Minnesota
16.08	Delaware
15.87	New Jersey
15.31	Vermont
15.25	Arizona
15.20	Illinois
15.19	Pennsylvania
15.02	Hawaii
14.97	New Hampshire
14.64	North Dakota
14.60	Nebraska
14.55	Missouri
14.43	Maine
14.31	Utah
14.26	Wisconsin
14.17	Georgia
13.99	Ohio
13.95	South Dakota
13.80	California
13.76	Montana
13.75	Iowa
13.66	Wyoming
13.55	North Carolina
13.44	Texas
13.40	Tennessee
13.36	Kansas
13.28	Washington
13.08	Michigan
13.05	Oregon
12.85	Oklahoma
12.58	Indiana
12.51	New Mexico
12.23	Louisiana
12.21	West Virginia
12.14	Kentucky
11.96	South Carolina
11.80	Alaska
11.45	Idaho
11.02	Arkansas
10.72	Alabama
9.70	Mississippi

Table G.149. UNEMPIST

Unemployment Insurance ($1,000) 1998

1,075	California
471	New York
419	Pennsylvania
408	Michigan
338	Texas
300	Illinois
266	New Jersey
263	Ohio
240	Florida
223	North Carolina
220	Wisconsin
183	Massachusetts
178	Washington
175	Georgia
165	Tennessee
148	Oregon
145	Alabama
140	Missouri
128	Indiana
110	Kentucky
109	Connecticut
107	Minnesota
102	South Carolina
101	Maryland
100	Virginia
86	Arkansas
72	Iowa
68	Louisiana
66	Arizona
63	Nevada
60	Mississippi
57	Colorado
52	West Virginia
49	Kansas
47	Rhode Island
47	Oklahoma
46	Idaho
44	Alaska
40	Maine
37	Hawaii
37	Utah
33	New Mexico
28	Nebraska
27	Montana
25	Delaware
19	Vermont
16	New Hampshire
12	North Dakota
11	Wyoming
8	South Dakota

Table G.150. UEMPAVR

Unemployment Weekly Benefits 1998

269	Hawaii
266	New Jersey
261	Massachusetts
260	Washington
257	Minnesota
238	Pennsylvania
235	Michigan
227	Illinois
227	Rhode Island
225	Colorado
215	Ohio
215	Wisconsin
215	Oregon
215	Kansas
214	Connecticut
214	Iowa
208	Texas
208	Nevada
207	North Carolina
206	New York
205	Florida
202	Maryland
201	Indiana
197	Delaware
195	Idaho
195	Utah
190	North Dakota
189	Oklahoma
189	Wyoming
187	West Virginia
183	Virginia
183	New Hampshire
181	Vermont
180	Georgia
177	Arkansas
176	Alaska
174	Tennessee
174	South Carolina
173	Montana
169	New Mexico
164	Missouri
164	Nebraska
162	South Dakota
154	California
152	Alabama
149	Arizona
149	Maine
148	Louisiana
146	Mississippi
86	Kentucky

Table G.151. WORKCOMP

Workers' Compensation 1998

7,374	California
2,557	New York
2,448	Pennsylvania
2,335	Ohio
2,208	Florida
1,687	Illinois
1,482	Washington
1,465	Texas
1,367	Michigan
955	New Jersey
808	Georgia
766	North Carolina
732	Minnesota
711	Connecticut
657	Colorado
641	Massachusetts
622	Wisconsin
615	Alabama
591	Virginia
528	Missouri
520	Oklahoma
518	Tennessee
511	Kentucky
511	Maryland
493	Oregon
484	South Carolina
464	West Virginia
439	Indiana
418	Arizona
365	Louisiana
318	Kansas
292	Iowa
288	Maine
288	Nevada
235	Mississippi
195	Hawaii
169	Utah
166	Idaho
164	Nebraska
164	New Hampshire
161	Arkansas
155	Montana
119	Delaware
117	New Mexico
111	Alaska
104	Rhode Island
88	Vermont
81	North Dakota
74	Wyoming
73	South Dakota

Table G.152. TEMPASST

Temporary Assistance ($1,000) 1999

616	California
290	New York
117	Illinois
111	Texas
110	Ohio
103	Pennsylvania
92	Michigan
79	Florida
62	Washington
61	New Jersey
60	Georgia
57	Tennessee
56	North Carolina
52	Massachusetts
50	Missouri
43	Minnesota
42	Kentucky
37	Indiana
37	Louisiana
36	Virginia
34	Connecticut
34	Arizona
33	Maryland
26	New Mexico
22	Iowa
20	Alabama
19	Oklahoma
18	South Carolina
18	Rhode Island
17	Oregon
16	Mississippi
16	Hawaii
14	Colorado
13	Kansas
13	Maine
12	Arkansas
11	West Virginia
11	Nebraska
10	Utah
8	Wisconsin
8	Nevada
8	Alaska
7	Vermont
6	New Hampshire
6	Delaware
5	Montana
3	North Dakota
3	South Dakota
1	Idaho
1	Wyoming

Table G.153. FOODSTAM

Food Stamp Program ($1,000) 1999

2,027	California
1,541	New York
1,401	Texas
933	Florida
835	Pennsylvania
820	Illinois
683	Michigan
640	Ohio
617	Georgia
516	Louisiana
511	Tennessee
505	North Carolina
408	Missouri
405	Alabama
396	Kentucky
385	New Jersey
362	Virginia
309	South Carolina
307	Washington
298	Indiana
288	Mississippi
271	Oklahoma
264	Maryland
261	Massachusetts
257	Arizona
253	Arkansas
247	West Virginia
224	Oregon
208	Minnesota
182	Wisconsin
178	Connecticut
178	New Mexico
173	Colorado
129	Iowa
125	Hawaii
115	Kansas
109	Maine
92	Nebraska
88	Utah
76	Rhode Island
62	Nevada
61	Montana
57	Idaho
44	Vermont
44	South Dakota
41	Alaska
39	Delaware
37	New Hampshire
33	North Dakota
23	Wyoming

Table G.154. CHILDCAR

Licensed Child Care Centers 1999

13,051	California
7,733	Texas
6,052	Florida
4,746	Michigan
3,825	North Carolina
3,760	Ohio
3,508	Pennsylvania
3,500	New Jersey
3,411	New York
3,033	Tennessee
2,907	Illinois
2,503	Colorado
2,402	Virginia
2,295	Massachusetts
2,295	Wisconsin
2,284	Maryland
1,974	Kentucky
1,935	Arkansas
1,912	Oklahoma
1,910	Arizona
1,883	Washington
1,808	Louisiana
1,731	South Carolina
1,638	Connecticut
1,574	Minnesota
1,555	Mississippi
1,526	Iowa
1,515	Missouri
1,385	Kansas
1,353	Alabama
1,244	Georgia
1,200	New Hampshire
970	Oregon
904	Maine
783	Nebraska
656	Indiana
600	New Mexico
526	Idaho
515	Vermont
399	Nevada
384	Hawaii
360	Rhode Island
320	West Virginia
320	Utah
267	Delaware
251	Montana
225	Alaska
218	Wyoming
164	South Dakota
109	North Dakota

Table G.155. MALABOR

Percent Males Labor Force 1999

81.8	Utah
80.6	Alaska
80.4	Minnesota
80.1	Colorado
80.0	Nebraska
78.7	New Hampshire
78.5	Wyoming
78.5	South Dakota
78.3	Kansas
77.9	Texas
77.9	Vermont
77.8	Iowa
77.6	Wisconsin
77.6	Washington
77.5	Idaho
76.9	Illinois
76.8	Georgia
76.6	Nevada
76.4	Missouri
76.3	Michigan
76.2	Oregon
76.1	North Dakota
76.0	Indiana
75.5	New Jersey
75.1	Virginia
75.1	Maryland
74.9	California
74.9	Montana
74.8	North Carolina
74.8	Massachusetts
74.8	Arizona
74.3	Rhode Island
74.1	Ohio
73.9	Connecticut
73.8	Maine
73.6	Tennessee
73.1	Delaware
72.9	South Carolina
72.6	Oklahoma
72.5	Kentucky
72.1	Pennsylvania
70.9	New York
70.7	Hawaii
70.5	Alabama
70.3	Florida
70.3	Louisiana
69.7	Arkansas
69.7	Mississippi
69.3	New Mexico
65.0	West Virginia

Table G.156. FEMLABOR

Percent Females Labor Force 1999

69.9	Minnesota
68.2	South Dakota
67.2	Wisconsin
66.9	Colorado
66.6	Alaska
66.6	Nebraska
66.5	Vermont
66.3	Kansas
66.2	New Hampshire
66.1	Iowa
65.2	North Dakota
64.9	Maryland
64.3	Wyoming
63.6	Montana
63.6	Hawaii
63.3	Utah
63.3	Washington
63.1	Georgia
63.0	Illinois
63.0	Massachusetts
62.4	Maine
62.0	Idaho
61.7	Nevada
61.7	Connecticut
61.5	Delaware
61.4	Missouri
61.2	Michigan
61.1	Indiana
60.8	Rhode Island
60.6	Oregon
60.6	Virginia
60.3	Texas
60.3	North Carolina
60.3	Ohio
59.7	Tennessee
59.5	New Jersey
59.2	South Carolina
58.4	Arizona
58.4	Oklahoma
58.1	California
57.5	Pennsylvania
56.7	Kentucky
56.7	Alabama
56.4	Arkansas
56.0	Louisiana
55.8	New York
55.4	Florida
55.3	New Mexico
53.9	Mississippi
49.1	West Virginia

Table G.157. TOTUNEMP

Percent Unemployed 1999

6.6	West Virginia
6.4	Alaska
5.7	Oregon
5.6	Hawaii
5.6	New Mexico
5.2	Montana
5.2	Idaho
5.2	California
5.2	New York
5.1	Louisiana
5.1	Mississippi
4.9	Wyoming
4.8	Alabama
4.7	Washington
4.6	Texas
4.6	New Jersey
4.5	South Carolina
4.5	Kentucky
4.5	Arkansas
4.4	Nevada
4.4	Arizona
4.4	Pennsylvania
4.3	Illinois
4.3	Ohio
4.1	Maine
4.1	Rhode Island
4.0	Georgia
4.0	Tennessee
3.9	Florida
3.8	Michigan
3.7	Utah
3.5	Maryland
3.5	Delaware
3.4	North Dakota
3.4	Missouri
3.4	Oklahoma
3.2	Massachusetts
3.2	Connecticut
3.2	North Carolina
3.0	Wisconsin
3.0	Vermont
3.0	Kansas
3.0	Indiana
2.9	South Dakota
2.9	Colorado
2.9	Nebraska
2.8	Minnesota
2.8	Virginia
2.7	New Hampshire
2.5	Iowa

Table G.158. INSUNEMP

Percent Unemployed, Insured 1999

5.0	Alaska
3.2	Washington
3.1	Rhode Island
2.9	Oregon
2.7	California
2.7	Pennsylvania
2.6	Idaho
2.6	New Jersey
2.5	West Virginia
2.5	Hawaii
2.5	Arkansas
2.4	Montana
2.2	New York
2.2	Vermont
2.1	Nevada
2.1	Maine
2.1	Michigan
2.1	Massachusetts
2.0	Connecticut
2.0	Wisconsin
1.9	Illinois
1.8	Mississippi
1.7	New Mexico
1.7	Alabama
1.7	Tennessee
1.7	Missouri
1.6	Kentucky
1.6	Maryland
1.6	Delaware
1.5	Wyoming
1.5	South Carolina
1.4	Ohio
1.4	North Carolina
1.3	Louisiana
1.3	Texas
1.3	Minnesota
1.2	Florida
1.2	North Dakota
1.2	Iowa
1.1	Kansas
1.1	Indiana
1.0	Arizona
1.0	Georgia
1.0	Utah
1.0	Oklahoma
.9	Colorado
.8	Nebraska
.8	Virginia
.7	South Dakota
.7	New Hampshire

Table G.159. AVRPAY

Average Annual Pay 1998

40,915	Connecticut
40,678	New York
37,787	Massachusetts
35,349	California
34,704	Illinois
34,542	Michigan
33,996	Delaware
33,839	Alaska
33,306	Maryland
33,076	Washington
32,246	Colorado
32,073	Minnesota
31,582	Pennsylvania
31,512	Texas
31,384	Virginia
30,943	New Hampshire
30,873	Georgia
30,395	Ohio
30,201	Nevada
30,148	Rhode Island
29,542	Oregon
29,317	Arizona
29,107	Indiana
29,029	Hawaii
28,907	Missouri
28,542	Wisconsin
28,457	Tennessee
28,143	Florida
28,107	North Carolina
27,035	Alabama
26,905	Louisiana
26,869	Utah
26,842	Kansas
26,689	Kentucky
26,615	Vermont
26,151	South Carolina
26,035	Iowa
25,875	Maine
25,716	New Mexico
25,535	Nebraska
25,269	West Virginia
25,122	Oklahoma
24,866	Idaho
24,747	Wyoming
24,422	Arkansas
23,822	Mississippi
22,990	North Dakota
22,754	South Dakota
22,644	Montana
*	New Jersey

*Incomplete data

Table G.160. PCUNION

Percent Workers in Union 1999

26.5	New York
25.0	Hawaii
23.6	Alaska
23.6	Washington
22.5	Michigan
22.4	New Jersey
20.9	Nevada
20.5	Minnesota
19.2	Connecticut
19.1	Illinois
19.1	Ohio
19.0	Wisconsin
18.8	Rhode Island
18.6	Pennsylvania
18.3	California
17.9	Maryland
17.2	Montana
17.1	Massachusetts
17.1	Maine
16.8	Indiana
16.5	Oregon
16.1	West Virginia
15.7	Iowa
15.5	Delaware
15.3	Missouri
12.9	Kentucky
12.3	Alabama
12.2	New Hampshire
12.2	Nebraska
11.8	New Mexico
11.5	Kansas
11.3	Idaho
10.8	Vermont
10.8	Wyoming
10.4	Colorado
10.1	North Dakota
10.0	Louisiana
10.0	Oklahoma
9.0	Georgia
8.8	Tennessee
8.7	Florida
8.6	Arkansas
8.6	Mississippi
8.2	Arizona
8.0	Virginia
7.8	South Dakota
7.5	Utah
7.0	Texas
3.9	North Carolina
3.8	South Carolina

Table G.161. PERINCOM

Personal Income (billions) 1999

988.3	California
617.7	New York
531.7	Texas
423.5	Florida
379.4	Illinois
343.9	Pennsylvania
304.8	Ohio
294.0	New Jersey
274.6	Michigan
220.7	Massachusetts
211.8	Georgia
202.6	Virginia
200.6	North Carolina
174.4	Washington
166.3	Maryland
155.1	Indiana
146.2	Minnesota
143.9	Wisconsin
143.2	Missouri
140.3	Tennessee
128.5	Connecticut
128.5	Colorado
120.9	Arizona
100.3	Alabama
99.6	Louisiana
91.7	Kentucky
91.3	South Carolina
90.0	Oregon
76.6	Oklahoma
73.8	Iowa
70.7	Kansas
56.8	Mississippi
56.4	Arkansas
54.9	Nevada
49.7	Utah
45.7	Nebraska
38.4	New Mexico
37.7	West Virginia
37.1	New Hampshire
33.0	Hawaii
31.3	Maine
29.4	Rhode Island
29.3	Idaho
23.1	Delaware
19.7	Montana
18.4	South Dakota
17.7	Alaska
15.4	Vermont
14.9	North Dakota
12.5	Wyoming

Table G.162. INCOMEPC

Personal Income per Capita 1999

39,167	Connecticut
36,106	New Jersey
35,733	Massachusetts
33,946	New York
32,166	Maryland
31,678	Colorado
31,278	Illinois
30,905	New Hampshire
30,685	Delaware
30,622	Minnesota
30,351	Nevada
30,295	Washington
29,819	California
29,720	Rhode Island
29,484	Virginia
28,676	Pennsylvania
28,523	Alaska
28,023	Florida
27,844	Michigan
27,842	Hawaii
27,437	Nebraska
27,412	Wisconsin
27,198	Georgia
27,135	Oregon
27,081	Ohio
26,633	Kansas
26,525	Texas
26,220	North Carolina
26,187	Missouri
26,092	Indiana
26,003	Wyoming
25,892	Vermont
25,727	Iowa
25,581	Tennessee
25,307	Arizona
25,107	South Dakota
24,960	Maine
23,518	North Dakota
23,496	South Carolina
23,445	Idaho
23,356	Utah
23,161	Kentucky
22,946	Alabama
22,801	Oklahoma
22,792	Louisiana
22,314	Montana
22,114	Arkansas
22,063	New Mexico
20,888	West Virginia
20,506	Mississippi

Table G.163. STATPROD

Gross State Product (in billions) 1997

1,033.0	California
651.7	New York
601.6	Texas
393.5	Illinois
380.6	Florida
339.9	Pennsylvania
320.5	Ohio
294.1	New Jersey
272.6	Michigan
229.5	Georgia
221.0	Massachusetts
218.9	North Carolina
211.3	Virginia
172.3	Washington
161.7	Indiana
153.8	Maryland
152.1	Missouri
149.4	Minnesota
147.3	Wisconsin
147.0	Tennessee
134.6	Connecticut
126.1	Colorado
124.4	Louisiana
121.2	Arizona
103.1	Alabama
100.1	Kentucky
98.4	Oregon
93.3	South Carolina
80.5	Iowa
76.6	Oklahoma
71.7	Kansas
58.5	Arkansas
58.3	Mississippi
57.4	Nevada
55.4	Utah
48.8	Nebraska
45.2	New Mexico
38.2	West Virginia
38.1	New Hampshire
38.0	Hawaii
31.6	Delaware
30.2	Maine
29.1	Idaho
27.8	Rhode Island
24.5	Alaska
20.2	South Dakota
19.2	Montana
17.6	Wyoming
15.8	North Dakota
15.2	Vermont

Table G.164. BANKRPPC

Bankruptcy Percent Population 1999

.88	Tennessee
.86	Nevada
.76	Georgia
.71	Alabama
.66	Maryland
.66	Arkansas
.66	Utah
.65	Indiana
.65	Mississippi
.63	Oklahoma
.60	California
.60	Virginia
.58	Idaho
.56	Washington
.55	Illinois
.55	Oregon
.54	New Jersey
.54	Kentucky
.53	Rhode Island
.52	Florida
.52	Delaware
.51	Louisiana
.51	Missouri
.50	Hawaii
.50	Arizona
.49	Ohio
.46	West Virginia
.46	Kansas
.46	Wyoming
.44	New Mexico
.43	Colorado
.42	Montana
.41	New York
.40	Connecticut
.39	Michigan
.38	Pennsylvania
.37	New Hampshire
.36	Minnesota
.36	Wisconsin
.36	Maine
.35	North Carolina
.35	Nebraska
.35	North Dakota
.34	Texas
.34	Massachusetts
.32	Vermont
.31	South Dakota
.31	Iowa
.30	South Carolina
.24	Alaska

Table G.165. MEDINC98

Household Median Income 1998

50,692	Alaska
50,016	Maryland
49,826	New Jersey
47,926	Minnesota
47,241	Washington
46,599	Colorado
46,508	Connecticut
44,958	New Hampshire
44,299	Utah
43,354	Virginia
43,178	Illinois
42,345	Massachusetts
41,821	Michigan
41,458	Delaware
41,327	Wisconsin
40,934	California
40,827	Hawaii
40,686	Rhode Island
40,201	Missouri
39,756	Nevada
39,731	Indiana
39,372	Vermont
39,067	Oregon
39,015	Pennsylvania
38,925	Ohio
38,665	Georgia
37,394	New York
37,090	Arizona
37,019	Iowa
36,711	Kansas
36,680	Idaho
36,413	Nebraska
36,266	Alabama
36,252	Kentucky
35,838	North Carolina
35,783	Texas
35,640	Maine
35,250	Wyoming
34,909	Florida
34,091	Tennessee
33,727	Oklahoma
33,267	South Carolina
32,786	South Dakota
31,735	Louisiana
31,577	Montana
31,543	New Mexico
30,304	North Dakota
29,120	Mississippi
27,665	Arkansas
26,704	West Virginia

Table G.166. PERBELPV

Percent below Poverty 1998

20.4	New Mexico
19.1	Louisiana
17.8	West Virginia
17.6	Mississippi
16.7	New York
16.6	Arizona
16.6	Montana
15.4	California
15.1	Texas
15.1	North Dakota
15.0	Oregon
14.8	Arkansas
14.5	Alabama
14.1	Oklahoma
14.0	North Carolina
13.7	South Carolina
13.6	Georgia
13.5	Kentucky
13.4	Tennessee
13.1	Florida
13.0	Idaho
12.3	Nebraska
11.6	Rhode Island
11.2	Pennsylvania
11.2	Ohio
11.0	Michigan
10.9	Hawaii
10.8	South Dakota
10.6	Nevada
10.6	Wyoming
10.4	Minnesota
10.4	Maine
10.3	Delaware
10.1	Illinois
9.9	Vermont
9.8	New Hampshire
9.8	Missouri
9.6	Kansas
9.5	Connecticut
9.4	Alaska
9.4	Indiana
9.2	Colorado
9.1	Iowa
9.0	Utah
8.9	Washington
8.8	Virginia
8.8	Wisconsin
8.7	Massachusetts
8.6	New Jersey
7.2	Maryland

Table G.167. REFGASPR

Refiner Sales Price Gasoline (cents/gallon) 1998

97.5	Hawaii
75.5	Alaska
62.5	California
60.4	Idaho
60.0	Arizona
60.0	Montana
59.5	Utah
59.5	Washington
58.7	Vermont
58.4	Nevada
57.7	Maryland
57.1	Oregon
56.8	Wyoming
56.8	New Hampshire
56.3	West Virginia
56.3	New York
56.2	Connecticut
55.9	Minnesota
55.8	Massachusetts
54.2	Illinois
54.1	Colorado
53.9	Rhode Island
53.8	New Mexico
53.5	Maine
53.4	Delaware
53.2	Ohio
53.1	New Jersey
52.9	Virginia
52.8	South Dakota
52.4	Kentucky
52.0	North Dakota
51.9	Michigan
51.9	Missouri
51.8	Wisconsin
51.5	Florida
51.5	Indiana
51.4	Iowa
51.1	Nebraska
51.1	Pennsylvania
51.0	Alabama
50.3	Tennessee
50.0	North Carolina
49.8	Georgia
49.3	Arkansas
49.2	Mississippi
49.0	Kansas
48.9	South Carolina
48.0	Louisiana
47.2	Oklahoma
46.7	Texas

Table G.168. BANKASST

Assets Insured Banks (in Billions) 1999

1,170.3	New York
936.9	North Carolina
328.7	Illinois
309.3	Ohio
288.8	California
195.3	Pennsylvania
181.2	Texas
177.8	Alabama
169.7	Massachusetts
157.4	Minnesota
133.2	Delaware
123.3	Michigan
107.9	New Jersey
103.0	Rhode Island
90.4	Tennessee
86.3	Florida
86.2	Georgia
80.7	Virginia
80.4	Missouri
74.2	Wisconsin
65.0	Indiana
59.2	Utah
51.4	Kentucky
50.8	Louisiana
47.7	Arizona
45.4	Maryland
44.9	Iowa
41.6	Colorado
39.6	Oklahoma
34.8	Kansas
32.2	Nevada
32.0	South Dakota
29.5	Mississippi
28.5	Nebraska
26.7	Arkansas
23.6	Hawaii
23.1	West Virginia
22.0	New Hampshire
20.8	South Carolina
16.0	New Mexico
13.4	Washington
11.6	North Dakota
10.1	Montana
7.6	Vermont
7.5	Wyoming
7.2	Oregon
5.4	Alaska
5.1	Maine
3.2	Connecticut
2.1	Idaho

Table G.169. BANKDEP

Deposits Insured Banks (in Billions) 1999

729.8	New York
604.0	North Carolina
228.4	Illinois
226.3	California
187.0	Ohio
143.2	Texas
135.3	Pennsylvania
122.5	Alabama
115.6	Massachusetts
105.6	Minnesota
88.1	Michigan
82.3	New Jersey
64.9	Florida
64.8	Tennessee
64.3	Delaware
61.7	Missouri
54.5	Virginia
53.5	Wisconsin
50.8	Georgia
50.6	Rhode Island
45.3	Indiana
40.5	Louisiana
37.2	Kentucky
35.8	Iowa
34.4	Maryland
33.8	Colorado
31.0	Oklahoma
29.9	Utah
29.0	Kansas
25.9	Arizona
23.0	Nebraska
22.8	Mississippi
22.5	Arkansas
17.3	West Virginia
16.8	Hawaii
16.3	South Carolina
15.5	New Hampshire
12.0	South Dakota
11.4	Nevada
11.1	New Mexico
10.9	Washington
8.4	North Dakota
8.2	Montana
6.1	Vermont
6.1	Wyoming
5.7	Oregon
4.0	Alaska
3.8	Maine
2.5	Connecticut
1.8	Idaho

Table G.170. INCOMEUP

Increase Median Income 1990–1998

7,035.00	Alaska
6,335.00	Minnesota
5,746.00	Colorado
5,699.00	Missouri
5,526.00	Washington
5,476.00	Alabama
5,415.00	Utah
4,727.00	Maryland
4,522.00	Kentucky
4,162.00	Vermont
3,987.00	Rhode Island
3,725.00	Oklahoma
3,145.00	Virginia
3,068.00	Idaho
2,938.00	Michigan
2,935.00	New Hampshire
2,896.00	Ohio
2,500.00	Maine
2,339.00	Arizona
2,293.00	Georgia
2,053.00	Wyoming
2,044.00	Tennessee
2,032.00	Florida
1,999.00	Illinois
1,923.00	New Jersey
1,905.00	Montana
1,822.00	Indiana
1,783.00	Oregon
1,748.00	Pennsylvania
1,592.00	Iowa
1,527.00	Wisconsin
1,432.00	South Dakota
1,339.00	California
1,305.00	Texas
1,269.00	Louisiana
1,076.00	Nebraska
1,025.00	New York
707.00	New Mexico
593.00	Mississippi
518.00	North Carolina
476.00	Nevada
223.00	Kansas
143.00	Delaware
−58.00	South Carolina
−140.00	Connecticut
−210.00	Arkansas
−670.00	Massachusetts
−728.00	West Virginia
−1,460.00	North Dakota
−2,800.00	Hawaii

Table G.171. CARINSUR

Cost of Car Insurance (per Vehicle) 1998

1,138	New Jersey
960	New York
901	Connecticut
852	Rhode Island
845	Delaware
843	Nevada
830	Louisiana
818	Arizona
816	Massachusetts
797	Hawaii
771	Alaska
771	Florida
769	Maryland
764	Colorado
737	Michigan
731	Texas
725	West Virginia
722	Pennsylvania
718	California
710	Washington
680	Minnesota
676	New Mexico
672	Georgia
655	South Carolina
653	Mississippi
632	Alabama
630	Oregon
622	New Hampshire
619	Utah
617	Kentucky
611	Missouri
607	Illinois
589	Arkansas
587	Tennessee
583	Indiana
581	Ohio
575	Oklahoma
564	Virginia
564	North Carolina
552	Wisconsin
534	Vermont
532	Kansas
518	Nebraska
494	Idaho
492	Maine
492	Wyoming
479	South Dakota
471	Montana
459	Iowa
452	North Dakota

Table G.172. BANKRUPT

Bankruptcy Cases Filed (1,000) 1999

200.2	California
79.2	Florida
74.4	New York
68.6	Texas
66.6	Illinois
59.3	Georgia
55.3	Ohio
48.2	Tennessee
45.7	Pennsylvania
44.1	New Jersey
41.2	Virginia
38.9	Indiana
38.8	Michigan
34.1	Maryland
32.4	Washington
31.2	Alabama
27.9	Missouri
26.8	North Carolina
23.7	Arizona
22.5	Louisiana
21.4	Kentucky
21.3	Oklahoma
20.9	Massachusetts
18.9	Wisconsin
18.2	Oregon
18.1	Mississippi
17.4	Minnesota
17.3	Colorado
16.8	Arkansas
15.5	Nevada
14.0	Utah
13.2	Connecticut
12.3	Kansas
11.6	South Carolina
8.9	Iowa
8.4	West Virginia
7.7	New Mexico
7.3	Idaho
5.9	Hawaii
5.8	Nebraska
5.3	Rhode Island
4.5	New Hampshire
4.5	Maine
3.9	Delaware
3.7	Montana
2.3	South Dakota
2.2	Wyoming
2.2	North Dakota
1.9	Vermont
1.5	Alaska

Table G.173. PATENTS

Number of Patents 1998

17,821	California
7,113	New York
5,972	Texas
4,364	Illinois
4,198	New Jersey
3,890	Ohio
3,825	Michigan
3,759	Pennsylvania
3,735	Massachusetts
3,114	Florida
2,779	Minnesota
2,071	Connecticut
1,998	Washington
1,916	Colorado
1,878	Wisconsin
1,840	North Carolina
1,677	Arizona
1,569	Maryland
1,561	Indiana
1,560	Oregon
1,495	Georgia
1,157	Virginia
1,049	Missouri
912	Tennessee
897	Idaho
731	Utah
720	Iowa
682	South Carolina
649	New Hampshire
543	Louisiana
542	Oklahoma
422	Alabama
422	Delaware
404	Kentucky
404	Kansas
363	New Mexico
357	Rhode Island
343	Vermont
332	Nevada
233	Nebraska
210	West Virginia
202	Mississippi
184	Arkansas
149	Montana
143	Maine
93	Hawaii
76	Alaska
69	North Dakota
57	South Dakota
49	Wyoming

Table G.174. PATENTPC

Patents (per 100,000) Persons 1998

71.66	Idaho
63.10	Connecticut
60.48	Massachusetts
58.19	Minnesota
57.77	Vermont
56.00	Delaware
54.03	New Hampshire
53.77	California
51.55	New Jersey
47.24	Colorado
47.04	Oregon
39.09	New York
38.78	Michigan
36.03	Rhode Island
35.98	Illinois
35.77	Wisconsin
35.10	Arizona
34.71	Washington
34.56	Ohio
34.32	Utah
31.34	Pennsylvania
30.34	Maryland
29.79	Texas
26.27	Indiana
25.09	Iowa
24.05	North Carolina
20.86	New Mexico
20.61	Florida
19.20	Georgia
19.18	Missouri
18.35	Nevada
17.55	South Carolina
16.88	Montana
16.83	Virginia
16.63	Tennessee
16.14	Oklahoma
15.22	Kansas
13.99	Nebraska
12.42	Louisiana
12.27	Alaska
11.62	West Virginia
11.41	Maine
10.89	North Dakota
10.22	Wyoming
10.20	Kentucky
9.66	Alabama
7.84	Hawaii
7.77	South Dakota
7.30	Mississippi
7.21	Arkansas

Table G.175. COMPUTER

Percent Households Computers 2000

62.4	Alaska
60.1	Utah
56.3	Washington
55.3	Colorado
54.2	New Hampshire
51.3	Oregon
50.0	Idaho
48.7	Vermont
48.1	New Jersey
47.6	Minnesota
47.5	California
46.4	Virginia
46.3	Maryland
46.1	Wyoming
44.3	Arizona
44.0	Michigan
43.8	Connecticut
43.7	Kansas
43.5	Indiana
43.4	Massachusetts
43.4	Maine
43.0	Wisconsin
42.9	Nebraska
42.7	Illinois
42.3	Hawaii
42.2	New Mexico
41.8	Missouri
41.6	Nevada
41.6	South Dakota
41.4	Iowa
41.0	Rhode Island
40.9	Texas
40.9	Montana
40.7	Ohio
40.5	Delaware
40.2	North Dakota
39.5	Florida
39.3	Pennsylvania
37.8	Oklahoma
37.5	Tennessee
37.3	New York
35.9	Kentucky
35.8	Georgia
35.7	South Carolina
35.0	North Carolina
34.3	Alabama
31.1	Louisiana
29.8	Arkansas
28.3	West Virginia
25.7	Mississippi

Table G.176. INTERNET

Percent Households Internet 2000

44.1	Alaska
37.1	New Hampshire
36.6	Washington
35.8	Utah
34.5	Colorado
32.7	Oregon
31.8	Vermont
31.8	Connecticut
31.3	New Jersey
31.0	Maryland
30.7	California
29.3	Arizona
29.0	Minnesota
28.1	Massachusetts
27.9	Virginia
27.9	Hawaii
27.8	Florida
27.4	Idaho
27.1	Rhode Island
26.5	Illinois
26.5	Nevada
26.1	Indiana
26.0	Maine
25.8	New Mexico
25.7	Kansas
25.4	Michigan
25.1	Wisconsin
25.1	Delaware
24.9	Pennsylvania
24.6	Ohio
24.5	Texas
24.3	Missouri
23.9	South Dakota
23.9	Georgia
23.7	New York
22.9	Nebraska
22.7	Wyoming
21.8	Iowa
21.6	Alabama
21.5	Montana
21.4	South Carolina
21.3	Tennessee
21.1	Kentucky
20.6	North Dakota
20.4	Oklahoma
19.9	North Carolina
17.8	Louisiana
17.6	West Virginia
14.7	Arkansas
13.6	Mississippi

Table G.177. RDINDTOT

R&D by Industry (millions) 1998

43,919	California
13,655	Michigan
13,514	New York
13,382	Massachusetts
11,368	New Jersey
10,774	Texas
8,830	Illinois
8,762	Pennsylvania
8,466	Washington
8,019	Maryland
6,970	Ohio
4,934	Virginia
4,773	Florida
4,565	Colorado
4,560	North Carolina
3,818	Minnesota
3,559	Connecticut
3,089	Indiana
3,032	New Mexico
2,556	Delaware
2,503	Tennessee
2,501	Wisconsin
2,492	Georgia
2,318	Arizona
1,926	Alabama
1,910	Oregon
1,868	Missouri
1,677	Rhode Island
1,518	Kansas
1,495	Utah
1,340	New Hampshire
1,127	Idaho
1,054	Iowa
989	South Carolina
645	Kentucky
571	Nevada
542	Louisiana
513	Oklahoma
421	West Virginia
366	Mississippi
315	Nebraska
283	Arkansas
242	Hawaii
191	Montana
175	Vermont
159	Maine
119	North Dakota
65	Wyoming
60	South Dakota
*	Alaska

*Incomplete data

Table G.178　　RDUNITOT

R&D by Universities (millions) 1998

3,345	California
1,925	New York
1,698	Texas
1,343	Massachusetts
1,342	Pennsylvania
1,330	Maryland
1,046	Illinois
899	North Carolina
878	Michigan
808	Ohio
802	Georgia
713	Florida
536	Wisconsin
534	Washington
491	Virginia
489	Colorado
485	New Jersey
484	Missouri
442	Alabama
425	Indiana
406	Arizona
404	Connecticut
365	Minnesota
358	Iowa
352	Louisiana
346	Tennessee
310	Oregon
249	Utah
246	South Carolina
229	New Mexico
213	Kansas
210	Kentucky
209	Oklahoma
186	Nebraska
153	Mississippi
148	Hawaii
117	New Hampshire
117	Arkansas
112	Rhode Island
84	Nevada
76	Alaska
73	Delaware
72	Idaho
72	Montana
63	West Virginia
58	Vermont
57	North Dakota
49	Wyoming
35	Maine
25	South Dakota

Table G.179.　RDINDPC

R&D by Industry, per Capita 1998

3,392.00	Delaware
2,167.07	Massachusetts
1,742.68	New Mexico
1,692.54	Rhode Island
1,550.57	Maryland
1,470.72	Washington
1,395.98	New Jersey
1,384.36	Michigan
1,325.05	California
1,125.46	Colorado
1,115.61	New Hampshire
1,084.39	Connecticut
900.38	Idaho
799.50	Minnesota
742.67	New York
730.53	Pennsylvania
728.05	Illinois
717.89	Virginia
701.93	Utah
619.19	Ohio
596.02	North Carolina
575.97	Oregon
571.96	Kansas
537.51	Texas
519.78	Indiana
485.11	Arizona
476.34	Wisconsin
456.46	Tennessee
440.75	Alabama
367.32	Iowa
341.60	Missouri
319.97	Georgia
315.86	Florida
315.60	Nevada
294.74	Vermont
254.52	South Carolina
232.99	West Virginia
216.36	Montana
204.13	Hawaii
189.07	Nebraska
187.80	North Dakota
162.84	Kentucky
152.77	Oklahoma
135.53	Wyoming
132.20	Mississippi
126.89	Maine
123.97	Louisiana
110.92	Arkansas
81.84	South Dakota
*	Alaska

*Incomplete data

Table G.180.　RDUNIPC

R&D by Universities, per Capita 1998

257.17	Maryland
217.48	Massachusetts
131.62	New Mexico
124.84	Hawaii
124.76	Iowa
123.09	Connecticut
122.68	Alaska
120.56	Colorado
117.50	North Carolina
116.91	Utah
113.04	Rhode Island
111.89	Pennsylvania
111.64	Nebraska
105.79	New York
102.98	Georgia
102.17	Wyoming
102.09	Wisconsin
101.15	Alabama
100.92	California
97.69	Vermont
97.41	New Hampshire
96.88	Delaware
93.48	Oregon
92.77	Washington
89.95	North Dakota
89.01	Michigan
88.51	Missouri
86.24	Illinois
84.97	Arizona
84.71	Texas
81.56	Montana
80.51	Louisiana
80.25	Kansas
76.43	Minnesota
71.78	Ohio
71.51	Indiana
71.44	Virginia
63.31	South Carolina
63.10	Tennessee
62.24	Oklahoma
59.56	New Jersey
57.52	Idaho
55.26	Mississippi
53.02	Kentucky
47.18	Florida
46.43	Nevada
45.86	Arkansas
34.87	West Virginia
34.10	South Dakota
27.93	Maine

Table G.181. NUMBRIDG

Number of Bridges 1998

47,173	Texas
27,832	Ohio
25,962	Kansas
25,267	Illinois
24,735	Iowa
23,267	California
22,856	Missouri
22,827	Oklahoma
21,956	Pennsylvania
19,122	Tennessee
17,908	Indiana
17,282	New York
16,656	Mississippi
16,493	North Carolina
15,591	Alabama
15,541	Nebraska
14,339	Georgia
13,515	Louisiana
13,326	Wisconsin
13,273	Kentucky
12,614	Minnesota
12,584	Virginia
12,523	Arkansas
11,028	Florida
10,631	Michigan
9,039	South Carolina
7,882	Colorado
7,440	Washington
7,215	Oregon
6,713	Arizona
6,640	West Virginia
6,317	New Jersey
6,055	South Dakota
5,000	Montana
4,974	Massachusetts
4,814	Maryland
4,568	North Dakota
4,146	Connecticut
4,035	Idaho
3,647	New Mexico
3,024	Wyoming
2,697	Vermont
2,692	Utah
2,354	Maine
2,339	New Hampshire
1,368	Alaska
1,307	Nevada
1,060	Hawaii
799	Delaware
751	Rhode Island

Table G.182. BRIDGDEF

Percent Bridges Deficient 1998

38.7	New York
35.1	Oklahoma
30.3	Missouri
25.1	Pennsylvania
25.0	Mississippi
24.2	Rhode Island
21.4	Vermont
20.9	North Dakota
20.5	Louisiana
20.4	West Virginia
19.4	Michigan
19.1	South Dakota
19.0	Iowa
18.3	Nebraska
17.7	Alabama
17.7	New Hampshire
17.5	Maine
17.1	North Carolina
17.0	New Jersey
14.6	Wisconsin
14.5	Kansas
14.3	Indiana
13.7	Georgia
13.6	Ohio
13.4	Wyoming
13.3	Illinois
13.3	Massachusetts
13.2	Arkansas
12.1	Minnesota
12.1	Utah
12.0	Hawaii
11.5	South Carolina
11.5	Montana
11.5	Alaska
11.0	Tennessee
10.0	Virginia
9.6	Kentucky
9.6	Maryland
9.0	Connecticut
8.4	Idaho
8.3	Colorado
8.1	Texas
8.1	New Mexico
8.1	Delaware
6.9	Washington
6.3	California
5.6	Nevada
5.5	Oregon
3.0	Arizona
2.8	Florida

Table G.183. BRIDGOBS

Percent Bridges Obsolete 1998

39.1	Hawaii
36.3	Massachusetts
24.5	Rhode Island
22.6	West Virginia
22.2	New Jersey
21.7	Kentucky
20.8	California
20.0	Maryland
19.9	Connecticut
19.5	Maine
19.4	Virginia
19.1	Washington
18.4	Florida
17.6	New Hampshire
17.5	Alaska
16.9	Oregon
16.7	Vermont
16.6	Pennsylvania
16.3	North Carolina
16.0	Louisiana
14.5	Tennessee
14.4	Texas
14.1	Alabama
13.7	Georgia
13.6	Kansas
13.5	Michigan
13.4	Ohio
13.3	Arkansas
13.0	New York
12.1	Nebraska
11.6	Montana
11.6	Nevada
11.2	Indiana
11.1	Missouri
11.0	Idaho
10.5	Delaware
10.4	Colorado
10.3	New Mexico
9.6	South Carolina
9.4	Iowa
9.4	Utah
8.5	Mississippi
8.5	Wyoming
8.2	Illinois
7.4	Wisconsin
6.8	Arizona
6.7	South Dakota
6.4	Oklahoma
6.3	North Dakota
5.9	Minnesota

Table G.184. HIWAYFND

State Highway Funds 1998

6,574	California
6,051	New York
4,295	Texas
4,024	Florida
3,902	Pennsylvania
3,351	Massachusetts
3,327	Ohio
3,306	Illinois
2,745	Michigan
2,619	Virginia
2,513	New Jersey
2,352	North Carolina
1,805	Washington
1,652	Indiana
1,613	Georgia
1,492	Maryland
1,481	Kentucky
1,438	Missouri
1,430	Arizona
1,427	Connecticut
1,420	Tennessee
1,400	Louisiana
1,398	Wisconsin
1,377	Minnesota
1,306	Kansas
1,177	Iowa
1,166	Colorado
1,129	Utah
1,053	Alabama
1,051	Oregon
944	Oklahoma
893	West Virginia
843	Mississippi
815	Arkansas
766	South Carolina
647	Delaware
589	Nebraska
570	New Mexico
485	Maine
446	Nevada
414	Idaho
404	Alaska
378	Montana
371	New Hampshire
339	Rhode Island
326	Hawaii
321	Wyoming
306	North Dakota
305	South Dakota
222	Vermont

Table G.185. HIWAYFED

Federal Grants (FTA) per Capita 1998

50.6	Oregon
43.7	New Jersey
41.4	New York
36.8	Massachusetts
23.6	Illinois
21.9	Connecticut
21.3	Pennsylvania
20.9	California
20.9	Utah
17.6	Maryland
16.3	Washington
15.8	Georgia
13.3	Nevada
12.5	Vermont
11.5	Missouri
11.1	Louisiana
10.5	Florida
8.9	Texas
8.4	Ohio
8.1	Hawaii
7.7	Arizona
7.7	Wisconsin
7.6	Delaware
7.4	Tennessee
7.1	West Virginia
7.1	Rhode Island
6.9	Michigan
6.9	Iowa
6.8	Indiana
6.8	North Dakota
6.6	New Mexico
6.6	South Dakota
5.5	Virginia
5.2	Colorado
4.8	North Carolina
4.1	Kentucky
4.0	Oklahoma
3.6	Arkansas
3.3	Nebraska
3.2	Idaho
2.9	Alaska
2.9	Montana
2.9	New Hampshire
2.9	Wyoming
2.8	South Carolina
2.8	Maine
2.7	Minnesota
2.6	Mississippi
2.4	Alabama
2.1	Kansas

Table G.186. HIWAYTRS

Federal Grants (HTF) per Capita 1998

394.0	Alaska
279.2	Wyoming
220.5	North Dakota
197.3	South Dakota
195.1	Montana
174.2	Hawaii
167.5	Massachusetts
151.6	Vermont
133.0	Idaho
120.3	West Virginia
116.9	Delaware
116.3	New Mexico
113.1	Arkansas
112.7	Connecticut
107.4	Rhode Island
104.7	Oregon
101.0	Nebraska
94.9	Maine
89.3	New Hampshire
88.5	Nevada
83.2	Washington
82.3	Maryland
82.2	Missouri
81.4	Oklahoma
80.3	Iowa
80.0	New Jersey
77.7	Pennsylvania
74.9	Kentucky
74.4	Utah
73.2	Arizona
73.1	Indiana
71.7	Kansas
71.4	Mississippi
70.5	Tennessee
69.3	Alabama
68.2	Ohio
67.0	South Carolina
66.2	New York
65.6	Virginia
65.0	California
64.5	Minnesota
63.7	Wisconsin
63.2	Georgia
61.9	Michigan
60.7	Texas
60.3	North Carolina
59.1	Illinois
58.8	Louisiana
53.3	Colorado
50.3	Florida

Table G.187. GASTAX

State Gasoline Tax (cents/gallon) 1998

36.0	Connecticut
35.4	West Virginia
29.0	Rhode Island
27.0	Montana
25.9	Pennsylvania
25.4	Wisconsin
25.0	Idaho
24.8	Nevada
24.6	Nebraska
24.5	Utah
24.0	Oregon
23.5	Maryland
23.0	Delaware
23.0	Washington
22.7	New York
22.3	North Carolina
22.0	Ohio
22.0	Colorado
21.0	South Dakota
21.0	Massachusetts
20.0	North Dakota
20.0	Vermont
20.0	Iowa
20.0	Tennessee
20.0	Minnesota
20.0	Texas
20.0	Louisiana
19.5	New Hampshire
19.0	Maine
19.0	Michigan
19.0	Illinois
18.9	New Mexico
18.6	Arkansas
18.4	Mississippi
18.0	Arizona
18.0	Kansas
18.0	Alabama
18.0	California
17.5	Virginia
17.0	Missouri
17.0	Oklahoma
16.4	Kentucky
16.0	Hawaii
16.0	South Carolina
15.0	Indiana
13.0	Florida
10.5	New Jersey
9.0	Wyoming
8.0	Alaska
7.5	Georgia

Table G.188. AUTOREG

Auto Registration (1,000) 1998

16,174	California
7,664	New York
7,456	Texas
7,438	Florida
6,664	Ohio
6,425	Illinois
6,132	Pennsylvania
5,105	Michigan
4,215	New Jersey
4,033	Georgia
3,783	Massachusetts
3,774	Virginia
3,531	North Carolina
3,273	Indiana
2,776	Washington
2,696	Tennessee
2,622	Maryland
2,601	Missouri
2,544	Wisconsin
2,412	Minnesota
2,063	Alabama
1,998	Connecticut
1,967	Louisiana
1,843	Colorado
1,823	South Carolina
1,738	Iowa
1,728	Arizona
1,716	Kentucky
1,588	Oregon
1,549	Oklahoma
1,250	Mississippi
1,127	Kansas
929	Arkansas
850	Utah
834	Nebraska
821	New Mexico
777	West Virginia
688	New Hampshire
666	Nevada
565	Maine
522	Rhode Island
502	Idaho
458	Montana
450	Hawaii
417	Delaware
382	South Dakota
330	North Dakota
296	Vermont
232	Alaska
219	Wyoming

Table G.189. FATALCOH

Percent Fatal Accidents Alcohol 1998

50	Texas
49	Nevada
48	Rhode Island
47	Massachusetts
47	New Hampshire
47	Hawaii
47	North Dakota
46	Washington
46	Louisiana
45	Missouri
45	New Mexico
44	Montana
44	Alaska
44	Wyoming
43	Illinois
43	Minnesota
43	Connecticut
43	Arizona
43	Oregon
42	Pennsylvania
42	Wisconsin
41	Tennessee
41	West Virginia
41	South Dakota
39	Michigan
39	Indiana
39	Delaware
38	California
38	Alabama
38	Nebraska
37	Virginia
37	Colorado
37	Mississippi
37	Vermont
36	New Jersey
36	Iowa
35	Kansas
34	Maryland
34	Idaho
33	Florida
33	Ohio
33	Kentucky
33	Oklahoma
32	Georgia
32	North Carolina
31	Arkansas
30	South Carolina
28	Maine
24	New York
14	Utah

Table G.190.	TRAFATAL		Table G.191.	FARMINCO		Table G.192.	MINERAL

Traffic Fatalities 1998		Farm Income (millions) 1998		Value Nonfuel Minerals (millions) 1999

3,577	Texas	5,366	California	3,200	California
3,494	California	3,125	Texas	2,780	Nevada
2,824	Florida	2,361	North Carolina	2,510	Arizona
1,596	North Carolina	2,277	Iowa	1,930	Florida
1,569	Georgia	2,226	Florida	1,840	Georgia
1,498	New York	1,901	Georgia	1,780	Texas
1,481	Pennsylvania	1,759	Nebraska	1,660	Michigan
1,422	Ohio	1,595	Arkansas	1,580	Minnesota
1,393	Illinois	1,496	Kansas	1,380	Missouri
1,367	Michigan	1,484	Illinois	1,270	Pennsylvania
1,216	Tennessee	1,313	Kentucky	1,260	Utah
1,169	Missouri	1,299	Ohio	1,090	Alaska
1,071	Alabama	1,260	Minnesota	1,080	Alabama
1,002	South Carolina	1,209	Alabama	1,040	Ohio
980	Arizona	1,158	South Dakota	956	Wyoming
978	Indiana	1,050	Washington	935	New York
948	Mississippi	927	Mississippi	913	Illinois
935	Virginia	908	Wisconsin	761	North Carolina
922	Louisiana	901	Oklahoma	717	Indiana
858	Kentucky	840	Idaho	710	Tennessee
755	Oklahoma	802	Indiana	671	New Mexico
743	New Jersey	763	Missouri	667	Virginia
714	Wisconsin	760	Colorado	631	Washington
660	Washington	746	North Dakota	574	South Carolina
650	Minnesota	700	Arizona	566	Kansas
628	Colorado	662	Pennsylvania	555	Colorado
625	Arkansas	571	New Mexico	537	Iowa
606	Maryland	515	Oregon	518	Arkansas
538	Oregon	496	Virginia	491	Montana
493	Kansas	447	New York	483	Kentucky
449	Iowa	374	Louisiana	475	Oklahoma
424	New Mexico	355	Montana	420	Idaho
406	Massachusetts	343	Tennessee	374	Louisiana
361	Nevada	330	South Carolina	336	Maryland
354	West Virginia	310	Maryland	334	Wisconsin
350	Utah	308	Michigan	303	Oregon
329	Connecticut	219	Utah	300	New Jersey
315	Nebraska	142	Vermont	226	South Dakota
265	Idaho	130	Massachusetts	204	Massachusetts
237	Montana	129	Connecticut	190	Mississippi
192	Maine	118	Delaware	180	West Virginia
165	South Dakota	117	New Jersey	163	Nebraska
154	Wyoming	63	Maine	103	Connecticut
128	New Hampshire	60	Wyoming	101	Maine
120	Hawaii	47	Nevada	89	Hawaii
115	Delaware	35	West Virginia	83	Vermont
104	Vermont	34	Hawaii	64	New Hampshire
92	North Dakota	24	Rhode Island	38	North Dakota
74	Rhode Island	20	Alaska	25	Rhode Island
71	Alaska	12	New Hampshire	10	Delaware

Table G.193. TRAFATPT

Traffic Fatalities per 1,000 1998

.3424	Mississippi
.3211	Wyoming
.2685	Montana
.2579	South Carolina
.2451	Alabama
.2450	Arkansas
.2437	New Mexico
.2251	South Dakota
.2248	Oklahoma
.2218	Tennessee
.2166	Kentucky
.2138	Missouri
.2117	Idaho
.2109	Louisiana
.2086	North Carolina
.2051	Arizona
.2015	Georgia
.1995	Nevada
.1959	West Virginia
.1891	Nebraska
.1869	Florida
.1858	Kansas
.1785	Texas
.1752	Vermont
.1646	Indiana
.1643	Utah
.1622	Oregon
.1565	Iowa
.1548	Colorado
.1532	Maine
.1526	Delaware
.1452	North Dakota
.1386	Michigan
.1361	Minnesota
.1360	Virginia
.1360	Wisconsin
.1263	Ohio
.1235	Pennsylvania
.1172	Maryland
.1149	Illinois
.1147	Washington
.1146	Alaska
.1066	New Hampshire
.1054	California
.1012	Hawaii
.1002	Connecticut
.0912	New Jersey
.0823	New York
.0747	Rhode Island
.0657	Massachusetts

Table G.194. DEATHOMI

Homicides (per 100,000) 1997

16.1	Louisiana
14.2	Mississippi
12.0	Alabama
11.8	Arkansas
10.9	Maryland
10.5	Nevada
10.4	Tennessee
9.8	Illinois
9.5	South Carolina
9.5	New Mexico
9.5	Arizona
9.2	North Carolina
9.0	Alaska
8.8	California
8.7	Oklahoma
8.7	Georgia
8.1	Michigan
8.0	Missouri
7.7	Florida
7.6	Texas
7.6	Virginia
7.4	Indiana
6.6	Kentucky
6.5	Pennsylvania
6.3	New York
6.1	Kansas
5.3	West Virginia
4.7	Colorado
4.7	Washington
4.5	New Jersey
4.4	Wyoming
4.4	Delaware
4.4	Ohio
4.2	Montana
4.1	Oregon
4.1	Wisconsin
4.0	Hawaii
3.9	Nebraska
3.9	Connecticut
3.6	Idaho
3.1	Utah
3.0	South Dakota
2.8	Minnesota
2.8	Rhode Island
2.5	Iowa
2.3	Massachusetts
2.2	New Hampshire
1.8	Maine
*	Vermont
*	North Dakota

*Incomplete data

Table G.195. FARMINPP

Farm Income per Person 1998

1,579.52	South Dakota
1,177.28	North Dakota
1,055.80	Nebraska
793.54	Iowa
671.09	Idaho
625.15	Arkansas
563.67	Kansas
402.14	Montana
334.82	Mississippi
331.50	Kentucky
328.19	New Mexico
308.60	North Carolina
276.67	Alabama
268.31	Oklahoma
263.85	Minnesota
244.09	Georgia
239.16	Vermont
187.37	Colorado
182.41	Washington
172.94	Wisconsin
161.89	California
156.59	Delaware
155.91	Texas
155.30	Oregon
147.31	Florida
146.49	Arizona
139.53	Missouri
134.95	Indiana
125.10	Wyoming
122.36	Illinois
115.40	Ohio
102.82	Utah
85.54	Louisiana
84.93	South Carolina
72.17	Virginia
62.55	Tennessee
59.94	Maryland
55.19	Pennsylvania
50.28	Maine
39.30	Connecticut
32.28	Alaska
31.23	Michigan
28.68	Hawaii
25.98	Nevada
24.57	New York
24.22	Rhode Island
21.05	Massachusetts
19.37	West Virginia
14.37	New Jersey
9.99	New Hampshire

Table G.196. MINERLPP

Minerals Income per Person 1999

1,993.32	Wyoming
1,759.48	Alaska
1,536.55	Nevada
591.59	Utah
556.20	Montana
525.29	Arizona
385.67	New Mexico
335.54	Idaho
330.85	Minnesota
308.27	South Dakota
252.36	Missouri
247.15	Alabama
236.25	Georgia
213.26	Kansas
203.03	Arkansas
187.15	Iowa
168.29	Michigan
147.72	South Carolina
141.45	Oklahoma
139.79	Vermont
136.83	Colorado
129.48	Tennessee
127.72	Florida
121.94	Kentucky
120.65	Indiana
109.62	Washington
105.89	Pennsylvania
99.62	West Virginia
99.47	North Carolina
97.84	Nebraska
97.05	Virginia
96.55	California
92.39	Ohio
91.37	Oregon
88.80	Texas
85.54	Louisiana
80.60	Maine
75.28	Illinois
75.07	Hawaii
68.63	Mississippi
64.97	Maryland
63.61	Wisconsin
59.97	North Dakota
53.28	New Hampshire
51.38	New York
36.84	New Jersey
33.04	Massachusetts
31.38	Connecticut
25.23	Rhode Island
13.27	Delaware

Table G.197. CONCONTR

Construction Contracts (millions) 1999

45,949	California
40,157	Texas
32,343	Florida
19,306	New York
18,592	Georgia
17,100	Ohio
17,080	North Carolina
16,823	Illinois
14,709	Michigan
14,188	Pennsylvania
13,500	Arizona
12,776	Virginia
11,775	Colorado
10,714	Washington
10,437	Indiana
10,101	Tennessee
9,574	New Jersey
8,922	Massachusetts
8,775	Minnesota
7,862	Missouri
7,659	Maryland
7,472	Wisconsin
7,236	South Carolina
6,676	Kentucky
5,907	Oregon
5,626	Nevada
5,482	Alabama
5,045	Louisiana
4,489	Utah
4,448	Connecticut
4,404	Oklahoma
4,388	Kansas
3,873	Mississippi
3,825	Iowa
3,353	Arkansas
2,872	Nebraska
2,380	Idaho
2,378	New Mexico
1,837	Hawaii
1,666	New Hampshire
1,653	Maine
1,537	West Virginia
1,391	North Dakota
1,353	Alaska
1,083	Rhode Island
1,036	Delaware
931	South Dakota
927	Montana
721	Wyoming
648	Vermont

Table G.198. MANPEMP

Earnings Manufacturing Employee 1996

47,178	Delaware
43,230	Michigan
42,802	Connecticut
42,419	New Jersey
40,071	Massachusetts
38,610	Washington
37,533	New York
37,124	Illinois
37,065	Ohio
36,724	California
36,309	Maryland
36,071	Minnesota
34,849	Pennsylvania
34,812	Indiana
34,686	Colorado
34,554	Arizona
34,439	Louisiana
34,131	Texas
33,859	Oregon
33,293	New Hampshire
33,083	West Virginia
32,994	Kansas
32,910	Wisconsin
32,712	Missouri
32,152	Idaho
31,474	Virginia
31,307	Iowa
30,969	Vermont
30,933	Kentucky
30,873	Alaska
30,870	Rhode Island
30,554	Florida
30,175	Maine
30,100	Georgia
30,053	New Mexico
29,789	Hawaii
29,576	Utah
29,299	Nevada
29,112	South Carolina
29,098	Oklahoma
28,877	Tennessee
28,033	Nebraska
27,815	North Carolina
27,679	Alabama
27,608	Wyoming
26,746	South Dakota
26,584	Montana
25,796	North Dakota
24,410	Arkansas
23,666	Mississippi

TABLE G.199. RETAIL

Retail Sales per Household 1998

34,289	New Hampshire
34,142	Hawaii
33,148	Alaska
30,991	Delaware
30,507	South Dakota
29,871	Nevada
29,466	Connecticut
29,313	Florida
29,249	Oregon
29,091	Idaho
29,029	North Dakota
28,714	Virginia
28,691	Utah
28,690	Wisconsin
28,429	Michigan
28,183	Ohio
28,053	New Jersey
27,916	Georgia
27,725	Wyoming
27,668	North Carolina
27,601	Minnesota
27,542	Iowa
27,497	New Mexico
27,301	Nebraska
27,204	Missouri
26,982	Tennessee
26,901	Massachusetts
26,861	Arizona
26,707	Maine
26,598	Texas
26,434	Vermont
26,385	Indiana
26,298	Pennsylvania
26,290	Montana
26,173	Colorado
25,976	Louisiana
25,950	Maryland
25,901	South Carolina
25,598	Illinois
25,313	Washington
25,178	California
25,047	Kansas
24,527	Arkansas
24,389	Kentucky
23,859	Alabama
22,730	Oklahoma
22,171	New York
21,798	Rhode Island
21,008	West Virginia
20,470	Mississippi

Table G.200. INVESTUS

Foreign Investment (millions) 1997

91,788	California
77,906	Texas
53,711	New York
37,649	Illinois
35,095	Ohio
30,488	New Jersey
29,598	Florida
25,922	Alaska
25,671	Pennsylvania
25,403	Georgia
25,151	Louisiana
24,019	North Carolina
20,914	Michigan
20,158	Virginia
18,367	Indiana
17,123	Tennessee
16,909	Kentucky
16,847	South Carolina
15,473	Massachusetts
15,157	Hawaii
13,006	Alabama
12,275	Washington
10,945	Missouri
10,578	Maryland
9,972	Minnesota
9,833	Colorado
9,797	Arizona
8,784	Nevada
8,703	Connecticut
8,003	Wisconsin
7,719	Utah
7,269	Oregon
6,714	West Virginia
5,723	Oklahoma
5,696	Kansas
5,444	Iowa
4,956	Wyoming
4,945	New Mexico
3,960	Maine
3,934	Arkansas
3,323	Delaware
2,967	Mississippi
2,628	Rhode Island
2,546	New Hampshire
2,041	Montana
2,027	Nebraska
1,407	Idaho
1,166	North Dakota
1,031	Vermont
986	South Dakota

Table G.201. FOREMPLY

Work for Foreign Firms (1,000s) 1997

569.4	California
351.5	New York
350.6	Texas
240.9	Florida
234.1	Ohio
225.0	Pennsylvania
225.0	North Carolina
224.5	Illinois
212.4	New Jersey
188.9	Georgia
171.4	Michigan
159.5	Massachusetts
149.4	Tennessee
143.3	Virginia
128.3	Indiana
116.9	South Carolina
96.6	Minnesota
92.0	Maryland
89.5	Kentucky
86.6	Washington
84.0	Missouri
83.8	Connecticut
80.3	Colorado
76.5	Wisconsin
65.0	Alabama
59.4	Arizona
58.0	Louisiana
52.0	Oregon
50.1	Hawaii
45.4	Kansas
37.8	Iowa
36.7	Utah
35.2	Arkansas
34.4	Oklahoma
31.6	Maine
31.6	New Hampshire
27.2	West Virginia
25.5	Nevada
21.7	Mississippi
20.8	Nebraska
19.1	Delaware
18.5	Rhode Island
17.4	New Mexico
12.4	Idaho
10.4	South Dakota
9.6	Vermont
8.7	Alaska
6.9	Wyoming
4.4	Montana
3.5	North Dakota

Table G.202. IMMIGRNT

Immigrants Admitted 1998

170,126	California
96,559	New York
59,965	Florida
44,428	Texas
35,091	New Jersey
33,163	Illinois
16,920	Washington
15,869	Massachusetts
15,686	Virginia
15,561	Maryland
13,943	Michigan
11,942	Pennsylvania
10,445	Georgia
7,780	Connecticut
7,697	Ohio
6,981	Minnesota
6,513	Colorado
6,415	North Carolina
6,211	Arizona
6,106	Nevada
5,909	Oregon
5,465	Hawaii
3,981	Indiana
3,724	Wisconsin
3,588	Missouri
3,360	Utah
3,184	Kansas
2,806	Tennessee
2,273	Oklahoma
2,199	New Mexico
2,193	Louisiana
2,125	South Carolina
2,017	Kentucky
1,976	Rhode Island
1,655	Iowa
1,608	Alabama
1,504	Idaho
1,267	Nebraska
1,063	Delaware
1,010	New Hampshire
1,008	Alaska
914	Arkansas
709	Maine
701	Mississippi
513	Vermont
472	North Dakota
375	West Virginia
356	South Dakota
299	Montana
159	Wyoming

Table G.203. METROPOP

Percent Metropolitan 2000

100.0	New Jersey
96.7	California
96.1	Massachusetts
95.6	Connecticut
93.8	Rhode Island
93.0	Florida
92.7	Maryland
91.9	New York
87.8	Arizona
86.1	Nevada
84.5	Texas
84.5	Illinois
84.5	Pennsylvania
84.0	Colorado
82.9	Washington
82.6	Michigan
81.6	Delaware
81.0	Ohio
78.1	Virginia
76.7	Utah
75.2	Louisiana
73.1	Hawaii
72.7	Oregon
71.7	Indiana
70.1	Minnesota
70.1	Alabama
70.0	South Carolina
68.9	Georgia
68.0	Missouri
67.8	Wisconsin
67.8	Tennessee
67.1	North Carolina
60.5	Oklahoma
60.2	New Hampshire
57.0	New Mexico
56.4	Kansas
51.8	Nebraska
48.6	Arkansas
48.3	Kentucky
44.6	Iowa
43.1	North Dakota
41.9	West Virginia
41.5	Alaska
38.3	Idaho
35.9	Mississippi
35.8	Maine
34.0	South Dakota
33.4	Montana
29.6	Wyoming
27.9	Vermont

Table G.204. HOUSHOLD

Households in State (1,000s) 2000

11,446	California
7,113	Texas
6,766	New York
5,881	Florida
4,593	Pennsylvania
4,438	Illinois
4,285	Ohio
3,693	Michigan
2,957	New Jersey
2,883	North Carolina
2,843	Georgia
2,579	Virginia
2,349	Massachusetts
2,231	Indiana
2,211	Washington
2,100	Tennessee
2,089	Missouri
1,973	Wisconsin
1,906	Maryland
1,791	Minnesota
1,762	Arizona
1,663	Alabama
1,599	Louisiana
1,561	Colorado
1,497	Kentucky
1,441	South Carolina
1,288	Oklahoma
1,286	Oregon
1,238	Connecticut
1,103	Iowa
999	Kansas
997	Mississippi
970	Arkansas
716	West Virginia
677	Utah
676	Nevada
636	Nebraska
632	New Mexico
490	Maine
450	New Hampshire
448	Idaho
401	Hawaii
376	Rhode Island
346	Montana
284	Delaware
277	South Dakota
247	North Dakota
231	Vermont
215	Alaska
185	Wyoming

Table G.205.   CHRISTAN

Percent Population Christian 1990

79.6	Utah
75.9	North Dakota
75.1	Rhode Island
70.7	Alabama
70.1	Louisiana
70.1	Mississippi
68.1	South Dakota
66.5	Oklahoma
64.2	Minnesota
63.9	Wisconsin
63.5	Texas
63.4	Nebraska
61.7	South Carolina
60.9	Massachusetts
60.8	Tennessee
60.5	Arkansas
60.3	Iowa
60.1	Kentucky
59.6	North Carolina
58.9	Connecticut
58.6	Pennsylvania
58.3	New Mexico
57.5	Illinois
56.6	Missouri
56.5	Georgia
55.7	New Jersey
55.5	New York
54.3	Kansas
50.4	Idaho
49.2	Michigan
48.9	Ohio
47.6	Wyoming
47.1	Indiana
46.8	Virginia
44.6	Delaware
43.9	Maryland
42.7	Montana
41.3	West Virginia
41.1	Arizona
40.4	Vermont
39.5	Florida
39.2	California
38.9	New Hampshire
37.8	Colorado
36.1	Maine
35.3	Hawaii
32.4	Washington
31.8	Oregon
31.8	Alaska
29.6	Nevada

Table G.206.   JEWISH

Percent Population Jewish 1990

9.1	New York
5.8	New Jersey
4.5	Massachusetts
4.3	Florida
4.2	Maryland
3.4	Nevada
3.1	Connecticut
3.0	California
2.3	Pennsylvania
2.3	Illinois
1.8	Delaware
1.8	Arizona
1.8	Colorado
1.6	Rhode Island
1.3	Ohio
1.2	Missouri
1.1	Georgia
1.1	Michigan
1.1	Virginia
1.0	Vermont
.9	Minnesota
.8	New Hampshire
.7	Oregon
.6	Texas
.6	New Mexico
.6	Kansas
.6	Maine
.6	Hawaii
.6	Washington
.6	Alaska
.5	Wisconsin
.4	Louisiana
.4	Nebraska
.3	South Carolina
.3	Tennessee
.3	Kentucky
.3	North Carolina
.3	Indiana
.2	Utah
.2	Alabama
.2	Oklahoma
.2	Iowa
.1	North Dakota
.1	Mississippi
.1	South Dakota
.1	Arkansas
.1	Idaho
.1	Wyoming
.1	Montana
.1	West Virginia

Table G.207.   LOWBIRWT

Percent Low Birth Weight 1998

10.1	Louisiana
10.1	Mississippi
9.5	South Carolina
9.3	Alabama
9.1	Tennessee
8.9	Arkansas
8.9	Wyoming
8.8	North Carolina
8.7	Maryland
8.6	Colorado
8.5	Georgia
8.4	Delaware
8.1	Florida
8.1	Kentucky
8.0	New Jersey
8.0	Illinois
8.0	West Virginia
7.9	Virginia
7.9	Indiana
7.8	New York
7.8	Connecticut
7.8	Missouri
7.8	Michigan
7.7	Ohio
7.6	Nevada
7.6	Pennsylvania
7.6	Rhode Island
7.6	New Mexico
7.5	Hawaii
7.4	Texas
7.2	Oklahoma
7.0	Kansas
7.0	Montana
6.9	Massachusetts
6.8	Arizona
6.7	Utah
6.5	Vermont
6.5	Wisconsin
6.5	Nebraska
6.5	North Dakota
6.4	Iowa
6.2	California
6.0	Alaska
6.0	Idaho
5.8	Minnesota
5.8	Maine
5.8	South Dakota
5.7	New Hampshire
5.7	Washington
5.4	Oregon

Table G.208. TEENBRTH

Percent Births Unmarried Teens 1998

21.5	Utah
17.3	Texas
16.8	Arizona
16.4	Nevada
16.2	Alaska
16.0	Georgia
16.0	California
15.8	Idaho
15.7	New Mexico
15.6	Mississippi
15.3	Louisiana
15.2	Illinois
15.0	Colorado
14.8	North Carolina
14.8	Oklahoma
14.7	Hawaii
14.6	Kansas
14.5	Arkansas
14.4	Indiana
14.3	Alabama
14.3	Tennessee
14.2	Delaware
14.2	New York
14.2	Nebraska
14.1	New Jersey
14.0	South Carolina
14.0	Maryland
14.0	Washington
13.9	Virginia
13.9	Missouri
13.9	South Dakota
13.8	Kentucky
13.8	Minnesota
13.8	Oregon
13.6	Michigan
13.6	Ohio
13.4	Connecticut
13.2	Massachusetts
13.1	Florida
13.0	Wyoming
13.0	Iowa
12.9	Wisconsin
12.7	Rhode Island
12.4	North Dakota
12.3	Montana
12.2	Pennsylvania
12.2	New Hampshire
11.5	West Virginia
11.1	Vermont
11.0	Maine

Table G.209. UNMARRBR

Percent Births to Unmarried 1998

45.4	Mississippi
44.9	Louisiana
44.0	New Mexico
38.8	South Carolina
38.4	Arizona
37.1	Delaware
36.6	Florida
36.2	Georgia
35.0	Nevada
35.0	Arkansas
34.9	Tennessee
34.9	New York
34.4	Maryland
34.1	Illinois
34.1	Alabama
34.1	Missouri
34.0	Ohio
33.9	Michigan
33.9	Rhode Island
33.5	Indiana
33.2	Oklahoma
32.8	California
32.8	North Carolina
32.8	Pennsylvania
32.4	West Virginia
32.0	South Dakota
31.5	Texas
31.5	Hawaii
31.2	Connecticut
31.1	Alaska
30.6	Maine
30.1	Kentucky
29.9	Montana
29.8	Virginia
29.7	Oregon
29.6	Wyoming
28.5	Wisconsin
28.3	New Jersey
28.0	Vermont
27.9	Washington
27.8	Kansas
27.2	Iowa
27.0	North Dakota
26.2	Nebraska
26.1	Massachusetts
25.6	Colorado
25.6	Minnesota
24.1	New Hampshire
22.0	Idaho
17.1	Utah

Table G.210. ABORTION

Abortion Rates per 1,000 1996

44.6	Nevada
41.4	New York
35.8	New Jersey
33.0	California
32.0	Florida
29.3	Massachusetts
27.3	Hawaii
26.3	Maryland
26.1	Illinois
24.4	Rhode Island
24.1	Delaware
22.5	Connecticut
22.3	Michigan
21.6	Oregon
21.1	Georgia
20.9	Washington
20.9	Colorado
20.7	Texas
20.2	North Carolina
19.8	Arizona
18.9	Virginia
18.9	Kansas
17.1	Vermont
17.0	Ohio
15.6	Alabama
15.6	Montana
15.2	Pennsylvania
14.8	Tennessee
14.7	Louisiana
14.6	Alaska
14.4	New Mexico
13.9	Minnesota
12.7	New Hampshire
12.3	Wisconsin
12.3	Nebraska
11.8	Oklahoma
11.6	South Carolina
11.4	Arkansas
11.2	Indiana
9.7	Maine
9.6	Kentucky
9.4	Iowa
9.4	North Dakota
9.1	Missouri
7.8	Utah
7.2	Mississippi
6.6	West Virginia
6.5	South Dakota
6.1	Idaho
2.7	Wyoming

Table G.211.   DEATHS

Death Rate per 1,000 Population 1997

11.5	West Virginia
10.8	Arkansas
10.6	Florida
10.6	Pennsylvania
10.2	Oklahoma
10.1	Alabama
10.1	Missouri
10.1	Mississippi
10.0	Tennessee
9.9	Iowa
9.8	Maine
9.7	Rhode Island
9.6	Kentucky
9.5	Ohio
9.3	North Dakota
9.3	South Dakota
9.2	Louisiana
9.1	Connecticut
9.1	Nebraska
9.1	South Carolina
9.0	Massachusetts
9.0	Oregon
9.0	North Carolina
9.0	Montana
8.9	Delaware
8.9	Indiana
8.8	New Jersey
8.8	Wisconsin
8.7	Illinois
8.7	Michigan
8.6	New York
8.4	Vermont
8.3	Nevada
8.2	Maryland
8.2	Arizona
8.1	New Hampshire
8.0	Virginia
8.0	Wyoming
7.9	Georgia
7.9	Minnesota
7.7	New Mexico
7.5	Washington
7.5	Idaho
7.2	Texas
6.9	California
6.8	Hawaii
6.7	Colorado
5.6	Utah
4.2	Alaska
*	Kansas

*Incomplete data

Table G.212.   INFMORTT

Infant Mortality per 1,000 Births 1997

10.6	Mississippi
9.6	West Virginia
9.6	South Carolina
9.5	Alabama
9.5	Louisiana
9.2	North Carolina
8.8	Maryland
8.7	Arkansas
8.6	Tennessee
8.6	Georgia
8.4	Illinois
8.2	Indiana
8.2	Michigan
7.8	Ohio
7.8	Delaware
7.8	Virginia
7.7	South Dakota
7.6	Pennsylvania
7.6	Missouri
7.5	Oklahoma
7.5	Alaska
7.4	Nebraska
7.4	Kansas
7.3	Kentucky
7.2	Connecticut
7.1	Florida
7.1	Arizona
7.0	Rhode Island
7.0	Colorado
6.9	Montana
6.8	Idaho
6.7	New York
6.6	Hawaii
6.5	Wisconsin
6.5	Nevada
6.4	Texas
6.3	New Jersey
6.2	Iowa
6.2	North Dakota
6.1	Vermont
6.1	New Mexico
5.9	Minnesota
5.9	California
5.8	Oregon
5.8	Wyoming
5.8	Utah
5.6	Washington
5.2	Massachusetts
5.1	Maine
4.3	New Hampshire

Table G.213.   INFMORTW

Infant Mortality White per 1,000 Births 1997

9.1	West Virginia
7.5	Alabama
7.4	Arkansas
7.3	Indiana
7.1	Mississippi
7.0	Kentucky
7.0	Rhode Island
6.9	North Carolina
6.9	Idaho
6.8	Alaska
6.8	Nebraska
6.8	Arizona
6.7	Oklahoma
6.7	Colorado
6.6	Louisiana
6.6	Kansas
6.5	Tennessee
6.5	Ohio
6.4	South Carolina
6.4	Illinois
6.3	Connecticut
6.2	Nevada
6.1	Georgia
6.1	Michigan
6.1	Missouri
6.1	Vermont
6.0	Virginia
6.0	Pennsylvania
6.0	Montana
5.9	Texas
5.9	Iowa
5.9	North Dakota
5.8	Utah
5.7	Delaware
5.7	Florida
5.7	New York
5.7	Wisconsin
5.7	Oregon
5.6	New Mexico
5.6	California
5.6	Wyoming
5.3	South Dakota
5.3	Washington
5.3	Maine
5.1	Maryland
5.1	Minnesota
5.0	Massachusetts
4.9	New Jersey
4.3	New Hampshire
*	Hawaii

*Incomplete data

Table G.214. INFMORTB	**Table G.215. DEATHALL**	**Table G.216. DEATHART**
Infant Mortality Black per 1,000 Births 1997	*All Deaths Rate per 100,000 1997*	*Heart Death Rate per 100,000 1997*

19.2	Nebraska	1,150.0	West Virginia	381.3	West Virginia
18.2	Iowa	1,103.7	Arkansas	355.3	Mississippi
17.6	Pennsylvania	1,064.3	Pennsylvania	350.5	Pennsylvania
17.5	Michigan	1,054.3	Florida	341.7	Missouri
17.1	Kansas	1,023.3	Oklahoma	339.8	Florida
17.1	Illinois	1,007.3	Mississippi	339.8	Oklahoma
16.5	Minnesota	1,005.6	Missouri	335.9	New York
16.3	Colorado	1,001.5	Alabama	335.5	Arkansas
16.3	Tennessee	994.5	Rhode Island	330.7	Rhode Island
16.3	Missouri	981.1	Tennessee	319.4	Iowa
16.2	Maryland	972.3	Kentucky	318.8	Kentucky
15.8	Indiana	970.9	Iowa	314.2	Alabama
15.7	North Carolina	965.6	Maine	310.3	Tennessee
15.6	Ohio	941.7	Ohio	306.8	Ohio
15.4	South Carolina	930.3	South Dakota	298.0	Nebraska
15.4	Washington	922.3	Nebraska	297.8	Connecticut
15.0	Oklahoma	919.5	North Dakota	292.8	Maine
14.9	Mississippi	919.3	Louisiana	290.5	New Jersey
14.5	Delaware	915.3	Kansas	288.6	South Dakota
14.4	Arizona	906.0	Indiana	285.1	North Dakota
14.3	Connecticut	899.6	Connecticut	284.1	Indiana
14.2	Virginia	896.0	South Carolina	280.4	Kansas
13.9	Alabama	895.8	New Jersey	278.8	Michigan
13.9	Wisconsin	893.9	Massachusetts	274.3	Illinois
13.8	Arkansas	889.9	Delaware	272.7	Louisiana
13.8	Louisiana	889.2	North Carolina	272.3	Delaware
13.8	Georgia	887.0	Oregon	269.8	Massachusetts
13.6	Nevada	884.0	Montana	264.9	Wisconsin
13.4	New Jersey	874.7	New York	263.2	South Carolina
13.1	California	868.4	Wisconsin	260.0	North Carolina
12.3	Florida	865.1	Illinois	255.7	Vermont
11.0	Kentucky	857.9	Vermont	239.9	Montana
10.9	Texas	852.3	Michigan	238.9	New Hampshire
10.9	New York	820.4	Maryland	236.0	Georgia
8.8	Massachusetts	813.7	Arizona	235.7	Maryland
*	West Virginia	806.5	New Hampshire	232.4	Nevada
*	Rhode Island	799.7	Virginia	232.1	Virginia
*	Idaho	797.7	Nevada	231.8	Oregon
*	Alaska	792.8	Georgia	224.4	Texas
*	Vermont	787.8	Minnesota	223.4	Arizona
*	Montana	780.6	Wyoming	216.8	Wyoming
*	North Dakota	741.7	Idaho	212.8	California
*	Utah	739.0	Washington	208.1	Idaho
*	Oregon	734.5	Texas	205.1	Minnesota
*	New Mexico	731.5	New Mexico	200.6	Hawaii
*	Wyoming	696.0	California	198.1	Washington
*	South Dakota	665.1	Hawaii	189.3	New Mexico
*	Maine	658.3	Colorado	166.6	Colorado
*	New Hampshire	562.3	Utah	146.0	Utah
*	Hawaii	422.6	Alaska	91.4	Alaska

*Incomplete data

Table G.217. DEATHCAN

Cancer Death Rate per 100,000 1997

262.0	West Virginia
260.0	Florida
251.1	Pennsylvania
249.7	Rhode Island
240.3	Arkansas
239.9	Maine
229.5	Kentucky
228.1	Delaware
225.5	New Jersey
223.7	Massachusetts
222.0	Iowa
221.7	Alabama
221.4	Missouri
220.9	Tennessee
220.7	Ohio
218.3	Connecticut
218.1	Oklahoma
214.9	Louisiana
214.2	Mississippi
210.3	Indiana
209.8	South Dakota
208.8	Vermont
208.7	Oregon
206.3	North Dakota
206.0	New York
205.8	Illinois
205.8	New Hampshire
204.6	Wisconsin
204.3	North Carolina
203.5	Montana
203.2	South Carolina
201.1	Kansas
200.6	Michigan
198.8	Maryland
195.4	Nebraska
192.0	Virginia
189.6	Nevada
187.3	Minnesota
185.5	Arizona
178.9	Washington
175.9	Wyoming
174.0	Georgia
165.6	Texas
161.1	California
160.9	Idaho
159.9	New Mexico
155.6	Hawaii
145.1	Colorado
103.6	Utah
102.1	Alaska

Table G.218. DEATHCER

Cerebral Death Rate per 100,000 1997

97.5	Arkansas
79.2	Oregon
77.4	South Dakota
75.7	Iowa
75.7	South Carolina
75.2	North Dakota
74.9	Tennessee
72.1	Oklahoma
71.2	Wisconsin
70.4	North Carolina
69.6	Pennsylvania
69.3	Rhode Island
68.6	Missouri
68.4	Florida
68.1	West Virginia
68.0	Mississippi
66.8	Alabama
66.5	Nebraska
66.2	Kansas
65.3	Indiana
64.0	Kentucky
64.0	Minnesota
63.5	Maine
61.9	Montana
61.5	Ohio
60.7	Illinois
60.0	Virginia
60.0	Washington
59.8	Hawaii
58.9	Vermont
58.9	Michigan
58.8	New Hampshire
58.7	Idaho
58.2	Connecticut
58.1	Louisiana
57.0	Georgia
55.7	Massachusetts
54.5	Arizona
52.2	Texas
51.8	California
51.3	New Jersey
51.2	Maryland
48.6	Wyoming
47.6	Nevada
47.4	Delaware
44.4	New Mexico
44.2	New York
43.9	Colorado
42.5	Utah
21.7	Alaska

Table G.219. DEATHACC

Accidents Death Rate per 100,000 1997

58.2	Mississippi
57.9	New Mexico
53.3	Arkansas
53.2	Alabama
51.3	Wyoming
51.2	Montana
48.4	Oklahoma
47.1	Arizona
47.0	Tennessee
46.1	Kentucky
45.6	South Carolina
45.1	Idaho
44.2	West Virginia
44.1	Missouri
44.1	Alaska
43.8	Louisiana
41.5	South Dakota
41.2	North Carolina
41.2	Georgia
40.2	Oregon
40.2	Nebraska
39.8	Pennsylvania
39.6	Delaware
39.5	Nevada
39.0	Kansas
38.2	North Dakota
38.1	Iowa
37.9	Florida
36.9	Texas
36.8	Colorado
36.4	Minnesota
35.7	Indiana
35.6	Wisconsin
34.5	Maine
34.3	Virginia
34.2	Washington
34.1	Vermont
33.3	Utah
32.4	Michigan
30.9	Connecticut
30.8	Ohio
29.9	Hawaii
29.5	New Jersey
29.2	Illinois
28.0	California
27.4	New Hampshire
27.3	New York
26.9	Maryland
24.5	Rhode Island
21.0	Massachusetts

Table G.220. DEATHMV

Auto Death Rate per 100,000 1997

32.0	Mississippi
28.9	Arkansas
28.8	Alabama
26.6	Montana
25.8	Oklahoma
25.0	Wyoming
24.7	New Mexico
24.0	South Carolina
23.4	Tennessee
21.8	Kentucky
21.7	Missouri
21.5	Georgia
21.4	Nevada
21.3	West Virginia
21.3	Louisiana
21.0	North Carolina
20.9	Arizona
20.6	Idaho
20.5	South Dakota
20.2	Kansas
19.3	Texas
18.9	Delaware
18.9	Florida
18.5	Nebraska
18.3	Utah
17.2	Iowa
16.9	Oregon
16.7	Indiana
16.5	North Dakota
16.2	Colorado
15.8	Michigan
15.2	Maine
14.5	Wisconsin
14.3	Virginia
13.8	Alaska
13.8	Pennsylvania
13.6	Washington
13.1	Vermont
12.9	Ohio
12.8	Minnesota
12.7	Maryland
12.1	Illinois
11.9	Hawaii
11.9	California
11.3	New Hampshire
11.2	Connecticut
10.4	New Jersey
10.1	New York
10.1	Rhode Island
8.2	Massachusetts

Table G.221. DEATHPUL

Pulmonary Death Rate per 100,000 1997

62.7	West Virginia
60.8	Montana
56.3	Wyoming
56.0	Maine
55.2	Florida
52.2	Arizona
52.1	Oklahoma
51.8	Nevada
50.5	Oregon
49.8	Kentucky
49.7	Arkansas
49.0	Kansas
48.7	Vermont
47.8	Nebraska
47.7	Missouri
46.7	New Hampshire
46.3	Ohio
46.0	Tennessee
45.6	Indiana
45.5	South Dakota
45.2	Iowa
44.3	Pennsylvania
43.6	Rhode Island
43.2	Idaho
43.0	North Carolina
42.9	Alabama
42.7	New Mexico
42.6	Colorado
41.8	Washington
40.7	Mississippi
40.5	Delaware
39.8	South Carolina
39.8	Massachusetts
39.0	Wisconsin
38.7	Connecticut
37.2	Michigan
36.7	North Dakota
36.5	California
35.8	Virginia
35.8	Illinois
35.6	Maryland
35.4	New Jersey
34.8	Minnesota
34.5	Texas
33.9	Louisiana
33.6	New York
33.5	Georgia
21.6	Hawaii
21.5	Utah
19.5	Alaska

Table G.222. DEATHDIA

Diabetes Death Rate per 100,000 1997

38.7	Louisiana
37.6	West Virginia
29.9	Ohio
29.5	Pennsylvania
29.1	New Jersey
28.6	North Dakota
28.1	Oklahoma
27.9	Delaware
27.7	Rhode Island
27.4	South Carolina
27.4	Maryland
27.2	Alabama
26.6	South Dakota
26.2	Florida
25.9	Kentucky
25.3	Arkansas
25.3	Indiana
25.0	Oregon
24.9	Michigan
24.7	North Carolina
24.5	Tennessee
24.5	Texas
24.4	Maine
24.3	Vermont
24.1	Missouri
23.7	Iowa
23.6	New Hampshire
23.1	New Mexico
23.0	Illinois
22.7	Wisconsin
22.4	Minnesota
22.3	Kansas
22.2	Massachusetts
21.0	Utah
20.9	Mississippi
20.8	Arizona
20.1	New York
20.0	Idaho
19.5	Washington
19.2	Montana
19.0	Nebraska
19.0	Connecticut
18.5	Virginia
17.4	California
17.0	Georgia
17.0	Hawaii
16.7	Wyoming
14.5	Nevada
13.4	Colorado
13.3	Alaska

Table G.223. DEATHIV

HIV Death Rate per 100,000 1997

16.0	New York
12.8	Florida
12.5	New Jersey
11.6	Maryland
9.9	Georgia
9.2	Louisiana
8.4	South Carolina
8.2	Delaware
6.6	North Carolina
6.2	Texas
6.1	Connecticut
5.8	California
5.7	Mississippi
5.2	Tennessee
5.2	Nevada
4.9	Virginia
4.8	Pennsylvania
4.5	Alabama
4.3	Illinois
4.2	Rhode Island
4.0	Massachusetts
3.6	Arizona
3.3	Oklahoma
3.2	Michigan
3.2	Colorado
3.1	Washington
3.0	Hawaii
2.7	Missouri
2.6	Ohio
2.6	Arkansas
2.6	Indiana
2.5	Oregon
2.5	New Mexico
2.2	Maine
1.9	Kentucky
1.9	Nebraska
1.7	West Virginia
1.7	Kansas
1.5	Wisconsin
1.5	Minnesota
1.2	Utah
.9	Iowa
*	North Dakota
*	South Dakota
*	Vermont
*	New Hampshire
*	Idaho
*	Montana
*	Wyoming
*	Alaska

*Incomplete data

Table G.224. DEATHSUI

Suicide Rate per 100,000 1997

24.5	Nevada
21.0	Alaska
20.8	Montana
19.8	Wyoming
17.3	New Mexico
17.3	Idaho
17.2	South Dakota
16.6	Arizona
16.5	Oregon
15.7	Colorado
15.0	Oklahoma
14.6	Utah
14.4	West Virginia
14.3	Florida
14.1	Arkansas
13.6	Tennessee
13.1	Missouri
13.0	Washington
12.5	Kentucky
12.5	North Dakota
12.4	Mississippi
12.4	Indiana
12.4	Vermont
12.3	Kansas
12.2	North Carolina
12.1	Georgia
12.1	Louisiana
12.1	Iowa
11.9	Delaware
11.9	Alabama
11.7	Pennsylvania
11.6	Hawaii
11.6	New Hampshire
11.5	South Carolina
11.3	Virginia
11.1	Wisconsin
11.0	Texas
11.0	Maine
10.6	California
10.6	Nebraska
10.3	Michigan
10.2	Maryland
10.1	Ohio
10.1	Minnesota
8.0	Massachusetts
7.9	Connecticut
7.6	New York
7.6	Illinois
7.3	New Jersey
7.3	Rhode Island

Table G.225. MEDCAREE

Enrollment in Medicare (1,000s) 1999

3,822	California
2,764	Florida
2,677	New York
2,219	Texas
2,081	Pennsylvania
1,686	Ohio
1,621	Illinois
1,384	Michigan
1,188	New Jersey
1,112	North Carolina
950	Massachusetts
897	Georgia
875	Virginia
852	Missouri
843	Indiana
814	Tennessee
775	Wisconsin
723	Washington
675	Alabama
659	Arizona
647	Minnesota
632	Maryland
614	Kentucky
596	Louisiana
556	South Carolina
510	Connecticut
502	Oklahoma
483	Oregon
475	Iowa
458	Colorado
435	Arkansas
413	Mississippi
388	Kansas
334	West Virginia
252	Nebraska
229	Nevada
229	New Mexico
213	Maine
201	Utah
170	Rhode Island
167	New Hampshire
162	Idaho
161	Hawaii
135	Montana
119	South Dakota
110	Delaware
103	North Dakota
88	Vermont
64	Wyoming
40	Alaska

Table G.226.   MEDCAREP

Payments in Medicare (millions) 1999

23,306	California
18,389	Florida
16,838	New York
14,228	Texas
12,953	Pennsylvania
9,305	Ohio
7,606	Illinois
7,475	New Jersey
6,716	Michigan
5,809	North Carolina
4,855	Tennessee
4,833	Massachusetts
4,730	Indiana
4,258	Louisiana
4,096	Maryland
4,062	Missouri
4,050	Virginia
3,895	Georgia
3,817	Alabama
3,356	Wisconsin
3,120	Kentucky
2,992	Minnesota
2,986	Connecticut
2,828	Arizona
2,801	South Carolina
2,505	Washington
2,328	Colorado
2,231	Mississippi
2,066	Oklahoma
2,044	Arkansas
1,739	Kansas
1,653	West Virginia
1,649	Oregon
1,417	Iowa
1,056	Nebraska
1,048	Nevada
973	Rhode Island
836	Utah
795	New Mexico
660	Maine
600	Hawaii
580	Idaho
557	New Hampshire
509	Montana
487	South Dakota
459	North Dakota
386	Delaware
254	Vermont
211	Wyoming
133	Alaska

Table G.227.   PAYENROL

Dollars Each Medicare Enrollee 1999

7,144	Louisiana
6,653	Florida
6,481	Maryland
6,412	Texas
6,292	New Jersey
6,290	New York
6,224	Pennsylvania
6,098	California
5,964	Tennessee
5,855	Connecticut
5,724	Rhode Island
5,655	Alabama
5,611	Indiana
5,519	Ohio
5,402	Mississippi
5,224	North Carolina
5,087	Massachusetts
5,083	Colorado
5,081	Kentucky
5,038	South Carolina
4,949	West Virginia
4,853	Michigan
4,768	Missouri
4,699	Arkansas
4,692	Illinois
4,629	Virginia
4,624	Minnesota
4,576	Nevada
4,482	Kansas
4,456	North Dakota
4,342	Georgia
4,330	Wisconsin
4,291	Arizona
4,190	Nebraska
4,159	Utah
4,116	Oklahoma
4,092	South Dakota
3,770	Montana
3,727	Hawaii
3,580	Idaho
3,509	Delaware
3,472	New Mexico
3,465	Washington
3,414	Oregon
3,335	New Hampshire
3,325	Alaska
3,297	Wyoming
3,099	Maine
2,983	Iowa
2,886	Vermont

Table G.228.   MEDCAIDR

Recipients Medicaid (1,000s) 1998

7,082	California
3,073	New York
2,325	Texas
1,905	Florida
1,844	Tennessee
1,523	Pennsylvania
1,413	Washington
1,364	Illinois
1,363	Michigan
1,291	Ohio
1,222	Georgia
1,168	North Carolina
908	Massachusetts
813	New Jersey
734	Missouri
721	Louisiana
653	Virginia
644	Kentucky
607	Indiana
595	South Carolina
561	Maryland
538	Minnesota
527	Alabama
519	Wisconsin
511	Oregon
508	Arizona
486	Mississippi
425	Arkansas
381	Connecticut
345	Colorado
343	West Virginia
342	Oklahoma
329	New Mexico
315	Iowa
242	Kansas
216	Utah
211	Nebraska
185	Hawaii
170	Maine
153	Rhode Island
128	Nevada
124	Vermont
123	Idaho
101	Montana
101	Delaware
94	New Hampshire
90	South Dakota
75	Alaska
62	North Dakota
46	Wyoming

Table G.229. MEDCAIDP

Medicaid Payments (millions) 1998

24,299	New York
14,237	California
7,140	Texas
6,173	Illinois
6,121	Ohio
6,080	Pennsylvania
5,686	Florida
4,609	Massachusetts
4,345	Michigan
4,219	New Jersey
4,014	North Carolina
3,167	Tennessee
3,012	Georgia
2,924	Minnesota
2,570	Missouri
2,564	Indiana
2,489	Maryland
2,425	Kentucky
2,421	Connecticut
2,384	Louisiana
2,206	Wisconsin
2,118	Virginia
2,044	Washington
2,019	South Carolina
1,902	Alabama
1,644	Arizona
1,442	Mississippi
1,439	Colorado
1,378	Oregon
1,376	Arkansas
1,289	Iowa
1,243	West Virginia
1,178	Oklahoma
919	Rhode Island
916	Kansas
862	New Mexico
753	Nebraska
747	Maine
619	Utah
606	New Hampshire
507	Hawaii
462	Nevada
425	Idaho
420	Delaware
361	Montana
356	South Dakota
351	Vermont
341	North Dakota
330	Alaska
192	Wyoming

Table G.230. PAYRECIP

Dollars Medicaid Each Recipient 1998

7,907	New York
6,447	New Hampshire
6,354	Connecticut
6,007	Rhode Island
5,500	North Dakota
5,435	Minnesota
5,189	New Jersey
5,076	Massachusetts
4,741	Ohio
4,526	Illinois
4,437	Maryland
4,400	Alaska
4,394	Maine
4,250	Wisconsin
4,224	Indiana
4,174	Wyoming
4,171	Colorado
4,158	Delaware
4,092	Iowa
3,992	Pennsylvania
3,956	South Dakota
3,785	Kansas
3,766	Kentucky
3,624	West Virginia
3,609	Nevada
3,609	Alabama
3,574	Montana
3,569	Nebraska
3,501	Missouri
3,455	Idaho
3,444	Oklahoma
3,437	North Carolina
3,393	South Carolina
3,307	Louisiana
3,243	Virginia
3,238	Arkansas
3,236	Arizona
3,188	Michigan
3,071	Texas
2,985	Florida
2,967	Mississippi
2,866	Utah
2,831	Vermont
2,741	Hawaii
2,697	Oregon
2,620	New Mexico
2,465	Georgia
2,010	California
1,717	Tennessee
1,447	Washington

Table G.231. NOCOVER

Percent No Health Insurance 1998

24.5	Texas
24.2	Arizona
22.1	California
21.2	Nevada
21.1	New Mexico
20.0	Mississippi
19.6	Montana
19.0	Louisiana
18.7	Arkansas
18.3	Oklahoma
17.7	Idaho
17.5	Florida
17.5	Georgia
17.3	New York
17.3	Alaska
17.2	West Virginia
17.0	Alabama
16.9	Wyoming
16.6	Maryland
16.4	New Jersey
15.4	South Carolina
15.1	Colorado
15.0	Illinois
15.0	North Carolina
14.7	Delaware
14.4	Indiana
14.3	South Dakota
14.3	Oregon
14.2	North Dakota
14.1	Kentucky
14.1	Virginia
13.9	Utah
13.2	Michigan
13.0	Tennessee
12.7	Maine
12.6	Connecticut
12.3	Washington
11.8	Wisconsin
11.3	New Hampshire
10.5	Pennsylvania
10.5	Missouri
10.4	Ohio
10.3	Massachusetts
10.3	Kansas
10.0	Rhode Island
10.0	Hawaii
9.9	Vermont
9.3	Minnesota
9.3	Iowa
9.0	Nebraska

Table G.232. CHINOCOV

Percent Children No Insurance 1998

26.3	Arizona
25.4	Texas
23.1	Nevada
22.5	Oklahoma
21.2	Mississippi
20.4	California
19.8	Montana
19.1	Georgia
19.0	Arkansas
18.4	Louisiana
18.0	Florida
17.9	Alabama
17.6	Idaho
17.6	Delaware
17.5	Maryland
17.1	New Mexico
16.4	Wyoming
16.4	North Dakota
15.3	South Dakota
15.2	Indiana
14.8	South Carolina
14.6	Illinois
14.0	Kentucky
13.8	New York
13.7	Alaska
13.4	New Jersey
13.2	North Carolina
12.9	Virginia
12.5	Colorado
11.8	Oregon
11.5	Utah
10.7	Michigan
10.7	Tennessee
10.4	Maine
10.1	Connecticut
10.0	Minnesota
9.7	Wisconsin
9.6	West Virginia
9.6	New Hampshire
9.5	Hawaii
9.4	Washington
9.1	Pennsylvania
9.1	Ohio
8.9	Missouri
8.7	Iowa
8.0	Massachusetts
8.0	Kansas
7.6	Rhode Island
6.3	Vermont
5.5	Nebraska

Table G.233. DOCTORS

Physicians per 100,000 Population 1998

412	Massachusetts
387	New York
374	Maryland
354	Connecticut
338	Rhode Island
305	Vermont
295	New Jersey
291	Pennsylvania
265	Hawaii
260	Illinois
249	Minnesota
247	California
246	Louisiana
246	Tennessee
241	Virginia
238	Florida
238	Colorado
237	New Hampshire
235	Washington
235	Ohio
234	Delaware
232	North Carolina
230	Missouri
227	Wisconsin
225	Oregon
224	Michigan
223	Maine
222	North Dakota
218	Nebraska
215	West Virginia
212	New Mexico
211	Georgia
209	Kentucky
207	South Carolina
203	Texas
203	Kansas
202	Arizona
200	Utah
198	Alabama
195	Indiana
190	Montana
190	Arkansas
184	South Dakota
173	Nevada
173	Iowa
171	Wyoming
169	Oklahoma
167	Alaska
163	Mississippi
154	Idaho

Table G.234. TAXRECD

Percent Taxes Received for Costs of Substance Abuse 1998

33.66	Florida
30.09	North Dakota
28.66	Washington
27.10	South Carolina
25.79	Michigan
24.43	Oregon
24.11	South Dakota
24.00	Arkansas
24.00	Rhode Island
23.31	Arizona
21.41	Nebraska
21.29	Kansas
21.07	Wisconsin
20.88	Connecticut
20.81	Mississippi
20.79	New Jersey
20.73	Vermont
19.93	Oklahoma
18.34	Illinois
16.99	Nevada
16.97	Hawaii
16.93	Tennessee
16.09	Iowa
15.98	Alabama
15.17	West Virginia
15.15	Idaho
14.52	Pennsylvania
14.00	Georgia
13.94	New Mexico
13.90	Alaska
13.63	Ohio
13.47	Massachusetts
13.25	Louisiana
13.01	Montana
12.93	Utah
12.14	Minnesota
11.83	Maryland
11.45	Colorado
10.31	Missouri
10.24	New York
9.10	Delaware
8.77	Kentucky
8.72	California
7.47	Virginia
6.36	Wyoming
*	New Hampshire
*	North Carolina
*	Maine
*	Texas
*	Indiana

*Incomplete data

Table G.235.   AIDS

AIDS Cases Reported 1998

8,714	New York
5,654	California
5,448	Florida
3,967	Texas
2,134	New Jersey
1,740	Pennsylvania
1,639	Maryland
1,304	Illinois
1,295	Georgia
998	Virginia
951	Louisiana
924	Massachusetts
788	North Carolina
777	South Carolina
714	Michigan
695	Tennessee
685	Ohio
666	Connecticut
645	Arizona
484	Alabama
484	Indiana
443	Missouri
441	Washington
415	Mississippi
314	Colorado
285	Oklahoma
280	Kentucky
258	Nevada
209	New Mexico
204	Oregon
203	Arkansas
203	Wisconsin
190	Minnesota
174	Delaware
161	Hawaii
139	Utah
128	Rhode Island
126	Kansas
86	West Virginia
75	Iowa
72	Nebraska
42	New Hampshire
32	Idaho
31	Maine
29	Alaska
29	Montana
20	Vermont
15	South Dakota
6	North Dakota
6	Wyoming

Table G.236.   AIDSPT

AIDS per 1,000 Population 1998

.48	New York
.36	Florida
.32	Maryland
.26	New Jersey
.23	Delaware
.22	Louisiana
.20	Connecticut
.20	South Carolina
.20	Texas
.17	California
.17	Georgia
.15	Mississippi
.15	Massachusetts
.15	Virginia
.15	Pennsylvania
.14	Nevada
.14	Hawaii
.13	Arizona
.13	Rhode Island
.13	Tennessee
.12	New Mexico
.11	Alabama
.11	Illinois
.10	North Carolina
.08	Oklahoma
.08	Indiana
.08	Missouri
.08	Arkansas
.08	Colorado
.08	Washington
.07	Michigan
.07	Kentucky
.07	Utah
.06	Oregon
.06	Ohio
.05	West Virginia
.05	Kansas
.05	Alaska
.04	Nebraska
.04	Minnesota
.04	Wisconsin
.03	New Hampshire
.03	Vermont
.03	Montana
.03	Iowa
.03	Idaho
.02	Maine
.02	South Dakota
.01	Wyoming
.01	North Dakota

Table G.237.   SYPHILIS

Syphilis Cases Reported 1998

5,145	New York
3,965	Texas
3,028	Illinois
2,618	California
2,539	Florida
2,156	Maryland
2,133	North Carolina
1,836	Georgia
1,750	Tennessee
1,651	Louisiana
1,161	Mississippi
1,133	Alabama
910	Pennsylvania
871	South Carolina
826	New Jersey
707	Virginia
697	Arizona
686	Michigan
568	Massachusetts
509	Indiana
506	Arkansas
474	Ohio
375	Missouri
363	Oklahoma
339	Kentucky
208	Wisconsin
177	Connecticut
141	Washington
136	Nevada
118	Colorado
114	Delaware
113	Kansas
76	New Mexico
74	Minnesota
55	Rhode Island
55	Utah
48	Iowa
33	Nebraska
32	Oregon
15	Hawaii
15	Idaho
14	New Hampshire
13	Alaska
11	West Virginia
6	Vermont
4	Maine
2	South Dakota
2	Wyoming
*	Montana
*	North Dakota

*Incomplete data

Table G.238. SYPHILPT

Syphilis Cases per 1,000 1998

.42	Mississippi
.42	Maryland
.38	Louisiana
.32	Tennessee
.28	New York
.28	North Carolina
.26	Alabama
.25	Illinois
.24	Georgia
.22	South Carolina
.20	Arkansas
.20	Texas
.17	Florida
.15	Delaware
.15	Arizona
.11	Oklahoma
.10	Virginia
.10	New Jersey
.09	Massachusetts
.09	Indiana
.09	Kentucky
.08	California
.08	Pennsylvania
.08	Nevada
.07	Michigan
.07	Missouri
.06	Rhode Island
.05	Connecticut
.04	New Mexico
.04	Kansas
.04	Ohio
.04	Wisconsin
.03	Colorado
.03	Utah
.02	Washington
.02	Alaska
.02	Nebraska
.02	Iowa
.02	Minnesota
.01	Hawaii
.01	Idaho
.01	New Hampshire
.01	Vermont
.01	Oregon
.01	West Virginia
.00	Wyoming
.00	Maine
.00	South Dakota
*	Montana
*	North Dakota

*Incomplete data

Table G.239. TB

Tuberculosis Cases 1998

3,852	California
2,000	New York
1,820	Texas
1,302	Florida
850	Illinois
640	New Jersey
631	Georgia
498	North Carolina
448	Pennsylvania
439	Tennessee
385	Michigan
381	Alabama
380	Louisiana
339	Virginia
324	Maryland
286	South Carolina
282	Massachusetts
265	Washington
254	Arizona
230	Ohio
225	Mississippi
198	Oklahoma
188	Indiana
184	Missouri
181	Hawaii
179	Kentucky
171	Arkansas
161	Minnesota
156	Oregon
128	Nevada
128	Connecticut
109	Wisconsin
79	Colorado
68	New Mexico
63	Rhode Island
56	Kansas
55	Alaska
55	Iowa
52	Utah
42	West Virginia
36	Delaware
31	Nebraska
23	South Dakota
20	Montana
14	Idaho
14	New Hampshire
13	Maine
10	North Dakota
5	Vermont
4	Wyoming

Table G.240. TBPT

Tuberculosis Cases per 1,000 1998

.15	Hawaii
.12	California
.11	New York
.09	Texas
.09	Alaska
.09	Alabama
.09	Louisiana
.09	Florida
.08	Mississippi
.08	Georgia
.08	Tennessee
.08	New Jersey
.07	South Carolina
.07	Nevada
.07	Illinois
.07	Arkansas
.07	North Carolina
.06	Rhode Island
.06	Maryland
.06	Oklahoma
.05	Arizona
.05	Virginia
.05	Delaware
.05	Oregon
.05	Washington
.05	Massachusetts
.05	Kentucky
.04	New Mexico
.04	Michigan
.04	Connecticut
.04	Pennsylvania
.03	Minnesota
.03	Missouri
.03	Indiana
.03	South Dakota
.02	Utah
.02	West Virginia
.02	Montana
.02	Kansas
.02	Wisconsin
.02	Ohio
.02	Colorado
.02	Iowa
.02	Nebraska
.02	North Dakota
.01	New Hampshire
.01	Idaho
.01	Maine
.01	Vermont
.01	Wyoming

Table G.241. MCIGARET

Percent Males Who Smoke 1998

36.5	South Dakota
33.3	Kentucky
32.6	Nevada
30.3	Tennessee
30.3	Michigan
29.8	South Carolina
29.7	Ohio
29.6	Indiana
29.6	West Virginia
29.4	Missouri
28.6	Arkansas
28.3	Alaska
28.2	Louisiana
28.0	Georgia
27.4	North Carolina
27.3	Delaware
27.2	Alabama
26.9	Mississippi
26.7	Oklahoma
26.4	Colorado
26.0	Illinois
25.9	New York
25.8	Virginia
25.8	Iowa
25.7	New Hampshire
25.3	Texas
25.2	Nebraska
25.1	New Mexico
24.7	Arizona
24.3	Maryland
24.1	Rhode Island
24.0	Pennsylvania
24.0	Wisconsin
23.9	Wyoming
23.6	Vermont
23.5	Florida
23.0	Kansas
22.5	Massachusetts
22.4	Washington
22.3	Hawaii
21.9	California
21.9	Idaho
21.8	North Dakota
21.7	Connecticut
21.6	Oregon
21.5	Montana
21.2	Maine
20.9	New Jersey
19.7	Minnesota
15.9	Utah

Table G.242. FCIGARET

Percent Females Who Smoke 1998

28.5	Kentucky
28.1	Nevada
26.4	West Virginia
24.8	Michigan
23.7	Arkansas
23.6	Missouri
23.6	Pennsylvania
23.5	Alaska
23.5	Maine
23.1	Louisiana
23.0	Ohio
22.9	New York
22.9	Wisconsin
22.7	Indiana
22.4	Tennessee
22.3	North Carolina
22.3	Alabama
21.9	Delaware
21.7	Mississippi
21.7	Wyoming
21.5	Rhode Island
21.5	Montana
21.1	Oklahoma
21.1	Iowa
21.0	New Hampshire
21.0	Vermont
20.6	Illinois
20.6	Maryland
20.6	Florida
20.6	Connecticut
20.6	Oregon
20.3	Washington
20.2	South Carolina
20.2	Virginia
20.2	New Mexico
19.7	Georgia
19.5	Colorado
19.5	Kansas
19.5	Massachusetts
19.2	Arizona
19.1	Nebraska
18.9	Texas
18.8	Idaho
18.5	South Dakota
18.3	North Dakota
17.6	New Jersey
16.7	Hawaii
16.6	California
16.4	Minnesota
12.5	Utah

Table G.243. HSGRAD

Percent High School Graduates 1999

92.8	Alaska
91.2	Washington
91.1	Minnesota
91.0	Utah
90.7	Wyoming
90.4	Colorado
89.7	Iowa
89.3	Vermont
89.3	Nebraska
88.9	Maine
88.8	Montana
88.7	South Dakota
88.0	Hawaii
87.6	Kansas
87.4	New Jersey
87.3	Virginia
86.8	Wisconsin
86.5	New Hampshire
86.4	Nevada
86.2	Oregon
86.1	Pennsylvania
86.1	Ohio
85.5	Michigan
85.4	Illinois
85.1	Massachusetts
85.0	Missouri
84.9	North Dakota
84.8	Idaho
84.7	Maryland
84.5	Delaware
83.7	Connecticut
83.5	Oklahoma
83.1	Arizona
82.9	Indiana
82.7	Florida
81.9	New York
81.1	Alabama
80.9	Rhode Island
80.9	New Mexico
80.7	Georgia
80.4	California
79.8	North Carolina
79.1	Tennessee
78.9	Arkansas
78.6	South Carolina
78.3	Louisiana
78.2	Kentucky
78.2	Texas
78.0	Mississippi
75.1	West Virginia

Table G.244. COLLGRAD

Percent College Graduates 1999

38.7	Colorado
34.7	Maryland
33.5	Connecticut
32.0	Minnesota
31.6	Virginia
31.0	Massachusetts
30.5	New Jersey
28.6	Washington
28.3	Vermont
27.9	Utah
27.2	New Hampshire
27.1	California
26.9	New York
26.8	Oregon
26.8	Rhode Island
26.5	Kansas
26.2	Hawaii
25.6	South Dakota
25.6	Illinois
25.5	Alaska
25.5	Ohio
24.5	New Mexico
24.4	Texas
24.2	Arizona
24.0	Montana
24,0	Delaware
23.9	Pennsylvania
23.9	North Carolina
23.7	Oklahoma
23.6	Wisconsin
23.0	Missouri
22.9	Maine
22.3	Wyoming
22.3	North Dakota
21.8	Alabama
21.7	Iowa
21.6	Florida
21.5	Georgia
21.3	Michigan
20.9	South Carolina
20.8	Idaho
20.7	Louisiana
20.4	Nebraska
20.2	Nevada
19.8	Kentucky
19.2	Mississippi
18.4	Indiana
17.9	West Virginia
17.7	Tennessee
17.3	Arkansas

Table G.245. K8ENROLL

Grades K–8 Enrollment (1,000s) 1998

4,270	California
2,868	Texas
2,028	New York
1,704	Florida
1,452	Illinois
1,301	Ohio
1,267	Pennsylvania
1,245	Michigan
1,029	Georgia
936	New Jersey
921	North Carolina
815	Virginia
705	Massachusetts
697	Indiana
696	Washington
665	Tennessee
651	Missouri
623	Arizona
607	Maryland
601	Wisconsin
586	Minnesota
558	Louisiana
542	Alabama
501	Colorado
478	South Carolina
465	Kentucky
448	Oklahoma
399	Connecticut
380	Oregon
365	Mississippi
337	Iowa
329	Utah
327	Kansas
319	Arkansas
232	New Mexico
229	Nevada
206	West Virginia
200	Nebraska
169	Idaho
151	Maine
147	New Hampshire
135	Hawaii
112	Rhode Island
110	Montana
97	Alaska
91	South Dakota
80	Delaware
77	North Dakota
73	Vermont
64	Wyoming

Table G.246. HSENROLL

Grades 9–12 Enrollment (1,000s) 1998

1,656	California
1,077	Texas
849	New York
634	Florida
560	Illinois
549	Pennsylvania
541	Ohio
475	Michigan
372	Georgia
334	North Carolina
333	New Jersey
309	Virginia
302	Washington
291	Indiana
279	Wisconsin
270	Minnesota
262	Missouri
258	Massachusetts
241	Tennessee
235	Maryland
226	Arizona
210	Louisiana
206	Alabama
198	Colorado
191	Kentucky
187	South Carolina
181	Oklahoma
163	Oregon
162	Iowa
153	Utah
145	Connecticut
145	Kansas
137	Mississippi
133	Arkansas
96	New Mexico
92	West Virginia
91	Nebraska
82	Nevada
76	Idaho
60	Maine
58	New Hampshire
53	Hawaii
50	Montana
42	Rhode Island
42	South Dakota
38	Alaska
38	North Dakota
33	Delaware
32	Vermont
31	Wyoming

Table G.247.   ADAPP

Expenditures per Pupil ADA 1999

10,611	Alaska
10,420	New Jersey
9,786	New York
9,589	Connecticut
8,658	Delaware
8,239	Rhode Island
8,139	Michigan
7,904	Vermont
7,854	Massachusetts
7,716	Pennsylvania
7,694	Wisconsin
7,592	Oregon
7,584	Maine
7,553	Maryland
7,424	Minnesota
7,401	West Virginia
7,305	Wyoming
7,207	Indiana
6,839	New Hampshire
6,816	Ohio
6,704	Montana
6,694	Hawaii
6,662	Kentucky
6,633	Washington
6,588	Kansas
6,550	Virginia
6,475	Texas
6,404	Illinois
6,404	Nebraska
6,296	Georgia
6,272	North Carolina
6,203	Florida
6,182	Nevada
6,100	Iowa
6,005	South Carolina
5,757	Louisiana
5,697	Colorado
5,614	Missouri
5,593	Oklahoma
5,579	Tennessee
5,545	Arkansas
5,462	California
5,429	New Mexico
5,366	Idaho
5,281	South Dakota
4,918	Arizona
4,818	Alabama
4,704	North Dakota
4,658	Mississippi
4,059	Utah

Table G.248.   COLENROL

Total College Enrollment (1,000s) 1997

1,958	California
1,024	New York
969	Texas
726	Illinois
658	Florida
588	Pennsylvania
550	Michigan
537	Ohio
413	Massachusetts
374	North Carolina
365	Virginia
326	New Jersey
315	Washington
306	Georgia
303	Missouri
298	Wisconsin
296	Indiana
293	Arizona
270	Minnesota
261	Maryland
252	Colorado
250	Tennessee
219	Louisiana
219	Alabama
181	Iowa
179	Kentucky
178	Kansas
177	Oklahoma
176	South Carolina
170	Oregon
158	Utah
153	Connecticut
131	Mississippi
112	Nebraska
112	Arkansas
109	New Mexico
88	West Virginia
76	Nevada
72	Rhode Island
64	New Hampshire
62	Hawaii
62	Idaho
56	Maine
45	Delaware
44	Montana
39	South Dakota
39	North Dakota
36	Vermont
30	Wyoming
28	Alaska

Table G.249.   COLLEGPC

Percent Enrolled in College 1997

7.42	Utah
7.27	Rhode Island
6.72	Nebraska
6.71	Kansas
6.69	Massachusetts
6.31	Iowa
6.26	New Mexico
6.26	Wyoming
6.21	Colorado
6.15	North Dakota
6.13	Arizona
6.06	Vermont
5.99	Illinois
5.97	Delaware
5.91	California
5.68	Wisconsin
5.65	Minnesota
5.63	New York
5.58	Michigan
5.54	Missouri
5.47	Washington
5.33	New Hampshire
5.32	South Dakota
5.31	Virginia
5.27	Oklahoma
5.23	Hawaii
5.13	Oregon
5.05	Maryland
5.01	Alabama
5.01	Louisiana
4.98	Montana
4.98	Indiana
4.95	Idaho
4.90	Pennsylvania
4.89	North Carolina
4.87	West Virginia
4.83	Texas
4.77	Ohio
4.73	Mississippi
4.66	Connecticut
4.56	Tennessee
4.53	South Carolina
4.52	Alaska
4.52	Kentucky
4.47	Maine
4.39	Arkansas
4.35	Florida
4.20	Nevada
4.00	New Jersey
3.93	Georgia

Table G.250. CHILDPOV

Percent Children 5–17 in Poverty 1998

29.8	Louisiana
28.9	New York
25.7	West Virginia
24.7	Georgia
23.6	Arizona
23.5	New Mexico
22.3	California
21.8	Alabama
21.3	North Carolina
21.2	Montana
20.5	Rhode Island
20.5	Florida
20.1	Texas
19.9	Oklahoma
19.4	Oregon
19.3	Mississippi
18.0	Pennsylvania
17.6	South Carolina
17.4	Idaho
17.2	North Dakota
16.7	Kentucky
16.0	Ohio
15.7	Delaware
15.0	Massachusetts
14.8	Nebraska
14.8	Michigan
14.5	Hawaii
14.5	Tennessee
14.4	Missouri
14.2	Iowa
13.4	Connecticut
13.3	New Hampshire
13.2	Kansas
13.2	New Jersey
13.1	Arkansas
13.0	Wyoming
12.8	Nevada
12.6	Minnesota
12.6	Indiana
12.5	Colorado
12.2	Vermont
12.1	Illinois
12.0	Maine
11.8	Utah
11.5	Wisconsin
10.8	Washington
9.2	South Dakota
9.0	Alaska
8.1	Maryland
7.9	Virginia

Table G.251. SCHAGE

School-Age Children (1,000s) 1999

6,424	California
4,080	Texas
3,227	New York
2,618	Florida
2,304	Illinois
2,140	Pennsylvania
2,104	Ohio
1,906	Michigan
1,477	Georgia
1,460	New Jersey
1,407	North Carolina
1,214	Virginia
1,115	Indiana
1,096	Washington
1,076	Massachusetts
1,036	Missouri
1,016	Wisconsin
974	Tennessee
963	Maryland
950	Minnesota
949	Arizona
876	Louisiana
777	Colorado
775	Alabama
706	Kentucky
702	South Carolina
649	Oklahoma
610	Connecticut
608	Oregon
550	Mississippi
537	Iowa
515	Kansas
497	Utah
483	Arkansas
364	New Mexico
348	Nevada
329	Nebraska
303	West Virginia
258	Idaho
231	New Hampshire
223	Maine
209	Hawaii
179	Rhode Island
171	Montana
148	South Dakota
147	Alaska
132	Delaware
121	North Dakota
107	Vermont
96	Wyoming

Table G.252. COLUNIPC

Per Capita Expenditures for Colleges 1995–1996

626	Delaware
600	Utah
583	New Mexico
579	North Dakota
575	Wyoming
547	Iowa
529	Vermont
521	Alaska
520	Michigan
493	Indiana
492	Colorado
491	Kansas
489	Wisconsin
489	Hawaii
487	Nebraska
468	Washington
464	North Carolina
463	Oregon
437	Alabama
432	Montana
429	Idaho
424	Mississippi
412	South Carolina
411	Arizona
406	Maryland
404	Minnesota
392	Virginia
384	Oklahoma
375	California
371	Texas
370	West Virginia
364	Kentucky
359	Louisiana
357	Ohio
356	Tennessee
350	Illinois
342	Pennsylvania
338	Arkansas
329	New Jersey
326	Rhode Island
324	Georgia
321	South Dakota
315	Maine
314	Missouri
310	New Hampshire
299	Nevada
298	New York
273	Connecticut
257	Florida
248	Massachusetts

Table G.253. TOBALCRV

Tax Revenue Tobacco Alcohol per Capita 2000

77.19	Washington
73.95	Alaska
72.80	Rhode Island
72.62	Michigan
72.26	Florida
67.99	Oregon
62.49	Hawaii
59.48	Massachusetts
57.59	Wisconsin
55.80	Connecticut
52.60	Minnesota
52.42	New Jersey
49.34	Arkansas
48.93	New York
47.98	Nevada
47.68	Arizona
47.56	Kansas
47.49	Vermont
46.52	North Dakota
45.51	Delaware
44.28	Alabama
43.79	Illinois
42.86	South Carolina
42.55	South Dakota
42.42	Oklahoma
42.37	Pennsylvania
41.38	Iowa
37.87	Montana
37.83	New Mexico
37.64	Nebraska
37.07	Mississippi
35.87	Ohio
32.23	Louisiana
31.30	Utah
29.94	Maryland
29.67	Idaho
29.63	California
29.37	Georgia
29.32	Tennessee
28.30	West Virginia
26.16	Missouri
24.89	Colorado
21.48	Kentucky
19.96	Virginia
15.26	Wyoming
*	Indiana
*	North Carolina
*	Texas
*	Maine
*	New Hampshire

*Incomplete data

Table G.254. SUBABUPC

Spending re Substance Abuse per Capita 2000

531.95	Alaska
500.11	Delaware
478.04	New York
441.67	Massachusetts
433.30	Minnesota
368.13	Hawaii
339.63	California
303.37	Rhode Island
291.81	Pennsylvania
291.13	Montana
282.32	Nevada
281.53	Michigan
278.25	Oregon
277.09	Alabama
273.37	Wisconsin
271.36	New Mexico
269.32	Washington
267.21	Connecticut
267.10	Virginia
263.19	Ohio
257.10	Iowa
253.74	Missouri
253.09	Maryland
252.08	New Jersey
244.88	Kentucky
243.33	Louisiana
242.05	Utah
240.06	Wyoming
238.81	Illinois
229.05	Vermont
223.42	Kansas
217.39	Colorado
214.70	Florida
212.86	Oklahoma
209.72	Georgia
205.58	Arkansas
204.55	Arizona
195.79	Idaho
186.61	West Virginia
178.12	Mississippi
176.49	South Dakota
175.78	Nebraska
173.20	Tennessee
158.13	South Carolina
154.58	North Dakota
*	Indiana
*	North Carolina
*	Texas
*	Maine
*	New Hampshire

*Incomplete data

Table G.255. HOSPBEDS

Number Hospital Beds (1,000s) 1998

74.5	California
68.5	New York
56.6	Texas
49.2	Florida
44.7	Pennsylvania
39.2	Illinois
35.2	Ohio
27.2	Michigan
26.4	New Jersey
25.2	Georgia
23.3	North Carolina
20.7	Missouri
20.7	Tennessee
19.4	Indiana
17.9	Virginia
17.8	Louisiana
17.0	Alabama
16.7	Wisconsin
16.5	Massachusetts
16.5	Minnesota
15.2	Kentucky
13.0	Mississippi
12.7	Maryland
12.2	Iowa
11.5	South Carolina
11.0	Oklahoma
10.9	Kansas
10.9	Arizona
10.7	Washington
9.9	Arkansas
9.2	Colorado
8.1	West Virginia
8.1	Nebraska
6.9	Connecticut
6.8	Oregon
4.4	Montana
4.4	South Dakota
4.0	Utah
4.0	North Dakota
3.8	Maine
3.5	Nevada
3.5	New Mexico
3.4	Idaho
2.8	Hawaii
2.8	New Hampshire
2.6	Rhode Island
2.0	Delaware
1.9	Wyoming
1.7	Vermont
1.2	Alaska

Table G.256. HOSPBEDP

Hospital Beds per 1,000 1998

6.31	North Dakota
6.00	South Dakota
4.98	Montana
4.86	Nebraska
4.70	Mississippi
4.48	West Virginia
4.25	Iowa
4.11	Kansas
4.07	Louisiana
3.96	Wyoming
3.89	Alabama
3.88	Arkansas
3.84	Kentucky
3.79	Missouri
3.77	Tennessee
3.76	New York
3.73	Pennsylvania
3.46	Minnesota
3.28	Oklahoma
3.26	Indiana
3.26	Florida
3.24	New Jersey
3.24	Georgia
3.23	Illinois
3.18	Wisconsin
3.13	Ohio
3.05	North Carolina
3.03	Maine
2.96	South Carolina
2.86	Vermont
2.82	Texas
2.76	Michigan
2.72	Idaho
2.67	Massachusetts
2.65	Delaware
2.62	Rhode Island
2.60	Virginia
2.46	Maryland
2.36	Hawaii
2.33	New Hampshire
2.28	Arizona
2.27	Colorado
2.25	California
2.10	Connecticut
2.05	Oregon
2.01	New Mexico
1.94	Alaska
1.93	Nevada
1.88	Utah
1.86	Washington

Table G.257. EXPCOLL

Expenditures for Colleges (in millions) 1995–1996

11,954	California
7,095	Texas
5,413	New York
4,993	Michigan
4,143	Illinois
4,120	Pennsylvania
3,990	Ohio
3,705	Florida
3,401	North Carolina
2,879	Indiana
2,629	New Jersey
2,615	Virginia
2,588	Washington
2,525	Wisconsin
2,384	Georgia
2,060	Maryland
1,896	Tennessee
1,882	Colorado
1,881	Minnesota
1,867	Alabama
1,819	Arizona
1,683	Missouri
1,562	Louisiana
1,561	Iowa
1,525	South Carolina
1,511	Massachusetts
1,482	Oregon
1,413	Kentucky
1,268	Oklahoma
1,263	Kansas
1,199	Utah
1,150	Mississippi
998	New Mexico
892	Connecticut
847	Arkansas
805	Nebraska
675	West Virginia
579	Hawaii
510	Idaho
480	Nevada
454	Delaware
392	Maine
380	Montana
373	North Dakota
360	New Hampshire
323	Rhode Island
316	Alaska
312	Vermont
276	Wyoming
235	South Dakota

Table G.258. ELESECPC

Expenditures Public Schools per Capita 1995–1996

1,942	Alaska
1,440	New York
1,423	New Jersey
1,358	Wyoming
1,295	Minnesota
1,285	Connecticut
1,221	Wisconsin
1,194	Michigan
1,169	Nebraska
1,158	Washington
1,123	Vermont
1,122	Oregon
1,116	Montana
1,107	Delaware
1,099	Kansas
1,083	Rhode Island
1,069	Georgia
1,065	Ohio
1,052	Texas
1,052	Maryland
1,048	Utah
1,048	Maine
1,043	New Hampshire
1,041	Pennsylvania
1,022	Indiana
1,019	Colorado
1,008	Illinois
1,001	Virginia
996	Iowa
996	Massachusetts
993	West Virginia
991	Idaho
967	Missouri
948	Florida
942	Nevada
940	Oklahoma
938	California
935	South Carolina
935	North Dakota
923	Arizona
919	South Dakota
886	Kentucky
878	New Mexico
872	North Carolina
867	Louisiana
849	Mississippi
835	Alabama
800	Tennessee
800	Hawaii
797	Arkansas

Table G.259. VIOL39

Total Number Violent Crimes 1960–1998

6,867,103	California
5,171,423	New York
3,201,917	Florida
2,955,530	Illinois
2,803,367	Texas
2,081,954	Michigan
1,473,912	Ohio
1,389,817	Pennsylvania
1,245,451	New Jersey
1,175,178	Maryland
1,051,106	Georgia
1,047,134	North Carolina
997,254	Massachusetts
934,682	Louisiana
911,251	Missouri
782,300	Tennessee
732,368	South Carolina
663,164	Indiana
660,392	Alabama
637,948	Virginia
579,132	Washington
568,769	Arizona
456,994	Colorado
427,662	Oklahoma
387,927	Oregon
370,045	Kentucky
368,222	Connecticut
346,440	Minnesota
300,125	Wisconsin
299,430	New Mexico
299,139	Arkansas
280,474	Mississippi
275,999	Kansas
219,411	Nevada
187,412	Iowa
136,941	Nebraska
131,234	Utah
106,163	West Virginia
105,357	Rhode Island
102,771	Delaware
82,972	Alaska
76,971	Hawaii
73,424	Idaho
45,960	Montana
55,231	Maine
37,342	Wyoming
36,497	New Hampshire
35,430	South Dakota
19,781	Vermont
13,836	North Dakota

Table G.260. VIOLEN39

Average Number of Violent Crimes per 100,000 1960–1998

845.83	New York
754.61	Florida
683.80	Maryland
682.77	California
666.13	Illinois
587.88	Nevada
584.24	Michigan
576.04	Louisiana
572.60	South Carolina
546.09	New Mexico
484.42	Arizona
469.29	Missouri
467.97	Texas
456.55	Georgia
446.60	Alaska
440.43	North Carolina
435.61	Massachusetts
431.60	Alabama
425.46	Tennessee
424.46	New Jersey
415.79	Delaware
395.66	Colorado
376.15	Oregon
358.08	Oklahoma
349.36	Ohio
338.43	Washington
336.48	Arkansas
310.07	Indiana
299.86	Pennsylvania
299.57	Virginia
297.52	Connecticut
291.50	Kansas
286.06	Mississippi
279.84	Rhode Island
263.46	Kentucky
221.84	Nebraska
217.49	Utah
215.25	Wyoming
211.11	Minnesota
196.21	Hawaii
194.63	Idaho
168.77	Iowa
160.11	Wisconsin
150.12	Montana
147.56	West Virginia
129.58	South Dakota
125.41	Maine
97.30	Vermont
96.19	New Hampshire
54.79	North Dakota

Table G.261. VIOL6098

Average Violent Crimes per 1,000 over 39 Years 1960–1998

8.4583	New York
7.5461	Florida
6.8380	Maryland
6.8277	California
6.6613	Illinois
5.8788	Nevada
5.8424	Michigan
5.7604	Louisiana
5.7260	South Carolina
5.4609	New Mexico
4.8442	Arizona
4.6929	Missouri
4.6797	Texas
4.5655	Georgia
4.4660	Alaska
4.4043	North Carolina
4.3561	Massachusetts
4.3160	Alabama
4.2546	Tennessee
4.2446	New Jersey
4.1579	Delaware
3.9566	Colorado
3.7615	Oregon
3.5808	Oklahoma
3.4936	Ohio
3.3843	Washington
3.3648	Arkansas
3.1007	Indiana
2.9986	Pennsylvania
2.9957	Virginia
2.9752	Connecticut
2.9150	Kansas
2.8606	Mississippi
2.7984	Rhode Island
2.6346	Kentucky
2.2184	Nebraska
2.1749	Utah
2.1525	Wyoming
2.1111	Minnesota
1.9621	Hawaii
1.9463	Idaho
1.6877	Iowa
1.6011	Wisconsin
1.5012	Montana
1.4756	West Virginia
1.2958	South Dakota
1.2541	Maine
.9730	Vermont
.9619	New Hampshire
.5479	North Dakota

Table G.262.   VIOLENT

Average Violent Crimes per 1,000 1998

9.3930	Florida
9.3124	New Mexico
9.1280	South Carolina
8.0773	Illinois
7.9388	Maryland
7.6818	Louisiana
7.3297	Tennessee
7.1277	Delaware
7.0366	California
6.4815	Michigan
6.4362	Nevada
6.2454	New York
6.0060	Alaska
5.9891	Massachusetts
5.9534	Missouri
5.8064	Arizona
5.7930	North Carolina
5.6485	Texas
5.6426	Georgia
5.3946	Oklahoma
5.0528	Alabama
4.8935	Arkansas
4.8212	Indiana
4.8150	Mississippi
4.4675	Nebraska
4.4014	New Jersey
4.2631	Connecticut
4.2504	Washington
4.1692	Oregon
4.1616	Pennsylvania
3.9703	Kansas
3.8856	Ohio
3.8782	Colorado
3.2606	Virginia
3.2265	Utah
3.0962	Rhode Island
3.0904	Minnesota
2.9138	Iowa
2.8416	Idaho
2.8399	Kentucky
2.4902	Wisconsin
2.4694	Hawaii
2.4367	West Virginia
2.4264	Wyoming
1.8454	South Dakota
1.7829	Montana
1.5291	New Hampshire
1.2559	Maine
1.0672	Vermont
.9023	North Dakota

Table G.263.   PROP39

Total Number Property Crimes 1960–1998

50,260,651	California
27,406,444	Texas
27,225,774	New York
22,982,027	Florida
17,823,318	Illinois
16,737,034	Michigan
14,910,467	Ohio
11,332,869	Pennsylvania
11,128,709	New Jersey
8,900,935	Georgia
8,500,038	Massachusetts
8,176,931	Washington
7,951,155	North Carolina
7,392,439	Missouri
7,314,791	Indiana
7,264,480	Maryland
7,060,275	Virginia
6,635,379	Arizona
6,288,034	Louisiana
5,908,921	Wisconsin
5,814,092	Tennessee
5,584,043	Colorado
5,582,200	Minnesota
4,935,668	Oregon
4,696,706	Alabama
4,614,796	South Carolina
4,541,586	Connecticut
4,502,725	Oklahoma
3,473,425	Kansas
3,408,866	Kentucky
3,392,587	Iowa
2,585,415	Utah
2,570,976	Arkansas
2,482,956	New Mexico
2,368,894	Mississippi
1,954,536	Hawaii
1,881,418	Nebraska
1,844,441	Nevada
1,507,428	Rhode Island
1,264,558	West Virginia
1,254,326	Maine
1,191,770	Idaho
1,101,901	Montana
1,018,726	Delaware
947,439	New Hampshire
745,541	Alaska
613,617	South Dakota
584,699	Vermont
568,011	Wyoming
546,080	North Dakota

Table G.264.   PROPER39

Average Number Property Crimes per 100,000 1960–1998

5,947.73	Arizona
5,691.57	Florida
5,563.31	Nevada
5,335.64	California
5,160.95	Hawaii
4,965.70	Washington
4,946.53	Colorado
4,914.81	Oregon
4,725.65	New Mexico
4,724.61	Michigan
4,691.11	Texas
4,453.02	New York
4,448.02	Utah
4,293.55	Maryland
4,288.24	Delaware
4,286.06	Alaska
4,044.37	Rhode Island
4,028.92	Illinois
3,892.37	Louisiana
3,876.20	Georgia
3,843.68	Missouri
3,833.24	Oklahoma
3,827.87	New Jersey
3,762.81	Massachusetts
3,718.18	Connecticut
3,701.97	Kansas
3,697.71	South Carolina
3,595.71	Montana
3,546.84	Ohio
3,467.69	Minnesota
3,460.67	Indiana
3,365.23	Wyoming
3,295.44	Virginia
3,290.52	North Carolina
3,289.73	Idaho
3,217.84	Tennessee
3,210.16	Wisconsin
3,075.84	Alabama
3,072.00	Nebraska
3,053.75	Iowa
2,903.15	Arkansas
2,894.55	Vermont
2,846.55	Maine
2,563.62	New Hampshire
2,452.22	Kentucky
2,448.99	Pennsylvania
2,386.79	Mississippi
2,247.60	South Dakota
2,158.11	North Dakota
1,752.72	West Virginia

Table G.265. PROP6098

Average Property Crimes per 1,000 over 39 Years 1960–1998

59.4773	Arizona
56.9157	Florida
55.6331	Nevada
53.3564	California
51.6095	Hawaii
49.6570	Washington
49.4653	Colorado
49.1481	Oregon
47.2565	New Mexico
47.2461	Michigan
46.9111	Texas
44.5302	New York
44.4802	Utah
42.9355	Maryland
42.8824	Delaware
42.8606	Alaska
40.4437	Rhode Island
40.2892	Illinois
38.9237	Louisiana
38.7620	Georgia
38.4368	Missouri
38.3324	Oklahoma
38.2787	New Jersey
37.6281	Massachusetts
37.1818	Connecticut
37.0197	Kansas
36.9771	South Carolina
35.9571	Montana
35.4684	Ohio
34.6769	Minnesota
34.6067	Indiana
33.6523	Wyoming
32.9544	Virginia
32.9052	North Carolina
32.8973	Idaho
32.1784	Tennessee
32.1016	Wisconsin
30.7584	Alabama
30.7200	Nebraska
30.5375	Iowa
29.0315	Arkansas
28.9455	Vermont
28.4655	Maine
25.6362	New Hampshire
24.5222	Kentucky
24.4899	Pennsylvania
23.8679	Mississippi
22.4760	South Dakota
21.5811	North Dakota
17.5272	West Virginia

Table G.266. PROPER

Average Property Crimes per 1,000 1998

60.3205	Arizona
59.5061	Florida
59.0865	New Mexico
53.2402	Washington
52.7099	Louisiana
52.2180	Utah
51.9645	Oregon
50.8608	Hawaii
49.2840	Mississippi
49.1415	South Carolina
48.2715	Georgia
47.3132	North Carolina
46.3686	Nevada
46.2499	Delaware
46.1248	Missouri
45.5055	Maryland
45.4696	Texas
44.6371	Oklahoma
44.6173	Kansas
43.6926	Tennessee
41.7029	Michigan
41.1278	Colorado
40.8864	Indiana
40.6502	Illinois
40.0937	Alabama
39.8120	Connecticut
39.5675	Ohio
38.8479	Nebraska
38.5152	Alaska
37.8039	Arkansas
37.1555	Minnesota
36.3823	California
35.3658	Wyoming
34.7236	Montana
34.2958	Idaho
33.3500	Virginia
32.9410	Wisconsin
32.1423	New Jersey
31.8967	Rhode Island
30.8875	Iowa
30.1184	Vermont
29.0931	Maine
28.3719	New Hampshire
27.8185	South Dakota
27.6187	New York
27.6184	Pennsylvania
27.1938	Massachusetts
26.2812	North Dakota
26.0531	Kentucky
22.9385	West Virginia

Table G.267. MURD39

Total Number of Murders 1960–1998

89,621	California
64,727	Texas
61,447	New York
39,557	Florida
39,454	Illinois
31,507	Michigan
25,888	Georgia
24,493	Ohio
24,253	Pennsylvania
22,496	North Carolina
20,953	Louisiana
17,840	Virginia
17,200	Alabama
16,628	Tennessee
16,389	Missouri
15,818	Maryland
14,632	New Jersey
13,080	South Carolina
12,937	Indiana
11,188	Mississippi
10,641	Kentucky
8,489	Arizona
8,378	Oklahoma
7,725	Arkansas
7,318	Massachusetts
6,905	Washington
6,234	Colorado
5,392	Wisconsin
4,824	New Mexico
4,666	Connecticut
4,555	Kansas
4,167	Oregon
3,884	West Virginia
3,797	Minnesota
3,740	Nevada
2,056	Iowa
1,825	Nebraska
1,661	Utah
1,628	Hawaii
1,603	Alaska
1,311	Delaware
1,206	Idaho
1,120	Rhode Island
1,110	Montana
967	Maine
808	Wyoming
757	New Hampshire
566	South Dakota
418	Vermont
293	North Dakota

Table G.268. MURDER39

Average Murder Rate per 100,000 over 39 Years 1960–1998

13.20	Louisiana
12.29	Georgia
11.68	Alabama
11.64	Texas
11.63	Mississippi
11.34	Nevada
11.17	South Carolina
10.79	Florida
10.04	Alaska
10.04	New York
9.90	North Carolina
9.54	Tennessee
9.41	Maryland
9.41	New Mexico
9.15	California
9.03	Arkansas
8.94	Illinois
8.87	Michigan
8.66	Virginia
8.55	Missouri
7.83	Kentucky
7.77	Arizona
7.29	Oklahoma
6.12	Indiana
5.85	Ohio
5.75	Delaware
5.70	Colorado
5.40	West Virginia
5.24	Pennsylvania
5.06	New Jersey
5.03	Wyoming
4.88	Kansas
4.41	Hawaii
4.24	Oregon
4.21	Washington
3.82	Connecticut
3.67	Montana
3.44	Idaho
3.25	Massachusetts
3.00	Nebraska
2.98	Rhode Island
2.93	Utah
2.93	Wisconsin
2.35	Minnesota
2.23	Maine
2.15	New Hampshire
2.11	Vermont
2.09	South Dakota
1.85	Iowa
1.16	North Dakota

Table G.269. MURD6098

Average Murder Rate per 1,000 over 39 Years 1960–1998

.1320	Louisiana
.1229	Georgia
.1168	Alabama
.1164	Texas
.1163	Mississippi
.1134	Nevada
.1117	South Carolina
.1079	Florida
.1004	Alaska
.1004	New York
.0990	North Carolina
.0954	Tennessee
.0941	Maryland
.0941	New Mexico
.0915	California
.0903	Arkansas
.0894	Illinois
.0887	Michigan
.0866	Virginia
.0855	Missouri
.0783	Kentucky
.0777	Arizona
.0729	Oklahoma
.0612	Indiana
.0585	Ohio
.0575	Delaware
.0570	Colorado
.0540	West Virginia
.0524	Pennsylvania
.0506	New Jersey
.0503	Wyoming
.0488	Kansas
.0441	Hawaii
.0424	Oregon
.0421	Washington
.0382	Connecticut
.0367	Montana
.0344	Idaho
.0325	Massachusetts
.0300	Nebraska
.0298	Rhode Island
.0293	Utah
.0293	Wisconsin
.0235	Minnesota
.0223	Maine
.0215	New Hampshire
.0211	Vermont
.0209	South Dakota
.0185	Iowa
.0116	North Dakota

Table G.270. MURDER

Murder Rate per 1,000 1998

.1292	Louisiana
.1205	Mississippi
.1023	New Mexico
.1000	Maryland
.0973	Nevada
.0899	Indiana
.0880	Tennessee
.0837	Illinois
.0813	North Carolina
.0813	Alabama
.0812	South Carolina
.0811	Georgia
.0808	Arizona
.0793	Arkansas
.0789	Missouri
.0774	Michigan
.0682	Texas
.0665	California
.0664	Alaska
.0650	Florida
.0612	Virginia
.0610	Oklahoma
.0586	Kansas
.0530	Pennsylvania
.0493	New York
.0480	Connecticut
.0467	Colorado
.0462	Kentucky
.0446	Ohio
.0431	West Virginia
.0396	New Jersey
.0385	Washington
.0372	Oregon
.0364	Wisconsin
.0312	Utah
.0309	Nebraska
.0309	Delaware
.0295	Idaho
.0293	Wyoming
.0265	Minnesota
.0243	Rhode Island
.0209	Maine
.0205	Massachusetts
.0201	Hawaii
.0190	Iowa
.0189	New Hampshire
.0143	Vermont
.0141	Montana
.0118	North Dakota
.0118	South Dakota

Table G.271. RAPES39

Total Number of Rapes 1960–1998

358,434	California
203,581	Texas
162,884	Michigan
158,668	Florida
154,852	New York
125,672	Illinois
119,450	Ohio
87,887	Pennsylvania
67,949	Georgia
65,992	Washington
62,871	New Jersey
56,361	Tennessee
53,189	Maryland
52,356	Indiana
50,906	Missouri
49,816	North Carolina
48,559	Louisiana
48,467	Virginia
47,264	Massachusetts
41,883	Colorado
40,882	South Carolina
40,669	Minnesota
36,470	Arizona
35,511	Oklahoma
35,311	Alabama
34,260	Oregon
27,393	Kentucky
25,628	Wisconsin
23,520	Kansas
22,855	Mississippi
22,725	Arkansas
20,580	Connecticut
20,418	New Mexico
17,048	Nevada
14,795	Utah
13,451	Iowa
11,078	Nebraska
10,057	Alaska
9,635	Delaware
9,403	West Virginia
9,127	Hawaii
6,746	New Hampshire
6,738	Idaho
5,982	Rhode Island
5,757	Maine
5,515	South Dakota
5,018	Montana
3,842	Vermont
3,605	Wyoming
2,774	North Dakota

Table G.272. RAPE39

Average Rape Rate per 100,000 over 39 Years 1960–1998

54.66	Alaska
45.55	Michigan
44.89	Nevada
37.99	Delaware
37.78	Washington
37.76	New Mexico
37.43	California
37.41	Florida
36.35	Colorado
33.80	Texas
33.18	Oregon
32.24	Arizona
32.08	South Carolina
31.01	Maryland
30.63	Tennessee
30.00	Louisiana
29.81	Georgia
29.79	Oklahoma
28.36	Illinois
28.23	Ohio
26.42	Missouri
25.52	Arkansas
25.34	New York
24.75	Kansas
24.52	Indiana
24.31	Minnesota
23.83	Utah
23.09	Alabama
22.98	Mississippi
22.95	Hawaii
22.31	Virginia
21.49	New Jersey
20.81	Wyoming
20.71	Massachusetts
20.54	North Carolina
19.99	South Dakota
19.38	Kentucky
18.97	Pennsylvania
18.72	Vermont
17.98	Nebraska
17.79	Idaho
16.85	New Hampshire
16.65	Connecticut
16.23	Montana
15.75	Rhode Island
13.67	Wisconsin
13.02	West Virginia
12.78	Maine
12.13	Iowa
11.00	North Dakota

Table G.273. RAPE6098

Average Rape Rate per 1,000 over 39 Years 1960–1998

.5466	Alaska
.4555	Michigan
.4489	Nevada
.3799	Delaware
.3778	Washington
.3776	New Mexico
.3743	California
.3741	Florida
.3635	Colorado
.3380	Texas
.3318	Oregon
.3224	Arizona
.3208	South Carolina
.3101	Maryland
.3063	Tennessee
.3000	Louisiana
.2981	Georgia
.2979	Oklahoma
.2836	Illinois
.2823	Ohio
.2642	Missouri
.2552	Arkansas
.2534	New York
.2475	Kansas
.2452	Indiana
.2431	Minnesota
.2383	Utah
.2309	Alabama
.2298	Mississippi
.2295	Hawaii
.2231	Virginia
.2149	New Jersey
.2081	Wyoming
.2071	Massachusetts
.2054	North Carolina
.1999	South Dakota
.1938	Kentucky
.1897	Pennsylvania
.1872	Vermont
.1798	Nebraska
.1779	Idaho
.1685	New Hampshire
.1665	Connecticut
.1623	Montana
.1575	Rhode Island
.1367	Wisconsin
.1302	West Virginia
.1278	Maine
.1213	Iowa
.1100	North Dakota

Table G.274. (also14) RAPE

Rape Rate per 1,000 1998

.6880	Alaska
.5493	Michigan
.5336	New Mexico
.5215	Nevada
.4974	Florida
.4955	Washington
.4940	Minnesota
.4802	Colorado
.4796	Tennessee
.4737	South Carolina
.4649	New Hampshire
.4554	Mississippi
.4523	Oklahoma
.4293	Ohio
.4256	Kansas
.4237	Utah
.4010	Texas
.4005	South Dakota
.3971	Oregon
.3721	Indiana
.3678	Louisiana
.3513	Arkansas
.3502	Rhode Island
.3400	Illinois
.3309	Maryland
.3296	Alabama
.3278	North Dakota
.3244	Idaho
.3112	Arizona
.3064	North Carolina
.2996	Georgia
.2994	California
.2951	Hawaii
.2929	Kentucky
.2850	Missouri
.2824	Vermont
.2766	Wyoming
.2702	Massachusetts
.2672	Virginia
.2642	Pennsylvania
.2588	Connecticut
.2560	Iowa
.2522	Nebraska
.2261	Montana
.2061	New York
.2001	New Jersey
.1985	Wisconsin
.1862	West Virginia
.1811	Maine
.0000	Delaware

Table G.275. ROB39

Total Number of Robberies 1960–1998

2,865,595	New York
2,641,568	California
1,277,446	Illinois
1,023,140	Florida
921,339	Texas
812,506	Michigan
621,527	Ohio
613,678	Pennsylvania
592,307	New Jersey
497,009	Maryland
349,548	Georgia
331,701	Missouri
328,172	Massachusetts
270,810	Louisiana
254,289	Tennessee
217,318	North Carolina
216,621	Indiana
211,964	Virginia
174,090	Washington
161,093	Connecticut
150,767	Arizona
148,520	Alabama
135,807	Minnesota
126,957	South Carolina
126,632	Colorado
121,538	Oregon
112,562	Wisconsin
104,549	Kentucky
102,182	Oklahoma
92,313	Nevada
74,541	Kansas
65,431	Arkansas
64,020	Mississippi
56,458	New Mexico
39,786	Iowa
35,232	Hawaii
32,390	Nebraska
32,213	Utah
30,740	Rhode Island
29,882	Delaware
24,638	West Virginia
14,819	Alaska
9,440	Maine
8,213	Idaho
8,033	Montana
7,794	New Hampshire
4,464	South Dakota
4,175	Wyoming
2,785	Vermont
2,272	North Dakota

Table G.276. ROBBER39

Average Robbery Rate per 100,000 1960–1998

468.78	New York
289.47	Maryland
289.37	Illinois
266.58	California
255.97	Nevada
243.88	Florida
229.41	Michigan
201.91	New Jersey
172.50	Missouri
167.18	Louisiana
154.65	Texas
150.21	Georgia
147.54	Ohio
144.38	Massachusetts
139.11	Tennessee
132.41	Pennsylvania
131.83	Arizona
130.77	Connecticut
122.62	Delaware
119.56	Oregon
115.30	Colorado
105.70	New Mexico
103.81	Washington
102.46	Indiana
99.41	South Carolina
97.40	Virginia
96.42	Alabama
90.52	Hawaii
87.68	North Carolina
86.50	Oklahoma
84.04	Minnesota
82.20	Alaska
81.82	Rhode Island
79.18	Kansas
75.30	Kentucky
73.66	Arkansas
64.15	Mississippi
59.96	Wisconsin
55.82	Utah
52.99	Nebraska
35.80	Iowa
34.18	West Virginia
26.63	Montana
25.75	Wyoming
23.00	Idaho
21.40	Maine
20.72	New Hampshire
16.39	South Dakota
13.90	Vermont
9.00	North Dakota

Table G.277. ROB6098

Average Robbery Rate per 1,000 1960–1998

4.6878	New York
2.8947	Maryland
2.8937	Illinois
2.6658	California
2.5597	Nevada
2.4388	Florida
2.2941	Michigan
2.0191	New Jersey
1.7250	Missouri
1.6718	Louisiana
1.5465	Texas
1.5021	Georgia
1.4754	Ohio
1.4438	Massachusetts
1.3911	Tennessee
1.3241	Pennsylvania
1.3183	Arizona
1.3077	Connecticut
1.2262	Delaware
1.1956	Oregon
1.1530	Colorado
1.0570	New Mexico
1.0381	Washington
1.0246	Indiana
.9941	South Carolina
.9740	Virginia
.9642	Alabama
.9052	Hawaii
.8768	North Carolina
.8650	Oklahoma
.8404	Minnesota
.8220	Alaska
.8182	Rhode Island
.7918	Kansas
.7530	Kentucky
.7366	Arkansas
.6415	Mississippi
.5996	Wisconsin
.5582	Utah
.5299	Nebraska
.3580	Iowa
.3418	West Virginia
.2663	Montana
.2575	Wyoming
.2300	Idaho
.2140	Maine
.2072	New Hampshire
.1639	South Dakota
.1390	Vermont
.0900	North Dakota

Table G.278. ROBBERY

Robbery Rate per 1,000 1998

2.9803	Maryland
2.6580	New York
2.5489	Nevada
2.4846	Illinois
2.4302	Florida
2.1056	California
2.0026	Louisiana
1.9973	Delaware
1.9235	Tennessee
1.8790	Georgia
1.8620	New Jersey
1.7341	New Mexico
1.6960	Mississippi
1.6930	Missouri
1.6708	Arizona
1.6648	Pennsylvania
1.6151	Michigan
1.6093	North Carolina
1.5651	South Carolina
1.5565	Connecticut
1.4678	Ohio
1.4527	Texas
1.3995	Indiana
1.3119	Alabama
1.1475	Washington
1.0629	Virginia
1.0508	Oregon
1.0268	Hawaii
.9614	Arkansas
.9522	Massachusetts
.9240	Minnesota
.9201	Oklahoma
.8684	Kansas
.8670	Alaska
.8564	Wisconsin
.8365	Colorado
.7796	Nebraska
.7536	Kentucky
.6999	Utah
.6650	Rhode Island
.4177	Iowa
.4106	New Hampshire
.3723	West Virginia
.2690	South Dakota
.2484	Montana
.2146	Idaho
.2109	Maine
.1613	Wyoming
.1014	North Dakota
.0965	Vermont

Table G.279. ASLT39

Total Number of Assaults 1960–1998

3,777,480	California
2,089,529	New York
1,980,552	Florida
1,613,720	Texas
1,512,958	Illinois
1,075,057	Michigan
757,504	North Carolina
708,442	Ohio
663,999	Pennsylvania
614,500	Massachusetts
609,162	Maryland
607,721	Georgia
594,360	Louisiana
575,641	New Jersey
551,449	South Carolina
512,255	Missouri
459,361	Alabama
455,022	Tennessee
381,250	Indiana
373,043	Arizona
359,677	Virginia
332,148	Washington
282,245	Colorado
281,591	Oklahoma
227,962	Oregon
227,462	Kentucky
217,730	New Mexico
203,258	Arkansas
182,411	Mississippi
181,883	Connecticut
173,383	Kansas
166,167	Minnesota
156,543	Wisconsin
132,119	Iowa
106,310	Nevada
91,648	Nebraska
82,565	Utah
68,238	West Virginia
67,515	Rhode Island
61,943	Delaware
57,267	Idaho
56,493	Alaska
39,067	Maine
31,799	Montana
30,984	Hawaii
28,754	Wyoming
24,885	South Dakota
21,200	New Hampshire
12,736	Vermont
8,497	North Dakota

Table G.280. ASSAUL39

Average Assault Rate per 100,000 1960–1998

462.53	Florida
429.94	South Carolina
393.21	New Mexico
369.60	California
365.66	Louisiana
353.90	Maryland
341.66	New York
339.46	Illinois
322.31	North Carolina
312.59	Arizona
300.43	Alabama
300.41	Michigan
299.71	Alaska
275.68	Nevada
267.88	Texas
267.27	Massachusetts
264.27	Georgia
261.81	Missouri
249.43	Delaware
245.98	Tennessee
238.31	Colorado
234.51	Oklahoma
228.26	Arkansas
219.17	Oregon
195.97	New Jersey
192.63	Washington
187.29	Mississippi
182.69	Kansas
179.28	Rhode Island
176.97	Indiana
171.22	Virginia
167.74	Ohio
163.67	Wyoming
160.96	Kentucky
150.39	Idaho
147.86	Nebraska
146.98	Connecticut
143.23	Pennsylvania
134.92	Utah
119.00	Iowa
103.60	Montana
100.39	Minnesota
94.94	West Virginia
91.11	South Dakota
88.98	Maine
83.57	Wisconsin
78.33	Hawaii
62.53	Vermont
56.47	New Hampshire
33.63	North Dakota

Table G.281. ASLT6098

Average Assault Rate per 1,000 1960–1998

4.6253	Florida
4.2994	South Carolina
3.9321	New Mexico
3.6960	California
3.6566	Louisiana
3.5390	Maryland
3.4166	New York
3.3946	Illinois
3.2231	North Carolina
3.1259	Arizona
3.0043	Alabama
3.0041	Michigan
2.9971	Alaska
2.7568	Nevada
2.6788	Texas
2.6727	Massachusetts
2.6427	Georgia
2.6181	Missouri
2.4943	Delaware
2.4598	Tennessee
2.3831	Colorado
2.3451	Oklahoma
2.2826	Arkansas
2.1917	Oregon
1.9597	New Jersey
1.9263	Washington
1.8729	Mississippi
1.8269	Kansas
1.7928	Rhode Island
1.7697	Indiana
1.7122	Virginia
1.6774	Ohio
1.6367	Wyoming
1.6096	Kentucky
1.5039	Idaho
1.4786	Nebraska
1.4698	Connecticut
1.4323	Pennsylvania
1.3492	Utah
1.1900	Iowa
1.0360	Montana
1.0039	Minnesota
.9494	West Virginia
.9111	South Dakota
.8898	Maine
.8357	Wisconsin
.7833	Hawaii
.6253	Vermont
.5647	New Hampshire
.3363	North Dakota

Table G.282. ASSAULT

Assault Rate per 1,000 1998

7.0079	South Carolina
6.9424	New Mexico
6.4003	Florida
5.1821	Louisiana
5.1690	Illinois
5.0995	Delaware
4.8386	Tennessee
4.7462	Massachusetts
4.5650	California
4.5276	Maryland
4.3846	Alaska
4.2396	Michigan
3.9612	Oklahoma
3.8964	Missouri
3.7960	North Carolina
3.7436	Arizona
3.7265	Texas
3.5015	Arkansas
3.4048	Nebraska
3.3828	Georgia
3.3321	New York
3.3301	Alabama
3.2685	Nevada
2.9598	Indiana
2.6840	Oregon
2.6177	Kansas
2.5688	Washington
2.5431	Mississippi
2.5148	Colorado
2.3998	Connecticut
2.2997	New Jersey
2.2731	Idaho
2.2211	Iowa
2.1797	Pennsylvania
2.0716	Utah
2.0567	Rhode Island
1.9592	Wyoming
1.9439	Ohio
1.8692	Virginia
1.8351	West Virginia
1.7472	Kentucky
1.6459	Minnesota
1.3989	Wisconsin
1.2943	Montana
1.1642	South Dakota
1.1274	Hawaii
.8429	Maine
.6739	Vermont
.6348	New Hampshire
.4613	North Dakota

Table G.283. BURG39

Total Number of Burglaries 1960–1998

14,498,479	California
7,943,222	New York
7,760,208	Texas
6,684,820	Florida
4,534,689	Michigan
4,389,174	Illinois
3,838,136	Ohio
3,095,572	Pennsylvania
3,018,003	New Jersey
2,559,100	Georgia
2,522,725	North Carolina
2,370,450	Massachusetts
2,107,063	Washington
2,084,391	Missouri
1,884,076	Indiana
1,869,364	Tennessee
1,826,435	Maryland
1,716,620	Louisiana
1,676,124	Arizona
1,641,596	Virginia
1,427,872	Alabama
1,427,779	South Carolina
1,422,137	Colorado
1,386,114	Oklahoma
1,382,705	Minnesota
1,270,362	Oregon
1,258,573	Connecticut
1,203,422	Wisconsin
1,000,845	Kentucky
924,921	Kansas
807,337	Mississippi
757,666	Iowa
746,576	Arkansas
702,615	New Mexico
529,519	Nevada
494,832	Utah
475,205	Hawaii
402,339	Rhode Island
380,692	Nebraska
369,473	West Virginia
346,075	Maine
275,121	Idaho
252,452	Delaware
229,145	New Hampshire
204,922	Montana
168,588	Vermont
153,595	Alaska
133,026	South Dakota
106,601	Wyoming
90,388	North Dakota

Table G.284. BURGLA39

Average Burglary Rate per 100,000
1960–1998

1,700.53	Florida
1,653.42	Nevada
1,567.23	California
1,553.31	Arizona
1,353.05	Texas
1,345.11	New Mexico
1,304.32	Washington
1,299.18	New York
1,290.68	Hawaii
1,287.59	Colorado
1,284.89	Michigan
1,283.65	Oregon
1,183.98	Oklahoma
1,164.18	South Carolina
1,148.93	Georgia
1,091.05	Maryland
1,090.36	Missouri
1,080.73	Rhode Island
1,078.82	Delaware
1,067.61	Louisiana
1,051.70	North Carolina
1,051.50	Massachusetts
1,050.39	Tennessee
1,045.73	New Jersey
1,035.02	Connecticut
994.04	Illinois
988.22	Kansas
944.41	Alabama
914.28	Ohio
907.59	Alaska
896.01	Indiana
878.51	Utah
867.45	Minnesota
850.11	Arkansas
848.95	Vermont
816.08	Mississippi
793.03	Maine
786.14	Virginia
761.87	Idaho
723.17	Kentucky
681.72	Iowa
676.23	Montana
670.07	Pennsylvania
655.80	Wisconsin
639.05	New Hampshire
638.14	Wyoming
623.68	Nebraska
511.85	West Virginia
488.33	South Dakota
357.28	North Dakota

Table G.285. BURG6098

Average Burglary Rate per 1,000
1960–1998

17.0053	Florida
16.5342	Nevada
15.6723	California
15.5331	Arizona
13.5305	Texas
13.4511	New Mexico
13.0432	Washington
12.9918	New York
12.9068	Hawaii
12.8759	Colorado
12.8489	Michigan
12.8365	Oregon
11.8398	Oklahoma
11.6418	South Carolina
11.4893	Georgia
10.9105	Maryland
10.9036	Missouri
10.8073	Rhode Island
10.7882	Delaware
10.6761	Louisiana
10.5170	North Carolina
10.5150	Massachusetts
10.5039	Tennessee
10.4573	New Jersey
10.3502	Connecticut
9.9404	Illinois
9.8822	Kansas
9.4441	Alabama
9.1428	Ohio
9.0759	Alaska
8.9601	Indiana
8.7851	Utah
8.6745	Minnesota
8.5011	Arkansas
8.4895	Vermont
8.1608	Mississippi
7.9303	Maine
7.8614	Virginia
7.6187	Idaho
7.2317	Kentucky
6.8172	Iowa
6.7623	Montana
6.7007	Pennsylvania
6.5580	Wisconsin
6.3905	New Hampshire
6.3814	Wyoming
6.2368	Nebraska
5.1185	West Virginia
4.8833	South Dakota
3.5728	North Dakota

Table G.286. BURGLARY		Table G.287. LARC39		Table G.288. LARCEN39	
Burglary Rate per 1,000 1998		*Total Number of Larcenies 1960–1998*		*Average Larceny Rate per 100,000 1960–1998*	
14.1747	New Mexico	29,003,336	California	3,847.93	Arizona
13.6210	Florida	16,764,361	Texas	3,500.61	Florida
13.2258	North Carolina	15,173,763	New York	3,426.81	Hawaii
13.1793	Mississippi	14,206,211	Florida	3,326.07	Nevada
12.1222	Arizona	11,118,723	Illinois	3,303.01	Washington
11.7142	South Carolina	10,206,707	Michigan	3,294.62	Utah
11.6141	Louisiana	9,518,068	Ohio	3,242.54	Oregon
11.4332	Oklahoma	6,678,422	Pennsylvania	3,237.07	Colorado
11.3755	Nevada	6,432,037	New Jersey	3,079.84	California
10.6870	Tennessee	5,470,887	Washington	3,022.27	New Mexico
10.4296	Washington	5,463,961	Georgia	2,879.59	Michigan
9.8569	Texas	4,942,272	North Carolina	2,854.95	Texas
9.7730	Georgia	4,903,071	Virginia	2,854.64	Alaska
9.3621	Hawaii	4,671,589	Indiana	2,825.47	Delaware
9.2679	Alabama	4,579,725	Maryland	2,697.66	Maryland
9.2616	Oregon	4,525,988	Missouri	2,670.79	Montana
9.2594	Arkansas	4,312,366	Arizona	2,542.45	Wyoming
9.1943	Maryland	4,280,707	Massachusetts	2,509.23	Illinois
9.1403	Missouri	4,252,208	Wisconsin	2,483.95	Kansas
8.9258	Kansas	3,948,955	Louisiana	2,482.26	New York
8.9078	Michigan	3,722,779	Minnesota	2,435.34	Louisiana
8.7182	Indiana	3,697,053	Colorado	2,355.42	Idaho
8.6895	Delaware	3,268,644	Oregon	2,346.68	Missouri
8.3512	Ohio	3,249,263	Tennessee	2,346.17	Georgia
8.2614	Illinois	2,895,151	Alabama	2,308.43	Wisconsin
8.2330	California	2,856,180	South Carolina	2,302.09	Minnesota
8.1743	Utah	2,692,719	Connecticut	2,287.92	Rhode Island
7.9192	Colorado	2,665,098	Oklahoma	2,267.55	South Carolina
7.7512	Connecticut	2,445,129	Iowa	2,267.29	Virginia
6.9176	Idaho	2,333,100	Kansas	2,266.38	Oklahoma
6.8436	Minnesota	2,099,327	Kentucky	2,262.87	Ohio
6.7112	New Jersey	1,935,140	Utah	2,222.25	Nebraska
6.6644	Maine	1,660,223	Arkansas	2,206.23	New Jersey
6.5768	Vermont	1,592,523	New Mexico	2,204.43	Indiana
6.5022	Alaska	1,397,627	Mississippi	2,200.99	Iowa
6.5000	Rhode Island	1,363,196	Nebraska	2,200.55	Connecticut
6.4877	Iowa	1,315,211	Hawaii	2,035.73	North Carolina
6.3740	Kentucky	1,113,652	Nevada	1,894.30	Maine
6.2014	Nebraska	854,658	Idaho	1,890.58	Massachusetts
6.1241	West Virginia	853,390	Rhode Island	1,885.81	Alabama
5.8591	Massachusetts	839,155	Maine	1,883.40	Vermont
5.6930	Wisconsin	821,889	Montana	1,868.63	Arkansas
5.6080	Virginia	794,965	West Virginia	1,784.88	Tennessee
5.5590	Wyoming	675,717	Delaware	1,739.62	New Hampshire
5.4480	New York	651,409	New Hampshire	1,676.21	North Dakota
5.2034	Pennsylvania	504,457	Alaska	1,645.13	South Dakota
5.1994	Montana	449,528	South Dakota	1,503.62	Kentucky
5.0120	South Dakota	431,101	Wyoming	1,442.09	Pennsylvania
4.3821	New Hampshire	424,225	North Dakota	1,405.87	Mississippi
3.5705	North Dakota	384,196	Vermont	1,102.12	West Virginia

Table G.289. LARC6098

Average Larceny Rate per 1,000 1960–1998

38.4793	Arizona
35.0061	Florida
34.2681	Hawaii
33.2607	Nevada
33.0301	Washington
32.9462	Utah
32.4254	Oregon
32.3707	Colorado
30.7984	California
30.2227	New Mexico
28.7959	Michigan
28.5495	Texas
28.5464	Alaska
28.2547	Delaware
26.9766	Maryland
26.7079	Montana
25.4245	Wyoming
25.0923	Illinois
24.8395	Kansas
24.8226	New York
24.3534	Louisiana
23.5542	Idaho
23.4668	Missouri
23.4617	Georgia
23.0843	Wisconsin
23.0209	Minnesota
22.8792	Rhode Island
22.6755	South Carolina
22.6729	Virginia
22.6638	Oklahoma
22.6287	Ohio
22.2225	Nebraska
22.0623	New Jersey
22.0443	Indiana
22.0099	Iowa
22.0055	Connecticut
20.3573	North Carolina
18.9430	Maine
18.9058	Massachusetts
18.8581	Alabama
18.8340	Vermont
18.6863	Arkansas
17.8488	Tennessee
17.3962	New Hampshire
16.7621	North Dakota
16.4513	South Dakota
15.0362	Kentucky
14.4209	Pennsylvania
14.0587	Mississippi
11.0212	West Virginia

Table G.290. LARCENY

Larceny Rate per 1,000 1998

40.2682	Utah
39.4336	Arizona
38.8872	Florida
38.3932	New Mexico
37.4575	Oregon
36.8097	Hawaii
36.6533	Washington
35.5996	Louisiana
33.4138	Kansas
33.1791	South Carolina
33.1035	Delaware
32.9568	Georgia
32.0156	Missouri
31.3837	Mississippi
30.8309	Maryland
30.8222	North Carolina
30.7193	Texas
29.1653	Nebraska
29.1505	Oklahoma
29.0879	Colorado
28.4217	Wyoming
28.0405	Indiana
27.9943	Illinois
27.9530	Alaska
27.6886	Tennessee
27.5438	Connecticut
27.4002	Alabama
27.2385	Montana
27.1133	Nevada
27.0734	Minnesota
27.0517	Ohio
26.6557	Michigan
25.7183	Arkansas
25.5441	Idaho
25.0318	Virginia
24.5279	Wisconsin
22.5405	Iowa
22.1647	California
22.0758	Vermont
21.6653	New Hampshire
21.6580	South Dakota
21.5344	Rhode Island
21.2162	Maine
21.0954	New Jersey
20.8148	North Dakota
18.8697	Pennsylvania
18.6070	New York
17.5010	Kentucky
17.2661	Massachusetts
14.9511	West Virginia

Table G.291. THEFT39

Total Number Auto Thefts 1960–1998

6,758,836	California
4,108,789	New York
2,881,875	Texas
2,315,421	Illinois
2,090,996	Florida
1,995,638	Michigan
1,848,881	Massachusetts
1,678,669	New Jersey
1,558,875	Pennsylvania
1,554,263	Ohio
877,874	Georgia
858,320	Maryland
782,060	Missouri
759,126	Indiana
695,465	Tennessee
646,889	Arizona
622,459	Louisiana
598,981	Washington
590,294	Connecticut
515,608	Virginia
486,158	North Carolina
476,716	Minnesota
464,853	Colorado
453,291	Wisconsin
451,513	Oklahoma
396,662	Oregon
373,683	Alabama
330,837	South Carolina
308,694	Kentucky
251,699	Rhode Island
215,404	Kansas
201,270	Nevada
189,792	Iowa
187,818	New Mexico
164,177	Arkansas
164,120	Hawaii
163,930	Mississippi
155,443	Utah
137,530	Nebraska
100,120	West Virginia
90,557	Delaware
87,489	Alaska
75,090	Montana
69,096	Maine
66,885	New Hampshire
61,991	Idaho
31,915	Vermont
31,467	North Dakota
31,063	South Dakota
30,309	Wyoming

Table G.292. MVT39

Average Number Auto Thefts per 100,000 1960–1998

820.72	Massachusetts
688.58	California
675.71	Rhode Island
671.57	New York
583.81	Nevada
575.93	New Jersey
560.11	Michigan
546.49	Arizona
525.65	Illinois
523.83	Alaska
504.84	Maryland
490.44	Florida
483.11	Texas
482.61	Connecticut
443.46	Hawaii
421.87	Colorado
406.65	Missouri
389.42	Louisiana
388.61	Oregon
383.95	Delaware
382.88	Oklahoma
382.57	Tennessee
381.09	Georgia
369.67	Ohio
360.23	Indiana
358.37	Washington
358.27	New Mexico
336.82	Pennsylvania
298.16	Minnesota
274.89	Utah
265.96	South Carolina
248.68	Montana
245.93	Wisconsin
245.63	Alabama
242.01	Virginia
229.82	Kansas
226.06	Nebraska
225.44	Kentucky
203.09	North Carolina
184.95	New Hampshire
184.64	Wyoming
184.42	Arkansas
172.45	Idaho
171.04	Iowa
164.87	Mississippi
162.19	Vermont
159.21	Maine
138.74	West Virginia
124.61	North Dakota
114.14	South Dakota

Table G.293. MVT6098

Average Auto Thefts per 1,000 1960–1998

8.2072	Massachusetts
6.8858	California
6.7571	Rhode Island
6.7157	New York
5.8381	Nevada
5.7593	New Jersey
5.6011	Michigan
5.4649	Arizona
5.2565	Illinois
5.2383	Alaska
5.0484	Maryland
4.9044	Florida
4.8311	Texas
4.8261	Connecticut
4.4346	Hawaii
4.2187	Colorado
4.0665	Missouri
3.8942	Louisiana
3.8861	Oregon
3.8395	Delaware
3.8288	Oklahoma
3.8257	Tennessee
3.8109	Georgia
3.6967	Ohio
3.6023	Indiana
3.5837	Washington
3.5827	New Mexico
3.3682	Pennsylvania
2.9816	Minnesota
2.7489	Utah
2.6596	South Carolina
2.4868	Montana
2.4593	Wisconsin
2.4563	Alabama
2.4201	Virginia
2.2982	Kansas
2.2606	Nebraska
2.2544	Kentucky
2.0309	North Carolina
1.8495	New Hampshire
1.8464	Wyoming
1.8442	Arkansas
1.7245	Idaho
1.7104	Iowa
1.6487	Mississippi
1.6219	Vermont
1.5921	Maine
1.3874	West Virginia
1.2461	North Dakota
1.1414	South Dakota

Table G.294. CARTHEFT

Auto Thefts per 1,000 1998

8.7647	Arizona
7.8798	Nevada
6.9978	Florida
6.5187	New Mexico
6.1573	Washington
6.1394	Michigan
5.9846	California
5.5418	Georgia
5.4962	Louisiana
5.4803	Maryland
5.3170	Tennessee
5.2453	Oregon
4.9689	Missouri
4.8934	Texas
4.7210	Mississippi
4.6890	Hawaii
4.5170	Connecticut
4.4570	Delaware
4.3945	Illinois
4.3358	New Jersey
4.2483	South Carolina
4.1645	Ohio
4.1277	Indiana
4.1208	Colorado
4.0685	Massachusetts
4.0600	Alaska
4.0533	Oklahoma
3.8623	Rhode Island
3.7754	Utah
3.5636	New York
3.5453	Pennsylvania
3.4811	Nebraska
3.4255	Alabama
3.2651	North Carolina
3.2385	Minnesota
2.8262	Arkansas
2.7201	Wisconsin
2.7102	Virginia
2.3244	New Hampshire
2.2857	Montana
2.2777	Kansas
2.1781	Kentucky
1.8959	North Dakota
1.8633	West Virginia
1.8593	Iowa
1.8341	Idaho
1.4659	Vermont
1.3850	Wyoming
1.2124	Maine
1.1485	South Dakota

Table G.295. TOTALFEM

Total Females Ages 15–19 1996

1,011,100	California
710,900	Texas
568,700	New York
421,100	Florida
400,000	Illinois
393,500	Ohio
388,800	Pennsylvania
345,400	Michigan
257,900	Georgia
244,400	New Jersey
240,300	North Carolina
217,200	Virginia
211,000	Indiana
191,200	Missouri
190,600	Washington
188,600	Wisconsin
181,800	Tennessee
178,600	Massachusetts
178,200	Louisiana
168,200	Minnesota
156,600	Alabama
155,000	Maryland
151,200	Arizona
142,600	Kentucky
133,900	South Carolina
131,700	Colorado
122,300	Oklahoma
111,700	Mississippi
111,300	Oregon
106,900	Iowa
104,300	Utah
95,400	Connecticut
95,200	Kansas
93,000	Arkansas
67,700	West Virginia
67,100	New Mexico
62,700	Nebraska
52,500	Idaho
48,800	Nevada
42,200	Maine
39,000	Hawaii
37,400	New Hampshire
34,200	Montana
30,300	South Dakota
30,100	Rhode Island
24,500	North Dakota
23,600	Alaska
23,400	Delaware
20,400	Wyoming
19,900	Vermont

Table G.296. NHWHITE

Non-Hispanic White Females Ages 15–19 1996

426,700	California
346,900	Texas
340,000	New York
328,100	Ohio
325,100	Pennsylvania
268,900	Michigan
263,900	Illinois
250,700	Florida
181,300	Indiana
164,600	Wisconsin
159,400	North Carolina
159,200	Missouri
154,200	Georgia
153,400	Washington
152,800	New Jersey
151,500	Minnesota
148,300	Virginia
144,100	Massachusetts
138,400	Tennessee
127,900	Kentucky
100,000	Iowa
99,600	Louisiana
99,400	Alabama
97,800	Colorado
95,400	Oregon
93,800	Utah
92,500	Maryland
91,200	Oklahoma
89,000	Arizona
80,300	Kansas
78,900	South Carolina
71,500	Connecticut
68,600	Arkansas
64,300	West Virginia
57,600	Mississippi
55,300	Nebraska
46,900	Idaho
41,000	Maine
35,900	New Hampshire
32,600	Nevada
30,500	Montana
26,800	New Mexico
26,500	South Dakota
25,100	Rhode Island
22,400	North Dakota
19,200	Vermont
18,200	Wyoming
16,500	Delaware
16,200	Alaska
9,800	Hawaii

Table G.297. NHBLACK

Non-Hispanic Black Females Ages 15–19 1996

102,100	New York
96,100	Texas
92,800	Florida
91,200	Georgia
79,900	California
74,100	Illinois
71,000	Louisiana
68,600	North Carolina
57,100	Michigan
53,900	Alabama
52,600	Ohio
52,200	Virginia
52,000	Mississippi
51,600	South Carolina
49,700	Maryland
43,200	Pennsylvania
41,800	New Jersey
39,100	Tennessee
25,700	Missouri
21,200	Arkansas
21,200	Indiana
13,100	Wisconsin
12,600	Kentucky
12,100	Oklahoma
11,800	Massachusetts
10,700	Connecticut
7,500	Washington
6,400	Kansas
6,100	Colorado
5,600	Minnesota
5,500	Arizona
5,500	Delaware
4,200	Nevada
2,800	Nebraska
2,600	Iowa
2,600	West Virginia
2,400	Oregon
1,600	Rhode Island
1,400	New Mexico
1,200	Hawaii
900	Alaska
600	Utah
300	New Hampshire
200	Idaho
200	Maine
200	South Dakota
200	Vermont
100	Montana
100	North Dakota
100	Wyoming

Table G.298. HISPANIC

Hispanic Females Ages 15–19 1996

382,800	California
249,400	Texas
96,600	New York
68,300	Florida
48,300	Illinois
43,100	Arizona
36,000	New Jersey
31,200	New Mexico
23,800	Colorado
14,800	Massachusetts
14,600	Washington
13,000	Pennsylvania
11,300	Michigan
10,600	Connecticut
9,100	Nevada
8,600	Virginia
8,000	Oregon
7,700	Ohio
7,500	Georgia
6,300	Maryland
6,300	Utah
6,100	Indiana
5,800	Wisconsin
5,800	Kansas
5,500	Oklahoma
5,300	North Carolina
4,500	Louisiana
4,300	Idaho
4,000	Hawaii
3,500	Missouri
3,400	Minnesota
3,000	Nebraska
2,400	Iowa
2,400	Rhode Island
2,200	Tennessee
2,000	Arkansas
1,800	South Carolina
1,500	Alabama
1,400	Wyoming
1,100	Kentucky
900	Mississippi
900	Delaware
900	Alaska
700	New Hampshire
700	Montana
400	West Virginia
400	Maine
300	South Dakota
300	North Dakota
200	Vermont

Table G.299. OTHERACE

Total Other Races Females Ages 15–19 1996

121,700	California
92,000	Florida
30,000	New York
24,100	Hawaii
18,500	Texas
15,100	Washington
13,800	New Jersey
13,600	Arizona
13,500	Illinois
13,400	Oklahoma
8,200	Michigan
8,200	Virginia
8,000	Massachusetts
7,800	New Mexico
7,700	Minnesota
7,600	Pennsylvania
7,000	North Carolina
6,500	Maryland
5,500	Alaska
5,400	Oregon
5,200	Ohio
5,200	Wisconsin
5,100	Georgia
4,000	Colorado
3,600	Utah
3,300	South Dakota
3,100	Louisiana
2,900	Missouri
2,900	Montana
2,900	Nevada
2,600	Connecticut
2,600	Kansas
2,400	Indiana
2,100	Tennessee
1,900	Alabama
1,900	Iowa
1,600	North Dakota
1,600	South Carolina
1,500	Nebraska
1,200	Arkansas
1,200	Idaho
1,200	Mississippi
1,100	Rhode Island
1,000	Kentucky
600	Maine
600	New Hampshire
600	Wyoming
500	Delaware
500	West Virginia
300	Vermont

Table G.300. TOTALBR

Birthrates per 1,000, all Females Ages 15–19 1996

76	Mississippi
75	Arkansas
74	Texas
74	Arizona
71	New Mexico
70	Nevada
69	Alabama
68	Georgia
67	Louisiana
66	Tennessee
64	North Carolina
63	California
63	Oklahoma
63	South Carolina
62	Kentucky
59	Florida
57	Illinois
57	Delaware
56	Indiana
54	Missouri
51	Oregon
50	Ohio
50	Colorado
50	Kansas
50	West Virginia
48	Hawaii
47	Michigan
47	Idaho
46	Virginia
46	Maryland
46	Alaska
45	Washington
44	Wyoming
43	Utah
43	Rhode Island
42	New York
40	South Dakota
39	Pennsylvania
39	Montana
39	Nebraska
38	Iowa
37	Wisconsin
37	Connecticut
35	New Jersey
32	Massachusetts
32	Minnesota
32	North Dakota
31	Maine
30	Vermont
29	New Hampshire

Table G.301. NHWHBR

Non-Hispanic White Birthrates per 1,000 Ages 15–19 1996

64	Arkansas
58	Kentucky
56	Tennessee
55	Oklahoma
54	Alabama
52	Mississippi
51	Georgia
50	Nevada
50	West Virginia
49	Indiana
48	South Carolina
47	Louisiana
47	North Carolina
45	Arizona
45	Missouri
45	Texas
44	Florida
44	Oregon
43	New Mexico
42	Idaho
42	Ohio
41	Kansas
40	Wyoming
37	Utah
37	Washington
35	Alaska
35	Delaware
35	Michigan
35	Virginia
34	Iowa
33	Colorado
32	California
32	Illinois
31	Maine
31	Montana
31	Nebraska
31	Vermont
30	Maryland
30	South Dakota
28	New Hampshire
28	Pennsylvania
28	Rhode Island
26	North Dakota
25	Wisconsin
24	Minnesota
24	New York
22	Hawaii
21	Massachusetts
19	Connecticut
15	New Jersey

Table G.302. BLACKBR

Black Birthrates per 1,000 Ages 15–19 1996

130	Wisconsin
121	Minnesota
118	Illinois
110	Delaware
108	Arkansas
108	Iowa
106	Missouri
106	Kansas
105	Indiana
103	Kentucky
102	Tennessee
102	Mississippi
101	Ohio
101	Pennsylvania
100	Nevada
100	Nebraska
98	Alabama
97	Louisiana
96	Florida
95	Georgia
94	Michigan
93	Oklahoma
91	North Carolina
88	Texas
86	Oregon
85	South Carolina
82	Rhode Island
81	West Virginia
81	New Jersey
80	Connecticut
79	Maryland
78	Virginia
77	California
75	Arizona
75	Colorado
72	Washington
72	Massachusetts
66	New York
55	New Mexico
36	Hawaii
*	Idaho
*	Wyoming
*	Utah
*	Alaska
*	Maine
*	Montana
*	Vermont
*	South Dakota
*	New Hampshire
*	North Dakota

*Incomplete data

Table G.303. HISPBR

Hispanic Birthrates per 1,000 Ages 15–19 1996

175	North Carolina
133	Arizona
132	Georgia
132	Minnesota
128	Oregon
127	Nevada
127	Pennsylvania
127	Rhode Island
126	Utah
121	Arkansas
114	Connecticut
113	Wisconsin
112	Colorado
112	Washington
111	Illinois
111	Kansas
109	Massachusetts
109	Texas
108	Iowa
105	Hawaii
104	California
104	Nebraska
104	Tennessee
103	Idaho
102	Oklahoma
96	Alabama
95	Michigan
94	Indiana
94	New Mexico
91	South Carolina
89	Kentucky
89	Ohio
84	Missouri
80	Wyoming
79	New Jersey
79	New York
68	Florida
67	Virginia
59	Maryland
41	Louisiana
*	Alaska
*	Delaware
*	Maine
*	Mississippi
*	Montana
*	New Hampshire
*	North Dakota
*	South Dakota
*	Vermont
*	West Virginia

*Incomplete data

Table G.304. BR151996

Total Births to Females Ages 15–19 1996

63,222	California
52,273	Texas
24,806	Florida
23,876	New York
22,831	Illinois
19,851	Ohio
17,648	Georgia
15,909	Michigan
15,300	Pennsylvania
15,296	North Carolina
12,061	Tennessee
11,945	Louisiana
11,875	Indiana
11,009	Arizona
10,807	Alabama
10,262	Missouri
9,912	Virginia
8,786	Kentucky
8,639	New Jersey
8,609	Washington
8,451	Mississippi
8,362	South Carolina
7,780	Oklahoma
7,186	Maryland
7,026	Arkansas
6,965	Wisconsin
6,541	Colorado
5,761	Massachusetts
5,681	Oregon
5,417	Minnesota
4,775	New Mexico
4,714	Kansas
4,438	Utah
4,047	Iowa
3,578	Connecticut
3,420	West Virginia
3,402	Nevada
2,486	Idaho
2,434	Nebraska
1,884	Hawaii
1,334	Delaware
1,333	Maine
1,326	Montana
1,285	Rhode Island
1,189	South Dakota
1,096	Alaska
1,072	New Hampshire
899	Wyoming
793	North Dakota
601	Vermont

Table G.305. TOTPCUN

Percent Births to Unmarried Teens Total 1996

92	Rhode Island
90	Maryland
90	Massachusetts
89	New Jersey
89	Pennsylvania
88	Connecticut
88	Delaware
88	New Hampshire
88	New York
87	Michigan
87	Minnesota
85	Vermont
84	Illinois
84	Ohio
84	Wisconsin
83	Louisiana
82	Hawaii
82	Maine
82	South Dakota
81	Iowa
81	Nebraska
80	Arizona
80	Indiana
80	Mississippi
80	North Dakota
80	South Carolina
79	Florida
79	New Mexico
78	Missouri
78	Montana
78	Virginia
77	Alaska
77	Nevada
76	Georgia
75	North Carolina
75	Washington
74	Kansas
74	Oregon
72	Colorado
70	Alabama
70	Tennessee
70	Wyoming
67	Arkansas
67	West Virginia
66	Oklahoma
66	Texas
65	Kentucky
62	California
60	Idaho
58	Utah

Table G.306. NHWPCUN

Percent Births to Unmarried Teens Non-Hispanic Whites 1996

92	Rhode Island
90	Massachusetts
88	New Hampshire
88	Minnesota
85	Pennsylvania
85	Vermont
84	Connecticut
83	New Jersey
83	Maine
82	Michigan
82	Wisconsin
81	Maryland
80	Delaware
80	Iowa
80	Nebraska
79	New York
79	North Dakota
78	Illinois
78	Ohio
78	South Dakota
75	Indiana
75	Washington
75	Oregon
73	Arizona
73	Montana
73	Nevada
71	Missouri
71	Kansas
70	Florida
68	Colorado
67	Wyoming
66	Alaska
66	West Virginia
65	New Mexico
65	Virginia
64	Louisiana
63	California
62	South Carolina
60	North Carolina
60	Texas
59	Oklahoma
59	Kentucky
59	Idaho
58	Georgia
57	Tennessee
54	Utah
53	Arkansas
50	Mississippi
46	Hawaii
46	Alabama

Table G.307. NHBPCUN

Percent Births to Unmarried Teens
Non-Hispanic Blacks 1996

98	Delaware
98	Illinois
98	Michigan
98	Missouri
98	Ohio
98	Pennsylvania
98	Rhode Island
98	West Virginia
98	Wisconsin
97	Georgia
97	Indiana
97	Kentucky
97	Maryland
97	Massachusetts
97	Mississippi
97	Nebraska
97	New Jersey
97	South Carolina
96	Arkansas
96	Connecticut
96	Florida
96	Louisiana
96	Minnesota
96	Nevada
96	New York
96	North Carolina
96	Oregon
96	Tennessee
95	Alabama
95	New Mexico
95	Virginia
94	Arizona
94	Iowa
94	Kansas
93	Oklahoma
93	Texas
90	Utah
90	Washington
88	Colorado
87	Alaska
82	California
74	Hawaii
*	Idaho
*	Maine
*	Montana
*	New Hampshire
*	North Dakota
*	South Dakota
*	Vermont
*	Wyoming

*Inadequate data

Table G.308. HISPPCUN

Percent Births to Unmarried Teens
Hispanics 1996

90	Rhode Island
89	New York
88	Pennsylvania
88	Massachusetts
88	Connecticut
85	New Jersey
85	Hawaii
84	Ohio
81	New Mexico
81	Arizona
81	Wyoming
79	New Hampshire
78	Michigan
78	Missouri
78	Montana
77	Delaware
77	Indiana
77	Minnesota
77	Nevada
76	Wisconsin
76	Iowa
74	Maryland
74	South Dakota
73	Illinois
73	Colorado
72	Louisiana
72	Virginia
72	Kansas
72	Alaska
71	Utah
70	Nebraska
70	Florida
68	Washington
67	Oregon
66	Mississippi
64	Arkansas
63	Oklahoma
61	Idaho
60	Tennessee
60	Texas
60	California
59	Kentucky
59	South Carolina
57	North Carolina
56	North Dakota
46	Alabama
45	Georgia
*	West Virginia
*	Maine
*	Vermont

*Inadequate data

Table G.309. TOTPCINC

Percent Teen Births Inadequate
Prenatal Care Total 1996

16	New Jersey
16	New Mexico
14	Arizona
14	Arkansas
14	Nevada
14	New York
13	Texas
12	Illinois
12	South Dakota
11	Colorado
11	Idaho
11	Minnesota
11	Oklahoma
11	South Carolina
10	Hawaii
10	Louisiana
10	North Dakota
10	Pennsylvania
10	Utah
10	Washington
10	Wisconsin
9	Alabama
9	Alaska
9	Florida
9	Georgia
9	Indiana
9	Massachusetts
9	Mississippi
9	Montana
9	Nebraska
9	Oregon
9	Tennessee
9	Virginia
9	Wyoming
8	California
8	Connecticut
8	Delaware
8	Maryland
8	Michigan
8	Missouri
8	North Carolina
8	Ohio
7	Kansas
7	Kentucky
7	West Virginia
6	Iowa
6	Vermont
5	Maine
5	New Hampshire
4	Rhode Island

Table G.310. NWHPCINC

Percent Teen Births Inadequate Prenatal Care, Non-Hispanic Whites 1996

12	New Jersey
11	New Mexico
10	Arkansas
9	New York
9	Idaho
9	Oklahoma
8	Arizona
8	Nevada
8	Texas
8	Colorado
8	Minnesota
8	Massachusetts
7	Illinois
7	South Dakota
7	South Carolina
7	North Dakota
7	Pennsylvania
7	Utah
7	Washington
7	Wisconsin
7	Alaska
7	Indiana
7	Nebraska
7	Oregon
7	Wyoming
7	Connecticut
7	West Virginia
6	Florida
6	Georgia
6	Montana
6	Tennessee
6	Virginia
6	California
6	Delaware
6	Michigan
6	Missouri
6	Ohio
6	Kentucky
6	Vermont
5	Louisiana
5	Alabama
5	Mississippi
5	Maryland
5	North Carolina
5	Kansas
5	Iowa
5	Maine
4	Hawaii
4	New Hampshire
3	Rhode Island

Table G.311. NHBPCINC

Percent Teen Births Inadequate Prenatal Care, Non-Hispanic Blacks 1996

20	Arkansas
20	New Jersey
18	Nevada
17	New York
16	New Mexico
16	Pennsylvania
15	Illinois
15	Minnesota
15	Oklahoma
15	Utah
15	Wisconsin
14	Arizona
14	Indiana
14	Missouri
14	South Carolina
14	Tennessee
14	Texas
13	Louisiana
13	Nebraska
13	Ohio
12	Alabama
11	Colorado
11	Florida
11	Georgia
11	Iowa
11	Massachusetts
11	Michigan
11	Mississippi
11	North Carolina
11	Virginia
10	Delaware
10	Washington
9	Kentucky
9	Maryland
8	California
8	Connecticut
8	Kansas
8	Oregon
8	West Virginia
6	Rhode Island
3	Hawaii
2	Alaska
*	Idaho
*	Maine
*	Montana
*	New Hampshire
*	North Dakota
*	South Dakota
*	Vermont
*	Wyoming

*Inadequate data

Table G.312. HISPCINC

Percent Teen Births Inadequate Prenatal Care, Hispanics 1996

26	Tennessee
23	Arkansas
21	Nevada
19	Utah
19	Idaho
18	Arizona
18	South Carolina
18	Kentucky
17	New Mexico
17	Wyoming
16	Minnesota
16	Texas
16	Alabama
16	Iowa
15	New Jersey
15	New York
15	Colorado
15	Virginia
15	Washington
15	Kansas
14	Oklahoma
14	Wisconsin
14	Indiana
14	North Carolina
14	Oregon
14	New Hampshire
13	Pennsylvania
13	Illinois
13	Louisiana
13	Georgia
12	Ohio
12	Michigan
12	Maryland
12	Alaska
11	Nebraska
11	Montana
11	North Dakota
10	Florida
10	Massachusetts
9	California
9	Connecticut
8	Delaware
7	Missouri
7	Mississippi
7	Hawaii
5	Rhode Island
5	South Dakota
*	West Virginia
*	Maine
*	Vermont

*Inadequate data

Table G.313. ABORT95

Teenage Abortion Rate per 1,000 1992–1995

95	Alabama
36	Rhode Island
32	North Carolina
30	Hawaii
30	Kansas
30	Oregon
28	Connecticut
28	Georgia
27	Washington
26	Massachusetts
26	Nevada
26	Vermont
24	New Jersey
23	Texas
23	Virginia
21	Maryland
21	Tennessee
20	Michigan
20	Montana
20	Pennsylvania
18	Colorado
18	Ohio
17	Arizona
17	Nebraska
17	New Mexico
16	Maine
16	Minnesota
16	New York
16	South Carolina
15	Arkansas
14	Louisiana
14	North Dakota
13	Indiana
13	Kentucky
13	Wisconsin
12	Missouri
10	South Dakota
10	West Virginia
9	Mississippi
8	Utah
5	Idaho
3	Wyoming
*	Alaska
*	California
*	Delaware
*	Florida
*	Illinois
*	Iowa
*	New Hampshire
*	Oklahoma

*Inadequate data

Table G.314. SMOK9596

Percent of Teen Births Occurring to Mothers Who Smoked 1995–1996

38	Vermont
35	New Hampshire
33	Maine
32	West Virginia
31	Kentucky
30	Montana
30	North Dakota
30	Alaska
29	Wyoming
29	Iowa
28	Oregon
27	Washington
27	Ohio
27	Wisconsin
25	Pennsylvania
25	Nebraska
25	Minnesota
25	Missouri
24	Rhode Island
24	Idaho
23	Massachusetts
22	Michigan
21	Utah
20	Tennessee
20	Arkansas
20	Oklahoma
18	North Carolina
18	Kansas
18	Colorado
16	Connecticut
16	Virginia
15	Nevada
15	South Carolina
15	Delaware
14	Alabama
14	Illinois
13	New Jersey
13	Maryland
13	Florida
12	Georgia
11	Hawaii
11	Arizona
11	New Mexico
10	Louisiana
10	Mississippi
9	Texas
*	New York
*	Indiana
*	South Dakota
*	California

*Inadequate data

Table G.315. LACKINSF

Percent Females Ages 12–19 Who Lack Health Insurance 1995

28	New Mexico
28	Texas
27	Arizona
27	Louisiana
26	Arkansas
25	Mississippi
24	Florida
22	California
21	Oklahoma
19	Colorado
19	Georgia
19	South Carolina
19	West Virginia
18	Alabama
18	Idaho
18	Nevada
17	Connecticut
17	Kentucky
17	New York
17	Oregon
16	Delaware
16	Montana
16	New Jersey
16	North Carolina
16	Rhode Island
16	Tennessee
15	Washington
14	Indiana
14	Missouri
14	Wyoming
13	Alaska
13	Kansas
13	Maine
13	Maryland
13	Virginia
12	Illinois
12	Iowa
12	Massachusetts
12	New Hampshire
11	Minnesota
11	Nebraska
11	North Dakota
11	Ohio
11	South Dakota
10	Utah
10	Vermont
9	Michigan
9	Pennsylvania
8	Hawaii
7	Wisconsin

Table G.316. LACKINSM

Percent Males Ages 12–19 Who Lack Health Insurance 1995

30	Texas
27	Louisiana
26	New Mexico
26	Arizona
26	Arkansas
26	Mississippi
23	California
23	Nevada
22	Florida
20	Oklahoma
20	Georgia
20	South Carolina
18	Delaware
18	North Carolina
17	Alabama
17	Idaho
17	Kentucky
17	New York
17	New Jersey
17	Tennessee
17	Washington
17	Wyoming
17	Maine
16	West Virginia
15	Connecticut
15	Oregon
15	Missouri
14	Indiana
14	Illinois
14	New Hampshire
13	Colorado
13	Rhode Island
13	Alaska
13	Kansas
13	Maryland
13	South Dakota
13	Utah
12	Iowa
12	Massachusetts
12	Nebraska
12	North Dakota
12	Ohio
12	Michigan
11	Montana
11	Virginia
10	Pennsylvania
9	Vermont
9	Wisconsin
7	Minnesota
5	Hawaii

Table G.317. PCCBR96

Percent Change in Birthrates per 1,000 Females Ages 15–19 1991–1996

−6	Arkansas
−6	Alabama
−6	Rhode Island
−7	Texas
−7	Delaware
−7	Indiana
−7	Oregon
−7	Connecticut
−8	Arizona
−8	Nevada
−9	New York
−9	Nebraska
−9	North Dakota
−10	North Carolina
−11	New Mexico
−11	Georgia
−11	Kentucky
−11	Kansas
−11	Utah
−11	Iowa
−12	Mississippi
−12	Louisiana
−12	Tennessee
−12	Oklahoma
−12	Illinois
−12	Idaho
−13	West Virginia
−14	South Carolina
−14	Florida
−14	Minnesota
−14	New Hampshire
−15	Colorado
−15	Maryland
−15	Virginia
−15	New Jersey
−15	Massachusetts
−16	California
−16	Washington
−16	Pennsylvania
−16	Wisconsin
−17	Missouri
−17	Ohio
−17	South Dakota
−17	Montana
−18	Hawaii
−19	Wyoming
−21	Michigan
−23	Vermont
−28	Maine
−29	Alaska

Table G.318. BRYT96

Birthrates per 1,000 Younger Teens Ages 15–17 1996

52	Mississippi
49	Arizona
49	Texas
46	New Mexico
45	Alabama
45	Arkansas
45	Georgia
43	Louisiana
42	Nevada
41	Delaware
41	North Carolina
41	South Carolina
40	Tennessee
39	California
37	Florida
37	Kentucky
37	Oklahoma
36	Illinois
33	Indiana
31	Missouri
30	Colorado
30	Maryland
30	Ohio
29	Oregon
29	West Virginia
28	Hawaii
28	Kansas
28	Michigan
28	Virginia
27	Alaska
27	Idaho
27	Rhode Island
26	New York
26	Washington
25	Pennsylvania
25	Wyoming
24	Connecticut
24	Utah
23	New Jersey
22	Nebraska
22	South Dakota
22	Wisconsin
21	Iowa
21	Montana
20	Massachusetts
19	Minnesota
17	Maine
16	North Dakota
15	New Hampshire
15	Vermont

Table G.319. GONTEEN

Gonorrhea Rate per 100,000 Females Ages 15–19 1996

1,784	Alabama
1,548	Delaware
1,502	Georgia
1,339	North Carolina
1,313	Maryland
1,267	South Carolina
1,220	Mississippi
1,183	Arkansas
1,132	Tennessee
974	Oklahoma
969	Illinois
941	Louisiana
931	Missouri
906	Ohio
878	Florida
852	Michigan
767	Virginia
752	Connecticut
653	New York
652	Indiana
629	Texas
600	Pennsylvania
582	Kentucky
576	Wisconsin
477	New Jersey
475	Kansas
427	Nebraska
385	Arizona
347	Alaska
336	California
328	Minnesota
317	Rhode Island
305	Colorado
299	Nevada
265	Iowa
244	West Virginia
233	New Mexico
231	Massachusetts
196	Washington
184	Hawaii
162	Oregon
116	South Dakota
115	New Hampshire
39	Wyoming
35	Vermont
30	Idaho
26	Maine
25	North Dakota
25	Utah
23	Montana

Table G.320. BUSFAIL

Number of Business Failures 1998

17,679	California
6,785	Texas
4,233	New York
3,291	Illinois
2,641	Pennsylvania
2,528	Washington
2,524	Ohio
2,483	Colorado
2,047	Florida
2,024	New Jersey
1,711	Minnesota
1,551	Michigan
1,369	Tennessee
1,321	Missouri
1,283	Maryland
1,225	Arizona
1,200	Massachusetts
1,140	Kansas
1,109	Oregon
1,005	Wisconsin
990	Oklahoma
860	Virginia
846	North Carolina
800	Georgia
781	Hawaii
748	Arkansas
677	Nevada
585	New Mexico
546	Alabama
530	Connecticut
473	Indiana
441	Idaho
410	South Carolina
388	Utah
383	Nebraska
377	Louisiana
322	New Hampshire
305	West Virginia
275	South Dakota
270	Kentucky
259	Maine
244	Iowa
201	Montana
177	Alaska
177	Mississippi
166	Wyoming
150	Rhode Island
144	North Dakota
80	Vermont
28	Delaware

Table G.321. PCTBRB96

Percent Teen Births That Are Repeat Births 1996

25	Mississippi
24	Alabama
24	Arkansas
24	Georgia
24	Illinois
24	Louisiana
24	Texas
23	Florida
23	North Carolina
23	Tennessee
22	Arizona
22	California
22	Indiana
22	Michigan
22	Rhode Island
21	Delaware
21	Kansas
21	Missouri
21	Nevada
21	Ohio
21	Pennsylvania
21	South Carolina
21	Wisconsin
20	Colorado
20	Connecticut
20	Kentucky
20	Maryland
20	New Jersey
20	New Mexico
20	New York
20	Oklahoma
20	Virginia
19	Alaska
19	Hawaii
19	Minnesota
19	Oregon
19	Washington
18	Idaho
18	Iowa
18	Massachusetts
18	West Virginia
17	Nebraska
17	South Dakota
17	Utah
16	Montana
15	Maine
15	North Dakota
15	Wyoming
14	Vermont
13	New Hampshire

Table G.322. PCTBAL96

Teen Births as Percent of All Births 1996

21	Mississippi
19	Arkansas
18	Alabama
18	Louisiana
18	New Mexico
17	Kentucky
17	Oklahoma
16	Texas
16	Tennessee
16	South Carolina
16	West Virginia
15	Georgia
15	North Carolina
15	Arizona
14	Indiana
14	Missouri
14	Wyoming
13	Florida
13	Delaware
13	Kansas
13	Nevada
13	Ohio
13	Oregon
13	Idaho
12	Illinois
12	California
12	Michigan
12	Colorado
12	Montana
11	Virginia
11	Alaska
11	Washington
11	Iowa
11	South Dakota
11	Utah
10	Rhode Island
10	Pennsylvania
10	Wisconsin
10	Maryland
10	Hawaii
10	Nebraska
10	Maine
10	North Dakota
9	New York
9	Minnesota
9	Vermont
8	Connecticut
8	New Jersey
7	Massachusetts
7	New Hampshire

Table G.323. VIOLENCE

Total Number of Violent Crimes 1998

229,754	California
139,601	Florida
113,038	New York
111,454	Texas
97,291	Illinois
60,676	Michigan
47,529	Pennsylvania
43,260	North Carolina
42,068	Georgia
40,739	Maryland
35,717	New Jersey
35,404	Massachusetts
35,076	Tennessee
34,952	South Carolina
32,160	Louisiana
31,165	Ohio
28,054	Missouri
26,217	Arizona
23,846	Washington
21,778	Virginia
21,387	Alabama
20,653	Indiana
18,035	Oklahoma
14,602	Minnesota
14,294	Colorado
13,660	Oregon
13,560	New Mexico
13,009	Wisconsin
12,399	Arkansas
11,991	Connecticut
11,244	Nevada
11,178	Kentucky
10,438	Kansas
7,513	Iowa
7,475	Mississippi
7,369	Nebraska
6,412	Utah
5,303	Delaware
4,411	West Virginia
3,469	Idaho
3,256	Alaska
3,059	Rhode Island
2,946	Hawaii
1,560	Maine
1,158	Wyoming
940	South Dakota
883	Montana
648	New Hampshire
597	Vermont
534	North Dakota

Table G.324. PROPERTY

Total Number of Property Crimes 1998

1,187,933	California
897,188	Texas
884,397	Florida
499,878	New York
489,632	Illinois
390,400	Michigan
359,882	Georgia
353,319	North Carolina
317,355	Ohio
315,426	Pennsylvania
298,693	Washington
272,358	Arizona
260,835	New Jersey
233,518	Maryland
222,750	Virginia
220,672	Louisiana
217,354	Missouri
209,088	Tennessee
188,168	South Carolina
175,560	Minnesota
175,148	Indiana
172,084	Wisconsin
170,258	Oregon
169,703	Alabama
160,755	Massachusetts
151,586	Colorado
149,229	Oklahoma
117,299	Kansas
111,980	Connecticut
103,774	Utah
102,545	Kentucky
95,786	Arkansas
86,037	New Mexico
81,006	Nevada
79,641	Iowa
76,510	Mississippi
64,078	Nebraska
60,677	Hawaii
41,868	Idaho
41,524	West Virginia
36,137	Maine
34,410	Delaware
31,514	Rhode Island
20,880	Alaska
17,197	Montana
16,878	Wyoming
16,848	Vermont
15,553	North Dakota
14,170	South Dakota
12,023	New Hampshire

Table G.325. VIOLENT		Table G.326. PROPER		Table G.327. RMURD609	
Violent Crime Rate per 1,000 1998		*Property Crime Rate per 1,000 1998*		*Rank-Order Murder Rate per 1,000 1960–1998*	
9.3930	Florida	60.3205	Arizona	1.000	Louisiana
9.3124	New Mexico	59.5061	Florida	2.000	Georgia
9.1280	South Carolina	59.0865	New Mexico	3.000	Alabama
8.0773	Illinois	53.2402	Washington	4.000	Texas
7.9388	Maryland	52.7099	Louisiana	5.000	Mississippi
7.6818	Louisiana	52.2180	Utah	6.000	Nevada
7.3297	Tennessee	51.9645	Oregon	7.000	South Carolina
7.1277	Delaware	50.8608	Hawaii	8.000	Florida
7.0366	California	49.2840	Mississippi	9.500	Alaska
6.4815	Michigan	49.1415	South Carolina	9.500	New York
6.4362	Nevada	48.2715	Georgia	11.000	North Carolina
6.2454	New York	47.3132	North Carolina	12.000	Tennessee
6.0060	Alaska	46.3686	Nevada	13.500	Maryland
5.9891	Massachusetts	46.2499	Delaware	13.500	New Mexico
5.9534	Missouri	46.1248	Missouri	15.000	California
5.8064	Arizona	45.5055	Maryland	16.000	Arkansas
5.7930	North Carolina	45.4696	Texas	17.000	Illinois
5.6485	Texas	44.6371	Oklahoma	18.000	Michigan
5.6426	Georgia	44.6173	Kansas	19.000	Virginia
5.3946	Oklahoma	43.6926	Tennessee	20.000	Missouri
5.0528	Alabama	41.7029	Michigan	21.000	Kentucky
4.8935	Arkansas	41.1278	Colorado	22.000	Arizona
4.8212	Indiana	40.8864	Indiana	23.000	Oklahoma
4.8150	Mississippi	40.6502	Illinois	24.000	Indiana
4.4675	Nebraska	40.0937	Alabama	25.000	Ohio
4.4014	New Jersey	39.8120	Connecticut	26.000	Delaware
4.2631	Connecticut	39.5675	Ohio	27.000	Colorado
4.2504	Washington	38.8479	Nebraska	28.000	West Virginia
4.1692	Oregon	38.5152	Alaska	29.000	Pennsylvania
4.1616	Pennsylvania	37.8039	Arkansas	30.000	New Jersey
3.9703	Kansas	37.1555	Minnesota	31.000	Wyoming
3.8856	Ohio	36.3823	California	32.000	Kansas
3.8782	Colorado	35.3658	Wyoming	33.000	Hawaii
3.2606	Virginia	34.7236	Montana	34.000	Oregon
3.2265	Utah	34.2958	Idaho	35.000	Washington
3.0962	Rhode Island	33.3500	Virginia	36.000	Connecticut
3.0904	Minnesota	32.9410	Wisconsin	37.000	Montana
2.9138	Iowa	32.1423	New Jersey	38.000	Idaho
2.8416	Idaho	31.8967	Rhode Island	39.000	Massachusetts
2.8399	Kentucky	30.8875	Iowa	40.000	Nebraska
2.4902	Wisconsin	30.1184	Vermont	41.000	Rhode Island
2.4694	Hawaii	29.0931	Maine	42.500	Utah
2.4367	West Virginia	28.3719	New Hampshire	42.500	Wisconsin
2.4264	Wyoming	27.8185	South Dakota	44.000	Minnesota
1.8454	South Dakota	27.6187	New York	45.000	Maine
1.7829	Montana	27.6184	Pennsylvania	46.000	New Hampshire
1.5291	New Hampshire	27.1938	Massachusetts	47.000	Vermont
1.2559	Maine	26.2812	North Dakota	48.000	South Dakota
1.0672	Vermont	26.0531	Kentucky	49.000	Iowa
.9023	North Dakota	22.9385	West Virginia	50.000	North Dakota

Table G.328. RRAPE609

Rank-Order Rape Rate per 1,000
1960–1998

1.000	Alaska
2.000	Michigan
3.000	Nevada
4.000	Delaware
5.000	Washington
6.000	New Mexico
7.000	California
8.000	Florida
9.000	Colorado
10.000	Texas
11.000	Oregon
12.000	Arizona
13.000	South Carolina
14.000	Maryland
15.000	Tennessee
16.000	Louisiana
17.000	Georgia
18.000	Oklahoma
19.000	Illinois
20.000	Ohio
21.000	Missouri
22.000	Arkansas
23.000	New York
24.000	Kansas
25.000	Indiana
26.000	Minnesota
27.000	Utah
28.000	Alabama
29.000	Mississippi
30.000	Hawaii
31.000	Virginia
32.000	New Jersey
33.000	Wyoming
34.000	Massachusetts
35.000	North Carolina
36.000	South Dakota
37.000	Kentucky
38.000	Pennsylvania
39.000	Vermont
40.000	Nebraska
41.000	Idaho
42.000	New Hampshire
43.000	Connecticut
44.000	Montana
45.000	Rhode Island
46.000	Wisconsin
47.000	West Virginia
48.000	Maine
49.000	Iowa
50.000	North Dakota

Table G.329. RROB6098

Rank-Order Robbery Rate per 1,000
1960–1998

1.000	New York
2.000	Maryland
3.000	Illinois
4.000	California
5.000	Nevada
6.000	Florida
7.000	Michigan
8.000	New Jersey
9.000	Missouri
10.000	Louisiana
11.000	Texas
12.000	Georgia
13.000	Ohio
14.000	Massachusetts
15.000	Tennessee
16.000	Pennsylvania
17.000	Arizona
18.000	Connecticut
19.000	Delaware
20.000	Oregon
21.000	Colorado
22.000	New Mexico
23.000	Washington
24.000	Indiana
25.000	South Carolina
26.000	Virginia
27.000	Alabama
28.000	Hawaii
29.000	North Carolina
30.000	Oklahoma
31.000	Minnesota
32.000	Alaska
33.000	Rhode Island
34.000	Kansas
35.000	Kentucky
36.000	Arkansas
37.000	Mississippi
38.000	Wisconsin
39.000	Utah
40.000	Nebraska
41.000	Iowa
42.000	West Virginia
43.000	Montana
44.000	Wyoming
45.000	Idaho
46.000	Maine
47.000	New Hampshire
48.000	South Dakota
49.000	Vermont
50.000	North Dakota

Table G.330. RASLT609

Rank-Order Assault Rate per 1,000
1960–1998

1.000	Florida
2.000	South Carolina
3.000	New Mexico
4.000	California
5.000	Louisiana
6.000	Maryland
7.000	New York
8.000	Illinois
9.000	North Carolina
10.000	Arizona
11.000	Alabama
12.000	Michigan
13.000	Alaska
14.000	Nevada
15.000	Texas
16.000	Massachusetts
17.000	Georgia
18.000	Missouri
19.000	Delaware
20.000	Tennessee
21.000	Colorado
22.000	Oklahoma
23.000	Arkansas
24.000	Oregon
25.000	New Jersey
26.000	Washington
27.000	Mississippi
28.000	Kansas
29.000	Rhode Island
30.000	Indiana
31.000	Virginia
32.000	Ohio
33.000	Wyoming
34.000	Kentucky
35.000	Idaho
36.000	Nebraska
37.000	Connecticut
38.000	Pennsylvania
39.000	Utah
40.000	Iowa
41.000	Montana
42.000	Minnesota
43.000	West Virginia
44.000	South Dakota
45.000	Maine
46.000	Wisconsin
47.000	Hawaii
48.000	Vermont
49.000	New Hampshire
50.000	North Dakota

Table G.331. RBURG609

*Rank-Order Burglary Rate per 1,000
1960–1998*

1.000	Florida
2.000	Nevada
3.000	California
4.000	Arizona
5.000	Texas
6.000	New Mexico
7.000	Washington
8.000	New York
9.000	Hawaii
10.000	Colorado
11.000	Michigan
12.000	Oregon
13.000	Oklahoma
14.000	South Carolina
15.000	Georgia
16.000	Maryland
17.000	Missouri
18.000	Rhode Island
19.000	Delaware
20.000	Louisiana
21.000	North Carolina
22.000	Massachusetts
23.000	Tennessee
24.000	New Jersey
25.000	Connecticut
26.000	Illinois
27.000	Kansas
28.000	Alabama
29.000	Ohio
30.000	Alaska
31.000	Indiana
32.000	Utah
33.000	Minnesota
34.000	Arkansas
35.000	Vermont
36.000	Mississippi
37.000	Maine
38.000	Virginia
39.000	Idaho
40.000	Kentucky
41.000	Iowa
42.000	Montana
43.000	Pennsylvania
44.000	Wisconsin
45.000	New Hampshire
46.000	Wyoming
47.000	Nebraska
48.000	West Virginia
49.000	South Dakota
50.000	North Dakota

Table G.332. RLARC609

*Rank-Order Larceny Rate per 1,000
1960–1998*

1.000	Arizona
2.000	Florida
3.000	Hawaii
4.000	Nevada
5.000	Washington
6.000	Utah
7.000	Oregon
8.000	Colorado
9.000	California
10.000	New Mexico
11.000	Michigan
12.000	Texas
13.000	Alaska
14.000	Delaware
15.000	Maryland
16.000	Montana
17.000	Wyoming
18.000	Illinois
19.000	Kansas
20.000	New York
21.000	Louisiana
22.000	Idaho
23.000	Missouri
24.000	Georgia
25.000	Wisconsin
26.000	Minnesota
27.000	Rhode Island
28.000	South Carolina
29.000	Virginia
30.000	Oklahoma
31.000	Ohio
32.000	Nebraska
33.000	New Jersey
34.000	Indiana
35.000	Iowa
36.000	Connecticut
37.000	North Carolina
38.000	Maine
39.000	Massachusetts
40.000	Alabama
41.000	Vermont
42.000	Arkansas
43.000	Tennessee
44.000	New Hampshire
45.000	North Dakota
46.000	South Dakota
47.000	Kentucky
48.000	Pennsylvania
49.000	Mississippi
50.000	West Virginia

Table G.333. RMVT6098

*Rank-Order Auto Theft Rate per 1,000
1960–1998*

1.000	Massachusetts
2.000	California
3.000	Rhode Island
4.000	New York
5.000	Nevada
6.000	New Jersey
7.000	Michigan
8.000	Arizona
9.000	Illinois
10.000	Alaska
11.000	Maryland
12.000	Florida
13.000	Texas
14.000	Connecticut
15.000	Hawaii
16.000	Colorado
17.000	Missouri
18.000	Louisiana
19.000	Oregon
20.000	Delaware
21.000	Oklahoma
22.000	Tennessee
23.000	Georgia
24.000	Ohio
25.000	Indiana
26.000	Washington
27.000	New Mexico
28.000	Pennsylvania
29.000	Minnesota
30.000	Utah
31.000	South Carolina
32.000	Montana
33.000	Wisconsin
34.000	Alabama
35.000	Virginia
36.000	Kansas
37.000	Nebraska
38.000	Kentucky
39.000	North Carolina
40.000	New Hampshire
41.000	Wyoming
42.000	Arkansas
43.000	Idaho
44.000	Iowa
45.000	Mississippi
46.000	Vermont
47.000	Maine
48.000	West Virginia
49.000	North Dakota
50.000	South Dakota

Table G.334. CRIME39

Average Total Crime Rankings per 1,000 1960–1998

5.43	Florida
5.57	Nevada
6.29	California
9.71	Michigan
10.00	Texas
10.36	New York
10.57	Arizona
11.07	Maryland
12.50	New Mexico
13.00	Louisiana
14.29	Illinois
15.50	Alaska
15.71	Georgia
16.00	Colorado
17.14	South Carolina
17.29	Delaware
17.86	Missouri
18.14	Oregon
18.14	Washington
21.43	Tennessee
22.43	Oklahoma
22.57	New Jersey
23.57	Massachusetts
23.57	Hawaii
24.43	Alabama
24.86	Ohio
25.86	North Carolina
27.57	Indiana
28.00	Rhode Island
28.57	Kansas
29.86	Connecticut
29.86	Virginia
30.71	Arkansas
30.79	Utah
32.57	Mississippi
33.00	Minnesota
34.29	Pennsylvania
35.00	Wyoming
36.00	Kentucky
36.43	Montana
37.57	Idaho
38.86	Nebraska
39.21	Wisconsin
42.71	Iowa
43.57	Vermont
43.71	Maine
43.71	West Virginia
44.71	New Hampshire
45.86	South Dakota
49.14	North Dakota

Table G.335. LGTRKINV

Large Trucks Involved in Fatal Crashes 1999

384	Texas
327	Florida
319	California
220	Georgia
207	Pennsylvania
200	Ohio
193	Illinois
191	Indiana
189	North Carolina
165	Tennessee
155	Missouri
149	New York
143	Alabama
131	Michigan
123	South Carolina
118	Louisiana
110	Mississippi
108	Arizona
107	Virginia
99	Iowa
94	Kentucky
92	Arkansas
86	Minnesota
82	Oklahoma
82	Kansas
74	Wisconsin
60	Colorado
59	Washington
59	New Jersey
58	Nebraska
57	Maryland
50	West Virginia
48	New Mexico
48	Oregon
41	Nevada
41	Utah
35	Massachusetts
25	Wyoming
25	Idaho
25	Maine
22	Connecticut
18	South Dakota
18	North Dakota
15	Montana
10	Delaware
9	Rhode Island
9	New Hampshire
8	Vermont
5	Alaska
3	Hawaii

Table G.336. LGTRKDEA

Large Trucks as Percent of Total Vehicles Involved in Fatalities 1999

14.5	Nebraska
14.1	Iowa
13.7	Indiana
12.5	North Dakota
11.8	Wyoming
11.7	Arkansas
11.6	Kansas
10.5	Georgia
10.3	Missouri
9.9	Ohio
9.7	Pennsylvania
9.7	Louisiana
9.7	West Virginia
9.7	Maine
9.5	Illinois
9.4	Tennessee
9.4	Alabama
9.4	Minnesota
9.4	Utah
9.2	Virginia
9.1	Mississippi
9.1	South Dakota
8.9	North Carolina
8.9	Nevada
8.8	Kentucky
8.7	South Carolina
8.6	New Mexico
8.5	Oklahoma
8.4	Oregon
8.0	Texas
7.8	Florida
7.7	Arizona
7.6	Rhode Island
7.3	Wisconsin
7.2	New York
7.2	Idaho
7.1	Colorado
7.1	Vermont
7.0	Washington
6.9	California
6.6	Maryland
6.5	Michigan
6.5	Delaware
6.1	Massachusetts
5.9	New Jersey
5.9	Montana
5.5	Connecticut
5.0	Alaska
4.8	New Hampshire
2.1	Hawaii

Table G.337. ALCOHOPC

Alcohol Consumption Per Capita in Gallons 1998

4.03	New Hampshire
3.90	Nevada
2.87	Delaware
2.77	Alaska
2.69	Wisconsin
2.64	Colorado
2.59	Arizona
2.58	Florida
2.47	Louisiana
2.46	Montana
2.44	Massachusetts
2.44	Wyoming
2.42	North Dakota
2.41	Minnesota
2.38	South Carolina
2.37	New Mexico
2.36	Vermont
2.35	Rhode Island
2.30	Oregon
2.30	Texas
2.29	Hawaii
2.29	Illinois
2.28	Idaho
2.28	South Dakota
2.24	Connecticut
2.21	Georgia
2.21	Missouri
2.21	Nebraska
2.21	Washington
2.18	California
2.17	New Jersey
2.16	Maine
2.11	Michigan
2.10	Maryland
2.10	Mississippi
1.98	Ohio
1.96	Virginia
1.95	North Carolina
1.94	Indiana
1.92	Iowa
1.92	New York
1.89	Pennsylvania
1.88	Tennessee
1.83	Alabama
1.80	Kansas
1.79	Arkansas
1.74	Kentucky
1.71	Oklahoma
1.63	West Virginia
1.25	Utah

Table G.338. PCUSLGTR

Percentage of Large Trucks in Crashes of All Crashes, United States 1999

7.8	Texas
6.7	Florida
6.5	California
4.5	Georgia
4.2	Pennsylvania
4.1	Ohio
3.9	Illinois
3.9	North Carolina
3.9	Indiana
3.4	Tennessee
3.2	Missouri
3.0	New York
2.9	Alabama
2.7	Michigan
2.5	South Carolina
2.4	Louisiana
2.2	Arizona
2.2	Mississippi
2.2	Virginia
2.0	Iowa
1.9	Arkansas
1.9	Kentucky
1.8	Minnesota
1.7	Kansas
1.7	Oklahoma
1.5	Wisconsin
1.2	Colorado
1.2	Nebraska
1.2	Washington
1.2	New Jersey
1.2	Maryland
1.0	New Mexico
1.0	Oregon
1.0	West Virginia
.8	Nevada
.8	Utah
.7	Massachusetts
.5	Wyoming
.5	Idaho
.5	Maine
.4	North Dakota
.4	South Dakota
.4	Connecticut
.3	Montana
.2	New Hampshire
.2	Delaware
.2	Vermont
.2	Rhode Island
.1	Alaska
.1	Hawaii

Table G.339. PEDEATH

Pedestrian Fatalities 1999 per 100,000 Population

3.7	Nevada
3.2	Florida
3.0	Arizona
3.0	New Mexico
2.9	South Carolina
2.9	Wyoming
2.4	Louisiana
2.2	Mississippi
2.2	Maryland
2.1	Texas
2.0	California
2.0	Georgia
2.0	North Carolina
2.0	Alabama
1.9	New York
1.9	New Jersey
1.9	Michigan
1.9	Oklahoma
1.9	Utah
1.9	Hawaii
1.6	Arkansas
1.6	Colorado
1.6	West Virginia
1.6	Connecticut
1.6	Delaware
1.5	Pennsylvania
1.5	South Dakota
1.4	Illinois
1.4	Oregon
1.4	Rhode Island
1.3	Tennessee
1.3	Kentucky
1.2	Missouri
1.2	Virginia
1.2	Kansas
1.2	Massachusetts
1.1	Ohio
1.1	Indiana
1.1	Minnesota
1.1	Idaho
1.1	Alaska
1.0	Wisconsin
1.0	Washington
.9	Maine
.8	Nebraska
.8	Montana
.7	Vermont
.6	Iowa
.6	North Dakota
.4	New Hampshire

Table G.340. TOTFATAL

Total Traffic Fatalities 1999

3,559	California
3,518	Texas
2,918	Florida
1,549	Pennsylvania
1,548	New York
1,508	Georgia
1,505	North Carolina
1,456	Illinois
1,430	Ohio
1,382	Michigan
1,285	Tennessee
1,138	Alabama
1,094	Missouri
1,065	South Carolina
1,024	Arizona
1,013	Indiana
927	Mississippi
924	Louisiana
877	Virginia
814	Kentucky
745	Wisconsin
739	Oklahoma
727	New Jersey
634	Washington
626	Colorado
625	Minnesota
604	Arkansas
590	Maryland
537	Kansas
490	Iowa
460	New Mexico
414	Oregon
414	Massachusetts
395	West Virginia
360	Utah
350	Nevada
301	Connecticut
295	Nebraska
278	Idaho
220	Montana
189	Wyoming
181	Maine
150	South Dakota
141	New Hampshire
119	North Dakota
100	Delaware
98	Hawaii
90	Vermont
88	Rhode Island
76	Alaska

Table G.341. TOTSPEED

Total Traffic Fatalities, Speeding 1999

1,332	Texas
1,307	California
589	Pennsylvania
568	North Carolina
524	Florida
502	South Carolina
480	Illinois
445	New York
407	Alabama
383	Arizona
373	Missouri
363	Ohio
363	Tennessee
318	Georgia
314	Michigan
276	Oklahoma
265	Colorado
233	Indiana
232	Virginia
226	Washington
215	Kentucky
206	Mississippi
203	Wisconsin
191	Maryland
171	Arkansas
166	New Mexico
155	Minnesota
139	Nevada
134	Kansas
133	Louisiana
128	Oregon
127	Massachusetts
114	West Virginia
113	Connecticut
97	Utah
95	Idaho
86	Montana
79	Maine
69	New Jersey
69	Nebraska
67	Wyoming
59	South Dakota
52	Iowa
50	New Hampshire
48	North Dakota
38	Alaska
37	Vermont
29	Hawaii
25	Rhode Island
21	Delaware

Table G.342. ANYALCOH

Percent of Total Traffic Fatalities, Any Alcohol 1999

53	Alaska
49	Texas
49	Massachusetts
47	Montana
47	New Hampshire
47	North Dakota
46	Louisiana
45	New Mexico
45	Nevada
45	Connecticut
44	Illinois
44	Hawaii
43	South Dakota
42	Washington
42	Nebraska
41	Wisconsin
41	Oregon
41	Rhode Island
40	Arizona
40	Missouri
40	Michigan
40	New Jersey
40	Delaware
39	Pennsylvania
39	Mississippi
38	California
38	Alabama
38	Tennessee
38	Vermont
37	West Virginia
37	Idaho
37	Wyoming
36	North Carolina
36	Florida
36	Virginia
35	Colorado
35	Kentucky
35	Kansas
34	Georgia
34	Indiana
33	Oklahoma
33	Iowa
32	Ohio
32	Minnesota
32	Maine
31	South Carolina
31	Arkansas
30	Maryland
22	New York
21	Utah

Table G.343. FATALPOP

Traffic Fatalities per 100,000 Population 1999

39.38	Wyoming
33.48	Mississippi
27.41	South Carolina
26.44	New Mexico
26.04	Alabama
24.92	Montana
23.68	Arkansas
23.43	Tennessee
22.20	Idaho
22.01	Oklahoma
21.86	West Virginia
21.43	Arizona
21.13	Louisiana
20.55	Kentucky
20.46	South Dakota
20.23	Kansas
20.01	Missouri
19.67	North Carolina
19.36	Georgia
19.35	Nevada
19.31	Florida
18.77	North Dakota
17.71	Nebraska
17.55	Texas
17.08	Iowa
17.05	Indiana
16.90	Utah
15.43	Colorado
15.15	Vermont
14.45	Maine
14.19	Wisconsin
14.01	Michigan
13.26	Delaware
13.09	Minnesota
12.91	Pennsylvania
12.76	Virginia
12.70	Ohio
12.48	Oregon
12.26	Alaska
12.01	Illinois
11.74	New Hampshire
11.41	Maryland
11.01	Washington
10.74	California
9.17	Connecticut
8.93	New Jersey
8.88	Rhode Island
8.51	New York
8.27	Hawaii
6.70	Massachusetts

Table G.344. BUSFAIL

Business Failures per 1,000 Population 1998

.6588	Hawaii
.6122	Colorado
.5334	California
.4392	Washington
.4295	Kansas
.3751	South Dakota
.3742	Nevada
.3583	Minnesota
.3523	Idaho
.3461	Wyoming
.3385	Texas
.3362	New Mexico
.3344	Oregon
.2948	Oklahoma
.2932	Arkansas
.2857	Alaska
.2713	Illinois
.2681	New Hampshire
.2564	Arizona
.2497	Tennessee
.2485	New Jersey
.2481	Maryland
.2416	Missouri
.2326	New York
.2299	Nebraska
.2277	Montana
.2272	North Dakota
.2242	Ohio
.2202	Pennsylvania
.2067	Maine
.1943	Massachusetts
.1914	Wisconsin
.1822	Utah
.1688	West Virginia
.1615	Connecticut
.1572	Michigan
.1514	Rhode Island
.1355	Florida
.1347	Vermont
.1251	Virginia
.1249	Alabama
.1106	North Carolina
.1055	South Carolina
.1027	Georgia
.0862	Louisiana
.0850	Iowa
.0796	Indiana
.0682	Kentucky
.0639	Mississippi
.0372	Delaware

Table G.345. PCFATCH

Percent Change Traffic Fatalities 1975–1999

70	Mississippi
61	Nevada
53	Arizona
46	Florida
32	Utah
30	South Carolina
26	Alabama
14	Tennessee
11	Georgia
8	Colorado
8	Arkansas
6	Kansas
5	Missouri
4	Texas
0	North Carolina
−1	Idaho
−1	Louisiana
−2	Oklahoma
−6	Kentucky
−7	New Hampshire
−10	Indiana
−10	Wyoming
−12	Maryland
−12	Virginia
−13	California
−14	West Virginia
−16	Washington
−17	Minnesota
−17	New Mexico
−18	Delaware
−19	Ohio
−19	Maine
−20	Wisconsin
−20	Nebraska
−20	Rhode Island
−22	Michigan
−23	Connecticut
−23	South Dakota
−24	Montana
−25	Pennsylvania
−26	Oregon
−27	Iowa
−29	Illinois
−29	North Dakota
−30	New Jersey
−32	Hawaii
−32	Alaska
−35	New York
−37	Vermont
−52	Massachusetts

Table G.346. NOBELT

Percent Passenger Car Occupants Killed, Wore No Seat Belt 1999

72.3	Montana
71.3	Mississippi
68.8	South Dakota
68.3	Wyoming
66.7	Tennessee
66.7	Delaware
66.1	Idaho
66.0	Rhode Island
63.6	Kentucky
61.6	South Carolina
60.9	Arkansas
60.0	Utah
59.7	Alabama
59.7	Nebraska
59.1	West Virginia
58.6	Alaska
57.3	Massachusetts
56.8	Oklahoma
56.7	North Dakota
56.5	Virginia
56.2	Florida
55.4	New Jersey
55.1	Wisconsin
54.3	New Hampshire
54.1	Missouri
53.9	New Mexico
53.2	Ohio
53.1	Connecticut
53.1	Vermont
53.0	Colorado
52.8	Washington
51.8	Pennsylvania
51.4	Nevada
50.6	Arizona
50.0	Louisiana
50.0	Hawaii
48.3	Indiana
47.7	Kansas
47.2	Georgia
46.1	New York
45.1	Texas
45.1	Minnesota
45.0	Illinois
43.1	Michigan
41.4	Maine
41.3	Maryland
39.4	Iowa
38.4	North Carolina
37.9	Oregon
33.5	California

Table G.347. PCINCOME

Per Capita Income (thousands) 1999

39,543	Connecticut
35,612	New Jersey
35,527	Massachusetts
33,901	New York
32,517	Maryland
31,533	Colorado
31,325	New Hampshire
31,138	Illinois
31,004	Nevada
30,742	Minnesota
30,701	Delaware
30,380	Washington
29,856	California
29,794	Virginia
29,335	Rhode Island
28,629	Alaska
28,619	Pennsylvania
28,104	Michigan
27,781	Florida
27,533	Hawaii
27,370	Wisconsin
27,324	Georgia
27,171	Ohio
27,047	Nebraska
26,958	Oregon
26,834	Texas
26,705	Kansas
26,417	North Carolina
26,404	Missouri
26,363	Wyoming
26,157	Indiana
25,845	Vermont
25,598	Iowa
25,548	Tennessee
25,173	Arizona
25,041	South Dakota
24,582	Maine
23,538	South Carolina
23,276	Utah
23,273	North Dakota
23,227	Kentucky
22,972	Alabama
22,958	Oklahoma
22,871	Idaho
22,839	Louisiana
22,233	Arkansas
21,997	Montana
21,836	New Mexico
20,921	West Virginia
20,686	Mississippi

Table G.348. PCDISPIN

Per Capita Disposable Income (thousands) 1999

31,940	Connecticut
29,744	New Jersey
29,270	Massachusetts
28,031	New York
27,185	New Hampshire
27,169	Maryland
26,667	Nevada
26,662	Colorado
26,376	Illinois
26,063	Minnesota
26,028	Washington
25,944	Delaware
25,300	Rhode Island
25,144	Virginia
25,141	California
25,074	Alaska
24,471	Pennsylvania
24,064	Hawaii
23,981	Florida
23,828	Michigan
23,519	Texas
23,368	Nebraska
23,362	Georgia
23,169	Ohio
23,143	Wisconsin
23,026	Kansas
22,937	Oregon
22,773	Missouri
22,648	Tennessee
22,641	North Carolina
22,621	Wyoming
22,459	South Dakota
22,293	Indiana
22,280	Iowa
22,274	Vermont
21,706	Arizona
21,144	Maine
20,652	North Dakota
20,548	South Carolina
20,210	Utah
20,164	Louisiana
20,155	Alabama
20,028	Oklahoma
20,024	Kentucky
19,918	Idaho
19,521	Arkansas
19,282	Montana
19,212	New Mexico
18,465	Mississippi
18,453	West Virginia

Table G.349. TAXTOFED

Personal Income and Nontax Payments to Federal Government (in thousands) 1999

115,829,124	California
78,854,802	New York
62,806,304	Texas
53,936,841	Florida
47,903,438	Illinois
39,631,788	New Jersey
38,273,305	Pennsylvania
32,636,639	Michigan
32,329,909	Ohio
29,295,501	Massachusetts
23,816,356	Virginia
23,662,291	Washington
23,592,941	Georgia
20,688,686	North Carolina
20,469,236	Connecticut
19,949,658	Maryland
16,969,544	Indiana
16,666,305	Minnesota
15,930,540	Wisconsin
15,661,337	Colorado
14,917,765	Missouri
14,873,317	Tennessee
13,576,351	Arizona
9,642,221	Alabama
9,453,855	Louisiana
9,064,796	Oregon
8,921,663	South Carolina
8,713,525	Kentucky
7,439,709	Nevada
7,437,135	Kansas
7,081,894	Iowa
6,890,748	Oklahoma
5,008,729	Arkansas
4,781,061	Mississippi
4,748,857	New Hampshire
4,619,862	Nebraska
4,546,112	Utah
3,431,120	New Mexico
3,141,852	West Virginia
3,051,528	Rhode Island
2,993,822	Maine
2,881,682	Hawaii
2,661,765	Delaware
2,612,327	Idaho
1,993,696	Alaska
1,786,119	South Dakota
1,708,549	Montana
1,655,239	Wyoming
1,607,919	Vermont
1,346,018	North Dakota

Table G.350. STATETAX

Personal Income Tax Payments to State Government (in thousands) 1999

32,426,463	California
21,944,560	New York
8,425,907	Massachusetts
7,427,252	Illinois
7,426,257	Ohio
7,012,471	Michigan
6,822,488	North Carolina
6,506,181	Virginia
6,487,282	New Jersey
6,441,527	Pennsylvania
5,914,348	Georgia
5,250,899	Wisconsin
4,556,614	Indiana
4,457,147	Maryland
4,063,255	Minnesota
3,799,665	Connecticut
3,692,240	Missouri
3,585,810	Oregon
3,133,232	Colorado
2,540,405	Kentucky
2,088,821	Arizona
2,049,034	Oklahoma
1,975,428	South Carolina
1,921,716	Alabama
1,721,786	Kansas
1,721,786	Iowa
1,532,797	Louisiana
1,512,903	Utah
1,489,031	Arkansas
1,088,176	Nebraska
1,048,389	Hawaii
1,040,432	Maine
964,836	Mississippi
936,986	West Virginia
863,379	Idaho
831,550	New Mexico
772,864	Rhode Island
748,992	Delaware
487,392	Montana
395,881	Vermont
186,005	North Dakota
159,148	Tennessee
62,665	New Hampshire
0	Texas
0	Florida
0	Washington
0	Nevada
0	Alaska
0	South Dakota
0	Wyoming

Table G.351. CARPLATE

State Motor Vehicle Licenses (thousands of dollars) 1999

1,266,192	California
746,527	Texas
734,698	Florida
663,056	Illinois
613,725	Michigan
564,444	Pennsylvania
494,127	Minnesota
473,644	Ohio
448,451	New York
447,994	Oklahoma
369,480	North Carolina
344,121	New Jersey
249,379	Massachusetts
247,237	Iowa
239,458	Wisconsin
221,442	Washington
218,275	Virginia
204,518	Missouri
200,276	Connecticut
196,337	Georgia
177,844	Tennessee
149,709	Maryland
131,038	Colorado
130,086	Alabama
106,075	Kansas
103,450	Arizona
101,403	Mississippi
98,362	Oregon
92,705	South Carolina
86,296	Nevada
81,214	Arkansas
78,492	Kentucky
77,012	Louisiana
73,438	Indiana
67,966	Idaho
62,294	West Virginia
56,665	New Mexico
53,693	Nebraska
52,739	Utah
51,336	New Hampshire
45,027	Maine
40,880	Rhode Island
32,864	Wyoming
32,850	Hawaii
32,692	North Dakota
31,343	Vermont
27,362	Alaska
23,819	Delaware
23,199	South Dakota
21,766	Montana

Table G.352. LOCARPLT

Local Motor Vehicle Licenses (thousands of dollars) 1999

146,389	Texas
72,486	New York
68,334	Illinois
62,970	Virginia
58,591	Washington
54,888	Ohio
44,479	Tennessee
24,857	Hawaii
18,957	Florida
17,459	Maine
17,043	Colorado
13,213	North Carolina
12,369	Kentucky
12,221	Alabama
8,630	Nebraska
8,572	South Dakota
6,715	Iowa
6,572	Missouri
6,093	Oregon
6,030	Wyoming
5,968	South Carolina
5,608	Montana
3,794	Alaska
3,210	Minnesota
2,485	Idaho
2,222	Louisiana
1,580	Arizona
1,296	Oklahoma
1,127	Kansas
787	New Mexico
690	Mississippi
510	Michigan
354	West Virginia
350	Wisconsin
162	Georgia
0	California
0	Pennsylvania
0	New Jersey
0	Massachusetts
0	Connecticut
0	Maryland
0	Nevada
0	Arkansas
0	Indiana
0	Utah
0	New Hampshire
0	Rhode Island
0	North Dakota
0	Vermont
0	Delaware

Table G.353. TAXTOLOC

Personal Tax and Nontax Payments to Local Governments (in thousands) 1999

7,339,595	New York
4,209,174	Ohio
3,775,809	Pennsylvania
3,757,857	California
2,780,742	Maryland
1,513,978	Texas
1,509,543	Florida
1,262,423	Michigan
1,017,437	Illinois
1,012,712	Kentucky
877,360	Indiana
624,592	Missouri
566,464	Georgia
536,948	Minnesota
521,586	New Jersey
516,284	Washington
452,910	Virginia
435,689	North Carolina
390,409	Colorado
355,632	Alabama
350,430	Tennessee
329,004	Arizona
309,993	Oregon
306,041	Louisiana
299,361	Wisconsin
227,648	Kansas
220,111	Iowa
197,632	South Carolina
186,959	Massachusetts
183,995	Oklahoma
171,474	Nevada
168,250	Utah
145,733	Mississippi
144,808	West Virginia
142,265	Nebraska
139,398	Arkansas
103,875	Connecticut
101,474	Alaska
100,581	New Mexico
78,845	Delaware
65,378	Hawaii
62,236	Idaho
55,752	Maine
54,119	Wyoming
49,048	Montana
41,259	North Dakota
41,026	South Dakota
32,124	New Hampshire
20,271	Rhode Island
15,735	Vermont

Table G.354. LOCINTAX

Income Tax Payments to Local Governments (in thousands) 1999

5,623,417	New York
3,373,485	Ohio
2,685,192	Pennsylvania
2,473,119	Maryland
599,987	Kentucky
559,579	Michigan
532,518	Indiana
319,991	Missouri
83,439	Alabama
41,735	Delaware
32,800	New Jersey
30,957	Iowa
0	California
0	Texas
0	Florida
0	Illinois
0	Georgia
0	Minnesota
0	Washington
0	Virginia
0	North Carolina
0	Colorado
0	Tennessee
0	Arizona
0	Oregon
0	Louisiana
0	Wisconsin
0	Kansas
0	South Carolina
0	Massachusetts
0	Oklahoma
0	Nevada
0	Utah
0	Mississippi
0	West Virginia
0	Nebraska
0	Arkansas
0	Connecticut
0	Alaska
0	New Mexico
0	Hawaii
0	Idaho
0	Maine
0	Wyoming
0	Montana
0	North Dakota
0	South Dakota
0	New Hampshire
0	Rhode Island
0	Vermont

Table G.355. LOCTAXOT

Local Government, Other Taxes (in thousands) 1999

359,544	California
170,640	Pennsylvania
151,534	New York
79,603	Texas
76,903	Virginia
66,606	Florida
60,484	Oregon
60,441	Maryland
56,586	Washington
52,257	Illinois
49,656	Ohio
44,192	Alabama
36,131	Georgia
35,792	Kentucky
34,144	Nevada
31,649	Missouri
30,775	Michigan
29,361	North Carolina
26,040	South Carolina
25,709	New Jersey
25,532	Louisiana
25,480	Tennessee
22,872	Colorado
19,145	Arizona
19,105	Nebraska
18,981	Massachusetts
18,548	West Virginia
16,659	Wisconsin
15,349	Minnesota
10,698	Utah
9,042	Connecticut
8,818	Indiana
7,830	Kansas
6,872	Mississippi
5,062	New Mexico
4,805	Delaware
4,685	Oklahoma
4,467	Idaho
3,884	Iowa
3,193	New Hampshire
3,115	Arkansas
3,003	Hawaii
2,917	Montana
2,505	Maine
2,318	Rhode Island
2,038	Wyoming
2,006	South Dakota
1,711	Alaska
1,114	North Dakota
992	Vermont

Table G.356. LOCNOTAX

Local Government, Nontaxes (in thousands) 1999

3,398,313	California
1,492,158	New York
1,423,980	Florida
1,287,986	Texas
919,977	Pennsylvania
896,846	Illinois
731,145	Ohio
671,559	Michigan
530,171	Georgia
518,389	Minnesota
463,077	New Jersey
401,107	Washington
393,115	North Carolina
364,564	Kentucky
350,494	Colorado
335,991	Indiana
313,037	Virginia
308,279	Arizona
282,352	Wisconsin
280,471	Tennessee
278,287	Louisiana
266,380	Missouri
247,182	Maryland
243,416	Oregon
218,691	Kansas
215,780	Alabama
178,555	Iowa
178,014	Oklahoma
167,978	Massachusetts
165,624	South Carolina
157,552	Utah
138,171	Mississippi
137,330	Nevada
136,283	Arkansas
125,906	West Virginia
114,530	Nebraska
95,969	Alaska
94,833	Connecticut
94,732	New Mexico
55,284	Idaho
46,051	Wyoming
40,523	Montana
40,145	North Dakota
37,518	Hawaii
35,788	Maine
32,305	Delaware
30,448	South Dakota
28,931	New Hampshire
17,953	Rhode Island
14,743	Vermont

Table G.357. STALOPER

State and Local Personal Property Taxes (in thousands) 1999

1,622,002	California
355,088	Virginia
267,140	Washington
257,859	Florida
245,141	Georgia
194,747	Arizona
182,717	Connecticut
179,202	South Carolina
173,404	North Carolina
162,548	Missouri
150,650	Minnesota
134,601	Texas
125,294	Colorado
122,060	Kansas
108,010	Indiana
91,261	Kentucky
89,552	Oklahoma
79,040	Nebraska
78,066	Utah
57,477	Nevada
55,861	Rhode Island
53,290	Alabama
40,300	Mississippi
37,650	Maine
36,327	Arkansas
34,263	Tennessee
30,698	Ohio
27,280	Montana
16,155	West Virginia
3,317	Alaska
0	New York
0	Pennsylvania
0	Maryland
0	Michigan
0	Delaware
0	New Jersey
0	Iowa
0	Illinois
0	Oregon
0	Louisiana
0	Wisconsin
0	Massachusetts
0	New Mexico
0	Hawaii
0	Idaho
0	Wyoming
0	North Dakota
0	South Dakota
0	New Hampshire
0	Vermont

Table G.358. PERSINCO

Personal Income (in thousands) 1999

989,590,237	California
616,878,287	New York
537,857,064	Texas
419,800,453	Florida
377,649,677	Illinois
343,262,714	Pennsylvania
305,855,474	Ohio
290,004,020	New Jersey
277,213,854	Michigan
219,385,942	Massachusetts
212,806,472	Georgia
204,769,186	Virginia
202,108,514	North Carolina
174,876,529	Washington
168,167,999	Maryland
155,448,448	Indiana
146,810,202	Minnesota
144,388,701	Missouri
143,704,954	Wisconsin
140,093,866	Tennessee
129,780,036	Connecticut
127,903,519	Colorado
120,287,327	Arizona
100,385,369	Alabama
99,854,509	Louisiana
91,999,744	Kentucky
91,462,503	South Carolina
89,397,520	Oregon
77,093,344	Oklahoma
73,452,523	Iowa
70,876,368	Kansas
57,272,226	Mississippi
56,724,374	Arkansas
56,093,775	Nevada
49,573,035	Utah
45,060,994	Nebraska
37,990,750	New Mexico
37,802,421	West Virginia
37,625,713	New Hampshire
32,640,570	Hawaii
30,802,685	Maine
29,066,144	Rhode Island
28,627,034	Idaho
23,134,604	Delaware
19,418,790	Montana
18,358,337	South Dakota
17,735,548	Alaska
15,345,290	Vermont
14,747,353	North Dakota
12,643,647	Wyoming

Table G.359. PCTAXALL

Percent of Per Capita Income for All Taxes: Federal, State, Local 1999

18.81	Connecticut
17.20	Massachusetts
16.92	New York
16.13	New Jersey
16.12	Maryland
15.41	California
15.26	Virginia
15.15	Delaware
15.07	Wisconsin
15.05	Colorado
14.90	Illinois
14.88	Minnesota
14.87	Michigan
14.52	Oregon
14.44	Indiana
14.40	Ohio
14.16	Georgia
14.13	Pennsylvania
13.96	North Carolina
13.90	Washington
13.59	Maine
13.58	Wyoming
13.48	Nevada
13.45	Kentucky
13.42	Rhode Island
13.41	Kansas
13.39	Missouri
13.39	Vermont
13.36	Arizona
13.19	Nebraska
13.15	Florida
12.81	New Hampshire
12.80	Utah
12.60	Iowa
12.50	Idaho
12.42	Oklahoma
12.36	South Carolina
12.29	Hawaii
12.11	Alaska
11.98	Texas
11.91	Alabama
11.89	Montana
11.82	Arkansas
11.64	New Mexico
11.46	West Virginia
11.38	Louisiana
11.00	Tennessee
10.88	North Dakota
10.41	Mississippi
9.92	South Dakota

Table G.360. OBESITY

Percent at Risk of Being Overweight 1999

41.8	Mississippi
41.3	West Virginia
38.0	Arkansas
37.7	Louisiana
37.7	Alaska
37.5	Alabama
37.3	South Carolina
37.2	Oklahoma
36.8	Michigan
36.7	Kentucky
36.6	Iowa
36.3	North Dakota
36.1	Texas
36.1	South Dakota
36.0	Illinois
35.9	Ohio
35.9	Georgia
35.7	Nebraska
35.5	Pennsylvania
35.5	Missouri
35.0	Virginia
34.9	North Carolina
34.5	Tennessee
34.1	Indiana
33.8	Wisconsin
33.6	Florida
33.5	California
33.5	Idaho
33.4	Kansas
33.0	New Mexico
32.8	Oregon
32.7	Maryland
32.7	Maine
32.3	Rhode Island
32.0	Delaware
31.9	New York
31.8	Washington
31.8	Wyoming
31.4	New Jersey
31.1	Vermont
30.0	Utah
29.8	Montana
29.2	Minnesota
28.9	Nevada
28.8	Hawaii
28.6	Connecticut
28.3	Massachusetts
27.8	New Hampshire
26.7	Colorado
22.9	Arizona

Table G.361. TAXNONTX

Personal Tax and Nontax Payments to State Governments (in thousands) 1999

35,085,200	California
23,615,454	New York
9,156,071	Massachusetts
8,826,094	Illinois
8,478,266	Ohio
8,280,269	Michigan
7,713,746	Pennsylvania
7,632,330	New Jersey
7,589,154	North Carolina
7,334,571	Virginia
6,453,965	Georgia
5,966,562	Wisconsin
5,009,860	Indiana
4,993,935	Minnesota
4,928,526	Maryland
4,196,901	Connecticut
4,152,919	Missouri
3,958,866	Oregon
3,583,660	Colorado
2,870,712	Kentucky
2,674,375	Oklahoma
2,470,909	Arizona
2,319,322	South Carolina
2,259,026	Alabama
2,220,404	Iowa
1,979,909	Texas
1,976,460	Kansas
1,937,106	Louisiana
1,737,134	Utah
1,733,465	Arkansas
1,712,162	Florida
1,287,557	Nebraska
1,220,894	Maine
1,182,434	Mississippi
1,165,754	Hawaii
1,155,647	West Virginia
1,032,529	New Mexico
1,020,605	Idaho
870,615	Rhode Island
844,226	Delaware
644,222	Tennessee
612,224	Montana
603,751	Washington
496,626	Vermont
273,519	North Dakota
192,202	New Hampshire
178,486	Nevada
103,983	Alaska
85,212	Wyoming
65,907	South Dakota

Table G.362. DISPERIN

Disposal Personal Income (in thousands) 1999

833,296,054	California
510,068,436	New York
471,422,272	Texas
362,384,048	Florida
319,902,708	Illinois
293,499,854	Pennsylvania
260,807,427	Ohio
242,218,316	New Jersey
235,034,523	Michigan
181,947,961	Georgia
180,747,411	Massachusetts
173,221,581	North Carolina
172,810,261	Virginia
149,827,063	Washington
140,509,073	Maryland
132,483,674	Indiana
124,530,877	Missouri
124,462,364	Minnesota
124,191,634	Tennessee
121,508,491	Wisconsin
108,142,819	Colorado
104,827,307	Connecticut
103,716,316	Arizona
88,157,507	Louisiana
88,075,200	Alabama
79,844,684	South Carolina
79,311,534	Kentucky
76,063,865	Oregon
67,254,674	Oklahoma
63,930,114	Iowa
61,113,065	Kansas
51,122,698	Mississippi
49,806,455	Arkansas
48,246,629	Nevada
43,043,473	Utah
38,932,270	Nebraska
33,426,520	New Mexico
33,343,959	West Virginia
32,652,530	New Hampshire
28,527,756	Hawaii
26,494,567	Maine
25,067,869	Rhode Island
24,931,866	Idaho
19,549,768	Delaware
17,021,689	Montana
16,465,285	South Dakota
15,533,078	Alaska
13,225,010	Vermont
13,086,557	North Dakota
10,849,077	Wyoming

Table G.363. PERTXNO

Personal Tax and Nontax Payments to Federal Government (in thousands) 1999

156,294,183	California
106,809,851	New York
66,434,792	Texas
57,746,969	Illinois
57,416,405	Florida
49,762,860	Pennsylvania
47,785,704	New Jersey
45,048,047	Ohio
42,179,331	Michigan
38,638,531	Massachusetts
31,958,925	Virginia
30,858,511	Georgia
28,886,933	North Carolina
27,658,926	Maryland
25,049,466	Washington
24,952,729	Connecticut
22,964,774	Indiana
22,347,838	Minnesota
22,196,463	Wisconsin
19,857,824	Missouri
19,760,700	Colorado
16,571,011	Arizona
15,902,232	Tennessee
13,333,655	Oregon
12,688,210	Kentucky
12,310,169	Alabama
11,697,002	Louisiana
11,617,819	South Carolina
9,838,670	Oklahoma
9,763,303	Kansas
9,522,409	Iowa
7,847,146	Nevada
6,917,919	Arkansas
6,529,562	Utah
6,149,528	Mississippi
6,128,724	Nebraska
4,973,183	New Hampshire
4,564,230	New Mexico
4,458,462	West Virginia
4,308,118	Maine
4,112,814	Hawaii
3,998,275	Rhode Island
3,695,168	Idaho
3,584,836	Delaware
2,397,101	Montana
2,202,470	Alaska
2,120,280	Vermont
1,893,052	South Dakota
1,794,570	Wyoming
1,660,796	North Dakota

Table G.364. INDINTAX

Individual Income Taxes to Federal Government (in thousands) 1999

112,066,780	California
73,433,047	New York
60,806,096	Texas
51,722,030	Florida
46,416,024	Illinois
38,626,975	New Jersey
37,008,908	Pennsylvania
31,679,205	Michigan
31,312,109	Ohio
28,398,570	Massachusetts
23,107,368	Virginia
22,928,544	Washington
22,862,971	Georgia
20,010,388	North Carolina
19,924,169	Connecticut
19,390,942	Maryland
16,448,112	Indiana
16,160,785	Minnesota
15,394,496	Wisconsin
15,154,173	Colorado
14,391,809	Missouri
14,375,598	Tennessee
13,079,700	Arizona
9,291,742	Alabama
9,118,942	Louisiana
8,711,888	Oregon
8,604,597	South Carolina
8,396,883	Kentucky
7,178,566	Kansas
7,153,328	Nevada
6,813,531	Iowa
6,626,115	Oklahoma
4,795,728	Arkansas
4,595,240	New Hampshire
4,591,295	Mississippi
4,433,287	Nebraska
4,361,653	Utah
3,288,673	New Mexico
3,016,889	West Virginia
2,952,532	Rhode Island
2,872,715	Maine
2,779,643	Hawaii
2,581,000	Delaware
2,496,807	Idaho
1,939,175	Alaska
1,713,657	South Dakota
1,620,056	Montana
1,577,942	Wyoming
1,541,597	Vermont
1,290,248	North Dakota

Table G.365. FIDUCTAX

Fiduciary Income Taxes Paid to Federal Government (in thousands) 1999

2,605,936	California
1,784,647	New York
1,687,578	Florida
1,301,609	Texas
1,063,195	Illinois
844,116	Pennsylvania
719,717	New Jersey
680,617	Massachusetts
623,477	Ohio
611,749	Michigan
533,745	Washington
472,921	Virginia
459,279	Georgia
430,270	Connecticut
413,543	North Carolina
378,725	Maryland
366,047	Colorado
352,026	Wisconsin
338,199	Minnesota
334,750	Missouri
329,901	Arizona
313,155	Indiana
305,943	Tennessee
236,722	Oregon
223,237	Nevada
197,771	Alabama
182,309	Louisiana
182,196	South Carolina
178,760	Kentucky
167,800	Iowa
166,141	Kansas
147,846	Oklahoma
128,463	Nebraska
123,735	Arkansas
111,534	New Hampshire
109,964	Utah
93,263	Mississippi
81,867	New Mexico
77,325	Maine
71,799	Idaho
64,379	Rhode Island
61,932	Hawaii
61,646	West Virginia
60,609	Wyoming
57,678	Montana
54,489	Delaware
46,878	South Dakota
45,515	Vermont
33,789	North Dakota
33,443	Alaska

Table G.366. FEDNONTX

Nontaxes Paid by Individuals to Federal Government (in thousands) 1999

1,156,408	California
698,599	Texas
637,108	New York
527,233	Florida
424,219	Illinois
420,281	Pennsylvania
394,323	Ohio
345,685	Michigan
285,096	New Jersey
270,691	Georgia
264,755	North Carolina
236,067	Virginia
216,314	Massachusetts
208,277	Indiana
200,002	Washington
191,776	Tennessee
191,206	Missouri
184,018	Wisconsin
179,991	Maryland
167,321	Minnesota
166,750	Arizona
152,708	Alabama
152,604	Louisiana
141,117	Colorado
137,882	Kentucky
134,870	South Carolina
116,787	Oklahoma
116,186	Oregon
114,797	Connecticut
100,563	Iowa
96,503	Mississippi
92,428	Kansas
89,266	Arkansas
74,495	Utah
63,317	West Virginia
63,144	Nevada
60,580	New Mexico
58,112	Nebraska
43,782	Maine
43,721	Idaho
42,083	New Hampshire
40,107	Hawaii
34,617	Rhode Island
30,815	Montana
26,276	Delaware
25,584	South Dakota
21,981	North Dakota
21,078	Alaska
20,807	Vermont
16,688	Wyoming

Table G.367. TXNONSTA

Personal Tax and Nontax Payments to State Governments (in thousands) 1999

35,085,200	California
23,615,454	New York
9,156,071	Massachusetts
8,826,094	Illinois
8,478,266	Ohio
8,280,269	Michigan
7,713,746	Pennsylvania
7,632,330	New Jersey
7,589,154	North Carolina
7,334,571	Virginia
6,453,965	Georgia
5,966,562	Wisconsin
5,009,860	Indiana
4,993,935	Minnesota
4,928,526	Maryland
4,196,901	Connecticut
4,152,919	Missouri
3,958,866	Oregon
3,583,660	Colorado
2,870,712	Kentucky
2,674,375	Oklahoma
2,470,909	Arizona
2,319,322	South Carolina
2,259,026	Alabama
2,220,404	Iowa
1,979,909	Texas
1,976,460	Kansas
1,937,106	Louisiana
1,737,134	Utah
1,733,465	Arkansas
1,712,162	Florida
1,287,557	Nebraska
1,220,894	Maine
1,182,434	Mississippi
1,165,754	Hawaii
1,155,647	West Virginia
1,032,529	New Mexico
1,020,605	Idaho
870,615	Rhode Island
844,226	Delaware
644,222	Tennessee
612,224	Montana
603,751	Washington
496,626	Vermont
273,519	North Dakota
192,202	New Hampshire
178,486	Nevada
103,983	Alaska
85,212	Wyoming
65,907	South Dakota

Table G.368. STAOTAX

Other Taxes Paid to State Governments (in thousands) 1999

69,557	California
67,058	Texas
66,508	Wisconsin
55,933	Pennsylvania
55,911	Michigan
54,764	Colorado
45,280	Georgia
43,796	Minnesota
43,278	Montana
39,168	Virginia
36,845	Washington
35,931	South Carolina
28,449	Ohio
28,224	Tennessee
27,423	Oregon
27,413	Missouri
25,476	New York
23,788	Illinois
23,303	Massachusetts
23,024	Idaho
22,047	Maryland
21,930	Arkansas
20,341	Wyoming
19,300	Louisiana
18,996	Iowa
17,595	Nebraska
17,257	Oklahoma
17,056	Kentucky
16,380	Alabama
16,302	Arizona
16,227	Florida
16,167	Alaska
16,131	North Carolina
15,687	Utah
15,493	South Dakota
15,446	West Virginia
15,302	New Mexico
13,993	Kansas
13,078	Indiana
12,043	New Jersey
11,949	Maine
10,833	Mississippi
10,540	Vermont
8,244	North Dakota
7,436	Nevada
7,088	New Hampshire
5,454	Connecticut
5,305	Delaware
1,816	Rhode Island
435	Hawaii

Table G.369. PCFEDTAX

Per Capita Taxes Paid to Federal Government 1999

6,070.68	Connecticut
4,743.34	New Jersey
4,598.83	Massachusetts
4,035.54	New York
3,983.17	Washington
3,953.75	Nevada
3,827.06	Illinois
3,825.75	New Hampshire
3,749.48	Maryland
3,736.11	Colorado
3,425.18	Delaware
3,422.75	Florida
3,384.10	Minnesota
3,381.09	California
3,362.09	Virginia
3,290.11	Wyoming
3,211.67	Michigan
3,130.23	Alaska
3,085.61	Pennsylvania
3,033.61	Texas
2,979.89	Rhode Island
2,935.58	Georgia
2,932.04	Wisconsin
2,781.65	Ohio
2,767.69	Indiana
2,737.29	Arizona
2,704.76	Kansas
2,660.99	Nebraska
2,631.84	Missouri
2,627.11	Oregon
2,621.59	Tennessee
2,615.47	North Carolina
2,596.42	Vermont
2,374.54	Iowa
2,344.71	Hawaii
2,337.44	South Dakota
2,292.60	Maine
2,214.41	South Carolina
2,126.32	Alabama
2,119.98	Kentucky
2,085.74	Louisiana
2,047.88	Utah
2,036.16	North Dakota
1,994.73	Idaho
1,973.21	Oklahoma
1,890.21	New Mexico
1,879.67	Arkansas
1,835.18	Montana
1,669.62	West Virginia
1,658.33	Mississippi

Table G.370. PCSTATAX

Per Capita Taxes Paid to State Governments 1999

1,482.72	Massachusetts
1,297.79	New York
1,278.75	Connecticut
1,193.81	Oregon
1,136.39	Wisconsin
1,120.35	Delaware
1,067.17	Virginia
1,058.53	California
1,045.74	Minnesota
991.94	North Carolina
983.35	Hawaii
974.35	Maine
952.99	Maryland
937.24	New Jersey
883.52	Colorado
878.68	Rhode Island
843.00	Indiana
839.46	Michigan
836.44	Vermont
828.68	Georgia
815.62	Utah
815.38	Idaho
796.41	Oklahoma
773.82	Iowa
772.83	Nebraska
759.45	Missouri
753.18	Ohio
744.70	Kansas
727.72	Illinois
724.78	Kentucky
693.52	Montana
679.42	Arkansas
643.13	Pennsylvania
639.56	West Virginia
596.88	South Carolina
593.46	New Mexico
517.11	Arizona
516.96	Alabama
443.07	Louisiana
431.65	North Dakota
427.08	Mississippi
177.67	Wyoming
167.85	Alaska
160.02	New Hampshire
117.48	Tennessee
113.30	Florida
104.88	Washington
98.78	Texas
98.65	Nevada
89.90	South Dakota

Table G.371. PCLOCTAX

Per Capita Taxes (not Including Property) Paid to Local Governments 1999

537.69	Maryland
403.35	New York
373.93	Ohio
314.81	Pennsylvania
255.68	Kentucky
163.80	Alaska
147.63	Indiana
127.99	Michigan
114.22	Missouri
113.38	California
112.84	Wyoming
112.44	Minnesota
104.63	Delaware
99.90	Florida
96.25	Colorado
94.78	Nevada
93.48	Oregon
89.69	Washington
85.77	Kansas
85.39	Nebraska
83.89	Illinois
81.38	Alabama
80.14	West Virginia
79.00	Utah
76.71	Iowa
75.53	Texas
72.73	Georgia
70.00	Louisiana
68.85	Arizona
65.90	Virginia
65.11	North Dakota
64.05	New Jersey
63.91	Tennessee
57.81	New Mexico
57.02	Wisconsin
56.95	North Carolina
55.96	South Dakota
55.56	Montana
55.15	Hawaii
54.79	Oklahoma
54.64	Arkansas
52.64	Mississippi
50.86	South Carolina
49.72	Idaho
44.49	Maine
31.65	Connecticut
30.28	Massachusetts
26.74	New Hampshire
26.50	Vermont
20.46	Rhode Island

Table G.372. PCFSLTAX

Per Capita Taxes Paid to Federal, State, and Local Governments 1999

7,436.76	Connecticut
6,111.83	Massachusetts
5,744.63	New Jersey
5,736.68	New York
5,240.16	Maryland
4,746.77	Colorado
4,650.16	Delaware
4,638.67	Illinois
4,601.94	California
4,573.82	Minnesota
4,546.83	Virginia
4,224.15	Washington
4,179.12	Michigan
4,178.94	Nevada
4,125.44	Wisconsin
4,043.55	Pennsylvania
4,012.51	New Hampshire
3,935.41	Rhode Island
3,914.40	Oregon
3,911.49	Ohio
3,868.47	Georgia
3,776.50	Indiana
3,687.02	North Carolina
3,653.01	Florida
3,581.22	Kansas
3,580.62	Wyoming
3,566.66	Nebraska
3,535.24	Missouri
3,467.23	Alaska
3,459.36	Vermont
3,383.20	Hawaii
3,364.01	Arizona
3,341.48	Maine
3,225.07	Iowa
3,214.63	Texas
3,123.48	Kentucky
2,979.15	Utah
2,908.27	South Carolina
2,859.83	Idaho
2,851.08	Oklahoma
2,809.23	Tennessee
2,736.86	Alabama
2,627.96	Arkansas
2,615.16	Montana
2,598.81	Louisiana
2,541.48	New Mexico
2,532.92	North Dakota
2,483.30	South Dakota
2,398.27	West Virginia
2,152.61	Mississippi

Table G.373. STANONTX

Nontaxes Paid to State Governments (in thousands) 1999

1,322,988	California
1,196,967	New York
1,166,324	Texas
961,237	Florida
788,884	New Jersey
711,998	Illinois
651,842	Pennsylvania
598,162	Michigan
570,947	Virginia
549,916	Ohio
457,482	Massachusetts
409,697	Wisconsin
392,757	Minnesota
381,055	North Carolina
366,730	Indiana
345,464	Washington
307,997	Louisiana
299,623	Maryland
298,000	Georgia
279,006	Tennessee
264,626	Colorado
262,336	Arizona
247,271	Oregon
234,759	Kentucky
232,385	Iowa
228,748	Missouri
215,258	South Carolina
191,506	Connecticut
190,844	Alabama
160,090	Oklahoma
155,805	Utah
141,290	Arkansas
140,921	West Virginia
134,606	Kansas
129,012	New Mexico
128,093	Nebraska
123,486	Maine
105,362	Mississippi
84,754	Nevada
84,080	Hawaii
71,113	New Hampshire
66,236	Idaho
66,110	Delaware
60,454	Alaska
59,788	Montana
58,862	Vermont
55,055	Rhode Island
46,578	North Dakota
32,007	Wyoming
27,215	South Dakota

Table G.374. PCSTALOP

Per Capita Personal Property Taxes Paid to State and Local Governments 1999

56.38	Rhode Island
55.67	Connecticut
51.66	Virginia
48.94	California
47.44	Nebraska
46.41	Washington
46.12	South Carolina
45.99	Kansas
40.76	Arizona
36.65	Utah
31.77	Nevada
31.55	Minnesota
31.48	Georgia
30.90	Montana
30.89	Colorado
30.05	Maine
29.73	Missouri
26.67	Oklahoma
23.04	Kentucky
22.66	North Carolina
18.17	Indiana
17.06	Florida
14.56	Mississippi
14.24	Arkansas
12.19	Alabama
8.94	West Virginia
6.72	Texas
6.25	Tennessee
5.35	Alaska
2.73	Ohio
.00	New York
.00	New Jersey
.00	Illinois
.00	Pennsylvania
.00	Michigan
.00	Massachusetts
.00	Wisconsin
.00	Louisiana
.00	Maryland
.00	Oregon
.00	Iowa
.00	New Mexico
.00	Hawaii
.00	New Hampshire
.00	Idaho
.00	Delaware
.00	Vermont
.00	North Dakota
.00	Wyoming
.00	South Dakota

Table G.375. WHATLEFT

Per Capita Income after All Taxes Paid 1999

32,106	Connecticut
29,867	New Jersey
29,415	Massachusetts
28,164	New York
27,312	New Hampshire
27,277	Maryland
26,825	Nevada
26,786	Colorado
26,499	Illinois
26,168	Minnesota
26,156	Washington
26,051	Delaware
25,400	Rhode Island
25,254	California
25,247	Virginia
25,162	Alaska
24,575	Pennsylvania
24,150	Hawaii
24,128	Florida
23,925	Michigan
23,619	Texas
23,480	Nebraska
23,456	Georgia
23,260	Ohio
23,245	Wisconsin
23,124	Kansas
23,044	Oregon
22,869	Missouri
22,782	Wyoming
22,739	Tennessee
22,730	North Carolina
22,558	South Dakota
22,386	Vermont
22,381	Indiana
22,373	Iowa
21,809	Arizona
21,241	Maine
20,740	North Dakota
20,630	South Carolina
20,297	Utah
20,240	Louisiana
20,235	Alabama
20,107	Oklahoma
20,104	Kentucky
20,011	Idaho
19,605	Arkansas
19,382	Montana
19,295	New Mexico
18,533	Mississippi
18,523	West Virginia

Table G.376.   TAXRATE

Proportion of Income Paid in Taxes to Federal, State, and Local Governments 1999

.1881	Connecticut
.1720	Massachusetts
.1692	New York
.1613	New Jersey
.1612	Maryland
.1541	California
.1526	Virginia
.1515	Delaware
.1507	Wisconsin
.1505	Colorado
.1490	Illinois
.1488	Minnesota
.1487	Michigan
.1452	Oregon
.1444	Indiana
.1440	Ohio
.1416	Georgia
.1413	Pennsylvania
.1396	North Carolina
.1390	Washington
.1359	Maine
.1358	Wyoming
.1348	Nevada
.1345	Kentucky
.1342	Rhode Island
.1341	Kansas
.1339	Missouri
.1339	Vermont
.1336	Arizona
.1319	Nebraska
.1315	Florida
.1281	New Hampshire
.1280	Utah
.1260	Iowa
.1250	Idaho
.1242	Oklahoma
.1236	South Carolina
.1229	Hawaii
.1211	Alaska
.1198	Texas
.1191	Alabama
.1189	Montana
.1182	Arkansas
.1164	New Mexico
.1146	West Virginia
.1138	Louisiana
.1100	Tennessee
.1088	North Dakota
.1041	Mississippi
.0992	South Dakota

Table G.377.   TOTSTALO

Total Paid in State and Local Taxes and Nontaxes (in thousands) 1999

40,465,059	California
30,955,049	New York
12,718,138	Ohio
11,489,555	Pennsylvania
9,843,531	Illinois
9,542,692	Michigan
9,343,030	Massachusetts
8,198,247	North Carolina
8,153,916	New Jersey
8,142,569	Virginia
7,709,268	Maryland
7,265,570	Georgia
6,265,923	Wisconsin
5,995,230	Indiana
5,681,533	Minnesota
4,940,059	Missouri
4,483,493	Connecticut
4,268,859	Oregon
4,099,363	Colorado
3,974,685	Kentucky
3,628,488	Texas
3,479,564	Florida
2,994,660	Arizona
2,947,922	Oklahoma
2,696,156	South Carolina
2,667,948	Alabama
2,440,515	Iowa
2,326,168	Kansas
2,243,147	Louisiana
1,983,450	Utah
1,909,190	Arkansas
1,508,862	Nebraska
1,387,175	Washington
1,368,467	Mississippi
1,316,610	West Virginia
1,314,296	Maine
1,231,132	Hawaii
1,133,110	New Mexico
1,082,841	Idaho
1,028,915	Tennessee
946,747	Rhode Island
923,071	Delaware
688,552	Montana
512,361	Vermont
407,437	Nevada
314,778	North Dakota
224,326	New Hampshire
208,774	Alaska
139,331	Wyoming
106,933	South Dakota

Table G.378.   PCSTALO

Per Capita in State and Local Taxes and Nontaxes 1999

1,701.14	New York
1,513.00	Massachusetts
1,490.68	Maryland
1,366.07	Connecticut
1,287.29	Oregon
1,224.98	Delaware
1,220.85	California
1,193.41	Wisconsin
1,189.72	Minnesota
1,184.73	Virginia
1,129.83	Ohio
1,071.56	North Carolina
1,048.89	Maine
1,038.49	Hawaii
1,010.66	Colorado
1,008.81	Indiana
1,003.50	Kentucky
1,001.29	New Jersey
967.45	Michigan
957.94	Pennsylvania
955.52	Rhode Island
932.89	Georgia
931.27	Utah
905.66	Nebraska
903.39	Missouri
877.87	Oklahoma
876.46	Kansas
865.10	Idaho
862.94	Vermont
850.53	Iowa
811.61	Illinois
779.98	Montana
748.30	Arkansas
728.65	West Virginia
693.86	South Carolina
651.27	New Mexico
626.72	Arizona
610.53	Alabama
513.07	Louisiana
496.76	North Dakota
494.28	Mississippi
337.00	Alaska
290.51	Wyoming
240.98	Washington
230.26	Florida
225.20	Nevada
187.64	Tennessee
186.76	New Hampshire
181.02	Texas
145.86	South Dakota

Table G.379. MOTCYDEA

Number of Motorcycle Deaths 1999

236	California
182	Texas
177	Florida
120	Ohio
111	Pennsylvania
107	New York
106	North Carolina
103	Illinois
83	Michigan
73	Arizona
67	Indiana
66	Wisconsin
65	South Carolina
60	Colorado
59	Georgia
59	Tennessee
44	Maryland
42	Kentucky
42	New Jersey
38	Connecticut
38	Virginia
38	Washington
38	Louisiana
37	Missouri
35	Massachusetts
33	Oklahoma
32	Alabama
32	New Hampshire
30	Minnesota
30	Iowa
23	Utah
23	West Virginia
23	New Mexico
22	Arkansas
18	Mississippi
18	Oregon
17	Nevada
17	Hawaii
16	Maine
15	Kansas
15	Montana
13	Idaho
12	Rhode Island
10	South Dakota
9	Alaska
9	Wyoming
8	Nebraska
7	Delaware
7	Vermont
3	North Dakota

Table G.380. PCHELMET

Percent of Motorcycle Deaths with Helmet 1999

94.4	Oregon
92.9	New Jersey
87.6	Florida
87.5	Alabama
85.7	Delaware
82.9	Massachusetts
81.1	Missouri
80.2	North Carolina
79.7	Georgia
79.7	Tennessee
79.5	Maryland
78.9	Washington
78.3	West Virginia
75.8	California
72.0	New York
71.2	Pennsylvania
71.1	Michigan
64.7	Nevada
57.1	Vermont
55.6	Alaska
55.3	Louisiana
50.0	Nebraska
45.2	Kentucky
40.0	Montana
38.9	Mississippi
37.5	New Hampshire
36.9	South Carolina
35.2	Texas
33.3	Wyoming
33.3	North Dakota
31.6	Connecticut
30.4	New Mexico
30.0	Colorado
26.7	Minnesota
26.0	Arizona
25.8	Wisconsin
25.0	Maine
23.3	Iowa
23.1	Idaho
20.0	Kansas
20.0	South Dakota
19.4	Indiana
18.2	Arkansas
16.7	Rhode Island
16.5	Illinois
15.8	Virginia
11.8	Hawaii
9.2	Ohio
9.1	Oklahoma
4.3	Utah

Table G.381. JUSTICE

Per Capita Expenditures for Total State and Local Justice System 1996

738.08	Alaska
573.57	New York
531.86	California
498.93	Nevada
488.20	New Jersey
468.18	Florida
431.31	Delaware
424.56	Maryland
402.92	Arizona
396.17	Connecticut
390.22	Massachusetts
386.23	Michigan
379.90	New Mexico
379.12	Oregon
373.61	Hawaii
373.20	Rhode Island
366.21	Wisconsin
362.51	Washington
359.04	Illinois
357.22	Ohio
356.34	Colorado
356.24	Wyoming
354.60	Texas
353.29	Pennsylvania
338.02	Virginia
336.15	Georgia
331.64	North Carolina
324.28	Utah
316.78	Louisiana
311.70	Minnesota
304.13	Idaho
293.46	South Carolina
291.70	Kansas
282.07	Tennessee
265.98	New Hampshire
262.50	Missouri
261.42	Oklahoma
260.79	Montana
251.94	South Dakota
247.44	Iowa
242.94	Alabama
239.58	Vermont
238.66	Nebraska
233.59	Indiana
233.02	Mississippi
224.15	Kentucky
219.65	Arkansas
212.67	Maine
178.99	West Virginia
174.09	North Dakota

Table G.382. POLICE

Per Capita Expenditures of Justice Costs for Police Protection 1996

256.44	New York
240.16	Alaska
226.13	California
225.00	New Jersey
213.41	Nevada
210.69	Florida
192.30	Illinois
183.18	Massachusetts
176.40	Maryland
176.09	Delaware
175.46	Arizona
171.10	Connecticut
169.28	Wisconsin
166.17	Oregon
165.76	Rhode Island
164.77	New Mexico
161.40	Wyoming
156.96	Colorado
156.70	Louisiana
154.25	Ohio
152.76	Hawaii
152.25	Michigan
145.70	Washington
143.90	Pennsylvania
141.52	Kansas
140.02	Minnesota
136.74	Georgia
136.40	Virginia
136.28	North Carolina
134.96	Texas
134.38	Missouri
132.27	Utah
129.84	Idaho
125.78	New Hampshire
123.98	Tennessee
121.66	Oklahoma
121.12	South Carolina
117.51	Alabama
116.84	Iowa
115.58	Montana
114.48	Vermont
109.57	South Dakota
106.90	Nebraska
106.25	Indiana
105.51	Mississippi
103.71	Maine
101.14	Arkansas
95.82	Kentucky
83.22	North Dakota
72.71	West Virginia

Table G.383. JUDICIAL

Per Capita Expenditures of Justice Costs for Judicial and Legal 1996

255.82	Alaska
131.32	Hawaii
122.19	New Jersey
118.17	California
107.61	New York
107.25	Nevada
99.96	Delaware
93.63	Arizona
90.04	Rhode Island
86.08	Wyoming
85.12	Massachusetts
83.23	Connecticut
82.35	Florida
81.91	Utah
79.34	Washington
78.29	Michigan
77.12	Ohio
77.08	Oregon
75.67	Maryland
75.00	New Mexico
74.16	Minnesota
73.03	Wisconsin
70.57	Colorado
69.96	Idaho
69.74	Pennsylvania
64.67	Illinois
64.43	Iowa
64.39	New Hampshire
63.29	Kansas
61.73	South Dakota
61.54	Montana
59.50	Louisiana
58.11	Tennessee
54.05	Georgia
52.99	Texas
52.23	Virginia
51.87	Vermont
51.10	North Carolina
50.97	North Dakota
50.92	Alabama
49.49	West Virginia
48.95	Kentucky
47.41	Nebraska
46.09	Oklahoma
42.58	Indiana
42.30	Missouri
40.27	South Carolina
38.00	Arkansas
37.56	Mississippi
36.52	Maine

Table G.384. CORRECT

Per Capita Expenditures of Justice Costs for Corrections 1996

242.10	Alaska
209.52	New York
187.56	California
178.27	Nevada
175.14	Florida
172.49	Maryland
166.65	Texas
155.70	Michigan
155.26	Delaware
149.39	Virginia
145.36	Georgia
144.25	North Carolina
141.83	Connecticut
141.01	New Jersey
140.13	New Mexico
139.66	Pennsylvania
137.47	Washington
135.87	Oregon
133.84	Arizona
132.06	South Carolina
128.81	Colorado
125.85	Ohio
123.90	Wisconsin
121.92	Massachusetts
117.40	Rhode Island
110.10	Utah
108.77	Wyoming
104.33	Idaho
102.07	Illinois
100.59	Louisiana
99.97	Tennessee
97.52	Minnesota
93.67	Oklahoma
89.96	Mississippi
89.52	Hawaii
86.89	Kansas
85.82	Missouri
84.76	Indiana
84.35	Nebraska
83.68	Montana
80.64	South Dakota
80.50	Arkansas
79.38	Kentucky
75.81	New Hampshire
74.50	Alabama
73.23	Vermont
72.43	Maine
66.17	Iowa
56.79	West Virginia
39.90	North Dakota

Table G.385. JUSTCOST

Percent of State and Local Payrolls Devoted to Justice System Costs 1996

18.9	Nevada
18.9	Florida
16.7	New York
16.2	New Jersey
15.9	California
15.9	Illinois
15.3	Arizona
14.4	Rhode Island
14.2	Delaware
14.2	Hawaii
13.7	Maryland
13.3	Pennsylvania
13.3	Massachusetts
13.1	Texas
12.8	Connecticut
12.6	Virginia
12.6	New Mexico
12.5	Michigan
12.5	Colorado
12.4	Georgia
12.4	Ohio
12.0	Idaho
11.6	Louisiana
11.6	Tennessee
11.6	New Hampshire
11.5	Oregon
11.1	Missouri
10.8	Alaska
10.8	Washington
10.8	South Carolina
10.8	Wisconsin
10.8	Oklahoma
10.4	North Carolina
10.4	Kansas
10.3	Utah
10.1	Alabama
9.9	Minnesota
9.4	Arkansas
9.4	Vermont
9.2	Indiana
9.0	Wyoming
9.0	South Dakota
8.8	Kentucky
8.7	Mississippi
8.7	Nebraska
8.6	Maine
8.6	Iowa
7.5	North Dakota
7.3	Montana
6.2	West Virginia

Table G.386. POLICOST

Percent of Justice System Payrolls Devoted to Police Protection 1996

61.6	Missouri
59.0	Illinois
57.6	New Hampshire
54.7	Vermont
54.0	Maine
53.9	West Virginia
53.6	Nebraska
53.5	Massachusetts
53.4	Connecticut
53.1	New Jersey
52.7	Wyoming
52.4	Montana
51.7	Oklahoma
51.6	Wisconsin
50.9	Indiana
50.7	Mississippi
50.2	Iowa
50.0	Alabama
49.7	Arkansas
49.2	New York
49.2	Pennsylvania
49.2	North Carolina
49.0	Kansas
48.9	Idaho
48.9	Utah
48.6	Oregon
48.4	California
48.4	South Dakota
48.3	Maryland
48.1	Washington
48.0	Ohio
47.8	Colorado
47.5	North Dakota
47.4	South Carolina
47.2	Alaska
47.0	Rhode Island
46.6	Tennessee
46.2	Louisiana
46.2	Minnesota
46.1	Hawaii
45.7	Florida
44.7	Arizona
44.4	Texas
44.3	Delaware
43.7	Michigan
43.4	Virginia
42.9	Nevada
41.9	Kentucky
40.4	Georgia
39.1	New Mexico

Table G.387. JUDICOST

Percent of Justice System Payrolls Devoted to Judicial and Legal Costs 1996

33.3	Hawaii
31.0	West Virginia
30.3	North Dakota
26.6	Wyoming
26.4	Alaska
25.9	Iowa
25.9	South Dakota
25.1	Delaware
24.7	Kentucky
24.3	Minnesota
23.8	New Jersey
23.8	Nevada
23.7	Washington
23.4	Arizona
22.7	Colorado
22.2	Louisiana
22.1	Utah
21.7	Idaho
21.6	Montana
21.6	Alabama
21.5	Vermont
21.1	New Mexico
20.9	Mississippi
20.9	Oregon
20.7	Ohio
20.7	Florida
20.4	California
20.0	Wisconsin
19.9	Kansas
19.8	Nebraska
19.8	Tennessee
19.4	Pennsylvania
18.6	Massachusetts
18.5	Rhode Island
18.5	Michigan
18.4	Oklahoma
18.3	Arkansas
17.8	Indiana
17.6	Illinois
17.6	New York
17.3	North Carolina
16.9	Maryland
16.8	Georgia
15.8	Texas
15.4	New Hampshire
15.3	Virginia
15.1	Connecticut
14.7	South Carolina
14.6	Missouri
14.4	Maine

Table G.388. CORRCOST

Percent of Justice System Payrolls Devoted to Corrections Costs 1996

42.8	Georgia
41.3	Virginia
39.8	New Mexico
39.8	Texas
37.9	South Carolina
37.8	Michigan
34.8	Maryland
34.5	Rhode Island
33.6	Florida
33.6	Tennessee
33.5	North Carolina
33.4	Kentucky
33.3	Nevada
33.2	New York
32.0	Arkansas
31.8	Arizona
31.6	Louisiana
31.6	Maine
31.5	Connecticut
31.4	Pennsylvania
31.3	Ohio
31.3	Indiana
31.2	California
31.2	Kansas
30.5	Delaware
30.5	Oregon
29.9	Oklahoma
29.5	Minnesota
29.4	Colorado
29.4	Idaho
29.0	Utah
28.4	Mississippi
28.4	Wisconsin
28.3	Alabama
28.2	Washington
27.9	Massachusetts
27.0	New Hampshire
26.6	Nebraska
26.4	Alaska
26.1	Montana
25.7	South Dakota
23.9	Iowa
23.9	Vermont
23.8	Missouri
23.4	Illinois
23.1	New Jersey
22.2	North Dakota
20.7	Wyoming
20.6	Hawaii
15.0	West Virginia

Table G.389. JUSTEMPL

Percent State/Local Government Employees Devoted to Total Justice System 1996

16.3	Florida
15.8	Nevada
15.7	New Jersey
14.6	New York
14.1	Arizona
13.9	Illinois
13.8	Maryland
13.5	Pennsylvania
13.5	California
12.8	Delaware
12.6	Texas
12.6	Connecticut
12.4	Hawaii
12.2	Georgia
12.0	Ohio
12.0	Massachusetts
11.9	Rhode Island
11.8	Michigan
11.5	Louisiana
11.4	Virginia
11.3	South Carolina
11.2	New Mexico
11.2	Missouri
11.1	Oklahoma
11.0	Tennessee
11.0	Colorado
10.7	Idaho
10.6	North Carolina
10.6	Wisconsin
10.6	Washington
10.2	Oregon
10.1	New Hampshire
9.9	Indiana
9.8	Kansas
9.7	Kentucky
9.4	Arkansas
9.4	Utah
9.4	Alaska
8.9	Alabama
8.6	Mississippi
8.4	Wyoming
8.3	Minnesota
8.2	South Dakota
8.1	Vermont
8.0	Maine
8.0	Nebraska
7.6	Iowa
7.4	Montana
7.3	North Dakota
6.6	West Virginia

Table G.390. POLIEMPL

Percent of Total Justice System Employees Devoted to Police Protection 1996

54.7	New Hampshire
53.7	Illinois
53.5	Missouri
52.8	Maine
52.4	West Virginia
51.5	Iowa
51.4	Montana
51.0	Wyoming
50.7	Mississippi
50.6	Massachusetts
50.3	Wisconsin
49.7	Alabama
49.6	Rhode Island
49.0	Nebraska
48.5	Arkansas
47.9	North Dakota
47.5	Indiana
47.5	South Dakota
47.4	North Carolina
47.3	New York
47.3	Utah
47.1	Colorado
46.8	New Jersey
46.6	Vermont
46.5	Idaho
46.4	Connecticut
46.4	Kansas
45.2	California
45.2	Tennessee
44.9	Maryland
44.8	Pennsylvania
44.7	South Carolina
44.5	Minnesota
44.3	Louisiana
44.0	Oklahoma
43.6	Ohio
43.5	Oregon
42.4	Michigan
42.0	Florida
41.5	Washington
41.2	Alaska
40.5	Hawaii
40.5	Virginia
40.4	Nevada
40.2	Texas
39.2	New Mexico
38.6	Arizona
38.6	Georgia
38.5	Kentucky
37.7	Delaware

Table G.391. JUDIEMPL

Percent of Total Justice System Employees Devoted to Judicial and Legal 1995

33.2	Hawaii
29.7	New Jersey
28.6	Alaska
28.2	West Virginia
27.6	Delaware
26.4	North Dakota
24.0	Kentucky
23.7	Wyoming
23.7	Ohio
23.5	Nevada
23.3	Iowa
23.3	Minnesota
22.9	Oregon
22.7	South Dakota
22.3	Arizona
21.9	Rhode Island
21.9	Washington
21.8	Pennsylvania
21.6	Vermont
21.3	Colorado
21.0	Louisiana
20.8	Idaho
20.4	Montana
20.3	Utah
19.7	Kansas
19.7	Florida
19.5	Illinois
19.4	Alabama
19.3	Indiana
19.2	California
19.0	Michigan
18.8	Nebraska
18.7	Massachusetts
18.5	New Mexico
18.3	Wisconsin
17.6	Connecticut
17.6	Maryland
17.5	New Hampshire
17.3	Mississippi
17.0	Missouri
17.0	New York
17.0	Tennessee
15.8	Arkansas
15.1	Oklahoma
14.7	Georgia
14.6	Texas
14.5	North Carolina
13.6	Virginia
13.4	South Carolina
13.0	Maine

Table G.392. CORREMPL

Percent of Total Justice System Employees Devoted to Corrections 1995

46.5	Georgia
45.9	Virginia
45.2	Texas
42.3	New Mexico
41.9	South Carolina
40.9	Oklahoma
39.1	Arizona
38.6	Michigan
38.3	Florida
38.1	North Carolina
37.8	Tennessee
37.5	Kentucky
37.5	Maryland
36.6	Washington
36.1	Nevada
35.9	Connecticut
35.7	New York
35.7	Arkansas
35.5	California
34.7	Delaware
34.7	Louisiana
34.2	Maine
33.9	Kansas
33.6	Oregon
33.4	Pennsylvania
33.3	Indiana
32.7	Ohio
32.7	Idaho
32.4	Utah
32.3	Minnesota
32.2	Nebraska
32.0	Mississippi
31.7	Vermont
31.6	Colorado
31.5	Wisconsin
30.9	Alabama
30.7	Massachusetts
30.2	Alaska
29.8	South Dakota
29.5	Missouri
28.5	Rhode Island
28.2	Montana
27.8	New Hampshire
26.9	Illinois
26.3	Hawaii
25.7	North Dakota
25.2	Wyoming
25.1	Iowa
23.5	New Jersey
19.5	West Virginia

Table G.393. JUSTRATE

Rate (per 10,000 population) of Total Justice System Employees 1995

89.5	New York
86.1	New Jersey
80.4	Florida
74.1	Georgia
73.9	Texas
73.1	Delaware
72.2	New Mexico
72.2	Nevada
70.8	Alaska
69.9	Arizona
69.6	Louisiana
69.0	Maryland
68.6	Hawaii
68.4	Illinois
66.5	Wyoming
65.7	Oklahoma
65.1	South Carolina
63.3	Connecticut
63.2	Kansas
62.7	California
61.8	Virginia
60.9	Ohio
60.3	Idaho
59.4	Massachusetts
58.9	Colorado
58.6	Rhode Island
58.3	Pennsylvania
57.4	Michigan
57.1	North Carolina
56.8	Missouri
56.3	Tennessee
54.8	Wisconsin
54.5	Mississippi
54.1	Washington
53.1	Oregon
52.1	Indiana
51.6	Arkansas
51.5	Kentucky
51.3	Alabama
51.2	Nebraska
49.4	Utah
47.8	New Hampshire
47.6	Minnesota
47.2	Montana
46.5	Vermont
45.8	South Dakota
45.1	Iowa
43.3	North Dakota
42.8	Maine
33.9	West Virginia

Table G.394. POLTOTRA

Rate (per 10,000 population) of Police Protection Employees 1995

42.4	New York
40.3	New Jersey
36.7	Illinois
34.0	Wyoming
33.8	Florida
31.0	Maryland
30.8	Louisiana
30.4	Missouri
30.0	Massachusetts
29.7	Texas
29.4	Connecticut
29.4	Kansas
29.2	Alaska
29.1	Nevada
29.1	South Carolina
29.1	Rhode Island
28.9	Oklahoma
28.8	Georgia
28.4	California
28.3	New Mexico
28.0	Idaho
27.8	Hawaii
27.8	Colorado
27.7	Mississippi
27.6	Delaware
27.5	Wisconsin
27.1	North Carolina
27.0	Arizona
26.6	Ohio
26.2	New Hampshire
26.1	Pennsylvania
25.5	Tennessee
25.5	Alabama
25.1	Arkansas
25.1	Nebraska
25.0	Virginia
24.7	Indiana
24.3	Michigan
24.3	Montana
23.4	Utah
23.2	Iowa
23.1	Oregon
22.6	Maine
22.4	Washington
21.8	South Dakota
21.7	Vermont
21.2	Minnesota
20.7	North Dakota
19.8	Kentucky
17.7	West Virginia

Table G.395. POLSWORA

Rate (per 10,000 population) of Police Protection Sworn Employees 1995

36.5	New York
28.3	New Jersey
27.5	Illinois
25.0	Maryland
24.9	Massachusetts
23.9	Louisiana
23.0	Wyoming
22.8	Rhode Island
22.7	Connecticut
22.3	Florida
21.9	Texas
21.9	Georgia
21.6	South Carolina
21.6	North Carolina
21.5	Missouri
21.5	Hawaii
21.5	Wisconsin
21.0	Colorado
20.9	Kansas
20.8	Oklahoma
20.6	Pennsylvania
20.4	New Mexico
20.2	Mississippi
20.1	Delaware
20.0	California
19.7	Alaska
19.7	Nevada
19.7	Ohio
19.7	New Hampshire
19.7	Alabama
19.6	Idaho
19.5	Tennessee
19.3	Arkansas
19.2	Virginia
19.1	Michigan
18.5	Nebraska
18.1	Arizona
17.9	Indiana
17.4	Iowa
17.3	Maine
16.9	Oregon
16.6	Montana
16.5	South Dakota
16.0	Washington
15.9	Utah
15.9	Minnesota
15.7	North Dakota
15.3	Vermont
14.3	Kentucky
13.9	West Virginia

Table G.396. JUDIRATE

Rate (per 10,000 population) of Judicial and Legal Employees 1995

25.6	New Jersey
22.8	Hawaii
20.2	Delaware
20.2	Alaska
17.0	Nevada
15.8	Wyoming
15.8	Florida
15.6	Arizona
15.2	New York
14.6	Louisiana
14.5	Ohio
13.3	Illinois
13.3	New Mexico
12.8	Rhode Island
12.7	Pennsylvania
12.5	Colorado
12.5	Idaho
12.4	Kansas
12.4	Kentucky
12.2	Oregon
12.1	Maryland
12.1	California
11.9	Washington
11.4	North Dakota
11.2	Connecticut
11.1	Massachusetts
11.1	Minnesota
10.9	Georgia
10.9	Michigan
10.8	Texas
10.5	Iowa
10.4	South Dakota
10.1	Vermont
10.0	Wisconsin
10.0	Indiana
10.0	Utah
9.9	Oklahoma
9.9	Alabama
9.7	Missouri
9.6	Tennessee
9.6	Nebraska
9.6	Montana
9.6	West Virginia
9.4	Mississippi
8.8	South Carolina
8.4	New Hampshire
8.4	Virginia
8.3	North Carolina
8.2	Arkansas
5.6	Maine

Table G.397. CORRATE

Rate (per 10,000 population) of Corrections Employees 1995

34.5	Georgia
33.4	Texas
31.9	New York
30.8	Florida
30.5	New Mexico
28.4	Virginia
27.3	Arizona
27.2	South Carolina
26.9	Oklahoma
26.1	Nevada
25.9	Maryland.
25.4	Delaware
24.2	Louisiana
22.7	Connecticut
22.3	California
22.1	Michigan
21.7	North Carolina
21.4	Alaska
21.4	Kansas
21.3	Tennessee
20.2	New Jersey
19.9	Ohio
19.8	Washington
19.7	Idaho
19.5	Pennsylvania
19.3	Kentucky
18.6	Colorado
18.4	Illinois
18.4	Arkansas
18.2	Massachusetts
18.0	Hawaii
17.8	Oregon
17.4	Mississippi
17.3	Indiana
17.2	Wisconsin
16.8	Wyoming
16.8	Missouri
16.7	Rhode Island
16.5	Nebraska
16.0	Utah
15.8	Alabama
15.4	Minnesota
14.7	Vermont
14.6	Maine
13.6	South Dakota
13.3	Montana
13.3	New Hampshire
11.3	Iowa
11.1	North Dakota
6.6	West Virginia

Table G.398. STAPOLTO

Total Personnel in State Law Enforcement Agencies 1997

9,533	California
6,563	Texas
5,318	Pennsylvania
4,681	New York
3,660	Illinois
3,521	New Jersey
2,950	Michigan
2,588	Massachusetts
2,382	Ohio
2,251	Virginia
2,202	Maryland
2,067	Florida
2,056	Missouri
2,016	Washington
1,910	Georgia
1,877	Indiana
1,731	Tennessee
1,719	North Carolina
1,678	Arizona
1,606	Kentucky
1,459	Connecticut
1,375	Louisiana
1,340	Alabama
1,339	Oregon
1,290	Oklahoma
1,110	South Carolina
925	West Virginia
803	Colorado
763	Delaware
741	Kansas
735	Arkansas
718	Minnesota
679	Alaska
658	Wisconsin
624	Nebraska
592	New Mexico
554	Iowa
547	Nevada
520	Mississippi
475	Maine
421	Utah
404	Vermont
393	New Hampshire
290	Wyoming
278	Montana
265	Idaho
234	South Dakota
225	Rhode Island
195	North Dakota
*	Hawaii

*Inadequate data

Table G.399. STAPOLSW

State Police Officers, Sworn 1997

6,532	California
4,098	Pennsylvania
3,979	New York
2,757	Texas
2,555	New Jersey
2,270	Massachusetts
2,054	Michigan
1,980	Illinois
1,658	Virginia
1,637	Florida
1,516	Maryland
1,354	Ohio
1,298	North Carolina
1,222	Indiana
1,056	Missouri
966	Arizona
945	Connecticut
935	Washington
918	Kentucky
913	Tennessee
909	Louisiana
891	South Carolina
853	Oregon
826	Georgia
747	Oklahoma
716	Alabama
608	West Virginia
568	Colorado
561	Delaware
526	Kansas
520	Mississippi
505	Arkansas
499	Minnesota
495	Wisconsin
466	Nebraska
435	New Mexico
432	Iowa
389	Utah
375	Nevada
337	Maine
321	Alaska
289	New Hampshire
263	Vermont
212	Montana
195	Idaho
184	Rhode Island
156	Wyoming
154	South Dakota
131	North Dakota
*	Hawaii

*Incomplete data

Table G.400. STAPOLPC

Percent of State Police Officers, Sworn 1997

100	Mississippi
92	Utah
88	Massachusetts
85	New York
82	Rhode Island
80	South Carolina
79	Florida
78	Iowa
77	Pennsylvania
76	North Carolina
76	Montana
75	Wisconsin
75	Nebraska
74	Virginia
74	Delaware
74	New Hampshire
74	Idaho
73	New Jersey
73	New Mexico
71	Colorado
71	Kansas
71	Maine
70	Michigan
69	California
69	Maryland
69	Arkansas
69	Minnesota
69	Nevada
67	North Dakota
66	Louisiana
66	West Virginia
66	South Dakota
65	Indiana
65	Connecticut
65	Vermont
64	Oregon
58	Arizona
58	Oklahoma
57	Ohio
57	Kentucky
54	Illinois
54	Wyoming
53	Tennessee
53	Alabama
51	Missouri
47	Alaska
46	Washington
43	Georgia
42	Texas
*	Hawaii

*Incomplete data

Table G.401. OFFPPOP

Sworn State Police Officers (per 10,000 residents) 1997

7.4449	Delaware
5.1816	Alaska
4.4295	Vermont
3.6760	Massachusetts
3.4167	Pennsylvania
3.3648	West Virginia
3.2527	Wyoming
3.1375	New Jersey
2.9314	Maryland
2.8793	Connecticut
2.7971	Nebraska
2.6895	Maine
2.5723	Oregon
2.5002	New Mexico
2.4124	Virginia
2.4061	New Hampshire
2.4015	Montana
2.3177	Kentucky
2.2930	South Carolina
2.2245	Oklahoma
2.1867	New York
2.1006	South Dakota
2.0824	Michigan
2.0791	Louisiana
2.0727	Nevada
2.0673	North Dakota
2.0562	Indiana
2.0216	Arizona
1.9819	Kansas
1.9793	Arkansas
1.9707	California
1.9311	Missouri
1.8782	Mississippi
1.8570	Rhode Island
1.8264	Utah
1.6966	North Carolina
1.6650	Tennessee
1.6385	Alabama
1.6325	Illinois
1.6243	Washington
1.5579	Idaho
1.5055	Iowa
1.4003	Colorado
1.3755	Texas
1.2028	Ohio
1.0833	Florida
1.0606	Georgia
1.0449	Minnesota
.9428	Wisconsin
*	Hawaii

*Incomplete data

Table G.402. ROBRATE

Robberies (per 100,000 population) 1998

298.7	Maryland
270.3	New York
254.9	Nevada
248.5	Illinois
242.7	Florida
210.6	California
198.0	Louisiana
194.2	Delaware
187.2	Georgia
186.2	New Jersey
178.0	Tennessee
165.2	Arizona
164.9	Pennsylvania
163.4	New Mexico
160.8	North Carolina
155.8	Michigan
154.9	South Carolina
149.2	Missouri
145.1	Texas
133.8	Connecticut
133.5	Ohio
130.9	Alabama
123.3	Mississippi
115.6	Washington
111.2	Indiana
105.6	Virginia
105.2	Oregon
102.7	Hawaii
96.6	Massachusetts
96.2	Arkansas
92.5	Minnesota
92.0	Oklahoma
86.8	Kansas
86.6	Alaska
85.6	Wisconsin
81.5	Colorado
77.6	Nebraska
75.4	Kentucky
66.7	Rhode Island
66.0	Utah
50.9	Iowa
37.3	West Virginia
21.5	New Hampshire
21.5	Idaho
21.1	Maine
20.2	South Dakota
19.9	Montana
16.2	Wyoming
10.2	North Dakota
9.5	Vermont

Table G.403. ROBGUN

Percent of All Robberies with a Gun 1998

58.4	Louisiana
57.3	Mississippi
55.7	Wisconsin
55.4	Tennessee
51.6	Alabama
51.4	Kansas
50.9	Arkansas
50.1	Georgia
48.6	Maryland
48.6	New Mexico
48.4	Indiana
47.3	Virginia
47.0	North Carolina
45.8	Michigan
44.6	Alaska
42.9	South Carolina
42.8	Kentucky
42.7	Nebraska
42.5	Texas
41.9	Missouri
41.4	Oklahoma
41.0	Arizona
40.8	Pennsylvania
39.6	Nevada
39.5	Florida
39.3	Ohio
37.7	Delaware
36.7	Utah
35.6	Connecticut
34.6	California
33.1	Idaho
32.9	Washington
32.6	West Virginia
31.9	Colorado
31.6	Vermont
30.5	Oregon
30.4	New Jersey
27.3	Minnesota
26.7	Wyoming
25.5	Iowa
22.5	North Dakota
22.4	Massachusetts
22.2	South Dakota
20.7	Rhode Island
20.4	New York
17.9	Montana
16.7	New Hampshire
13.8	Maine
11.7	Hawaii
*	Illinois

*Incomplete data

Table G.404. ROBKNIFE

Percent of All Robberies with a Knife 1998

17.8	Massachusetts
13.8	Maine
13.7	Idaho
12.2	Alaska
11.9	Rhode Island
11.6	New Mexico
11.4	Iowa
11.4	New York
11.1	South Dakota
10.3	New Hampshire
10.2	Nevada
10.2	Oregon
10.1	Arizona
10.0	California
9.9	New Jersey
9.8	Connecticut
9.7	South Carolina
9.5	Texas
9.2	Colorado
9.1	West Virginia
9.0	Delaware
8.9	Washington
8.8	Utah
8.7	Minnesota
8.4	Nebraska
8.3	Oklahoma
7.9	Maryland
7.9	North Carolina
7.7	Tennessee
7.7	Alabama
7.1	Wisconsin
7.1	Indiana
7.1	Montana
7.0	Kentucky
6.9	Michigan
6.9	Hawaii
6.8	Florida
6.7	Pennsylvania
6.7	Wyoming
6.4	Missouri
6.0	Virginia
5.9	Arkansas
5.8	Louisiana
5.8	Ohio
5.0	North Dakota
4.7	Georgia
4.5	Kansas
4.1	Mississippi
.0	Vermont
*	Illinois

*Incomplete data

Table G.405. ROBFIST

Percent of Robberies That Were Fist Related 1998

78.2	Hawaii
63.2	New Hampshire
62.5	Maine
59.0	Rhode Island
56.0	Wyoming
53.6	Minnesota
51.8	Oregon
51.1	New Jersey
49.4	Washington
48.9	South Dakota
47.9	Iowa
47.3	West Virginia
47.0	Pennsylvania
46.8	Delaware
45.7	Utah
45.7	Ohio
45.6	California
44.9	Connecticut
43.9	Massachusetts
43.8	Kentucky
43.5	Colorado
43.4	Oklahoma
43.0	Nevada
43.0	Missouri
42.5	Florida
41.1	Nebraska
39.3	Montana
38.6	Alaska
38.3	Arizona
38.1	Indiana
37.9	Texas
36.8	Vermont
36.5	Idaho
35.9	Arkansas
35.3	Maryland
34.7	South Carolina
34.6	North Carolina
34.5	Virginia
34.1	Kansas
33.0	Wisconsin
32.6	Alabama
32.4	New Mexico
31.6	Georgia
30.0	New York
29.5	Mississippi
29.4	Michigan
29.2	Louisiana
27.8	Tennessee
25.0	North Dakota
*	Illinois

*Incomplete data

Table G.406. ASLRATE

Assaults per 100,000 Population 1998

732.0	New Mexico
694.6	South Carolina
639.9	Florida
531.9	Louisiana
516.9	Illinois
498.3	Delaware
495.2	Massachusetts
492.0	Alaska
482.8	Tennessee
456.6	California
454.5	Maryland
407.3	Michigan
396.1	Oklahoma
379.9	North Carolina
373.6	Arizona
372.6	Texas
372.2	Missouri
350.9	Arkansas
347.0	Georgia
345.7	Nebraska
341.3	New York
339.9	Alabama
326.8	Nevada
279.0	Indiana
271.0	Oregon
261.8	Kansas
260.8	Washington
244.4	Colorado
238.6	Mississippi
233.3	Iowa
230.0	New Jersey
226.4	Idaho
223.5	Pennsylvania
207.5	Rhode Island
206.2	Connecticut
203.5	Utah
199.0	Wyoming
188.3	West Virginia
187.2	Virginia
184.5	Ohio
174.7	Kentucky
165.2	Minnesota
139.9	Wisconsin
112.7	Hawaii
97.8	South Dakota
96.9	Montana
84.6	Maine
67.0	Vermont
50.4	New Hampshire
44.8	North Dakota

Table G.407. ASLGUN

Percent of All Assaults That Were Gun Related 1998

36.4	Mississippi
31.2	Wisconsin
29.7	Tennessee
29.7	North Carolina
28.0	Arizona
26.7	New Mexico
26.3	Missouri
25.8	Georgia
25.1	Alabama
25.1	Kansas
24.8	Idaho
24.7	Louisiana
24.6	Michigan
23.8	South Carolina
22.8	Texas
22.2	Arkansas
20.4	Pennsylvania
20.2	Kentucky
20.2	Minnesota
19.9	Alaska
19.8	Montana
19.0	Maryland
18.8	Oklahoma
18.8	Washington
18.4	West Virginia
18.3	Indiana
17.4	Florida
17.4	Ohio
16.8	Utah
16.6	Colorado
16.4	Vermont
15.9	Oregon
15.0	Nevada
14.8	Delaware
14.6	Nebraska
14.5	California
13.9	Rhode Island
13.6	Virginia
13.2	South Dakota
12.7	New Jersey
12.0	Hawaii
11.1	Wyoming
10.4	Connecticut
10.2	New York
10.1	Iowa
7.5	New Hampshire
5.4	Massachusetts
3.1	Maine
1.6	North Dakota
*	Illinois

*Incomplete data

Table G.408. ASLKNIFE

Percent of all Assaults That Were Knife Related 1998

29.7	South Dakota
28.5	Minnesota
25.3	New York
24.3	Alaska
23.5	New Hampshire
22.9	Delaware
22.8	South Carolina
22.8	Maryland
22.7	Texas
22.5	Idaho
21.3	Louisiana
20.9	Tennessee
20.8	Mississippi
20.7	New Jersey
20.4	Vermont
20.2	Michigan
20.0	Utah
19.8	Wyoming
19.7	North Carolina
19.4	Rhode Island
18.9	Washington
18.8	Wisconsin
18.7	Nevada
18.7	Virginia
18.5	Georgia
18.4	Florida
18.2	New Mexico
18.2	Colorado
18.0	Missouri
17.0	Montana
16.9	Alabama
16.9	Kansas
16.6	Ohio
16.3	Oregon
15.9	Arkansas
15.8	Iowa
15.7	Arizona
15.4	Connecticut
15.2	Oklahoma
15.0	Pennsylvania
15.0	West Virginia
13.8	Massachusetts
13.1	North Dakota
13.0	California
12.4	Kentucky
11.9	Indiana
11.9	Nebraska
11.6	Maine
10.9	Hawaii
*	Illinois

*Incomplete data

Table G.409. ASLFIST

Percent of All Assaults That Were Fist Related 1998

58.8	Maine
53.0	Hawaii
47.8	Iowa
45.3	North Dakota
44.4	Nebraska
43.4	West Virginia
41.6	Indiana
41.4	California
41.2	Pennsylvania
40.8	Wyoming
40.5	Montana
40.5	Arkansas
39.7	Kentucky
39.4	Massachusetts
38.9	Virginia
36.9	New Hampshire
36.4	Nevada
36.0	Connecticut
34.7	Ohio
33.7	New Jersey
33.2	Oregon
31.4	Vermont
31.4	Alabama
30.0	Wisconsin
29.4	Oklahoma
28.7	Alaska
28.5	South Dakota
28.3	Washington
28.1	Colorado
26.4	Arizona
25.9	Utah
25.1	Minnesota
23.8	New Mexico
21.5	Louisiana
20.8	Missouri
20.5	Rhode Island
20.3	North Carolina
19.8	South Carolina
18.9	Texas
18.8	Georgia
18.4	Mississippi
18.4	Florida
16.9	New York
16.5	Idaho
15.3	Tennessee
13.5	Maryland
11.4	Delaware
10.4	Michigan
4.9	Kansas
*	Illinois

*Incomplete data

Table G.410. BANKROB

Number of Bank Robberies 1998

1,451	California
631	Florida
418	New York
351	Washington
329	Ohio
289	North Carolina
288	Michigan
255	Illinois
243	Arizona
234	Oregon
230	Pennsylvania
210	Virginia
204	Texas
199	Maryland
158	Georgia
154	Massachusetts
154	Tennessee
136	Colorado
124	New Jersey
124	Wisconsin
118	Nevada
113	Missouri
111	South Carolina
93	Indiana
84	Louisiana
83	Kentucky
81	Nebraska
81	Minnesota
77	Mississippi
75	Alabama
63	Utah
49	Iowa
48	Oklahoma
43	New Mexico
40	Hawaii
35	Connecticut
27	Kansas
26	Arkansas
22	Delaware
19	Rhode Island
14	New Hampshire
9	Idaho
8	West Virginia
7	Alaska
6	Maine
4	Wyoming
4	Vermont
3	North Dakota
2	South Dakota
1	Montana

Table G.411. MARPLANT

Number Marijuana Plants Eradicated 1999

918,212	California
629,312	Hawaii
526,388	Kentucky
518,265	Tennessee
79,403	Arkansas
60,687	Texas
56,838	Florida
48,685	Alabama
44,439	Michigan
42,677	Iowa
42,198	Georgia
40,726	Ohio
36,991	West Virginia
32,083	Missouri
30,196	Minnesota
29,639	North Carolina
28,888	Indiana
27,020	Illinois
22,108	Wisconsin
20,056	Oregon
18,910	Oklahoma
18,261	Alaska
14,904	Virginia
14,767	Kansas
13,152	Washington
12,514	New York
10,129	Utah
9,426	Maine
9,273	Pennsylvania
7,208	Idaho
7,000	Vermont
5,566	Massachusetts
4,785	Colorado
4,764	South Carolina
4,718	Connecticut
3,610	Maryland
3,502	New Jersey
3,329	Arizona
2,773	Louisiana
2,635	Mississippi
1,340	Delaware
1,305	New Hampshire
987	Nevada
727	Nebraska
721	North Dakota
615	Montana
611	Rhode Island
416	New Mexico
255	South Dakota
69	Wyoming

Table G.412. MARBULK

Bulk-Processed Marijuana Seized 1999

42,303	California
11,889	Pennsylvania
5,793	Alabama
4,883	Tennessee
3,511	New Jersey
1,686	Mississippi
1,066	Missouri
1,033	Colorado
1,011	Iowa
994	Arizona
691	New York
657	Florida
629	Kentucky
593	Nevada
429	Indiana
415	Michigan
362	Virginia
315	Minnesota
299	Texas
297	Oregon
292	Wisconsin
179	Ohio
177	Arkansas
156	Illinois
152	Delaware
141	Hawaii
88	Vermont
87	Wyoming
85	Maine
84	Nebraska
80	Kansas
69	West Virginia
69	Oklahoma
52	South Dakota
44	Alaska
30	Maryland
28	Washington
22	Georgia
18	South Carolina
17	Montana
14	Rhode Island
12	Utah
5	Massachusetts
3	Idaho
0	North Carolina
0	Connecticut
0	Louisiana
0	New Hampshire
0	North Dakota
0	New Mexico

Table G.413. MARARRES

Arrests for Marijuana 1999

1,880	New Jersey
1,457	California
1,100	Hawaii
977	Tennessee
822	Missouri
576	Kentucky
466	Florida
413	Arizona
399	Indiana
371	Pennsylvania
274	Colorado
224	Michigan
211	Alaska
210	Virginia
195	Wisconsin
168	New York
161	Maine
151	Oregon
149	Georgia
145	Alabama
143	Maryland
139	West Virginia
119	Washington
117	Illinois
113	Louisiana
112	North Carolina
96	Nevada
86	Vermont
73	Arkansas
71	Ohio
70	Utah
61	Texas
54	Montana
36	Oklahoma
32	Nebraska
31	Iowa
30	Minnesota
30	New Hampshire
25	Mississippi
21	Kansas
20	Idaho
17	Delaware
17	South Carolina
16	Massachusetts
13	North Dakota
10	Connecticut
9	South Dakota
8	Rhode Island
4	Wyoming
0	New Mexico

Table G.414. MARWEAP

Weapons Seized during Marijuana Arrests 1999

931	California
268	Michigan
210	Washington
195	Oregon
184	Pennsylvania
183	Alaska
155	Kentucky
107	Tennessee
102	New Jersey
94	Missouri
94	Minnesota
89	Florida
87	Arizona
86	Maryland
75	Oklahoma
68	Ohio
66	Arkansas
64	New York
63	Hawaii
57	Illinois
51	Colorado
48	Maine
45	Wisconsin
44	Nevada
42	Texas
40	Montana
40	Massachusetts
37	Indiana
33	Alabama
24	Virginia
20	West Virginia
19	Vermont
18	Georgia
17	Utah
10	Kansas
9	New Hampshire
8	Louisiana
6	North Carolina
6	Nebraska
4	Rhode Island
3	Mississippi
3	South Carolina
2	Delaware
0	Iowa
0	Idaho
0	North Dakota
0	Connecticut
0	South Dakota
0	Wyoming
0	New Mexico

Table G.415. PROBRATE

Adults on Probation State and Federal Jurisdiction (per 100,000) 1999

5,368	Georgia
4,073	Idaho
3,705	Washington
3,673	Delaware
3,121	Texas
2,986	Minnesota
2,902	Rhode Island
2,533	Florida
2,399	Indiana
2,341	Michigan
2,320	Vermont
2,224	Connecticut
2,198	Ohio
2,105	Maryland
2,095	New Jersey
1,841	North Carolina
1,828	Oregon
1,753	Hawaii
1,674	Nebraska
1,657	Arizona
1,612	Arkansas
1,534	South Carolina
1,516	Colorado
1,501	Illinois
1,387	Wisconsin
1,372	California
1,335	New York
1,298	Pennsylvania
1,290	Missouri
1,264	Alabama
1,131	Oklahoma
1,104	Louisiana
1,089	Wyoming
1,069	Alaska
983	Massachusetts
967	Tennessee
915	Iowa
909	Kansas
907	New Mexico
896	Montana
894	Nevada
782	Maine
663	Utah
647	South Dakota
634	Kentucky
618	Mississippi
616	Virginia
576	North Dakota
427	West Virginia
*	New Hampshire

*Incomplete data

Table G.416. PRISENT

Prisoners (per 100,000 population) State and Federal Authorities 1999

715	Texas
672	Louisiana
617	Oklahoma
536	South Carolina
526	Nevada
500	Alabama
499	Mississippi
484	Arizona
473	Georgia
470	California
457	Michigan
443	Delaware
443	Missouri
437	Florida
429	Ohio
420	Alaska
413	Maryland
407	Virginia
392	Arkansas
381	New York
372	Kentucky
368	North Carolina
364	Connecticut
351	New Jersey
342	Colorado
342	Illinois
323	Wyoming
320	Idaho
309	Tennessee
304	Kansas
304	South Dakota
302	Wisconsin
301	Indiana
291	Pennsylvania
290	Hawaii
286	Montana
256	New Mexico
243	Iowa
234	Washington
232	Oregon
213	Rhode Island
206	Utah
200	Nebraska
184	New Hampshire
177	Massachusetts
174	West Virginia
140	Vermont
124	Maine
113	Minnesota
112	North Dakota

Table G.417. TREATFAC

Number Drug and Alcohol Treatment Facilities 1997

1,184	New York
1,179	California
597	Michigan
526	Florida
504	Texas
484	Ohio
475	Pennsylvania
468	Illinois
310	Massachusetts
304	Maryland
298	Washington
269	Wisconsin
251	Indiana
239	Minnesota
237	New Jersey
231	Kentucky
209	Connecticut
160	Oregon
153	Virginia
152	Georgia
145	Kansas
143	Arizona
143	Colorado
142	Missouri
139	North Carolina
138	Louisiana
132	Tennessee
132	Maine
112	Utah
108	Oklahoma
97	Nebraska
81	West Virginia
78	Iowa
77	Alabama
72	New Mexico
71	Nevada
71	Mississippi
69	Hawaii
64	South Carolina
60	Alaska
59	Rhode Island
55	Arkansas
54	New Hampshire
51	South Dakota
47	Wyoming
45	Montana
41	Delaware
40	North Dakota
39	Idaho
20	Vermont

Table G.418. CLIENTS

Number Clients in Treatment for Drug or Alcohol Abuse 1997

88,876	California
49,788	Michigan
41,663	Florida
40,693	Texas
40,401	Ohio
39,040	Illinois
36,382	Pennsylvania
33,219	Massachusetts
31,260	Washington
27,272	New York
23,794	Maryland
22,627	Oregon
21,039	Virginia
20,594	New Jersey
18,458	Indiana
17,379	North Carolina
16,535	Wisconsin
16,118	Georgia
15,592	Connecticut
13,621	Utah
13,530	Colorado
13,166	Tennessee
12,307	Arizona
12,185	Louisiana
12,119	Kentucky
11,090	Missouri
10,862	South Carolina
10,664	Alabama
8,288	Kansas
8,188	Maine
7,593	Minnesota
7,572	Oklahoma
6,452	New Mexico
5,373	Iowa
5,334	Mississippi
5,279	Nevada
5,261	Alaska
5,084	Rhode Island
4,704	West Virginia
4,197	Nebraska
4,129	Arkansas
3,567	Delaware
2,507	New Hampshire
2,464	Idaho
2,298	Montana
2,177	Hawaii
2,091	Wyoming
2,086	North Dakota
1,880	South Dakota
1,638	Vermont

Table G.419. PCLIENTS

Percent of State Population in Treatment for Drugs or Alcohol Abuse 1997

.85	Alaska
.68	Oregon
.65	Maine
.64	Utah
.54	Washington
.54	Massachusetts
.51	Rhode Island
.50	Michigan
.48	Connecticut
.47	Delaware
.46	Maryland
.44	Wyoming
.37	New Mexico
.36	Ohio
.33	Colorado
.33	North Dakota
.32	Illinois
.31	Wisconsin
.31	Kansas
.31	Indiana
.31	Virginia
.31	Kentucky
.30	Pennsylvania
.29	Nevada
.28	South Carolina
.28	Louisiana
.28	Vermont
.28	Florida
.27	California
.26	West Virginia
.26	Montana
.26	Arizona
.26	South Dakota
.25	New Jersey
.25	Nebraska
.24	Alabama
.24	Tennessee
.23	North Carolina
.23	Oklahoma
.21	New Hampshire
.21	Georgia
.20	Texas
.20	Missouri
.20	Idaho
.19	Mississippi
.19	Iowa
.18	Hawaii
.16	Arkansas
.16	Minnesota
.15	New York

Table G.420. PCALCABU

Percent of Clients in Treatment for Alcohol Abuse 1997

59.5	West Virginia
48.5	South Dakota
47.4	North Dakota
46.0	Wyoming
45.6	Wisconsin
44.2	New Mexico
43.1	Alaska
42.9	Vermont
40.6	South Carolina
40.4	New Hampshire
38.5	Kentucky
38.4	Nebraska
35.8	Colorado
35.8	Iowa
35.5	Minnesota
35.4	Indiana
35.2	Michigan
34.9	Oklahoma
33.5	Maine
33.1	Kansas
32.2	North Carolina
30.6	Washington
30.4	Utah
29.8	Oregon
29.6	Montana
28.7	Ohio
28.2	Texas
27.6	Arizona
27.1	Massachusetts
27.0	Nevada
26.8	Mississippi
26.2	Illinois
25.6	Virginia
25.5	Rhode Island
24.4	Georgia
23.2	Alabama
23.1	Missouri
23.0	Hawaii
22.7	Tennessee
22.5	Pennsylvania
21.9	New York
21.5	Arkansas
20.3	Maryland
20.2	Florida
19.3	Delaware
19.0	Louisiana
17.1	New Jersey
15.7	Connecticut
15.7	Idaho
14.4	California

Table G.421. PCDRUGAB

Percent of Clients in Treatment for Drug Abuse 1997

54.5	Alabama
50.5	New York
46.2	Connecticut
44.6	California
40.9	Nevada
38.5	Arkansas
38.5	New Jersey
37.6	Rhode Island
37.5	Arizona
37.3	Maryland
36.0	Hawaii
35.3	Texas
33.4	Florida
31.9	Oklahoma
31.8	Colorado
30.9	Tennessee
30.8	Massachusetts
30.3	Georgia
29.5	Louisiana
28.4	Michigan
28.1	Pennsylvania
27.8	Kentucky
27.8	Illinois
27.2	Utah
26.1	Mississippi
24.7	Missouri
23.5	Indiana
23.1	South Carolina
22.9	Virginia
22.8	Oregon
21.0	Montana
19.8	Kansas
19.7	North Carolina
19.7	Ohio
18.5	New Hampshire
18.3	Maine
17.5	New Mexico
17.5	Delaware
17.0	Alaska
16.8	Minnesota
16.2	Iowa
16.1	Wisconsin
15.9	West Virginia
14.6	Idaho
14.0	Washington
13.6	Wyoming
13.1	Vermont
12.2	South Dakota
11.6	North Dakota
10.6	Nebraska

Table G.422. PCDRUALC

Percent of Clients in Treatment for Drug and Alcohol Abuse 1997

69.7	Idaho
63.2	Delaware
55.3	Washington
52.2	Missouri
51.6	Ohio
51.5	Louisiana
51.5	Virginia
51.0	Nebraska
49.4	Pennsylvania
49.4	Montana
48.2	Maine
48.1	North Carolina
48.0	Iowa
47.7	Minnesota
47.4	Oregon
47.2	Mississippi
47.1	Kansas
46.5	Florida
46.4	Tennessee
46.0	Illinois
45.3	Georgia
44.4	New Jersey
44.0	Vermont
42.4	Utah
42.1	Massachusetts
41.2	Indiana
41.0	California
41.0	Hawaii
41.0	New Hampshire
41.0	North Dakota
40.4	Wyoming
40.0	Arkansas
39.9	Alaska
39.3	South Dakota
38.3	New Mexico
38.3	Wisconsin
38.2	Connecticut
36.9	Rhode Island
36.5	Texas
36.4	Michigan
36.3	South Carolina
34.9	Arizona
33.8	Kentucky
33.2	Oklahoma
32.4	Maryland
32.4	Colorado
32.1	Nevada
27.6	New York
24.6	West Virginia
22.4	Alabama

Table G.423. ONPAROLE

Number of Adults on Parole State and Federal Jurisdiction 1999

114,046	California
109,310	Texas
83,702	Pennsylvania
57,956	New York
30,484	Illinois
22,003	Georgia
21,904	Louisiana
17,874	Oregon
15,776	Ohio
15,541	Michigan
15,007	Maryland
12,968	New Jersey
11,448	Missouri
8,530	Wisconsin
7,645	Arkansas
7,338	Tennessee
6,418	Florida
5,909	Kansas
5,860	Virginia
5,263	Colorado
5,005	Alabama
4,868	Kentucky
4,539	Indiana
4,389	North Carolina
4,304	Massachusetts
3,944	South Carolina
3,893	Nevada
3,715	Arizona
3,388	Utah
3,151	Minnesota
2,514	Iowa
2,252	Hawaii
1,922	New Mexico
1,527	Oklahoma
1,526	Connecticut
1,360	South Dakota
1,356	Mississippi
1,310	Idaho
1,158	West Virginia
1,146	New Hampshire
794	Vermont
634	Delaware
612	Nebraska
549	Montana
493	Alaska
458	Wyoming
413	Rhode Island
200	Washington
157	North Dakota
31	Maine

Table G.424. PCPAROLE

Percent of State Population on Parole
1999

.70	Pennsylvania
.55	Texas
.54	Oregon
.50	Louisiana
.34	California
.32	New York
.30	Arkansas
.29	Maryland
.28	Georgia
.25	Illinois
.22	Kansas
.22	Nevada
.21	Missouri
.19	Hawaii
.19	South Dakota
.16	Wisconsin
.16	New Jersey
.16	Utah
.16	Michigan
.14	Ohio
.13	Tennessee
.13	Vermont
.13	Colorado
.12	Kentucky
.11	Alabama
.11	New Mexico
.10	Idaho
.10	South Carolina
.10	Wyoming
.10	New Hampshire
.09	Iowa
.09	Virginia
.08	Delaware
.08	Alaska
.08	Arizona
.08	Indiana
.07	Massachusetts
.07	Minnesota
.06	West Virginia
.06	Montana
.06	North Carolina
.05	Mississippi
.05	Connecticut
.05	Oklahoma
.04	Florida
.04	Rhode Island
.04	Nebraska
.02	North Dakota
.00	Washington
.00	Maine

Table G.425. POPEST89

Resident Population (in thousands)
1989

29,063	California
17,950	New York
16,991	Texas
12,671	Florida
12,040	Pennsylvania
11,658	Illinois
10,907	Ohio
9,273	Michigan
7,736	New Jersey
6,571	North Carolina
6,436	Georgia
6,098	Virginia
5,913	Massachusetts
5,593	Indiana
5,159	Missouri
4,940	Tennessee
4,867	Wisconsin
4,761	Washington
4,694	Maryland
4,382	Louisiana
4,353	Minnesota
4,118	Alabama
3,727	Kentucky
3,556	Arizona
3,512	South Carolina
3,317	Colorado
3,239	Connecticut
3,224	Oklahoma
2,840	Iowa
2,820	Oregon
2,621	Mississippi
2,513	Kansas
2,406	Arkansas
1,857	West Virginia
1,707	Utah
1,611	Nebraska
1,528	New Mexico
1,222	Maine
1,112	Hawaii
1,111	Nevada
1,107	New Hampshire
1,014	Idaho
998	Rhode Island
806	Montana
715	South Dakota
673	Delaware
660	North Dakota
567	Vermont
527	Alaska
475	Wyoming

Table G.426. POPEST90

Resident Population (in thousands)
1990

29,811	California
17,991	New York
16,986	Texas
12,938	Florida
11,883	Pennsylvania
11,431	Illinois
10,847	Ohio
9,295	Michigan
7,748	New Jersey
6,632	North Carolina
6,478	Georgia
6,189	Virginia
6,016	Massachusetts
5,544	Indiana
5,117	Missouri
4,877	Tennessee
4,867	Washington
4,781	Maryland
4,692	Wisconsin
4,376	Minnesota
4,222	Louisiana
4,040	Alabama
3,687	Kentucky
3,665	Arizona
3,486	South Carolina
3,294	Colorado
3,287	Connecticut
3,146	Oklahoma
2,842	Oregon
2,777	Iowa
2,575	Mississippi
2,478	Kansas
2,351	Arkansas
1,793	West Virginia
1,723	Utah
1,578	Nebraska
1,515	New Mexico
1,228	Maine
1,202	Nevada
1,109	New Hampshire
1,108	Hawaii
1,007	Idaho
1,003	Rhode Island
799	Montana
696	South Dakota
666	Delaware
639	North Dakota
563	Vermont
550	Alaska
454	Wyoming

Table G.427. POPEST91

Resident Population (in thousands)
1991

30,414	California
18,030	New York
17,340	Texas
13,289	Florida
11,943	Pennsylvania
11,536	Illinois
10,934	Ohio
9,395	Michigan
7,784	New Jersey
6,748	North Carolina
6,621	Georgia
6,284	Virginia
5,999	Massachusetts
5,602	Indiana
5,158	Missouri
5,013	Washington
4,953	Wisconsin
4,947	Tennessee
4,856	Maryland
4,427	Minnesota
4,241	Louisiana
4,091	Alabama
3,762	Arizona
3,715	Kentucky
3,559	South Carolina
3,368	Colorado
3,289	Connecticut
3,166	Oklahoma
2,919	Oregon
2,791	Iowa
2,591	Mississippi
2,495	Kansas
2,371	Arkansas
1,798	West Virginia
1,772	Utah
1,591	Nebraska
1,547	New Mexico
1,285	Nevada
1,235	Maine
1,131	Hawaii
1,107	New Hampshire
1,039	Idaho
1,004	Rhode Island
808	Montana
701	South Dakota
680	Delaware
634	North Dakota
569	Alaska
567	Vermont
458	Wyoming

Table G.428. POPEST92

Resident Population (in thousands)
1992

30,876	California
18,082	New York
17,650	Texas
13,505	Florida
11,981	Pennsylvania
11,635	Illinois
11,008	Ohio
9,470	Michigan
7,828	New Jersey
6,832	North Carolina
6,759	Georgia
6,383	Virginia
5,993	Massachusetts
5,649	Indiana
5,194	Missouri
5,139	Washington
5,014	Tennessee
5,005	Wisconsin
4,903	Maryland
4,472	Minnesota
4,271	Louisiana
4,139	Alabama
3,867	Arizona
3,756	Kentucky
3,601	South Carolina
3,460	Colorado
3,275	Connecticut
3,204	Oklahoma
2,974	Oregon
2,807	Iowa
2,610	Mississippi
2,526	Kansas
2,394	Arkansas
1,821	Utah
1,805	West Virginia
1,602	Nebraska
1,581	New Mexico
1,331	Nevada
1,236	Maine
1,150	Hawaii
1,113	New Hampshire
1,066	Idaho
1,001	Rhode Island
822	Montana
709	South Dakota
690	Delaware
635	North Dakota
587	Alaska
570	Vermont
463	Wyoming

Table G.429. POPEST93

Resident Population (in thousands)
1993

31,147	California
18,141	New York
17,997	Texas
13,714	Florida
12,022	Pennsylvania
11,726	Illinois
11,070	Ohio
9,529	Michigan
7,875	New Jersey
6,947	North Carolina
6,894	Georgia
6,465	Virginia
6,011	Massachusetts
5,702	Indiana
5,248	Washington
5,238	Missouri
5,086	Tennessee
5,055	Wisconsin
4,943	Maryland
4,522	Minnesota
4,285	Louisiana
4,193	Alabama
3,993	Arizona
3,792	Kentucky
3,635	South Carolina
3,561	Colorado
3,272	Connecticut
3,229	Oklahoma
3,034	Oregon
2,821	Iowa
2,636	Mississippi
2,546	Kansas
2,424	Arkansas
1,876	Utah
1,816	West Virginia
1,615	New Mexico
1,612	Nebraska
1,380	Nevada
1,238	Maine
1,162	Hawaii
1,122	New Hampshire
1,101	Idaho
998	Rhode Island
840	Montana
716	South Dakota
699	Delaware
637	North Dakota
597	Alaska
574	Vermont
469	Wyoming

Table G.430. POPEST94

Resident Population (in thousands)
1994

31,317	California
18,338	Texas
18,157	New York
13,962	Florida
12,043	Pennsylvania
11,805	Illinois
11,111	Ohio
9,584	Michigan
7,919	New Jersey
7,061	North Carolina
7,046	Georgia
6,537	Virginia
6,031	Massachusetts
5,746	Indiana
5,335	Washington
5,281	Missouri
5,163	Tennessee
5,096	Wisconsin
4,985	Maryland
4,566	Minnesota
4,307	Louisiana
4,233	Alabama
4,148	Arizona
3,823	Kentucky
3,666	South Carolina
3,654	Colorado
3,268	Connecticut
3,246	Oklahoma
3,087	Oregon
2,829	Iowa
2,663	Mississippi
2,569	Kansas
2,451	Arkansas
1,930	Utah
1,818	West Virginia
1,653	New Mexico
1,622	Nebraska
1,456	Nevada
1,238	Maine
1,174	Hawaii
1,135	Idaho
1,133	New Hampshire
993	Rhode Island
855	Montana
723	South Dakota
708	Delaware
640	North Dakota
601	Alaska
579	Vermont
475	Wyoming

Table G.431. POPEST95

Resident Population (in thousands)
1995

31,494	California
18,680	Texas
18,151	New York
14,185	Florida
12,045	Pennsylvania
11,885	Illinois
11,155	Ohio
9,660	Michigan
7,966	New Jersey
7,189	Georgia
7,185	North Carolina
6,601	Virginia
6,062	Massachusetts
5,792	Indiana
5,431	Washington
5,325	Missouri
5,241	Tennessee
5,137	Wisconsin
5,024	Maryland
4,605	Minnesota
4,328	Louisiana
4,307	Arizona
4,263	Alabama
3,855	Kentucky
3,738	Colorado
3,700	South Carolina
3,266	Oklahoma
3,265	Connecticut
3,141	Oregon
2,841	Iowa
2,691	Mississippi
2,587	Kansas
2,480	Arkansas
1,977	Utah
1,821	West Virginia
1,682	New Mexico
1,635	Nebraska
1,526	Nevada
1,237	Maine
1,180	Hawaii
1,165	Idaho
1,146	New Hampshire
989	Rhode Island
869	Montana
728	South Dakota
718	Delaware
642	North Dakota
601	Alaska
583	Vermont
478	Wyoming

Table G.432. POPEST96

Resident Population (in thousands)
1996

31,781	California
19,006	Texas
18,144	New York
14,427	Florida
12,038	Pennsylvania
11,953	Illinois
11,187	Ohio
9,739	Michigan
8,010	New Jersey
7,332	Georgia
7,308	North Carolina
6,665	Virginia
6,085	Massachusetts
5,835	Indiana
5,510	Washington
5,368	Missouri
5,314	Tennessee
5,174	Wisconsin
5,057	Maryland
4,648	Minnesota
4,432	Arizona
4,339	Louisiana
4,290	Alabama
3,881	Kentucky
3,813	Colorado
3,739	South Carolina
3,290	Oklahoma
3,267	Connecticut
3,195	Oregon
2,848	Iowa
2,710	Mississippi
2,598	Kansas
2,505	Arkansas
2,022	Utah
1,819	West Virginia
1,706	New Mexico
1,648	Nebraska
1,596	Nevada
1,241	Maine
1,188	Idaho
1,184	Hawaii
1,161	New Hampshire
988	Rhode Island
877	Montana
731	South Dakota
727	Delaware
643	North Dakota
605	Alaska
586	Vermont
480	Wyoming

Table G.433.   POPEST97

Resident Population (in thousands)
1997

32,218	California
19,355	Texas
18,143	New York
14,683	Florida
12,016	Pennsylvania
12,012	Illinois
11,212	Ohio
9,785	Michigan
8,054	New Jersey
7,486	Georgia
7,429	North Carolina
6,733	Virginia
6,115	Massachusetts
5,872	Indiana
5,604	Washington
5,407	Missouri
5,378	Tennessee
5,200	Wisconsin
5,093	Maryland
4,688	Minnesota
4,552	Arizona
4,351	Louisiana
4,320	Alabama
3,908	Kentucky
3,891	Colorado
3,790	South Carolina
3,314	Oklahoma
3,269	Connecticut
3,243	Oregon
2,854	Iowa
2,732	Mississippi
2,616	Kansas
2,524	Arkansas
2,065	Utah
1,816	West Virginia
1,723	New Mexico
1,676	Nevada
1,656	Nebraska
1,245	Maine
1,211	Idaho
1,189	Hawaii
1,173	New Hampshire
987	Rhode Island
879	Montana
735	Delaware
731	South Dakota
641	North Dakota
609	Alaska
589	Vermont
480	Wyoming

Table G.434.   POPEST98

Resident Population (in thousands)
1998 (1999 figures in G.28)

32,683	California
19,712	Texas
18,159	New York
14,908	Florida
12,070	Illinois
12,002	Pennsylvania
11,238	Ohio
9,820	Michigan
8,096	New Jersey
7,637	Georgia
7,546	North Carolina
6,789	Virginia
6,144	Massachusetts
5,908	Indiana
5,688	Washington
5,438	Missouri
5,433	Tennessee
5,222	Wisconsin
5,130	Maryland
4,726	Minnesota
4,667	Arizona
4,363	Louisiana
4,351	Alabama
3,969	Colorado
3,934	Kentucky
3,840	South Carolina
3,339	Oklahoma
3,282	Oregon
3,273	Connecticut
2,861	Iowa
2,751	Mississippi
2,639	Kansas
2,538	Arkansas
2,101	Utah
1,812	West Virginia
1,744	Nevada
1,734	New Mexico
1,661	Nebraska
1,248	Maine
1,231	Idaho
1,190	Hawaii
1,186	New Hampshire
988	Rhode Island
880	Montana
744	Delaware
731	South Dakota
638	North Dakota
615	Alaska
591	Vermont
480	Wyoming

Table G.435.   POPEST00

Resident Population (in thousands)
2000

33,872	California
20,852	Texas
18,976	New York
15,982	Florida
12,419	Illinois
12,281	Pennsylvania
11,353	Ohio
9,938	Michigan
8,414	New Jersey
8,186	Georgia
8,049	North Carolina
7,079	Virginia
6,349	Massachusetts
6,080	Indiana
5,894	Washington
5,689	Tennessee
5,595	Missouri
5,364	Wisconsin
5,296	Maryland
5,131	Arizona
4,919	Minnesota
4,469	Louisiana
4,447	Alabama
4,301	Colorado
4,042	Kentucky
4,012	South Carolina
3,451	Oklahoma
3,421	Oregon
3,406	Connecticut
2,926	Iowa
2,845	Mississippi
2,688	Kansas
2,673	Arkansas
2,233	Utah
1,988	Nevada
1,819	New Mexico
1,808	West Virginia
1,711	Nebraska
1,294	Idaho
1,275	Maine
1,236	New Hampshire
1,212	Hawaii
1,048	Rhode Island
902	Montana
784	Delaware
755	South Dakota
642	North Dakota
627	Alaska
609	Vermont
493	Wyoming

Table G.436. EXPSTA89

State Funds, Total Expenditures (in millions) 1989

43,962	California
34,336	New York
17,229	Florida
15,514	Pennsylvania
15,505	Illinois
15,464	Ohio
14,203	Texas
13,971	Massachusetts
13,017	New Jersey
12,155	Michigan
9,538	Virginia
8,478	Maryland
8,368	Washington
8,323	North Carolina
8,187	Wisconsin
7,566	Minnesota
7,464	Georgia
7,412	Connecticut
6,262	Indiana
5,884	Louisiana
5,859	Missouri
5,814	Oregon
5,493	Kentucky
5,347	Iowa
5,236	South Carolina
4,792	Tennessee
4,129	Oklahoma
4,053	Arizona
3,804	Colorado
3,588	Alabama
3,256	Hawaii
3,082	Arkansas
3,028	Kansas
2,880	Alaska
2,708	Mississippi
2,481	West Virginia
2,395	New Mexico
2,210	Utah
1,876	Nebraska
1,815	Maine
1,781	Delaware
1,675	Rhode Island
1,353	Montana
1,266	Nevada
1,163	New Hampshire
1,136	North Dakota
1,024	Idaho
938	Wyoming
828	Vermont
793	South Dakota

Table G.437. EXPFED89

Federal Funds, Total Expenditures (in millions) 1989

17,280	California
9,114	New York
4,986	Pennsylvania
4,324	Texas
4,126	Ohio
4,027	Florida
3,826	Michigan
3,368	Alabama
3,105	Illinois
2,881	New Jersey
2,667	Massachusetts
2,611	Louisiana
2,499	Georgia
2,320	North Carolina
2,058	Wisconsin
1,971	Tennessee
1,963	Indiana
1,856	Virginia
1,853	Minnesota
1,842	Washington
1,763	Maryland
1,701	Kentucky
1,694	South Carolina
1,485	Oklahoma
1,426	Missouri
1,397	Mississippi
1,338	Iowa
1,314	Colorado
1,257	Kansas
1,227	Arizona
1,082	Connecticut
1,044	Arkansas
857	West Virginia
845	Oregon
677	Maine
638	New Mexico
631	Utah
539	Nebraska
525	Idaho
447	Montana
416	Rhode Island
393	Hawaii
390	North Dakota
384	South Dakota
322	New Hampshire
320	Vermont
315	Alaska
307	Nevada
266	Wyoming
244	Delaware

Table G.438. EXPTOT89

All Funds, Total Expenditures (in millions) 1989

61,242	California
43,450	New York
21,256	Florida
20,500	Pennsylvania
19,589	Ohio
18,610	Illinois
18,527	Texas
16,637	Massachusetts
15,981	Michigan
15,898	New Jersey
11,393	Virginia
10,643	North Carolina
10,244	Wisconsin
10,241	Maryland
10,209	Washington
9,962	Georgia
9,419	Minnesota
8,495	Louisiana
8,494	Connecticut
8,225	Indiana
7,285	Missouri
7,193	Kentucky
6,955	Alabama
6,930	South Carolina
6,763	Tennessee
6,684	Iowa
6,659	Oregon
5,614	Oklahoma
5,280	Arizona
5,118	Colorado
4,285	Kansas
4,125	Arkansas
4,105	Mississippi
3,649	Hawaii
3,338	West Virginia
3,195	Alaska
3,033	New Mexico
2,840	Utah
2,492	Maine
2,415	Nebraska
2,091	Rhode Island
2,025	Delaware
1,800	Montana
1,573	Nevada
1,549	Idaho
1,526	North Dakota
1,484	New Hampshire
1,205	Wyoming
1,177	South Dakota
1,148	Vermont

Table G.439. EXPSTA90

State Funds, Total Expenditures (in millions) 1990

47,322	California
35,508	New York
18,544	Florida
17,830	Texas
16,299	Pennsylvania
15,464	Ohio
15,342	Illinois
13,452	Michigan
12,986	New Jersey
12,911	Massachusetts
10,341	Virginia
9,242	North Carolina
9,171	Georgia
8,909	Maryland
8,872	Washington
8,551	Wisconsin
7,908	Minnesota
7,446	Connecticut
6,599	Indiana
6,378	Missouri
5,944	Oregon
5,821	Louisiana
5,711	Kentucky
5,580	Iowa
5,517	South Carolina
5,137	Tennessee
4,593	Oklahoma
4,156	Arizona
3,922	Colorado
3,839	Kansas
3,654	Alabama
3,450	Hawaii
3,367	Arkansas
2,965	New Mexico
2,838	Alaska
2,769	Mississippi
2,641	West Virginia
2,425	Utah
2,149	Nebraska
1,953	Maine
1,797	Delaware
1,684	Rhode Island
1,558	Nevada
1,276	Idaho
1,267	Montana
1,127	North Dakota
1,085	Wyoming
993	New Hampshire
858	Vermont
720	South Dakota

Table G.440. EXPFED90

Federal Funds, Total Expenditures (in millions) 1990

18,659	California
9,815	New York
5,655	Texas
5,108	Pennsylvania
4,791	Ohio
4,028	Michigan
3,937	Florida
3,721	Alabama
3,088	Massachusetts
3,016	New Jersey
2,958	Illinois
2,523	North Carolina
2,468	Wisconsin
2,432	Georgia
2,397	Louisiana
2,211	Tennessee
2,198	Indiana
2,160	Washington
2,071	South Carolina
1,879	Minnesota
1,876	Maryland
1,838	Kentucky
1,813	Virginia
1,648	Arizona
1,622	Missouri
1,421	Iowa
1,370	Colorado
1,327	Oklahoma
1,313	Mississippi
1,246	Connecticut
1,177	Arkansas
1,043	Oregon
920	West Virginia
893	Kansas
888	Alaska
805	New Mexico
715	Utah
642	Maine
592	Nebraska
539	Idaho
508	Hawaii
480	Rhode Island
446	Montana
442	South Dakota
389	North Dakota
369	Nevada
345	New Hampshire
320	Vermont
274	Wyoming
258	Delaware

Table G.441. EXPTOT90

All Funds, Total Expenditures (in millions) 1990

65,981	California
45,323	New York
23,485	Texas
22,481	Florida
21,407	Pennsylvania
20,255	Ohio
18,300	Illinois
17,480	Michigan
16,002	New Jersey
15,999	Massachusetts
12,154	Virginia
11,765	North Carolina
11,603	Georgia
11,032	Washington
11,019	Wisconsin
10,785	Maryland
9,787	Minnesota
8,797	Indiana
8,692	Connecticut
8,218	Louisiana
8,000	Missouri
7,588	South Carolina
7,549	Kentucky
7,375	Alabama
7,348	Tennessee
7,001	Iowa
6,987	Oregon
5,920	Oklahoma
5,804	Arizona
5,292	Colorado
4,732	Kansas
4,544	Arkansas
4,082	Mississippi
3,958	Hawaii
3,770	New Mexico
3,726	Alaska
3,561	West Virginia
3,140	Utah
2,741	Nebraska
2,595	Maine
2,164	Rhode Island
2,055	Delaware
1,927	Nevada
1,815	Idaho
1,713	Montana
1,516	North Dakota
1,359	Wyoming
1,338	New Hampshire
1,178	Vermont
1,162	South Dakota

Table G.442. EXPSTA91

State Funds, Total Expenditures (in millions) 1991

48,901	California
35,670	New York
21,887	Florida
20,200	Texas
17,371	Pennsylvania
17,331	Ohio
16,356	Illinois
15,322	Massachusetts
14,177	New Jersey
13,337	Michigan
10,927	Virginia
10,750	Washington
9,868	North Carolina
9,398	Georgia
9,315	Maryland
8,993	Minnesota
7,685	Oregon
7,115	Indiana
6,837	Connecticut
6,793	Louisiana
6,607	Kentucky
6,215	Missouri
5,774	Iowa
5,613	South Carolina
5,385	Tennessee
5,151	Wisconsin
5,022	Oklahoma
4,801	Arizona
4,062	Kansas
4,045	Colorado
3,881	Alabama
3,787	Hawaii
3,688	Arkansas
3,133	Mississippi
3,089	Alaska
2,985	New Mexico
2,836	West Virginia
2,660	Utah
2,432	Nebraska
1,961	Maine
1,840	Nevada
1,789	Delaware
1,655	Rhode Island
1,637	Montana
1,369	Idaho
1,128	North Dakota
1,092	Wyoming
1,087	New Hampshire
910	Vermont
777	South Dakota

Table G.443. EXPFED91

Federal Funds, Total Expenditures (in millions 1991

21,484	California
11,458	New York
6,550	Texas
6,053	Pennsylvania
5,373	Ohio
4,783	Michigan
4,717	Florida
4,501	Alabama
4,015	Massachusetts
3,353	Illinois
3,257	New Jersey
3,180	Louisiana
2,964	Georgia
2,930	North Carolina
2,779	Wisconsin
2,583	Indiana
2,459	Washington
2,452	Tennessee
2,250	South Carolina
2,128	Kentucky
2,086	Virginia
2,022	Minnesota
1,989	Maryland
1,924	Missouri
1,897	Arizona
1,590	Iowa
1,590	Oklahoma
1,584	Mississippi
1,421	Connecticut
1,332	Colorado
1,331	Arkansas
1,082	Oregon
1,049	West Virginia
990	Kansas
871	New Mexico
731	Utah
727	Maine
686	Nebraska
681	Alaska
606	Hawaii
603	Idaho
534	Rhode Island
518	Montana
472	New Hampshire
471	South Dakota
442	North Dakota
431	Nevada
380	Vermont
357	Delaware
334	Wyoming

Table G.444. EXPTOT91

All Funds, Total Expenditures (in millions) 1991

70,385	California
47,128	New York
26,750	Texas
26,604	Florida
23,424	Pennsylvania
22,704	Ohio
19,709	Illinois
19,337	Massachusetts
18,120	Michigan
17,434	New Jersey
13,209	Washington
13,013	Virginia
12,798	North Carolina
12,362	Georgia
11,304	Maryland
11,015	Minnesota
9,973	Louisiana
9,698	Indiana
8,767	Oregon
8,735	Kentucky
8,382	Alabama
8,258	Connecticut
8,139	Missouri
7,930	Wisconsin
7,863	South Carolina
7,837	Tennessee
7,364	Iowa
6,698	Arizona
6,612	Oklahoma
5,377	Colorado
5,052	Kansas
5,019	Arkansas
4,717	Mississippi
4,393	Hawaii
3,885	West Virginia
3,856	New Mexico
3,770	Alaska
3,391	Utah
3,118	Nebraska
2,688	Maine
2,271	Nevada
2,189	Rhode Island
2,155	Montana
2,146	Delaware
1,972	Idaho
1,570	North Dakota
1,559	New Hampshire
1,426	Wyoming
1,290	Vermont
1,248	South Dakota

Table G.445. EXPSTA92

State Funds, Total Expenditures (in millions) 1992

54,520	California
37,047	New York
23,195	Florida
21,292	Texas
19,611	Pennsylvania
18,005	Ohio
17,487	New Jersey
17,044	Illinois
14,344	Michigan
12,194	Wisconsin
11,650	Massachusetts
11,429	Washington
11,117	Virginia
10,140	North Carolina
9,271	Georgia
9,025	Minnesota
8,991	Maryland
7,541	Louisiana
7,359	Kentucky
7,326	Oregon
7,129	Connecticut
6,994	Indiana
6,541	Missouri
6,019	Iowa
5,766	South Carolina
5,510	Tennessee
5,377	Arizona
5,205	Oklahoma
4,476	Colorado
4,160	Arkansas
4,070	Kansas
4,008	Alabama
3,956	Hawaii
3,730	Alaska
3,235	New Mexico
3,115	Mississippi
3,057	West Virginia
2,810	Utah
2,642	Nebraska
2,510	Maine
2,132	Nevada
2,029	Rhode Island
2,003	Delaware
1,507	Montana
1,470	Idaho
1,458	Wyoming
1,286	New Hampshire
1,059	North Dakota
939	Vermont
876	South Dakota

Table G.446. EXPFED92

Federal Funds, Total Expenditures (in millions) 1992

26,722	California
13,584	New York
7,654	Texas
6,983	Pennsylvania
5,728	Florida
5,474	Alabama
5,426	Ohio
5,331	Michigan
4,561	Illinois
4,165	New Jersey
3,693	Georgia
3,644	Louisiana
3,501	North Carolina
3,128	Tennessee
3,107	Wisconsin
3,079	Indiana
3,020	Massachusetts
2,811	Washington
2,636	South Carolina
2,554	Kentucky
2,379	Missouri
2,302	Maryland
2,256	Virginia
2,249	Minnesota
2,215	Arizona
2,002	Mississippi
1,800	Oklahoma
1,620	Arkansas
1,604	Colorado
1,582	Iowa
1,437	West Virginia
1,403	Oregon
1,397	Kansas
1,350	Connecticut
1,063	Maine
1,024	New Mexico
855	Utah
807	Nebraska
762	Alaska
704	Rhode Island
690	Hawaii
664	Idaho
654	New Hampshire
581	Montana
533	South Dakota
501	North Dakota
493	Nevada
426	Vermont
384	Wyoming
343	Delaware

Table G.447. EXPTOT92

All Funds, Total Expenditures (in millions) 1992

81,242	California
50,631	New York
28,946	Texas
28,923	Florida
26,594	Pennsylvania
23,431	Ohio
21,652	New Jersey
21,605	Illinois
19,675	Michigan
15,301	Wisconsin
14,670	Massachusetts
14,240	Washington
13,641	North Carolina
13,373	Virginia
12,964	Georgia
11,293	Maryland
11,274	Minnesota
11,185	Louisiana
10,073	Indiana
9,913	Kentucky
9,482	Alabama
8,920	Missouri
8,729	Oregon
8,638	Tennessee
8,479	Connecticut
8,402	South Carolina
7,601	Iowa
7,592	Arizona
7,005	Oklahoma
6,080	Colorado
5,780	Arkansas
5,467	Kansas
5,117	Mississippi
4,646	Hawaii
4,494	West Virginia
4,492	Alaska
4,259	New Mexico
3,665	Utah
3,573	Maine
3,449	Nebraska
2,733	Rhode Island
2,625	Nevada
2,346	Delaware
2,134	Idaho
2,088	Montana
1,940	New Hampshire
1,842	Wyoming
1,560	North Dakota
1,409	South Dakota
1,365	Vermont

Table G.448. EXPSTA93

State Funds, Total Expenditures (in millions) 1993

52,599	California
37,993	New York
26,158	Florida
23,470	Texas
19,583	Pennsylvania
18,770	Ohio
17,165	Illinois
16,839	New Jersey
14,959	Michigan
12,023	Massachusetts
11,541	Virginia
11,117	North Carolina
10,221	Washington
10,210	Georgia
9,965	Wisconsin
9,363	Connecticut
9,223	Minnesota
9,185	Maryland
8,134	Indiana
8,068	Louisiana
7,661	Oregon
7,403	Kentucky
7,062	Missouri
6,769	Alabama
6,528	Tennessee
6,288	Iowa
6,044	South Carolina
5,375	Oklahoma
5,334	Arizona
4,992	Colorado
4,561	Hawaii
4,495	Arkansas
4,326	Kansas
3,485	New Mexico
3,467	Alaska
3,265	Mississippi
3,262	West Virginia
3,002	Utah
2,798	Nebraska
2,540	Rhode Island
2,424	Nevada
2,354	Maine
2,137	Delaware
1,597	Montana
1,587	Idaho
1,376	Wyoming
1,364	New Hampshire
1,123	North Dakota
935	Vermont
904	South Dakota

Table G.449. EXPFED93

Federal Funds, Total Expenditures (in millions) 1993

29,582	California
15,186	New York
9,451	Texas
7,341	Florida
7,250	Pennsylvania
6,419	Ohio
5,859	Michigan
5,354	Illinois
4,379	New Jersey
4,323	Louisiana
4,155	North Carolina
4,009	Georgia
3,512	Massachusetts
3,437	Tennessee
3,358	Wisconsin
3,226	Indiana
3,213	Alabama
2,964	Washington
2,752	South Carolina
2,749	Kentucky
2,667	Arizona
2,509	Minnesota
2,449	Virginia
2,445	Missouri
2,382	Maryland
2,149	Mississippi
1,893	Oklahoma
1,814	Arkansas
1,797	Iowa
1,715	West Virginia
1,649	Colorado
1,593	Connecticut
1,570	Kansas
1,380	Oregon
1,177	New Mexico
1,063	Maine
964	Utah
863	Nebraska
860	Alaska
794	Hawaii
771	Rhode Island
758	Idaho
740	New Hampshire
651	Montana
566	South Dakota
555	Nevada
551	North Dakota
500	Delaware
492	Vermont
389	Wyoming

Table G.450. EXPTOT93

All Funds, Total Expenditures (in millions) 1993

82,181	California
53,179	New York
33,499	Florida
32,921	Texas
26,833	Pennsylvania
25,189	Ohio
22,519	Illinois
21,218	New Jersey
20,818	Michigan
15,535	Massachusetts
15,272	North Carolina
14,219	Georgia
13,990	Virginia
13,323	Wisconsin
13,185	Washington
12,391	Louisiana
11,732	Minnesota
11,567	Maryland
11,360	Indiana
10,956	Connecticut
10,152	Kentucky
9,982	Alabama
9,965	Tennessee
9,507	Missouri
9,041	Oregon
8,796	South Carolina
8,085	Iowa
8,001	Arizona
7,268	Oklahoma
6,641	Colorado
6,309	Arkansas
5,896	Kansas
5,414	Mississippi
5,355	Hawaii
4,977	West Virginia
4,662	New Mexico
4,327	Alaska
3,966	Utah
3,661	Nebraska
3,417	Maine
3,311	Rhode Island
2,979	Nevada
2,637	Delaware
2,345	Idaho
2,248	Montana
2,104	New Hampshire
1,765	Wyoming
1,674	North Dakota
1,470	South Dakota
1,427	Vermont

Table G.451. EXPSTA94

State Funds, Total Expenditures (in millions) 1994

52,265	California
40,149	New York
28,833	Florida
24,850	Texas
20,894	Pennsylvania
20,301	Ohio
19,019	Illinois
16,963	New Jersey
15,855	Michigan
12,619	Massachusetts
12,595	Virginia
12,264	North Carolina
11,268	Washington
11,186	Wisconsin
10,892	Georgia
10,589	Connecticut
10,374	Minnesota
9,516	Maryland
9,206	Louisiana
8,649	Indiana
8,485	Oregon
7,762	Kentucky
7,663	Missouri
7,319	Tennessee
7,245	Alabama
6,789	South Carolina
6,652	Iowa
6,193	Colorado
5,625	Arizona
5,456	Oklahoma
5,296	Kansas
4,771	Arkansas
4,552	Hawaii
4,012	Alaska
3,800	Mississippi
3,735	New Mexico
3,428	West Virginia
3,255	Utah
3,045	Nebraska
2,716	Nevada
2,496	Maine
2,433	Rhode Island
2,393	Delaware
1,720	Idaho
1,608	Montana
1,528	New Hampshire
1,379	Wyoming
1,088	North Dakota
967	South Dakota
962	Vermont

Table G.452. EXPFED94

Federal Funds, Total Expenditures (in millions) 1994

32,436	California
16,456	New York
10,274	Texas
8,657	Pennsylvania
7,501	Ohio
7,006	Florida
6,659	Michigan
5,927	Illinois
5,167	Louisiana
4,646	Georgia
4,485	New Jersey
4,423	North Carolina
4,010	Massachusetts
3,947	Tennessee
3,816	Indiana
3,638	Wisconsin
3,574	Alabama
3,442	Washington
3,184	Kentucky
3,124	South Carolina
2,999	Arizona
2,872	Missouri
2,708	Minnesota
2,628	Mississippi
2,573	Virginia
2,511	Maryland
1,999	Iowa
1,917	Oklahoma
1,911	Arkansas
1,887	Connecticut
1,855	West Virginia
1,681	Kansas
1,668	Colorado
1,651	Oregon
1,330	New Mexico
1,047	Maine
1,015	Utah
974	Nebraska
968	Alaska
858	New Hampshire
837	Idaho
831	Hawaii
825	Rhode Island
662	Montana
636	South Dakota
617	Nevada
549	North Dakota
523	Vermont
468	Delaware
410	Wyoming

Table G.453. EXPTOT94

All Funds, Total Expenditures (in millions) 1994

84,701	California
56,605	New York
35,839	Florida
35,124	Texas
29,551	Pennsylvania
27,802	Ohio
24,946	Illinois
22,514	Michigan
21,448	New Jersey
16,687	North Carolina
16,629	Massachusetts
15,538	Georgia
15,168	Virginia
14,824	Wisconsin
14,710	Washington
14,373	Louisiana
13,082	Minnesota
12,476	Connecticut
12,465	Indiana
12,027	Maryland
11,266	Tennessee
10,946	Kentucky
10,819	Alabama
10,535	Missouri
10,136	Oregon
9,913	South Carolina
8,651	Iowa
8,624	Arizona
7,861	Colorado
7,373	Oklahoma
6,977	Kansas
6,682	Arkansas
6,428	Mississippi
5,383	Hawaii
5,283	West Virginia
5,065	New Mexico
4,980	Alaska
4,270	Utah
4,019	Nebraska
3,543	Maine
3,363	Nevada
3,258	Rhode Island
2,861	Delaware
2,557	Idaho
2,386	New Hampshire
2,270	Montana
1,789	Wyoming
1,637	North Dakota
1,603	South Dakota
1,485	Vermont

Table G.454. EXPSTA95

State Funds, Total Expenditures (in millions) 1995

53,905	California
44,375	New York
27,490	Florida
26,304	Texas
24,418	Ohio
21,644	Pennsylvania
21,236	Michigan
19,566	Illinois
17,723	New Jersey
14,050	North Carolina
13,826	Massachusetts
13,648	Virginia
12,976	Georgia
12,481	Washington
12,467	Wisconsin
11,049	Minnesota
10,683	Maryland
10,406	Louisiana
10,133	Connecticut
9,385	Indiana
8,626	Missouri
8,506	Kentucky
8,099	Alabama
7,649	Tennessee
7,515	Oregon
6,837	South Carolina
6,672	Arizona
6,349	Colorado
6,223	Iowa
5,557	Kansas
5,500	Oklahoma
5,182	Arkansas
4,845	Hawaii
4,253	Mississippi
3,985	New Mexico
3,546	Utah
3,387	Alaska
3,065	West Virginia
3,064	Nebraska
3,007	Nevada
2,680	Delaware
2,678	Maine
2,495	Rhode Island
1,950	Idaho
1,532	Montana
1,473	New Hampshire
1,340	Wyoming
1,145	North Dakota
1,012	Vermont
990	South Dakota

Table G.455. EXPFED95

Federal Funds, Total Expenditures (in millions) 1995

31,497	California
20,480	New York
10,406	Texas
8,727	Pennsylvania
8,417	Florida
6,235	Michigan
6,137	Illinois
4,875	Georgia
4,733	Louisiana
4,709	New Jersey
4,527	North Carolina
4,286	Massachusetts
4,214	Ohio
4,020	Washington
3,720	Tennessee
3,608	Wisconsin
3,386	Indiana
3,288	Alabama
3,185	Arizona
3,160	South Carolina
2,917	Virginia
2,907	Kentucky
2,884	Missouri
2,883	Minnesota
2,845	Maryland
2,368	Oregon
2,242	Iowa
2,224	Mississippi
2,164	Connecticut
2,131	Oklahoma
1,846	Arkansas
1,772	Colorado
1,772	West Virginia
1,605	Kansas
1,487	New Mexico
1,207	Alaska
1,096	Utah
1,072	Maine
989	Nebraska
980	Rhode Island
904	Hawaii
793	Idaho
788	New Hampshire
747	Montana
679	Nevada
655	South Dakota
624	North Dakota
533	Vermont
506	Delaware
453	Wyoming

Table G.456. EXPTOT95

All Funds, Total Expenditures (in millions) 1995

85,402	California
64,855	New York
36,710	Texas
35,907	Florida
30,371	Pennsylvania
28,632	Ohio
27,471	Michigan
25,703	Illinois
22,432	New Jersey
18,577	North Carolina
18,112	Massachusetts
17,851	Georgia
16,565	Virginia
16,501	Washington
16,075	Wisconsin
15,139	Louisiana
13,932	Minnesota
13,528	Maryland
12,771	Indiana
12,297	Connecticut
11,510	Missouri
11,413	Kentucky
11,387	Alabama
11,369	Tennessee
9,997	South Carolina
9,883	Oregon
9,857	Arizona
8,465	Iowa
8,121	Colorado
7,631	Oklahoma
7,162	Kansas
7,028	Arkansas
6,477	Mississippi
5,749	Hawaii
5,472	New Mexico
4,837	West Virginia
4,642	Utah
4,594	Alaska
4,053	Nebraska
3,750	Maine
3,686	Nevada
3,475	Rhode Island
3,186	Delaware
2,743	Idaho
2,279	Montana
2,261	New Hampshire
1,793	Wyoming
1,769	North Dakota
1,645	South Dakota
1,545	Vermont

Table G.457. EXPSTA96

State Funds, Total Expenditures (in millions) 1996

57,934	California
45,670	New York
28,595	Texas
27,823	Florida
25,626	Ohio
23,313	Michigan
22,154	Pennsylvania
20,156	Illinois
18,283	New Jersey
14,674	Georgia
14,571	Massachusetts
13,978	Virginia
13,576	North Carolina
13,287	Washington
12,914	Wisconsin
11,457	Minnesota
11,226	Maryland
10,824	Indiana
10,048	Connecticut
9,661	Kentucky
9,540	Louisiana
9,540	Missouri
9,487	Arizona
9,437	Oregon
8,629	Tennessee
8,256	Alabama
7,432	South Carolina
6,968	Colorado
6,761	Iowa
5,889	Oklahoma
5,864	Kansas
5,577	Arkansas
4,987	Hawaii
4,506	Mississippi
4,249	New Mexico
3,736	Nevada
3,707	Utah
3,219	Alaska
3,187	Nebraska
3,018	Delaware
2,963	West Virginia
2,684	Maine
2,510	Rhode Island
2,042	Idaho
1,545	Montana
1,384	New Hampshire
1,175	North Dakota
1,096	Wyoming
1,005	South Dakota
995	Vermont

Table G.458. EXPFED96

Federal Funds, Total Expenditures (in millions) 1996

30,340	California
21,277	New York
11,357	Texas
9,155	Pennsylvania
8,636	Florida
7,461	Michigan
6,344	Illinois
4,875	Tennessee
4,793	New Jersey
4,749	Georgia
4,594	North Carolina
4,257	Massachusetts
4,209	Louisiana
4,045	Ohio
3,764	Wisconsin
3,507	Washington
3,447	Indiana
3,382	Alabama
3,276	South Carolina
3,212	Arizona
2,951	Minnesota
2,943	Maryland
2,930	Virginia
2,928	Kentucky
2,842	Missouri
2,631	Connecticut
2,463	Oregon
2,340	Mississippi
2,183	Oklahoma
2,106	Iowa
2,000	Colorado
1,962	Arkansas
1,854	New Mexico
1,808	West Virginia
1,704	Kansas
1,216	Utah
1,162	Maine
1,055	Nebraska
997	Rhode Island
949	Alaska
948	Hawaii
823	Idaho
819	New Hampshire
788	Montana
716	Nevada
648	South Dakota
596	North Dakota
583	Wyoming
565	Delaware
549	Vermont

Table G.459. EXPTOT96

All Funds, Total Expenditures (in millions) 1996

88,274	California
66,947	New York
39,952	Texas
36,459	Florida
31,309	Pennsylvania
30,774	Michigan
29,671	Ohio
26,500	Illinois
23,076	New Jersey
19,423	Georgia
18,828	Massachusetts
18,170	North Carolina
16,908	Virginia
16,794	Washington
16,678	Wisconsin
14,408	Minnesota
14,271	Indiana
14,169	Maryland
13,749	Louisiana
13,504	Tennessee
12,699	Arizona
12,679	Connecticut
12,589	Kentucky
12,382	Missouri
11,900	Oregon
11,638	Alabama
10,708	South Carolina
8,968	Colorado
8,867	Iowa
8,072	Oklahoma
7,568	Kansas
7,539	Arkansas
6,846	Mississippi
6,103	New Mexico
5,935	Hawaii
4,923	Utah
4,771	West Virginia
4,452	Nevada
4,242	Nebraska
4,168	Alaska
3,846	Maine
3,583	Delaware
3,507	Rhode Island
2,865	Idaho
2,333	Montana
2,203	New Hampshire
1,771	North Dakota
1,679	Wyoming
1,653	South Dakota
1,544	Vermont

Table G.460. EXPSTA97

State Funds, Total Expenditures (in millions) 1997

63,080	California
45,032	New York
28,750	Florida
28,680	Texas
27,426	Ohio
23,045	Pennsylvania
22,116	Michigan
21,383	Illinois
18,603	New Jersey
16,073	Massachusetts
15,197	Georgia
14,632	Virginia
14,497	North Carolina
14,060	Wisconsin
13,559	Washington
12,160	Minnesota
11,393	Maryland
10,983	Connecticut
10,495	Indiana
10,210	Louisiana
10,010	Missouri
9,621	Oregon
9,033	Arizona
8,864	Tennessee
8,610	Alabama
8,527	Kentucky
7,825	South Carolina
7,356	Iowa
6,463	Colorado
6,282	Oklahoma
6,154	Arkansas
6,046	Kansas
5,070	Hawaii
4,776	Mississippi
4,465	Nevada
4,454	New Mexico
4,197	Utah
3,430	Nebraska
3,298	Delaware
3,244	Alaska
3,162	West Virginia
2,680	Maine
2,525	Rhode Island
2,084	Idaho
1,608	Montana
1,533	Wyoming
1,457	New Hampshire
1,302	North Dakota
1,112	South Dakota
1,036	Vermont

Table G.461. EXPFED97

Federal Funds, Total Expenditures (in millions) 1997

31,775	California
20,318	New York
11,497	Texas
9,304	Pennsylvania
8,553	Florida
7,096	Michigan
6,312	Illinois
5,551	North Carolina
5,343	New Jersey
5,261	Massachusetts
5,188	Tennessee
4,789	Georgia
4,629	Ohio
4,357	Washington
4,260	Louisiana
3,786	Wisconsin
3,525	Alabama
3,508	Indiana
3,436	Arizona
3,396	Maryland
3,308	South Carolina
3,281	Kentucky
3,139	Minnesota
3,097	Virginia
2,814	Missouri
2,761	Colorado
2,527	Oregon
2,468	Mississippi
2,364	Connecticut
2,180	Oklahoma
2,055	Iowa
2,053	Arkansas
1,975	New Mexico
1,942	West Virginia
1,732	Kansas
1,280	Utah
1,215	Maine
1,112	Nebraska
1,088	Hawaii
1,047	Rhode Island
990	Alaska
874	Idaho
806	New Hampshire
794	Montana
753	Nevada
695	North Dakota
603	South Dakota
601	Delaware
583	Vermont
472	Wyoming

Table G.462. EXPTOT97

All Funds, Total Expenditures (in millions) 1997

94,855	California
65,350	New York
40,177	Texas
37,303	Florida
32,349	Pennsylvania
32,055	Ohio
29,212	Michigan
27,695	Illinois
23,946	New Jersey
21,334	Massachusetts
20,048	North Carolina
19,986	Georgia
17,916	Washington
17,846	Wisconsin
17,729	Virginia
15,299	Minnesota
14,789	Maryland
14,470	Louisiana
14,052	Tennessee
14,003	Indiana
13,347	Connecticut
12,824	Missouri
12,469	Arizona
12,135	Alabama
11,808	Kentucky
11,133	South Carolina
9,411	Iowa
9,224	Colorado
8,462	Oklahoma
8,207	Arkansas
7,778	Kansas
7,244	Mississippi
6,429	New Mexico
6,158	Hawaii
5,477	Utah
5,218	Nevada
5,104	West Virginia
4,542	Nebraska
4,234	Alaska
3,899	Delaware
3,895	Maine
3,572	Rhode Island
2,958	Idaho
2,402	Montana
2,263	New Hampshire
2,005	Wyoming
1,997	North Dakota
1,715	South Dakota
1,619	Vermont
1,248	Oregon

Table G.463. EXPSTA98

State Funds, Total Expenditures (in millions) 1998

67,076	California
48,243	New York
31,628	Florida
30,395	Texas
29,727	Ohio
25,050	Michigan
24,237	Pennsylvania
22,727	Illinois
19,301	New Jersey
17,309	Wisconsin
16,440	Massachusetts
15,490	North Carolina
15,366	Georgia
15,315	Virginia
14,040	Washington
12,854	Minnesota
12,096	Maryland
11,697	Connecticut
11,091	Indiana
10,521	Missouri
10,412	Oregon
10,381	Louisiana
9,699	Arizona
9,459	Kentucky
9,110	Tennessee
9,046	South Carolina
8,115	Alabama
7,611	Iowa
6,709	Oklahoma
6,667	Arkansas
5,779	Kansas
5,292	Mississippi
5,197	New Mexico
5,195	Nevada
5,100	Hawaii
4,514	Colorado
4,429	Utah
3,604	Delaware
3,562	West Virginia
3,560	Nebraska
3,249	Alaska
2,776	Maine
2,655	Rhode Island
2,184	Idaho
1,585	Montana
1,515	New Hampshire
1,486	Wyoming
1,218	North Dakota
1,186	South Dakota
1,098	Vermont

Table G.464. EXPFED98

Federal Funds, Total Expenditures (in millions) 1998

31,649	California
21,923	New York
12,154	Texas
9,385	Pennsylvania
8,810	Florida
7,097	Michigan
6,324	Illinois
5,929	North Carolina
5,924	Georgia
5,622	Massachusetts
5,374	Tennessee
5,110	New Jersey
4,801	Alabama
4,479	Washington
4,220	Ohio
4,120	Louisiana
3,906	Kentucky
3,843	Wisconsin
3,757	South Carolina
3,643	Indiana
3,450	Maryland
3,411	Minnesota
3,352	Missouri
3,314	Arizona
3,269	Virginia
2,670	Mississippi
2,516	Oklahoma
2,291	Iowa
2,229	Oregon
2,136	Arkansas
1,983	West Virginia
1,830	Kansas
1,716	New Mexico
1,519	Colorado
1,325	Maine
1,292	Utah
1,259	Connecticut
1,224	Nebraska
1,036	Alaska
1,028	Rhode Island
976	Hawaii
885	Idaho
847	Montana
833	New Hampshire
809	North Dakota
789	Nevada
771	South Dakota
648	Vermont
540	Delaware
476	Wyoming

Table G.465. EXPTOT98

All Funds, Total Expenditures (in millions) 1998

98,725	California
70,166	New York
42,549	Texas
40,438	Florida
33,947	Ohio
33,622	Pennsylvania
32,147	Michigan
29,051	Illinois
24,411	New Jersey
22,062	Massachusetts
21,419	North Carolina
21,290	Georgia
21,152	Wisconsin
18,584	Virginia
18,519	Washington
16,265	Minnesota
15,546	Maryland
14,734	Indiana
14,501	Louisiana
14,484	Tennessee
13,873	Missouri
13,365	Kentucky
13,013	Arizona
12,956	Connecticut
12,916	Alabama
12,803	South Carolina
12,641	Oregon
9,902	Iowa
9,225	Oklahoma
8,803	Arkansas
7,962	Mississippi
7,609	Kansas
6,913	New Mexico
6,076	Hawaii
6,033	Colorado
5,984	Nevada
5,721	Utah
5,545	West Virginia
4,784	Nebraska
4,285	Alaska
4,144	Delaware
4,101	Maine
3,683	Rhode Island
3,069	Idaho
2,432	Montana
2,348	New Hampshire
2,027	North Dakota
1,962	Wyoming
1,957	South Dakota
1,746	Vermont

Table G.466. EXPSTA99

State Funds, Total Expenditures (in millions) 1999

72,563	California
51,639	New York
34,673	Florida
31,488	Texas
30,674	Ohio
25,524	Pennsylvania
24,393	Michigan
24,226	Illinois
20,719	New Jersey
18,448	Wisconsin
17,811	Massachusetts
17,662	Virginia
17,238	North Carolina
16,527	Georgia
14,953	Washington
13,841	Minnesota
13,140	Maryland
12,276	Connecticut
11,265	Missouri
10,714	Indiana
10,665	Louisiana
10,658	Arizona
10,434	Oregon
10,415	Kentucky
9,576	Tennessee
8,337	Alabama
8,133	Iowa
7,446	South Carolina
7,316	Arkansas
6,853	Oklahoma
6,136	Kansas
5,948	Nevada
5,582	New Mexico
5,497	Mississippi
5,162	Hawaii
4,791	Colorado
4,775	Utah
4,003	Nebraska
3,920	West Virginia
3,886	Delaware
3,542	Alaska
3,051	Maine
2,849	Rhode Island
2,349	Idaho
1,661	Montana
1,618	Wyoming
1,571	New Hampshire
1,310	North Dakota
1,260	Vermont
1,251	South Dakota

Table G.467. EXPFED99

Federal Funds, Total Expenditures (in millions) 1999

34,375	California
20,937	New York
13,098	Texas
10,679	Pennsylvania
9,349	Florida
8,471	Michigan
6,675	Illinois
6,414	Georgia
6,122	North Carolina
5,793	Tennessee
5,456	Massachusetts
5,371	New Jersey
5,152	Alabama
4,738	Washington
4,413	Ohio
4,349	Wisconsin
4,220	Kentucky
4,204	Louisiana
4,115	Indiana
3,899	Missouri
3,785	Arizona
3,533	Maryland
3,504	Virginia
3,444	Minnesota
3,443	South Carolina
3,094	Oklahoma
2,643	Mississippi
2,516	Iowa
2,457	Oregon
2,089	Kansas
2,050	Arkansas
1,980	West Virginia
1,959	New Mexico
1,732	Colorado
1,479	Utah
1,356	Maine
1,355	Nebraska
1,351	Connecticut
1,350	Alaska
1,120	Rhode Island
1,018	Idaho
1,015	Hawaii
954	Montana
928	Nevada
923	New Hampshire
810	North Dakota
722	Vermont
706	South Dakota
682	Delaware
536	Wyoming

Table G.468. EXPTOT99

All Funds, Total Expenditures (in millions) 1999

106,938	California
72,576	New York
44,586	Texas
44,022	Florida
36,203	Pennsylvania
35,087	Ohio
32,864	Michigan
30,901	Illinois
26,090	New Jersey
23,360	North Carolina
23,267	Massachusetts
22,941	Georgia
22,797	Wisconsin
21,166	Virginia
19,691	Washington
17,285	Minnesota
16,673	Maryland
15,369	Tennessee
15,164	Missouri
14,869	Louisiana
14,829	Indiana
14,635	Kentucky
14,443	Arizona
13,627	Connecticut
13,489	Alabama
12,891	Oregon
10,889	South Carolina
10,649	Iowa
9,947	Oklahoma
9,366	Arkansas
8,225	Kansas
8,140	Mississippi
7,541	New Mexico
6,876	Nevada
6,523	Colorado
6,254	Utah
6,177	Hawaii
5,900	West Virginia
5,358	Nebraska
4,892	Alaska
4,568	Delaware
4,407	Maine
3,969	Rhode Island
3,367	Idaho
2,615	Montana
2,494	New Hampshire
2,154	Wyoming
2,120	North Dakota
1,982	Vermont
1,957	South Dakota

Table G.469. EXPSTA00

State Funds, Total Expenditures (in millions) 2000

82,281	California
48,577	New York
36,759	Florida
35,065	Texas
32,792	Ohio
26,879	Pennsylvania
26,739	Illinois
26,582	Michigan
23,207	New Jersey
21,150	Wisconsin
19,821	Massachusetts
18,695	North Carolina
18,356	Virginia
15,972	Georgia
15,584	Washington
14,396	Minnesota
14,087	Maryland
13,818	Connecticut
12,554	Indiana
11,512	Missouri
11,128	Arizona
11,123	Louisiana
10,585	South Carolina
10,324	Alabama
9,905	Tennessee
9,162	Colorado
8,849	Iowa
8,020	Kentucky
7,790	Arkansas
7,634	Oregon
7,547	Oklahoma
6,305	Mississippi
6,000	New Mexico
5,866	Kansas
5,476	Hawaii
4,899	Utah
4,298	Nebraska
4,095	Delaware
4,039	West Virginia
3,565	Nevada
3,401	Alaska
3,303	Maine
2,886	Rhode Island
2,532	Idaho
2,369	New Hampshire
1,756	Montana
1,750	Wyoming
1,363	Vermont
1,322	South Dakota
1,300	North Dakota

Table G.470. EXPFED00

Federal Funds, Total Expenditures (in millions) 2000

37,303	California
23,470	New York
14,400	Texas
11,024	Pennsylvania
10,737	Florida
9,328	Georgia
7,965	Michigan
7,405	Illinois
6,942	North Carolina
5,987	South Carolina
5,780	Tennessee
5,721	Massachusetts
5,597	New Jersey
5,295	Washington
5,035	Wisconsin
4,800	Ohio
4,633	Kentucky
4,421	Missouri
4,406	Alabama
4,295	Louisiana
4,091	Indiana
3,780	Maryland
3,738	Minnesota
3,721	Virginia
3,545	Arizona
3,105	Colorado
3,092	Mississippi
2,985	Connecticut
2,822	Oklahoma
2,770	Iowa
2,419	Oregon
2,269	New Mexico
2,224	Arkansas
2,187	West Virginia
2,169	Kansas
1,844	Alaska
1,539	Utah
1,503	Nebraska
1,495	Maine
1,291	Rhode Island
1,099	Idaho
1,029	Nevada
1,027	Montana
1,017	Hawaii
974	New Hampshire
917	North Dakota
831	Vermont
783	South Dakota
749	Delaware
596	Wyoming

Table G.471. EXPTOT00

All Funds, Total Expenditures (in millions) 2000

119,584	California
72,047	New York
49,465	Texas
47,496	Florida
37,903	Pennsylvania
37,592	Ohio
34,547	Michigan
34,144	Illinois
28,804	New Jersey
26,185	Wisconsin
25,637	North Carolina
25,542	Massachusetts
25,300	Georgia
22,077	Virginia
20,879	Washington
18,134	Minnesota
17,867	Maryland
16,803	Connecticut
16,645	Indiana
16,572	South Carolina
15,933	Missouri
15,685	Tennessee
15,418	Louisiana
14,730	Alabama
14,673	Arizona
12,653	Kentucky
12,267	Colorado
11,619	Iowa
10,369	Oklahoma
10,053	Oregon
10,014	Arkansas
9,397	Mississippi
8,269	New Mexico
8,035	Kansas
6,493	Hawaii
6,438	Utah
6,226	West Virginia
5,801	Nebraska
5,245	Alaska
4,844	Delaware
4,798	Maine
4,594	Nevada
4,177	Rhode Island
3,631	Idaho
3,343	New Hampshire
2,783	Montana
2,346	Wyoming
2,217	North Dakota
2,194	Vermont
2,105	South Dakota

Table G.472. STAPC89

Expenditures of Funds from State (per capita) 1989

5,464.90	Alaska
2,928.06	Hawaii
2,646.36	Delaware
2,362.76	Massachusetts
2,288.36	Connecticut
2,061.70	Oregon
1,974.74	Wyoming
1,912.87	New York
1,882.75	Iowa
1,806.14	Maryland
1,757.61	Washington
1,738.11	Minnesota
1,721.21	North Dakota
1,682.65	New Jersey
1,682.15	Wisconsin
1,678.66	Montana
1,678.36	Rhode Island
1,567.41	New Mexico
1,564.12	Virginia
1,512.64	California
1,490.89	South Carolina
1,485.27	Maine
1,473.84	Kentucky
1,460.32	Vermont
1,417.81	Ohio
1,359.72	Florida
1,342.77	Louisiana
1,336.03	West Virginia
1,329.99	Illinois
1,310.79	Michigan
1,294.67	Utah
1,288.54	Pennsylvania
1,280.96	Arkansas
1,280.71	Oklahoma
1,266.63	North Carolina
1,204.93	Kansas
1,164.49	Nebraska
1,159.73	Georgia
1,146.82	Colorado
1,139.76	Arizona
1,139.51	Nevada
1,135.69	Missouri
1,119.61	Indiana
1,109.09	South Dakota
1,050.59	New Hampshire
1,033.19	Mississippi
1,009.86	Idaho
970.04	Tennessee
871.30	Alabama
835.91	Texas

Table G.473. FEDPC89

Expenditures of Funds from Federal (per capita) 1989

817.87	Alabama
597.72	Alaska
595.85	Louisiana
594.57	California
590.91	North Dakota
564.37	Vermont
560.00	Wyoming
554.59	Montana
554.01	Maine
537.06	South Dakota
533.00	Mississippi
517.75	Idaho
507.74	New York
500.20	Kansas
482.35	South Carolina
471.13	Iowa
461.50	West Virginia
460.61	Oklahoma
456.40	Kentucky
451.04	Massachusetts
433.92	Arkansas
425.68	Minnesota
422.85	Wisconsin
417.54	New Mexico
416.83	Rhode Island
414.12	Pennsylvania
412.60	Michigan
398.99	Tennessee
396.14	Colorado
388.28	Georgia
386.89	Washington
378.29	Ohio
375.59	Maryland
372.41	New Jersey
369.65	Utah
362.56	Delaware
353.42	Hawaii
353.07	North Carolina
350.97	Indiana
345.05	Arizona
334.57	Nebraska
334.05	Connecticut
317.81	Florida
304.36	Virginia
299.65	Oregon
290.88	New Hampshire
276.41	Missouri
276.33	Nevada
266.34	Illinois
254.49	Texas

Table G.474. TOTPC89

Expenditures of Funds from All Sources (per capita) 1989

5,157.38	Alaska
3,078.03	Hawaii
2,694.18	Massachusetts
2,687.32	Delaware
2,588.03	Connecticut
2,512.50	Wyoming
2,408.21	North Dakota
2,387.81	New York
2,329.40	Iowa
2,110.38	Rhode Island
2,039.02	Montana
2,008.05	Oregon
1,988.76	Maine
1,980.23	Maryland
1,972.36	Minnesota
1,952.25	New Jersey
1,951.07	Wisconsin
1,943.03	Louisiana
1,933.51	Vermont
1,847.69	California
1,847.33	West Virginia
1,816.04	Kentucky
1,783.45	South Carolina
1,773.52	Washington
1,743.26	New Mexico
1,740.22	Ohio
1,709.19	Pennsylvania
1,671.81	Oklahoma
1,657.67	Virginia
1,620.17	Michigan
1,616.78	Arkansas
1,614.51	Kansas
1,605.44	South Dakota
1,591.58	Alabama
1,534.42	Illinois
1,482.69	Mississippi
1,449.56	Nebraska
1,406.63	Florida
1,391.10	North Carolina
1,384.00	Indiana
1,333.44	Utah
1,332.21	Missouri
1,279.11	Georgia
1,261.79	Colorado
1,237.52	Idaho
1,235.50	New Hampshire
1,233.33	Tennessee
1,104.99	Arizona
924.31	Texas
869.42	Nevada

Table G.475. STAPC90

Expenditures of Funds from State (per capita) 1990

5,160.00	Alaska
3,113.72	Hawaii
2,698.20	Delaware
2,389.87	Wyoming
2,265.29	Connecticut
2,146.11	Massachusetts
2,091.48	Oregon
2,009.36	Iowa
1,973.65	New York
1,957.10	New Mexico
1,863.42	Maryland
1,822.89	Washington
1,822.46	Wisconsin
1,807.13	Minnesota
1,763.69	North Dakota
1,678.96	Rhode Island
1,676.05	New Jersey
1,670.87	Virginia
1,590.39	Maine
1,587.40	California
1,585.73	Montana
1,582.62	South Carolina
1,549.23	Kansas
1,548.96	Kentucky
1,523.98	Vermont
1,472.95	West Virginia
1,459.95	Oklahoma
1,447.23	Michigan
1,433.30	Florida
1,432.16	Arkansas
1,425.65	Ohio
1,415.71	Georgia
1,407.43	Utah
1,393.55	North Carolina
1,378.73	Louisiana
1,371.62	Pennsylvania
1,361.85	Nebraska
1,342.14	Illinois
1,296.17	Nevada
1,267.13	Idaho
1,246.43	Missouri
1,190.65	Colorado
1,190.30	Indiana
1,133.97	Arizona
1,075.34	Mississippi
1,053.31	Tennessee
1,049.69	Texas
1,034.48	South Dakota
904.46	Alabama
895.40	New Hampshire

Table G.476. FEDPC90

Expenditures of Funds from Federal (per capita) 1990

1,614.55	Alaska
921.04	Alabama
635.06	South Dakota
625.91	California
608.76	North Dakota
603.52	Wyoming
594.09	South Carolina
568.38	Vermont
567.74	Louisiana
558.20	Montana
545.55	New York
535.25	Idaho
531.35	New Mexico
526.00	Wisconsin
522.80	Maine
513.30	Massachusetts
513.11	West Virginia
511.70	Iowa
509.90	Mississippi
500.64	Arkansas
498.51	Kentucky
478.56	Rhode Island
458.48	Hawaii
453.35	Tennessee
449.66	Arizona
443.81	Washington
441.69	Ohio
433.35	Michigan
429.86	Pennsylvania
429.39	Minnesota
421.81	Oklahoma
415.91	Colorado
414.97	Utah
396.46	Indiana
392.39	Maryland
389.26	New Jersey
387.39	Delaware
380.43	North Carolina
379.07	Connecticut
375.42	Georgia
375.16	Nebraska
367.00	Oregon
360.37	Kansas
332.92	Texas
316.98	Missouri
311.09	New Hampshire
306.99	Nevada
304.30	Florida
292.94	Virginia
258.77	Illinois

Table G.477. TOTPC90

Expenditures of Funds from All Sources (per capita) 1990

6,774.55	Alaska
3,572.20	Hawaii
3,085.59	Delaware
2,993.39	Wyoming
2,659.41	Massachusetts
2,644.36	Connecticut
2,521.07	Iowa
2,519.20	New York
2,488.45	New Mexico
2,458.48	Oregon
2,372.46	North Dakota
2,348.47	Wisconsin
2,266.69	Washington
2,255.80	Maryland
2,236.52	Minnesota
2,213.31	California
2,176.71	South Carolina
2,157.53	Rhode Island
2,143.93	Montana
2,113.19	Maine
2,092.36	Vermont
2,065.31	New Jersey
2,047.46	Kentucky
1,986.06	West Virginia
1,963.81	Virginia
1,946.47	Louisiana
1,932.79	Arkansas
1,909.60	Kansas
1,881.75	Oklahoma
1,880.58	Michigan
1,867.34	Ohio
1,825.50	Alabama
1,822.40	Utah
1,802.38	Idaho
1,801.48	Pennsylvania
1,791.14	Georgia
1,773.97	North Carolina
1,737.59	Florida
1,737.01	Nebraska
1,669.54	South Dakota
1,606.56	Colorado
1,603.16	Nevada
1,600.91	Illinois
1,586.76	Indiana
1,585.24	Mississippi
1,583.63	Arizona
1,563.42	Missouri
1,506.66	Tennessee
1,382.61	Texas
1,206.49	New Hampshire

Table G.478. STAPC91

Expenditures of Funds from State (per capita) 1991

5,428.82	Alaska
3,348.36	Hawaii
2,632.75	Oregon
2,630.88	Delaware
2,554.09	Massachusetts
2,384.28	Wyoming
2,144.42	Washington
2,078.75	Connecticut
2,068.79	Iowa
2,031.40	Minnesota
2,025.99	Montana
1,978.37	New York
1,929.54	New Mexico
1,918.25	Maryland
1,821.30	New Jersey
1,779.18	North Dakota
1,778.47	Kentucky
1,738.86	Virginia
1,648.41	Rhode Island
1,647.00	Florida
1,628.06	Kansas
1,607.85	California
1,604.94	Vermont
1,601.74	Louisiana
1,587.85	Maine
1,586.23	Oklahoma
1,585.06	Ohio
1,577.31	West Virginia
1,577.13	South Carolina
1,555.46	Arkansas
1,528.60	Nebraska
1,501.13	Utah
1,462.36	North Carolina
1,454.49	Pennsylvania
1,431.91	Nevada
1,419.58	Michigan
1,419.42	Georgia
1,417.82	Illinois
1,317.61	Idaho
1,276.18	Arizona
1,270.08	Indiana
1,209.19	Mississippi
1,204.92	Missouri
1,201.01	Colorado
1,164.94	Texas
1,108.42	South Dakota
1,088.54	Tennessee
1,039.98	Wisconsin
981.93	New Hampshire
948.67	Alabama

Table G.479. FEDPC91

Expenditures of Funds from Federal (per capita) 1991

1,196.84	Alaska
1,100.22	Alabama
749.82	Louisiana
729.26	Wyoming
706.39	California
697.16	North Dakota
671.90	South Dakota
670.19	Vermont
669.28	Massachusetts
641.09	Montana
635.50	New York
632.20	South Carolina
611.35	Mississippi
588.66	Maine
583.43	West Virginia
580.37	Idaho
572.81	Kentucky
569.69	Iowa
563.03	New Mexico
561.37	Arkansas
561.07	Wisconsin
535.81	Hawaii
531.87	Rhode Island
525.00	Delaware
509.10	Michigan
506.82	Pennsylvania
504.25	Arizona
502.21	Oklahoma
495.65	Tennessee
491.40	Ohio
490.52	Washington
461.09	Indiana
456.74	Minnesota
447.67	Georgia
434.20	North Carolina
432.05	Connecticut
431.18	Nebraska
426.38	New Hampshire
418.42	New Jersey
412.53	Utah
409.60	Maryland
396.79	Kansas
395.49	Colorado
377.74	Texas
373.01	Missouri
370.67	Oregon
354.96	Florida
335.41	Nevada
331.95	Virginia
290.66	Illinois

Table G.480. TOTPC91

Expenditures of Funds from All Sources (per capita) 1991

6,625.66	Alaska
3,884.17	Hawaii
3,223.37	Massachusetts
3,155.88	Delaware
3,113.54	Wyoming
3,003.43	Oregon
2,667.08	Montana
2,638.48	Iowa
2,634.95	Washington
2,613.87	New York
2,510.79	Connecticut
2,492.57	New Mexico
2,488.14	Minnesota
2,476.34	North Dakota
2,351.57	Louisiana
2,351.28	Kentucky
2,327.84	Maryland
2,314.23	California
2,275.13	Vermont
2,239.72	New Jersey
2,209.33	South Carolina
2,180.28	Rhode Island
2,176.52	Maine
2,160.73	West Virginia
2,116.83	Arkansas
2,088.44	Oklahoma
2,076.46	Ohio
2,070.81	Virginia
2,048.89	Alabama
2,024.85	Kansas
2,001.96	Florida
1,961.32	Pennsylvania
1,959.77	Nebraska
1,928.69	Michigan
1,913.66	Utah
1,897.98	Idaho
1,896.56	North Carolina
1,867.09	Georgia
1,820.53	Mississippi
1,780.44	Arizona
1,780.31	South Dakota
1,767.32	Nevada
1,731.17	Indiana
1,708.48	Illinois
1,601.05	Wisconsin
1,596.50	Colorado
1,584.19	Tennessee
1,577.94	Missouri
1,542.68	Texas
1,408.31	New Hampshire

Table G.481. STAPC92

Expenditures of Funds from State (per capita) 1992

6,354.34	Alaska
3,440.00	Hawaii
3,149.03	Wyoming
2,902.90	Delaware
2,463.35	Oregon
2,436.36	Wisconsin
2,233.90	New Jersey
2,223.97	Washington
2,176.79	Connecticut
2,144.28	Iowa
2,048.83	New York
2,046.17	New Mexico
2,030.74	Maine
2,026.97	Rhode Island
2,018.11	Minnesota
1,959.27	Kentucky
1,943.93	Massachusetts
1,833.78	Maryland
1,833.33	Montana
1,765.77	California
1,765.63	Louisiana
1,741.66	Virginia
1,737.68	Arkansas
1,717.51	Florida
1,693.63	West Virginia
1,667.72	North Dakota
1,649.19	Nebraska
1,647.37	Vermont
1,636.84	Pennsylvania
1,635.63	Ohio
1,624.53	Oklahoma
1,611.24	Kansas
1,601.80	Nevada
1,601.22	South Carolina
1,543.11	Utah
1,514.68	Michigan
1,484.19	North Carolina
1,464.89	Illinois
1,390.48	Arizona
1,378.99	Idaho
1,371.65	Georgia
1,293.64	Colorado
1,259.34	Missouri
1,238.10	Indiana
1,235.54	South Dakota
1,206.35	Texas
1,193.49	Mississippi
1,155.44	New Hampshire
1,098.92	Tennessee
968.35	Alabama

Table G.482. FEDPC92

Expenditures of Funds from Federal (per capita) 1992

1,322.54	Alabama
1,298.13	Alaska
865.46	California
860.03	Maine
853.20	Louisiana
829.37	Wyoming
796.12	West Virginia
788.98	North Dakota
767.05	Mississippi
751.76	South Dakota
751.24	New York
747.37	Vermont
732.02	South Carolina
706.81	Montana
703.30	Rhode Island
679.98	Kentucky
676.69	Arkansas
647.69	New Mexico
623.85	Tennessee
622.89	Idaho
620.78	Wisconsin
600.00	Hawaii
587.60	New Hampshire
582.84	Pennsylvania
572.80	Arizona
563.59	Iowa
562.94	Michigan
561.80	Oklahoma
553.05	Kansas
546.99	Washington
546.38	Georgia
545.05	Indiana
532.06	New Jersey
512.44	North Carolina
503.92	Massachusetts
503.75	Nebraska
502.91	Minnesota
497.10	Delaware
492.91	Ohio
471.76	Oregon
469.52	Utah
469.51	Maryland
463.58	Colorado
458.03	Missouri
433.65	Texas
424.14	Florida
412.21	Connecticut
392.01	Illinois
370.40	Nevada
353.44	Virginia

Table G.483. TOTPC92

Expenditures of Funds from All Sources (per capita) 1992

7,652.47	Alaska
4,040.00	Hawaii
3,978.40	Wyoming
3,400.00	Delaware
3,057.14	Wisconsin
2,935.10	Oregon
2,890.78	Maine
2,800.08	New York
2,770.97	Washington
2,765.97	New Jersey
2,730.27	Rhode Island
2,707.87	Iowa
2,693.86	New Mexico
2,639.24	Kentucky
2,631.23	California
2,618.82	Louisiana
2,589.01	Connecticut
2,540.15	Montana
2,521.02	Minnesota
2,489.75	West Virginia
2,456.69	North Dakota
2,447.86	Massachusetts
2,414.37	Arkansas
2,394.74	Vermont
2,333.24	South Carolina
2,303.28	Maryland
2,290.89	Alabama
2,219.68	Pennsylvania
2,186.33	Oklahoma
2,164.29	Kansas
2,152.93	Nebraska
2,141.65	Florida
2,128.54	Ohio
2,095.10	Virginia
2,077.61	Michigan
2,012.63	Utah
2,001.88	Idaho
1,996.63	North Carolina
1,987.31	South Dakota
1,972.20	Nevada
1,963.28	Arizona
1,960.54	Mississippi
1,918.04	Georgia
1,856.90	Illinois
1,783.15	Indiana
1,757.23	Colorado
1,743.04	New Hampshire
1,722.78	Tennessee
1,717.37	Missouri
1,640.00	Texas

Table G.484. STAPC93

Expenditures of Funds from State (per capita) 1993

5,807.37	Alaska
3,925.13	Hawaii
3,057.22	Delaware
2,933.90	Wyoming
2,861.55	Connecticut
2,545.09	Rhode Island
2,525.05	Oregon
2,229.00	Iowa
2,157.89	New Mexico
2,138.29	New Jersey
2,094.32	New York
2,039.58	Minnesota
2,000.17	Massachusetts
1,971.32	Wisconsin
1,952.27	Kentucky
1,947.60	Washington
1,907.39	Florida
1,901.45	Maine
1,901.19	Montana
1,882.85	Louisiana
1,858.18	Maryland
1,854.37	Arkansas
1,796.26	West Virginia
1,785.15	Virginia
1,762.95	North Dakota
1,756.52	Nevada
1,735.73	Nebraska
1,699.14	Kansas
1,695.57	Ohio
1,688.73	California
1,664.60	Oklahoma
1,662.72	South Carolina
1,628.93	Pennsylvania
1,628.92	Vermont
1,614.36	Alabama
1,600.26	North Carolina
1,600.21	Utah
1,569.84	Michigan
1,481.00	Georgia
1,463.84	Illinois
1,441.42	Idaho
1,426.52	Indiana
1,401.85	Colorado
1,348.22	Missouri
1,335.84	Arizona
1,304.11	Texas
1,283.52	Tennessee
1,262.57	South Dakota
1,238.62	Mississippi
1,215.69	New Hampshire

Table G.485. FEDPC93

Expenditures of Funds from Federal (per capita) 1993

1,440.54	Alaska
1,008.87	Louisiana
949.75	California
944.38	West Virginia
864.99	North Dakota
858.64	Maine
857.14	Vermont
837.11	New York
829.42	Wyoming
815.25	Mississippi
790.50	South Dakota
775.00	Montana
772.55	Rhode Island
766.28	Alabama
757.08	South Carolina
748.35	Arkansas
728.79	New Mexico
724.95	Kentucky
715.31	Delaware
688.47	Idaho
683.30	Hawaii
675.78	Tennessee
667.92	Arizona
664.29	Wisconsin
659.54	New Hampshire
637.01	Iowa
616.65	Kansas
614.86	Michigan
603.06	Pennsylvania
598.10	North Carolina
586.25	Oklahoma
584.26	Massachusetts
581.52	Georgia
579.86	Ohio
565.77	Indiana
564.79	Washington
556.06	New Jersey
554.84	Minnesota
535.36	Nebraska
535.29	Florida
525.14	Texas
513.86	Utah
486.86	Connecticut
481.89	Maryland
466.78	Missouri
463.07	Colorado
456.59	Illinois
454.85	Oregon
402.17	Nevada
378.81	Virginia

Table G.486. TOTPC93

Expenditures of Funds from All Sources (per capita) 1993

7,247.91	Alaska
4,608.43	Hawaii
3,772.53	Delaware
3,763.33	Wyoming
3,348.41	Connecticut
3,317.64	Rhode Island
2,979.89	Oregon
2,931.43	New York
2,891.72	Louisiana
2,886.69	New Mexico
2,866.00	Iowa
2,760.10	Maine
2,740.64	West Virginia
2,694.35	New Jersey
2,677.22	Kentucky
2,676.19	Montana
2,638.49	California
2,635.61	Wisconsin
2,627.94	North Dakota
2,602.72	Arkansas
2,594.43	Minnesota
2,584.43	Massachusetts
2,512.39	Washington
2,486.06	Vermont
2,442.69	Florida
2,419.81	South Carolina
2,380.63	Alabama
2,340.08	Maryland
2,315.79	Kansas
2,275.43	Ohio
2,271.09	Nebraska
2,250.85	Oklahoma
2,231.99	Pennsylvania
2,198.36	North Carolina
2,184.70	Michigan
2,163.96	Virginia
2,158.70	Nevada
2,129.88	Idaho
2,114.07	Utah
2,062.52	Georgia
2,053.87	Mississippi
2,053.07	South Dakota
2,003.76	Arizona
1,992.28	Indiana
1,959.30	Tennessee
1,920.43	Illinois
1,875.22	New Hampshire
1,864.93	Colorado
1,829.25	Texas
1,815.01	Missouri

Table G.487. STAPC94

Expenditures of Funds from State (per capita) 1994

6,675.54	Alaska
3,877.34	Hawaii
3,379.94	Delaware
3,240.21	Connecticut
2,903.16	Wyoming
2,748.62	Oregon
2,450.15	Rhode Island
2,351.36	Iowa
2,272.01	Minnesota
2,259.53	New Mexico
2,211.21	New York
2,195.05	Wisconsin
2,142.06	New Jersey
2,137.45	Louisiana
2,112.09	Washington
2,092.36	Massachusetts
2,065.11	Florida
2,061.50	Kansas
2,030.34	Kentucky
2,016.16	Maine
1,946.55	Arkansas
1,926.72	Virginia
1,908.93	Maryland
1,885.59	West Virginia
1,880.70	Montana
1,877.31	Nebraska
1,865.38	Nevada
1,851.88	South Carolina
1,827.11	Ohio
1,736.86	North Carolina
1,734.95	Pennsylvania
1,711.55	Alabama
1,700.00	North Dakota
1,694.85	Colorado
1,686.53	Utah
1,680.84	Oklahoma
1,668.90	California
1,661.49	Vermont
1,654.32	Michigan
1,611.10	Illinois
1,545.84	Georgia
1,515.42	Idaho
1,505.22	Indiana
1,451.05	Missouri
1,426.96	Mississippi
1,417.59	Tennessee
1,356.08	Arizona
1,355.11	Texas
1,348.63	New Hampshire
1,337.48	South Dakota

Table G.488. FEDPC94

Expenditures of Funds from Federal (per capita) 1994

1,610.65	Alaska
1,199.67	Louisiana
1,035.73	California
1,020.35	West Virginia
986.86	Mississippi
906.32	New York
903.28	Vermont
879.67	South Dakota
863.16	Wyoming
857.81	North Dakota
852.15	South Carolina
845.72	Maine
844.32	Alabama
832.85	Kentucky
830.82	Rhode Island
804.60	New Mexico
779.68	Arkansas
774.27	Montana
764.48	Tennessee
757.28	New Hampshire
737.44	Idaho
723.00	Arizona
718.84	Pennsylvania
713.89	Wisconsin
707.84	Hawaii
706.61	Iowa
694.80	Michigan
675.10	Ohio
664.90	Massachusetts
664.11	Indiana
661.02	Delaware
659.38	Georgia
654.34	Kansas
645.17	Washington
626.40	North Carolina
600.49	Nebraska
593.08	Minnesota
590.57	Oklahoma
577.42	Connecticut
566.36	New Jersey
560.26	Texas
543.84	Missouri
534.82	Oregon
525.91	Utah
503.71	Maryland
502.08	Illinois
501.79	Florida
456.49	Colorado
423.76	Nevada
393.61	Virginia

Table G.489. TOTPC94

Expenditures of Funds from All Sources (per capita) 1994

8,286.19	Alaska
4,585.18	Hawaii
4,040.96	Delaware
3,817.63	Connecticut
3,766.32	Wyoming
3,337.13	Louisiana
3,283.45	Oregon
3,280.97	Rhode Island
3,117.53	New York
3,064.13	New Mexico
3,057.97	Iowa
2,908.95	Wisconsin
2,905.94	West Virginia
2,865.09	Minnesota
2,863.20	Kentucky
2,861.87	Maine
2,757.26	Washington
2,757.25	Massachusetts
2,726.23	Arkansas
2,715.84	Kansas
2,708.42	New Jersey
2,704.63	California
2,704.04	South Carolina
2,654.97	Montana
2,566.90	Florida
2,564.77	Vermont
2,557.81	North Dakota
2,555.87	Alabama
2,502.21	Ohio
2,477.81	Nebraska
2,453.79	Pennsylvania
2,413.82	Mississippi
2,412.64	Maryland
2,363.26	North Carolina
2,349.12	Michigan
2,320.33	Virginia
2,309.75	Nevada
2,271.41	Oklahoma
2,252.86	Idaho
2,217.15	South Dakota
2,212.44	Utah
2,205.22	Georgia
2,182.06	Tennessee
2,169.34	Indiana
2,151.34	Colorado
2,113.17	Illinois
2,105.91	New Hampshire
2,079.07	Arizona
1,994.89	Missouri
1,915.37	Texas

Table G.490. STAPC95

Expenditures of Funds from State (per capita) 1995

5,635.61	Alaska
4,105.93	Hawaii
3,732.59	Delaware
3,103.52	Connecticut
2,803.35	Wyoming
2,522.75	Rhode Island
2,444.77	New York
2,426.90	Wisconsin
2,404.34	Louisiana
2,399.35	Minnesota
2,392.55	Oregon
2,369.20	New Mexico
2,298.10	Washington
2,280.77	Massachusetts
2,224.83	New Jersey
2,206.49	Kentucky
2,198.34	Michigan
2,190.43	Iowa
2,188.97	Ohio
2,164.92	Maine
2,148.05	Kansas
2,126.39	Maryland
2,089.52	Arkansas
2,067.57	Virginia
1,970.51	Nevada
1,955.46	North Carolina
1,937.96	Florida
1,899.84	Alabama
1,874.01	Nebraska
1,847.84	South Carolina
1,804.98	Georgia
1,796.93	Pennsylvania
1,793.63	Utah
1,783.49	North Dakota
1,762.95	Montana
1,735.85	Vermont
1,711.60	California
1,698.50	Colorado
1,684.02	Oklahoma
1,683.14	West Virginia
1,673.82	Idaho
1,646.28	Illinois
1,620.34	Indiana
1,619.91	Missouri
1,580.45	Mississippi
1,549.11	Arizona
1,459.45	Tennessee
1,408.14	Texas
1,359.89	South Dakota
1,285.34	New Hampshire

Table G.491. FEDPC95

Expenditures of Funds from Federal (per capita) 1995

2,008.32	Alaska
1,128.31	New York
1,093.58	Louisiana
1,000.10	California
990.90	Rhode Island
973.09	West Virginia
971.96	North Dakota
947.70	Wyoming
914.24	Vermont
899.73	South Dakota
884.07	New Mexico
866.61	Maine
859.61	Montana
854.05	South Carolina
826.46	Mississippi
789.16	Iowa
771.29	Alabama
766.10	Hawaii
754.09	Kentucky
753.90	Oregon
744.35	Arkansas
740.20	Washington
739.49	Arizona
724.53	Pennsylvania
709.79	Tennessee
707.03	Massachusetts
704.74	Delaware
702.36	Wisconsin
687.61	New Hampshire
680.69	Idaho
678.12	Georgia
662.79	Connecticut
652.48	Oklahoma
645.45	Michigan
630.06	North Carolina
626.06	Minnesota
620.41	Kansas
604.89	Nebraska
593.37	Florida
591.14	New Jersey
584.60	Indiana
566.28	Maryland
557.07	Texas
554.38	Utah
541.60	Missouri
516.37	Illinois
474.05	Colorado
444.95	Nevada
441.90	Virginia
377.77	Ohio

Table G.492. TOTPC95

Expenditures of Funds from All Sources (per Capita) 1995

7,643.93	Alaska
4,872.03	Hawaii
4,437.33	Delaware
3,766.31	Connecticut
3,751.05	Wyoming
3,573.08	New York
3,513.65	Rhode Island
3,497.92	Louisiana
3,253.27	New Mexico
3,146.45	Oregon
3,129.26	Wisconsin
3,038.30	Washington
3,031.53	Maine
3,025.41	Minnesota
2,987.79	Massachusetts
2,979.58	Iowa
2,960.57	Kentucky
2,843.79	Michigan
2,833.87	Arkansas
2,815.97	New Jersey
2,768.46	Kansas
2,755.45	North Dakota
2,711.69	California
2,701.89	South Carolina
2,692.68	Maryland
2,671.12	Alabama
2,656.23	West Virginia
2,650.09	Vermont
2,622.55	Montana
2,585.53	North Carolina
2,566.74	Ohio
2,531.34	Florida
2,521.46	Pennsylvania
2,509.47	Virginia
2,483.10	Georgia
2,478.90	Nebraska
2,415.47	Nevada
2,406.91	Mississippi
2,354.51	Idaho
2,348.00	Utah
2,336.50	Oklahoma
2,288.60	Arizona
2,259.62	South Dakota
2,204.94	Indiana
2,172.55	Colorado
2,169.24	Tennessee
2,162.64	Illinois
2,161.50	Missouri
1,972.95	New Hampshire
1,965.20	Texas

Table G.493. STAPC96

Expenditures of Funds from State (per capita) 1996

5,320.66	Alaska
4,211.99	Hawaii
4,151.31	Delaware
3,075.60	Connecticut
2,953.68	Oregon
2,540.49	Rhode Island
2,517.09	New York
2,495.94	Wisconsin
2,490.62	New Mexico
2,489.31	Kentucky
2,464.93	Minnesota
2,411.43	Washington
2,394.58	Massachusetts
2,393.78	Michigan
2,373.95	Iowa
2,340.85	Nevada
2,290.69	Ohio
2,283.33	Wyoming
2,282.52	New Jersey
2,257.12	Kansas
2,226.35	Arkansas
2,219.89	Maryland
2,198.66	Louisiana
2,162.77	Maine
2,140.57	Arizona
2,097.22	Virginia
2,001.36	Georgia
1,987.70	South Carolina
1,933.86	Nebraska
1,928.54	Florida
1,924.48	Alabama
1,857.69	North Carolina
1,855.01	Indiana
1,840.34	Pennsylvania
1,833.33	Utah
1,827.43	Colorado
1,827.37	North Dakota
1,822.91	California
1,789.97	Oklahoma
1,777.20	Missouri
1,761.69	Montana
1,718.86	Idaho
1,697.95	Vermont
1,686.27	Illinois
1,662.73	Mississippi
1,628.92	West Virginia
1,623.82	Tennessee
1,504.52	Texas
1,374.83	South Dakota
1,192.08	New Hampshire

Table G.494. FEDPC96

Expenditures of Funds from Federal (per capita) 1996

1,568.60	Alaska
1,214.58	Wyoming
1,172.67	New York
1,086.75	New Mexico
1,009.11	Rhode Island
993.95	West Virginia
970.04	Louisiana
954.66	California
936.86	Vermont
936.34	Maine
926.91	North Dakota
917.39	Tennessee
898.52	Montana
886.46	South Dakota
876.17	South Carolina
863.47	Mississippi
805.33	Connecticut
800.68	Hawaii
788.34	Alabama
783.23	Arkansas
777.17	Delaware
770.89	Oregon
766.10	Michigan
760.51	Pennsylvania
754.44	Kentucky
739.47	Iowa
727.48	Wisconsin
724.73	Arizona
705.43	New Hampshire
699.59	Massachusetts
692.76	Idaho
663.53	Oklahoma
655.89	Kansas
647.71	Georgia
640.17	Nebraska
636.48	Washington
634.90	Minnesota
628.63	North Carolina
601.38	Utah
598.60	Florida
598.38	New Jersey
597.55	Texas
590.75	Indiana
581.97	Maryland
530.75	Illinois
529.43	Missouri
524.52	Colorado
448.62	Nevada
439.61	Virginia
361.58	Ohio

Table G.495. TOTPC96

Expenditures of Funds from All Sources (per capita) 1996

6,889.26	Alaska
5,012.67	Hawaii
4,928.47	Delaware
3,880.93	Connecticut
3,724.57	Oregon
3,689.76	New York
3,577.37	New Mexico
3,549.60	Rhode Island
3,497.92	Wyoming
3,243.75	Kentucky
3,223.42	Wisconsin
3,168.70	Louisiana
3,159.87	Michigan
3,113.41	Iowa
3,099.83	Minnesota
3,099.11	Maine
3,094.17	Massachusetts
3,047.91	Washington
3,009.58	Arkansas
2,913.01	Kansas
2,880.90	New Jersey
2,865.30	Arizona
2,863.87	South Carolina
2,801.86	Maryland
2,789.47	Nevada
2,777.57	California
2,754.28	North Dakota
2,712.82	Alabama
2,660.21	Montana
2,652.27	Ohio
2,649.07	Georgia
2,634.81	Vermont
2,622.87	West Virginia
2,600.85	Pennsylvania
2,574.03	Nebraska
2,541.21	Tennessee
2,536.83	Virginia
2,527.14	Florida
2,526.20	Mississippi
2,486.32	North Carolina
2,453.50	Oklahoma
2,445.76	Indiana
2,434.72	Utah
2,411.62	Idaho
2,351.95	Colorado
2,306.63	Missouri
2,261.29	South Dakota
2,217.02	Illinois
2,102.07	Texas
1,897.50	New Hampshire

Table G.496. STAPC97

Expenditures of Funds from State (per capita) 1997

5,326.77	Alaska
4,487.07	Delaware
4,264.09	Hawaii
3,359.74	Connecticut
3,193.75	Wyoming
2,966.70	Oregon
2,703.85	Wisconsin
2,664.08	Nevada
2,628.45	Massachusetts
2,593.86	Minnesota
2,585.03	New Mexico
2,577.44	Iowa
2,558.26	Rhode Island
2,482.06	New York
2,446.13	Ohio
2,438.19	Arkansas
2,419.52	Washington
2,346.59	Louisiana
2,311.16	Kansas
2,309.78	New Jersey
2,260.19	Michigan
2,236.99	Maryland
2,181.93	Kentucky
2,173.18	Virginia
2,152.61	Maine
2,071.26	Nebraska
2,064.64	South Carolina
2,032.45	Utah
2,031.20	North Dakota
2,030.06	Georgia
1,993.06	Alabama
1,984.40	Arizona
1,958.05	Florida
1,957.91	California
1,951.41	North Carolina
1,917.86	Pennsylvania
1,895.59	Oklahoma
1,851.30	Missouri
1,829.35	Montana
1,787.30	Indiana
1,780.14	Illinois
1,758.91	Vermont
1,748.17	Mississippi
1,741.19	West Virginia
1,720.89	Idaho
1,661.01	Colorado
1,648.20	Tennessee
1,521.20	South Dakota
1,481.79	Texas
1,242.11	New Hampshire

Table G.497. FEDPC97

Expenditures of Funds from Federal (per capita) 1997

1,625.62	Alaska
1,146.26	New Mexico
1,119.88	New York
1,084.24	North Dakota
1,069.38	West Virginia
1,060.79	Rhode Island
989.81	Vermont
986.25	California
983.33	Wyoming
979.09	Louisiana
975.90	Maine
964.67	Tennessee
915.05	Hawaii
903.37	Mississippi
903.30	Montana
872.82	South Carolina
860.34	Massachusetts
839.56	Kentucky
824.90	South Dakota
817.69	Delaware
815.97	Alabama
813.39	Arkansas
779.22	Oregon
777.48	Washington
774.30	Pennsylvania
754.83	Arizona
747.21	North Carolina
728.08	Wisconsin
725.19	Michigan
723.16	Connecticut
721.72	Idaho
720.04	Iowa
709.59	Colorado
687.13	New Hampshire
671.50	Nebraska
669.58	Minnesota
666.80	Maryland
663.40	New Jersey
662.08	Kansas
657.82	Oklahoma
639.73	Georgia
619.85	Utah
597.41	Indiana
594.01	Texas
582.51	Florida
525.47	Illinois
520.44	Missouri
459.97	Virginia
449.28	Nevada
412.86	Ohio

Table G.498. TOTPC97

Expenditures of Funds from All Sources (per capita) 1997

6,952.38	Alaska
5,304.76	Delaware
5,179.14	Hawaii
4,177.08	Wyoming
4,082.90	Connecticut
3,745.92	Oregon
3,731.28	New Mexico
3,619.05	Rhode Island
3,601.94	New York
3,488.80	Massachusetts
3,431.92	Wisconsin
3,325.67	Louisiana
3,297.48	Iowa
3,263.44	Minnesota
3,251.58	Arkansas
3,197.00	Washington
3,128.51	Maine
3,115.44	North Dakota
3,113.37	Nevada
3,021.49	Kentucky
2,985.39	Michigan
2,973.24	Kansas
2,973.18	New Jersey
2,944.16	California
2,937.47	South Carolina
2,903.79	Maryland
2,858.99	Ohio
2,810.57	West Virginia
2,809.03	Alabama
2,748.73	Vermont
2,742.75	Nebraska
2,739.24	Arizona
2,732.65	Montana
2,698.61	North Carolina
2,692.16	Pennsylvania
2,669.78	Georgia
2,652.30	Utah
2,651.54	Mississippi
2,633.15	Virginia
2,612.87	Tennessee
2,553.41	Oklahoma
2,540.56	Florida
2,442.61	Idaho
2,384.71	Indiana
2,371.74	Missouri
2,370.60	Colorado
2,346.10	South Dakota
2,305.61	Illinois
2,075.79	Texas
1,929.24	New Hampshire

Table G.499. STAPC98

Expenditures of Funds from State (per capita) 1998

5,282.93	Alaska
4,844.09	Delaware
4,285.71	Hawaii
3,573.79	Connecticut
3,314.63	Wisconsin
3,172.46	Oregon
3,095.83	Wyoming
2,997.12	New Mexico
2,978.78	Nevada
2,719.85	Minnesota
2,687.25	Rhode Island
2,675.78	Massachusetts
2,660.26	Iowa
2,656.70	New York
2,645.22	Ohio
2,626.87	Arkansas
2,550.92	Michigan
2,468.35	Washington
2,404.42	Kentucky
2,384.02	New Jersey
2,379.33	Louisiana
2,357.89	Maryland
2,355.73	South Carolina
2,255.86	Virginia
2,224.36	Maine
2,189.84	Kansas
2,143.29	Nebraska
2,121.55	Florida
2,108.04	Utah
2,078.21	Arizona
2,052.74	North Carolina
2,052.32	California
2,019.41	Pennsylvania
2,012.05	Georgia
2,009.28	Oklahoma
1,965.78	West Virginia
1,934.72	Missouri
1,923.66	Mississippi
1,909.09	North Dakota
1,882.93	Illinois
1,877.29	Indiana
1,865.09	Alabama
1,857.87	Vermont
1,801.14	Montana
1,774.17	Idaho
1,676.79	Tennessee
1,622.44	South Dakota
1,541.95	Texas
1,277.40	New Hampshire
1,137.31	Colorado

Table G.500. FEDPC98

Expenditures of Funds from Federal (per capita) 1998

1,684.55	Alaska
1,268.03	North Dakota
1,207.28	New York
1,103.42	Alabama
1,096.45	Vermont
1,094.37	West Virginia
1,061.70	Maine
1,054.72	South Dakota
1,040.49	Rhode Island
992.88	Kentucky
991.67	Wyoming
989.62	New Mexico
989.14	Tennessee
978.39	South Carolina
970.56	Mississippi
968.36	California
962.50	Montana
944.30	Louisiana
915.04	Massachusetts
841.61	Arkansas
820.17	Hawaii
800.77	Iowa
787.45	Washington
785.71	North Carolina
781.95	Pennsylvania
775.70	Georgia
753.52	Oklahoma
736.91	Nebraska
735.92	Wisconsin
725.81	Delaware
722.71	Michigan
721.75	Minnesota
718.93	Idaho
710.09	Arizona
702.36	New Hampshire
693.44	Kansas
679.16	Oregon
672.51	Maryland
631.18	New Jersey
616.62	Indiana
616.58	Texas
616.40	Missouri
614.95	Utah
590.96	Florida
523.94	Illinois
481.51	Virginia
452.41	Nevada
384.66	Connecticut
382.72	Colorado
375.51	Ohio

Table G.501. TOTPC98

Expenditures of Funds from All Sources (per capita) 1998

6,967.48	Alaska
5,569.89	Delaware
5,105.88	Hawaii
4,087.50	Wyoming
4,050.56	Wisconsin
3,986.74	New Mexico
3,958.45	Connecticut
3,863.98	New York
3,851.61	Oregon
3,727.73	Rhode Island
3,590.82	Massachusetts
3,468.48	Arkansas
3,461.03	Iowa
3,441.60	Minnesota
3,431.19	Nevada
3,397.31	Kentucky
3,334.11	South Carolina
3,323.63	Louisiana
3,286.06	Maine
3,273.63	Michigan
3,255.80	Washington
3,177.12	North Dakota
3,060.15	West Virginia
3,030.41	Maryland
3,020.73	Ohio
3,020.68	California
3,015.19	New Jersey
2,968.51	Alabama
2,954.31	Vermont
2,894.22	Mississippi
2,883.29	Kansas
2,880.19	Nebraska
2,838.46	North Carolina
2,801.37	Pennsylvania
2,788.30	Arizona
2,787.74	Georgia
2,763.64	Montana
2,762.80	Oklahoma
2,737.37	Virginia
2,722.99	Utah
2,712.50	Florida
2,677.15	South Dakota
2,665.93	Tennessee
2,551.12	Missouri
2,493.91	Indiana
2,493.10	Idaho
2,406.88	Illinois
2,158.53	Texas
1,979.76	New Hampshire
1,520.03	Colorado

Table G.502.   STAPC99

Expenditures of Funds from State (per capita) 1999

5,717.51	Alaska
5,157.01	Delaware
4,354.29	Hawaii
3,740.37	Connecticut
3,513.61	Wisconsin
3,373.63	Wyoming
3,287.54	Nevada
3,208.33	New Mexico
3,146.42	Oregon
2,898.33	Minnesota
2,884.29	Massachusetts
2,875.40	Rhode Island
2,867.48	Arkansas
2,837.84	New York
2,834.38	Iowa
2,724.97	Ohio
2,629.50	Kentucky
2,597.65	Washington
2,569.80	Virginia
2,544.27	New Jersey
2,540.78	Maryland
2,472.99	Michigan
2,439.37	Louisiana
2,434.88	Maine
2,402.72	Nebraska
2,311.94	Kansas
2,294.52	Florida
2,253.10	North Carolina
2,241.96	Utah
2,230.49	Arizona
2,189.25	California
2,169.43	West Virginia
2,128.06	Pennsylvania
2,122.14	Vermont
2,122.05	Georgia
2,067.34	North Dakota
2,060.04	Missouri
2,040.77	Oklahoma
1,997.47	Illinois
1,985.47	Mississippi
1,916.24	South Carolina
1,907.84	Alabama
1,881.56	Montana
1,876.65	Idaho
1,802.82	Indiana
1,746.32	Tennessee
1,706.38	South Dakota
1,570.93	Texas
1,307.93	New Hampshire
1,181.17	Colorado

Table G.503.   FEDPC99

Expenditures of Funds from Federal (per capita) 1999

2,179.18	Alaska
1,278.28	North Dakota
1,216.02	Vermont
1,178.98	Alabama
1,150.60	New York
1,130.38	Rhode Island
1,125.96	New Mexico
1,117.59	Wyoming
1,095.78	West Virginia
1,082.17	Maine
1,080.68	Montana
1,065.43	Kentucky
1,056.44	Tennessee
1,037.11	California
962.99	South Dakota
961.57	Louisiana
954.63	Mississippi
921.37	Oklahoma
905.06	Delaware
890.36	Pennsylvania
886.06	South Carolina
883.54	Massachusetts
876.83	Iowa
858.80	Michigan
856.18	Hawaii
828.31	Wisconsin
823.55	Georgia
823.09	Washington
813.31	Nebraska
813.29	Idaho
803.49	Arkansas
800.18	North Carolina
792.12	Arizona
787.10	Kansas
768.44	New Hampshire
740.92	Oregon
721.18	Minnesota
713.01	Missouri
694.42	Utah
692.42	Indiana
683.15	Maryland
659.55	New Jersey
653.46	Texas
618.68	Florida
550.36	Illinois
512.92	Nevada
509.83	Virginia
427.01	Colorado
411.64	Connecticut
392.03	Ohio

Table G.504.   TOTPC99

Expenditures of Funds from All Sources (per capita) 1999

7,896.69	Alaska
6,062.07	Delaware
5,210.47	Hawaii
4,491.22	Wyoming
4,341.92	Wisconsin
4,334.30	New Mexico
4,152.00	Connecticut
4,005.78	Rhode Island
3,988.44	New York
3,887.33	Oregon
3,800.46	Nevada
3,767.83	Massachusetts
3,711.21	Iowa
3,694.94	Kentucky
3,670.96	Arkansas
3,619.51	Minnesota
3,517.05	Maine
3,420.74	Washington
3,400.93	Louisiana
3,345.61	North Dakota
3,338.16	Vermont
3,331.79	Michigan
3,265.21	West Virginia
3,226.36	California
3,223.93	Maryland
3,216.03	Nebraska
3,203.82	New Jersey
3,117.00	Ohio
3,099.03	Kansas
3,086.83	Alabama
3,079.63	Virginia
3,053.28	North Carolina
3,022.60	Arizona
3,018.42	Pennsylvania
2,962.24	Montana
2,962.14	Oklahoma
2,945.59	Georgia
2,940.09	Mississippi
2,936.38	Utah
2,913.19	Florida
2,802.75	Tennessee
2,802.30	South Carolina
2,773.05	Missouri
2,689.94	Idaho
2,669.37	South Dakota
2,547.83	Illinois
2,495.25	Indiana
2,224.39	Texas
2,076.37	New Hampshire
1,608.18	Colorado

Table G.505.   STAPC00

Expenditures of Funds from State (per capita) 2000

5,424.24	Alaska
5,223.21	Delaware
4,518.15	Hawaii
4,056.96	Connecticut
3,942.95	Wisconsin
3,549.70	Wyoming
3,298.52	New Mexico
3,121.91	Massachusetts
3,024.27	Iowa
2,926.61	Minnesota
2,914.33	Arkansas
2,888.40	Ohio
2,758.14	New Jersey
2,753.82	Rhode Island
2,674.78	Michigan
2,659.93	Maryland
2,644.04	Washington
2,638.33	South Carolina
2,593.02	Virginia
2,590.59	Maine
2,559.92	New York
2,511.98	Nebraska
2,488.92	Louisiana
2,429.17	California
2,322.65	North Carolina
2,321.57	Alabama
2,300.03	Florida
2,238.10	Vermont
2,233.96	West Virginia
2,231.51	Oregon
2,216.17	Mississippi
2,193.91	Utah
2,188.67	Pennsylvania
2,186.90	Oklahoma
2,182.29	Kansas
2,168.78	Arizona
2,153.07	Illinois
2,130.20	Colorado
2,064.80	Indiana
2,057.55	Missouri
2,024.92	North Dakota
1,984.17	Kentucky
1,956.72	Idaho
1,951.14	Georgia
1,946.78	Montana
1,916.67	New Hampshire
1,793.26	Nevada
1,750.99	South Dakota
1,741.08	Tennessee
1,681.61	Texas

Table G.506.   FEDPC00

Expenditures of Funds from Federal (per capita) 2000

2,940.99	Alaska
1,492.27	South Carolina
1,428.35	North Dakota
1,364.53	Vermont
1,247.39	New Mexico
1,236.83	New York
1,231.87	Rhode Island
1,209.62	West Virginia
1,208.92	Wyoming
1,172.55	Maine
1,146.21	Kentucky
1,139.51	Georgia
1,138.58	Montana
1,101.29	California
1,086.82	Mississippi
1,037.09	South Dakota
1,016.00	Tennessee
990.78	Alabama
961.07	Louisiana
955.36	Delaware
946.68	Iowa
938.67	Wisconsin
901.09	Massachusetts
898.37	Washington
897.65	Pennsylvania
878.43	Nebraska
876.39	Connecticut
862.47	North Carolina
849.30	Idaho
839.11	Hawaii
832.02	Arkansas
817.73	Oklahoma
806.92	Kansas
801.47	Michigan
790.17	Missouri
788.03	New Hampshire
759.91	Minnesota
721.93	Colorado
713.75	Maryland
707.10	Oregon
690.90	Arizona
690.58	Texas
689.21	Utah
672.86	Indiana
671.82	Florida
665.20	New Jersey
596.26	Illinois
525.64	Virginia
517.61	Nevada
422.80	Ohio

Table G.507.   TOTPC00

Expenditures of Funds from Federal (per capita) 2000

8,365.23	Alaska
6,178.57	Delaware
5,357.26	Hawaii
4,933.35	Connecticut
4,881.62	Wisconsin
4,758.62	Wyoming
4,545.90	New Mexico
4,130.61	South Carolina
4,023.00	Massachusetts
3,985.69	Rhode Island
3,970.95	Iowa
3,796.74	New York
3,763.14	Maine
3,746.35	Arkansas
3,686.52	Minnesota
3,602.63	Vermont
3,542.42	Washington
3,530.47	California
3,476.25	Michigan
3,453.27	North Dakota
3,449.99	Louisiana
3,443.58	West Virginia
3,423.34	New Jersey
3,390.41	Nebraska
3,373.68	Maryland
3,312.35	Alabama
3,311.20	Ohio
3,302.99	Mississippi
3,185.12	North Carolina
3,130.38	Kentucky
3,118.66	Virginia
3,090.64	Georgia
3,086.31	Pennsylvania
3,085.37	Montana
3,004.64	Oklahoma
2,989.21	Kansas
2,971.84	Florida
2,938.61	Oregon
2,883.12	Utah
2,859.68	Arizona
2,852.13	Colorado
2,847.72	Missouri
2,806.03	Idaho
2,788.08	South Dakota
2,757.08	Tennessee
2,749.34	Illinois
2,737.66	Indiana
2,704.69	New Hampshire
2,372.19	Texas
2,310.87	Nevada

Table G.508.   ELESEC89

Percent of All Expenditures Devoted to Elementary and Secondary Education 1989

36.7	Texas
31.0	North Carolina
30.6	Missouri
29.4	New Mexico
28.9	Indiana
28.0	Utah
27.8	Idaho
27.7	Alabama
26.9	California
26.7	Georgia
26.7	Delaware
26.7	Washington
26.1	Mississippi
25.7	West Virginia
25.4	Maine
25.3	Florida
24.8	Kentucky
24.3	Arizona
24.2	New York
24.1	Kansas
23.5	New Jersey
23.0	Wyoming
23.0	Tennessee
22.3	Louisiana
22.3	Pennsylvania
22.1	Alaska
22.1	Arkansas
21.9	Nevada
21.7	Colorado
21.6	Oklahoma
21.5	South Carolina
20.4	Ohio
20.2	Michigan
19.7	Connecticut
19.4	Virginia
19.3	Montana
19.2	Vermont
19.0	Rhode Island
18.8	Wisconsin
18.6	Illinois
18.5	Minnesota
18.4	Maryland
18.0	North Dakota
15.4	Iowa
15.0	Hawaii
13.4	South Dakota
12.5	Massachusetts
12.1	Nebraska
11.0	Oregon
7.0	New Hampshire

Table G.509.   HIGHED89

Percent of All Expenditures Devoted to Higher Education 1989

26.2	Nebraska
26.0	Alabama
20.9	Iowa
20.6	Kansas
19.5	South Carolina
18.9	North Carolina
18.9	Wyoming
18.3	Wisconsin
18.1	Colorado
18.1	Virginia
17.6	Kentucky
16.6	South Dakota
16.2	Georgia
16.0	New Hampshire
15.8	Oregon
15.6	California
15.0	Arizona
14.8	West Virginia
14.7	Oklahoma
14.4	Mississippi
14.4	Tennessee
14.2	Texas
14.2	New Mexico
14.2	Maryland
14.0	Arkansas
13.2	Minnesota
12.9	Washington
12.8	Utah
11.9	North Dakota
11.5	Montana
11.3	Hawaii
11.0	Louisiana
10.6	Indiana
10.5	Connecticut
10.1	Nevada
10.0	Idaho
10.0	New York
9.9	Illinois
9.2	Missouri
8.8	Florida
8.5	Michigan
8.3	Alaska
8.0	Ohio
7.2	Delaware
7.0	Rhode Island
6.9	Pennsylvania
6.3	Maine
6.1	New Jersey
5.3	Vermont
5.3	Massachusetts

Table G.510.   ASSIST89

Percent of All Expenditures Devoted to Cash Assistance 1989

10.1	California
10.0	Michigan
8.0	Arkansas
6.9	Ohio
6.4	Massachusetts
6.3	Wisconsin
6.0	New York
5.6	Illinois
5.6	Vermont
5.4	Rhode Island
5.4	Maine
5.3	Pennsylvania
4.5	Connecticut
4.2	Washington
3.7	Minnesota
3.6	Montana
3.4	Hawaii
3.4	New Jersey
3.2	West Virginia
3.2	Texas
3.1	Idaho
3.1	Missouri
3.0	South Dakota
3.0	Oklahoma
3.0	Maryland
2.8	Georgia
2.7	Nebraska
2.7	Kansas
2.7	Colorado
2.7	Alaska
2.5	Kentucky
2.5	Utah
2.4	Iowa
2.3	Mississippi
2.2	Tennessee
2.2	Louisiana
2.1	North Carolina
2.1	Oregon
2.0	Wyoming
2.0	New Hampshire
2.0	Arizona
2.0	New Mexico
2.0	Indiana
1.8	North Dakota
1.7	Florida
1.6	Virginia
1.6	Nevada
1.5	South Carolina
1.4	Delaware
1.2	Alabama

Table G.511. MEDIC89

Percent of All Expenditures Devoted to Medicaid 1989

17.8	New York
16.6	Rhode Island
15.7	Maine
15.3	Tennessee
13.8	Indiana
13.3	Montana
13.1	Minnesota
13.1	New Hampshire
12.7	New Jersey
12.3	South Dakota
12.2	Wisconsin
12.0	Louisiana
11.9	Pennsylvania
11.9	Georgia
11.9	Kentucky
11.6	Ohio
11.6	North Dakota
11.5	Arkansas
11.3	Illinois
11.3	Oklahoma
11.3	Mississippi
10.8	Massachusetts
10.4	Nebraska
10.3	Missouri
10.0	California
10.0	Michigan
9.9	Vermont
9.9	North Carolina
9.7	Maryland
9.6	Connecticut
9.4	West Virginia
9.4	Florida
9.3	Colorado
9.0	Washington
8.4	New Mexico
8.0	South Carolina
7.9	Virginia
7.7	Alabama
7.3	Idaho
7.3	Utah
7.3	Nevada
7.2	Kansas
7.0	Iowa
6.7	Hawaii
6.3	Oregon
6.1	Texas
5.3	Delaware
4.5	Wyoming
3.5	Alaska
.0	Arizona

Table G.512. CORREC89

Percent of All Expenditures Devoted to Corrections 1989

7.6	Nevada
7.3	Virginia
5.4	Maryland
5.1	New York
5.1	Arizona
4.2	Michigan
4.2	South Carolina
4.0	Tennessee
3.6	California
3.4	Georgia
3.4	New Mexico
3.3	North Carolina
3.2	New Jersey
3.2	Utah
3.1	Florida
3.1	Kansas
3.0	Ohio
3.0	Colorado
3.0	Delaware
3.0	Alaska
2.8	New Hampshire
2.8	Oklahoma
2.8	Texas
2.7	Illinois
2.6	Rhode Island
2.5	Indiana
2.5	Louisiana
2.5	Massachusetts
2.4	Maine
2.4	Missouri
2.4	Oregon
2.2	Vermont
2.1	Montana
2.1	Washington
2.1	Wyoming
2.0	Nebraska
2.0	Connecticut
1.9	South Dakota
1.9	Kentucky
1.9	Mississippi
1.9	Alabama
1.9	Hawaii
1.8	Wisconsin
1.8	Idaho
1.5	Minnesota
1.5	Arkansas
1.4	Pennsylvania
1.3	Iowa
1.2	North Dakota
.7	West Virginia

Table G.513. TRANS89

Percent of All Expenditures Devoted to Transportation 1989

19.6	Wyoming
19.5	Nevada
18.9	Maryland
18.0	Montana
16.9	New Hampshire
16.8	South Dakota
16.7	Virginia
16.3	West Virginia
15.7	Alaska
15.0	Hawaii
14.9	Idaho
14.8	Mississippi
14.5	North Dakota
14.4	Vermont
14.4	Nebraska
14.0	New Mexico
14.0	Pennsylvania
13.7	Texas
13.6	Minnesota
13.2	Utah
13.2	Oklahoma
13.0	Delaware
12.9	Arkansas
12.4	Rhode Island
11.9	Tennessee
11.3	Arizona
11.3	Florida
11.3	Kansas
11.2	North Carolina
10.9	Illinois
10.8	Maine
10.7	Washington
10.4	South Carolina
10.4	Indiana
10.2	New Jersey
9.7	Missouri
9.6	Colorado
9.5	Connecticut
9.4	Wisconsin
9.2	Alabama
9.0	Michigan
9.0	Louisiana
8.4	Oregon
8.2	New York
8.1	Georgia
7.7	Iowa
7.3	Kentucky
6.6	Ohio
5.8	California
5.4	Massachusetts

Table G.514. OTHER89

Percent of All Expenditures Devoted to All Other Expenditures 1989

57.2	Massachusetts
53.8	Oregon
46.7	Hawaii
45.2	Iowa
44.7	Alaska
44.1	Connecticut
43.5	Vermont
43.5	Ohio
43.3	Delaware
42.4	Arizona
42.2	New Hampshire
41.2	North Dakota
41.0	Illinois
41.0	Louisiana
40.8	New Jersey
40.3	Florida
38.2	Pennsylvania
38.2	Michigan
37.0	Rhode Island
36.5	Minnesota
36.0	South Dakota
35.6	Colorado
35.1	Idaho
34.9	South Carolina
34.8	Missouri
34.4	Washington
34.0	Kentucky
33.9	Maine
33.3	Oklahoma
33.1	Wisconsin
32.9	Utah
32.2	Montana
32.1	Nebraska
32.0	Nevada
31.9	Indiana
31.0	Kansas
31.0	Georgia
30.5	Maryland
30.0	West Virginia
30.0	Arkansas
29.8	Wyoming
29.2	Mississippi
29.2	Tennessee
28.9	Virginia
28.8	New Mexico
28.7	New York
28.1	California
26.3	Alabama
23.6	North Carolina
23.3	Texas

Table G.515. ELESEC90

Percent of All Expenditures Devoted to Elementary and Secondary Education 1990

30.1	Utah
28.9	North Carolina
28.9	Texas
28.8	New Mexico
28.2	Missouri
27.5	Indiana
27.3	Idaho
26.9	Delaware
26.3	Georgia
26.2	Alabama
25.9	West Virginia
25.4	Mississippi
25.2	Washington
25.2	Maine
25.2	Oklahoma
25.0	California
24.7	Kentucky
24.5	Florida
24.0	New Jersey
23.8	New York
23.7	Arizona
23.7	Colorado
23.2	Kansas
22.9	Louisiana
22.8	Arkansas
22.6	Pennsylvania -
22.3	Alaska
21.6	Nevada
21.4	Tennessee
20.9	Wyoming
20.7	Vermont
20.3	Illinois
20.1	Virginia
20.0	Michigan
19.9	Ohio
19.5	South Carolina
19.3	Rhode Island
18.9	Wisconsin
17.8	North Dakota
17.5	Minnesota
17.0	Maryland
16.7	Iowa
15.9	Connecticut
14.7	South Dakota
14.5	Montana
13.5	Hawaii
12.1	Massachusetts
11.1	Oregon
11.0	Nebraska
7.8	New Hampshire

Table G.516. HIGHED90

Percent of All Expenditures Devoted to Higher Education 1990

25.2	Alabama
24.9	Nebraska
24.1	Iowa
20.1	Kansas
19.9	Colorado
18.9	South Carolina
18.8	North Carolina
18.4	Wisconsin
18.1	Kentucky
17.2	South Dakota
17.2	New Hampshire
16.8	Virginia
15.5	Wyoming
15.2	Mississippi
15.2	Oregon
15.1	Georgia
15.0	Washington
14.7	New Mexico
14.4	West Virginia
14.4	Oklahoma
14.3	Maryland
14.0	Arizona
14.0	Arkansas
13.9	Utah
13.4	Tennessee
13.1	Nevada
12.1	Texas
12.1	Indiana
11.9	North Dakota
11.6	Minnesota
11.2	Louisiana
11.1	Montana
10.9	Illinois
10.8	California
9.9	Florida
9.9	Connecticut
9.6	Alaska
9.5	Hawaii
9.1	New York
8.5	Missouri
8.4	Michigan
7.9	Idaho
7.7	Ohio
7.4	Delaware
6.8	Pennsylvania
6.6	Rhode Island
6.3	Maine
6.1	New Jersey
5.1	Vermont
4.1	Massachusetts

Table G.517. ASSIST90

Percent of All Expenditures Devoted to Cash Assistance 1990

9.7	Arkansas
9.5	California
8.9	Michigan
8.0	New York
7.0	Ohio
6.3	Massachusetts
6.0	Pennsylvania
6.0	Maine
5.6	Rhode Island
5.5	Illinois
5.1	Wisconsin
5.0	Connecticut
4.6	Vermont
4.3	Washington
3.5	Maryland
3.5	Nevada
3.2	West Virginia
3.1	Hawaii
3.0	New Jersey
2.9	Kansas
2.9	Oklahoma
2.8	Colorado
2.8	Oregon
2.8	Minnesota
2.8	Alaska
2.8	Missouri
2.7	South Dakota
2.7	Utah
2.6	Georgia
2.6	Montana
2.4	North Carolina
2.4	Kentucky
2.3	Iowa
2.3	Arizona
2.2	Nebraska
2.2	New Hampshire
2.1	Mississippi
2.1	Tennessee
2.1	Louisiana
1.9	North Dakota
1.9	Idaho
1.8	Indiana
1.7	Virginia
1.7	Texas
1.6	New Mexico
1.6	Florida
1.5	Wyoming
1.3	South Carolina
1.3	Delaware
.9	Alabama

Table G.518. MEDIC90

Percent of All Expenditures Devoted to Medicaid 1990

19.3	Tennessee
18.5	Rhode Island
17.7	New York
15.8	Indiana
14.4	Louisiana
14.1	Maine
14.1	North Dakota
14.0	Texas
13.5	Michigan
13.5	Georgia
13.4	South Dakota
13.3	Massachusetts
13.3	Mississippi
12.8	Ohio
12.8	Oklahoma
12.7	Minnesota
12.6	Arizona
12.4	New Jersey
12.3	Wisconsin
12.2	Arkansas
12.1	Vermont
12.0	Illinois
11.9	New Hampshire
11.7	Kentucky
11.5	Pennsylvania
11.5	West Virginia
11.4	Missouri
11.4	North Carolina
11.2	Nevada
10.9	Colorado
10.9	Montana
10.7	California
10.5	Connecticut
10.5	Nebraska
10.4	Florida
9.9	Washington
9.9	South Carolina
9.4	Maryland
8.9	Utah
8.5	Idaho
8.2	Kansas
8.2	New Mexico
7.7	Alabama
7.5	Iowa
7.2	Virginia
5.9	Delaware
5.7	Oregon
5.2	Hawaii
3.9	Alaska
3.6	Wyoming

Table G.519. CORREC90

Percent of All Expenditures Devoted to Corrections 1990

6.0	Maryland
5.6	Tennessee
5.0	New York
4.9	California
4.6	Utah
4.4	Arizona
4.3	Michigan
4.3	South Carolina
4.2	Georgia
4.2	Virginia
3.8	Texas
3.8	Florida
3.7	Massachusetts
3.6	New Mexico
3.6	Alaska
3.4	New Jersey
3.4	North Carolina
3.2	Delaware
3.1	Rhode Island
3.1	Kansas
3.0	Oklahoma
2.9	Illinois
2.9	Nevada
2.8	Colorado
2.7	Indiana
2.7	Ohio
2.7	Vermont
2.6	Missouri
2.5	New Hampshire
2.5	Connecticut
2.5	Washington
2.3	Louisiana
2.3	Alabama
2.3	Oregon
2.2	Maine
2.1	Idaho
2.0	Kentucky
1.9	Wisconsin
1.9	Montana
1.9	Nebraska
1.9	Hawaii
1.7	South Dakota
1.7	Mississippi
1.7	Pennsylvania
1.6	Arkansas
1.5	Wyoming
1.4	Iowa
1.3	Minnesota
1.0	North Dakota
.7	West Virginia

Table G.520. TRANS90

Percent of All Expenditures Devoted to Transportation 1990

25.3	Hawaii
20.0	Montana
17.9	Maryland
17.5	Minnesota
17.1	West Virginia
17.0	South Dakota
16.7	Wyoming
15.4	Alaska
15.3	Virginia
15.2	Connecticut
14.4	Vermont
14.1	Idaho
13.8	New Hampshire
13.3	Mississippi
13.2	Pennsylvania
13.1	Kansas
13.0	New Mexico
12.8	Utah
12.8	North Dakota
12.5	Nebraska
12.4	Arizona
12.2	Kentucky
12.0	Tennessee
12.0	North Carolina
11.9	Illinois
11.9	Nevada
11.8	South Carolina
11.8	Rhode Island
11.2	Oklahoma
11.1	Texas
10.9	Delaware
10.8	Indiana
10.6	Maine
10.5	Louisiana
9.3	Michigan
9.3	Wisconsin
9.2	Colorado
8.5	Missouri
8.5	Iowa
8.4	Georgia
8.2	New Jersey
8.2	Washington
8.0	New York
7.6	Arkansas
7.3	Florida
7.2	Oregon
7.0	Alabama
6.5	Ohio
6.1	Massachusetts
5.0	California

Table G.521. OTHER90

Percent of All Expenditures Devoted to All Other Expenditures 1990

55.7	Oregon
54.4	Massachusetts
44.6	New Hampshire
44.3	Delaware
43.5	Ohio
42.9	New Jersey
42.4	Alaska
42.4	Florida
41.5	Hawaii
41.1	Connecticut
40.5	North Dakota
40.4	Vermont
40.2	Wyoming
39.5	Iowa
39.0	Montana
38.2	Pennsylvania
38.1	Idaho
38.0	Missouri
37.0	Nebraska
36.6	Minnesota
36.6	Louisiana
36.5	Illinois
35.7	Nevada
35.7	Maine
35.6	Michigan
35.1	Rhode Island
34.8	Washington
34.7	Virginia
34.4	South Carolina
34.2	Wisconsin
34.2	California
33.3	South Dakota
32.0	Maryland
32.0	Arkansas
30.7	Colorado
30.7	Alabama
30.6	Oklahoma
30.5	Arizona
30.0	New Mexico
29.9	Georgia
29.3	Kansas
29.3	Indiana
29.0	Mississippi
29.0	Kentucky
28.4	Texas
28.4	New York
27.2	West Virginia
27.0	Utah
26.4	Tennessee
23.0	North Carolina

Table G.522. ELESEC91

Percent of All Expenditures Devoted to Elementary and Secondary Education 1991

32.5	West Virginia
29.1	North Carolina
28.8	Alabama
28.2	New Mexico
27.8	Utah
27.7	Idaho
27.6	Indiana
27.5	Missouri
27.0	Texas
26.6	Delaware
26.2	Georgia
25.9	Maine
25.9	Oklahoma
25.8	Mississippi
25.3	California
25.1	Washington
24.8	Florida
24.1	Louisiana
23.3	Arkansas
23.3	Colorado
22.8	New Jersey
22.6	Wyoming
22.5	Kentucky
22.2	Kansas
22.0	New York
21.9	Nevada
21.5	Minnesota
21.4	Pennsylvania
21.3	Arizona
20.8	Tennessee
20.7	Alaska
20.6	Michigan
20.4	Montana
20.0	Vermont
19.5	Illinois
19.1	North Dakota
19.1	South Carolina
19.0	Virginia
18.8	Wisconsin
18.8	Maryland
18.5	Iowa
18.2	Ohio
16.8	Connecticut
16.6	Rhode Island
15.5	Nebraska
14.1	Hawaii
14.0	South Dakota
10.7	Oregon
10.7	Massachusetts
10.6	New Hampshire

Table G.523. HIGHED91

Percent of All Expenditures Devoted to Higher Education 1991

25.7	Iowa
25.6	Alabama
24.4	Nebraska
20.4	South Carolina
19.5	Kentucky
19.5	Kansas
17.9	Wisconsin
17.7	New Mexico
17.4	Colorado
17.1	Wyoming
16.9	South Dakota
16.6	North Carolina
16.0	Virginia
16.0	Oregon
15.7	Texas
15.4	Oklahoma
15.3	Georgia
15.2	Arkansas
15.0	Mississippi
15.0	Maryland
14.7	West Virginia
13.9	Tennessee
13.7	Washington
13.2	Arizona
13.0	Utah
13.0	Minnesota
12.9	Nevada
11.5	Louisiana
11.4	California
10.7	North Dakota
10.4	Illinois
10.2	Indiana
10.0	Connecticut
9.6	Idaho
9.3	Florida
9.2	Montana
8.9	Alaska
8.8	New York
8.2	Michigan
8.2	Hawaii
7.9	Missouri
7.5	Ohio
7.3	Delaware
7.1	Maine
6.6	Pennsylvania
6.5	New Hampshire
5.9	Rhode Island
5.6	New Jersey
4.7	Vermont
4.1	Massachusetts

Table G.524. ASSIST91

Percent of All Expenditures Devoted to Cash Assistance 1991

9.6	California
9.1	New York
8.4	Michigan
7.2	Ohio
6.0	Massachusetts
5.9	Connecticut
5.9	Rhode Island
5.8	Maine
5.6	Vermont
5.4	Illinois
5.2	Pennsylvania
4.5	Wisconsin
4.3	Arkansas
4.1	Washington
3.5	New Hampshire
3.4	Nevada
3.3	Maryland
3.3	New Jersey
3.2	Minnesota
3.0	West Virginia
2.9	Oklahoma
2.9	Missouri
2.8	Georgia
2.7	Alaska
2.6	Kansas
2.6	Colorado
2.6	Hawaii
2.5	South Dakota
2.4	Iowa
2.4	Tennessee
2.4	Utah
2.3	Oregon
2.2	New Mexico
2.2	Arizona
2.2	Louisiana
2.2	Montana
2.1	Kentucky
2.1	Mississippi
1.9	Nebraska
1.9	Texas
1.9	North Dakota
1.9	Florida
1.8	North Carolina
1.7	Wyoming
1.7	Virginia
1.7	Indiana
1.7	Idaho
1.5	Delaware
1.3	South Carolina
1.0	Alabama

Table G.525. MEDIC91

Percent of All Expenditures Devoted to Medicaid 1991

20.2	Rhode Island
20.0	Tennessee
19.6	New York
17.8	Louisiana
17.8	Indiana
17.7	New Hampshire
16.4	Texas
15.9	Pennsylvania
15.9	Georgia
15.3	Maine
15.0	Massachusetts
15.0	Missouri
15.0	Mississippi
14.9	Vermont
14.6	Ohio
14.6	New Jersey
14.5	Minnesota
13.9	Michigan
13.9	Alabama
13.8	South Dakota
13.3	Arkansas
13.0	Wisconsin
12.9	Colorado
12.7	Nevada
12.7	Arizona
12.4	North Dakota
12.4	North Carolina
12.3	Illinois
12.2	Oklahoma
12.2	Kentucky
12.1	Connecticut
12.1	Florida
11.9	West Virginia
11.9	South Carolina
11.4	California
10.7	Washington
10.4	Maryland
10.0	Iowa
10.0	Montana
9.9	Kansas
9.9	Virginia
9.8	Idaho
9.5	Nebraska
9.4	Utah
9.3	Oregon
8.9	New Mexico
6.8	Delaware
5.3	Alaska
4.9	Hawaii
4.6	Wyoming

Table G.526. CORREC91

Percent of All Expenditures Devoted to Corrections 1991

5.5	Maryland
5.4	Texas
5.3	New York
4.7	South Carolina
4.7	Virginia
4.4	California
4.3	Tennessee
4.0	Georgia
3.8	Rhode Island
3.8	New Jersey
3.8	Arizona
3.8	North Carolina
3.7	Massachusetts
3.7	Michigan
3.7	Florida
3.6	Indiana
3.6	Connecticut
3.5	Delaware
3.4	Colorado
3.3	Kansas
3.2	Illinois
3.0	Ohio
3.0	Nevada
3.0	Oregon
3.0	Alaska
2.9	Oklahoma
2.9	Idaho
2.8	Louisiana
2.8	New Hampshire
2.8	Maine
2.8	Utah
2.7	New Mexico
2.6	Alabama
2.5	Vermont
2.5	Washington
2.3	Missouri
2.2	Kentucky
2.1	South Dakota
2.1	Wyoming
2.0	Pennsylvania
2.0	Nebraska
1.9	Mississippi
1.9	Wisconsin
1.8	Arkansas
1.8	Iowa
1.5	Minnesota
1.5	North Dakota
1.5	Montana
1.5	Hawaii
.7	West Virginia

Table G.527. TRANS91

Percent of All Expenditures Devoted to Transportation 1991

26.2	Hawaii
18.7	Alaska
17.9	Wyoming
17.2	Maryland
16.6	New Hampshire
16.6	South Dakota
16.2	Arizona
14.9	North Dakota
14.7	West Virginia
14.3	Virginia
14.2	Connecticut
13.7	Montana
13.2	Kentucky
12.5	Kansas
12.5	Vermont
12.5	Mississippi
12.5	Minnesota
12.2	Illinois
12.2	Idaho
11.8	North Carolina
11.8	Nebraska
11.7	Tennessee
11.7	Nevada
11.4	Pennsylvania
11.2	Indiana
11.1	Rhode Island
11.1	Delaware
10.8	New Mexico
10.6	Utah
10.3	Maine
10.2	Florida
10.1	Oklahoma
9.4	Colorado
9.3	Oregon
9.3	Iowa
9.1	Michigan
9.0	New Jersey
8.9	Wisconsin
8.8	Texas
8.8	Georgia
8.5	Louisiana
8.4	South Carolina
8.4	Washington
8.2	Missouri
8.1	New York
8.0	Ohio
7.8	California
7.8	Alabama
7.8	Arkansas
6.7	Massachusetts

Table G.528. OTHER91

Percent of All Expenditures Devoted to All Other Expenditures 1991

53.7	Massachusetts
49.6	Oregon
43.3	Delaware
43.0	Montana
42.5	Hawaii
42.3	New Hampshire
41.6	Ohio
40.9	New Jersey
40.7	Alaska
40.1	Vermont
39.6	North Dakota
38.1	Florida
37.7	Pennsylvania
37.4	Connecticut
37.0	Illinois
36.6	Rhode Island
36.3	Missouri
36.2	Idaho
36.1	Michigan
35.5	Washington
35.1	Wisconsin
35.0	Nebraska
34.5	Virginia
34.5	Arkansas
34.3	South Dakota
34.3	South Carolina
34.2	Nevada
34.1	Wyoming
34.1	Utah
33.7	Minnesota
33.2	Louisiana
32.9	Maine
32.3	Iowa
31.1	Colorado
30.7	Arizona
30.6	Oklahoma
30.2	California
30.0	Kansas
29.8	Maryland
29.5	New Mexico
28.3	Kentucky
27.9	Indiana
27.7	Mississippi
27.1	Georgia
27.1	New York
27.0	Tennessee
24.9	Texas
24.5	North Carolina
22.5	West Virginia
20.4	Alabama

Table G.529. ELESEC92

Percent of All Expenditures Devoted to Elementary and Secondary Education 1992

30.3	Wisconsin
28.8	West Virginia
28.3	New Mexico
28.1	Idaho
28.1	Utah
26.8	North Carolina
26.3	Indiana
26.0	Missouri
25.9	Texas
25.8	Washington
25.1	Oklahoma
24.9	Delaware
24.9	Kentucky
24.5	Georgia
23.7	Florida
23.6	Wyoming
23.2	New Jersey
23.0	Alabama
22.8	California
22.5	Arkansas
22.5	Arizona
22.0	Colorado
21.9	New York
21.8	Kansas
21.6	North Dakota
21.1	Nevada
21.1	Mississippi
20.6	Minnesota
20.4	Pennsylvania
19.6	Louisiana
19.5	Alaska
19.3	Michigan
19.2	Connecticut
19.1	Maine
19.0	Vermont
19.0	South Carolina
18.8	Virginia
18.4	Montana
17.6	Maryland
17.3	Iowa
17.2	Tennessee
17.0	Illinois
16.9	Nebraska
16.8	Ohio
14.5	South Dakota
14.4	Hawaii
14.2	Rhode Island
12.6	Oregon
8.9	Massachusetts
8.2	New Hampshire

Table G.530. HIGHED92

Percent of All Expenditures Devoted to Higher Education 1992

26.4	Wisconsin
26.2	Alabama
23.6	Nebraska
22.3	Iowa
19.6	Kansas
19.6	South Carolina
19.1	New Mexico
17.6	Wyoming
17.2	Colorado
16.5	Arkansas
16.4	South Dakota
15.9	Washington
15.6	Oregon
15.5	Oklahoma
15.5	Kentucky
15.0	Georgia
14.9	North Carolina
14.9	Virginia
14.7	Maryland
13.4	West Virginia
13.1	Texas
13.0	Arizona
12.6	Nevada
12.6	Mississippi
12.5	Utah
12.5	North Dakota
12.4	Minnesota
12.3	California
12.0	Connecticut
11.5	Tennessee
11.1	Idaho
10.2	Indiana
9.6	Louisiana
9.5	Illinois
8.8	New York
8.5	Alaska
8.0	Michigan
8.0	Montana
7.8	Ohio
7.6	Hawaii
7.4	Florida
7.3	Delaware
7.0	Missouri
6.0	Pennsylvania
5.8	Maine
5.4	New Hampshire
4.9	New Jersey
4.1	Vermont
4.1	Rhode Island
2.9	Massachusetts

Table G.531. ASSIST92

Percent of All Expenditures Devoted to Cash Assistance 1992

10.3	Ohio
9.7	California
9.0	New York
7.3	Connecticut
7.2	Maine
7.0	Michigan
5.9	Wisconsin
5.9	Vermont
5.3	Illinois
5.3	Massachusetts
5.2	Rhode Island
5.0	Pennsylvania
4.1	Arkansas
4.1	Washington
3.6	Nevada
3.6	Mississippi
3.5	Alaska
3.4	Maryland
3.4	New Jersey
3.3	Arizona
3.1	North Carolina
3.1	Minnesota
3.0	Georgia
3.0	Missouri
3.0	New Hampshire
2.9	Oregon
2.7	Kansas
2.7	Oklahoma
2.7	Kentucky
2.7	West Virginia
2.7	Hawaii
2.6	Colorado
2.5	New Mexico
2.5	Wyoming
2.5	Florida
2.3	Iowa
2.3	South Dakota
2.3	Utah
2.3	Tennessee
2.0	Nebraska
2.0	Montana
1.9	Virginia
1.8	Texas
1.8	North Dakota
1.8	Indiana
1.8	Delaware
1.5	Louisiana
1.4	Alabama
1.4	South Carolina
1.4	Idaho

Table G.532. MEDIC92

Percent of All Expenditures Devoted to Medicaid 1992

34.4	New Hampshire
27.5	Rhode Island
23.6	Tennessee
23.2	Louisiana
22.6	New York
21.6	Maine
21.6	Wisconsin
21.5	Pennsylvania
21.2	Texas
21.0	Missouri
20.5	Indiana
20.2	New Jersey
19.4	Michigan
18.5	Georgia
18.5	West Virginia
17.5	Illinois
17.5	Kentucky
17.1	Vermont
16.3	California
16.3	Colorado
16.3	Alabama
16.1	South Dakota
15.9	Ohio
15.9	Minnesota
15.8	Nevada
15.8	Mississippi
15.6	Maryland
15.4	North Carolina
14.7	Arkansas
14.5	South Carolina
14.3	Florida
14.1	Connecticut
13.8	Massachusetts
13.7	Oklahoma
13.2	North Dakota
12.4	Arizona
12.0	Washington
11.6	New Mexico
11.6	Nebraska
11.2	Virginia
10.7	Utah
10.4	Montana
10.3	Iowa
10.1	Kansas
9.7	Idaho
9.1	Oregon
8.3	Wyoming
7.3	Delaware
6.6	Hawaii
4.5	Alaska

Table G.533. CORREC92

Percent of All Expenditures Devoted to Corrections 1992

6.1	Texas
4.7	New York
4.6	Michigan
4.4	Connecticut
4.4	Virginia
4.3	Arizona
4.3	Delaware
4.2	California
4.2	North Carolina
4.2	South Carolina
3.9	Maryland
3.8	Colorado
3.7	Washington
3.6	Georgia
3.6	Tennessee
3.5	Alaska
3.3	Idaho
3.3	Indiana
3.3	New Jersey
3.2	Florida
3.2	Ohio
3.1	Kansas
2.9	Mississippi
2.9	Nevada
2.9	Rhode Island
2.9	Wisconsin
2.8	Illinois
2.8	Utah
2.7	Massachusetts
2.7	New Mexico
2.7	Oklahoma
2.4	Maine
2.3	Louisiana
2.2	Vermont
2.1	Missouri
2.1	Oregon
2.1	South Dakota
2.0	Pennsylvania
2.0	Wyoming
1.9	New Hampshire
1.8	Kentucky
1.7	Alabama
1.7	Arkansas
1.7	Hawaii
1.7	Nebraska
1.6	Iowa
1.5	Minnesota
1.5	Montana
1.2	North Dakota
1.0	West Virginia

Table G.534. TRANS92

Percent of All Expenditures Devoted to Transportation 1992

23.4	Hawaii
19.4	Wyoming
16.8	Alaska
16.4	South Dakota
15.0	Maryland
13.9	North Dakota
13.8	West Virginia
13.7	Virginia
13.6	Tennessee
13.5	Minnesota
13.4	Iowa
13.4	Montana
13.1	Wisconsin
13.0	Kansas
12.6	Vermont
12.5	Connecticut
12.5	Kentucky
12.4	Arizona
12.3	New Hampshire
11.7	Idaho
11.7	Illinois
11.1	North Carolina
11.1	Indiana
11.1	Mississippi
11.1	Nevada
10.7	Pennsylvania
10.7	Nebraska
10.6	Florida
10.5	Delaware
10.3	Utah
9.6	Ohio
9.6	Rhode Island
9.3	Oklahoma
9.2	Texas
9.2	New Mexico
9.0	Missouri
8.7	Maine
8.6	Michigan
8.1	Georgia
7.8	Colorado
7.7	Washington
7.7	Massachusetts
7.7	Alabama
7.6	South Carolina
7.6	Louisiana
7.5	Arkansas
7.3	New York
6.8	Oregon
6.0	New Jersey
4.7	California

Table G.535. OTHER92

Percent of All Expenditures Devoted to All Other Expenditures 1992

58.8	Massachusetts
50.9	Oregon
46.2	Montana
43.9	Delaware
43.6	Hawaii
43.6	Alaska
39.2	Vermont
39.0	New Jersey
38.3	Florida
36.6	Rhode Island
36.4	Ohio
36.2	Illinois
36.1	Louisiana
36.0	North Dakota
35.2	Virginia
35.2	Maine
34.8	New Hampshire
34.8	Idaho
34.5	Pennsylvania
33.8	South Carolina
33.6	Nebraska
33.3	Utah
33.2	Michigan
33.0	Arkansas
32.9	Minnesota
32.9	Iowa
32.9	Mississippi
32.9	Nevada
32.2	South Dakota
32.0	Arizona
31.9	Missouri
31.0	Oklahoma
30.8	Washington
30.5	Connecticut
30.4	Colorado
29.9	California
29.8	Maryland
29.8	Kansas
28.2	Tennessee
27.3	Georgia
26.8	Wyoming
26.8	Indiana
26.6	New Mexico
25.7	New York
25.2	Kentucky
24.4	North Carolina
23.8	Alabama
22.7	Texas
21.8	West Virginia
.0	Wisconsin

Table G.536. ELESEC93

Percent of All Expenditures Devoted to Elementary and Secondary Education 1993

34.4	Utah
27.9	Washington
27.8	Idaho
27.3	Oklahoma
26.8	West Virginia
26.4	North Carolina
25.5	Texas
25.3	Missouri
24.9	Indiana
24.8	Delaware
24.7	Kansas
24.4	California
24.4	Alabama
24.3	Georgia
24.3	Kentucky
23.4	New Jersey
22.4	Mississippi
22.3	Colorado
21.3	Arkansas
20.9	Pennsylvania
20.8	Wisconsin
20.7	Montana
20.7	Michigan
20.7	Nevada
20.7	Arizona
20.7	New Mexico
20.6	Louisiana
20.5	Minnesota
19.3	Maryland
19.2	New York
18.9	Wyoming
18.8	South Carolina
18.7	Alaska
18.7	Iowa
18.6	Virginia
18.6	Tennessee
18.5	North Dakota
17.6	Florida
17.6	Ohio
17.4	Rhode Island
17.1	Vermont
16.8	Maine
16.8	Connecticut
16.7	Nebraska
16.5	Illinois
14.9	Oregon
14.8	South Dakota
13.6	Hawaii
10.2	Massachusetts
7.0	New Hampshire

Table G.537. HIGHED93

Percent of All Expenditures Devoted to Higher Education 1993

25.1	Alabama
24.8	Iowa
23.7	Nebraska
20.5	South Carolina
17.8	Wisconsin
17.7	Kansas
17.5	Georgia
16.6	Arkansas
16.1	Colorado
16.0	South Dakota
15.7	Maryland
15.4	Washington
15.2	Oklahoma
15.1	North Carolina
15.0	Oregon
14.2	Virginia
13.8	Kentucky
13.8	Mississippi
13.3	Tennessee
12.5	Texas
12.5	Minnesota
11.9	Louisiana
11.9	North Dakota
11.9	Nevada
11.8	New Mexico
11.8	Wyoming
11.7	Utah
11.7	Arizona
11.4	West Virginia
10.9	Connecticut
10.6	Idaho
8.9	Montana
8.9	Illinois
8.7	Indiana
8.3	Alaska
7.9	Florida
7.7	Michigan
7.7	New York
7.3	California
7.3	Ohio
6.9	Delaware
6.9	Hawaii
6.7	Missouri
5.9	Pennsylvania
5.2	New Hampshire
5.0	New Jersey
4.9	Maine
4.3	Rhode Island
4.1	Vermont
3.4	Massachusetts

Table G.538. ASSIST93

Percent of All Expenditures Devoted to Cash Assistance 1993

10.0	New York
9.8	California
7.0	Michigan
6.8	Massachusetts
6.7	Connecticut
5.7	Rhode Island
5.6	Vermont
5.3	Pennsylvania
5.2	Maine
4.9	Washington
4.6	Ohio
4.2	Illinois
4.1	Wisconsin
3.8	Minnesota
3.6	New Jersey
3.5	Arkansas
3.5	Nevada
3.5	New Mexico
3.5	Alaska
3.4	Arizona
3.1	North Carolina
3.0	Maryland
3.0	Kentucky
2.9	Georgia
2.9	Oklahoma
2.9	Hawaii
2.9	Missouri
2.9	New Hampshire
2.8	Oregon
2.5	Iowa
2.5	Colorado
2.5	West Virginia
2.5	Florida
2.4	Tennessee
2.3	Kansas
2.3	Texas
2.3	Utah
2.2	South Dakota
2.2	Montana
2.0	Virginia
2.0	Delaware
1.8	Nebraska
1.8	Louisiana
1.8	Wyoming
1.8	Indiana
1.7	South Carolina
1.5	Mississippi
1.4	North Dakota
1.4	Idaho
1.3	Alabama

Table G.539. MEDIC93

Percent of All Expenditures Devoted to Medicaid 1993

33.8	New Hampshire
30.7	Rhode Island
26.5	Tennessee
26.5	Louisiana
25.0	Indiana
24.4	New York
23.9	Michigan
23.1	West Virginia
22.0	Mississippi
21.9	Maine
21.3	New Jersey
21.1	Georgia
21.0	Texas
20.6	Pennsylvania
20.6	Missouri
20.4	Illinois
20.3	Kentucky
19.6	Massachusetts
19.5	Colorado
18.2	Vermont
18.2	Minnesota
17.8	South Carolina
17.5	Nevada
17.5	New Mexico
17.2	North Carolina
16.6	South Dakota
16.4	Ohio
16.2	Arkansas
16.1	California
15.7	Alabama
15.5	Wisconsin
15.4	Oklahoma
15.2	Washington
15.2	Maryland
15.2	Florida
14.9	North Dakota
14.4	Nebraska
14.3	Connecticut
13.9	Arizona
13.4	Montana
12.7	Idaho
12.2	Virginia
12.1	Iowa
11.5	Utah
10.2	Oregon
10.2	Kansas
8.6	Delaware
7.9	Wyoming
6.3	Hawaii
4.8	Alaska

Table G.540. CORREC93

Percent of All Expenditures Devoted to Corrections 1993

5.8	Texas
4.9	Michigan
4.3	Maryland
4.2	South Carolina
3.9	California
3.9	Connecticut
3.8	Rhode Island
3.8	Tennessee
3.8	Georgia
3.8	Virginia
3.7	New York
3.6	North Carolina
3.6	Arizona
3.5	Colorado
3.5	Ohio
3.3	Delaware
3.1	Indiana
3.1	Idaho
2.9	New Jersey
2.9	Massachusetts
2.9	Kansas
2.8	Illinois
2.8	Nevada
2.8	New Mexico
2.8	Florida
2.8	Alaska
2.7	Vermont
2.7	Utah
2.6	Louisiana
2.6	Oklahoma
2.5	Washington
2.2	Pennsylvania
2.2	South Dakota
2.1	Wisconsin
2.1	Oregon
2.0	Maine
2.0	Missouri
1.9	New Hampshire
1.9	Nebraska
1.9	Iowa
1.8	Kentucky
1.8	Montana
1.8	Wyoming
1.7	West Virginia
1.7	Arkansas
1.7	Alabama
1.6	Mississippi
1.6	Minnesota
1.5	Hawaii
1.0	North Dakota

Table G.541. TRANS93

Percent of All Expenditures Devoted to Transportation 1993

18.5	Hawaii
17.8	Wyoming
16.3	Maryland
15.8	Alaska
15.2	South Dakota
14.2	Connecticut
13.3	Florida
13.2	Montana
13.1	New Hampshire
12.6	Vermont
12.5	West Virginia
11.8	Virginia
11.8	North Dakota
11.7	Kentucky
11.3	North Carolina
11.3	Louisiana
11.2	Idaho
11.2	Mississippi
11.0	Nebraska
10.8	Iowa
10.7	Delaware
10.5	New Mexico
10.4	Nevada
10.3	Kansas
10.2	Rhode Island
10.1	Indiana
10.1	Illinois
10.0	Massachusetts
9.9	Utah
9.9	Maine
9.8	Arizona
9.8	Pennsylvania
9.8	Minnesota
9.5	Tennessee
9.0	Texas
9.0	Michigan
8.9	Oklahoma
8.7	Wisconsin
8.6	Missouri
8.4	Washington
8.2	Arkansas
7.7	South Carolina
7.4	Colorado
7.3	Georgia
7.3	Alabama
6.5	Oregon
5.8	New York
5.7	Ohio
5.4	California
4.7	New Jersey

Table G.542. OTHER93

Percent of All Expenditures Devoted to All Other Expenditures 1993

50.3	Hawaii
48.4	Oregon
47.2	Massachusetts
46.2	Alaska
44.9	Ohio
43.7	Delaware
40.7	Florida
40.5	North Dakota
40.0	Wyoming
39.9	Montana
39.7	Vermont
39.5	Maine
39.2	New Jersey
37.5	Virginia
37.1	Illinois
36.7	Arizona
36.2	New Hampshire
35.3	Pennsylvania
33.8	Missouri
33.7	Minnesota
33.3	Idaho
33.2	New Mexico
33.2	Nevada
33.1	Connecticut
33.0	South Dakota
33.0	California
32.5	Arkansas
31.8	Kansas
31.1	Wisconsin
30.6	Nebraska
29.3	Iowa
29.3	South Carolina
29.3	New York
28.8	Colorado
28.0	Rhode Island
27.7	Oklahoma
27.6	Mississippi
27.5	Utah
26.7	Michigan
26.5	Indiana
26.1	Maryland
25.9	Tennessee
25.7	Washington
25.3	Louisiana
25.2	Kentucky
24.6	Alabama
23.8	Texas
23.3	North Carolina
23.1	Georgia
22.0	West Virginia

Table G.543. ELESEC94

Percent of All Expenditures Devoted to Elementary and Secondary Education 1994

34.4	Utah
28.9	Texas
28.3	Oklahoma
28.3	Washington
26.3	Idaho
25.4	Kansas
25.4	Kentucky
25.1	Delaware
25.1	West Virginia
24.5	Missouri
24.4	Indiana
24.0	New Jersey
23.6	Alabama
23.4	Michigan
23.4	North Carolina
23.1	Georgia
22.5	Minnesota
22.3	Arizona
22.1	Mississippi
21.9	Wyoming
21.1	Arkansas
20.7	Colorado
20.5	Montana
20.5	Pennsylvania
20.3	New Mexico
20.3	Nevada
20.1	Wisconsin
19.6	New York
18.8	North Dakota
18.6	Florida
18.6	Maryland
18.5	South Carolina
18.4	Iowa
18.4	Tennessee
18.1	California
17.9	Louisiana
17.4	Virginia
17.2	Illinois
16.9	Alaska
16.9	Vermont
16.3	Maine
16.1	Ohio
16.0	Nebraska
14.4	Rhode Island
14.1	Hawaii
14.0	South Dakota
13.8	Oregon
13.5	Connecticut
10.4	Massachusetts
6.6	New Hampshire

Table G.544. HIGHED94

Percent of All Expenditures Devoted to Higher Education 1994

27.3	Alabama
25.3	Iowa
22.9	Nebraska
21.0	South Carolina
19.3	North Carolina
17.7	Wisconsin
17.5	Kansas
16.3	South Dakota
16.1	Maryland
16.0	Arkansas
16.0	Colorado
15.4	Georgia
15.3	Oklahoma
14.8	Kentucky
14.6	Virginia
14.5	Oregon
13.9	Texas
13.0	Tennessee
12.6	Utah
12.4	North Dakota
11.9	Arizona
11.8	West Virginia
11.7	Minnesota
11.7	New Mexico
11.7	Nevada
11.1	Mississippi
10.1	Louisiana
9.6	Illinois
9.5	Rhode Island
9.4	Wyoming
9.0	Montana
8.9	Idaho
8.7	Washington
8.4	Connecticut
8.1	Indiana
8.1	Alaska
7.8	New York
7.8	Florida
7.1	Michigan
7.1	Ohio
6.7	California
6.3	Hawaii
6.1	Delaware
6.1	Missouri
5.9	Pennsylvania
5.1	New Jersey
5.0	New Hampshire
4.9	Maine
3.9	Massachusetts
3.8	Vermont

Table G.545. ASSIST94

Percent of All Expenditures Devoted to Cash Assistance 1994

9.6	New York
9.4	California
6.2	Michigan
5.7	Massachusetts
5.4	Vermont
5.2	Washington
5.1	Maine
4.9	Connecticut
4.8	Pennsylvania
4.4	Rhode Island
4.2	Ohio
4.1	Illinois
3.7	Wisconsin
3.7	Arkansas
3.7	Alaska
3.6	Minnesota
3.6	New Jersey
3.4	Hawaii
3.2	Arizona
3.2	New Mexico
3.2	Nevada
3.0	New Hampshire
2.9	Maryland
2.8	Oklahoma
2.8	Missouri
2.7	North Carolina
2.7	Kentucky
2.6	Georgia
2.4	Iowa
2.4	West Virginia
2.4	Florida
2.3	Montana
2.2	South Dakota
2.2	Oregon
2.2	Utah
2.0	Kansas
2.0	Colorado
2.0	Tennessee
1.9	Virginia
1.7	Nebraska
1.6	Idaho
1.6	Indiana
1.5	Texas
1.5	Mississippi
1.5	Delaware
1.3	South Carolina
1.3	Wyoming
1.2	North Dakota
1.2	Louisiana
1.1	Alabama

Table G. 546. MEDIC94

Percent of All Expenditures Devoted to Medicaid 1994

38.3	New Hampshire
30.2	Louisiana
29.2	New York
26.1	Tennessee
24.8	Indiana
23.7	New Jersey
23.5	Maine
23.3	Rhode Island
22.8	Texas
22.2	Georgia
22.0	West Virginia
21.0	Missouri
20.9	Mississippi
20.3	Illinois
20.0	California
19.6	Michigan
19.4	Pennsylvania
19.3	Vermont
19.1	Massachusetts
18.9	South Carolina
18.4	Minnesota
17.8	Colorado
17.7	New Mexico
17.7	Nevada
17.7	South Dakota
17.0	Kentucky
16.8	North Carolina
16.5	Arkansas
16.4	Alabama
16.3	Washington
15.9	Florida
15.8	Ohio
15.8	Wisconsin
15.4	Arizona
14.7	Maryland
14.5	Nebraska
14.3	Connecticut
14.1	Oklahoma
13.5	Montana
13.5	Idaho
13.1	North Dakota
12.6	Iowa
11.9	Virginia
11.4	Utah
10.2	Oregon
10.1	Kansas
8.8	Wyoming
8.3	Delaware
8.2	Hawaii
5.3	Alaska

Table G.547.   CORREC94

Percent of All Expenditures Devoted to Corrections 1994

7.0	Texas
5.0	Colorado
4.8	Michigan
4.0	North Carolina
4.0	Arizona
3.8	California
3.8	South Carolina
3.8	Maryland
3.8	Virginia
3.7	New York
3.7	Georgia
3.7	Ohio
3.5	Tennessee
3.2	Rhode Island
3.2	Florida
3.1	New Jersey
3.0	Connecticut
3.0	Idaho
2.9	Illinois
2.9	Utah
2.9	Delaware
2.8	New Mexico
2.8	Nevada
2.8	Alaska
2.7	Indiana
2.6	Pennsylvania
2.6	Washington
2.6	Oklahoma
2.6	Kansas
2.5	Vermont
2.4	Louisiana
2.2	Wisconsin
2.1	South Dakota
1.9	New Hampshire
1.9	Missouri
1.9	Montana
1.9	Oregon
1.8	Arkansas
1.8	Iowa
1.7	Maine
1.7	Massachusetts
1.7	Minnesota
1.7	Kentucky
1.6	Alabama
1.6	Nebraska
1.5	Mississippi
1.5	Hawaii
1.3	West Virginia
1.3	North Dakota
1.3	Wyoming

Table G.548.   TRANS94

Percent of All Expenditures Devoted to Transportation 1994

16.8	South Dakota
16.5	Alaska
15.8	Hawaii
15.7	Wyoming
14.4	Maryland
14.2	West Virginia
13.9	Montana
13.2	Connecticut
13.2	Idaho
13.1	North Dakota
12.4	Vermont
12.4	Massachusetts
12.2	Kentucky
12.1	New Hampshire
12.0	Virginia
11.8	Florida
10.6	Nebraska
10.5	Tennessee
10.4	Arizona
10.3	New Mexico
10.3	Nevada
10.2	Pennsylvania
10.2	Kansas
10.0	North Carolina
10.0	Illinois
9.8	Indiana
9.8	Wisconsin
9.7	Delaware
9.6	Washington
9.6	Minnesota
9.5	Mississippi
9.3	Missouri
8.9	Utah
8.8	Texas
8.8	Oklahoma
8.8	Iowa
8.6	Colorado
8.6	Michigan
8.1	Maine
7.9	Arkansas
7.8	Rhode Island
7.6	Oregon
7.1	Georgia
7.1	Alabama
6.7	South Carolina
5.9	New York
5.8	Ohio
5.8	Louisiana
5.7	California
5.1	New Jersey

Table G.549.   OTHER94

Percent of All Expenditures Devoted to All Other Expenditures 1994

50.8	Hawaii
49.9	Oregon
47.2	Ohio
46.9	Massachusetts
46.8	Alaska
46.4	Delaware
42.8	Connecticut
41.6	Wyoming
40.3	Florida
40.3	Maine
40.1	North Dakota
39.8	Vermont
38.9	Montana
38.5	Virginia
37.3	Rhode Island
36.7	Pennsylvania
36.2	California
36.0	Illinois
35.5	New Jersey
34.4	Missouri
34.1	New Mexico
34.1	Nevada
33.6	Idaho
33.4	Mississippi
33.0	New Hampshire
32.9	Arizona
32.9	Arkansas
32.8	Nebraska
32.6	Minnesota
32.4	Louisiana
32.3	Kansas
31.0	South Dakota
30.7	Wisconsin
30.7	Iowa
30.2	Michigan
29.9	South Carolina
29.8	Colorado
29.4	Maryland
29.3	Washington
28.6	Indiana
28.0	Oklahoma
27.6	Utah
26.5	Tennessee
26.1	Kentucky
26.1	Georgia
24.2	New York
23.7	North Carolina
23.0	West Virginia
22.8	Alabama
17.0	Texas

Table G.550. ELESEC95

Percent of All Expenditures Devoted to Elementary and Secondary Education 1995

33.8	Utah
33.0	Michigan
28.1	Texas
27.7	Idaho
27.7	Indiana
26.5	Oklahoma
26.4	Wyoming
26.2	Washington
26.0	Kentucky
24.6	Georgia
24.5	Missouri
24.4	Kansas
24.3	Mississippi
24.3	North Carolina
24.2	Delaware
22.8	Alabama
21.8	New Mexico
21.8	Minnesota
21.7	New Jersey
21.6	Arkansas
21.3	Colorado
21.1	Arizona
20.7	West Virginia
20.2	Wisconsin
20.1	Montana
20.1	California
20.0	Pennsylvania
19.3	New York
19.1	Iowa
19.1	Tennessee
19.0	Alaska
18.8	Louisiana
18.4	North Dakota
18.2	South Carolina
17.2	Florida
17.1	Illinois
17.0	Virginia
17.0	Maryland
16.7	Vermont
16.5	Ohio
16.5	Nebraska
15.3	Connecticut
15.1	Oregon
14.9	Rhode Island
14.6	Hawaii
14.4	South Dakota
13.9	Maine
12.8	Massachusetts
12.4	Nevada
6.9	New Hampshire

Table G.551. HIGHED95

Percent of All Expenditures Devoted to Higher Education 1995

26.7	Alabama
24.1	Iowa
22.1	Nebraska
20.4	South Carolina
18.9	New Mexico
18.0	Kansas
17.4	North Carolina
16.9	Oklahoma
16.8	South Dakota
16.8	Wisconsin
16.1	Mississippi
16.0	Arkansas
15.5	Colorado
15.2	Oregon
14.9	Tennessee
14.5	Maryland
14.4	Georgia
14.2	Virginia
13.3	Kentucky
12.4	Texas
12.2	Utah
11.4	Arizona
11.4	North Dakota
11.3	Minnesota
10.6	Idaho
9.9	Wyoming
9.8	Alaska
9.7	Louisiana
9.5	Illinois
9.4	Connecticut
9.3	Rhode Island
8.9	Montana
8.5	Indiana
8.1	Washington
7.7	Nevada
7.4	Ohio
7.3	New York
7.0	California
7.0	West Virginia
6.6	Florida
6.4	Hawaii
6.2	Delaware
6.1	Michigan
6.1	Missouri
5.8	Pennsylvania
5.6	New Hampshire
4.8	Massachusetts
4.4	Maine
4.4	New Jersey
3.9	Vermont

Table G.552. ASSIST95

Percent of All Expenditures Devoted to Cash Assistance 1995

10.0	California
6.3	New York
5.6	Massachusetts
5.4	Connecticut
4.9	Maine
4.9	Vermont
4.6	Pennsylvania
4.4	Alaska
4.4	Michigan
4.1	Washington
4.0	Illinois
4.0	Rhode Island
3.7	Hawaii
3.5	Ohio
3.4	New Jersey
3.2	Arkansas
3.1	Wisconsin
3.1	New Hampshire
3.0	Arizona
2.9	Minnesota
2.8	Missouri
2.6	New Mexico
2.6	North Carolina
2.6	Maryland
2.5	Oklahoma
2.3	Georgia
2.2	Kentucky
2.1	Oregon
2.1	Tennessee
2.1	Montana
2.1	Florida
2.0	Iowa
1.9	South Dakota
1.7	Kansas
1.7	Colorado
1.7	Utah
1.6	Virginia
1.6	Idaho
1.5	Indiana
1.5	Nevada
1.5	Delaware
1.4	Nebraska
1.3	Texas
1.3	Louisiana
1.3	West Virginia
1.1	South Carolina
1.1	North Dakota
1.1	Wyoming
1.0	Mississippi
.7	Alabama

Table G.553. MEDIC95

Percent of All Expenditures Devoted to Medicaid 1995

32.0	New Hampshire
29.4	New York
26.2	Louisiana
24.7	Tennessee
24.0	Illinois
24.0	Rhode Island
23.7	Maine
22.1	New Jersey
22.1	Texas
21.7	Missouri
21.6	Ohio
21.5	Mississippi
20.5	Massachusetts
20.0	Vermont
19.6	California
19.6	Pennsylvania
19.2	South Dakota
19.1	Georgia
19.1	Indiana
18.6	Kentucky
18.5	Minnesota
18.1	Colorado
17.7	South Carolina
17.6	Michigan
17.0	Arkansas
16.9	Alabama
16.7	Connecticut
16.2	Washington
15.4	Montana
15.3	Florida
15.2	West Virginia
15.0	Nebraska
14.9	North Dakota
14.3	Wisconsin
14.3	Oklahoma
14.2	Arizona
14.2	Maryland
13.4	Oregon
12.6	Idaho
12.4	Virginia
12.3	Iowa
12.2	New Mexico
12.0	North Carolina
11.5	Utah
11.0	Nevada
10.4	Kansas
10.1	Delaware
9.0	Hawaii
8.4	Wyoming
6.1	Alaska

Table G.554. CORREC95

Percent of All Expenditures Devoted to Corrections 1995

9.3	Texas
6.0	Colorado
5.8	Nevada
4.9	Maryland
4.3	California
4.3	Michigan
4.3	Arizona
4.1	Ohio
4.1	Georgia
3.9	Virginia
3.8	New York
3.8	Tennessee
3.8	Florida
3.8	North Carolina
3.6	South Carolina
3.6	Idaho
3.2	Rhode Island
3.2	Connecticut
3.2	Utah
3.1	Illinois
3.1	New Jersey
3.1	Delaware
3.1	Alaska
3.0	Indiana
2.9	Washington
2.8	Mississippi
2.8	Pennsylvania
2.8	Oklahoma
2.8	Kansas
2.7	Vermont
2.6	Louisiana
2.3	Wisconsin
2.3	New Mexico
2.2	Alabama
2.2	Oregon
2.1	New Hampshire
2.1	Missouri
2.1	South Dakota
1.9	Minnesota
1.9	Iowa
1.8	Maine
1.8	Kentucky
1.8	Arkansas
1.8	Montana
1.7	Nebraska
1.7	Hawaii
1.6	Wyoming
1.5	Massachusetts
1.1	North Dakota
.6	West Virginia

Table G.555. TRANS95

Percent of All Expenditures Devoted to Transportation 1995

18.1	Alaska
18.0	Wyoming
15.5	South Dakota
14.5	Maryland
14.0	Hawaii
13.7	Montana
13.6	Idaho
13.5	North Dakota
13.4	Virginia
12.1	Massachusetts
12.0	New Hampshire
11.9	Florida
11.9	Kansas
11.6	Iowa
11.3	Arizona
11.1	Vermont
11.0	Nebraska
10.5	Illinois
10.4	North Carolina
10.3	Washington
10.2	Connecticut
10.2	Pennsylvania
10.0	Kentucky
9.6	Nevada
9.5	Minnesota
9.4	Utah
9.4	Indiana
9.1	Missouri
9.1	West Virginia
8.9	Wisconsin
8.8	Oklahoma
8.7	Maine
8.6	Delaware
8.4	Rhode Island
8.4	Mississippi
8.2	Tennessee
8.1	Texas
8.0	New Mexico
8.0	Oregon
7.6	Arkansas
7.3	Georgia
7.2	Michigan
7.0	Colorado
6.9	Alabama
6.8	Louisiana
6.7	Ohio
6.6	New York
5.6	South Carolina
5.6	New Jersey
4.8	California

Table G.556. OTHER95

Percent of All Expenditures Devoted to All Other Expenditures 1995

52.1	Nevada
50.7	Hawaii
46.3	Delaware
46.1	West Virginia
44.0	Oregon
43.0	Florida
42.6	Massachusetts
42.5	Maine
40.9	Vermont
40.2	Ohio
39.7	Alaska
39.7	North Dakota
39.7	Connecticut
39.7	New Jersey
38.3	New Hampshire
38.0	Montana
37.4	Virginia
37.0	Pennsylvania
36.1	Rhode Island
34.7	Wyoming
34.6	Arizona
34.6	Louisiana
34.5	Wisconsin
34.2	Minnesota
34.2	New Mexico
34.1	California
33.6	Missouri
33.4	South Carolina
32.7	Arkansas
32.3	Maryland
32.2	Nebraska
32.1	Washington
31.8	Illinois
31.0	Kansas
30.8	Indiana
30.4	Colorado
30.3	Idaho
30.1	South Dakota
29.6	North Carolina
29.1	Iowa
28.2	Utah
28.2	Oklahoma
28.1	Georgia
28.0	Kentucky
27.4	Michigan
27.3	New York
27.2	Tennessee
25.8	Mississippi
23.7	Alabama
18.7	Texas

Table G.557. ELESEC96

Percent of All Expenditures Devoted to Elementary and Secondary Education 1996

33.7	Utah
32.9	Michigan
32.3	West Virginia
30.5	Texas
28.6	Idaho
27.1	Washington
25.9	Oklahoma
25.4	Georgia
25.1	Indiana
24.6	Minnesota
24.5	Kansas
24.5	Kentucky
24.4	North Carolina
24.1	Missouri
23.5	Alabama
23.4	Mississippi
23.1	Delaware
22.9	Montana
22.5	New Mexico
22.1	New Jersey
21.9	Wyoming
21.2	Wisconsin
21.1	Nevada
21.1	Alaska
21.1	Colorado
20.8	Arkansas
20.5	Iowa
20.3	Pennsylvania
20.2	California
19.9	Louisiana
19.4	Tennessee
18.7	North Dakota
18.7	South Carolina
18.7	New York
17.9	Florida
17.8	Oregon
17.8	Illinois
17.5	Arizona
17.4	Vermont
17.3	Ohio
17.1	Virginia
16.9	Maryland
16.9	Nebraska
15.3	Rhode Island
15.3	South Dakota
14.9	Connecticut
14.2	Hawaii
13.5	Maine
13.4	Massachusetts
6.9	New Hampshire

Table G.558. HIGHED96

Percent of All Expenditures Devoted to Higher Education 1996

25.7	Iowa
25.3	Alabama
21.9	Nebraska
20.4	New Mexico
18.7	South Carolina
18.3	Kentucky
18.2	North Carolina
16.8	Wisconsin
16.7	South Dakota
16.6	Oklahoma
16.4	Kansas
16.3	Georgia
16.2	Mississippi
16.1	Arkansas
15.4	Colorado
14.9	Maryland
14.2	Virginia
13.9	West Virginia
13.3	Texas
13.3	Arizona
13.0	Tennessee
12.6	Washington
12.2	North Dakota
12.1	Nevada
12.1	Alaska
11.8	Utah
11.4	Oregon
11.1	Rhode Island
11.0	Minnesota
10.5	Idaho
9.8	Louisiana
9.6	Montana
9.6	Wyoming
9.6	Illinois
9.5	Connecticut
8.2	Indiana
7.8	California
7.6	Ohio
7.3	New York
7.2	Florida
6.2	Missouri
6.1	Michigan
5.9	Pennsylvania
5.7	Delaware
5.7	Hawaii
5.5	New Hampshire
5.1	Massachusetts
4.8	New Jersey
4.2	Vermont
4.2	Maine

Table G.559. ASSIST96

Percent of All Expenditures Devoted to Cash Assistance 1996

8.8	California
5.3	New York
4.9	Vermont
4.7	Massachusetts
4.7	Maine
4.1	Connecticut
4.1	Pennsylvania
3.8	Washington
3.8	Rhode Island
3.7	Illinois
3.7	Michigan
3.6	Hawaii
2.8	New Mexico
2.8	Arkansas
2.8	New Hampshire
2.8	New Jersey
2.7	Wisconsin
2.7	Ohio
2.6	Minnesota
2.5	Nevada
2.5	Alaska
2.4	Missouri
2.3	North Carolina
2.2	Arizona
2.1	Oklahoma
2.1	Georgia
2.1	West Virginia
2.0	Kentucky
2.0	Maryland
2.0	Montana
2.0	Florida
1.9	Iowa
1.9	Oregon
1.8	South Dakota
1.8	Tennessee
1.7	Colorado
1.6	Utah
1.5	Delaware
1.4	Kansas
1.4	Virginia
1.4	Idaho
1.3	Nebraska
1.3	Louisiana
1.3	Indiana
1.2	Texas
1.1	South Carolina
.9	Mississippi
.9	North Dakota
.9	Wyoming
.6	Alabama

Table G.560. MEDIC96

Percent of All Expenditures Devoted to Medicaid 1996

38.8	New Hampshire
33.6	New York
25.9	West Virginia
25.9	Tennessee
25.3	Pennsylvania
24.9	Illinois
24.3	Rhode Island
23.5	Missouri
23.0	New Jersey
22.5	Louisiana
21.9	Vermont
21.6	Maine
21.4	Mississippi
21.0	Texas
20.7	Ohio
20.1	Massachusetts
19.5	Minnesota
19.3	Michigan
19.3	South Dakota
19.0	North Carolina
18.9	South Carolina
18.6	California
18.6	Washington
18.6	Georgia
18.6	Indiana
18.5	Nevada
18.5	Alaska
18.0	Alabama
17.7	Kentucky
17.7	Maryland
17.5	Connecticut
16.9	Arkansas
16.7	Colorado
16.3	Montana
15.8	Nebraska
15.6	Florida
14.4	North Dakota
14.2	Wisconsin
14.2	Oklahoma
13.9	Iowa
13.5	Oregon
13.4	New Mexico
13.1	Idaho
12.8	Arizona
12.6	Virginia
11.9	Utah
10.5	Kansas
10.0	Delaware
9.5	Hawaii
8.8	Wyoming

Table G.561. CORREC96

Percent of All Expenditures Devoted to Corrections 1996

6.6	Texas
5.2	Maryland
5.0	Oregon
5.0	Idaho
4.5	Michigan
4.4	North Carolina
4.4	California
4.3	Ohio
4.3	Arizona
4.2	Virginia
4.1	New York
4.0	Georgia
3.8	Tennessee
3.8	Colorado
3.7	South Carolina
3.6	Pennsylvania
3.6	Florida
3.6	Utah
3.3	Rhode Island
3.3	Louisiana
3.2	Illinois
3.1	New Jersey
3.1	Indiana
3.1	Nevada
3.1	Alaska
3.0	Connecticut
2.9	Vermont
2.8	Missouri
2.8	Oklahoma
2.7	Montana
2.7	Kansas
2.7	Delaware
2.4	Washington
2.4	Wisconsin
2.4	New Mexico
2.3	Mississippi
2.2	South Dakota
2.2	Alabama
2.1	New Hampshire
2.1	Minnesota
2.0	Nebraska
2.0	Iowa
1.8	Kentucky
1.8	Arkansas
1.7	Maine
1.7	Massachusetts
1.7	Hawaii
1.5	Wyoming
1.2	North Dakota
1.1	West Virginia

Table G.562. TRANS96

Percent of All Expenditures Devoted to Transportation 1996

16.3	Wyoming
16.2	West Virginia
15.7	South Dakota
15.2	Kansas
14.9	Maryland
14.7	Montana
14.6	Hawaii
13.6	Virginia
13.1	New Hampshire
12.7	North Dakota
12.1	Idaho
12.1	Florida
11.9	Vermont
11.2	Massachusetts
10.8	Nebraska
10.5	Connecticut
10.4	Mississippi
10.3	Pennsylvania
10.2	Indiana
10.2	Nevada
10.2	Alaska
10.1	Minnesota
9.9	Illinois
9.8	North Carolina
9.8	Kentucky
9.5	Oklahoma
9.4	Washington
9.4	Maine
9.2	Utah
9.0	Texas
9.0	Arizona
8.7	Colorado
8.7	Wisconsin
8.6	Iowa
8.5	Ohio
8.5	Missouri
8.4	Delaware
8.2	Tennessee
8.2	Louisiana
8.2	Arkansas
8.1	New Mexico
7.8	New Jersey
7.6	Oregon
7.4	Rhode Island
7.1	Alabama
7.0	Michigan
6.9	Georgia
6.6	California
5.6	New York
5.6	South Carolina

Table G.563. OTHER96

Percent of All Expenditures Devoted to All Other Expenditures 1996

50.6	Hawaii
48.7	Delaware
44.9	Maine
43.8	Massachusetts
42.8	Oregon
41.6	Florida
41.0	Wyoming
40.8	Arizona
40.5	Connecticut
39.9	North Dakota
38.9	Ohio
37.0	Vermont
36.9	Virginia
36.5	New Jersey
35.0	Louisiana
34.7	Rhode Island
34.0	Wisconsin
33.7	California
33.6	Indiana
33.3	Arkansas
33.3	South Carolina
32.6	Colorado
32.5	Nevada
32.5	Alaska
32.5	Missouri
31.7	Montana
31.4	Nebraska
30.9	Illinois
30.8	New Hampshire
30.5	Pennsylvania
30.4	New Mexico
30.0	Minnesota
29.3	Kansas
29.3	Idaho
29.1	South Dakota
29.1	Oklahoma
28.4	Maryland
28.4	Utah
27.9	Tennessee
27.4	Iowa
26.8	Georgia
26.5	Michigan
26.1	Washington
26.0	Kentucky
25.5	New York
25.3	Mississippi
23.2	Alabama
22.0	North Carolina
18.4	Texas
8.5	West Virginia

Table G.564. ELESEC97

Percent of All Expenditures Devoted to Elementary and Secondary Education 1997

34.2	Utah
31.2	West Virginia
30.8	Michigan
29.5	Texas
29.4	Kansas
28.7	Idaho
26.4	Kentucky
26.3	Oklahoma
25.9	Washington
25.6	Alabama
25.4	Missouri
25.3	Georgia
25.1	Minnesota
25.1	North Carolina
24.5	Wisconsin
24.1	Indiana
23.3	Delaware
23.0	California
22.7	New Jersey
22.5	Montana
21.5	Wyoming
21.5	Mississippi
21.4	Iowa
21.2	Colorado
21.2	Nevada
21.1	New Mexico
20.5	Arkansas
20.2	Alaska
19.9	Pennsylvania
19.2	Louisiana
18.9	New York
18.8	Florida
18.3	Illinois
17.9	Arizona
17.9	Vermont
17.8	Virginia
17.7	Maryland
17.5	South Dakota
17.4	Tennessee
17.3	South Carolina
17.1	Ohio
17.0	North Dakota
16.7	Oregon
16.3	Nebraska
15.8	Rhode Island
14.3	Maine
14.2	Massachusetts
14.0	Hawaii
13.4	Connecticut
7.4	New Hampshire

Table G.565. HIGHED97

Percent of All Expenditures Devoted to Higher Education 1997

25.1	Iowa
24.7	Alabama
23.0	Nebraska
20.3	New Mexico
19.3	South Carolina
17.4	Kansas
17.4	Mississippi
17.2	West Virginia
16.9	Oklahoma
16.3	Georgia
16.2	South Dakota
15.6	Arkansas
15.5	Maryland
15.0	Colorado
14.8	Wisconsin
14.5	Kentucky
14.2	North Carolina
14.2	Virginia
13.6	Texas
12.8	Arizona
12.6	Tennessee
11.9	Utah
11.9	Nevada
11.8	Louisiana
10.9	Washington
10.6	Minnesota
10.6	Rhode Island
10.5	North Dakota
10.5	Oregon
10.4	Alaska
10.0	Montana
9.7	Idaho
9.6	Wyoming
8.8	California
8.5	Connecticut
8.3	Illinois
7.7	Florida
7.4	Missouri
7.4	Indiana
7.4	Ohio
7.1	New York
7.0	Hawaii
6.0	Pennsylvania
5.9	New Hampshire
5.8	Michigan
5.7	Delaware
5.0	Massachusetts
4.6	New Jersey
4.5	Maine
3.7	Vermont

Table G.566. ASSIST97

Percent of All Expenditures Devoted to Cash Assistance 1997

8.0	California
5.1	Maine
5.0	New York
4.3	Alaska
4.2	Vermont
4.0	Massachusetts
3.7	Pennsylvania
3.6	South Dakota
3.6	Connecticut
3.4	Rhode Island
3.4	New Hampshire
3.3	Illinois
3.3	Hawaii
3.2	West Virginia
2.9	Washington
2.8	New Mexico
2.8	Michigan
2.7	Arkansas
2.7	Ohio
2.6	New Jersey
2.4	Nevada
2.3	Minnesota
2.1	Utah
2.1	Missouri
2.0	Kentucky
2.0	Oregon
1.9	Georgia
1.9	Wisconsin
1.8	North Carolina
1.7	Maryland
1.7	Montana
1.7	Delaware
1.6	Oklahoma
1.6	Colorado
1.5	Iowa
1.5	Kansas
1.5	Arizona
1.5	Florida
1.3	Idaho
1.2	Tennessee
1.1	Nebraska
1.1	Virginia
1.0	Mississippi
1.0	Texas
1.0	Indiana
.8	Louisiana
.7	South Carolina
.7	North Dakota
.5	Alabama
.5	Wyoming

Table G.567. MEDIC97

Percent of All Expenditures Devoted to Medicaid 1997

33.4	New York
30.7	New Hampshire
26.2	Pennsylvania
25.0	Texas
24.9	Rhode Island
24.1	Maine
24.1	West Virginia
23.7	Illinois
23.2	New Jersey
22.8	Mississippi
22.2	Tennessee
21.8	Louisiana
21.7	Vermont
21.2	Massachusetts
21.1	Kentucky
21.0	Ohio
20.6	South Dakota
20.2	Missouri
20.1	North Carolina
19.5	Alabama
18.8	Minnesota
18.6	Michigan
18.3	Georgia
18.2	Nevada
18.1	Maryland
17.7	Indiana
17.4	Connecticut
17.2	California
17.0	South Carolina
16.9	Colorado
16.5	North Dakota
16.3	Arkansas
16.0	Montana
15.9	Nebraska
15.8	Washington
15.7	New Mexico
15.7	Florida
14.1	Oklahoma
14.0	Idaho
13.7	Wisconsin
13.4	Iowa
12.5	Virginia
12.4	Oregon
12.4	Arizona
11.7	Utah
11.3	Hawaii
11.1	Kansas
9.9	Delaware
7.8	Wyoming
6.9	Alaska

Table G.568. CORREC97

Percent of All Expenditures Devoted to Corrections 1997

7.1	Texas
5.0	Maryland
4.7	Virginia
4.7	Oregon
4.5	Michigan
4.5	California
4.4	Ohio
4.4	Arizona
4.3	North Carolina
4.1	New York
4.1	Colorado
4.0	South Carolina
3.8	Missouri
3.7	Pennsylvania
3.7	Idaho
3.7	Utah
3.7	Alaska
3.6	Rhode Island
3.6	Georgia
3.6	Florida
3.5	Tennessee
3.4	New Jersey
3.4	Wisconsin
3.3	Illinois
3.2	Nevada
3.2	Indiana
3.2	Oklahoma
3.1	Connecticut
3.0	Louisiana
2.9	South Dakota
2.9	Montana
2.8	Vermont
2.8	Kansas
2.8	Delaware
2.5	Mississippi
2.5	Washington
2.3	Alabama
2.3	Minnesota
2.3	New Mexico
2.2	New Hampshire
2.2	Kentucky
2.2	Nebraska
2.1	Arkansas
2.1	Iowa
2.1	Wyoming
1.8	Hawaii
1.7	Maine
1.6	Massachusetts
1.4	North Dakota
1.1	West Virginia

Table G.569. TRANS97

Percent of All Expenditures Devoted to Transportation 1997

16.4	Alaska
16.4	Wyoming
16.2	South Dakota
16.1	West Virginia
15.1	Maryland
14.6	Montana
14.1	Hawaii
13.9	Idaho
13.9	New Hampshire
13.7	Kansas
13.6	Virginia
12.7	North Dakota
11.9	Massachusetts
11.8	Florida
11.8	Vermont
11.4	Colorado
11.0	North Carolina
10.8	Utah
10.5	Connecticut
10.4	Nebraska
10.3	Nevada
10.3	Mississippi
10.1	Pennsylvania
10.1	Minnesota
10.0	Illinois
9.5	Kentucky
9.4	Maine
9.3	Iowa
9.1	Arizona
9.1	Washington
9.0	Oklahoma
8.8	Missouri
8.6	Ohio
8.6	Arkansas
8.5	Wisconsin
8.5	Indiana
8.2	Texas
7.8	Delaware
7.7	Michigan
7.4	Alabama
7.4	New Mexico
7.3	Tennessee
7.1	Oregon
6.8	Louisiana
6.7	New Jersey
6.6	California
6.3	Georgia
6.1	South Carolina
6.0	Rhode Island
5.8	New York

Table G.570. OTHER97

Percent of All Expenditures Devoted to All Other Expenditures 1997

48.9	Delaware
48.5	Hawaii
46.6	Oregon
43.4	Connecticut
42.1	Massachusetts
42.0	Wyoming
41.8	Arizona
41.4	North Dakota
40.8	Florida
39.8	Maine
38.8	Ohio
38.2	Alaska
38.1	Vermont
38.1	Indiana
36.9	New Jersey
36.6	Louisiana
36.5	New Hampshire
36.1	Virginia
35.7	Tennessee
35.7	Rhode Island
35.6	South Carolina
34.3	Arkansas
33.2	Illinois
33.2	Wisconsin
32.9	Washington
32.8	Nevada
32.4	Montana
32.3	Missouri
31.9	California
31.0	Nebraska
30.8	Minnesota
30.4	Pennsylvania
30.4	New Mexico
29.9	Colorado
29.8	Michigan
29.0	Oklahoma
28.7	Idaho
28.2	Georgia
27.2	Iowa
26.8	Maryland
25.7	Utah
25.6	New York
24.4	Mississippi
24.3	Kentucky
24.1	Kansas
23.4	North Carolina
23.1	South Dakota
20.0	Alabama
15.6	Texas
7.0	West Virginia

Table G.571.   ELESEC98

Percent of All Expenditures Devoted to Elementary and Secondary Education 1998

34.2	Michigan
31.9	West Virginia
31.4	Utah
28.7	Texas
28.5	Idaho
26.1	Kansas
25.9	North Carolina
25.7	Indiana
25.5	Missouri
25.5	Georgia
25.4	Washington
25.3	Oklahoma
24.9	Wisconsin
24.3	California
23.8	Minnesota
23.7	Alabama
23.1	New Jersey
23.1	Delaware
22.0	Montana
21.9	Wyoming
21.8	Mississippi
21.5	Nevada
21.2	Colorado
21.1	Maine
21.0	Iowa
21.0	Kentucky
20.7	New Mexico
20.2	Alaska
20.1	Louisiana
20.0	Pennsylvania
19.9	Arkansas
19.9	Illinois
19.6	Arizona
18.8	Oregon
18.6	New York
18.5	Tennessee
18.4	South Dakota
18.1	Vermont
17.8	South Carolina
17.7	Virginia
17.6	North Dakota
17.6	Florida
17.6	Ohio
17.5	Maryland
16.9	Hawaii
16.7	Nebraska
16.2	Rhode Island
15.1	Massachusetts
13.5	Connecticut
9.2	New Hampshire

Table G.572.   HIGHED98

Percent of All Expenditures Devoted to Higher Education 1998

24.7	Iowa
24.6	Alabama
24.1	Nebraska
19.7	Mississippi
19.2	West Virginia
19.0	South Carolina
17.8	New Mexico
17.5	Kansas
16.7	Georgia
16.4	Oklahoma
15.7	Washington
15.5	Maryland
15.3	Colorado
15.1	Arkansas
14.7	North Carolina
14.7	Wisconsin
14.7	Virginia
14.4	Arizona
13.9	South Dakota
12.6	Kentucky
12.6	Oregon
12.4	Texas
12.1	Nevada
11.8	Louisiana
11.8	Tennessee
11.8	North Dakota
11.2	Utah
10.7	Minnesota
10.6	Rhode Island
10.5	Alaska
9.9	Idaho
9.6	Montana
9.2	Hawaii
8.9	Wyoming
8.7	California
8.7	Connecticut
8.6	Florida
8.4	Indiana
7.9	Illinois
7.8	New Jersey
7.4	Ohio
6.7	Missouri
6.5	New York
6.4	Pennsylvania
6.2	Michigan
6.0	New Hampshire
5.8	Delaware
5.2	Massachusetts
4.2	Maine
3.2	Vermont

Table G.573.   ASSIST98

Percent of All Expenditures Devoted to Cash Assistance 1998

7.2	New York
6.5	California
5.9	Connecticut
4.5	Maine
4.5	Vermont
4.0	Alaska
3.7	Rhode Island
3.5	Hawaii
3.4	Washington
3.4	Massachusetts
3.0	Pennsylvania
2.7	Arkansas
2.7	Illinois
2.4	New Mexico
2.3	Ohio
2.3	Michigan
2.2	Minnesota
2.1	Nevada
2.1	New Jersey
2.0	Georgia
1.9	Colorado
1.9	New Hampshire
1.7	Iowa
1.7	Maryland
1.7	Wisconsin
1.7	Oregon
1.7	Missouri
1.6	Kentucky
1.5	North Carolina
1.5	Utah
1.5	Delaware
1.4	Montana
1.3	West Virginia
1.2	Nebraska
1.2	Oklahoma
1.2	Arizona
1.2	South Dakota
1.1	North Dakota
1.0	Louisiana
1.0	Tennessee
1.0	Florida
1.0	Indiana
.8	Mississippi
.8	Virginia
.7	Kansas
.7	Texas
.6	South Carolina
.6	Idaho
.5	Wyoming
.3	Alabama

Table G.574. MEDIC98

Percent of All Expenditures Devoted to Medicaid 1998

33.0	New York
30.8	New Hampshire
27.2	Rhode Island
26.4	Pennsylvania
25.8	Maine
24.4	West Virginia
24.1	Texas
23.9	Tennessee
23.0	Illinois
22.1	Vermont
22.1	Mississippi
21.9	New Jersey
20.9	Ohio
20.9	Louisiana
20.5	Massachusetts
19.6	Michigan
19.4	North Carolina
18.9	Kentucky
18.8	Alabama
18.5	New Mexico
18.4	South Dakota
18.3	Minnesota
18.2	Missouri
18.0	Nevada
17.5	South Carolina
17.2	Colorado
17.0	Indiana
16.9	Georgia
16.4	Arkansas
16.4	Nebraska
16.1	North Dakota
16.0	California
16.0	Washington
15.7	Montana
15.2	Connecticut
15.2	Florida
14.9	Arizona
14.3	Oklahoma
13.9	Iowa
13.2	Wisconsin
13.2	Idaho
13.1	Maryland
13.1	Oregon
12.9	Kansas
12.3	Virginia
11.0	Utah
9.7	Delaware
9.4	Hawaii
9.1	Wyoming
6.9	Alaska

Table G.575. CORREC98

Percent of All Expenditures Devoted to Corrections 1998

5.8	Arizona
5.6	Texas
5.1	Michigan
4.7	Maryland
4.6	Ohio
4.6	Indiana
4.6	Virginia
4.5	Georgia
4.4	Colorado
4.3	Idaho
4.0	Missouri
3.9	North Carolina
3.8	Pennsylvania
3.8	New Jersey
3.7	New York
3.7	Florida
3.7	Alaska
3.6	South Carolina
3.6	California
3.6	Oklahoma
3.6	Wisconsin
3.5	Rhode Island
3.5	Louisiana
3.5	Delaware
3.4	Illinois
3.4	Oregon
3.4	Utah
3.3	Nevada
3.3	Montana
3.2	Tennessee
3.0	Kansas
2.9	Vermont
2.7	Mississippi
2.7	Connecticut
2.5	South Dakota
2.5	Nebraska
2.4	Washington
2.3	Kentucky
2.3	New Mexico
2.3	Minnesota
2.3	Iowa
2.2	Alabama
2.1	New Hampshire
2.0	Arkansas
2.0	Wyoming
1.9	Hawaii
1.8	Maine
1.7	North Dakota
1.6	Massachusetts
1.1	West Virginia

Table G.576. TRANS98

Percent of All Expenditures Devoted to Transportation 1998

17.5	Wyoming
17.1	Utah
16.7	South Dakota
15.0	Maryland
15.0	Alaska
15.0	North Dakota
15.0	West Virginia
14.0	Virginia
14.0	Montana
13.7	New Hampshire
12.9	Idaho
12.4	Florida
12.4	Hawaii
12.1	Massachusetts
11.9	Vermont
11.5	North Carolina
11.2	Kansas
10.7	Pennsylvania
10.7	Mississippi
10.6	Louisiana
10.2	Nevada
10.1	Indiana
9.9	Arizona
9.8	New Mexico
9.5	Connecticut
9.2	Minnesota
9.1	Oklahoma
9.1	Illinois
9.1	Nebraska
8.9	Maine
8.7	Ohio
8.7	Kentucky
8.4	Michigan
8.3	Wisconsin
8.2	Texas
8.2	Delaware
8.2	Iowa
8.0	Washington
7.9	Missouri
7.9	Arkansas
7.7	Colorado
7.5	Tennessee
7.4	New Jersey
7.1	Georgia
6.4	South Carolina
6.4	Alabama
6.3	California
6.1	Oregon
5.4	New York
5.2	Rhode Island

Table G.577. OTHER98

Percent of All Expenditures Devoted to All Other Expenditures 1998

48.1	Delaware
46.6	Hawaii
44.4	Connecticut
44.3	Oregon
42.1	Massachusetts
41.5	Florida
40.2	Wyoming
39.7	Alaska
38.6	Ohio
37.3	Vermont
36.6	North Dakota
36.3	New Hampshire
36.1	Arkansas
35.9	Missouri
35.8	Virginia
35.1	South Carolina
34.9	Kentucky
34.8	California
34.3	Arizona
34.2	Tennessee
34.0	Montana
34.0	New Jersey
33.9	Illinois
33.7	Maine
33.7	Rhode Island
33.6	Wisconsin
33.5	Minnesota
33.1	Indiana
32.8	Nevada
32.7	Maryland
32.3	Colorado
32.1	Louisiana
30.6	Idaho
30.2	Oklahoma
30.0	Nebraska
29.7	Pennsylvania
29.1	Washington
28.8	South Dakota
28.6	New Mexico
28.5	Kansas
28.2	Iowa
27.3	Georgia
25.6	New York
24.3	Utah
24.2	Michigan
23.9	Alabama
23.1	North Carolina
22.3	Mississippi
20.4	Texas
7.1	West Virginia

Table G. 578. ELESEC99

Percent of All Expenditures Devoted to Elementary and Secondary Education 1999

34.3	Colorado
31.5	Michigan
31.3	Utah
29.0	Idaho
28.5	Kansas
27.6	Texas
27.5	Indiana
27.2	West Virginia
25.4	North Carolina
25.0	Washington
24.8	Georgia
24.7	Oklahoma
24.6	California
24.6	New Mexico
24.5	Alabama
24.1	Minnesota
24.0	Missouri
23.7	New Jersey
23.3	Wyoming
22.8	Mississippi
22.0	Kentucky
21.9	Delaware
21.3	South Carolina
21.2	Wisconsin
20.8	Montana
20.8	Illinois
20.4	Maine
20.4	Iowa
20.2	Louisiana
20.1	Vermont
19.7	Arkansas
19.3	New York
19.1	Hawaii
19.1	Pennsylvania
18.9	Florida
18.5	Arizona
18.4	Oregon
18.4	Ohio
18.1	Tennessee
18.0	Nebraska
17.9	Virginia
17.9	Maryland
17.5	Alaska
17.2	North Dakota
16.2	Rhode Island
15.2	Connecticut
15.1	Massachusetts
14.6	South Dakota
11.1	Nevada
8.6	New Hampshire

Table G.579. HIGHED99

Percent of All Expenditures Devoted to Higher Education 1999

25.4	Iowa
22.2	Nebraska
18.9	New Mexico
18.7	Georgia
18.7	Kentucky
18.2	West Virginia
16.7	South Dakota
16.6	Kansas
16.4	Arkansas
15.8	Washington
15.2	Maryland
15.0	Mississippi
13.8	Virginia
13.4	Oklahoma
13.4	Louisiana
13.2	North Carolina
13.2	Arizona
13.1	Tennessee
12.9	Wisconsin
12.1	Texas
11.9	Alabama
11.9	North Dakota
11.5	Oregon
10.9	Utah
10.7	Minnesota
10.6	Montana
10.6	Rhode Island
10.3	Alaska
10.1	Hawaii
10.0	Idaho
9.8	Indiana
9.8	Florida
8.6	Connecticut
8.4	Wyoming
8.3	New Jersey
8.0	Illinois
7.9	California
7.8	Colorado
7.3	Missouri
7.2	South Carolina
7.1	Ohio
6.9	Nevada
6.5	New York
6.2	Pennsylvania
5.9	Michigan
5.7	Delaware
5.4	New Hampshire
5.2	Massachusetts
4.3	Maine
3.1	Vermont

Table G.580. ASSIST99

Percent of All Expenditures Devoted to Cash Assistance 1999

7.4	California
5.4	Colorado
4.6	New Mexico
4.3	New York
4.3	Maine
3.8	Connecticut
3.6	Rhode Island
3.3	Vermont
3.0	Hawaii
2.8	Arkansas
2.8	Alaska
2.7	Pennsylvania
2.7	Massachusetts
2.4	Washington
2.4	New Hampshire
2.3	North Carolina
2.1	Oregon
1.9	Minnesota
1.8	Indiana
1.8	Illinois
1.7	New Jersey
1.6	Michigan
1.5	South Dakota
1.4	Maryland
1.4	Utah
1.4	Missouri
1.3	Kentucky
1.3	Ohio
1.3	Delaware
1.2	Montana
1.1	Iowa
1.0	Nebraska
1.0	Oklahoma
.9	Arizona
.9	Wisconsin
.9	North Dakota
.8	Georgia
.8	Mississippi
.8	Idaho
.7	Virginia
.7	Tennessee
.6	West Virginia
.6	Kansas
.6	Texas
.6	Florida
.5	Louisiana
.5	Wyoming
.5	South Carolina
.5	Nevada
.3	Alabama

Table G.581. MEDIC99

Percent of All Expenditures Devoted to Medicaid 1999

32.2	New York
30.2	New Hampshire
27.9	Colorado
27.4	Pennsylvania
26.5	Rhode Island
25.3	Tennessee
24.7	Maine
23.6	Mississippi
23.2	Texas
22.3	West Virginia
21.8	New Jersey
21.8	Louisiana
21.7	Vermont
21.6	South Carolina
21.1	Illinois
20.9	Ohio
20.7	North Carolina
20.1	Massachusetts
19.9	South Dakota
19.0	Connecticut
18.9	Michigan
18.9	Kentucky
18.9	Alabama
18.5	Indiana
18.4	Missouri
17.8	Minnesota
16.9	California
16.9	Washington
16.9	Nebraska
16.8	North Dakota
16.6	Maryland
16.1	Arkansas
15.9	Oregon
15.9	Georgia
15.1	Montana
15.1	Idaho
15.0	Florida
14.8	Oklahoma
14.7	Kansas
13.9	Arizona
13.8	New Mexico
13.2	Iowa
11.4	Wisconsin
11.4	Virginia
10.9	Utah
9.5	Delaware
9.4	Hawaii
8.1	Wyoming
8.0	Alaska
7.8	Nevada

Table G.582. CORREC99

Percent of All Expenditures Devoted to Corrections 1999

5.8	Texas
5.0	Arizona
4.9	Michigan
4.9	Maryland
4.6	Ohio
4.3	Oregon
4.3	Virginia
4.1	Idaho
4.0	California
3.9	New York
3.9	North Carolina
3.9	Indiana
3.8	Delaware
3.7	Pennsylvania
3.7	New Jersey
3.7	Illinois
3.7	Utah
3.6	Florida
3.6	Oklahoma
3.5	Georgia
3.5	Alaska
3.4	Louisiana
3.4	Washington
3.4	Montana
3.4	Kansas
3.4	Wisconsin
3.3	Rhode Island
3.2	South Carolina
3.1	Massachusetts
3.1	Nevada
3.0	Vermont
3.0	Missouri
2.8	Connecticut
2.7	New Hampshire
2.7	Mississippi
2.6	Tennessee
2.6	South Dakota
2.6	Kentucky
2.5	Nebraska
2.4	Iowa
2.4	Hawaii
2.3	Minnesota
2.2	New Mexico
2.1	Wyoming
2.0	Arkansas
1.9	Maine
1.7	North Dakota
1.6	Alabama
1.4	West Virginia
.1	Colorado

Table G.583. TRANS99

Percent of All Expenditures Devoted to Transportation 1999

21.9	Alaska
18.3	Wyoming
15.9	Alabama
15.5	Montana
15.4	South Dakota
14.7	Utah
14.3	New Hampshire
13.8	West Virginia
13.7	Virginia
13.6	Maryland
13.6	Colorado
13.3	North Dakota
12.0	Florida
11.9	Vermont
11.7	Hawaii
11.6	Idaho
11.3	Kansas
11.3	Mississippi
11.0	Massachusetts
10.9	Arizona
10.6	Pennsylvania
10.6	Kentucky
10.3	North Carolina
9.6	Oklahoma
9.6	Nebraska
9.4	Minnesota
9.2	Iowa
9.1	Ohio
9.0	New Mexico
8.8	Texas
8.8	Maine
8.6	Indiana
8.3	Illinois
8.2	Michigan
8.1	Wisconsin
8.1	Rhode Island
8.0	Delaware
7.8	Missouri
7.7	Georgia
7.5	New Jersey
7.5	Connecticut
7.1	Washington
6.8	Oregon
6.6	Arkansas
6.5	California
6.1	Nevada
6.0	Tennessee
3.9	South Carolina
3.7	New York
3.1	Louisiana

Table G.584. OTHER99

Percent of All Expenditures Devoted to All Other Expenditures 1999

64.5	Nevada
49.8	Delaware
44.3	Hawaii
43.1	Connecticut
42.8	Massachusetts
42.5	Oregon
42.3	South Carolina
42.2	Wisconsin
40.1	Florida
39.3	Wyoming
38.6	Ohio
38.3	Virginia
38.1	North Dakota
38.0	Missouri
37.7	Louisiana
37.6	Arizona
36.9	Vermont
36.5	Arkansas
36.4	New Hampshire
36.4	Illinois
36.1	Alaska
35.6	Maine
34.1	Tennessee
33.8	Minnesota
33.4	Montana
33.2	New Jersey
32.8	Oklahoma
32.7	California
31.7	Rhode Island
30.4	Maryland
30.3	Pennsylvania
30.1	New York
29.9	Indiana
29.8	Nebraska
29.4	South Dakota
29.4	Idaho
29.4	Washington
29.1	Michigan
28.7	Georgia
28.4	Iowa
27.1	Utah
27.0	Alabama
26.9	New Mexico
26.0	Kentucky
24.9	Kansas
24.2	North Carolina
23.7	Mississippi
21.9	Texas
16.4	West Virginia
10.8	Colorado

Table G.585. ELESEC00

Percent of All Expenditures Devoted to Elementary and Secondary Education 2000

31.6	Michigan
30.3	Texas
29.5	Oregon
29.5	Kansas
28.7	New Hampshire
28.6	Idaho
27.4	California
27.2	Utah
26.3	Kentucky
26.0	West Virginia
25.6	Indiana
25.0	Alabama
24.9	Minnesota
24.7	Georgia
24.3	Oklahoma
24.1	Missouri
24.1	New Mexico
23.9	Washington
23.6	North Carolina
22.5	New Jersey
22.3	Delaware
21.7	Wyoming
21.1	Mississippi
20.9	Illinois
20.7	New York
20.6	Montana
20.5	Vermont
19.9	Maine
19.7	Iowa
19.6	Arizona
19.5	Wisconsin
19.5	Louisiana
19.5	Arkansas
19.0	Colorado
18.8	Pennsylvania
18.7	Florida
18.6	Tennessee
18.2	Ohio
18.1	Virginia
17.8	Alaska
17.5	Maryland
17.3	North Dakota
17.1	Hawaii
17.0	Nevada
16.9	South Carolina
16.7	Nebraska
16.6	Rhode Island
14.4	Massachusetts
13.8	Connecticut
13.7	South Dakota

Table G.586. HIGHED00

Percent of All Expenditures Devoted to Higher Education 2000

25.1	Iowa
24.3	Alabama
22.6	Nebraska
21.0	New Mexico
18.5	Mississippi
18.4	Kentucky
18.3	West Virginia
17.3	Kansas
16.3	Washington
16.1	South Carolina
15.9	Arkansas
15.8	Maryland
15.7	South Dakota
15.6	Oklahoma
14.5	Georgia
14.3	Virginia
13.9	Arizona
13.6	Texas
13.4	Louisiana
13.0	North Carolina
12.5	Tennessee
12.2	Utah
12.0	Wyoming
11.9	Wisconsin
11.5	Colorado
10.8	North Dakota
10.7	Minnesota
10.5	Montana
10.4	Rhode Island
9.8	Oregon
9.5	California
9.5	Indiana
9.5	Florida
9.4	Idaho
9.4	Nevada
9.4	Connecticut
8.3	Hawaii
8.2	Alaska
7.6	New Jersey
7.4	Illinois
7.0	New York
7.0	Ohio
6.8	Michigan
6.8	Missouri
5.5	Delaware
5.3	Massachusetts
5.2	Pennsylvania
4.4	New Hampshire
4.3	Maine
3.1	Vermont

Table G.587. ASSIST00

Percent of All Expenditures Devoted to Cash Assistance 2000

7.3	California
4.8	New York
4.7	Rhode Island
4.5	Maine
3.5	New Mexico
3.0	Connecticut
3.0	Vermont
2.9	Arkansas
2.8	Colorado
2.8	Pennsylvania
2.7	Washington
2.7	Oregon
2.6	Hawaii
2.5	Alaska
2.3	Massachusetts
2.2	Minnesota
1.8	North Carolina
1.8	Wyoming
1.8	Illinois
1.7	Kentucky
1.6	Oklahoma
1.5	Georgia
1.4	Utah
1.3	Michigan
1.3	Delaware
1.3	New Hampshire
1.2	Iowa
1.2	Idaho
1.2	Missouri
1.1	New Jersey
1.0	Montana
1.0	Ohio
.9	Nebraska
.9	Wisconsin
.8	Mississippi
.8	West Virginia
.8	Maryland
.8	Arizona
.8	Nevada
.7	Tennessee
.7	Indiana
.6	Kansas
.6	Virginia
.6	North Dakota
.5	South Dakota
.5	Texas
.5	Florida
.4	Louisiana
.3	South Carolina
.2	Alabama

Table G.588. MEDIC00

Percent of All Expenditures Devoted to Medicaid 2000

34.5	New York
28.7	Tennessee
27.9	Pennsylvania
26.2	Connecticut
25.8	Rhode Island
24.8	Maine
24.3	Kentucky
24.2	New Hampshire
23.5	Vermont
22.8	Texas
22.0	Louisiana
21.5	Illinois
21.5	West Virginia
21.4	Oregon
21.2	Mississippi
20.0	Washington
19.4	North Carolina
19.4	Michigan
19.4	South Dakota
19.3	Massachusetts
19.3	Alabama
18.9	Ohio
18.5	Minnesota
18.4	Missouri
18.2	Wyoming
17.6	Indiana
17.3	North Dakota
17.1	Colorado
16.8	Nebraska
16.6	Idaho
16.5	California
16.5	Maryland
16.2	Arkansas
16.1	South Carolina
15.9	Montana
15.7	Florida
15.5	Oklahoma
14.5	New Mexico
14.3	Georgia
14.1	New Jersey
13.9	Arizona
13.0	Iowa
12.6	Nevada
12.2	Virginia
11.8	Utah
11.0	Wisconsin
10.1	Delaware
9.3	Alaska
8.5	Hawaii
7.2	Kansas

Table G.589. CORREC00

Percent of All Expenditures Devoted to Corrections 2000

8.1	Oregon
5.7	Texas
5.3	Michigan
4.8	Ohio
4.6	Maryland
4.6	Arizona
4.5	Georgia
4.5	Virginia
4.1	California
4.1	Utah
4.0	New York
4.0	Delaware
3.9	Pennsylvania
3.9	Idaho
3.8	Illinois
3.8	Oklahoma
3.7	Louisiana
3.7	Indiana
3.6	North Carolina
3.6	Colorado
3.6	Nevada
3.6	Alaska
3.6	Kansas
3.5	Wyoming
3.5	Montana
3.5	New Jersey
3.4	Rhode Island
3.4	Washington
3.4	Florida
3.3	Wisconsin
3.2	Kentucky
3.1	Vermont
3.1	Nebraska
3.1	South Carolina
2.9	Massachusetts
2.9	Missouri
2.8	Mississippi
2.7	Tennessee
2.7	Connecticut
2.6	Iowa
2.5	South Dakota
2.3	New Hampshire
2.1	Alabama
2.1	Minnesota
2.1	New Mexico
2.1	Hawaii
2.0	Maine
2.0	Arkansas
1.8	North Dakota
1.4	West Virginia

Table G.590. TRANS00

Percent of All Expenditures Devoted to Transportation 2000

23.9	Alaska
17.1	South Dakota
16.3	Colorado
16.2	Montana
15.9	West Virginia
14.6	North Dakota
13.2	Maryland
13.0	Florida
12.9	Virginia
12.2	Vermont
12.0	New Hampshire
11.9	Utah
11.6	Hawaii
11.4	Nevada
11.3	North Carolina
11.0	Arizona
10.7	Massachusetts
10.3	Idaho
10.3	Iowa
10.1	Wyoming
10.0	Pennsylvania
10.0	Nebraska
9.8	Mississippi
9.6	Oklahoma
9.6	Indiana
9.3	Texas
9.3	Illinois
9.2	Minnesota
9.1	Missouri
9.1	Maine
9.0	Kansas
8.5	New Mexico
8.4	Ohio
8.2	Michigan
8.1	Delaware
7.7	South Carolina
7.4	Louisiana
7.3	Wisconsin
7.1	New Jersey
7.0	Georgia
7.0	Rhode Island
6.9	Alabama
6.8	Oregon
6.8	Tennessee
6.7	Arkansas
6.6	Washington
6.2	Connecticut
6.0	New York
5.9	California
4.2	Kentucky

Table G.591. OTHER00

Percent of All Expenditures Devoted to All Other Expenditures 2000

49.7	Hawaii
48.8	Delaware
46.2	Wisconsin
45.2	Nevada
45.1	Massachusetts
44.2	New Jersey
41.7	Ohio
39.8	South Carolina
39.1	Florida
38.8	Connecticut
37.7	North Dakota
37.5	Missouri
37.4	Virginia
36.8	Arkansas
36.1	Arizona
35.5	Maine
35.3	Illinois
34.8	Alaska
34.6	Vermont
33.7	Louisiana
33.5	Indiana
33.4	Georgia
32.9	Wyoming
32.8	Kansas
32.5	Minnesota
32.3	Montana
32.2	Rhode Island
31.6	Maryland
31.5	Pennsylvania
31.4	Utah
31.1	South Dakota
30.0	Idaho
29.9	Nebraska
29.9	Tennessee
29.7	Colorado
29.6	Oklahoma
29.4	California
28.2	Iowa
27.4	Michigan
27.3	North Carolina
27.2	New Hampshire
27.0	Washington
26.3	New Mexico
25.9	Mississippi
23.2	Oregon
22.9	New York
22.2	Alabama
21.9	Kentucky
17.8	Texas
16.2	West Virginia

Table G.592. SCHOOL89

Per Capita Expenditures of Total Funds Devoted to Elementary and Secondary Education 1989

1,139.78	Alaska
717.52	Delaware
577.87	Wyoming
577.85	New York
512.52	New Mexico
509.84	Connecticut
505.15	Maine
497.03	California
474.76	West Virginia
473.53	Washington
461.71	Hawaii
458.78	New Jersey
450.38	Kentucky
440.87	Alabama
433.48	North Dakota
433.30	Louisiana
431.24	North Carolina
407.66	Missouri
400.97	Rhode Island
399.98	Indiana
393.53	Montana
389.10	Kansas
386.98	Mississippi
383.44	South Carolina
381.15	Pennsylvania
373.36	Utah
371.23	Vermont
366.80	Wisconsin
364.89	Minnesota
364.36	Maryland
361.11	Oklahoma
358.73	Iowa
357.31	Arkansas
355.88	Florida
355.00	Ohio
344.03	Idaho
341.52	Georgia
339.22	Texas
336.77	Massachusetts
327.27	Michigan
321.59	Virginia
285.40	Illinois
283.67	Tennessee
273.81	Colorado
268.51	Arizona
220.89	Oregon
215.13	South Dakota
190.40	Nevada
175.40	Nebraska
86.48	New Hampshire

Table G.593. COLLEG89

Per Capita Expenditures of Total Funds Devoted to Higher Education 1989

486.84	Iowa
474.86	Wyoming
428.06	Alaska
413.81	Alabama
379.78	Nebraska
357.05	Wisconsin
347.82	Hawaii
347.77	South Carolina
332.59	Kansas
319.62	Kentucky
317.27	Oregon
300.04	Virginia
288.24	California
286.58	North Dakota
281.19	Maryland
273.41	West Virginia
271.74	Connecticut
266.50	South Dakota
262.92	North Carolina
260.35	Minnesota
247.54	New Mexico
245.76	Oklahoma
238.78	New York
234.49	Montana
228.78	Washington
228.38	Colorado
226.35	Arkansas
213.73	Louisiana
213.51	Mississippi
207.22	Georgia
197.68	New Hampshire
193.49	Delaware
177.60	Tennessee
170.68	Utah
165.75	Arizona
151.91	Illinois
147.73	Rhode Island
146.70	Indiana
142.79	Massachusetts
139.22	Ohio
137.71	Michigan
131.25	Texas
125.29	Maine
123.78	Florida
123.75	Idaho
122.56	Missouri
119.09	New Jersey
117.93	Pennsylvania
102.48	Vermont
87.81	Nevada

Table G.594. HELP89

Per Capita Expenditures of Total Funds Devoted to Cash Assistance 1989

186.62	California
172.43	Massachusetts
162.02	Michigan
143.27	New York
139.25	Alaska
129.34	Arkansas
122.92	Wisconsin
120.07	Ohio
116.46	Connecticut
113.96	Rhode Island
108.28	Vermont
107.39	Maine
104.65	Hawaii
90.59	Pennsylvania
85.93	Illinois
74.49	Washington
73.40	Montana
72.98	Minnesota
66.38	New Jersey
59.41	Maryland
59.11	West Virginia
55.91	Iowa
50.25	Wyoming
50.15	Oklahoma
48.16	South Dakota
45.40	Kentucky
43.59	Kansas
43.35	North Dakota
42.75	Louisiana
42.17	Oregon
41.30	Missouri
39.14	Nebraska
38.36	Idaho
37.62	Delaware
35.82	Georgia
34.87	New Mexico
34.10	Mississippi
34.07	Colorado
33.34	Utah
29.58	Texas
29.21	North Carolina
27.68	Indiana
27.13	Tennessee
26.75	South Carolina
26.52	Virginia
24.71	New Hampshire
23.91	Florida
22.10	Arizona
19.10	Alabama
13.91	Nevada

Table G.595. MEDICA89

Per Capita Expenditures of Total Funds Devoted to Medicaid 1989

425.03	New York
350.32	Rhode Island
312.24	Maine
290.97	Massachusetts
279.35	North Dakota
271.19	Montana
258.38	Minnesota
248.45	Connecticut
247.94	New Jersey
238.03	Wisconsin
233.16	Louisiana
216.11	Kentucky
206.23	Hawaii
203.39	Pennsylvania
201.86	Ohio
197.47	South Dakota
192.08	Maryland
191.42	Vermont
190.99	Indiana
188.91	Oklahoma
188.70	Tennessee
185.93	Arkansas
184.77	California
180.51	Alaska
173.65	West Virginia
173.39	Illinois
167.54	Mississippi
163.06	Iowa
162.02	Michigan
161.85	New Hampshire
159.62	Washington
152.21	Georgia
150.75	Nebraska
146.43	New Mexico
142.68	South Carolina
142.43	Delaware
137.72	North Carolina
137.22	Missouri
132.22	Florida
130.96	Virginia
126.51	Oregon
122.55	Alabama
117.35	Colorado
116.24	Kansas
113.06	Wyoming
97.34	Utah
90.34	Idaho
63.47	Nevada
56.38	Texas
.00	Arizona

Table G.596. PRISON89

Per Capita Expenditures of Total Funds Devoted to Corrections 1989

154.72	Alaska
121.78	New York
121.01	Virginia
106.93	Maryland
80.62	Delaware
74.90	South Carolina
68.05	Michigan
67.35	Massachusetts
66.52	California
66.08	Nevada
62.47	New Jersey
59.27	New Mexico
58.48	Hawaii
56.35	Arizona
54.87	Rhode Island
52.76	Wyoming
52.21	Ohio
51.76	Connecticut
50.05	Kansas
49.33	Tennessee
48.58	Louisiana
48.19	Oregon
47.73	Maine
46.81	Oklahoma
45.91	North Carolina
43.61	Florida
43.49	Georgia
42.82	Montana
42.67	Utah
42.54	Vermont
41.43	Illinois
37.85	Colorado
37.24	Washington
35.12	Wisconsin
34.60	Indiana
34.59	New Hampshire
34.50	Kentucky
31.97	Missouri
30.50	South Dakota
30.28	Iowa
30.24	Alabama
29.59	Minnesota
28.99	Nebraska
28.90	North Dakota
28.17	Mississippi
25.88	Texas
24.25	Arkansas
23.93	Pennsylvania
22.28	Idaho
12.93	West Virginia

Table G.597. HIWAY89

Per Capita Expenditures of Total Funds Devoted to Transportation 1989

809.71	Alaska
492.45	Wyoming
461.71	Hawaii
374.26	Maryland
367.02	Montana
349.35	Delaware
349.19	North Dakota
301.12	West Virginia
278.42	Vermont
276.83	Virginia
269.71	South Dakota
268.24	Minnesota
261.69	Rhode Island
245.86	Connecticut
244.06	New Mexico
239.29	Pennsylvania
220.68	Oklahoma
219.44	Mississippi
214.79	Maine
208.80	New Hampshire
208.74	Nebraska
208.56	Arkansas
199.13	New Jersey
195.80	New York
189.77	Washington
185.48	South Carolina
184.39	Idaho
183.40	Wisconsin
182.44	Kansas
179.36	Iowa
176.01	Utah
174.87	Louisiana
169.54	Nevada
168.68	Oregon
167.25	Illinois
158.95	Florida
155.80	North Carolina
146.77	Tennessee
146.43	Alabama
145.82	Michigan
145.49	Massachusetts
143.94	Indiana
132.57	Kentucky
129.22	Missouri
126.63	Texas
124.86	Arizona
121.13	Colorado
114.85	Ohio
107.17	California
103.61	Georgia

Table G.598. ELSE89

Per Capita Expenditures of Total Funds Devoted to All Other Expenditures 1989

2,305.35	Alaska
1,541.07	Massachusetts
1,437.44	Hawaii
1,163.61	Delaware
1,141.32	Connecticut
1,080.33	Oregon
1,052.89	Iowa
992.18	North Dakota
841.08	Vermont
796.64	Louisiana
796.52	New Jersey
780.84	Rhode Island
756.99	Ohio
748.72	Wyoming
719.91	Minnesota
685.30	New York
674.19	Maine
656.56	Montana
652.91	Pennsylvania
645.80	Wisconsin
629.11	Illinois
622.42	South Carolina
618.91	Michigan
617.45	Kentucky
610.09	Washington
603.97	Maryland
577.96	South Dakota
566.87	Florida
556.71	Oklahoma
554.20	West Virginia
521.38	New Hampshire
519.20	California
502.06	New Mexico
500.50	Kansas
485.03	Arkansas
479.07	Virginia
468.51	Arizona
465.31	Nebraska
463.61	Missouri
449.20	Colorado
441.50	Indiana
438.70	Utah
434.37	Idaho
432.95	Mississippi
418.59	Alabama
396.52	Georgia
360.13	Tennessee
328.30	North Carolina
278.21	Nevada
215.36	Texas

Table G.599. SCHOOL90

Per Capita Expenditures of Total Funds Devoted to Elementary and Secondary Education 1990

1,510.72	Alaska
830.02	Delaware
716.67	New Mexico
625.62	Wyoming
599.57	New York
571.21	Washington
553.33	California
548.54	Utah
532.52	Maine
514.39	West Virginia
512.68	North Carolina
505.72	Kentucky
495.67	New Jersey
492.05	Idaho
482.25	Hawaii
478.28	Alabama
474.20	Oklahoma
471.07	Georgia
445.74	Louisiana
443.86	Wisconsin
443.03	Kansas
440.88	Missouri
440.68	Arkansas
436.36	Indiana
433.12	Vermont
425.71	Florida
424.46	South Carolina
422.30	North Dakota
421.02	Iowa
420.45	Connecticut
416.40	Rhode Island
407.13	Pennsylvania
402.65	Mississippi
399.57	Texas
394.73	Virginia
391.39	Minnesota
383.49	Maryland
380.75	Colorado
376.12	Michigan
375.32	Arizona
371.60	Ohio
346.28	Nevada
324.98	Illinois
322.43	Tennessee
321.79	Massachusetts
310.87	Montana
272.89	Oregon
245.42	South Dakota
191.07	Nebraska
94.11	New Hampshire

Table G.600. COLLEG90

Per Capita Expenditures of Total Funds Devoted to Higher Education 1990

650.36	Alaska
607.58	Iowa
463.98	Wyoming
460.02	Alabama
432.52	Nebraska
432.12	Wisconsin
411.40	South Carolina
383.83	Kansas
373.69	Oregon
370.59	Kentucky
365.80	New Mexico
340.00	Washington
339.36	Hawaii
333.51	North Carolina
329.92	Virginia
322.58	Maryland
319.70	Colorado
287.16	South Dakota
285.99	West Virginia
282.32	North Dakota
270.97	Oklahoma
270.59	Arkansas
270.46	Georgia
261.79	Connecticut
259.44	Minnesota
253.31	Utah
240.96	Mississippi
239.04	California
237.98	Montana
229.25	New York
228.33	Delaware
221.71	Arizona
218.00	Louisiana
210.01	Nevada
207.52	New Hampshire
201.89	Tennessee
192.00	Indiana
174.50	Illinois
172.02	Florida
167.30	Texas
157.97	Michigan
143.78	Ohio
142.40	Rhode Island
142.39	Idaho
133.13	Maine
132.89	Missouri
125.98	New Jersey
122.50	Pennsylvania
109.04	Massachusetts
106.71	Vermont

Table G.601. HELP90

Per Capita Expenditures of Total Funds Devoted to Cash Assistance 1990

210.26	California
201.54	New York
189.69	Alaska
187.48	Arkansas
167.54	Massachusetts
167.37	Michigan
132.22	Connecticut
130.71	Ohio
126.79	Maine
120.82	Rhode Island
119.77	Wisconsin
110.74	Hawaii
108.09	Pennsylvania
97.47	Washington
96.25	Vermont
88.05	Illinois
78.95	Maryland
68.84	Oregon
63.55	West Virginia
62.62	Minnesota
61.96	New Jersey
57.98	Iowa
56.11	Nevada
55.74	Montana
55.38	Kansas
54.57	Oklahoma
49.20	Utah
49.14	Kentucky
46.57	Georgia
45.08	South Dakota
45.08	North Dakota
44.98	Colorado
44.90	Wyoming
43.78	Missouri
42.58	North Carolina
40.88	Louisiana
40.11	Delaware
39.82	New Mexico
38.21	Nebraska
36.42	Arizona
34.25	Idaho
33.38	Virginia
33.29	Mississippi
31.64	Tennessee
28.56	Indiana
28.30	South Carolina
27.80	Florida
26.54	New Hampshire
23.50	Texas
16.43	Alabama

Table G.602. MEDICA90

Per Capita Expenditures of Total Funds Devoted to Medicaid 1990

445.90	New York
399.14	Rhode Island
353.70	Massachusetts
334.52	North Dakota
297.96	Maine
290.79	Tennessee
288.86	Wisconsin
284.04	Minnesota
280.29	Louisiana
277.66	Connecticut
264.21	Alaska
256.10	New Jersey
253.88	Michigan
253.18	Vermont
250.71	Indiana
241.80	Georgia
240.86	Oklahoma
239.55	Kentucky
239.02	Ohio
236.82	California
235.80	Arkansas
233.69	Montana
228.40	West Virginia
224.40	Washington
223.72	South Dakota
215.49	South Carolina
212.05	Maryland
210.84	Mississippi
207.17	Pennsylvania
204.05	New Mexico
202.23	North Carolina
199.54	Arizona
193.57	Texas
192.11	Illinois
189.08	Iowa
185.75	Hawaii
182.39	Nebraska
182.05	Delaware
180.71	Florida
179.55	Nevada
178.23	Missouri
175.11	Colorado
162.19	Utah
156.59	Kansas
153.20	Idaho
143.57	New Hampshire
141.39	Virginia
140.56	Alabama
140.13	Oregon
107.76	Wyoming

Table G.603. PRISON90

Per Capita Expenditures of Total Funds Devoted to Corrections 1990

243.88	Alaska
135.35	Maryland
125.96	New York
108.45	California
98.74	Delaware
98.40	Massachusetts
93.60	South Carolina
89.58	New Mexico
84.37	Tennessee
83.83	Utah
82.48	Virginia
80.86	Michigan
75.23	Georgia
70.22	New Jersey
69.68	Arizona
67.87	Hawaii
66.88	Rhode Island
66.11	Connecticut
66.03	Florida
60.32	North Carolina
59.20	Kansas
56.67	Washington
56.55	Oregon
56.49	Vermont
56.45	Oklahoma
52.54	Texas
50.42	Ohio
46.49	Nevada
46.49	Maine
46.43	Illinois
44.98	Colorado
44.90	Wyoming
44.77	Louisiana
44.62	Wisconsin
42.84	Indiana
41.99	Alabama
40.95	Kentucky
40.73	Montana
40.65	Missouri
37.85	Idaho
35.29	Iowa
33.00	Nebraska
30.92	Arkansas
30.63	Pennsylvania
30.16	New Hampshire
29.07	Minnesota
28.38	South Dakota
26.95	Mississippi
23.72	North Dakota
13.90	West Virginia

Table G.604. HIWAY90

Per Capita Expenditures of Total Funds Devoted to Transportation 1990

1,043.28	Alaska
903.77	Hawaii
499.90	Wyoming
428.79	Montana
403.79	Maryland
401.94	Connecticut
391.39	Minnesota
339.62	West Virginia
336.33	Delaware
323.50	New Mexico
303.67	North Dakota
301.30	Vermont
300.46	Virginia
283.82	South Dakota
256.85	South Carolina
254.59	Rhode Island
254.14	Idaho
250.16	Kansas
249.79	Kentucky
237.80	Pennsylvania
233.27	Utah
224.00	Maine
218.41	Wisconsin
217.13	Nebraska
214.29	Iowa
212.88	North Carolina
210.84	Mississippi
210.76	Oklahoma
204.38	Louisiana
201.54	New York
196.37	Arizona
190.78	Nevada
190.51	Illinois
185.87	Washington
180.80	Tennessee
177.01	Oregon
174.89	Michigan
171.37	Indiana
169.36	New Jersey
166.50	New Hampshire
162.22	Massachusetts
153.47	Texas
150.46	Georgia
147.80	Colorado
146.89	Arkansas
132.89	Missouri
127.78	Alabama
126.84	Florida
121.38	Ohio
110.67	California

Table G.605. ELSE90

Per Capita Expenditures of Total Funds Devoted to All Other Expenditures 1990

2,872.41	Alaska
1,482.46	Hawaii
1,446.72	Massachusetts
1,369.37	Oregon
1,366.91	Delaware
1,203.34	Wyoming
1,086.83	Connecticut
995.82	Iowa
960.85	North Dakota
886.02	New Jersey
845.31	Vermont
836.13	Montana
818.57	Minnesota
812.29	Ohio
803.18	Wisconsin
788.81	Washington
757.29	Rhode Island
756.95	California
754.41	Maine
748.79	South Carolina
746.53	New Mexico
736.74	Florida
721.86	Maryland
715.45	New York
712.41	Louisiana
688.17	Pennsylvania
686.71	Idaho
681.44	Virginia
669.49	Michigan
642.69	Nebraska
618.49	Arkansas
594.10	Missouri
593.76	Kentucky
584.33	Illinois
575.82	Oklahoma
572.33	Nevada
560.43	Alabama
559.51	Kansas
555.96	South Dakota
540.21	West Virginia
538.10	New Hampshire
535.55	Georgia
493.21	Colorado
492.05	Utah
483.01	Arizona
464.92	Indiana
459.72	Mississippi
408.01	North Carolina
397.76	Tennessee
392.66	Texas

Table G.606. SCHOOL91

Per Capita Expenditures of Total Funds Devoted to Elementary and Secondary Education 1991

1,371.51	Alaska
839.46	Delaware
703.66	Wyoming
702.90	New Mexico
702.24	West Virginia
661.37	Washington
590.08	Alabama
585.50	California
575.05	New York
566.73	Louisiana
563.72	Maine
551.90	North Carolina
547.67	Hawaii
544.08	Montana
540.91	Oklahoma
534.95	Minnesota
532.00	Utah
529.04	Kentucky
525.74	Idaho
510.66	New Jersey
496.49	Florida
493.22	Arkansas
489.18	Georgia
488.12	Iowa
477.80	Indiana
472.98	North Dakota
469.70	Mississippi
455.03	Vermont
449.52	Kansas
437.63	Maryland
433.93	Missouri
421.98	South Carolina
421.81	Connecticut
419.72	Pennsylvania
416.52	Texas
397.31	Michigan
393.45	Virginia
387.04	Nevada
379.23	Arizona
377.92	Ohio
371.98	Colorado
361.93	Rhode Island
344.90	Massachusetts
333.15	Illinois
329.51	Tennessee
321.37	Oregon
303.76	Nebraska
301.00	Wisconsin
249.24	South Dakota
149.28	New Hampshire

Table G.607.   COLLEG91

Per Capita Expenditures of Total Funds Devoted to Higher Education 1991

678.09	Iowa
589.68	Alaska
532.41	Wyoming
524.52	Alabama
480.55	Oregon
478.18	Nebraska
458.50	Kentucky
450.70	South Carolina
441.18	New Mexico
394.85	Kansas
360.99	Washington
349.18	Maryland
331.33	Virginia
323.46	Minnesota
321.76	Arkansas
321.62	Oklahoma
318.50	Hawaii
317.63	West Virginia
314.83	North Carolina
300.87	South Dakota
286.59	Wisconsin
285.66	Georgia
277.79	Colorado
273.08	Mississippi
270.43	Louisiana
264.97	North Dakota
263.82	California
251.08	Connecticut
248.78	Utah
245.37	Montana
242.20	Texas
235.02	Arizona
230.38	Delaware
230.02	New York
227.98	Nevada
220.20	Tennessee
186.18	Florida
182.21	Idaho
177.68	Illinois
176.58	Indiana
158.15	Michigan
155.73	Ohio
154.53	Maine
132.16	Massachusetts
129.45	Pennsylvania
128.64	Rhode Island
125.42	New Jersey
124.66	Missouri
106.93	Vermont
91.54	New Hampshire

Table G.608.   HELP91

Per Capita Expenditures of Total Funds Devoted to Cash Assistance 1991

237.86	New York
222.17	California
193.40	Massachusetts
178.89	Alaska
162.01	Michigan
149.51	Ohio
148.14	Connecticut
128.64	Rhode Island
127.41	Vermont
126.24	Maine
108.03	Washington
101.99	Pennsylvania
100.99	Hawaii
92.26	Illinois
91.02	Arkansas
79.62	Minnesota
76.82	Maryland
73.91	New Jersey
72.05	Wisconsin
69.08	Oregon
64.82	West Virginia
63.32	Iowa
60.56	Oklahoma
60.09	Nevada
58.68	Montana
54.84	New Mexico
52.93	Wyoming
52.65	Kansas
52.28	Georgia
51.73	Louisiana
49.38	Kentucky
49.29	New Hampshire
47.34	Delaware
47.05	North Dakota
45.93	Utah
45.76	Missouri
44.51	South Dakota
41.51	Colorado
39.17	Arizona
38.23	Mississippi
38.04	Florida
38.02	Tennessee
37.24	Nebraska
35.20	Virginia
34.14	North Carolina
32.27	Idaho
29.43	Indiana
29.31	Texas
28.72	South Carolina
20.49	Alabama

Table G.609.   MEDICA91

Per Capita Expenditures of Total Funds Devoted to Medicaid 1991

512.32	New York
483.51	Massachusetts
440.42	Rhode Island
418.58	Louisiana
360.78	Minnesota
351.16	Alaska
338.99	Vermont
333.01	Maine
327.00	New Jersey
316.84	Tennessee
311.85	Pennsylvania
308.15	Indiana
307.07	North Dakota
303.81	Connecticut
303.16	Ohio
296.87	Georgia
286.86	Kentucky
284.80	Alabama
281.94	Washington
281.54	Arkansas
279.32	Oregon
273.08	Mississippi
268.09	Michigan
266.71	Montana
263.85	Iowa
263.82	California
262.91	South Carolina
257.13	West Virginia
254.79	Oklahoma
253.00	Texas
249.27	New Hampshire
245.68	South Dakota
242.24	Florida
242.10	Maryland
236.69	Missouri
235.17	North Carolina
226.12	Arizona
224.45	Nevada
221.84	New Mexico
214.60	Delaware
210.14	Illinois
208.14	Wisconsin
205.95	Colorado
205.01	Virginia
200.46	Kansas
190.32	Hawaii
186.18	Nebraska
186.00	Idaho
179.88	Utah
143.22	Wyoming

Table G.610.   PRISON91

Per Capita Expenditures of Total Funds Devoted to Corrections 1991

198.77	Alaska
138.53	New York
128.03	Maryland
119.26	Massachusetts
110.46	Delaware
103.84	South Carolina
101.83	California
97.33	Virginia
90.39	Connecticut
90.10	Oregon
85.11	New Jersey
83.30	Texas
82.85	Rhode Island
74.68	Georgia
74.07	Florida
72.07	North Carolina
71.36	Michigan
68.12	Tennessee
67.66	Arizona
67.30	New Mexico
66.82	Kansas
65.87	Washington
65.84	Louisiana
65.38	Wyoming
62.32	Indiana
62.29	Ohio
60.94	Maine
60.56	Oklahoma
58.26	Hawaii
56.88	Vermont
55.04	Idaho
54.67	Illinois
54.28	Colorado
53.58	Utah
53.27	Alabama
53.02	Nevada
51.73	Kentucky
47.49	Iowa
40.01	Montana
39.43	New Hampshire
39.23	Pennsylvania
39.20	Nebraska
38.10	Arkansas
37.39	South Dakota
37.32	Minnesota
37.15	North Dakota
36.29	Missouri
34.59	Mississippi
30.42	Wisconsin
15.13	West Virginia

Table G.611.   HIWAY91

Per Capita Expenditures of Total Funds Devoted to Transportation 1991

1,239.00	Alaska
1,017.65	Hawaii
557.32	Wyoming
400.39	Maryland
368.97	North Dakota
365.39	Montana
356.53	Connecticut
350.30	Delaware
317.63	West Virginia
311.02	Minnesota
310.37	Kentucky
296.13	Virginia
295.53	South Dakota
288.43	Arizona
284.39	Vermont
279.32	Oregon
269.20	New Mexico
253.11	Kansas
245.38	Iowa
242.01	Rhode Island
233.78	New Hampshire
231.55	Idaho
231.25	Nebraska
227.57	Mississippi
224.18	Maine
223.79	North Carolina
223.59	Pennsylvania
221.34	Washington
215.97	Massachusetts
211.72	New York
210.93	Oklahoma
208.43	Illinois
206.78	Nevada
204.20	Florida
202.85	Utah
201.58	New Jersey
199.88	Louisiana
193.89	Indiana
185.58	South Carolina
185.35	Tennessee
180.51	California
175.51	Michigan
166.12	Ohio
165.11	Arkansas
164.30	Georgia
159.81	Alabama
150.07	Colorado
142.49	Wisconsin
135.76	Texas
129.39	Missouri

Table G.612.   ELSE91

Per Capita Expenditures of Total Funds Devoted to All Other Expenditures 1991

2,696.64	Alaska
1,730.95	Massachusetts
1,650.77	Hawaii
1,489.70	Oregon
1,366.50	Delaware
1,146.84	Montana
1,061.72	Wyoming
980.63	North Dakota
939.04	Connecticut
935.41	Washington
916.05	New Jersey
912.33	Vermont
863.81	Ohio
852.23	Iowa
838.50	Minnesota
797.98	Rhode Island
780.72	Louisiana
762.75	Florida
757.80	South Carolina
739.42	Pennsylvania
735.31	New Mexico
730.31	Arkansas
716.07	Maine
714.43	Virginia
708.36	New York
698.90	California
696.26	Michigan
693.70	Maryland
687.07	Idaho
685.92	Nebraska
665.41	Kentucky
652.56	Utah
639.06	Oklahoma
632.14	Illinois
610.65	South Dakota
607.45	Kansas
604.42	Nevada
595.72	New Hampshire
572.79	Missouri
561.97	Wisconsin
546.59	Arizona
505.98	Georgia
504.29	Mississippi
496.51	Colorado
486.17	West Virginia
483.00	Indiana
464.66	North Carolina
427.73	Tennessee
417.97	Alabama
384.13	Texas

Table G.613.   SCHOOL92

Per Capita Expenditures of Total Funds Devoted to Elementary and Secondary Education 1992

1,492.23	Alaska
938.90	Wyoming
926.31	Wisconsin
846.60	Delaware
762.36	New Mexico
717.05	West Virginia
714.91	Washington
657.17	Kentucky
641.70	New Jersey
613.22	New York
599.92	California
581.76	Hawaii
565.55	Utah
562.53	Idaho
552.14	Maine
548.77	Oklahoma
543.23	Arkansas
535.10	North Carolina
530.65	North Dakota
526.91	Alabama
519.33	Minnesota
513.29	Louisiana
507.57	Florida
497.09	Connecticut
471.82	Kansas
469.92	Georgia
468.97	Indiana
468.46	Iowa
467.39	Montana
455.00	Vermont
452.81	Pennsylvania
446.52	Missouri
443.32	South Carolina
441.74	Arizona
424.76	Texas
416.13	Nevada
413.67	Mississippi
405.38	Maryland
400.98	Michigan
393.88	Virginia
387.70	Rhode Island
386.59	Colorado
369.82	Oregon
363.85	Nebraska
357.60	Ohio
315.67	Illinois
296.32	Tennessee
288.16	South Dakota
217.86	Massachusetts
142.93	New Hampshire

Table G.614.   COLLEG92

Per Capita Expenditures of Total Funds Devoted to Higher Education 1992

807.09	Wisconsin
700.20	Wyoming
650.46	Alaska
603.86	Iowa
600.21	Alabama
514.53	New Mexico
508.09	Nebraska
457.88	Oregon
457.32	South Carolina
440.58	Washington
424.20	Kansas
409.08	Kentucky
398.37	Arkansas
338.88	Oklahoma
338.58	Maryland
333.63	West Virginia
325.92	South Dakota
323.64	California
312.61	Minnesota
312.17	Virginia
310.68	Connecticut
307.09	North Dakota
307.04	Hawaii
302.24	Colorado
297.50	North Carolina
287.71	Georgia
255.23	Arizona
251.58	Utah
251.41	Louisiana
248.50	Nevada
248.20	Delaware
247.03	Mississippi
246.41	New York
222.21	Idaho
214.84	Texas
203.21	Montana
198.12	Tennessee
181.88	Indiana
176.41	Illinois
167.67	Maine
166.21	Michigan
166.03	Ohio
158.48	Florida
135.53	New Jersey
133.18	Pennsylvania
120.22	Missouri
111.94	Rhode Island
98.18	Vermont
94.12	New Hampshire
70.99	Massachusetts

Table G.615.   HELP92

Per Capita Expenditures of Total Funds Devoted to Cash Assistance 1992

267.84	Alaska
255.23	California
252.01	New York
219.24	Ohio
208.14	Maine
189.00	Connecticut
180.37	Wisconsin
145.43	Michigan
141.97	Rhode Island
141.29	Vermont
129.74	Massachusetts
113.61	Washington
110.98	Pennsylvania
109.08	Hawaii
99.46	Wyoming
98.99	Arkansas
98.42	Illinois
94.04	New Jersey
85.12	Oregon
78.31	Maryland
78.15	Minnesota
71.26	Kentucky
71.00	Nevada
70.58	Mississippi
67.35	New Mexico
67.22	West Virginia
64.79	Arizona
62.28	Iowa
61.90	North Carolina
61.20	Delaware
59.03	Oklahoma
58.44	Kansas
57.54	Georgia
53.54	Florida
52.29	New Hampshire
51.52	Missouri
50.80	Montana
46.29	Utah
45.71	South Dakota
45.69	Colorado
44.22	North Dakota
43.06	Nebraska
39.81	Virginia
39.62	Tennessee
39.28	Louisiana
32.67	South Carolina
32.10	Indiana
32.07	Alabama
29.52	Texas
28.03	Idaho

Table G.616. MEDICA92

Per Capita Expenditures of Total Funds Devoted to Medicaid 1992

750.82	Rhode Island
660.34	Wisconsin
632.82	New York
624.41	Maine
607.57	Louisiana
599.60	New Hampshire
558.73	New Jersey
477.23	Pennsylvania
461.87	Kentucky
460.60	West Virginia
428.89	California
409.50	Vermont
406.58	Tennessee
403.06	Michigan
400.84	Minnesota
373.42	Alabama
365.55	Indiana
365.05	Connecticut
360.65	Missouri
359.31	Maryland
354.91	Arkansas
354.84	Georgia
347.68	Texas
344.36	Alaska
338.44	Ohio
338.32	South Carolina
337.80	Massachusetts
332.52	Washington
330.21	Wyoming
324.96	Illinois
324.28	North Dakota
319.96	South Dakota
312.49	New Mexico
311.61	Nevada
309.76	Mississippi
307.48	North Carolina
306.26	Florida
299.53	Oklahoma
286.43	Colorado
278.91	Iowa
267.09	Oregon
266.64	Hawaii
264.18	Montana
249.74	Nebraska
248.20	Delaware
243.45	Arizona
234.65	Virginia
218.59	Kansas
215.35	Utah
194.18	Idaho

Table G.617. PRISN92

Per Capita Expenditures of Total Funds Devoted to Corrections 1992

268	Alaska
146	Delaware
132	New York
114	Connecticut
111	California
103	Washington
100	Texas
98	South Carolina
96	Michigan
92	Virginia
91	New Jersey
90	Maryland
89	Wisconsin
84	Arizona
84	North Carolina
80	Wyoming
79	Rhode Island
73	New Mexico
69	Maine
69	Georgia
69	Hawaii
69	Florida
68	Ohio
67	Kansas
67	Colorado
66	Massachusetts
66	Idaho
62	Tennessee
62	Oregon
60	Louisiana
59	Oklahoma
59	Indiana
57	Nevada
57	Mississippi
56	Utah
53	Vermont
52	Illinois
48	Kentucky
44	Pennsylvania
43	Iowa
42	South Dakota
41	Arkansas
39	Alabama
38	Montana
38	Minnesota
37	Nebraska
36	Missouri
33	New Hampshire
29	North Dakota
25	West Virginia

Table G.618. HIWAY92

Per Capita Expenditures of Total Funds Devoted to Transportation 1992

1,285.61	Alaska
945.36	Hawaii
771.81	Wyoming
400.49	Wisconsin
362.86	Iowa
357.00	Delaware
345.49	Maryland
343.59	West Virginia
341.48	North Dakota
340.38	Montana
340.34	Minnesota
329.91	Kentucky
325.92	South Dakota
323.63	Connecticut
301.74	Vermont
287.03	Virginia
281.36	Kansas
262.11	Rhode Island
251.50	Maine
247.84	New Mexico
243.45	Arizona
237.51	Pennsylvania
234.30	Tennessee
234.22	Idaho
230.36	Nebraska
227.02	Florida
221.63	North Carolina
218.91	Nevada
217.62	Mississippi
217.26	Illinois
214.39	New Hampshire
213.36	Washington
207.30	Utah
204.41	New York
204.34	Ohio
203.33	Oklahoma
199.59	Oregon
199.03	Louisiana
197.93	Indiana
188.48	Massachusetts
181.08	Arkansas
178.67	Michigan
177.33	South Carolina
176.40	Alabama
165.96	New Jersey
155.36	Georgia
154.56	Missouri
150.88	Texas
137.06	Colorado
123.67	California

Table G.619. ELSE92

Per Capita Expenditures of Total Funds Devoted to All Other Expenditures 1992

3,336.48	Alaska
1,761.44	Hawaii
1,493.97	Oregon
1,492.60	Delaware
1,439.34	Massachusetts
1,173.55	Montana
1,078.73	New Jersey
1,066.21	Wyoming
1,017.55	Maine
999.28	Rhode Island
945.40	Louisiana
938.74	Vermont
890.89	Iowa
884.41	North Dakota
853.46	Washington
829.42	Minnesota
820.25	Florida
796.74	Arkansas
789.65	Connecticut
788.64	South Carolina
786.74	California
774.79	Ohio
765.79	Pennsylvania
737.47	Virginia
723.39	Nebraska
719.62	New York
716.57	New Mexico
696.65	Idaho
689.77	Michigan
686.38	Maryland
677.76	Oklahoma
672.20	Illinois
670.21	Utah
665.09	Kentucky
648.85	Nevada
645.02	Mississippi
644.96	Kansas
639.91	South Dakota
628.25	Arizona
606.58	New Hampshire
547.84	Missouri
545.23	Alabama
542.77	West Virginia
534.20	Colorado
523.62	Georgia
487.18	North Carolina
485.82	Tennessee
477.88	Indiana
372.28	Texas
.00	Wisconsin

Table G.620. SCHOOL93

Per Capita Expenditures of Total Funds Devoted to Elementary and Secondary Education 1993

1,355.36	Alaska
935.59	Delaware
734.49	West Virginia
727.24	Utah
711.27	Wyoming
700.96	Washington
650.56	Kentucky
643.79	California
630.48	New Jersey
626.75	Hawaii
614.48	Oklahoma
597.54	New Mexico
595.69	Louisiana
592.11	Idaho
580.87	Alabama
580.37	North Carolina
577.27	Rhode Island
572.00	Kansas
562.83	New York
562.53	Connecticut
554.38	Arkansas
553.97	Montana
548.21	Wisconsin
535.94	Iowa
531.86	Minnesota
501.19	Georgia
496.08	Indiana
486.17	North Dakota
466.49	Pennsylvania
466.46	Texas
463.70	Maine
460.07	Mississippi
459.20	Missouri
454.92	South Carolina
452.23	Michigan
451.63	Maryland
446.85	Nevada
444.00	Oregon
429.91	Florida
425.12	Vermont
415.88	Colorado
414.78	Arizona
402.50	Virginia
400.48	Ohio
379.27	Nebraska
364.43	Tennessee
316.87	Illinois
303.85	South Dakota
263.61	Massachusetts
131.27	New Hampshire

Table G.621. COLLEG93

Per Capita Expenditures of Total Funds Devoted to Higher Education 1993

710.77	Iowa
601.58	Alaska
597.54	Alabama
538.25	Nebraska
496.06	South Carolina
469.14	Wisconsin
446.98	Oregon
444.07	Wyoming
432.05	Arkansas
409.89	Kansas
386.91	Washington
369.46	Kentucky
367.39	Maryland
364.98	Connecticut
360.94	Georgia
344.11	Louisiana
342.13	Oklahoma
340.63	New Mexico
331.95	North Carolina
328.49	South Dakota
324.30	Minnesota
317.98	Hawaii
312.73	North Dakota
312.43	West Virginia
307.28	Virginia
300.25	Colorado
283.43	Mississippi
260.59	Tennessee
260.30	Delaware
256.45	Nevada
247.35	Utah
238.18	Montana
234.44	Arizona
228.66	Texas
225.77	Idaho
225.72	New York
192.97	Florida
192.61	California
173.33	Indiana
170.92	Illinois
168.22	Michigan
166.11	Ohio
142.66	Rhode Island
135.24	Maine
134.72	New Jersey
131.69	Pennsylvania
121.61	Missouri
101.93	Vermont
97.51	New Hampshire
87.87	Massachusetts

Table G.622. HELP93

Per Capita Expenditures of Total Funds Devoted to Cash Assistance 1993

293.14	New York
258.57	California
253.68	Alaska
224.34	Connecticut
189.11	Rhode Island
175.74	Massachusetts
152.93	Michigan
143.53	Maine
139.22	Vermont
133.64	Hawaii
123.11	Washington
118.30	Pennsylvania
108.06	Wisconsin
104.67	Ohio
101.03	New Mexico
98.59	Minnesota
97.00	New Jersey
91.10	Arkansas
83.44	Oregon
80.66	Illinois
80.32	Kentucky
75.55	Nevada
75.45	Delaware
71.65	Iowa
70.20	Maryland
68.52	West Virginia
68.15	North Carolina
68.13	Arizona
67.74	Wyoming
65.27	Oklahoma
61.07	Florida
59.81	Georgia
58.88	Montana
54.38	New Hampshire
53.26	Kansas
52.64	Missouri
52.05	Louisiana
48.62	Utah
47.02	Tennessee
46.62	Colorado
45.17	South Dakota
43.28	Virginia
42.07	Texas
41.14	South Carolina
40.88	Nebraska
36.79	North Dakota
35.86	Indiana
30.95	Alabama
30.81	Mississippi
29.82	Idaho

Table G.623. MEDICA93

Per Capita Expenditures of Total Funds Devoted to Medicaid 1993

1,018.51	Rhode Island
766.30	Louisiana
715.27	New York
633.83	New Hampshire
633.09	West Virginia
604.46	Maine
573.90	New Jersey
543.47	Kentucky
522.14	Michigan
519.21	Tennessee
506.55	Massachusetts
505.17	New Mexico
498.07	Indiana
478.82	Connecticut
472.19	Minnesota
459.79	Pennsylvania
452.46	Vermont
451.85	Mississippi
435.19	Georgia
430.73	South Carolina
424.80	California
421.64	Arkansas
408.52	Wisconsin
391.77	Illinois
391.56	North Dakota
384.14	Texas
381.88	Washington
378.12	North Carolina
377.77	Nevada
373.89	Missouri
373.76	Alabama
373.17	Ohio
371.29	Florida
363.66	Colorado
358.61	Montana
355.69	Maryland
347.90	Alaska
346.79	Iowa
346.63	Oklahoma
340.81	South Dakota
327.04	Nebraska
324.44	Delaware
303.95	Oregon
297.30	Wyoming
290.33	Hawaii
278.52	Arizona
270.50	Idaho
264.00	Virginia
243.12	Utah
236.21	Kansas

Table G.624. PRISON93

Per Capita Expenditures of Total Funds Devoted to Corrections 1993

202.94	Alaska
130.59	Connecticut
126.07	Rhode Island
124.49	Delaware
108.46	New York
107.05	Michigan
106.10	Texas
102.90	California
101.63	South Carolina
100.62	Maryland
82.23	Virginia
80.83	New Mexico
79.64	Ohio
79.14	North Carolina
78.38	Georgia
78.14	New Jersey
75.18	Louisiana
74.95	Massachusetts
74.45	Tennessee
72.14	Arizona
69.13	Hawaii
68.40	Florida
67.74	Wyoming
67.16	Kansas
67.12	Vermont
66.03	Idaho
65.27	Colorado
62.81	Washington
62.58	Oregon
61.76	Indiana
60.44	Nevada
58.52	Oklahoma
57.08	Utah
55.35	Wisconsin
55.20	Maine
54.45	Iowa
53.77	Illinois
49.10	Pennsylvania
48.19	Kentucky
48.17	Montana
46.59	West Virginia
45.17	South Dakota
44.25	Arkansas
43.15	Nebraska
41.51	Minnesota
40.47	Alabama
36.30	Missouri
35.63	New Hampshire
32.86	Mississippi
26.28	North Dakota

Table G.625   HIWAY93

Per Capita Expenditures of Total Funds Devoted to Transportation 1993

1,145.17	Alaska
852.56	Hawaii
669.87	Wyoming
475.47	Connecticut
403.66	Delaware
381.43	Maryland
353.26	Montana
342.58	West Virginia
338.40	Rhode Island
326.76	Louisiana
324.88	Florida
313.24	Vermont
313.23	Kentucky
312.07	South Dakota
310.10	North Dakota
309.53	Iowa
303.10	New Mexico
273.25	Maine
258.44	Massachusetts
255.35	Virginia
254.25	Minnesota
249.82	Nebraska
248.41	North Carolina
245.65	New Hampshire
238.55	Idaho
238.53	Kansas
230.03	Mississippi
229.30	Wisconsin
224.50	Nevada
218.74	Pennsylvania
213.42	Arkansas
211.04	Washington
209.29	Utah
201.22	Indiana
200.33	Oklahoma
196.62	Michigan
196.37	Arizona
193.96	Illinois
193.69	Oregon
186.33	South Carolina
186.13	Tennessee
173.79	Alabama
170.02	New York
164.63	Texas
156.09	Missouri
150.56	Georgia
142.48	California
138.00	Colorado
129.70	Ohio
126.63	New Jersey

Table G.626.   ELSE93

Per Capita Expenditures of Total Funds Devoted to All Other Expenditures 1993

3,348.53	Alaska
2,318.04	Hawaii
1,648.60	Delaware
1,505.33	Wyoming
1,442.27	Oregon
1,219.85	Massachusetts
1,108.32	Connecticut
1,090.24	Maine
1,067.80	Montana
1,064.32	North Dakota
1,056.18	New Jersey
1,021.67	Ohio
994.17	Florida
986.97	Vermont
958.38	New Mexico
928.94	Rhode Island
874.32	Minnesota
870.70	California
858.91	New York
845.88	Arkansas
839.74	Iowa
819.67	Wisconsin
811.48	Virginia
787.89	Pennsylvania
736.42	Kansas
735.38	Arizona
731.60	Louisiana
716.69	Nevada
712.48	Illinois
709.25	Idaho
709.00	South Carolina
694.95	Nebraska
678.83	New Hampshire
677.51	South Dakota
674.66	Kentucky
645.68	Washington
623.49	Oklahoma
613.47	Missouri
610.76	Maryland
602.94	West Virginia
585.64	Alabama
583.31	Michigan
581.37	Utah
566.87	Mississippi
537.10	Colorado
527.96	Indiana
512.22	North Carolina
507.46	Tennessee
476.44	Georgia
435.36	Texas

Table G.627.   SCHOOL94

Per Capita Expenditures of Total Funds Devoted to Elementary and Secondary Education 1994

1,400.37	Alaska
1,014.28	Delaware
824.82	Wyoming
780.31	Washington
761.08	Utah
729.39	West Virginia
727.25	Kentucky
689.82	Kansas
650.02	New Jersey
646.51	Hawaii
644.65	Minnesota
642.81	Oklahoma
622.02	New Mexico
611.04	New York
603.19	Alabama
597.35	Louisiana
592.50	Idaho
584.70	Wisconsin
575.24	Arkansas
562.67	Iowa
553.54	Texas
553.00	North Carolina
549.69	Michigan
544.27	Montana
533.45	Mississippi
529.32	Indiana
515.38	Connecticut
509.41	Georgia
503.03	Pennsylvania
500.25	South Carolina
489.54	California
488.75	Missouri
480.87	North Dakota
477.44	Florida
472.46	Rhode Island
468.88	Nevada
466.49	Maine
463.63	Arizona
453.12	Oregon
448.75	Maryland
445.33	Colorado
433.45	Vermont
403.74	Virginia
402.86	Ohio
401.50	Tennessee
396.45	Nebraska
363.47	Illinois
310.40	South Dakota
286.75	Massachusetts
138.99	New Hampshire

Table G.628. COLLEG94

Per Capita Expenditures of Total Funds Devoted to Higher Education 1994

773.67	Iowa
697.75	Alabama
671.18	Alaska
567.85	South Carolina
567.42	Nebraska
514.88	Wisconsin
476.10	Oregon
475.27	Kansas
456.11	North Carolina
436.20	Arkansas
423.75	Kentucky
388.43	Maryland
361.40	South Dakota
358.50	New Mexico
354.03	Wyoming
347.53	Oklahoma
344.21	Colorado
342.90	West Virginia
339.60	Georgia
338.77	Virginia
337.05	Louisiana
335.22	Minnesota
320.68	Connecticut
317.17	North Dakota
311.69	Rhode Island
288.87	Hawaii
283.67	Tennessee
278.77	Utah
270.24	Nevada
267.93	Mississippi
266.24	Texas
247.41	Arizona
246.50	Delaware
243.17	New York
239.88	Washington
238.95	Montana
202.86	Illinois
200.50	Idaho
200.22	Florida
181.21	California
177.66	Ohio
175.72	Indiana
166.79	Michigan
144.77	Pennsylvania
140.23	Maine
138.13	New Jersey
121.69	Missouri
107.53	Massachusetts
105.30	New Hampshire
97.46	Vermont

Table G.629. HELP94

Per Capita Expenditures of Total Funds Devoted to Cash Assistance 1994

306.59	Alaska
299.28	New York
254.24	California
187.06	Connecticut
157.16	Massachusetts
155.90	Hawaii
145.96	Maine
145.65	Michigan
144.36	Rhode Island
143.38	Washington
138.50	Vermont
117.78	Pennsylvania
107.63	Wisconsin
105.09	Ohio
103.14	Minnesota
100.87	Arkansas
98.05	New Mexico
97.50	New Jersey
86.64	Illinois
77.31	Kentucky
73.91	Nevada
73.39	Iowa
72.24	Oregon
69.97	Maryland
69.74	West Virginia
66.53	Arizona
63.81	North Carolina
63.60	Oklahoma
63.18	New Hampshire
61.61	Florida
61.06	Montana
60.61	Delaware
57.34	Georgia
55.86	Missouri
54.32	Kansas
48.96	Wyoming
48.78	South Dakota
48.67	Utah
44.09	Virginia
43.64	Tennessee
43.03	Colorado
42.12	Nebraska
40.05	Louisiana
36.21	Mississippi
36.05	Idaho
35.15	South Carolina
34.71	Indiana
30.69	North Dakota
28.73	Texas
28.11	Alabama

Table G.630. MEDICA94

Per Capita Expenditures of Total Funds Devoted to Medicaid 1994

1,007.81	Louisiana
910.32	New York
806.56	New Hampshire
764.47	Rhode Island
672.54	Maine
641.90	New Jersey
639.31	West Virginia
569.52	Tennessee
545.92	Connecticut
542.35	New Mexico
540.93	California
538.00	Indiana
527.18	Minnesota
526.64	Massachusetts
511.06	South Carolina
504.49	Mississippi
495.00	Vermont
489.56	Georgia
486.74	Kentucky
476.04	Pennsylvania
460.43	Michigan
459.61	Wisconsin
449.83	Arkansas
449.43	Washington
439.17	Alaska
436.70	Texas
428.97	Illinois
419.16	Alabama
418.93	Missouri
408.83	Nevada
408.14	Florida
397.03	North Carolina
395.35	Ohio
392.44	South Dakota
385.30	Iowa
382.94	Colorado
375.98	Hawaii
359.28	Nebraska
358.42	Montana
354.66	Maryland
335.40	Delaware
335.07	North Dakota
334.91	Oregon
331.44	Wyoming
320.27	Oklahoma
320.18	Arizona
304.14	Idaho
276.12	Virginia
274.30	Kansas
252.22	Utah

Table G.631. PRISON94

Per Capita Expenditures of Total Funds Devoted to Corrections 1994

232.01	Alaska
134.08	Texas
117.19	Delaware
115.35	New York
114.53	Connecticut
112.76	Michigan
107.57	Colorado
104.99	Rhode Island
102.78	California
102.75	South Carolina
94.53	North Carolina
92.58	Ohio
91.68	Maryland
88.17	Virginia
85.80	New Mexico
83.96	New Jersey
83.16	Arizona
82.14	Florida
81.59	Georgia
80.09	Louisiana
76.37	Tennessee
71.69	Washington
70.61	Kansas
68.78	Hawaii
67.59	Idaho
64.67	Nevada
64.16	Utah
64.12	Vermont
64.00	Wisconsin
63.80	Pennsylvania
62.39	Oregon
61.28	Illinois
59.06	Oklahoma
58.57	Indiana
55.04	Iowa
50.44	Montana
49.07	Arkansas
48.96	Wyoming
48.71	Minnesota
48.67	Kentucky
48.65	Maine
46.87	Massachusetts
46.56	South Dakota
40.89	Alabama
40.01	New Hampshire
39.64	Nebraska
37.90	Missouri
37.78	West Virginia
36.21	Mississippi
33.25	North Dakota

Table G.632. HIWAY94

Per Capita Expenditures of Total Funds Devoted to Transportation 1994

1,367.22	Alaska
724.46	Hawaii
591.31	Wyoming
503.93	Connecticut
412.64	West Virginia
391.97	Delaware
372.48	South Dakota
369.04	Montana
349.31	Kentucky
347.42	Maryland
341.90	Massachusetts
335.07	North Dakota
318.03	Vermont
315.60	New Mexico
302.89	Florida
297.38	Idaho
285.08	Wisconsin
278.44	Virginia
277.02	Kansas
275.05	Minnesota
269.10	Iowa
264.70	Washington
262.65	Nebraska
255.92	Rhode Island
254.82	New Hampshire
250.29	Pennsylvania
249.54	Oregon
237.90	Nevada
236.33	North Carolina
231.81	Maine
229.31	Mississippi
229.12	Tennessee
216.22	Arizona
215.37	Arkansas
212.59	Indiana
211.32	Illinois
202.02	Michigan
199.88	Oklahoma
196.91	Utah
193.55	Louisiana
185.52	Missouri
185.02	Colorado
183.93	New York
181.47	Alabama
181.17	South Carolina
168.55	Texas
156.57	Georgia
154.16	California
145.13	Ohio
138.13	New Jersey

Table G.633. ELSE94

Per Capita Expenditures of Total Funds Devoted to All Other Expenditures 1994

3,877.94	Alaska
2,329.27	Hawaii
1,875.01	Delaware
1,638.44	Oregon
1,633.94	Connecticut
1,566.79	Wyoming
1,293.15	Massachusetts
1,223.80	Rhode Island
1,181.04	Ohio
1,153.34	Maine
1,081.23	Louisiana
1,044.87	New Mexico
1,034.46	Florida
1,032.78	Montana
1,025.68	North Dakota
1,020.78	Vermont
979.08	California
961.49	New Jersey
938.80	Iowa
934.02	Minnesota
900.54	Pennsylvania
896.93	Arkansas
893.33	Virginia
893.05	Wisconsin
877.22	Kansas
812.72	Nebraska
808.51	South Carolina
807.88	Washington
806.22	Mississippi
787.63	Nevada
760.74	Illinois
756.96	Idaho
754.44	New York
747.29	Kentucky
709.44	Michigan
709.32	Maryland
694.95	New Hampshire
687.32	South Dakota
686.24	Missouri
684.02	Arizona
668.37	West Virginia
641.10	Colorado
636.00	Oklahoma
620.43	Indiana
610.63	Utah
582.74	Alabama
578.25	Tennessee
575.56	Georgia
560.09	North Carolina
325.61	Texas

Table G.634. SCHOOL95

Per Capita Expenditures of Total Funds Devoted to Elementary and Secondary 1995

1,452.35	Alaska
1,073.83	Delaware
990.28	Wyoming
938.45	Michigan
796.03	Washington
793.62	Utah
769.75	Kentucky
711.32	Hawaii
709.21	New Mexico
689.60	New York
675.50	Kansas
659.54	Minnesota
657.61	Louisiana
652.20	Idaho
632.11	Wisconsin
628.28	North Carolina
619.17	Oklahoma
612.12	Arkansas
611.07	New Jersey
610.84	Georgia
610.77	Indiana
609.02	Alabama
584.88	Mississippi
576.25	Connecticut
569.10	Iowa
552.22	Texas
549.84	West Virginia
545.05	California
529.57	Missouri
527.13	Montana
523.53	Rhode Island
507.00	North Dakota
504.29	Pennsylvania
491.74	South Carolina
482.89	Arizona
475.11	Oregon
462.75	Colorado
457.75	Maryland
442.56	Vermont
435.39	Florida
426.61	Virginia
423.51	Ohio
421.38	Maine
414.33	Tennessee
409.02	Nebraska
382.44	Massachusetts
369.81	Illinois
325.38	South Dakota
299.52	Nevada
136.13	New Hampshire

Table G.635. COLLEG95

Per Capita Expenditures of Total Funds Devoted to Higher Education 1995

749.10	Alaska
718.08	Iowa
713.19	Alabama
614.87	New Mexico
551.19	South Carolina
547.84	Nebraska
525.72	Wisconsin
498.32	Kansas
478.26	Oregon
453.42	Arkansas
449.88	North Carolina
394.87	Oklahoma
393.76	Kentucky
390.44	Maryland
387.51	Mississippi
379.62	South Dakota
371.35	Wyoming
357.57	Georgia
356.34	Virginia
354.03	Connecticut
341.87	Minnesota
339.30	Louisiana
336.75	Colorado
326.77	Rhode Island
323.22	Tennessee
314.12	North Dakota
311.81	Hawaii
286.46	Utah
275.11	Delaware
260.90	Arizona
260.83	New York
249.58	Idaho
246.10	Washington
243.69	Texas
233.41	Montana
205.45	Illinois
189.94	Ohio
189.82	California
187.42	Indiana
185.99	Nevada
185.94	West Virginia
173.47	Michigan
167.07	Florida
146.24	Pennsylvania
143.41	Massachusetts
133.39	Maine
131.85	Missouri
123.90	New Jersey
110.49	New Hampshire
103.35	Vermont

Table G.636. HELP95

Per Capita Expenditures of Total Funds Devoted to Cash Assistance 1995

336.33	Alaska
271.17	California
225.10	New York
203.38	Connecticut
180.27	Hawaii
167.32	Massachusetts
148.54	Maine
140.55	Rhode Island
129.85	Vermont
125.13	Michigan
124.57	Washington
115.99	Pennsylvania
97.01	Wisconsin
95.74	New Jersey
90.68	Arkansas
89.84	Ohio
87.74	Minnesota
86.51	Illinois
84.59	New Mexico
70.01	Maryland
68.66	Arizona
67.22	North Carolina
66.56	Delaware
66.08	Oregon
65.13	Kentucky
61.16	New Hampshire
60.52	Missouri
59.59	Iowa
58.41	Oklahoma
57.11	Georgia
55.07	Montana
53.16	Florida
47.06	Kansas
45.55	Tennessee
45.47	Louisiana
42.93	South Dakota
41.26	Wyoming
40.15	Virginia
39.92	Utah
37.67	Idaho
36.93	Colorado
36.23	Nevada
34.70	Nebraska
34.53	West Virginia
33.07	Indiana
30.31	North Dakota
29.72	South Carolina
25.55	Texas
24.07	Mississippi
18.70	Alabama

Table G.637. MEDICA95

Per Capita Expenditures of Total Funds Devoted to Medicaid 1995

1,050.49	New York
916.46	Louisiana
843.28	Rhode Island
718.47	Maine
631.34	New Hampshire
628.97	Connecticut
622.33	New Jersey
612.50	Massachusetts
559.70	Minnesota
554.42	Ohio
550.67	Kentucky
535.80	Tennessee
531.49	California
530.02	Vermont
519.03	Illinois
517.49	Mississippi
500.51	Michigan
494.21	Pennsylvania
492.20	Washington
481.76	Arkansas
478.23	South Carolina
474.27	Georgia
469.05	Missouri
466.28	Alaska
451.42	Alabama
448.17	Delaware
447.48	Wisconsin
438.48	Hawaii
434.31	Texas
433.85	South Dakota
421.62	Oregon
421.14	Indiana
410.56	North Dakota
403.87	Montana
403.75	West Virginia
396.90	New Mexico
393.23	Colorado
387.29	Florida
382.36	Maryland
371.83	Nebraska
366.49	Iowa
334.12	Oklahoma
324.98	Arizona
315.09	Wyoming
311.17	Virginia
310.26	North Carolina
296.67	Idaho
287.92	Kansas
270.02	Utah
265.70	Nevada

Table G.638. PRISON95

Per Capita Expenditures of Total Funds Devoted to Corrections 1995

236.96	Alaska
182.76	Texas
140.10	Nevada
137.56	Delaware
135.78	New York
131.94	Maryland
130.35	Colorado
122.28	Michigan
120.52	Connecticut
116.60	California
112.44	Rhode Island
105.24	Ohio
101.81	Georgia
98.41	Arizona
98.25	North Carolina
97.87	Virginia
97.27	South Carolina
96.19	Florida
90.95	Louisiana
88.11	Washington
87.30	New Jersey
84.76	Idaho
82.82	Hawaii
82.43	Tennessee
77.52	Kansas
75.14	Utah
74.83	New Mexico
71.97	Wisconsin
71.55	Vermont
70.60	Pennsylvania
69.22	Oregon
67.39	Mississippi
67.04	Illinois
66.15	Indiana
65.42	Oklahoma
60.02	Wyoming
58.76	Alabama
57.48	Minnesota
56.61	Iowa
54.57	Maine
53.29	Kentucky
51.01	Arkansas
47.45	South Dakota
47.21	Montana
45.39	Missouri
44.82	Massachusetts
42.14	Nebraska
41.43	New Hampshire
30.31	North Dakota
15.94	West Virginia

Table G.639. HIWAY95

Per Capita Expenditures of Total Funds Devoted to Transportation 1995

1,383.55	Alaska
682.08	Hawaii
675.19	Wyoming
390.44	Maryland
384.16	Connecticut
381.61	Delaware
371.99	North Dakota
361.52	Massachusetts
359.29	Montana
350.24	South Dakota
345.63	Iowa
336.27	Virginia
329.45	Kansas
320.21	Idaho
312.94	Washington
301.23	Florida
296.06	Kentucky
295.15	Rhode Island
294.16	Vermont
287.41	Minnesota
278.50	Wisconsin
272.68	Nebraska
268.89	North Carolina
263.74	Maine
260.26	New Mexico
258.61	Arizona
257.19	Pennsylvania
251.72	Oregon
241.72	West Virginia
237.86	Louisiana
236.75	New Hampshire
235.82	New York
231.88	Nevada
227.08	Illinois
220.71	Utah
215.37	Arkansas
207.26	Indiana
205.61	Oklahoma
204.75	Michigan
202.18	Mississippi
196.70	Missouri
184.31	Alabama
181.27	Georgia
177.88	Tennessee
171.97	Ohio
159.18	Texas
157.69	New Jersey
152.08	Colorado
151.31	South Carolina
130.16	California

Table G.640. ELSE95

Per Capita Expenditures of Total Funds Devoted to All Other Expenditures 1995

3,034.64	Alaska
2,470.12	Hawaii
2,054.48	Delaware
1,495.22	Connecticut
1,384.44	Oregon
1,301.61	Wyoming
1,288.40	Maine
1,272.80	Massachusetts
1,268.43	Rhode Island
1,258.46	Nevada
1,224.52	West Virginia
1,210.28	Louisiana
1,117.94	New Jersey
1,112.62	New Mexico
1,093.91	North Dakota
1,088.47	Florida
1,083.89	Vermont
1,079.59	Wisconsin
1,034.69	Minnesota
1,031.83	Ohio
996.57	Montana
975.45	New York
975.29	Washington
938.54	Virginia
932.94	Pennsylvania
926.68	Arkansas
924.69	California
902.43	South Carolina
869.73	Maryland
867.06	Iowa
858.22	Kansas
828.96	Kentucky
798.21	Nebraska
791.86	Arizona
779.20	Michigan
765.32	North Carolina
755.64	New Hampshire
726.26	Missouri
713.42	Idaho
697.75	Georgia
687.72	Illinois
680.14	South Dakota
679.12	Indiana
662.14	Utah
660.46	Colorado
658.89	Oklahoma
633.06	Alabama
620.98	Mississippi
590.03	Tennessee
367.49	Texas

Table G.641. SCHOOL96

Per Capita Expenditures of Total Funds Devoted to Elementary and Secondary Education 1996

1,453.63	Alaska
1,138.48	Delaware
1,039.60	Michigan
847.19	West Virginia
825.98	Washington
820.50	Utah
804.91	New Mexico
794.72	Kentucky
766.04	Wyoming
762.56	Minnesota
713.69	Kansas
711.80	Hawaii
689.99	New York
689.72	Idaho
683.37	Wisconsin
672.86	Georgia
662.97	Oregon
641.13	Texas
638.25	Iowa
637.51	Alabama
636.68	New Jersey
635.46	Oklahoma
630.57	Louisiana
625.99	Arkansas
613.89	Indiana
609.19	Montana
606.66	North Carolina
591.13	Mississippi
588.58	Nevada
578.26	Connecticut
561.07	California
555.90	Missouri
543.09	Rhode Island
535.54	South Carolina
527.97	Pennsylvania
515.05	North Dakota
501.43	Arizona
496.26	Colorado
493.00	Tennessee
473.51	Maryland
458.84	Ohio
458.46	Vermont
452.36	Florida
435.01	Nebraska
433.80	Virginia
418.38	Maine
414.62	Massachusetts
394.63	Illinois
345.98	South Dakota
130.93	New Hampshire

Table G.642. COLLEG96

Per Capita Expenditures of Total Funds Devoted to Higher Education 1996

833.60	Alaska
800.15	Iowa
729.78	New Mexico
686.34	Alabama
593.61	Kentucky
563.71	Nebraska
541.54	Wisconsin
535.54	South Carolina
484.54	Arkansas
477.73	Kansas
452.51	North Carolina
431.80	Georgia
424.60	Oregon
417.48	Maryland
409.24	Mississippi
407.28	Oklahoma
394.01	Rhode Island
384.04	Washington
381.08	Arizona
377.63	South Dakota
368.69	Connecticut
364.58	West Virginia
362.20	Colorado
360.23	Virginia
340.98	Minnesota
337.53	Nevada
336.02	North Dakota
335.80	Wyoming
330.36	Tennessee
310.53	Louisiana
287.30	Utah
285.72	Hawaii
280.92	Delaware
279.58	Texas
269.35	New York
255.38	Montana
253.22	Idaho
216.65	California
212.83	Illinois
201.57	Ohio
200.55	Indiana
192.75	Michigan
181.95	Florida
157.80	Massachusetts
153.45	Pennsylvania
143.01	Missouri
138.28	New Jersey
130.16	Maine
110.66	Vermont
104.36	New Hampshire

Table G.643. HELP96

Per Capita Expenditures of Total Funds Devoted to Cash Assistance 1996

244.43	California
195.56	New York
180.46	Hawaii
172.23	Alaska
159.12	Connecticut
145.66	Maine
145.43	Massachusetts
134.88	Rhode Island
129.11	Vermont
116.92	Michigan
115.82	Washington
106.63	Pennsylvania
100.17	New Mexico
87.03	Wisconsin
84.27	Arkansas
82.03	Illinois
80.67	New Jersey
80.60	Minnesota
73.93	Delaware
71.61	Ohio
70.77	Oregon
69.74	Nevada
64.88	Kentucky
63.04	Arizona
59.15	Iowa
57.19	North Carolina
56.04	Maryland
55.63	Georgia
55.36	Missouri
55.08	West Virginia
53.20	Montana
53.13	New Hampshire
51.52	Oklahoma
50.54	Florida
45.74	Tennessee
41.19	Louisiana
40.78	Kansas
40.70	South Dakota
39.98	Colorado
38.96	Utah
35.52	Virginia
33.76	Idaho
33.46	Nebraska
31.79	Indiana
31.50	South Carolina
31.48	Wyoming
25.22	Texas
24.79	North Dakota
22.74	Mississippi
16.28	Alabama

Table G.644. MEDICA96

Per Capita Expenditures of Total Funds Devoted to Medicaid 1996

1,274.51	Alaska
1,239.76	New York
862.55	Rhode Island
736.23	New Hampshire
712.96	Louisiana
679.32	West Virginia
679.16	Connecticut
669.41	Maine
662.61	New Jersey
658.17	Tennessee
658.01	Pennsylvania
621.93	Massachusetts
609.86	Michigan
604.47	Minnesota
577.02	Vermont
574.14	Kentucky
566.91	Washington
552.04	Illinois
549.02	Ohio
542.06	Missouri
541.27	South Carolina
540.61	Mississippi
516.63	California
516.05	Nevada
508.62	Arkansas
502.82	Oregon
495.93	Maryland
492.85	Delaware
492.73	Georgia
488.31	Alabama
479.37	New Mexico
476.20	Hawaii
472.40	North Carolina
457.73	Wisconsin
454.91	Indiana
441.44	Texas
436.43	South Dakota
433.61	Montana
432.76	Iowa
406.70	Nebraska
396.62	North Dakota
394.23	Florida
392.78	Colorado
366.76	Arizona
348.40	Oklahoma
319.64	Virginia
315.92	Idaho
307.82	Wyoming
305.87	Kansas
289.73	Utah

Table G.645. PRISN96

Per Capita Expenditures of Total Funds Devoted to Corrections 1996

214	Alaska
186	Oregon
151	New York
146	Maryland
142	Michigan
139	Texas
133	Delaware
123	Arizona
122	California
121	Idaho
117	Rhode Island
116	Connecticut
114	Ohio
109	North Carolina
107	Virginia
106	South Carolina
106	Georgia
105	Louisiana
97	Tennessee
94	Pennsylvania
91	Florida
89	Colorado
89	New Jersey
88	Utah
86	Nevada
86	New Mexico
85	Hawaii
79	Kansas
77	Wisconsin
76	Vermont
76	Indiana
73	Washington
72	Montana
71	Illinois
69	Oklahoma
65	Minnesota
65	Missouri
62	Iowa
60	Alabama
58	Kentucky
58	Mississippi
54	Arkansas
53	Maine
53	Massachusetts
52	Wyoming
51	Nebraska
50	South Dakota
40	New Hampshire
33	North Dakota
29	West Virginia

Table G.646. HIWAY96

Per Capita Expenditures of Total Funds Devoted to Transportation 1996

731.85	Hawaii
702.70	Alaska
570.16	Wyoming
442.78	Kansas
424.90	West Virginia
417.48	Maryland
413.99	Delaware
407.50	Connecticut
391.05	Montana
355.02	South Dakota
349.79	North Dakota
346.55	Massachusetts
345.01	Virginia
317.89	Kentucky
313.54	Vermont
313.08	Minnesota
305.78	Florida
291.81	Idaho
291.32	Maine
289.77	New Mexico
286.50	Washington
284.53	Nevada
283.07	Oregon
280.44	Wisconsin
278.00	Nebraska
267.89	Pennsylvania
267.75	Iowa
262.72	Mississippi
262.67	Rhode Island
259.83	Louisiana
257.88	Arizona
249.47	Indiana
248.57	New Hampshire
246.79	Arkansas
243.66	North Carolina
233.08	Oklahoma
225.44	Ohio
224.71	New Jersey
223.99	Utah
221.19	Michigan
219.48	Illinois
208.38	Tennessee
206.63	New York
204.62	Colorado
196.06	Missouri
192.61	Alabama
189.19	Texas
183.32	California
182.79	Georgia
160.38	South Carolina

Table G.647. ELSE96

Per Capita Expenditures of Total Funds Devoted to All Other Expenditures 1996

2,536.41	Hawaii
2,400.17	Delaware
2,239.01	Alaska
1,594.12	Oregon
1,571.78	Connecticut
1,434.15	Wyoming
1,391.50	Maine
1,355.24	Massachusetts
1,231.71	Rhode Island
1,169.04	Arizona
1,109.05	Louisiana
1,098.96	North Dakota
1,095.96	Wisconsin
1,087.52	New Mexico
1,051.53	New Jersey
1,051.29	Florida
1,031.73	Ohio
1,002.19	Arkansas
974.88	Vermont
953.67	South Carolina
940.89	New York
936.09	Virginia
936.04	California
929.95	Minnesota
906.58	Nevada
853.51	Kansas
853.08	Iowa
843.38	Kentucky
843.29	Montana
837.37	Michigan
821.77	Indiana
808.25	Nebraska
795.73	Maryland
795.51	Washington
793.26	Pennsylvania
766.74	Colorado
749.66	Missouri
713.97	Oklahoma
709.95	Georgia
709.00	Tennessee
706.60	Idaho
691.46	Utah
685.06	Illinois
658.03	South Dakota
639.13	Mississippi
629.37	Alabama
584.43	New Hampshire
546.99	North Carolina
386.78	Texas
222.94	West Virginia

Table G.648. SCHOOL97

Per Capita Expenditures of Total Funds Devoted to Elementary and Secondary Education 1997

1,404.38	Alaska
1,236.01	Delaware
919.50	Michigan
907.09	Utah
898.07	Wyoming
876.90	West Virginia
874.13	Kansas
840.82	Wisconsin
828.02	Washington
819.12	Minnesota
797.67	Kentucky
787.30	New Mexico
725.08	Hawaii
719.11	Alabama
705.66	Iowa
701.03	Idaho
680.77	New York
677.35	North Carolina
677.16	California
675.46	Georgia
674.91	New Jersey
671.55	Oklahoma
666.57	Arkansas
660.03	Nevada
638.53	Louisiana
614.85	Montana
612.36	Texas
602.42	Missouri
574.71	Indiana
571.81	Rhode Island
570.08	Mississippi
547.11	Connecticut
535.74	Pennsylvania
529.63	North Dakota
513.97	Maryland
508.18	South Carolina
502.57	Colorado
495.41	Massachusetts
492.02	Vermont
490.32	Arizona
488.89	Ohio
477.62	Florida
468.70	Virginia
454.64	Tennessee
447.38	Maine
447.07	Nebraska
421.93	Illinois
410.57	South Dakota
142.76	New Hampshire
64.27	Oregon

Table G.649. COLLEG97

Per Capita Expenditures of Total Funds Devoted to Higher Education 1997

827.67	Iowa
757.45	New Mexico
723.05	Alaska
693.83	Alabama
630.83	Nebraska
566.93	South Carolina
517.34	Kansas
507.92	Wisconsin
507.25	Arkansas
483.42	West Virginia
461.37	Mississippi
450.09	Maryland
438.12	Kentucky
435.17	Georgia
431.53	Oklahoma
401.00	Wyoming
392.43	Louisiana
383.62	Rhode Island
383.20	North Carolina
380.07	South Dakota
373.91	Virginia
370.49	Nevada
362.54	Hawaii
355.59	Colorado
350.62	Arizona
348.47	Washington
347.05	Connecticut
345.92	Minnesota
329.22	Tennessee
327.12	North Dakota
315.62	Utah
302.37	Delaware
282.31	Texas
273.27	Montana
259.09	California
255.74	New York
236.93	Idaho
211.57	Ohio
195.62	Florida
191.37	Illinois
176.47	Indiana
175.51	Missouri
174.44	Massachusetts
173.15	Michigan
161.53	Pennsylvania
140.78	Maine
136.77	New Jersey
113.83	New Hampshire
101.70	Vermont
40.41	Oregon

Table G.650. HELP97

Per Capita Expenditures of Total Funds Devoted to Cash Assistance 1997

298.95	Alaska
235.53	California
180.10	New York
170.91	Hawaii
159.55	Maine
146.98	Connecticut
139.55	Massachusetts
123.05	Rhode Island
115.45	Vermont
104.48	New Mexico
99.61	Pennsylvania
92.71	Washington
90.18	Delaware
89.94	West Virginia
87.79	Arkansas
84.46	South Dakota
83.59	Michigan
77.30	New Jersey
77.19	Ohio
76.09	Illinois
75.06	Minnesota
74.72	Nevada
65.59	New Hampshire
65.21	Wisconsin
60.43	Kentucky
55.70	Utah
50.73	Georgia
49.81	Missouri
49.46	Iowa
49.36	Maryland
48.58	North Carolina
46.46	Montana
44.60	Kansas
41.09	Arizona
40.85	Oklahoma
38.11	Florida
37.93	Colorado
31.75	Idaho
31.35	Tennessee
30.17	Nebraska
28.96	Virginia
26.61	Louisiana
26.52	Mississippi
23.85	Indiana
21.81	North Dakota
20.89	Wyoming
20.76	Texas
20.56	South Carolina
14.05	Alabama
7.70	Oregon

Table G.651. MEDICA97

Per Capita Expenditures of Total Funds Devoted to Medicaid 1997

1,203.05	New York
901.14	Rhode Island
753.97	Maine
739.63	Massachusetts
725.00	Louisiana
710.42	Connecticut
705.35	Pennsylvania
689.78	New Jersey
677.35	West Virginia
637.54	Kentucky
613.53	Minnesota
604.55	Mississippi
600.39	Ohio
596.47	Vermont
592.28	New Hampshire
585.81	New Mexico
585.24	Hawaii
580.06	Tennessee
566.63	Nevada
555.28	Michigan
547.76	Alabama
546.43	Illinois
542.42	North Carolina
530.01	Arkansas
525.59	Maryland
525.17	Delaware
518.95	Texas
514.05	North Dakota
506.40	California
505.13	Washington
499.37	South Carolina
488.57	Georgia
483.30	South Dakota
479.71	Alaska
479.09	Missouri
470.17	Wisconsin
441.86	Iowa
437.22	Montana
436.10	Nebraska
422.09	Indiana
400.63	Colorado
398.87	Florida
360.03	Oklahoma
341.97	Idaho
339.67	Arizona
330.03	Kansas
329.14	Virginia
325.81	Wyoming
310.32	Utah
47.72	Oregon

Table G.652. PRISON97

Per Capita Expenditures of Total Funds Devoted to Corrections 1997

257.24	Alaska
148.53	Delaware
147.68	New York
147.38	Texas
145.19	Maryland
134.34	Michigan
132.49	California
130.29	Rhode Island
126.57	Connecticut
125.80	Ohio
123.76	Virginia
120.53	Arizona
117.50	South Carolina
116.69	Wisconsin
116.04	North Carolina
101.09	New Jersey
99.77	Louisiana
99.63	Nevada
99.61	Pennsylvania
98.14	Utah
97.19	Colorado
96.11	Georgia
93.22	Hawaii
91.46	Florida
91.45	Tennessee
90.38	Idaho
90.13	Missouri
87.72	Wyoming
85.82	New Mexico
83.25	Kansas
81.71	Oklahoma
79.93	Washington
79.25	Montana
76.96	Vermont
76.31	Indiana
76.09	Illinois
75.06	Minnesota
69.25	Iowa
68.28	Arkansas
68.04	South Dakota
66.47	Kentucky
66.29	Mississippi
64.61	Alabama
60.34	Nebraska
55.82	Massachusetts
53.18	Maine
43.62	North Dakota
42.44	New Hampshire
30.92	West Virginia
18.09	Oregon

Table G.653. HIWAY97

Per Capita Expenditures of Total Funds Devoted to Transportation 1997

1,140.19	Alaska
730.26	Hawaii
685.04	Wyoming
452.50	West Virginia
438.47	Maryland
428.70	Connecticut
415.17	Massachusetts
413.77	Delaware
407.33	Kansas
398.97	Montana
395.66	North Dakota
380.07	South Dakota
358.11	Virginia
339.52	Idaho
329.61	Minnesota
324.35	Vermont
320.68	Nevada
306.67	Iowa
299.79	Florida
296.85	North Carolina
294.08	Maine
291.71	Wisconsin
290.93	Washington
287.04	Kentucky
286.45	Utah
285.25	Nebraska
279.64	Arkansas
276.11	New Mexico
273.11	Mississippi
271.91	Pennsylvania
270.25	Colorado
268.16	New Hampshire
249.27	Arizona
245.87	Ohio
230.56	Illinois
229.87	Michigan
229.81	Oklahoma
226.15	Louisiana
217.14	Rhode Island
208.91	New York
208.71	Missouri
207.87	Alabama
202.70	Indiana
199.20	New Jersey
194.31	California
190.74	Tennessee
179.19	South Carolina
170.22	Texas
168.20	Georgia
27.32	Oregon

Table G.654. ELSE97

Per Capita Expenditures of Total Funds Devoted to All Other Expenditures 1997

2,655.81	Alaska
2,594.03	Delaware
2,511.88	Hawaii
1,771.98	Connecticut
1,754.37	Wyoming
1,468.78	Massachusetts
1,292.00	Rhode Island
1,289.79	North Dakota
1,245.15	Maine
1,217.20	Louisiana
1,145.00	Arizona
1,139.40	Wisconsin
1,134.31	New Mexico
1,115.29	Arkansas
1,109.29	Ohio
1,097.10	New Jersey
1,051.81	Washington
1,047.26	Vermont
1,045.74	South Carolina
1,036.55	Florida
1,021.18	Nevada
1,005.14	Minnesota
950.57	Virginia
939.19	California
932.79	Tennessee
922.10	New York
908.57	Indiana
896.91	Iowa
889.64	Michigan
885.38	Montana
850.25	Nebraska
818.42	Pennsylvania
778.22	Maryland
766.07	Missouri
765.46	Illinois
752.88	Georgia
740.49	Oklahoma
734.22	Kentucky
716.55	Kansas
708.81	Colorado
704.17	New Hampshire
701.03	Idaho
681.64	Utah
646.98	Mississippi
631.48	North Carolina
561.81	Alabama
541.95	South Dakota
323.82	Texas
196.74	West Virginia
179.33	Oregon

Table G.655.   SCHOOL98

Per Capita Expenditures of Total Funds Devoted to Elementary and Secondary Education 1998

1,407.43	Alaska
1,286.65	Delaware
1,119.58	Michigan
1,008.59	Wisconsin
976.19	West Virginia
895.16	Wyoming
862.89	Hawaii
855.02	Utah
826.97	Washington
825.25	New Mexico
819.10	Minnesota
752.54	Kansas
737.71	Nevada
735.16	North Carolina
734.03	California
726.82	Iowa
724.10	Oregon
718.70	New York
713.43	Kentucky
710.87	Georgia
710.53	Idaho
703.54	Alabama
698.99	Oklahoma
697.11	New Jersey
693.36	Maine
690.23	Arkansas
668.05	Louisiana
650.54	Missouri
640.93	Indiana
630.94	Mississippi
619.50	Texas
608.00	Montana
603.89	Rhode Island
593.47	South Carolina
560.27	Pennsylvania
559.17	North Dakota
546.51	Arizona
542.21	Massachusetts
534.73	Vermont
534.39	Connecticut
531.65	Ohio
530.32	Maryland
493.20	Tennessee
492.60	South Dakota
484.51	Virginia
480.99	Nebraska
478.97	Illinois
477.40	Florida
322.25	Colorado
182.14	New Hampshire

Table G.656.   COLLEG98

Per Capita Expenditures of Total Funds Devoted to Higher Education 1998

854.87	Iowa
731.59	Alaska
730.25	Alabama
709.64	New Mexico
694.13	Nebraska
633.48	South Carolina
595.43	Wisconsin
587.55	West Virginia
570.16	Mississippi
523.74	Arkansas
511.16	Washington
504.58	Kansas
485.30	Oregon
469.74	Hawaii
469.71	Maryland
465.55	Georgia
453.10	Oklahoma
428.06	Kentucky
417.25	North Carolina
415.17	Nevada
402.39	Virginia
401.52	Arizona
395.14	Rhode Island
392.19	Louisiana
374.90	North Dakota
372.12	South Dakota
368.25	Minnesota
363.79	Wyoming
344.38	Connecticut
323.05	Delaware
314.58	Tennessee
304.97	Utah
267.66	Texas
265.31	Montana
262.80	California
251.16	New York
246.82	Idaho
235.19	New Jersey
233.28	Florida
232.56	Colorado
223.53	Ohio
209.49	Indiana
202.96	Michigan
190.14	Illinois
186.72	Massachusetts
179.29	Pennsylvania
170.93	Missouri
138.01	Maine
118.79	New Hampshire
94.54	Vermont

Table G.657.   HELP98

Per Capita Expenditures of Total Funds Devoted to Cash Assistance 1998

278.70	Alaska
278.21	New York
233.55	Connecticut
196.34	California
178.71	Hawaii
147.87	Maine
137.93	Rhode Island
132.94	Vermont
122.09	Massachusetts
110.70	Washington
95.68	New Mexico
93.65	Arkansas
84.04	Pennsylvania
83.55	Delaware
75.72	Minnesota
75.29	Michigan
72.06	Nevada
69.48	Ohio
68.86	Wisconsin
65.48	Oregon
64.99	Illinois
63.32	New Jersey
58.84	Iowa
55.75	Georgia
54.36	Kentucky
51.52	Maryland
43.37	Missouri
42.58	North Carolina
40.84	Utah
39.78	West Virginia
38.69	Montana
37.62	New Hampshire
34.95	North Dakota
34.56	Nebraska
33.46	Arizona
33.24	Louisiana
33.15	Oklahoma
32.13	South Dakota
28.88	Colorado
27.13	Florida
26.66	Tennessee
24.94	Indiana
23.15	Mississippi
21.90	Virginia
20.44	Wyoming
20.18	Kansas
20.00	South Carolina
15.11	Texas
14.96	Idaho
8.91	Alabama

Table G.658. MEDICA98

Per Capita Expenditures of Total Funds Devoted to Medicaid 1998

1,275.11	New York
1,013.94	Rhode Island
847.80	Maine
746.68	West Virginia
739.56	Pennsylvania
737.55	New Mexico
736.12	Massachusetts
694.64	Louisiana
660.33	New Jersey
652.90	Vermont
642.09	Kentucky
641.63	Michigan
639.62	Mississippi
637.16	Tennessee
631.33	Ohio
629.81	Minnesota
617.61	Nevada
609.77	New Hampshire
601.68	Connecticut
583.47	South Carolina
568.83	Arkansas *
558.08	Alabama
553.58	Illinois
550.66	North Carolina
540.28	Delaware
534.67	Wisconsin
520.93	Washington
520.21	Texas
511.52	North Dakota
504.56	Oregon
492.60	South Dakota
483.31	California
481.08	Iowa
480.76	Alaska
479.95	Hawaii
472.35	Nebraska
471.13	Georgia
464.30	Missouri
433.89	Montana
423.96	Indiana
415.46	Arizona
412.30	Florida
396.98	Maryland
395.08	Oklahoma
371.96	Wyoming
371.94	Kansas
336.70	Virginia
329.09	Idaho
299.53	Utah
261.45	Colorado

Table G.659. PRISON98

Per Capita Expenditures of Total Funds Devoted to Corrections 1998

257.80	Alaska
194.95	Delaware
166.95	Michigan
161.72	Arizona
145.82	Wisconsin
142.97	New York
142.43	Maryland
138.95	Ohio
130.95	Oregon
130.47	Rhode Island
125.92	Virginia
125.45	Georgia
120.88	Texas
120.03	South Carolina
116.33	Louisiana
114.72	Indiana
114.58	New Jersey
113.23	Nevada
110.70	North Carolina
108.74	California
107.20	Idaho
106.88	Connecticut
106.45	Pennsylvania
102.04	Missouri
100.36	Florida
99.46	Oklahoma
97.01	Hawaii
92.58	Utah
91.69	New Mexico
91.20	Montana
86.50	Kansas
85.68	Vermont
85.31	Tennessee
81.83	Illinois
81.75	Wyoming
79.60	Iowa
79.16	Minnesota
78.14	Mississippi
78.14	Washington
78.14	Kentucky
72.00	Nebraska
69.37	Arkansas
66.93	South Dakota
66.88	Colorado
65.31	Alabama
59.15	Maine
57.45	Massachusetts
54.01	North Dakota
41.58	New Hampshire
33.66	West Virginia

Table G.660. HIWAY98

Per Capita Expenditures of Total Funds Devoted to Transportation 1998

1,045.12	Alaska
715.31	Wyoming
633.13	Hawaii
476.57	North Dakota
465.63	Utah
459.02	West Virginia
456.73	Delaware
454.56	Maryland
447.08	South Dakota
434.49	Massachusetts
390.70	New Mexico
386.91	Montana
383.23	Virginia
376.05	Connecticut
352.30	Louisiana
351.56	Vermont
349.98	Nevada
336.35	Florida
336.20	Wisconsin
326.42	North Carolina
322.93	Kansas
321.61	Idaho
316.63	Minnesota
309.68	Mississippi
299.75	Pennsylvania
295.57	Kentucky
292.46	Maine
283.80	Iowa
276.04	Arizona
274.98	Michigan
274.01	Arkansas
271.23	New Hampshire
262.80	Ohio
262.10	Nebraska
260.46	Washington
251.88	Indiana
251.42	Oklahoma
234.95	Oregon
223.12	New Jersey
219.03	Illinois
213.38	South Carolina
208.65	New York
201.54	Missouri
199.94	Tennessee
197.93	Georgia
193.84	Rhode Island
190.30	California
189.98	Alabama
177.00	Texas
117.04	Colorado

Table G.661. ELSE98

Per Capita Expenditures of Total Funds Devoted to All Other Expenditures 1998

2,766.09	Alaska
2,679.12	Delaware
2,379.34	Hawaii
1,757.55	Connecticut
1,706.27	Oregon
1,643.18	Wyoming
1,511.74	Massachusetts
1,360.99	Wisconsin
1,256.25	Rhode Island
1,252.12	Arkansas
1,185.66	Kentucky
1,170.27	South Carolina
1,166.00	Ohio
1,162.82	North Dakota
1,152.94	Minnesota
1,140.21	New Mexico
1,125.69	Florida
1,125.43	Nevada
1,107.40	Maine
1,101.96	Vermont
1,066.89	Louisiana
1,051.20	California
1,025.17	New Jersey
990.94	Maryland
989.18	New York
979.98	Virginia
976.01	Iowa
956.39	Arizona
947.44	Washington
939.64	Montana
915.85	Missouri
911.75	Tennessee
864.06	Nebraska
834.37	Oklahoma
832.01	Pennsylvania
825.48	Indiana
821.74	Kansas
815.93	Illinois
792.22	Michigan
771.02	South Dakota
762.89	Idaho
761.05	Georgia
718.65	New Hampshire
709.47	Alabama
661.69	Utah
655.68	North Carolina
645.41	Mississippi
490.97	Colorado
440.34	Texas
217.27	West Virginia

Table G.662. SCHOOL99

Per Capita Expenditures of Total Funds Devoted to Elementary and Secondary Education 1999

1,381.92	Alaska
1,327.59	Delaware
1,066.24	New Mexico
1,049.51	Michigan
1,046.46	Wyoming
995.20	Hawaii
920.49	Wisconsin
919.09	Utah
888.14	West Virginia
883.22	Kansas
872.30	Minnesota
855.18	Washington
812.89	Kentucky
793.68	California
780.08	Idaho
775.53	North Carolina
769.77	New York
759.30	New Jersey
757.09	Iowa
756.27	Alabama
731.65	Oklahoma
730.51	Georgia
723.18	Arkansas
717.48	Maine
715.27	Oregon
686.99	Louisiana
686.19	Indiana
670.97	Vermont
670.34	Mississippi
665.53	Missouri
648.94	Rhode Island
631.10	Connecticut
616.15	Montana
613.93	Texas
596.89	South Carolina
578.89	Nebraska
577.08	Maryland
576.52	Pennsylvania
575.45	North Dakota
573.53	Ohio
568.94	Massachusetts
559.18	Arizona
551.61	Colorado
551.25	Virginia
550.59	Florida
529.95	Illinois
507.30	Tennessee
421.85	Nevada
389.73	South Dakota
178.57	New Hampshire

Table G.663. COLLEG99

Per Capita Expenditures of Total Funds Devoted to Higher Education 1999

942.65	Iowa
819.18	New Mexico
813.36	Alaska
713.96	Nebraska
690.95	Kentucky
602.04	Arkansas
594.27	West Virginia
560.11	Wisconsin
550.83	Georgia
540.48	Washington
526.26	Hawaii
514.44	Kansas
490.04	Maryland
455.73	Louisiana
447.04	Oregon
445.78	South Dakota
441.01	Mississippi
424.99	Virginia
424.61	Rhode Island
403.03	North Carolina
398.98	Arizona
398.13	North Dakota
396.93	Oklahoma
387.29	Minnesota
377.26	Wyoming
367.33	Alabama
367.16	Tennessee
357.07	Connecticut
345.54	Delaware
320.07	Utah
314.00	Montana
285.49	Florida
269.15	Texas
268.99	Idaho
265.92	New Jersey
262.23	Nevada
259.25	New York
254.88	California
244.53	Indiana
221.31	Ohio
203.83	Illinois
202.43	Missouri
201.77	South Carolina
196.58	Michigan
195.93	Massachusetts
187.14	Pennsylvania
151.23	Maine
125.44	Colorado
112.12	New Hampshire
103.48	Vermont

Table G.664. HELP99

Per Capita Expenditures of Total Funds Devoted to Cash Assistance 1999

238.75	California
221.11	Alaska
199.38	New Mexico
171.50	New York
157.78	Connecticut
156.31	Hawaii
151.23	Maine
144.21	Rhode Island
110.16	Vermont
102.79	Arkansas
101.73	Massachusetts
86.84	Colorado
82.10	Washington
81.63	Oregon
81.50	Pennsylvania
78.81	Delaware
70.23	North Carolina
68.77	Minnesota
54.46	New Jersey
53.31	Michigan
49.83	New Hampshire
48.03	Kentucky
45.86	Illinois
45.14	Maryland
44.91	Indiana
41.11	Utah
40.82	Iowa
40.52	Ohio
40.04	South Dakota
39.08	Wisconsin
38.82	Missouri
35.55	Montana
32.16	Nebraska
30.11	North Dakota
29.62	Oklahoma
27.20	Arizona
23.56	Georgia
23.52	Mississippi
22.46	Wyoming
21.56	Virginia
21.52	Idaho
19.62	Tennessee
19.59	West Virginia
19.00	Nevada
18.59	Kansas
17.48	Florida
17.00	Louisiana
14.01	South Carolina
13.35	Texas
9.26	Alabama

Table G.665. MEDICA99

Per Capita Expenditures of Total Funds Devoted to Medicaid 1999

1,284.28	New York
1,061.53	Rhode Island
868.71	Maine
827.05	Pennsylvania
788.88	Connecticut
757.33	Massachusetts
741.40	Louisiana
728.14	West Virginia
724.38	Vermont
709.10	Tennessee
698.43	New Jersey
698.34	Kentucky
693.86	Mississippi
651.45	Ohio
644.27	Minnesota
632.03	North Carolina
631.74	Alaska
629.71	Michigan
627.06	New Hampshire
618.09	Oregon
605.30	South Carolina
598.13	New Mexico
591.03	Arkansas
583.41	Alabama
578.10	Washington
575.90	Delaware
562.06	North Dakota
545.25	California
543.51	Nebraska
537.59	Illinois
535.17	Maryland
531.20	South Dakota
516.06	Texas
510.24	Missouri
494.98	Wisconsin
489.88	Iowa
489.78	Hawaii
468.35	Georgia
461.62	Indiana
455.56	Kansas
448.68	Colorado
447.30	Montana
438.40	Oklahoma
436.98	Florida
420.14	Arizona
406.18	Idaho
363.79	Wyoming
351.08	Virginia
320.07	Utah
296.44	Nevada

Table G.666. PRISON99

Per Capita Expenditures of Total Funds Devoted to Corrections 1999

276.38	Alaska
230.36	Delaware
167.16	Oregon
163.26	Michigan
157.97	Maryland
155.55	New York
151.13	Arizona
147.63	Wisconsin
143.38	Ohio
132.42	Virginia
132.19	Rhode Island
129.05	California
129.01	Texas
125.05	Hawaii
119.08	North Carolina
118.54	New Jersey
117.81	Nevada
116.80	Massachusetts
116.31	Washington
116.26	Connecticut
115.63	Louisiana
111.68	Pennsylvania
110.29	Idaho
108.65	Utah
106.64	Oklahoma
105.37	Kansas
104.88	Florida
103.10	Georgia
100.72	Montana
100.14	Vermont
97.31	Indiana
96.07	Kentucky
95.35	New Mexico
94.32	Wyoming
94.27	Illinois
89.67	South Carolina
89.07	Iowa
83.25	Minnesota
83.19	Missouri
80.40	Nebraska
79.38	Mississippi
73.42	Arkansas
72.87	Tennessee
69.40	South Dakota
66.82	Maine
56.88	North Dakota
56.06	New Hampshire
49.39	Alabama
45.71	West Virginia
1.61	Colorado

Table G.667. HIWAY99

Per Capita Expenditures of Total Funds Devoted to Transportation 1999

1,729.38	Alaska
821.89	Wyoming
609.63	Hawaii
490.81	Alabama
484.97	Delaware
459.15	Montana
450.60	West Virginia
444.97	North Dakota
438.45	Maryland
431.65	Utah
421.91	Virginia
414.46	Massachusetts
411.08	South Dakota
397.24	Vermont
391.66	Kentucky
390.09	New Mexico
351.70	Wisconsin
350.19	Kansas
349.58	Florida
341.43	Iowa
340.23	Minnesota
332.23	Mississippi
329.46	Arizona
324.47	Rhode Island
319.95	Pennsylvania
314.49	North Carolina
312.03	Idaho
311.40	Connecticut
309.50	Maine
308.74	Nebraska
296.92	New Hampshire
284.37	Oklahoma
283.65	Ohio
273.21	Michigan
264.34	Oregon
242.87	Washington
242.28	Arkansas
240.29	New Jersey
231.83	Nevada
226.81	Georgia
218.71	Colorado
216.30	Missouri
214.59	Indiana
211.47	Illinois
209.71	California
195.75	Texas
168.17	Tennessee
147.57	New York
109.29	South Carolina
105.43	Louisiana

Table G.668. ELSE99

Per Capita Expenditures of Total Funds Devoted to All Other Expenditures 1999

3,018.91	Delaware
2,850.71	Alaska
2,451.30	Nevada
2,308.24	Hawaii
1,832.29	Wisconsin
1,789.51	Connecticut
1,765.05	Wyoming
1,652.12	Oregon
1,612.63	Massachusetts
1,339.90	Arkansas
1,282.15	Louisiana
1,274.68	North Dakota
1,269.83	Rhode Island
1,252.07	Maine
1,231.78	Vermont
1,223.39	Minnesota
1,203.16	Ohio
1,200.52	New York
1,185.37	South Carolina
1,179.50	Virginia
1,168.19	Florida
1,165.93	New Mexico
1,136.50	Arizona
1,063.67	New Jersey
1,055.02	California
1,053.98	Iowa
1,053.76	Missouri
1,005.70	Washington
989.39	Montana
980.08	Maryland
971.58	Oklahoma
969.55	Michigan
960.68	Kentucky
958.38	Nebraska
955.74	Tennessee
927.41	Illinois
914.58	Pennsylvania
845.39	Georgia
833.44	Alabama
795.76	Utah
790.84	Idaho
784.79	South Dakota
771.66	Kansas
755.80	New Hampshire
746.08	Indiana
738.89	North Carolina
696.80	Mississippi
535.49	West Virginia
487.14	Texas
173.68	Colorado

Table G.669. SCHOOL00

Per Capita Expenditures of Total Funds Devoted to Elementary and Secondary Education 2000

1,489.01	Alaska
1,377.82	Delaware
1,098.50	Michigan
1,095.56	New Mexico
1,032.62	Wyoming
967.35	California
951.92	Wisconsin
917.94	Minnesota
916.09	Hawaii
895.33	West Virginia
881.82	Kansas
866.89	Oregon
846.64	Washington
828.09	Alabama
823.29	Kentucky
802.52	Idaho
785.93	New York
784.21	Utah
782.28	Iowa
776.25	New Hampshire
770.25	New Jersey
763.39	Georgia
751.69	North Carolina
748.86	Maine
738.54	Vermont
730.54	Arkansas
730.13	Oklahoma
718.77	Texas
700.84	Indiana
698.07	South Carolina
696.93	Mississippi
686.30	Missouri
680.80	Connecticut
672.75	Louisiana
661.62	Rhode Island
635.59	Montana
602.64	Ohio
597.42	North Dakota
590.39	Maryland
580.23	Pennsylvania
579.31	Massachusetts
574.61	Illinois
566.20	Nebraska
564.48	Virginia
560.50	Arizona
555.73	Florida
541.90	Colorado
512.82	Tennessee
392.85	Nevada
381.97	South Dakota

Table G.670. COLLEG00

Per Capita Expenditures of Total Funds Devoted to Higher Education 2000

996.71	Iowa
954.64	New Mexico
804.90	Alabama
766.23	Nebraska
685.95	Alaska
665.03	South Carolina
630.18	West Virginia
611.05	Mississippi
595.67	Arkansas
580.91	Wisconsin
577.41	Washington
575.99	Kentucky
571.03	Wyoming
533.04	Maryland
517.13	Kansas
468.72	Oklahoma
463.74	Connecticut
462.30	Louisiana
448.14	Georgia
445.97	Virginia
444.65	Hawaii
437.73	South Dakota
414.51	Rhode Island
414.07	North Carolina
397.50	Arizona
394.46	Minnesota
372.95	North Dakota
351.74	Utah
344.63	Tennessee
339.82	Delaware
335.39	California
327.99	Colorado
323.96	Montana
322.62	Texas
287.98	Oregon
282.33	Florida
265.77	New York
263.77	Idaho
260.17	New Jersey
260.08	Indiana
236.39	Michigan
231.78	Ohio
217.22	Nevada
213.22	Massachusetts
203.45	Illinois
193.65	Missouri
161.81	Maine
160.49	Pennsylvania
119.01	New Hampshire
111.68	Vermont

Table G.671. HELP00

Per Capita Expenditures of Total Funds Devoted to Cash Assistance 2000

257.72	California
209.13	Alaska
187.33	Rhode Island
182.24	New York
169.34	Maine
159.11	New Mexico
148.00	Connecticut
139.29	Hawaii
108.64	Arkansas
108.08	Vermont
95.65	Washington
92.53	Massachusetts
86.42	Pennsylvania
85.66	Wyoming
81.10	Minnesota
80.32	Delaware
79.86	Colorado
79.34	Oregon
57.33	North Carolina
53.22	Kentucky
49.49	Illinois
48.07	Oklahoma
47.65	Iowa
46.36	Georgia
45.19	Michigan
43.93	Wisconsin
40.36	Utah
37.66	New Jersey
35.16	New Hampshire
34.17	Missouri
33.67	Idaho
33.11	Ohio
30.85	Montana
30.51	Nebraska
27.55	West Virginia
26.99	Maryland
26.42	Mississippi
22.88	Arizona
20.72	North Dakota
19.30	Tennessee
19.16	Indiana
18.71	Virginia
18.49	Nevada
17.94	Kansas
14.86	Florida
13.94	South Dakota
13.80	Louisiana
12.39	South Carolina
11.86	Texas
6.62	Alabama

Table G.672. MEDICA00

Per Capita Expenditures of Total Funds Devoted to Medicaid 2000

1,309.88	New York
1,292.54	Connecticut
1,028.31	Rhode Island
933.26	Maine
866.07	Wyoming
861.08	Pennsylvania
846.62	Vermont
791.28	Tennessee
777.97	Alaska
776.44	Massachusetts
760.68	Kentucky
759.00	Louisiana
740.37	West Virginia
708.48	Washington
700.23	Mississippi
682.01	Minnesota
674.39	Michigan
665.03	South Carolina
659.16	New Mexico
654.54	New Hampshire
639.28	Alabama
628.86	Oregon
625.82	Ohio
624.04	Delaware
617.91	North Carolina
606.91	Arkansas
597.42	North Dakota
591.11	Illinois
582.53	California
569.59	Nebraska
556.66	Maryland
540.89	South Dakota
540.86	Texas
536.98	Wisconsin
523.98	Missouri
516.22	Iowa
490.57	Montana
487.71	Colorado
482.69	New Jersey
481.83	Indiana
466.58	Florida
465.80	Idaho
465.72	Oklahoma
455.37	Hawaii
441.96	Georgia
397.50	Arizona
380.48	Virginia
340.21	Utah
291.17	Nevada
215.22	Kansas

Table G.673. PRISON00

Per Capita Expenditures of Total Funds Devoted to Corrections 2000

301.15	Alaska
247.14	Delaware
238.03	Oregon
184.24	Michigan
166.55	Wyoming
161.09	Wisconsin
158.94	Ohio
155.19	Maryland
151.87	New York
144.75	California
140.34	Virginia
139.08	Georgia
135.51	Rhode Island
135.22	Texas
133.20	Connecticut
131.55	Arizona
128.05	South Carolina
127.65	Louisiana
120.44	Washington
120.37	Pennsylvania
119.82	New Jersey
118.21	Utah
116.67	Massachusetts
114.66	North Carolina
114.18	Oklahoma
112.50	Hawaii
111.68	Vermont
109.44	Idaho
107.99	Montana
107.61	Kansas
105.10	Nebraska
104.47	Illinois
103.24	Iowa
102.68	Colorado
101.29	Indiana
101.04	Florida
100.17	Kentucky
95.46	New Mexico
92.48	Mississippi
83.19	Nevada
82.58	Missouri
77.42	Minnesota
75.26	Maine
74.93	Arkansas
74.44	Tennessee
69.70	South Dakota
69.56	Alabama
62.21	New Hampshire
62.16	North Dakota
48.21	West Virginia

Table G.674. HIWAY00

Per Capita Expenditures of Total Funds Devoted to Transportation 2000

1,999.29	Alaska
621.44	Hawaii
547.53	West Virginia
504.18	North Dakota
500.46	Delaware
499.83	Montana
480.62	Wyoming
476.76	South Dakota
464.90	Colorado
445.33	Maryland
439.52	Vermont
430.46	Massachusetts
409.01	Iowa
402.31	Virginia
386.40	New Mexico
386.34	Florida
359.92	North Carolina
356.36	Wisconsin
343.09	Utah
342.45	Maine
339.16	Minnesota
339.04	Nebraska
324.56	New Hampshire
323.69	Mississippi
318.06	South Carolina
314.56	Arizona
308.63	Pennsylvania
305.87	Connecticut
289.02	Idaho
288.45	Oklahoma
285.05	Michigan
279.00	Rhode Island
278.14	Ohio
269.03	Kansas
263.44	Nevada
262.82	Indiana
259.14	Missouri
255.69	Illinois
255.30	Louisiana
251.01	Arkansas
243.06	New Jersey
233.80	Washington
228.55	Alabama
227.80	New York
220.61	Texas
216.34	Georgia
208.30	California
199.83	Oregon
187.48	Tennessee
131.48	Kentucky

Table G.675. ELSE00

Per Capita Expenditures of Total Funds Devoted to All Other Expenditures 2000

3,015.14	Delaware
2,911.10	Alaska
2,662.56	Hawaii
2,255.31	Wisconsin
1,914.14	Connecticut
1,814.37	Massachusetts
1,643.98	South Carolina
1,565.59	Wyoming
1,513.12	New Jersey
1,380.77	Ohio
1,378.66	Arkansas
1,335.91	Maine
1,301.88	North Dakota
1,283.39	Rhode Island
1,246.51	Vermont
1,198.12	Minnesota
1,195.57	New Mexico
1,166.38	Virginia
1,162.65	Louisiana
1,161.99	Florida
1,119.81	Iowa
1,067.90	Missouri
1,066.08	Maryland
1,044.51	Nevada
1,037.96	California
1,032.34	Arizona
1,032.27	Georgia
1,013.73	Nebraska
996.57	Montana
980.46	Kansas
972.19	Pennsylvania
970.52	Illinois
956.45	Washington
952.49	Michigan
917.12	Indiana
905.30	Utah
889.37	Oklahoma
869.54	North Carolina
869.45	New York
867.09	South Dakota
855.47	Mississippi
847.08	Colorado
841.81	Idaho
824.37	Tennessee
735.68	New Hampshire
735.34	Alabama
685.55	Kentucky
681.76	Oregon
557.86	West Virginia
422.25	Texas

Table G.676. SCHOOL

Average per Capita Expenditure for Elementary and Secondary Education 1989–2000

1,404.89	Alaska
1,051.99	Delaware
834.23	Wyoming
766.87	New Mexico
742.16	West Virginia
740.09	Washington
722.40	Michigan
715.61	Utah
689.08	Hawaii
685.99	Kentucky
684.01	Wisconsin
656.19	New York
653.14	Minnesota
649.68	Kansas
637.29	California
628.05	New Jersey
622.81	Alabama
620.42	Idaho
611.58	North Carolina
605.77	Oklahoma
592.22	Louisiana
584.51	Iowa
584.39	Arkansas
578.85	Georgia
552.99	Indiana
544.21	Maine
539.59	Connecticut
535.42	Montana
534.24	Mississippi
530.60	Missouri
529.83	Texas
514.13	Rhode Island
509.18	North Dakota
504.36	South Carolina
492.95	Pennsylvania
492.52	Vermont
470.18	Florida
469.52	Maryland
465.89	Oregon
457.00	Arizona
446.34	Nevada
445.38	Ohio
436.60	Virginia
429.31	Colorado
406.09	Tennessee
396.22	Massachusetts
393.91	Nebraska
392.45	Illinois
329.87	South Dakota
190.82	New Hampshire

Table G.677. COLLEGE

Average per Capita Expenditure for Higher Education 1989–2000

750.08	Iowa
677.33	Alaska
607.48	Alabama
571.15	New Mexico
568.41	Nebraska
514.87	Wisconsin
490.42	South Carolina
455.96	Kentucky
454.18	Kansas
449.15	Wyoming
437.66	Arkansas
399.85	Maryland
393.01	Oregon
392.66	West Virginia
383.73	Washington
376.40	North Carolina
370.05	Georgia
368.28	Oklahoma
367.19	Mississippi
360.02	Hawaii
356.95	Virginia
355.27	South Dakota
334.66	Connecticut
332.85	Minnesota
332.27	Louisiana
324.51	North Dakota
295.85	Arizona
292.76	Colorado
279.27	Tennessee
276.98	Rhode Island
276.38	Utah
272.84	Delaware
257.47	Nevada
255.29	Montana
250.60	California
247.95	New York
242.96	Texas
218.01	Idaho
198.28	Florida
193.73	Indiana
188.45	Illinois
185.69	Ohio
177.53	Michigan
161.59	New Jersey
147.31	Pennsylvania
146.75	Missouri
143.49	Massachusetts
142.62	Maine
122.69	New Hampshire
103.26	Vermont

Table G.678. CASHHELP

Average per Capita Expenditure for Public Assistance 1989–2000

237.70	Alaska
235.92	California
221.65	New York
170.50	Connecticut
148.35	Maine
147.05	Massachusetts
143.41	Hawaii
142.23	Rhode Island
123.04	Vermont
119.57	Michigan
106.80	Washington
105.55	Arkansas
101.83	Pennsylvania
100.92	Ohio
94.95	New Mexico
92.66	Wisconsin
80.34	Minnesota
78.08	Illinois
75.00	New Jersey
66.31	Delaware
65.99	Oregon
61.06	Maryland
59.90	Kentucky
58.34	Iowa
54.95	West Virginia
53.57	North Carolina
53.40	Nevada
51.53	Montana
51.24	Oklahoma
49.87	Georgia
48.87	Wyoming
47.74	Missouri
47.74	New Hampshire
47.19	Colorado
46.12	Arizona
44.30	South Dakota
44.08	Utah
42.23	Kansas
38.94	Florida
37.00	Louisiana
36.35	Nebraska
34.61	Tennessee
34.16	North Dakota
32.47	Mississippi
32.42	Virginia
31.01	Idaho
30.51	Indiana
26.74	South Carolina
24.55	Texas
18.41	Alabama

Table G.679. MEDICAID

Average per Capita Expenditure for Medicaid 1989–2000

917.02	New York
786.20	Rhode Island
655.26	Louisiana
636.35	Maine
576.78	Connecticut
561.93	Massachusetts
537.16	New Hampshire
535.14	New Jersey
535.06	Pennsylvania
530.65	West Virginia
516.93	Tennessee
508.17	Kentucky
505.66	Vermont
503.19	Alaska
503.10	Minnesota
473.42	Michigan
467.83	Mississippi
455.29	Ohio
449.10	New Mexico
439.49	South Carolina
437.14	California
434.73	Arkansas
433.79	Wisconsin
433.46	Washington
418.43	Illinois
415.21	Alabama
413.67	North Dakota
401.42	Indiana
400.62	Georgia
398.62	North Carolina
391.19	Missouri
387.79	Delaware
386.94	Texas
386.53	South Dakota
384.05	Maryland
370.02	Hawaii
366.61	Montana
362.94	Iowa
354.62	Nebraska
347.97	Oregon
344.76	Florida
343.27	Nevada
332.73	Oklahoma
326.33	Colorado
322.79	Wyoming
294.36	Arizona
279.50	Idaho
273.36	Virginia
264.08	Kansas
248.33	Utah

Table G.680. PRISONS

Average per Capita Expenditure for Corrections 1989–2000

236.94	Alaska
147.44	Delaware
135.57	New York
127.57	Maryland
120.74	Michigan
112.99	Texas
112.24	California
107.52	Virginia
107.26	Connecticut
106.07	Rhode Island
102.77	South Carolina
101.66	Arizona
99.30	Ohio
99.26	Oregon
92.00	North Carolina
91.82	New Jersey
91.16	Georgia
86.56	Wisconsin
85.80	Louisiana
82.36	Nevada
82.31	Florida
82.25	Hawaii
82.04	New Mexico
79.41	Washington
78.17	Utah
78.12	Idaho
76.65	Kansas
76.48	Tennessee
76.42	Massachusetts
75.18	Wyoming
73.05	Oklahoma
72.07	Colorado
71.86	Vermont
71.12	Pennsylvania
70.88	Indiana
67.02	Illinois
63.21	Montana
60.49	Iowa
60.34	Kentucky
57.51	Maine
57.26	Missouri
55.12	Minnesota
54.79	Mississippi
52.67	Nebraska
51.57	Arkansas
51.09	Alabama
50.08	South Dakota
41.38	New Hampshire
38.23	North Dakota
29.54	West Virginia

Table G.681. HIGHWAYS

Average per Capita Expenditure for Transportation 1989–2000

1,240.85	Alaska
742.82	Hawaii
627.57	Wyoming
403.35	Delaware
403.13	Maryland
393.26	Montana
386.12	West Virginia
379.30	North Dakota
376.75	Connecticut
356.65	South Dakota
328.42	Virginia
326.46	Vermont
313.87	Minnesota
309.60	Massachusetts
308.05	New Mexico
300.36	Kansas
294.57	Iowa
283.74	Kentucky
279.51	Wisconsin
276.99	Florida
276.20	Idaho
267.76	Maine
266.43	Utah
265.58	Rhode Island
262.15	Nebraska
261.04	Pennsylvania
259.09	North Carolina
253.20	Mississippi
247.51	New Hampshire
245.96	Arizona
244.23	Nevada
242.80	Washington
228.22	Oklahoma
227.95	Louisiana
219.96	Arkansas
213.55	Michigan
212.67	Illinois
210.75	Oregon
209.14	Indiana
204.98	Alabama
200.23	New York
195.78	Ohio
192.22	Colorado
192.03	South Carolina
191.25	Tennessee
190.74	New Jersey
180.51	Missouri
171.18	Georgia
167.66	Texas
161.23	California

Table G.682. ALLOTHER

Average-per Capita Expenditure for All Other Expenditures 1989–2000

2,907.89	Alaska
2,154.00	Hawaii
2,056.26	Delaware
1,475.55	Massachusetts
1,398.31	Connecticut
1,384.67	Wyoming
1,309.34	Oregon
1,094.18	North Dakota
1,090.81	Rhode Island
1,085.52	Maine
1,046.96	New Jersey
1,040.60	Wisconsin
1,027.78	Ohio
1,019.29	Vermont
1,008.02	Louisiana
963.71	Montana
963.25	Minnesota
962.29	Florida
961.66	New Mexico
951.30	Nevada
949.02	Arkansas
944.77	Iowa
944.72	South Carolina
879.64	California
872.36	Virginia
864.46	Washington
861.64	New York
816.51	Pennsylvania
814.74	Arizona
792.23	Maryland
776.49	Nebraska
766.84	Kentucky
765.64	Michigan
744.02	Kansas
736.92	Illinois
729.80	Missouri
709.79	Oklahoma
707.30	Idaho
671.03	South Dakota
659.49	Indiana
657.49	New Hampshire
653.62	Utah
651.08	Georgia
640.07	Tennessee
626.65	Mississippi
601.09	Alabama
580.70	North Carolina
566.59	Colorado
529.12	West Virginia
379.44	Texas

Table G.683. SALESTAX

Sales Tax Collected in Millions 1996

15,753	California
10,766	Texas
10,456	Florida
5,851	Pennsylvania
5,208	New York
4,798	Illinois
4,740	Ohio
4,318	New Jersey
4,153	Washington
3,950	Georgia
3,674	Tennessee
3,105	North Carolina
2,942	Indiana
2,901	Minnesota
2,704	Wisconsin
2,460	Connecticut
2,103	Arizona
2,000	Maryland
1,897	Louisiana
1,784	Kentucky
1,722	Virginia
1,624	Missouri
1,556	Massachusetts
1,545	South Carolina
1,432	Hawaii
1,369	Arkansas
1,340	Michigan
1,275	Iowa
1,240	Kansas
1,230	New Mexico
1,219	Colorado
1,186	Alabama
1,158	Utah
1,125	Oklahoma
1,078	Mississippi
746	West Virginia
711	Nebraska
630	Maine
463	Rhode Island
463	Idaho
341	South Dakota
290	North Dakota
209	Wyoming
183	Vermont
0	Delaware
0	Oregon
0	Montana
0	New Hampshire
*	Alaska
*	Nevada

*Incomplete data

Table G.684. PERINTAX

Personal Income Tax Collected in Millions 1996

20,875	California
16,564	New York
5,669	Illinois
5,509	Pennsylvania
5,263	Ohio
5,099	North Carolina
4,734	New Jersey
4,572	Michigan
4,301	Virginia
4,222	Georgia
4,184	Wisconsin
4,135	Minnesota
3,865	Massachusetts
3,484	Maryland
3,317	Oregon
3,113	Missouri
2,966	Indiana
2,879	Connecticut
2,319	Colorado
2,109	Iowa
2,075	Kentucky
1,814	South Carolina
1,530	Alabama
1,496	Oklahoma
1,494	Arizona
1,416	Kansas
1,319	Arkansas
1,136	Utah
1,110	Louisiana
1,000	Hawaii
847	Nebraska
751	West Virginia
741	Mississippi
651	Idaho
645	New Mexico
640	Maine
632	Delaware
576	Rhode Island
383	Montana
281	Vermont
152	North Dakota
115	Tennessee
0	Texas
0	Florida
0	Washington
0	South Dakota
0	Wyoming
0	New Hampshire
*	Alaska
*	Nevada

*Incomplete data

Table G.685. CORPTAX

Corporate Income Tax Collected in Millions 1996

5,862	California
2,160	Michigan
1,944	New York
1,677	Pennsylvania
1,642	Texas
1,172	New Jersey
1,163	Florida
1,114	Ohio
982	Indiana
978	Illinois
748	Connecticut
738	Georgia
702	Minnesota
689	North Carolina
636	Wisconsin
541	Tennessee
526	Massachusetts
508	Louisiana
477	Missouri
448	Arizona
402	Virginia
294	Iowa
285	Kentucky
262	Mississippi
252	Maryland
234	South Carolina
224	Arkansas
222	Oregon
219	Kansas
203	Colorado
191	Alabama
177	Utah
163	Oklahoma
163	New Mexico
156	West Virginia
153	New Hampshire
152	Idaho
127	Nebraska
76	Delaware
76	Montana
63	Rhode Island
58	Maine
49	North Dakota
48	Hawaii
42	Vermont
0	Washington
0	South Dakota
0	Wyoming
*	Alaska
*	Nevada

*Incomplete data

Table G.686. GAMETAX

Gaming Tax Collected in Millions 1996

1,190	Texas
1,021	New Jersey
807	Illinois
558	Georgia
419	Connecticut
332	Virginia
285	Louisiana
147	Kentucky
111	Mississippi
96	Rhode Island
67	California
67	Minnesota
60	Iowa
50	New Hampshire
46	Florida
46	Maine
42	New York
19	Montana
18	Colorado
16	Massachusetts
14	Oklahoma
12	North Dakota
8	Michigan
7	Arkansas
5	Alabama
4	Wisconsin
0	Pennsylvania
0	Ohio
0	Indiana
0	North Carolina
0	Tennessee
0	Missouri
0	Arizona
0	Maryland
0	South Carolina
0	Oregon
0	Kansas
0	Utah
0	New Mexico
0	Idaho
0	Nebraska
0	Delaware
0	Hawaii
0	Vermont
0	Washington
0	South Dakota
0	Wyoming
*	West Virginia
*	Alaska
*	Nevada

*Incomplete data

Table G.687. GOVERNMT

General Factor Based on Eight Variables Related to Government Procurement of Funds

39.00	Arkansas
38.38	South Dakota
37.63	Mississippi
37.63	North Dakota
37.63	Tennessee
37.00	West Virginia
36.13	Idaho
36.00	Utah
35.25	Louisiana
34.88	South Carolina
34.50	Vermont
34.38	Montana
34.13	New Hampshire
32.75	New Mexico
32.00	Oklahoma
31.88	Texas
31.25	Hawaii
30.13	Alabama
29.75	Arizona
28.75	Iowa
27.50	Rhode Island
27.50	Nevada
26.25	Maine
25.75	Florida
25.63	Kentucky
24.50	North Carolina
24.25	Nebraska
24.13	Alaska
23.38	Washington
22.88	Missouri
22.63	Kansas
21.63	Oregon
20.88	Georgia
20.75	Michigan
20.63	Indiana
20.38	Wisconsin
19.75	Pennsylvania
19.25	Wyoming
18.63	Ohio
18.50	Illinois
17.25	Delaware
15.88	New Jersey
15.25	Minnesota
14.50	California
14.13	Connecticut
14.00	Colorado
13.38	Virginia
12.75	Massachusetts
8.75	Maryland
5.38	New York

Table G.688. EXPEND

General Factor Based on Seven Variables Related to Government Expenditures

42.00	Texas
37.14	Colorado
35.14	Arizona
34.14	Tennessee
33.71	Virginia
33.57	Indiana
33.29	Idaho
33.14	Missouri
32.14	Nevada
32.14	Georgia
32.00	Florida
31.29	Illinois
31.00	Utah
30.86	South Carolina
30.29	New Hampshire
29.86	Ohio
28.71	North Carolina
28.57	Oklahoma
27.86	Nebraska
27.86	Oregon
27.71	South Dakota
27.29	Michigan
27.29	California
27.14	Mississippi
27.00	Maryland
26.71	Alabama
26.29	Kansas
25.57	New Jersey
24.71	Pennsylvania
24.29	Louisiana
24.00	New York
23.29	Montana
21.71	Vermont
21.00	North Dakota
20.86	Rhode Island
20.71	Massachusetts
20.29	Delaware
20.14	Washington
19.57	Iowa
18.57	Arkansas
18.00	Maine
17.14	Wisconsin
17.00	Wyoming
16.43	Kentucky
16.43	Connecticut
15.86	West Virginia
15.43	Minnesota
15.00	Hawaii
14.86	New Mexico
10.00	Alaska

Table G.689. CRIME

General Factor Based on Eight Variables Related to Crime Rates over 39 Years

42.69	Florida
41.88	Nevada
41.13	Arizona
40.88	Michigan
40.88	California
40.38	Texas
39.31	New Mexico
38.56	Maryland
38.13	Louisiana
36.31	New York
36.25	Georgia
35.50	Illinois
34.94	Alaska
34.50	Missouri
34.25	South Carolina
33.13	Colorado
32.13	Washington
31.81	Tennessee
31.50	Delaware
31.00	Oregon
28.44	Alabama
28.38	Oklahoma
27.94	North Carolina
26.13	New Jersey
25.69	Ohio
25.13	Hawaii
24.81	Kansas
24.38	Massachusetts
23.50	Indiana
22.38	Mississippi
22.13	Arkansas
21.75	Rhode Island
20.31	Utah
20.00	Virginia
19.81	Minnesota
19.38	Connecticut
18.88	Pennsylvania
17.19	Kentucky
16.75	Idaho
16.50	Montana
16.44	Wisconsin
15.00	Wyoming
12.50	Nebraska
9.50	West Virginia
8.88	Vermont
7.88	Iowa
6.63	Maine
6.00	New Hampshire
5.88	South Dakota
1.75	North Dakota

Table G.690. PROTECT

General Factor Based on Five Variables Related to Funds for Police Protection

42.40	Kentucky
38.70	Minnesota
37.90	Georgia
35.60	Washington
34.60	Texas
34.60	North Dakota
34.20	Tennessee
33.50	Virginia
33.30	Michigan
32.40	Ohio
31.50	Arizona
30.80	South Dakota
30.60	Utah
30.40	Hawaii
29.30	Arkansas
29.20	New Mexico
29.20	Iowa
29.10	Idaho
28.30	Indiana
27.90	Alabama
27.70	Colorado
27.60	Florida
27.40	South Carolina
27.20	Nevada
26.60	North Carolina
26.40	Oregon
26.00	Delaware
25.60	Mississippi
24.50	Louisiana
24.20	Oklahoma
23.60	Vermont
23.40	West Virginia
23.20	Kansas
22.90	Montana
22.80	Rhode Island
22.80	Wisconsin
22.40	Pennsylvania
22.00	California
22.00	Maine
21.90	Nebraska
18.60	Alaska
16.80	New Hampshire
16.60	Maryland
15.20	Missouri
13.80	Connecticut
12.90	New York
10.80	Illinois
9.40	New Jersey
9.40	Wyoming
7.80	Massachusetts

Table G.691. PUNISH

General Factor Based on Eleven Variables Related to Punishment for Crimes

46.32	Texas
41.55	Georgia
40.27	Virginia
39.27	South Carolina
38.91	Nevada
38.50	Florida
37.36	Louisiana
36.45	Oklahoma
36.18	Arizona
35.55	North Carolina
32.50	Delaware
32.50	Maryland
32.14	Mississippi
31.14	California
31.05	New York
30.36	Arkansas
29.00	Connecticut
28.50	Kentucky
28.09	New Mexico
27.18	Alabama
26.91	Idaho
26.27	Michigan
26.18	Ohio
26.05	Tennessee
25.09	Pennsylvania
23.68	Missouri
23.55	Alaska
23.23	Colorado
23.05	Wyoming
22.36	Kansas
22.36	New Jersey
22.23	Oregon
21.59	Indiana
20.64	Utah
20.50	Illinois
20.36	Washington
18.45	Montana
18.09	Nebraska
17.50	Rhode Island
17.45	Wisconsin
17.18	Minnesota
16.68	Massachusetts
15.36	West Virginia
14.86	Hawaii
13.50	South Dakota
12.64	Maine
12.14	North Dakota
11.86	Iowa
11.77	Vermont
10.64	New Hampshire

Table G.692. DEATH

General Factor Based on Six Variables Related to Death from Natural Causes

47.25	West Virginia
44.25	Arkansas
43.92	Pennsylvania
40.50	Oklahoma
40.08	Alabama
40.00	Florida
39.08	Rhode Island
38.50	Tennessee
37.83	Mississippi
37.58	Missouri
36.67	Ohio
36.33	South Dakota
36.08	Kentucky
34.42	South Carolina
34.08	Louisiana
34.00	Iowa
32.67	Indiana
32.42	North Dakota
30.83	North Carolina
29.83	Delaware
29.17	Maine
28.83	New Jersey
26.58	Kansas
26.42	Illinois
26.33	Nebraska
25.83	Michigan
25.50	Oregon
25.42	Connecticut
24.42	Wisconsin
23.92	Maryland
21.50	New York
21.17	Massachusetts
21.00	Vermont
20.33	Montana
18.42	Virginia
16.92	New Hampshire
16.67	Georgia
15.25	Arizona
14.83	Minnesota
13.92	Texas
12.33	Idaho
11.42	Nevada
10.58	Washington
9.92	Hawaii
8.92	New Mexico
8.00	Wyoming
7.92	California
6.08	Colorado
5.92	Alaska
5.17	Utah

Table G.693. HIWAYDEA

General Factor Based on Eleven Variables Related to Highway Fatalities

36.45	Mississippi
35.91	Louisiana
34.95	Alabama
32.91	Wyoming
32.32	Missouri
32.32	Nevada
31.59	New Mexico
30.91	Texas
30.50	Florida
30.18	Arizona
30.05	South Carolina
29.95	West Virginia
29.95	Tennessee
29.05	Kentucky
28.77	Georgia
28.36	Oklahoma
28.32	Rhode Island
28.09	Arkansas
27.86	Alaska
27.77	Hawaii
27.18	New Jersey
26.68	South Dakota
26.45	Montana
26.18	New Hampshire
25.68	Massachusetts
25.50	Delaware
25.32	Michigan
24.14	North Carolina
23.45	Pennsylvania
23.45	Kansas
23.00	Connecticut
22.86	Nebraska
22.73	Virginia
22.64	Indiana
22.27	Washington
22.23	North Dakota
22.14	Colorado
22.09	California
21.36	Idaho
21.32	Utah
20.27	Oregon
20.23	Vermont
19.91	Maryland
19.23	Illinois
18.64	Wisconsin
17.73	New York
17.55	Maine
17.23	Minnesota
16.50	Ohio
14.82	Iowa

Table G.694.   TRAUMA

General Factor Based on Two
Variables Related to Traumatic Deaths

47.25	New Mexico
46.50	Wyoming
46.50	Montana
43.00	Arizona
42.75	Alaska
42.25	Idaho
42.00	Oklahoma
42.00	Arkansas
39.50	Mississippi
39.00	South Dakota
38.50	Nevada
38.50	Tennessee
38.00	West Virginia
36.25	Kentucky
36.25	Oregon
35.25	Missouri
34.25	Alabama
31.00	Colorado
30.00	Florida
29.50	Louisiana
29.25	North Carolina
28.50	South Carolina
28.25	Georgia
28.25	North Dakota
26.50	Kansas
26.00	Utah
24.75	Delaware
24.50	Pennsylvania
24.00	Indiana
24.00	Washington
24.00	Iowa
21.50	Vermont
21.00	Nebraska
17.75	Texas
16.50	Wisconsin
16.00	Virginia
15.25	Maine
13.75	Hawaii
13.75	Minnesota
11.75	New Hampshire
11.00	Michigan
8.75	California
8.75	Ohio
8.00	Connecticut
6.00	Maryland
5.25	Illinois
4.75	New Jersey
3.75	New York
3.50	Massachusetts
1.75	Rhode Island

Table G.695.   HEALTH

General Factor Based on Eight
Variables Related to Health Factors

42.94	Louisiana
38.88	Mississippi
38.50	Arkansas
37.63	Tennessee
37.13	South Carolina
35.38	Alabama
34.94	New York
34.19	Nevada
33.31	Kentucky
33.25	Illinois
33.19	Georgia
33.06	North Carolina
33.06	Michigan
32.88	Oklahoma
32.44	Texas
31.81	Indiana
31.63	Florida
31.63	Virginia
31.25	Delaware
30.38	Maryland
30.13	Alaska
30.00	Missouri
28.81	Ohio
27.50	West Virginia
26.69	Pennsylvania
25.06	New Jersey
25.00	California
24.00	New Mexico
23.94	Arizona
23.38	Rhode Island
22.31	Colorado
21.00	Iowa
19.63	Wyoming
19.56	Wisconsin
19.25	Hawaii
19.19	Connecticut
18.50	South Dakota
18.25	Oregon
18.00	Nebraska
18.00	Massachusetts
16.38	Washington
15.88	Utah
15.63	Kansas
15.31	Montana
14.50	Idaho
10.94	Vermont
10.75	New Hampshire
10.38	Maine
10.25	North Dakota
9.38	Minnesota

Table G.696.   MEDICAL

General Factor Based on Eight
Variables Related to Health Care Costs

40.50	Texas
39.50	Nevada
37.88	Arizona
35.31	Mississippi
35.06	California
34.00	Arkansas
33.88	Oklahoma
33.75	Louisiana
33.50	New Mexico
32.75	Florida
32.56	Idaho
31.88	Alabama
31.44	South Carolina
30.13	New York
30.00	Georgia
29.56	Alaska
29.31	New Jersey
29.25	Indiana
29.13	Colorado
29.00	Maryland
28.44	Delaware
28.19	Connecticut
27.44	North Carolina
27.38	Kentucky
26.94	Wyoming
25.88	West Virginia
25.44	Montana
24.13	Illinois
23.13	Oregon
22.63	Rhode Island
22.38	Maine
21.69	Utah
21.63	New Hampshire
21.38	North Dakota
21.31	South Dakota
20.94	Tennessee
20.19	Ohio
20.13	Virginia
19.81	Washington
18.94	Missouri
18.81	Michigan
18.50	Massachusetts
17.69	Kansas
17.06	Wisconsin
15.94	Pennsylvania
15.81	Minnesota
14.75	Iowa
11.81	Nebraska
10.81	Hawaii
7.50	Vermont

Table G.697. TEENPROB

General Factor Based on Nine Variables Related to Problems of Teenagers

42.22	Mississippi
41.22	Louisiana
40.22	Arkansas
39.00	Arizona
38.78	Georgia
37.22	South Carolina
37.11	Alabama
36.22	New Mexico
36.06	Texas
35.17	Nevada
35.17	Illinois
34.94	Tennessee
33.67	Delaware
33.50	Oklahoma
33.11	North Carolina
32.22	Indiana
31.00	Florida
29.11	Missouri
28.56	Ohio
27.22	Maryland
27.22	Michigan
26.83	New York
25.28	Kentucky
25.17	California
23.28	Pennsylvania
23.17	Alaska
23.06	Colorado
22.72	Virginia
22.61	Kansas
22.28	New Jersey
21.17	Hawaii
21.11	Rhode Island
20.72	Oregon
20.33	Idaho
20.06	West Virginia
20.00	Wisconsin
19.94	South Dakota
19.33	Washington
18.56	Connecticut
17.50	Nebraska
17.17	Minnesota
17.11	Utah
16.44	Wyoming
14.33	Iowa
13.94	Massachusetts
13.56	Montana
11.56	North Dakota
10.61	Maine
9.83	Vermont
8.39	New Hampshire

Table G.698. EDUCACHI

General Factor Based on Four Variables Related to Educational Achievement

47.50	Arkansas
45.75	Mississippi
45.38	Kentucky
43.75	West Virginia
42.00	Tennessee
39.75	South Carolina
39.25	Louisiana
39.25	Georgia
36.75	Alabama
36.75	Florida
35.50	Nevada
34.25	Indiana
32.63	Texas
32.63	North Carolina
32.25	Maine
30.50	Oklahoma
28.38	North Dakota
26.75	Missouri
26.13	Alaska
26.00	Pennsylvania
25.75	Hawaii
25.75	Idaho
25.38	South Dakota
25.13	Montana
24.75	Ohio
23.63	New Mexico
23.50	Michigan
23.13	Nebraska
22.63	Wyoming
21.25	Arizona
20.25	Maryland
20.00	New Jersey
19.75	New York
19.75	Virginia
19.75	Wisconsin
19.00	California
19.00	Connecticut
18.88	Delaware
18.50	Iowa
18.13	Oregon
17.75	Kansas
17.63	Illinois
17.25	Rhode Island
14.50	New Hampshire
12.25	Washington
9.75	Massachusetts
8.75	Utah
8.63	Vermont
7.00	Minnesota
6.50	Colorado

Table G.699. EDUCSUPP

General Factor Based on Nine Variables Related to Support for Education

43.61	Mississippi
42.78	Arkansas
41.50	Louisiana
39.00	Tennessee
36.89	North Carolina
36.44	Oklahoma
36.39	South Dakota
36.11	Alabama
34.83	Kentucky
32.61	South Carolina
32.44	West Virginia
32.17	Florida
31.83	North Dakota
31.78	Nevada
31.67	Arizona
30.22	Maine
30.11	Missouri
29.94	Idaho
29.28	Hawaii
28.67	Texas
28.56	Montana
28.11	Georgia
28.00	California
25.83	New Hampshire
25.28	Utah
25.06	New Mexico
23.17	Virginia
22.94	Rhode Island
22.78	Illinois
22.67	Massachusetts
21.22	Ohio
21.22	Pennsylvania
21.11	Nebraska
20.89	New York
20.83	Iowa
19.56	Kansas
17.94	Maryland
17.67	Colorado
17.39	Indiana
17.17	Washington
17.00	Minnesota
16.39	Wyoming
16.17	Oregon
15.11	Vermont
14.78	Connecticut
14.11	Delaware
13.94	Wisconsin
13.00	New Jersey
12.72	Michigan
6.00	Alaska

Table G.700. WORK

General Factor Based on Seventeen Variables Related to Work and Employment

38.94	Mississippi
37.71	West Virginia
35.00	Oklahoma
34.94	Louisiana
33.76	Arkansas
32.21	Kentucky
31.88	Alabama
31.47	South Carolina
31.21	New Mexico
31.15	Maine
30.56	Florida
29.35	Tennessee
27.62	Arizona
27.09	Rhode Island
26.76	California
26.32	North Carolina
26.26	New Hampshire
26.24	North Dakota
26.18	South Dakota
26.12	Virginia
26.06	Montana
25.88	Texas
25.82	Wyoming
25.68	New York
25.62	Hawaii
25.44	Indiana
25.38	Pennsylvania
24.68	Ohio
24.09	Vermont
24.06	Idaho
23.74	Michigan
23.32	Georgia
23.09	Utah
22.76	Missouri
22.68	Maryland
22.62	New Jersey
22.21	Nevada
22.06	Alaska
22.00	Oregon
21.91	Connecticut
21.71	Nebraska
20.91	Massachusetts
20.15	Illinois
19.85	Wisconsin
19.74	Iowa
19.65	Kansas
19.29	Delaware
16.74	Washington
15.00	Colorado
12.12	Minnesota

Table G.701. ECONOMIC

General Factor Based on Seven Variables Related to Economic Opportunities

43.79	West Virginia
43.71	New Mexico
43.07	Arkansas
41.43	Mississippi
39.29	Louisiana
38.71	Montana
36.79	Oklahoma
36.43	Texas
35.86	California
35.14	Alabama
33.43	Arizona
33.43	New York
33.07	South Carolina
32.14	Idaho
32.00	Kentucky
31.29	Tennessee
28.71	Oregon
27.64	North Dakota
27.50	Kansas
26.86	South Dakota
26.36	Wyoming
26.14	Rhode Island
25.43	Pennsylvania
25.14	Illinois
25.14	Maine
25.00	North Carolina
24.64	Florida
24.14	Ohio
23.86	Washington
23.71	Hawaii
23.07	Georgia
22.14	Missouri
21.07	Nebraska
20.00	Michigan
19.64	Nevada
19.14	Alaska
18.86	Indiana
17.79	Vermont
17.21	Colorado
15.29	Wisconsin
15.29	Minnesota
14.86	Iowa
14.71	Utah
14.57	Massachusetts
14.50	Maryland
13.43	Delaware
13.00	New Jersey
11.64	Virginia
11.07	New Hampshire
7.86	Connecticut

Table G.702. SUMMARY

SUMMARY Factor Based on Summation of 15 General Factor Scores

544.81	Mississippi
533.54	Arkansas
531.90	Louisiana
505.93	Tennessee
502.30	South Carolina
499.44	Oklahoma
493.89	Alabama
490.34	Texas
486.53	Florida
476.91	Arizona
467.84	Nevada
461.90	Kentucky
458.12	Georgia
449.29	New Mexico
447.44	West Virginia
441.97	North Carolina
414.37	Missouri
397.41	Idaho
396.11	Indiana
392.83	South Dakota
381.56	Montana
369.69	Michigan
369.41	California
367.02	Ohio
366.68	Delaware
366.64	Pennsylvania
358.24	Oregon
353.16	Virginia
347.27	North Dakota
345.71	Illinois
344.25	New York
343.92	Alaska
340.10	Rhode Island
336.20	Kansas
335.21	Maryland
325.31	Wyoming
325.29	Colorado
323.67	Hawaii
317.54	Utah
313.99	Washington
309.60	Maine
309.23	Nebraska
305.37	New Jersey
294.09	Iowa
279.22	Wisconsin
278.62	Connecticut
271.13	New Hampshire
257.07	Vermont
251.01	Massachusetts
245.94	Minnesota

References and Sources

The variables are listed in the order in which they appear on the database columns, from left to right. Each variable is labeled with an acronym (eight letters or less) which crudely describes what is included. The definition that follows elaborates on the name of each variable. Note: Not all of these variables are included in this copy of Rankings of the States.

STATE   This variable includes the names of all 50 states in the United States. All information for each state is included in variables listed to the right of STATE in the database. If a column is blank after the name of the state, that indicates that only partial data or no data are included under variables that derive from the *Crime by Counties* 1998 report prepared by the Federal Bureau of Investigation (FBI); thus some of the crime data must be interpreted very cautiously.

POP   Table G.1   This figure is the population (in thousands) for each state, as reported by the Federal Bureau of Investigation in *Crime by Counties* 1998 for each municipality within a state, and for the state as a whole. The figures differ somewhat from information available from the Census Bureau because the FBI information includes most but not all municipalities within a state, and the information reported under POP represents a summary for each state of those municipalities that provided the FBI with crime data for 1998. All numbers reported for each of the next nine variables were derived from the Federal Bureau of Investigation *Crime by Counties* 1998 report.

MODINDEX   Table G.2   This number represents the total number of crimes reported, including arson, for that state for 1998. In the FBI report, INDEX summarizes all crimes except arson, and the category MODINDEX includes all crime, including arson. From Federal Bureau of Investigation *Crime by Counties*, 1998.

MURD   Table G.3   This number represents the total number of murders that occurred in that state which were reported to the FBI as having occurred during 1998. Federal Bureau of Investigation, *Crime by Counties*, 1998.

RAPES   Table G.4   This number represents the total number of rapes that occurred in that state which were reported to the FBI as having occurred during 1998. Federal Bureau of Investigation, *Crime by Counties*, 1998.

ROB   Table G.5   This number represents the total number of robberies that occurred in that state which were reported to the FBI as having occurred during 1998. Federal Bureau of Investigation, *Crime by Counties*, 1998.

ASLT   Table G.6   This number represents the total number of assaults that occurred in that state which were reported to the FBI as having occurred during 1998. Federal Bureau of Investigation, *Crime by Counties*, 1998.

BURG   Table G.8   This number represents the total number of burglaries that occurred in that state which were reported to the FBI as having occurred during 1998. Federal Bureau of Investigation, *Crime by Counties*, 1998.

LARC   Table G.7   This number represents the total number of larcenies that occurred in that state which were reported to the FBI as having occurred during 1998. Federal Bureau of Investigation, *Crime by Counties*, 1998.

THEFT   Table G.9   This number represents the total number of automobile thefts that occurred in that state which were reported to the FBI during 1998. Federal Bureau of Investigation, *Crime by Counties*, 1998.

ARSN   Table G.10   This number represents the total number of incidents of arson that occurred in that state which were reported to the FBI during 1998. Federal Bureau of Investigation, *Crime by Counties*, 1998.

TOTINDEX   Table G.11   This number represents the total number of crimes that occurred in that state which were reported to the FBI during 1998, and corresponds precisely to the MODINDEX value. It is a redundant value. Federal Bureau of Investigation, *Crime by Counties*, 1998.

MURDER   Table G.12   This number represents the murder rate per 1,000 population in that state in 1998. The number was calculated by dividing MURD by POP, and makes the values for each of the states comparable. Calculated: MURD / POP

ASSAULT   Table G.13   This number represents the assault rate per 1,000 population in that state in 1998. The number was calculated by dividing ASLT by POP, and makes the values for each of the states comparable. Calculated: ASLT / POP

RAPE   Table G.14   This number represents the rape rate per 1,000 population in that state in 1998. The number was calculated by dividing RAPES by POP, and makes the values for each of the states comparable. Calculated: RAPES / POP

ROBBERY   Table G.15   This number represents the robbery rate per 1,000 population in that state in 1998. The number was calculated by dividing ROB by POP, and makes the values for each of the states comparable. Calculated: ROB / POP

ARSON   Table G.16   This number represents the arson rate per 1,000 population in that state in 1998. The number was calculated by dividing ARSN by POP, and makes the values for each of the states comparable.

Calculated: ARSN / POP

BURGLARY Table G.17 This number represents the burglary rate per 1,000 population in that state in 1998. The number was calculated by dividing BURG by POP, and makes the values for each of the states comparable.

Calculated: BURG / POP

LARCENY Table G.18 This number represents the larceny rate per 1,000 population in that state in 1998. The number was calculated by dividing LARC by POP, and makes the values for each of the states comparable.

Calculated: LARC / POP

CARTHEFT Table G.19 This number represents the auto theft rate per 1,000 population in that state in 1998. The number was calculated by dividing THEFT by POP, and makes the values for each of the states comparable.

Calculated: THEFT / POP

ABUSE Table G.20 Percentage of childen referred for investigation of alleged abuse and neglect in 1998. This information was provided by the Children's Rights Council (CRC), a national child advocacy organization. Internet: http://www.vix.com/crc/bestStates98.html. States are ranked from 1 to 50 (actual data from which rankings were made are included for this variable), resulting in a report titled "The Best States to Raise a Child." I contacted the source by phone (202-547-6227). They said the Annie E. Casey Foundation is doing the project in 1999.

NOIMMUNE Table G.21 Percentage of children not immunized by age two for 1998. This information was provided by the Children's Rights Council (CRC), a national child advocacy organization. Internet address: http://www.vix.com/crc/bestStates98.html. States are ranked from 1 to 50 (actual data from which rankings were made are included for this variable), resulting in a report titled "The Best States to Raise a Child." I contacted the source by phone (202-547-6227). They said the Annie E. Casey Foundation is doing the project in 1999.

STALOCPP Table G.22 Average state and local funding per pupil, 1997. This information was reported in *Education Week*, January 11, 2001, p. 105.

TOTINST Table G.23 Total instructional dollars per student, 1998. *Education Week*, January 11, 2001, p. 103.

SUPSERV Table G.24 Support services expenditures per pupil, 1998. *Education Week*, January 11, 2001, p. 103.

AVRSTART Table G.25 Average starting teacher salaries, adjusted for the cost of living, 1998. *Education Week*, January 11, 2001, p. 103.

AVRSALRY Table G.26 Average salary all teachers, adjusted for the cost of living, 1998. *Education Week*, January 11, 2001, p. 103.

STUMEDIA Table G.27 Number of students per instructional media computer, 1999. *Education Week*, January 11, 2001, p. 103.

POPEST99 Table G.28 Population of state, 1999 estimate, by thousands. U.S. Census Bureau, *QuickFacts*. On the Internet: http://quickfacts.census.gov/qfd/states/01,000.html.

PCCHANGE Table G.40 Population percent change, 1990–1999 estimate. U.S. Census Bureau, *QuickFacts*. On the Internet: http://quickfacts.census.gov/qfd/states/01,000.html.

MALEPOP Table G.29 Male population, 1999 estimate. U.S. Census Bureau, *QuickFacts*. On the Internet: http://quickfacts.census.gov/qfd/states/01,000.html.

FEMALPOP Table G.30 Female population, 1999 estimate. U.S. Census Bureau, *QuickFacts*. On the Internet: http://quickfacts.census.gov/qfd/states/01,000.html.

PCUND18 Table G.31 Percent population under 18 years old, 1999 estimate. U.S. Census Bureau, *QuickFacts*. On the Internet: http://quickfacts.census.gov/qfd/states/01,000.html.

PCOVER65 Table G.32 Percent population 65 years old and over, 1999 estimate. U.S. Census Bureau, *QuickFacts*. On the Internet: http://quickfacts.census.gov/qfd/states/01,000.html.

PCWHITE Table G.33 Percent white population, 1999 estimate. U.S. Census Bureau, *QuickFacts*. On the Internet: http://quickfacts.census.gov/qfd/states/01,000.html.

PCBLACK Table G.34 Percent black population, 1999 estimate. U.S. Census Bureau, *QuickFacts*. On the Internet: http://quickfacts.census.gov/qfd/states/01,000.html.

PCHISP Table G.35 Percent Hispanic population, 1999 estimate. U.S. Census Bureau, *QuickFacts*. On the Internet: http://quickfacts.census.gov/qfd/states/01,000.html.

PCWNHISP Table G.36 Percent white non-Hispanic population, 1999 estimate. U.S. Census Bureau, *QuickFacts*. On the Internet: http://quickfacts.census.gov/qfd/states/01,000.html.

PCHOME Table G.37 Home ownership rate, 1999. U.S. Census Bureau, *QuickFacts*. On the Internet: http://quickfacts.census.gov/qfd/states/01,000.html.

PERHOUSE Table G.38 Persons per household, 1999. U.S. Census Bureau, *QuickFacts*. On the Internet: http://quickfacts.census.gov/qfd/states/01,000.html.

MEDINCOM Table G.39 Median household money income, 1997 model-based estimate. U.S. Census Bureau, *QuickFacts*. On the Internet: http://quickfacts.census.gov/qfd/states/01,000.html.

PCBELPOV Table G.41 Persons below poverty, percent, 1997 model-based estimate. U.S. Census Bureau, *QuickFacts*. On the Internet: http://quickfacts.census.gov/qfd/states/01,000.html.

CHBELPOV   Table G.42 Children below poverty, percent, 1997 model-based estimate. U.S. Census Bureau, *QuickFacts*. On the Internet: http://quickfacts.census. gov/qfd/states/01,000.html.

PCEMPCHG   Table G.43 Private nonfarm employment, percent change 1990–1998. U.S. Census Bureau, *QuickFacts*. On the Internet: http://quickfacts.census. gov/qfd/states/01,000.html.

RETAILPC   Table G.44 Retail sales, per capita, 1997. U.S. Census Bureau, *QuickFacts*. On the Internet: http://quickfacts.census.gov/qfd/states/01,000.html.

MINFIRMS   Table G.45 Minority-owned firms, 1992. U.S. Census Bureau, *QuickFacts*. On the Internet: http://quickfacts.census.gov/qfd/states/01,000.html.

WOMFIRMS   Table G.46 Women-owned firms, 1992. U.S. Census Bureau, *QuickFacts*. On the Internet: http://quickfacts.census.gov/qfd/states/01,000.html.

FEDFUNDS   Table G.47 Federal funds and grants, 1999 ($1,000). U.S. Census Bureau, *QuickFacts*. On the Internet: http://quickfacts.census.gov/qfd/states/01,000. html.

LOCGOV   Table G.48 Local government employment—full-time equivalent, 1997. U.S. Census Bureau, *QuickFacts*. On the Internet: http://quickfacts.census. gov/qfd/states/01,000.html.

POPDENSE   Table G.49 Persons per square mile, 1999. U.S. Census Bureau, *QuickFacts*. On the Internet: http://quickfacts.census.gov/qfd/states/01,000.html.

CRIMESPP   Table G.50 Total number of crimes committed per 1,000 population, 1998.
Calculated: MODINDEX / POP / 1000

PCMINOR   Table G.51 Percent of total minority population, 1999.
Calculated: 100 − PCWNHISP

PCMAJOR   Table G.52 Percent of total minority population, 1999.
Calculated: 100 − PCMINOR

MAJORPOP   Table G.53 Total number of persons classified as majority in thousands, 1999.
Calculated: POPEST99 * PCMAJOR / 100

MINORPOP   Table G.54 Total number of persons classified as miniority in thousands, 1999.
Calculated: POPEST99 * PCMINOR / 100

FEDFUNPP   Table G.65 Total federal funds and grants, per person, in 1999.
Calculated: FEDFUNDS / POPEST99

PCMINFRM   Table G.55 Percentage minority-owned firms of total minority population, 1992.
Calculated: (MINFIRMS / (MINORPOP * 1,000)) * 100

PCWOMFRM   Table G.56 Percentage of women-owned firms of total female population, 1992.
Calculated: (WOMFIRMS / (FEMALPOP * 1,000)) * 100

PCLOCGOV   Table G.57 Percentage of total population that work full time in local government, 1998.
Calculated: (LOCGOV / (POPEST99 * 1,000)) * 100

MURPLOGV   Table G.58 Number of murders per number of persons that work full time in local government, 1998.
Calculated: MURD / LOCGOV

CRIMLOGV   Table G.66 Number of total crimes per number of persons that work full time in local government, 1998.
Calculated: MODINDEX / LOCGOV

EXEC5069   Table G.59 Total number of executions in the state between years 1950 and 1969. *Statistical Abstract of the United States*, 1994, Table G.347, page 218.

EXEC7700   Table G.60 Total number of executions in the state between years 1977 and 2000. Reported in "The Death Penalty" web page by the Clark County Prosecutor. On the Internet: http://www.clarkprosecutor. org/html/death/dpusa.htm.

PRISON92   Table G.61 Total number of persons in prison in the state in 1992. *Statistical Abstract of the United States*, 1994, Table G.342, page 216.

PRISON96   Table G.62 Estimated average daily number of inmates, 1995–1996, from *State Prison Expenditures*, 1996, Table 1, page 2, by James J. Stephan. On the Internet: http://www.ojp.usdoj.gov/bjs/.

PRRATE92   Table G.63 Number of prisoners per 1,000 total population of the state.
Calculated: PRISON92 / POPEST99

PRRATE96   Table G.64 Number of prisoners per 1,000 total population of the state.
Calculated: prison96 / popest99

PRISPI96   Table G.67 Operating expenditures in dollars, per inmate per year, reported for June 30 1995 to June 30 1996, from *State Prison Expenditures*, 1996, Table 1, page 2, by James J. Stephan. On the Internet: http:// www.ojp.usdoj.gov/bjs/.

TOTPRISN   Table G. 68 Total operating and capital expenditures (in $1,000), reported for June 30 1995 to June 30 1996, from *State Prison Expenditures*, 1996, Table 1, page 2, by James J. Stephan. On the Internet: http://www.ojp.usdoj.gov/bjs/.

MEDICPI   Table G.69 State prison expenditures for inmate medical care, fiscal year 1996, per inmate per day, reported for June 30 1995 to June 30 1996, from *State Prison Expenditures*, 1996, Table 5, page 7, by James J. Stephan. On the Internet:http://www.ojp. usdoj.gov/bjs/.

FOODPI   Table G.70 State prison expenditures for food services, fiscal year 1996, per inmate per day, reported for June 30 1995 to June 30 1996, from *State Prison Expenditures*, 1996, Table 6, page 6, by James J. Stephan. On the Internet:http://www.ojp.usdoj.gov/ bjs/.

PRISCOST   Table G.71 Cost in dollars to maintain one inmate in prison for one year, per person in the state.
Calculated: (TOTPRISN * 1,000) / (POPEST99 * 1,000)

PRCH9296 Table G.73 Percent change in prison population between 1992 and 1996.
Calculated: (PRISON96−PRISON92) / (PRISON92 * 100)

EXPT5069 Table G.75 Executions per 1,000 persons in the state over period 1950 to 1969, based on population estimate for 1999.
Calculated: EXEC5069 / POPEST99

EXPT7700 Table G.76 Executions per 1,000 persons in the state over period 1977 to 2000, based on population estimate for 1999.
Calculated: EXEC7700 / POPEST99

UTILPIPD Table G.72 State prison expenditures for utilities, fiscal year 1996, per inmate per day, reported for June 30 1995 to June 30 1996, from *State Prison Expenditures*, 1996, Table 8, page 10, by James J. Stephan. On the Internet: http://www.ojp.usdoj.gov/bjs/.

CIVLABOR Table G.77 Number of persons (in 1,000s) in the civilian labor force, from Bureau of Labor Statistics, "State at a Glance," as of July 2000. On the Internet: http://stats.bls.gov/eag/eag.ak.htm.

EMPLOYED Table G.78 Number of persons (in 1,000s) in the civilian labor force who are employed, from Bureau of Labor Statistics, "State at a Glance," as of July 2000. On the Internet: http://stats.bls.gov/eag/eag.ak.htm.

UNEMPLOY Table G.79 Number of persons (in 1,000s) in the civilian labor force who are unemployed, from Bureau of Labor Statistics, "State at a Glance," as of July 2000. On the Internet: http://stats.bls.gov/eag/eag.ak.htm.

UNEMRATE Table G.80 Percent of persons in the civilian labor force who are unemployed, from Bureau of Labor Statistics, "State at a Glance," as of July 2000. On the Internet: http://stats.bls.gov/eag/eag.ak.htm.

NONFARMT Table G.81 Number of persons (in 1,000s) in nonfarm wage and salary employment, from Bureau of Labor Statistics, "State at a Glance," as of July 2000. On the Internet: http://stats.bls.gov/eag/eag.ak.htm.

MINING Table G.82 Number of persons (in 1,000s) in mining, from Bureau of Labor Statistics, "State at a Glance," as of July 2000. On the Internet: http://stats.bls.gov/eag/eag.ak.htm.

CONSTRUC Table G.83 Number of persons (in 1,000s) in construction, from Bureau of Labor Statistics, "State at a Glance," as of July 2000. On the Internet: http://stats.bls.gov/eag/eag.ak.htm.

MANUFACT Table G.84 Number of persons (in 1,000s) in manufacturing, from Bureau of Labor Statistics, "State at a Glance," as of July 2000. On the Internet: http://stats.bls.gov/eag/eag.ak.htm.

TRANSPU Table G.85 Number of persons (in 1,000s) in transportation and public utilities, from Bureau of Labor Statistics, "State at a Glance," as of July 2000. On the Internet:http://stats.bls.gov/eag/eag.ak.htm.

TRADE Table G.86 Number of persons (in 1,000s) in trade (wholesale and retail), from Bureau of Labor Statistics, "State at a Glance," as of July 2000. On the Internet: http://stats.bls.gov/eag/eag.ak.htm.

FINANCE Table G.87 Number of persons (in 1,000s) in finance, insurance, and real estate, from Bureau of Labor Statistics, "State at a Glance," as of July 2000. On the Internet: http://stats.bls.gov/eag/eag.ak.htm.

SERVICES Table G.88 Number of persons (in 1,000s) in services, from Bureau of Labor Statistics, "State at a Glance," as of July 2000. On the Internet: http://stats.bls.gov/eag/eag.ak.htm.

GOVTFSL Table G.74 Number of persons (in 1,000s) in government (federal, state, and local), from Bureau of Labor Statistics, "State at a Glance," as of July 2000. On the Internet: http://stats.bls.gov/eag/eag.ak.htm.

WWALLDEA Table G.89 Women, white, all deaths, rates three-year averages per 100,000 estimated population 1994–1996. National Center for Health Statistics. On the Internet: http://www.cdc.gov/nchs/datawh/statab/useTables.htm.

WWMALIG Table G.91 Women, white, all malignant neoplasms deaths, rates three-year averages per 100,000 estimated population 1994–1996. National Center for Health Statistics. On the Internet: http://www.cdc.gov/nchs/datawh/statab/useTables.htm.

WWDIABET Table G.93 Women, white, diabetes deaths, rates three-year averages per 100,000 estimated population 1994–1996. National Center for Health Statistics. From Internet: http://www.cdc.gov/nchs/datawh/statab/useTables.htm.

WWNUTRI Table G.95 Women, white, nutritional deficiencies deaths, rates three-year averages per 100,000 estimated population 1994–1996. National Center for Health Statistics. On the Internet: http://www.cdc.gov/nchs/datawh/statab/useTables.htm.

WWCARDIO Table G.97 Women, white, major cardiovascular diseases deaths, rates three-year averages per 100,000 estimated population 1994–1996. National Center for Health Statistics. On the Internet: http://www.cdc.gov/nchs/datawh/statab/useTables.htm.

WWPNEUMO Table G.99 Women, white, pneumonia and influenza deaths, rates three-year averages per 100,000 estimated population 1994–1996. National Center for Health Statistics. On the Internet: http://www.cdc.gov/nchs/datawh/statab/useTables.htm.

WWACCID Table G.101 Women, white, accidents and adverse effects deaths, rates three-year averages per 100,000 estimated population 1994–1996. National Center for Health Statistics. On the Internet: http://www.cdc.gov/nchs/datawh/statab/useTables.htm.

WWMOTVEH Table G.103 Women, white, motor vehicle accidents deaths, rates three-year averages per 100,000 estimated population 1994–1996. National Center for Health Statistics. On the Internet: http://www.cdc.gov/nchs/datawh/statab/useTables.htm.

WWFALLS Table G.105 Women, white, falls deaths, rates three-year averages per 100,000 estimated population 1994–1996. National Center for Health Statistics. On the Internet: http://www.cdc.gov/nchs/statab/useTables.htm.

WWSUICID Table G.107 Women, white, suicides, rates three-year averages per 100,000 estimated population 1994–1996. National Center for Health Statistics. On the Internet: http://www.cdc.gov/nchs/datawh/statab/useTables.htm.

WWHOMICI Table G.109 Women, white, homicides, rates three-year averages per 100,000 estimated population 1994–1996. National Center for Health Statistics. On the Internet: http://www.cdc.gov/nchs/datawh/statab/useTables.htm.

WWDRUGIN Table G.111 Women, white, drug-induced deaths, rates three-year averages per 100,000 estimated population 1994–1996. National Center for Health Statistics. On the Internet: http://www.cdc.gov/nchs/datawh/statab/useTables.htm.

WWALCOHO Table G.113 Women, white, alcohol-induced deaths, rates three-year averages per 100,000 estimated population 1994–1996. National Center for Health Statistics. On the Internet: http://www.cdc.gov/nchs/datawh/statab/useTables.htm.

WBALLDEA Table G.90 Women, black, all deaths, rates three-year averages per 100,000 estimated population 1994–1996. National Center for Health Statistics. On the Internet: http://www.cdc.gov/nchs/datawh/statab/useTables.htm.

WBMALIG Table G.92 Women, black, all malignant neoplasms deaths, rates three-year averages per 100,000 estimated population 1994–1996. National Center for Health Statistics. On the Internet: http://www.cdc.gov/nchs/datawh/statab/useTables.htm.

WBDIABET Table G.94 Women, black, diabetes deaths, rates three-year averages per 100,000 estimated population 1994–1996. National Center for Health Statistics. On the Internet: http://www.cdc.gov/nchs/datawh/statab/useTables.htm.

WBNUTRI Table G.96 Women, black, nutritional deficiencies deaths, rates three-year averages per 100,000 estimated population 1994–1996. National Center for Health Statistics. On the Internet: http://www.cdc.gov/nchs/datawh/statab/useTables.htm.

WBCARDIO Table G.98 Women, black, major cardiovascular diseases deaths, rates three-year averages per 100,000 estimated population 1994–1996. National Center for Health Statistics. On the Internet: http://www.cdc.gov/nchs/datawh/statab/useTables.htm.

WBPNEUMO Table G.100 Women, black, pneumonia and influenza deaths, rates three-year averages per 100,000 estimated population 1994–1996. National Center for Health Statistics. On the Internet: http://www.cdc.gov/nchs/datawh/statab/useTables.htm.

WBACCID Table G.102 Women, black, accidents and adverse effects deaths, rates three-year averages per 100,000 estimated population 1994–1996. National Center for Health Statistics. On the Internet: http://www.cdc.gov/nchs/datawh/statab/useTables.htm.

WBMOTVEH Table G.104 Women, black, motor vehicle accidents deaths, rates three-year averages per 100,000 estimated population 1994–1996. National Center for Health Statistics. On the Internet: http://www.cdc.gov/nchs/datawh/statab/useTables.htm.

WBFALLS Table G.106 Women, black, falls deaths, rates three-year averages per 100,000 estimated population 1994–1996. National Center for Health Statistics. On the Internet: http://www.cdc.gov/nchs/datawh/statab/useTables.htm.

WBSUICID Table G.108 Women, black, suicides, rates three-year averages per 100,000 estimated population 1994–1996. National Center for Health Statistics. On the Internet: http://www.cdc.gov/nchs/datawh/statab/useTables.htm.

WBHOMICI Table G.110 Women, black, homicides rates three-year averages per 100,000 estimated population 1994–1996. National Center for Health Statistics. On the Internet: http://www.cdc.gov/nchs/datawh/statab/useTables.htm.

WBDRUGIN Table G.112 Women, black, drug-induced deaths, rates three-year averages per 100,000 estimated population 1994–1996. National Center for Health Statistics. On the Internet: http://www.cdc.gov/nchs/datawh/statab/useTables.htm.

WBALCOHO Table G.114 Women, black, alcohol-induced deaths, rates three-year averages per 100,000 estimated population 1994–1996. National Center for Health Statistics. On the Internet: http://www.cdc.gov/nchs/datawh/statab/useTables.htm.

MWALLDEA Table G.115 Men, white, all deaths, rates three-year averages per 100,000 estimated population 1994–1996. National Center for Health Statistics. On the Internet: http://www.cdc.gov/nchs/datawh/statab/useTables.htm.

MWMALIG Table G.117 Men, white, all malignant neoplasms deaths, rates three-year averages per 100,000 estimated population 1994–1996. National Center for Health Statistics. On the Internet: http://www.cdc.gov/nchs/datawh/statab/useTables.htm.

MWDIABET Table G.119 Men, white, diabetes deaths, rates three-year averages per 100,000 estimated population 1994–1996. National Center for Health Statistics. On the Internet: http://www.cdc.gov/nchs/datawh/statab/useTables.htm.

MWNUTRI Table G.121 Men, white, nutritional deficiencies deaths, rates three-year averages per 100,000 estimated population 1994–1996. National Center for Health Statistics. On the Internet: http://www.cdc.gov/nchs/datawh/statab/useTables.htm

MWCARDIO Table G.123 Men, white, major cardiovascular diseases deaths, rates three-year averages per 100,000 estimated population 1994–1996. National Center for Health Statistics. On the Internet: http://www.cdc.gov/nchs/datawh/statab/useTables.htm.

MWPNEUMO Table G.125 Men, white, pneumonia and influenza deaths, rates three-year averages per 100,000 estimated population 1994–1996. National Center for Health Statistics. On the Internet: http://www.cdc.gov/nchs/datawh/statab/useTables.htm.

MWACCID Table G.127 Men, white, accidents and adverse effects deaths, rates three-year averages per 100,000 estimated population 1994–1996. National Center for Health Statistics. On the Internet: http://www.cdc.gov/nchs/datawh/statab/useTables.htm.

MWMOTVEH Table G.129 Men, white, motor vehicle accidents deaths, rates three-year averages per 100,000 estimated population 1994–1996. National Center for Health Statistics. On the Internet: http://www.cdc.gov/nchs/datawh/statab/useTables.htm.

MWFALLS Table G.131 Men, white, falls, rates three-year averages per 100,000 estimated population 1994–1996. National Center for Health Statistics. On the Internet: http://www.cdc.gov/nchs/datawh/statab/useTables.htm.

MWSUICID Table G.133 Men, white, suicides, rates three-year averages per 100,000 estimated population 1994–1996. National Center for Health Statistics. On the Internet: http://www.cdc.gov/nchs/datawh/statab/useTables.htm.

MWHOMICI Table G.135 Men, white, homocides, rates three-year averages per 100,000 estimated population 1994–1996. National Center for Health Statistics. On the Internet: http://www.cdc.gov/nchs/datawh/statab/useTables.htm.

MWDRUGIN Table G.137 Men, white, drug-induced deaths, rates three-year averages per 100,000 estimated population 1994–1996. National Center for Health Statistics. On the Internet: http://www.cdc.gov/nchs/datawh/statab/useTables.htm.

MWALCOHO Table G.139 Men, white, alcohol-induced deaths, rates three-year averages per 100,000 estimated population 1994–1996. National Center for Health Statistics. On the Internet: http://www.cdc.gov/nchs/datawh/statab/useTables.htm.

MBALLDEA Table G.116 Men, black, all deaths, rates three-year averages per 100,000 estimated population 1994–1996. National Center for Health Statistics. On the Internet: http://www.cdc.gov/nchs/datawh/statab/useTables.htm.

MBMALIG Table G.118 Men, black, all malignant neoplasms deaths, rates three-year averages per 100,000 estimated population 1994–1996. National Center for Health Statistics. On the Internet: http://www.cdc.gov/nchs/datawh/statab/useTables.htm.

MBDIABET Table G.120 Men, black, diabetes deaths, rates three-year averages per 100,000 estimated population 1994–1996. National Center for Health Statistics. On the Internet: http://www.cdc.gov/nchs/datawh/statab/useTables.htm.

MBNUTRI Table G.122 Men, black, nutritional deficiencies deaths, rates three-year averages per 100,000 estimated population 1994–1996. National Center for Health Statistics. On the Internet: http://www.cdc.gov/nchs/datawh/statab/useTables.htm.

MBCARDIO Table G.124 Men, black, major cardiovascular diseases deaths, rates three-year averages per 100,000 estimated population 1994–1996. National Center for Health Statistics. On the Internet: http://www.cdc.gov/nchs/datawh/statab/useTables.htm.

MBPNEUMO Table G.126 Men, black, pneumonia and influenza deaths, rates three-year averages per 100,000 estimated population 1994–1996. National Center for Health Statistics. On the Internet: http://www.cdc.gov/nchs/datawh/statab/useTables.htm.

MBACCID Table G.128 Men, black, accidents and adverse effects deaths, rates three-year averages per 100,000 estimated population 1994–1996. National Center for Health Statistics. On the Internet: http://www.cdc.gov/nchs/datawh/statab/useTables.htm.

MBMOTVEH Table G.130 Men, black, motor vehicle accidents deaths, rates three-year averages per 100,000 estimated population 1994–1996. National Center for Health Statistics. On the Internet: http://www.cdc.gov/nchs/datawh/statab/useTables.htm.

MBFALLS Table G.132 Men, black, falls deaths, rates three-year averages per 100,000 estimated population 1994–1996. National Center for Health Statistics. On the Internet: http://www.cdc.gov/nchs/datawh/statab/useTables.htm.

MBSUICID Table G.134 Men, black, suicides, rates three-year averages per 100,000 estimated population 1994–1996. National Center for Health Statistics. On the Internet: http://www.cdc.gov/nchs/datawh/statab/useTables.htm.

MBHOMICI Table G.136 Men, black, homicides, rates three-year averages per 100,000 estimated population 1994–1996. National Center for Health Statistics. On the Internet: http://www.cdc.gov/nchs/datawh/statab/useTables.htm.

MBDRUGIN Table G.138 Men, black, drug-induced deaths, rates three-year averages per 100,000 estimated population 1994–1996. National Center for Health Statistics. On the Internet: http://www.cdc.gov/nchs/datawh/statab/useTables.htm.

MBALCOHO Table G.140 Men, black, alcohol-induced deaths, rates three-year averages per 100,000 estimated population 1994–1996. National Center for Health Statistics. On the Internet: http://www.cdc.gov/nchs/datawh/statab/useTables.htm.

BURDENPR Table G.141 Average cost to each person in the state (i.e., burden on each citizen) to fund the state prison system, including both operating and capital expenditures.
Calculated: TOTPRISN / POPEST99

CONSTRPC Table G.143 Percent of total population that works in construction.
Calculated: (CONSTRUC / POPEST99) * 100

MANUFAPC Table G.144 Percent of total population that works in manufacturing.
Calculated: (MANUFACT / POPEST99) * 100

TRANSPC Table G.145 Percent of total population that works in transportation and public utilities.
Calculated: (TRANSPU / POPEST99) * 100

TRADEPC Table G.146 Percent of total population that works in trade.
Calculated: (TRADE / POPEST99) * 100

FINANCPC Table G.147 Percent of total population that works in finance, insurance, and real estate.
Calculated: (FINANCE / POPEST99) * 100

SERVICPC Table G.148 Percent of total population that works in services.
Calculated: (SERVICES / POPEST99) * 100

GOVFSLPC Table G.142 Percent of total population that works in federal, state, and local government.
Calculated: (GOVTFSL / POPEST99) * 100

UNEMPIST Table G.149 State unemployment insurance, in thousands of dollars, 1998. From No. 617, page 388, *Statistical Abstract of the United States*, 2000.

UNEMPAVR Table G.150 Unemployment insurance average weekly employment benefits, 1998. From No. 617, page 388, *Statistical Abstract of the United States*, 2000.

WORKCOMP Table G.151 Workers' compensation payments, 1998. From No. 622, page 390, *Statistical Abstract of the United States*, 2000.

TEMPASST Table G.152 Temporary assistance for needy families, 1999, in thousands of dollars. From No. 626, page 392, *Statistical Abstract of the United States*, 2000.

FOODSTAM Table G.153 Federal food stamp program, 1999, in thousands of dollars. From No. 630, page 393, *Statistical Abstract of the United States*, 2000.

CHILDCAR Table G.154 Licensed child care centers, 1999. From No. 634, page 395, *Statistical Abstract of the United States*, 2000.

MALABOR Table G.155 Percent of males over the age of 16 participating in civilian labor force, 1999. From No. 648, page 406, *Statistical Abstract of the United States*, 2000.

FEMLABOR Table G.156 Percent of females over the age of 16 participating in civilian labor force, 1999. From No. 648, page 406, *Statistical Abstract of the United States*, 2000.

TOTUNEMP Table G.157 Percent of total population over the age of 16 participating in civilian labor force that was unemployed in 1999. From No. 680, page 425, *Statistical Abstract of the United States*, 2000.

INSUNEMP Table G.158 Percent of total population over the age of 16 participating in civilian labor force that was unemployed in 1999 and was insured. From No. 680, page 425, *Statistical Abstract of the United States*, 2000.

AVRPAY Table G.159 Average annual pay 1998 for workers covered by state unemployment insurance laws and for federal civilian workers (approximately 98 percent of wage and salary workers) in 1998. From No. 694, page 436, *Statistical Abstract of the United States*, 2000.

PCUNION Table G.160 Percent of workers who were covered by unions, 1999. From No. 714, page 446, *Statistical Abstract of the United States*, 2000.

STATPROD Table G.163 Gross state produce in current dollars (in billions) in 1997. From No. 719, page 454, *Statistical Abstract of the United States*, 2000.

PERINCOM Table G.161 Personal income in current dollars (in billions) in 1999. From No. 726, page 459, *Statistical Abstract of the United States*, 2000.

INCOMEPC Table G.162 Personal income per capita in 1999. From No. 727, page 460, *Statistical Abstract of the United States*, 2000.

MEDINC98 Table G.165 Median income of households, 1998. From No. 742, page 469, *Statistical Abstract of the United States*, 2000.

PERBELPV Table G.166 Percent of persons below poverty level, 1998. From No. 759, page 477, *Statistical Abstract of the United States*, 2000.

REFGASPR Table G.167 Refiner/reseller sales price of one gallon of gasoline, 1998. From No. 785, page 504, *Statistical Abstract of the United States*, 2000.

BANKASST Table G.168 Assets of insured commercial banks (in billions), 1999. From No. 806, page 514, *Statistical Abstract of the United States*, 2000.

BANKDEP Table G.169 Deposits of insured commercial banks (in billions), 1999. From No. 806, page 514, *Statistical Abstract of the United States*, 2000.

INCOMEUP Table G.170 Increase in median income per household from 1990 to 1998.
Calculated: MEDINC98–MEDINCOM

CARINSUR Table G.171 Auto insurance, average expenditure per vehicle, 1998. From No. 850, page 531, *Statistical Abstract of the United States*, 2000.

BANKRUPT Table G.172 Bankruptcy cases filed (in thousands), 1999. From No. 878, page 549, *Statistical Abstract of the United States*, 2000.

BANKRPPC Table G.164 Bankruptcy cases filed as percent of total population.
Calculated: (BANKRUPT / POPEST99) * 100

PATENTS Table G.173 Number of patents granted to residents of the state, 1998. From No. 885, page 552, *Statistical Abstract of the United States*, 2000.

PATENTPC Table G.174 Number of patents granted for each 100,000 residents of the state, 1998. Calculated: (PATENTS / POPEST99) * 100

COMPUTER Table G.175 Percent of households with computers. From No. 915, page 569, *Statistical Abstract of the United States*, 2000.

INTERNET Table G.176 Percent of households with access to the Internet. From No. 915, page 569, *Statistical Abstract of the United States*, 2000.

RDINDTOT Table G.177 Total R&D expenditures by industry, in millions, 1998. From No. 981, page 605, *Statistical Abstract of the United States*, 2000.

RDUNITOT Table G.178 Total R&D expenditures by universities and colleges, in millions, 1998. From No. 981, page 605, *Statistical Abstract of the United States*, 2000.

RDINDPC Table G.179 R&D expenditures by industry, per capita, 1998. Calculated: RDINDTOT / (POPEST99 / 1,000)

RDUNIPC Table G.180 R&D expenditures by universities and colleges, per capita, 1998. Calculated: RDUNITOT / (POPEST99 / 1,000)

NUMBRIDG Table G.181 Number of bridges in state, 1998. From No. 1016, page 623, *Statistical Abstract of the United States*, 2000.

BRIDGDEF Table G.182 Percent of bridges structurally deficient, 1998. From No. 1016, page 623, *Statistical Abstract of the United States*, 2000.

BRIDGOBS Table G.183 Percent of bridges functionally obsolete, 1998. From No. 1016, page 623, *Statistical Abstract of the United States*, 2000.

HIWAYFND Table G.184 Disbursement of state highway funds by state, 1998. From No. 1020, page 625, *Statistical Abstract of the United States*, 2000.

HIWAYFED Table G.185 Per capita federal grants to state and local governments for Federal Transit Administration 1999. From No. 1021, page 625, *Statistical Abstract of the United States*, 2000.

HIWAYTRS Table G.186 Per capita federal grants to state and local governments for Highway Trust Fund 1999. From No. 1021, page 625, *Statistical Abstract of the United States*, 2000.

GASTAX Table G.187 State gasoline tax rates, 1998. From No. 1022, page 625, *Statistical Abstract of the United States*, 2000.

AUTOREG Table G.188 Motor vehicle registration (automobiles) in thousands, 1998. From No. 1026, page 627, *Statistical Abstract of the United States*, 2000.

FATALCOH Table G.189 Percent of accidents in 1998 in which fatalities occurred and at least some alcohol was evident (> 0.01). From No. 1041, page 637, *Statistical Abstract of the United States*, 2000.

TRAFATAL Table G.190 Traffic fatalities, 1998. From No. 1041, page 637, *Statistical Abstract of the United States*, 2000.

TRAFATPT Table G.193 Number of traffic fatalities per 1,000 population. Calculated: TRAFATAL / POPEST99

FARMINCO Table G.191 Net farm income, 1998, in millions. From No. 1112, page 671, *Statistical Abstract of the United States*, 2000.

MINERAL Table G.192 Value of domestic non-fuel mineral production, in millions, 1999. From No. 1169, page 698, *Statistical Abstract of the United States*, 2000.

FARMINPP Table G.195 Farm income per person in total population, 1998. Calculated: FARMINCO / (POPEST99 / 1,000)

MINERLPP Table G.196 Income from minerals per person in total population, 1999. Calculated: MINERAL / (POPEST99 / 1,000)

CONCONTR Table G.197 Value of all construction contracts in which work was actually done, 1999. From No. 1193, page 712, *Statistical Abstract of the United States*, 2000.

MANPEMP Table G.198 Earnings per employee involved in manufacturing, 1996. From No. 1231, page 735, *Statistical Abstract of the United States*, 2000.

RETAIL Table G.199 Retail sales per household, 1998. From No. 1295, page 766, *Statistical Abstract of the United States*, 2000.

INVESTUS Table G.200 Foreign direct investment in the United States, 1997 (gross book value). From No. 1314, page 784, *Statistical Abstract of the United States*, 2000.

FOREMPLY Table G.201 Number of employees (in thousands) who work for foreign firms which have made direct investment in the United States, 1997. From No. 1314, page 784, *Statistical Abstract of the United States*, 2000.

IMMIGRNT Table G.202 Immigrants admitted by state, 1998. From No. 9, page 11, *Statistical Abstract of the United States*, 2000.

METROPOP Table G.203 Percent of state residing in one of 258 metropolitan statistical areas 1999. From No. 33, page 32, *Statistical Abstract of the United States*, 2000.

HOUSHOLD Table G.204 Number of households (in thousands), 1998. From No. 63, page 55, *Statistical Abstract of the United States*, 2000.

CHRISTAN Table G.205 Percent of population which is Christian, 1990. From No. 76, page 62, *Statistical Abstract of the United States*, 2000.

JEWISH Table G.206 Percent of population which is Jewish, 1990. From No. 76, page 62, *Statistical Abstract of the United States*, 2000.

LOWBIRWT Table G.207 Percent of children born who were low birth weight, 1998. From No. 88, page 71, *Statistical Abstract of the United States*, 2000.

TEENBRTH Table G.208 Percent of total children born to teenage mothers, 1998. From No. 88, page 71, *Statistical Abstract of the United States*, 2000.

UNMARRBR Table G.209 Percent of total children born to unmarried women, 1998. From No. 88, page 71, *Statistical Abstract of the United States*, 2000.

ABORTION Table G.210 Abortion rates (per 1,000 women 15 to 44 years of age), 1996. From No. 114, page 83, *Statistical Abstract of the United States*, 2000.

DEATHS Table G.211 Rate of death per 1,000 population 1999. From No. 121, page 87, *Statistical Abstract of the United States*, 2000.

INFMORTT Table G.212 Total infant mortality rates (deaths per 1,000 live births), 1997. From No. 125, page 89, *Statistical Abstract of the United States*, 2000.

INFMORTW Total 213 Total infant mortality rates, white (deaths per 1,000 live births), 1997. From No. 125, page 89, *Statistical Abstract of the United States*, 2000.

INFMORTB Table G.214 Total infant mortality rates, black (deaths per 1,000 live births), 1997. From No. 125, page 89, *Statistical Abstract of the United States*, 2000.

DEATHALL Table G.215 Death rate for all causes per 100,000 resident population, 1997. From No. 130, page 94, *Statistical Abstract of the United States*, 2000.

DEATHART Table G.216 Death rate for heart disease per 100,000 resident population, 1997. From No. 130, page 94, *Statistical Abstract of the United States*, 2000.

DEATHCAN Table G.217 Death rate for cancer per 100,000 resident population, 1997. From No. 130, page 94, *Statistical Abstract of the United States*, 2000.

DEATHCER Table G.218 Death rate from cerebrovascular diseases per 100,000 resident population, 1997. From No. 130, page 94, *Statistical Abstract of the United States*, 2000.

DEATHACC Table G.219 Death rate from general accidents and adverse effects per 100,000 resident population, 1997. From No. 130, page 94, *Statistical Abstract of the United States*, 2000.

DEATHMV Table G.220 Death rate from motor vehicle accidents per 100,000 resident population, 1997. From No. 130, page 94, *Statistical Abstract of the United States*, 2000.

DEATHPUL Table G.221 Death rate from chronic obstructive pulmonary diseases per 100,000 resident population, 1997. From No. 130, page 94, *Statistical Abstract of the United States*, 2000.

DEATHDIA Table G.222 Death rate from diabetes mellitus per 100,000 resident population, 1997. From No. 130, page 94, *Statistical Abstract of the United States*, 2000.

DEATHIV Table G.223 Death rate from human immunodeficiency virus per 100,000 resident population, 1997. From No. 130, page 94, *Statistical Abstract of the United States*, 2000.

DEATHSUI Table G.224 Death rate from suicide per 100,000 resident population, 1997. From No. 130, page 94, *Statistical Abstract of the United States*, 2000.

DEATHOMI Table G.194 Death rate from homicide per 100,000 resident population, 1997. From No. 130, page 94, *Statistical Abstract of the United States*, 2000.

MEDCAREE Table G.225 Enrollment in Medicare (in thousands), 1999. From No. 169, page 115, *Statistical Abstract of the United States*, 2000.

MEDCAREP Table G.226 Payments in Medicare (in millions), 1999. From No. 169, page 115, *Statistical Abstract of the United States*, 2000.

PAYENROL Table G.227 Dollars paid per each enrollee in Medicare, 1999.
Calculated: (MEDCAREP / MEDCAREE) * 1,000

MEDCAIDR Table G.228 Recipients of Medicaid (in thousands), 1998. From No. 173, page 116, *Statistical Abstract of the United States*, 2000.

MEDCAIDP Table G.229 Payments of Medicaid (in millions), 1998. From No. 173, page 116, *Statistical Abstract of the United States*, 2000.

PAYRECIP Table G.230 Dollars paid per each recipient in Medicaid, 1998.
Calculated: (MEDCAIDP / MEDCAIDR) * 1,000

NOCOVER Table G.231 Percent of persons without health insurance, 1998. From No. 178, page 118, *Statistical Abstract of the United States*, 2000.

CHINOCOV Table G.232 Percent of children without health insurance, 1998. From No. 178, page 118, *Statistical Abstract of the United States*, 2000.

DOCTORS Table G.233 Number of active physicians (per 100,000 resident population), 1998. From No. 187, page 123, *Statistical Abstract of the United States*, 2000.

AIDS Table G.235 Number of AIDS cases reported in the state, 1998. From No. 218, page 138, *Statistical Abstract of the United States*, 2000.

SYPHILIS Table G.237 Number of syphilis cases reported in the state, 1998. From No. 218, page 138, *Statistical Abstract of the United States*, 2000.

TB Table G.239 Number of tuberculosis cases reported in the state, 1998. From No. 218, page 138, *Statistical Abstract of the United States*, 2000.

AIDSPT Table G.236 Number of AIDS cases reported in the state, per 1,000 population.
Calculated: AIDS / POPEST99

SYPHILPT Table G.238 Number of syphilis cases reported in the state in 1998, per 1,000 population.
Calculated: SYPHILIS / POPEST99

TBPT Table G.240 Number of tuberculosis cases reported in the state in 1998, per 1,000 population.
Calculated: TB / POPEST99

MCIGARET Table G.241 Percent of males who reported smoking more than 100 cigarettes, 1998. From No. 227, page 142, *Statistical Abstract of the United States*, 2000.

FCIGARET Table G.242 Percent of females who reported smoking more than 100 cigarettes, 1998. From

No. 227, page 142, *Statistical Abstract of the United States,* 2000.

HSGRAD   Table G.243   Percent of persons 25 or older who reported that they had graduated from high school, 1999. From No. 253, page 159, *Statistical Abstract of the United States,* 2000.

COLLGRAD   Table G.244   Percent of persons 25 or older who reported that they had graduated from college, 1999. From No. 227, page 142, *Statistical Abstract of the United States,* 2000.

K8ENROLL   Table G.245   Number of persons (in thousands) enrolled in public school, grades K through 8, 1998. From No. 266, page 167, *Statistical Abstract of the United States,* 2000.

HSENROLL   Table G.246   Number of persons (in thousands) enrolled in public school, grades 9 through 12, 1998. From No. 266, page 167, *Statistical Abstract of the United States,* 2000.

ADAPP   Table G.247   Expenditures per pupil in average daily attendance for public school students, 1999. From No. 275, page 172, *Statistical Abstract of the United States,* 2000.

COLENROL   Table G.248   Total college student enrollment in degree-granting institutions, in thousands, 1997. From No. 299, page 185, *Statistical Abstract of the United States,* 2000.

COLLEGPC   Table G.249   Percent of total population of state enrolled in college, 1997.
Calculated: (COLENROL / POPEST99) * 100

CHILDPOV   Table G.250   Percent of children 5 to 17 in poverty, 1998. Digest of Education Statistics 2000. From the Internet: http://nces.ed.gov/pubs2001/digest/ch2/html Table 20, p. 27.

SCHAGE   Table G.251   Total number of 5 to 17 year olds (i.e., school-age children), in thousands, 1999. Digest of Education Statistics 2000. From the Internet: http://nces.ed.gov/pubs2001/digest/ch2/html Table 17, p. 24.

EXPCOLL   Table G.257   Total expenditures for colleges and universities (in millions), 1995–1996. Digest of Education Statistics 2000. From the Internet: http://nces.ed.gov/pubs2001/digest/ch2/html, Table 34, p. 37.

ELESECPC   Table G.258   Amount of per capita expenditures for elementary and secondary education, 1995–1996. Digest of Education Statistics 2000. From the Internet: http://nces.ed.gov/pubs2001/digest/ch2/html, Table 35, p. 38.

COLUNIPC   Table G.252   Amount of per capita expenditures for colleges and universities, 1995–1996. Digest of Education Statistics 2000. From the Internet: http://nces.ed.gov/pubs2001/digest/ch2/html, Table 35, p. 38.

TOBALCRV   Table G.253   Tobacco and alcohol tax revenue, per capita. From "Shoveling Up: The Impact of Substance Abuse on State Budgets," The National Center on Addiction and Substance Abuse at Columbia University, January 2001.

SUBABUPC   Table G.254   Total per capita spending related to substance abuse. From "Shoveling Up: The Impact of Substance Abuse on State Budgets," The National Center on Addiction and Substance Abuse at Columbia University, January 2001.

HOSPBEDS   Table G.255   Number of hospital beds (in thousands), 1998. From No. 196, page 128, *Statistical Abstract of the United States,* 2000.

HOSPBEDP   Table G.256   Number of hospital beds per 1,000 population, 1998.
Calculated: HOSPBEDS / POPEST99

TAXRECD   Table G.234   Total funds received through taxes from alcohol and tobacco as a percent of the total funds expended to maintain prisons and other services required to take care of problems created from substance abuse.
Calculated: (TOBALCRV / SUBABUPC) * 100

VIOL39   Table G.259   Total number of violent crimes (i.e., murder, assault, rape, and robbery) reported 1960 to 1998. Sum computed from data provided in annual reports to the Bureau of Justice Statistics in Uniform Crime Reports by the Federal Bureau of Investigation and organized into separate computer files for each state (e.g., UCRAL, for Alabama). On the Internet: http://www.ojp.usdoj/gov/bjs/datast.htm.

VIOL6098   Table G.261   Average number of violent crimes (i.e., murder, assault, rape, and robbery) per 1,000 total population reported 1960 to 1998.
Calculated: VIOLEN39 / 100

PROP6098   Table G.265   Average number of property crimes (i.e., burglary, auto theft, and larceny) per 1,000 total population reported 1960 to 1998.
Calculated: PROPER39 / 100

VIOLENT   Table G.262 (also G.325)   Average number of violent crimes (i.e., murder, assault, rape, and robbery; see G.323) per 1,000 total population in 1998.
Calculated: VIOLENCE / POP

PROPER   Table G.266 (also G.326)   Average number of property crimes (i.e., burglary, auto theft, and larceny; see G.324) per 1,000 total population in 1998.
Calculated: PROPERTY / POP

MURDER   Table G.270 (also G.12)   This number represents the murder rate per 1,000 population in that state for 1998. The number was calculated by dividing MURD by POP, and makes the values for each of the states comparable.
Calculated: MURD / POP

RAPE   Table G.274 (also G.14)   This number represents the rape rate per 1,000 population in that state for 1998. The number was calculated by dividing RAPES by POP, and makes the values for each of the states comparable.
Calculated: RAPES / POP

ASSAULT   Table G.282 (also G.13)   This number represents the assault rate per 1,000 population in that state in 1998. The number was calculated by dividing ASLT by POP, and makes the values for each of the states comparable.

Calculated: ASLT / POP

ROBBERY Table G.278 (also G.15) This number represents the robbery rate per 1,000 population in that state for 1998. The number was calculated by dividing ROB by POP, and makes the values for each of the states comparable.

Calculated: ROB / POP

BURGLARY Table G.286 (also G.17) This number represents the burglary rate per 1,000 population in that state for 1998. The number was calculated by dividing BURG by POP, and makes the values for each of the states comparable.

Calculated: BURG / POP

LARCENY Table G.290 (also G.18) This number represents the larceny rate per 1,000 population in that state for 1998. The number was calculated by dividing LARC by POP, and makes the values for each of the states comparable. Calculated: LARC / POP

CARTHEFT Table G.294 (also G.19) This number represents the auto theft rate per 1,000 population in that state for 1998. The number was calculated by dividing THEFT by POP, and makes the values for each of the states comparable.

Calculated: THEFT / POP

PROP39 Table G.263 Total number of property crimes (i.e., burglary, larceny, motor vehicle, theft) reported 1960 to 1998. Sum computed from data provided in annual reports to the Bureau of Justice Statistics in Uniform Crime Reports by the Federal Bureau of Investigation and organized into separate computer files for each state (e.g., UCRAL, for Uniform Crime Report Alabama). On the Internet: http://www.ojp.usdoj/gov/bjs/datast.htm.

MURD39 Table G.267 Total number of murders reported 1960 to 1998. Sum computed from data provided in annual reports to the Bureau of Justice Statistics in Uniform Crime Reports by the Federal Bureau of Investigation and organized into separate computer files for each state (e.g., UCRAL, for Uniform Crime Report Alabama). On the Internet: http://www.ojp.usdoj/gov/bjs/datast.htm.

RAPES39 Table G.271 Total number of forcible rapes reported 1960 to 1998. Sum computed from data provided in annual reports to the Bureau of Justice Statistics in Uniform Crime Reports by the Federal Bureau of Investigation and organized into separate computer files for each state (e.g., UCRAL, for Uniform Crime Report Alabama). On the Internet: http://www.ojp.usdoj/gov/bjs/datast.htm.

ROB39 Table G.275 Total number of robberies reported 1960 to 1998. Sum computed from data provided in annual reports to the Bureau of Justice Statistics in Uniform Crime Reports by the Federal Bureau of Investigation and organized into separate computer files

for each state (e.g., UCRAL, for Uniform Crime Report Alabama). On the Internet: http://www.ojp.usdoj/gov/bjs/datast.htm.

ASLT39 Table G.279 Total number of aggravated assaults reported 1960 to 1998. Sum computed from data provided in annual reports to the Bureau of Justice Statistics in Uniform Crime Reports by the Federal Bureau of Investigation and organized into separate computer files for each state (e.g., UCRAL, for Uniform Crime Report Alabama). On the Internet: http://www.ojp.usdoj/gov/bjs/datast.htm.

BURG39 Table G.283 Total number of burglaries reported 1960 to 1998. Sum computed from data provided in annual reports to the Bureau of Justice Statistics in Uniform Crime Reports by the Federal Bureau of Investigation and organized into separate computer files for each state (e.g., UCRAL, for Uniform Crime Report Alabama). On the Internet: http://www.ojp.usdoj/gov/bjs/datast.htm.

LARC39 Table G.287 Total number of larcenies reported 1960 to 1998. Sum computed from data provided in annual reports to the Bureau of Justice Statistics in Uniform Crime Reports by the Federal Bureau of Investigation and organized into separate computer files for each state (e.g., UCRAL, for Uniform Crime Report Alabama). On the Internet: http://www.ojp.usdoj/gov/bjs/datast.htm.

THEFT39 Table G.291 Total number of motor vehicle thefts reported 1960 to 1998. Sum computed from data provided in annual reports to the Bureau of Justice Statistics in Uniform Crime Reports by the Federal Bureau of Investigation and organized into separate computer files for each state (e.g., UCRAL, for Uniform Crime Report Alabama). On the Internet: http://www.ojp.usdoj/gov/bjs/datast.htm.

VIOLEN39 Table G.260 Average number of violent crimes (i.e., murder, assault, rape, and robbery) per 100,000 total population reported 1960 to 1998. Mean computed from data provided in annual reports to the Bureau of Justice Statistics in Uniform Crime Reports by the Federal Bureau of Investigation and organized into separate computer files for each state (e.g., UCRAL, for Uniform Crime Report Alabama). On the Internet: http://www.ojp.usdoj/gov/bjs/datast.htm.

PROPER39 Table G.264 Average number of property crimes (i.e., burglary, larceny, motor vehicle, theft) per 100,000 total population reported 1960 to 1998. Mean computed from data provided in annual reports to the Bureau of Justice Statistics in Uniform Crime Reports by the Federal Bureau of Investigation and organized into separate computer files for each state (e.g., UCRAL, for Uniform Crime Report Alabama). On the Internet: http://www.ojp.usdoj/gov/bjs/datast.htm.

MURDER39 Table G.268 Average number of murders per 100,000 total population reported 1960 to 1998. Mean computed from data provided in annual reports to the Bureau of Justice Statistics in Uniform Crime Reports by the Federal Bureau of Investigation and organized into separate computer files for each state (e.g., UCRAL, for Uniform Crime Report Alabama). On the Internet: http://www.ojp.usdoj/gov/bjs/datast.htm.

RAPE39 Table G.272 Average number of forcible rapes per 100,000 total population reported 1960 to 1998. Mean computed from data provided in annual reports to the Bureau of Justice Statistics in Uniform Crime Reports by the Federal Bureau of Investigation and organized into separate computer files for each state (e.g., UCRAL, for Uniform Crime Report Alabama). On the Internet: http://www.ojp.usdoj/gov/bjs/datast.htm.

ROBBER39 Table G.276 Average number of robberies per 100,000 total population reported 1960 to 1998. Mean computed from data provided in annual reports to the Bureau of Justice Statistics in Uniform Crime Reports by the Federal Bureau of Investigation and organized into separate computer files for each state (e.g., UCRAL, for Uniform Crime Report Alabama). On the Internet: http://www.ojp.usdoj/gov/bjs/datast.htm.

ASSAUL39 Table G.280 Average number of aggravated assaults per 100,000 total population reported 1960 to 1998. Mean computed from data provided in annual reports to the Bureau of Justice Statistics in Uniform Crime Reports by the Federal Bureau of Investigation and organized into separate computer files for each state (e.g., UCRAL, for Uniform Crime Report Alabama). On the Internet: http://www.ojp.usdoj/gov/bjs/datast.htm.

BURGLA39 Table G.284 Average number of burglaries per 100,000 total population reported 1960 to 1998. Mean computed from data provided in annual reports to the Bureau of Justice Statistics in Uniform Crime Reports by the Federal Bureau of Investigation and organized into separate computer files for each state (e.g., UCRAL, for Uniform Crime Report Alabama). On the Internet: http://www.ojp.usdoj/gov/bjs/datast.htm.

LARCEN39 Table G.288 Average number of larcenies per 100,000 total population reported 1960 to 1998. Mean computed from data provided in annual reports to the Bureau of Justice Statistics in Uniform Crime Reports by the Federal Bureau of Investigation and organized into separate computer files for each state (e.g., UCRAL, for Uniform Crime Report Alabama). On the Internet: http://www.ojp.usdoj/gov/bjs/datast.htm.

MVT39 Table G.292 Average number of motor vehicle thefts per 100,000 total population reported 1960 to 1998. Mean computed from data provided in annual reports to the Bureau of Justice Statistics in Uniform Crime Reports by the Federal Bureau of Investigation and organized into separate computer files for each state (e.g., UCRAL, for Uniform Crime Report Alabama). On the Internet:http://www.ojp.usdoj/gov/bjs/datast.htm.

MURD6098 Table G.269 Average number of murders per 1,000 total population reported 1960 to 1998.
Calculated: MURDER39 / 100

RAPE6098 Table G.273 Average number of rapes per 1,000 total population reported 1960 to 1998.
Calculated: RAPE39 / 100

ASLT6098 Table G.281 Average number of aggravated assaults per 1,000 total population reported 1960 to 1998.
Calculated: ASSAUE39 / 100

BURG6098 Table G.285 Average number of burglaries per 1,000 total population reported 1960 to 1998.
Calculated: BURGLA39 / 100

LARC6098 Table G.289 Average number of larcenies per 1,000 total population reported 1960 to 1998.
Calculated: LARENC39 / 100

MVT6098 Table G.293 Average number of motor vehicle thefts per 1,000 total population reported 1960 to 1998.
Calculated: MVT39 / 100

TOTALFEM Table G.295 Total number of females ages 15–19 in the state, 1996. "When Teens Have Sex: Issues and Trends," state profile. The Annie E. Casey Foundation, Baltimore, Md. On the Internet: http://www.aecf.org/cgi-bin/teen.cgi?DATASET=AL.

NHWHITE Table G.296 Number of non-Hispanic white females in the state, 1996. "When Teens Have Sex: Issues and Trends," state profile. The Annie E. Casey Foundation, Baltimore, Md. On the Internet: http://www.aecf.org/cgi-bin/teen.cgi?DATASET=AL.

NHBLACK Table G.297 Number of non-Hispanic black females in the state, 1996. "When Teens Have Sex: Issues and Trends," state profile. The Annie E. Casey Foundation, Baltimore, Md. On the Internet: http://www.aecf.org/cgi-bin/teen.cgi?DATASET=AL.

HISPANIC Table G.298 Number of Hispanic females in the state, 1996. "When Teens Have Sex: Issues and Trends," state profile. The Annie E. Casey Foundation, Baltimore, Md. On the Internet: http://www.aecf.org/cgi-bin/teen.cgi?DATASET=AL.

OTHERACE Table G.299 Number of American Indian, Asian, and Pacific Islander females in the state, 1996. "When Teens Have Sex: Issues and Trends," state profile. The Annie E. Casey Foundation, Baltimore, Md. On the Internet: http://www.aecf.org/cgi-bin/teen.cgi?DATASET=AL.

TOTALBR Table G.300 Birthrate per 1,000 to all females ages 15–19 by race/ethnicity in the state, 1996. "When Teens Have Sex: Issues and Trends," state profile. The Annie E. Casey Foundation, Baltimore, Md. On the Internet: http://www.aecf.org/cgi-bin/teen.cgi?DATASET=AL.

NHWHBR Table G.301 Birthrate per 1,000 to non-Hispanic white females ages 15–19 in the state, 1996. "When Teens Have Sex: Issues and Trends," state profile.

The Annie E. Casey Foundation, Baltimore, Md. On the Internet: http://www.aecf.org/cgi-bin/teen.cgi?DATASET =AL.

BLACKBR Table G.302 Birthrate per 1,000 to non-Hispanic black females ages 15–19 in the state, 1996. "When Teens Have Sex: Issues and Trends," state profile. The Annie E. Casey Foundation, Baltimore, Md. On the Internet: http://www.aecf.org/cgi-bin/teen.cgi?DATASET =AL.

HISPBR Table G.303 Birthrate per 1,000 to Hispanic females ages 15–19 in the state, 1996. "When Teens Have Sex: Issues and Trends," state profile. The Annie E. Casey Foundation, Baltimore, Md. On the Internet: http://www.aecf.org/cgi-bin/teen.cgi?DATASET=AL.

BR151996 Table G.304 Number of births to all females ages 15–19 in 1996. "When Teens Have Sex: Issues and Trends," state profile. The Annie E. Casey Foundation, Baltimore, Md. On the Internet: http://www.aecf.org/cgi-bin/teen.cgi?DATASET=AL.

TOTPCUN Table G.305 Percent of births that occurred to unmarried teens in 1996. "When Teens Have Sex: Issues and Trends," state profile. The Annie E. Casey Foundation, Baltimore, Md. On the Internet: http://www.aecf.org/cgi-bin/teen.cgi?DATASET=AL.

NHWPCUN Table G.306 Percent of births that occurred to unmarried non-Hispanic white teens in 1996. "When Teens Have Sex: Issues and Trends," state profile. The Annie E. Casey Foundation, Baltimore, Md. On the Internet: http://www.aecf.org/cgi-bin/teen.cgi? DATASET=AL.

NHBPCUN Table G.307 Percent of births that occurred to unmarried non-Hispanic black teens in 1996. "When Teens Have Sex: Issues and Trends," state profile. The Annie E. Casey Foundation, Baltimore, Md. On the Internet: http://www.aecf.org/cgi-bin/teen.cgi? DATASET=AL.

HISPPCUN Table G.308 Percent of births that occurred to unmarried Hispanic teens in 1996. "When Teens Have Sex: Issues and Trends," state profile. The Annie E. Casey Foundation, Baltimore, Md. On the Internet: http://www.aecf.org/cgi-bin/teen.cgi?DATASET =AL.

TOTPCINC Table G.309 Percent of births to teens receiving inadequate prenatal care in 1996. "When Teens Have Sex: Issues and Trends," state profile. The Annie E. Casey Foundation, Baltimore, Md. On the Internet: http://www.aecf.org/cgi-bin/teen.cgi? DATASET=AL.

NWHPCINC Table G.310 Percent of births to non-Hispanic white teens receiving inadequate prenatal care in 1996. "When Teens Have Sex: Issues and Trends," state profile. The Annie E. Casey Foundation, Baltimore, Md. On the Internet: http://www.aecf.org/cgi-bin/teen. cgi?DATASET=AL.

NHBPCINC Table G.311 Percent of births to non-Hispanic black teens receiving inadequate prenatal care in 1996. "When Teens Have Sex: Issues and Trends," state profile. The Annie E. Casey Foundation, Baltimore, Md. On the Internet: http://www.aecf.org/cgi-bin/teen. cgi?DATASET=AL.

HISPCINC Table G.312 Percent of births to Hispanic teens receiving inadequate prenatal care in 1996. "When Teens Have Sex: Issues and Trends," state profile. The Annie E. Casey Foundation, Baltimore, Md. On the Internet: http://www.aecf.org/cgi-bin/teen. cgi?DATASET=AL.

ABORT95 Table G.313 Number of abortions per 1,000 females ages 15–19, 1996. "When Teens Have Sex: Issues and Trends," state profile. The Annie E. Casey Foundation, Baltimore, Md. On the Internet: http://www. aecf.org/cgi-bin/teen.cgi?DATASET=AL.

SMOK9596 Table G.314 Percent of teen births occurring to mothers who smoked, 1995–1996. "When Teens Have Sex: Issues and Trends," state profile. The Annie E. Casey Foundation, Baltimore, Md. On the Internet: http://www.aecf.org/cgi-bin/teen.cgi?DATASET =AL.

LACKINSF Table G.315 Percent of females ages 12–19 lacking health insurance, 1995. "When Teens Have Sex: Issues and Trends," state profile. The Annie E. Casey Foundation, Baltimore, Md. On the Internet: http://www.aecf.org/cgi-bin/teen.cgi?DATASET=AL.

LACKINSM Table G.316 Percent of males ages 12–19 lacking health insurance, 1995. "When Teens Have Sex: Issues and Trends," state profile. The Annie E. Casey Foundation, Baltimore, Md. On the Internet: http://www.aecf.org/cgi-bin/teen.cgi?DATASET=AL.

PCCBR96 Table G.317 Percent change in teen birthrate 1991–1996 (births per 1,000 females ages 15–19). "When Teens Have Sex: Issues and Trends," state profile. The Annie E. Casey Foundation, Baltimore, Md. On the Internet: http://www.aecf.org/cgi-bin/teen. cgi?DATASET=AL.

BRYT96 Table G.318 Birthrate for younger teens (births per 100,000 females ages 15–17, 1996). "When Teens Have Sex: Issues and Trends," state profile. The Annie E. Casey Foundation, Baltimore, Md. On the Internet: http://www.aecf.org/cgi-bin/teen.cgi?DATASET =AL.

PCTBRB96 Table G.321 Percent of teen births that are repeat births, 1996. "When Teens Have Sex: Issues and Trends," state profile. The Annie E. Casey Foundation, Baltimore, Md. On the Internet: http://www. aecf.org/cgi-bin/teen.cgi?DATASET=AL.

PCTBAL96 Table G.322 Teen births as percent of all births, 1996. "When Teens Have Sex: Issues and Trends," state profile. The Annie E. Casey Foundation, Baltimore, Md. On the Internet: http://www.aecf.org/ cgi-bin/teen.cgi?DATASET=AL.

GONTEEN Table G.319 Gonorrhea rate, 1996 (cases per 100,000 females, ages 15–19) "When Teens Have Sex: Issues and Trends," state profile. The Annie E.

Casey Foundation, Baltimore, Md. On the Internet: http://www.aecf.org/cgi-bin/teen.cgi?DATASET=AL.

BUSFAIL **Table G.320** Number of business failures, 1998. From No. 876, page 548, *Statistical Abstract of the United States*, 2000.

VIOLENCE **Table G.323** This number represents the total number of violent crimes for 1998. The number was calculated by summing the number of violent crimes (i.e., murder, aggravated assault, forcible rape, and robbery) to make it comparable to VIOLEN39 (i.e., the sum of those crimes for 1960 through 1998).
Calculated: MURD + ASLT + RAPES + ROB

PROPERTY **Table G.324** This number represents the total number of property crimes for 1998. The number was calculated by summing the number of property crimes (i.e., burglary, larceny, and automobile theft, but not arson) to make it comparable to PROPER39 (i.e., the sum of those crimes for 1960 through 1998).
Calculated: BURG + LARC + THEFT

VIOLENT **Table G.325 (also G.262)** This number represents the violent crime rate per 1,000 population for violent crimes in 1998.
Calculated: VIOLENCE / POP

PROPER **Table G.326 (also G.325)** This number represents the property crime rate per 1,000 population for property crimes in 1998.
Calculated: PROPERTY / POP

RMURD609 **Table G.327** Actual rank-order of average number of murders per 1,000 total population reported 1960 to 1998. Low values (e.g., 1.000) represent high murder rates per 1,000 total population between 1960 and 1998, and high values (e.g., 50.000) represent low murder rates for that period.
Calculated: MURD6098 by Rank

RRAPE609 **Table G.328** Actual rank-order of average number of rapes per 1,000 total population reported 1960 to 1998. Low values (e.g., 1.000) represent high rape rates per 1,000 total population between 1960 and 1998, and high values (e.g., 50.000) represent low rape rates for that period.
Calculated: RAPE6098 by Rank

RROB6098 **Table G.329** Actual rank-order of average number of robberies per 1,000 total population reported 1960 to 1998. Low values (e.g., 1.000) represent high robbery rates per 1,000 total population between 1960 and 1998, and high values (e.g., 50.000) represent low robbery rates for that period.
Calculated: ROB6098 by Rank

RASLT609 **Table G.330** Actual rank-order of average number of assaults per 1,000 total population reported 1960 to 1998. Low values (e.g., 1.000) represent high assault rates per 1,000 total population between 1960 and 1998, and high values (e.g., 50.000) represent low assault rates for that period.
Calculated: ASLT6098 by Rank

BUSFAIL **Table G.344** Business failures per 1,000 population, 1998.
Calculated: BUSFAIL / POPEST99

RBURG609 **Table G.331** Actual rank-order of average number of burglaries per 1,000 total population reported 1960 to 1998. Low values (e.g., 1.000) represent high burglary rates per 1,000 total population between 1960 and 1998, and high values (e.g., 50.000) represent low burglary rates for that period.
Calculated: BURG6098 by Rank

RLARC609 **Table G.332** Actual rank-order of average number of larcenies per 1,000 total population reported 1960 to 1998. Low values (e.g., 1.000) represent high larceny rates per 1,000 total population between 1960 and 1998, and high values (e.g., 50.000) represent low larceny rates for that period.
Calculated: LARC6098 by Rank

RMVT6098 **Table G.333** Actual rank-order of average number of motor vehicle thefts per 1,000 total population reported 1960 to 1998. Low values (e.g., 1.000) represent high auto theft rates per 1,000 total population between 1960 and 1998, and high values (e.g., 50.000) represent low auto theft rates for that period.
Calculated: MVT6098 by Rank

CRIME39 **Table G.334** Arithmetical mean (i.e., average) of total crime rankings for the time period 1960 to 1998. Low scores (i.e., 1.000) represent high total crime rates for 1960 to 1998. High values (e.g., 50.000) represent low total crime rates for that 39 year period.
Calculated: (RMURD609 + RRAPE609 + RROB6098 + RASLT609 + RBURG609 + RLARC609 + RMVT6098) / 7

ALCOHOPC **Table G.337** Per capita ethanol consumption, in gallons, for all beverages, 1998. (Gallons of ethanol, based on population age 14 and older.) On the Internet: http://www.niaaa.nih.gov/databases/consum03.txt.

PEDEATH **Table G.339** Pedestrian fatalities per 100,000 population, 1999. National Center for Statistics and Analysis, National Highway Traffic Safety Administration report, *Traffic Safety Facts 1999*. U.S. Department of Transportation, "Pedestrians," p. 6. On the Internet: http://www.nhtsa.dot.gov.

LGTRKINV **Table G.335** Number of large trucks involved in fatal crashes, 1999. National Center for Statistics and Analysis, National Highway Traffic Safety Administration report, *Traffic Safety Facts 1999*. U.S. Department of Transportation, "Large Trucks," p. 5. On the Internet: http://www.nhtsa.dot.gov.

LGTRKDEA **Table G.336** Percentage of large trucks in fatal crashes of total vehicles involved, 1999. National Center for Statistics and Analysis, National Highway Traffic Safety Administration report, *Traffic Safety Facts 1999*. U.S. Department of Transportation, "Large Trucks," p. 5. On the Internet: http://www.nhtsa.dot.gov.

PCUSLGTR **Table G.338** Percentage of U.S. total large trucks involved in fatal crashes. National Center for

Statistics and Analysis, National Highway Traffic Safety Administration report, *Traffic Safety Facts 1999*. U.S. Department of Transportation, "Large Trucks," p. 5. On the Internet: http://www.nhtsa.dot.gov.

TOTFATAL   Table G.340 Total number of traffic fatalities, 1999. National Center for Statistics and Analysis, National Highway Traffic Safety Administration report, *Traffic Safety Facts 1999*. U.S. Department of Transportation, "Speeding," p. 6. On the Internet: http://www.nhtsa.dot.gov.

TOTSPEED   Table G.341 Total number of speeding-related traffic fatalities, 1999. National Center for Statistics and Analysis, National Highway Traffic Safety Administration report, *Traffic Safety Facts 1999*. U.S. Department of Transportation, "Speeding," p. 6. On the Internet: http://www.nhtsa.dot.gov.

ANYALCOH   Table G.342 Percent of traffic fatalities in which any amount of alcohol (BAC > 0.01 g/dl) was reported in blood alcohol concentration in the crash, 1999. National Center for Statistics and Analysis, National Highway Traffic Safety Administration report, *Traffic Safety Facts 1999*. U.S. Department of Transportation, "Alcohol," p. 7. On the Internet: http://www.nhtsa.dot.gov.

FATALPOP   Table G.343 Traffic fatality rates per 100,000 population, 1999. National Center for Statistics and Analysis, National Highway Traffic Safety Administration report, *Traffic Safety Facts 1999*. U.S. Department of Transportation, "State Traffic Data," p. 2. On the Internet: http://www.nhtsa.dot.gov.

PCFATCH   Table G.345 Percent change in traffic fatalities, 1975–1999. National Center for Statistics and Analysis, National Highway Traffic Safety Administration report, *Traffic Safety Facts 1999*. U.S. Department of Transportation, "State Traffic Data," p. 3. On the Internet: http://www.nhtsa.dot.gov.

NOBELT   Table G.346 Percent of passenger car occupants killed that were unrestrained (i.e., no seatbelt), 1999. National Center for Statistics and Analysis, National Highway Traffic Safety Administration report, *Traffic Safety Facts 1999*. U.S. Department of Transportation, "State Traffic Data," p. 7. On the Internet: http://www.nhtsa.dot.gov.

PERSINCO   Table G.358 Total personal income, in thousands of dollars, 1999. Bureau of Economic Analysis, Regional Accounts Data, Annual State Personal Income. On the Internet: http://www.bea.doc.gov/bea/regional/spi/drill.cfm?Table=SA50&lc.

PCINCOME   Table G.347 Per capita personal income, 1999. Bureau of Economic Analysis, Regional Accounts Data, Annual State Personal Income. On the Internet: http://www.bea.doc.gov/bea/regional/spi/drill.cfm?Table=SA50&lc.

PCDISPIN   Table G.348 Per capita disposable personal income, in thousands of dollars, 1999. Bureau

of Economic Analysis, Regional Accounts Data, Annual State Personal Income. On the Internet: http://www.bea.doc.gov/bea/regional/spi/drill.cfm?Table=SA50&lc.

TAXTOFED   Table G.349 Personal tax and nontax payments to federal government, in thousands of dollars, 1999. Bureau of Economic Analysis, Regional Accounts Data, Annual State Personal Income. On the Internet: http://www.bea.doc.gov/bea/regional/spi/drill.cfm?Table=SA50&lc.

STATETAX   Table G.350 Individual income taxes paid to state government, in thousands of dollars, 1999. Bureau of Economic Analysis, Regional Accounts Data, Annual State Personal Income. On the Internet: http://www.bea.doc.gov/bea/regional/spi/drill.cfm?Table=SA50&lc.

CARPLATE   Table G.351 Motor vehicle licenses, in thousands of dollars, 1999. Bureau of Economic Analysis, Regional Accounts Data, Annual State Personal Income. On the Internet: http://www.bea.doc.gov/bea/regional/spi/drill.cfm?Table=SA50&lc.

TAXTOLOC   Table G.353 Total personal tax and nontax payments to local government, in thousands of dollars, 1999. Bureau of Economic Analysis, Regional Accounts Data, Annual State Personal Income. On the Internet: http://www.bea.doc.gov/bea/regional/spi/drill.cfm?Table=SA50&lc.

LOCINTAX   Table G.354 Total individual income taxes paid to local government, in thousands of dollars, 1999. Bureau of Economic Analysis, Regional Accounts Data, Annual State Personal Income. On the Internet: http://www.bea.doc.gov/bea/regional/spi/drill.cfm?Table=SA50&lc.

LOCARPLT   Table G.352 Total of motor vehicle licenses paid to local government, in thousands of dollars, 1999. Bureau of Economic Analysis, Regional Accounts Data, Annual State Personal Income. On the Internet: http://www.bea.doc.gov/bea/regional/spi/drill.cfm?Table=SA50&lc.

LOCTAXOT   Table G.355 Total of other taxes paid to local government, in thousands of dollars, 1999. Bureau of Economic Analysis, Regional Accounts Data, Annual State Personal Income. On the Internet: http://www.bea.doc.gov/bea/regional/spi/drill.cfm?Table=SA50&lc.

LOCNOTAX   Table G.356 Total of nontaxes paid to local government, in thousands of dollars, 1999. Bureau of Economic Analysis, Regional Accounts Data, Annual State Personal Income. On the Internet: http://www.bea.doc.gov/bea/regional/spi/drill.cfm?Table=SA50&lc.

STALOPER   Table G.357 Total of State and Local personal property taxes, in thousands of dollars, 1999. Bureau of Economic Analysis, Regional Accounts Data, Annual State Personal Income. On the Internet:

http://www.bea.doc.gov/bea/regional/spi/drill.cfm?
Table=SA50&lc.

TAXNONTX   Table G.361   Personal tax and non-tax payments, in thousands of dollars, 1999. Bureau of Economic Analysis, Regional Accounts Data, Annual State Personal Income. On the Internet: http://www.bea.doc.gov/bea/regional/spi/drill.cfm?Table=SA50&lc.

DISPERIN   Table G.362   Total disposable personal income, in thousands of dollars, 1999. Bureau of Economic Analysis, Regional Accounts Data, Annual State Personal Income. On the Internet: http://www.bea.doc.gov/bea/regional/spi/drill.cfm?Table=SA50&lc.

PERTXNO   Table G.363   Personal tax and nontax payments, in thousands of dollars, 1999. Bureau of Economic Analysis, Regional Accounts Data, Annual State Personal Income. On the Internet: http://www.bea.doc.gov/bea/regional/spi/drill.cfm?Table=SA50&lc.

INDINTAX   Table G.364   Total of individual income taxes paid to federal government (net of refunds), in thousands of dollars, 1999. Bureau of Economic Analysis, Regional Accounts Data, Annual State Personal Income. On the Internet: http://www.bea.doc.gov/bea/regional/spi/drill.cfm?Table=SA50&lc.

FIDUCTAX   Table G.365   Total of fiduciary income taxes paid to federal government, in thousands of dollars, 1999. Bureau of Economic Analysis, Regional Accounts Data, Annual State Personal Income. On the Internet: http://www.bea.doc.gov/bea/regional/spi/drill.cfm?Table=SA50&lc.

FEDNONTX   Table G.366   Total of nontaxes (e.g., hunting licenses) paid to federal government, in thousands of dollars, 1999. Bureau of Economic Analysis, Regional Accounts Data, Annual State Personal Income. On the Internet: http://www.bea.doc.gov/bea/regional/spi/drill.cfm?Table=SA50&lc.

TXNONSTA   Table G.367   Total of tax and nontax payments to state government, in thousands of dollars, 1999. Bureau of Economic Analysis, Regional Accounts Data, Annual State Personal Income. On the Internet: http://www.bea.doc.gov/bea/regional/spi/drill.cfm?Table=SA50&lc.

STAOTAX   Table G.368   Total of other taxes paid to state government, in thousands of dollars, 1999. Bureau of Economic Analysis, Regional Accounts Data, Annual State Personal Income. On the Internet: http://www.bea.doc.gov/bea/regional/spi/drill.cfm?Table=SA50&lc.

STANONTX   Table G.373   Total of nontax payments (e.g., hunting licenses), to state government, in thousands of dollars, 1999. Bureau of Economic Analysis, Regional Accounts Data, Annual State Personal Income. On the Internet: http://www.bea.doc.gov/bea/regional/spi/drill.cfm?Table=SA50&lc.

PCFEDTAX   Table G.369   Per capita taxes paid to federal government, 1999.
Calculated: INDINTAX / POPEST99

PCSTATAX   Table G.370   Per capita taxes paid to state government, not including state and local personal property taxes, 1999.
Calculated: TXNONSTA / POPEST99

PCLOCTAX   Table G.371   Per capita taxes paid to local government, not including state and local personal property taxes, 1999.
Calculated: TAXTOLOC / POPEST99

PCSTALOP   Table G.374   Per capita personal property taxes paid to state and local governments, 1999.
Calculated: STALOPER / POPEST99

PCFSLTAX   Table G.372   Per capita taxes paid to federal, state, and local governments, including state and local personal property taxes, 1999.
Calculated: PCFEDTAX + PCSTATAX + PCLOCTAX + PCSTALOP

WHATLEFT   Table G.375   Per capita income, after all federal, state, and local taxes were paid, 1999.
Calculated: PCINCOME−PCFSLTAX

TAXRATE   Table G.376   Proportion of per capita income paid in taxes to all levels of government, Federal, State, and Local, 1999.
Calculated: PCFSLTAX / PCINCOME

PCTAXALL   Table G.359   Percent of per capita income paid for taxes from all levels of government: Federal, State, and Local, 1999.
Calculated: TAXRATE * 100

TOTSTALO   Table G.377   Total of all taxes and nontax payments paid to state and local governments, 1999, in thousands.
Calculated: TXNONSTA + TAXTOLOC + STALOPER

PCSTALO   Table G.378   Per capita taxes and nontax payments and personal property taxes paid to state and local governments, 1999.
Calculated: TOTSTALO / POPEST99

OBESITY   Table G.360   Percent of persons at risk for health problems related to being overweight (NHANES II definition). Based on responses to survey involving approximately 2,000 persons in each state. Prevalence Data. On the Internet: http//apps.nccd.cdc.gov/brfss/display.asp?cat=RF&yr=1999&qkey=4402&state=AL

MOTCYDEA   Table G.379   Number of motorcyclists killed, 1999. National Center for Statistics and Analysis, National Highway Traffic Safety Administration report, *Traffic Safety Facts 1999.* U.S. Department of Transportation, "State Traffic Data," p. 7. On the Internet: http://www.nhtsa.dot.gov.

PCHELMET   Table G.380   Percent of motorcyclists killed who were helmeted. National Center for Statistics and Analysis, National Highway Traffic Safety Administration report, *Traffic Safety Facts 1999.* U.S. Department of Transportation, "State Traffic Data," p. 2. On the Internet: http://www.nhtsa.dot.gov.

JUSTICE   Table G.381   Per capita expenditures for total state and local justice system (i.e., police protection, judicial and legal costs, and corrections), 1996. Ann L. Pastore and Kathleen Maguire, eds. *Sourcebook of Criminal Justice Statistics—1999*. (Washington, D.C.: U.S. Department of Justice, Bureau of Justice Statistics, USGPO 2000), Table 1.7, p. 10.

POLICE   Table G.382   Per capita expenditures of justice system costs for state and local police protection costs, 1996. Ann L. Pastore and Kathleen Maguire, eds. *Sourcebook of Criminal Justice Statistics—1999*. (Washington, D.C.: U.S. Department of Justice, Bureau of Justice Statistics, USGPO 2000), Table 1.7, p. 10.

JUDICIAL   Table G.383   Per capita expenditures of justice system costs for state and local judicial and legal costs, 1996. Ann L. Pastore and Kathleen Maguire, eds. *Sourcebook of Criminal Justice Statistics—1999*. (Washington, D.C.: U.S. Department of Justice, Bureau of Justice Statistics, USGPO 2000), Table 1.7, p. 10.

CORRECT   Table G.384   Per capita expenditures of justice system costs for state and local corrections costs, 1996. Ann L. Pastore and Kathleen Maguire, eds. *Sourcebook of Criminal Justice Statistics—1999*. (Washington, D.C.: U.S. Department of Justice, Bureau of Justice Statistics, USGPO 2000), Table 1.7, p. 10.

JUSTCOST   Table G.385   Percent of state and local payrolls devoted to total justice system costs (i.e., police protection, judicial and legal, and corrections), October 1996. Ann L. Pastore and Kathleen Maguire, eds. *Sourcebook of Criminal Justice Statistics—1999*. (Washington, D.C.: U.S. Department of Justice, Bureau of Justice Statistics, USGPO 2000), Table 1.17, pp. 19 ff.

POLICOST   Table G.386   Percent of state and local justice system payrolls to police protection costs, October 1996. Ann L. Pastore and Kathleen Maguire, eds. *Sourcebook of Criminal Justice Statistics—1999*. (Washington, D.C.: U.S. Department of Justice, Bureau of Justice Statistics, USGPO 2000), Table 1.17, pp. 19 ff.

JUDICOST   Table G.387   Percent of state and local justice system payrolls devoted to judicial and legal costs, October 1996. Ann L. Pastore and Kathleen Maguire, eds. *Sourcebook of Criminal Justice Statistics— 1999*. (Washington, D.C.: U.S. Department of Justice, Bureau of Justice Statistics, USGPO 2000), Table 1.17, pp. 19 ff.

CORRCOST   Table G.388   Percent of state and local justice system payrolls devoted to corrections costs, October 1996. Ann L. Pastore and Kathleen Maguire, eds. *Sourcebook of Criminal Justice Statistics—1999*. (Washington, D.C.: U.S. Department of Justice, Bureau of Justice Statistics, USGPO 2000), Table 1.17, pp. 19 ff.

JUSTEMPL   Table G.389   Percent of state and local government full-time equivalent employment devoted to total justice system (i.e., police protection, judicial and legal, and corrections), October 1996. Ann L. Pastore and Kathleen Maguire, eds. *Sourcebook of Crimi-*

nal Justice Statistics—1999. (Washington, D.C.: U.S. Department of Justice, Bureau of Justice Statistics, USGPO 2000), Table 1.20, pp. 26 ff.

POLIEMPL   Table G.390   Percent of state and local total justice system full-time equivalent employment devoted to police protection, October 1996. Ann L. Pastore and Kathleen Maguire, eds. *Sourcebook of Criminal Justice Statistics—1999*. (Washington, D.C.: U.S. Department of Justice, Bureau of Justice Statistics, USGPO 2000), Table 1.20, pp. 26 ff.

JUDIEMPL   Table G.391   Percent of state and local total justice system full-time equivalent employment devoted to judicial and legal, October 1995. Ann L. Pastore and Kathleen Maguire, eds. *Sourcebook of Criminal Justice Statistics—1999*. (Washington, D.C.: U.S. Department of Justice, Bureau of Justice Statistics, USGPO 2000), Table 1.20, pp. 26 ff.

CORREMPL   Table G.392   Percent of state and local total justice system full-time equivalent employment devoted to corrections, October 1995. Ann L. Pastore and Kathleen Maguire, eds. *Sourcebook of Criminal Justice Statistics—1999*. (Washington, D.C.: U.S. Department of Justice, Bureau of Justice Statistics, USGPO 2000), Table 1.20, pp. 26 ff.

JUSTRATE   Table G.393   Rate (per 10,000 population) of state and local justice system full-time equivalent employees, October 1995.   Ann L. Pastore and Kathleen Maguire, eds. *Sourcebook of Criminal Justice Statistics—1999*. (Washington, D.C.: U.S. Department of Justice, Bureau of Justice Statistics, USGPO 2000), Table 1.21, pp. 31 ff.

POLTOTRA   Table G.394   Rate (per 10,000 population) of state and local justice system full-time equivalent employees who work in police protection, total, October 1995. Ann L. Pastore and Kathleen Maguire, eds. *Sourcebook of Criminal Justice Statistics—1999*. (Washington, D.C.: U.S. Department of Justice, Bureau of Justice Statistics, USGPO 2000), Table 1.21, pp. 31 ff.

POLSWORA   Table G.395   Rate (per 10,000 population) of state and local justice system full-time equivalent employees who work in police protection, sworn, October 1995.   Ann L. Pastore and Kathleen Maguire, eds. *Sourcebook of Criminal Justice Statistics—1999*. (Washington, D.C.: U.S. Department of Justice, Bureau of Justice Statistics, USGPO 2000), Table 1.21, pp. 31 ff.

JUDIRATE   Table G.396   Rate (per 10,000 population) of state and local justice system full-time equivalent employees who work in judical and legal, October 1995. Ann L. Pastore and Kathleen Maguire, eds. *Sourcebook of Criminal Justice Statistics—1999*. (Washington, D.C.: U.S. Department of Justice, Bureau of Justice Statistics, USGPO 2000), Table 1.21, pp. 31 ff.

CORRATE   Table G.397   Rate (per 10,000 population) of state and local justice system full-time equivalent employees who work in corrections, October 1995. Ann L. Pastore and Kathleen Maguire, eds. *Sourcebook of*

Criminal Justice Statistics—1999. (Washington, D.C.: U.S. Department of Justice, Bureau of Justice Statistics, USGPO 2000), Table 1.21, pp. 31 ff.

STAPOLTO   Table G.398   Total full-time personnel in state law enforcement agencies, 1997. Ann L. Pastore and Kathleen Maguire, eds. *Sourcebook of Criminal Justice Statistics—1999.* (Washington, D.C.: U.S. Department of Justice, Bureau of Justice Statistics, USGPO 2000), Table 1.21, pp. 31 ff.

STAPOLSW   Table G.399   Total full-time personnel in state law enforcement agencies who are sworn officers, 1997. Ann L. Pastore and Kathleen Maguire, eds. *Sourcebook of Criminal Justice Statistics—1999.* (Washington, D.C.: U.S. Department of Justice, Bureau of Justice Statistics, USGPO 2000), Table 1.21, pp. 31 ff.

STAPOLPC   Table G.400   Percent of full-time personnel in state law enforcement agencies who are sworn officers, 1997. Ann L. Pastore and Kathleen Maguire, eds. *Sourcebook of Criminal Justice Statistics—1999.* (Washington, D.C.: U.S. Department of Justice, Bureau of Justice Statistics, USGPO 2000), Table 1.21, pp. 31 ff.

OFFPPOP   Table G.401   Sworn officers per 10,000 residents of the total state population, 1997.
Calculated: STAPOLSW / (POPEST99 / 10)

ROBRATE   Table G.402   Robberies per 100,000 population, 1998. Ann L. Pastore and Kathleen Maguire, eds. *Sourcebook of Criminal Justice Statistics—1999.* (Washington, D.C.: U.S. Department of Justice, Bureau of Justice Statistics, USGPO 2000), Table 3.126, p. 280.

ROBGUN   Table G.403   Percent of all robberies that were firearm related, 1998. Ann L. Pastore and Kathleen Maguire, eds. *Sourcebook of Criminal Justice Statistics—1999.* (Washington, D.C.: U.S. Department of Justice, Bureau of Justice Statistics, USGPO 2000), Table 3.126, p. 280.

ROBKNIFE   Table G.404   Percent of all robberies that were knife related, 1998. Ann L. Pastore and Kathleen Maguire, eds. *Sourcebook of Criminal Justice Statistics—1999.* (Washington, D.C.: U.S. Department of Justice, Bureau of Justice Statistics, USGPO 2000), Table 3.126, p. 280.

ROBFIST   Table G.405   Percent of all robberies that were fist related, 1998. Ann L. Pastore and Kathleen Maguire, eds. *Sourcebook of Criminal Justice Statistics—1999.* (Washington, D.C.: U.S. Department of Justice, Bureau of Justice Statistics, USGPO 2000), Table 3.126, p. 280.

ASLRATE   Table G.406   Assaults per 100,000 population, 1998. Ann L. Pastore and Kathleen Maguire, eds. *Sourcebook of Criminal Justice Statistics—1999.* (Washington, D.C.: U.S. Department of Justice, Bureau of Justice Statistics, USGPO 2000), Table 3.126, p. 280.

ASLGUN   Table G.407   Percent of all assaults that were firearm related, 1998. Ann L. Pastore and Kathleen Maguire, eds. *Sourcebook of Criminal Justice Statistics—*

1999. (Washington, D.C.: U.S. Department of Justice, Bureau of Justice Statistics, USGPO 2000), Table 3.126, p. 280.

ASLKNIFE   Table G.408   Percent of all assaults that were knife related, 1998. Ann L. Pastore and Kathleen Maguire, eds. *Sourcebook of Criminal Justice Statistics—1999.* (Washington, D.C.: U.S. Department of Justice, Bureau of Justice Statistics, USGPO 2000), Table 3.126, p. 280.

ASLFIST   Table G.409   Percent of all assaults that were fist related, 1998. Ann L. Pastore and Kathleen Maguire, eds. *Sourcebook of Criminal Justice Statistics—1999.* (Washington, D.C.: U.S. Department of Justice, Bureau of Justice Statistics, USGPO 2000), Table 3.126, p. 280.

BANKROB   Table G.410   Number of bank robberies in each state, 1998. Ann L. Pastore and Kathleen Maguire, eds. *Sourcebook of Criminal Justice Statistics—1999.* (Washington, D.C.: U.S. Department of Justice, Bureau of Justice Statistics, USGPO 2000), Table 3.166, p. 315.

MARPLANT   Table G.411   Number of cultivated marijuana plants eradicated in 1999. Ann L. Pastore and Kathleen Maguire, eds. *Sourcebook of Criminal Justice Statistics—1999.* (Washington, D.C.: U.S. Department of Justice, Bureau of Justice Statistics, USGPO 2000), Table 4.40, p. 389.

MARBULK   Table G.412   Bulk-processed marijuana seized in 1999. Ann L. Pastore and Kathleen Maguire, eds. *Sourcebook of Criminal Justice Statistics—1999.* (Washington, D.C.: U.S. Department of Justice, Bureau of Justice Statistics, USGPO 2000), Table 4.40, p. 389.

MARARRES   Table G.413   Number of arrests for marijuana in 1999. Ann L. Pastore and Kathleen Maguire, eds. *Sourcebook of Criminal Justice Statistics—1999.* (Washington, D.C.: U.S. Department of Justice, Bureau of Justice Statistics, USGPO 2000), Table 4.40, p. 389.

MARWEAPO   Table G.414   Number of weapons seized during marijuana arrests in 1999. Ann L. Pastore and Kathleen Maguire, eds. *Sourcebook of Criminal Justice Statistics—1999.* (Washington, D.C.: U.S. Department of Justice, Bureau of Justice Statistics, USGPO 2000), Table 4.40, p. 389.

PROBRATE   Table G.415   Number of adults on probation under state and federal jurisdiction on December 31, 1999, per 100,000 adult residents. Ann L. Pastore and Kathleen Maguire, eds. *Sourcebook of Criminal Justice Statistics—1999.* (Washington, D.C.: U.S. Department of Justice, Bureau of Justice Statistics, USGPO 2000), Table 6.3, p. 485.

PRISENT   Table G.416   Rate (per 100,000 resident population) of prisoners of state and federal correctional authorities, 1999. Ann L. Pastore and Kathleen Maguire, eds. *Sourcebook of Criminal Justice Statistics—1999.*

(Washington, D.C.: U.S. Department of Justice, Bureau of Justice Statistics, USGPO 2000), Table 6.32, p. 507.

TREATFAC   Table G.417   Number of drug and alcohol treatment facilities, 1997. Ann L. Pastore and Kathleen Maguire, eds. *Sourcebook of Criminal Justice Statistics—1999.* (Washington, D.C.: U.S. Department of Justice, Bureau of Justice Statistics, USGPO 2000), Table 6.64 p. 530.

CLIENTS   Table G.418   Number of clients in treatment for drug or alcohol abuse, 1997. Ann L. Pastore and Kathleen Maguire, eds. *Sourcebook of Criminal Justice Statistics—1999.* (Washington, D.C.: U.S. Department of Justice, Bureau of Justice Statistics, USGPO 2000), Table 6.64, p. 530.

PCLIENTS   Table G.419   Percent of state population in treatment for drug or alcohol abuse, 1997. Calculated: (CLIENTS / POPEST99) / 10

PCALCABU   Table G.420   Percent of clients in treatment for alcohol abuse, 1997. Ann L. Pastore and Kathleen Maguire, eds. *Sourcebook of Criminal Justice Statistics—1999.* (Washington, D.C.: U.S. Department of Justice, Bureau of Justice Statistics, USGPO 2000), Table 6.64, p. 530.

PCDRUGAB   Table G.421   Percent of clients in treatment for drug abuse, 1997. Ann L. Pastore and Kathleen Maguire, eds. *Sourcebook of Criminal Justice Statistics—1999.* (Washington, D.C.: U.S. Department of Justice, Bureau of Justice Statistics, USGPO 2000), Table 6.64, p. 530.

PCDRUALC   Table G.422   Percent of clients in treatment for both drug and alcohol abuse, 1997. Ann L. Pastore and Kathleen Maguire, eds. *Sourcebook of Criminal Justice Statistics—1999.* (Washington, D.C.: U.S. Department of Justice, Bureau of Justice Statistics, USGPO 2000), Table 6.64, p. 530.

ONPAROLE   Table G.423   Number of adults on parole under state and federal jurisdiction, 1999. Ann L. Pastore and Kathleen Maguire, eds. *Sourcebook of Criminal Justice Statistics—1999.* (Washington, D.C.: U.S. Department of Justice, Bureau of Justice Statistics, USGPO 2000), Table 6.70, p. 536.

PCPAROLE   Table G.424   Percent of state population on parole under state and federal jurisdiction, 1999. Calculated: (ONPAROLE / POPEST99) / 10

POPEST89   Table G.425   Resident population by state, in thousands, 1989. U.S. Census Bureau, *Statistical Abstract of the United States*: 1991. Table No. 28, p. 23.

POPEST90   Table G.426   Resident population by state, in thousands, 1990. U.S. Census Bureau, *Statistical Abstract of the United States*: 2000. Table No. 20, p. 23.

POPEST91   Table G.427   Resident population by state, in thousands, 1991. U.S. Census Bureau, *Statistical Abstract of the United States*: 2000. Table No. 20, p. 23.

POPEST92   Table G.428   Resident population by state, in thousands, 1992. U.S. Census Bureau, *Statistical Abstract of the United States*: 2000. Table No. 20, p. 23.

POPEST93   Table G.429   Resident population by state, in thousands, 1993. U.S. Census Bureau, *Statistical Abstract of the United States*: 2000. Table No. 20, p. 23.

POPEST94   Table G.430   Resident population by state, in thousands, 1994. U.S. Census Bureau, *Statistical Abstract of the United States*: 2000. Table No. 20, p. 23.

POPEST95   Table G.431   Resident population by state, in thousands, 1995 U.S. Census Bureau, *Statistical Abstract of the United States*: 2000. Table No. 20, p. 23.

POPEST96   Table G.432   Resident population by state, in thousands, 1996. U.S. Census Bureau, *Statistical Abstract of the United States*: 2000. Table No. 20, p. 23.

POPEST97   Table G.433   Resident population by state, in thousands, 1997. U.S. Census Bureau, *Statistical Abstract of the United States*: 2000. Table No. 20, p. 23.

POPEST98   Table G.434   Resident population by state, in thousands, 1998. U.S. Census Bureau, *Statistical Abstract of the United States*: 2000. Table No. 20, p. 23.

POPEST00   Table G.435   Resident population by state, in thousands, 2000. U.S. Census Bureau, *Statistical Abstract of the United States*: 2000. Table No. 20, p. 23.

EXPSTA89   Table G.436   State Funds, Total State Expenditures by Fund Source, in millions. Actual Fiscal 1989, State Expenditure Report, 1990. National Association of State Budget Officers, 400 North Capitol Street, Washington, D.C. Table 1-2, p. 10.

EXPFED89   Table G.437   Federal Funds, Total State Expenditures by Fund Source, in millions. Actual Fiscal 1989, State Expenditure Report, 1990. National Association of State Budget Officers, 400 North Capitol Street, Washington, D.C. Table 1-2, p. 10.

EXPTOT89   Table G.438   All Funds, Total State Expenditures by Fund Source, in millions. Actual Fiscal 1989, State Expenditure Report, 1990. National Association of State Budget Officers, 400 North Capitol Street, Washington, D.C. Table 1-2, p. 10.

EXPSTA90   Table G.439   State Funds, Total State Expenditures by Fund Source, in millions. Actual Fiscal 1990, State Expenditure Report, 1991. National Association of State Budget Officers, 400 North Capitol Street, Washington, D.C. Table 1-4, p. 11.

EXPFED90   Table G.440   Federal Funds, Total State Expenditures by Fund Source, in millions. Actual Fiscal 1990, State Expenditure Report, 1991. National Association of State Budget Officers, 400 North Capitol Street, Washington, D.C. Table 1-4, p. 11.

EXPTOT90   Table G.441   All Funds, Total State Expenditures by Fund Source, in millions. Actual Fiscal 1990, State Expenditure Report, 1991. National Association of State Budget Officers, 400 North Capitol Street, Washington, D.C. Table 1-4, p. 11.

EXPSTA91   Table G.442   State Funds, Total State Expenditures by Fund Source, in millions. Actual Fiscal 1991, State Expenditure Report, 1992. National

Association of State Budget Officers, 400 North Capitol Street, Washington, D.C. Table A-1, p. 54.

EXPFED91 **Table G.443** Federal Funds, Total State Expenditures by Fund Source, in millions. Actual Fiscal 1991, State Expenditure Report, 1992. National Association of State Budget Officers, 400 North Capitol Street, Washington, D.C. Table A-1, p. 54.

EXPTOT91 **Table G.444** All Funds, Total State Expenditures by Fund Source, in millions. Actual Fiscal 1991, State Expenditure Report, 1992. National Association of State Budget Officers, 400 North Capitol Street, Washington, D.C. Table A-1, p. 54.

EXPSTA92 **Table G.445** State Funds, Total State Expenditures by Fund Source, in millions. Actual Fiscal 1992, State Expenditure Report, 1993. National Association of State Budget Officers, 400 North Capitol Street, Washington, D.C. Table A-1, p. 62.

EXPFED92 **Table G.446** Federal Funds, Total State Expenditures by Fund Source, in millions. Actual Fiscal 1992, State Expenditure Report, 1993. National Association of State Budget Officers, 400 North Capitol Street, Washington, D.C. Table A-1, p. 62.

EXPTOT92 **Table G.447** All Funds, Total State Expenditures by Fund Source, in millions. Actual Fiscal 1992, State Expenditure Report, 1993. National Association of State Budget Officers, 400 North Capitol Street, Washington, D.C. Table A-1, p. 62.

EXPSTA93 **Table G.448** State Funds, Total State Expenditures by Fund Source, in millions. Actual Fiscal 1993, State Expenditure Report, 1994. National Association of State Budget Officers, 400 North Capitol Street, Washington, D.C. Table A-1, p. 70.

EXPFED93 **Table G.449** Federal Funds, Total State Expenditures by Fund Source, in millions. Actual Fiscal 1993, State Expenditure Report, 1994. National Association of State Budget Officers, 400 North Capitol Street, Washington, D.C. Table A-1, p. 70.

EXPTOT93 **Table G.450** All Funds, Total State Expenditures by Fund Source, in millions. Actual Fiscal 1993, State Expenditure Report, 1994. National Association of State Budget Officers, 400 North Capitol Street, Washington, D.C. Table A-1, p. 70.

EXPSTA94 **Table G.451** State Funds, Total State Expenditures by Fund Source, in millions. Actual Fiscal 1994, State Expenditure Report, 1995. National Association of State Budget Officers, 400 North Capitol Street, Washington, D.C. Table A-1, p. 70.

EXPFED94 **Table G.452** Federal Funds, Total State Expenditures by Fund Source, in millions. Actual Fiscal 1994, State Expenditure Report, 1995. National Association of State Budget Officers, 400 North Capitol Street, Washington, D.C. Table A-1, p. 70.

EXPTOT94 **Table G.453** All Funds, Total State Expenditures by Fund Source, in millions. Actual Fiscal 1994, State Expenditure Report, 1995. National Associa-

tion of State Budget Officers, 400 North Capitol Street, Washington, D.C. Table A-1, p. 70.

EXPSTA95 **Table G.454** State Funds, Total State Expenditures by Fund Source, in millions. Actual Fiscal 1995, State Expenditure Report, 1997. National Association of State Budget Officers, 400 North Capitol Street, Washington, D.C. Table A-1, p. 116.

EXPFED95 **Table G.455** Federal Funds, Total State Expenditures by Fund Source, in millions. Actual Fiscal 1995, State Expenditure Report, 1997. National Association of State Budget Officers, 400 North Capitol Street, Washington, D.C. Table A-1, p. 116.

EXPTOT95 **Table G.456** All Funds, Total State Expenditures by Fund Source, in millions. Actual Fiscal 1995, State Expenditure Report, 1997. National Association of State Budget Officers, 400 North Capitol Street, Washington, D.C. Table A-1, p. 116.

EXPSTA96 **Table G.457** State Funds, Total State Expenditures by Fund Source, in millions. Actual Fiscal 1996, State Expenditure Report, 1997. National Association of State Budget Officers, 400 North Capitol Street, Washington, D.C. Table A-1, p. 116.

EXPFED96 **Table G.458** Federal Funds, Total State Expenditures by Fund Source, in millions. Actual Fiscal 1996, State Expenditure Report, 1997. National Association of State Budget Officers, 400 North Capitol Street, Washington, D.C. Table A-1, p. 116.

EXPTOT96 **Table G.459** All Funds, Total State Expenditures by Fund Source, in millions. Actual Fiscal 1996, State Expenditure Report, 1997. National Association of State Budget Officers, 400 North Capitol Street, Washington, D.C. Table A-1, p. 116.

EXPSTA97 **Table G.460** State Funds, Total State Expenditures by Fund Source, in millions. Actual Fiscal 1997, State Expenditure Report, 1998. National Association of State Budget Officers, 400 North Capitol Street, Washington, D.C. Table A-1, p. 134.

EXPFED97 **Table G.461** Federal Funds, Total State Expenditures by Fund Source, in millions. Actual Fiscal 1997, State Expenditure Report, 1998. National Association of State Budget Officers, 400 North Capitol Street, Washington, D.C. Table A-1, p. 134.

EXPTOT97 **Table G.462** All Funds, Total State Expenditures by Fund Source, in millions. Actual Fiscal 1997, State Expenditure Report, 1998. National Association of State Budget Officers, 400 North Capitol Street, Washington, D.C. Table A-1, p. 134.

EXPSTA98 **Table G.463** State Funds, Total State Expenditures by Fund Source, in millions. Actual Fiscal 1998, State Expenditure Report, 1999. National Association of State Budget Officers, 400 North Capitol Street, Washington, D.C. Table A-1, p. 118.

EXPFED98 **Table G.464** Federal Funds, Total State Expenditures by Fund Source, in millions. Actual Fiscal 1998, State Expenditure Report, 1999. National

Association of State Budget Officers, 400 North Capitol Street, Washington, D.C. Table A-1, p. 118.

EXPTOT98 **Table G.465** All Funds, Total State Expenditures by Fund Source, in millions. Actual Fiscal 1998, State Expenditure Report, 1999. National Association of State Budget Officers, 400 North Capitol Street, Washington, D.C. Table A-1, p. 118.

EXPSTA99 **Table G.466** State Funds, Total State Expenditures by Fund Source, in millions. Actual Fiscal 1999, State Expenditure Report, 1999. National Association of State Budget Officers, 400 North Capitol Street, Washington, D.C. Table A-1, p. 118.

EXPFED99 **Table G.467** Federal Funds, Total State Expenditures by Fund Source, in millions. Actual Fiscal 1999, State Expenditure Report, 1999. National Association of State Budget Officers, 400 North Capitol Street, Washington, D.C. Table A-1, p. 118.

EXPTOT99 **Table G.468** All Funds, Total State Expenditures by Fund Source, in millions. Actual Fiscal 1999, State Expenditure Report, 1999. National Association of State Budget Officers, 400 North Capitol Street, Washington, D.C. Table A-1, p. 118.

EXPSTA00 **Table G.469** State Funds, Total State Expenditures by Fund Source, in millions. Actual Fiscal 2000, State Expenditure Report, 2000. National Association of State Budget Officers, 400 North Capitol Street, Washington, D.C. Table A-1, p. 108.

EXPFED00 **Table G.470** Federal Funds, Total State Expenditures by Fund Source, in millions. Actual Fiscal 2000, State Expenditure Report, 2000. National Association of State Budget Officers, 400 North Capitol Street, Washington, D.C. Table A-1, p. 108.

EXPTOT00 **Table G.471** All Funds, Total State Expenditures by Fund Source, in millions. Actual Fiscal 2000, State Expenditure Report, 2000. National Association of State Budget Officers, 400 North Capitol Street, Washington, D.C. Table A-1, p. 108.

STAPC89 **Table G.472** Expenditures of funds from state, per capita, 1989.
Calculated: (EXPSTA89 / POPEST89) * 1,000

FEDPC89 **Table G.473** Expenditures of funds from federal government, per capita, 1989.
Calculated: (EXPFED89 / POPEST89) * 1,000

TOTPC89 **Table G.474** Expenditures of funds from all sources, per capita, 1989.
Calculated: (EXPTOT89 / POPEST89) * 1,000

STAPC90 **Table G.475** Expenditures of funds from state, per capita, 1990.
Calculated: (EXPSTA90 / POPEST90) * 1,000

FEDPC90 **Table G.476** Expenditures of funds from federal government, per capita, 1990.
Calculated: (EXPFED90 / POPEST90) * 1,000

TOTPC90 **Table G.477** Expenditures of funds from all sources, per capita, 1990.
Calculated: (EXPTOT90 / POPEST90) * 1,000

STAPC91 **Table G.478** Expenditures of funds from state, per capita, 1991.
Calculated: (EXPSTA91 / POPEST91) * 1,000

FEDPC91 **Table G.479** Expenditures of funds from federal government, per capita, 1991.
Calculated: (EXPFED91 / POPEST91) * 1,000

TOTPC91 **Table G.480** Expenditures of funds from all sources, per capita, 1991.
Calculated: (EXPTOT91 / POPEST91) * 1,000

STAPC92 **Table G.481** Expenditures of funds from state, per capita, 1992.
Calculated: (EXPSTA92 / POPEST92) * 1,000

FEDPC92 **Table G.482** Expenditures of funds from federal government, per capita, 1992.
Calculated: (EXPFED92 / POPEST92) * 1,000

TOTPC92 **Table G.483** Expenditures of funds from all sources, per capita, 1992.
Calculated: (EXPTOT92 / POPEST92) * 1,000

STAPC93 **Table G.484** Expenditures of funds from state, per capita, 1993.
Calculated: (EXPSTA93 / POPEST93) * 1,000

FEDPC93 **Table G.485** Expenditures of funds from federal government, per capita, 1993.
Calculated: (EXPFED93 / POPEST93) * 1,000

TOTPC93 **Table G.486** Expenditures of funds from all sources, per capita, 1993.
Calculated: (EXPTOT93 / POPEST93) * 1,000

STAPC94 **Table G.487** Expenditures of funds from state, per capita, 1994.
Calculated: (EXPSTA94 / POPEST94) * 1,000

FEDPC94 **Table G.488** Expenditures of funds from federal government, per capita, 1994.
Calculated: (EXPFED94 / POPEST94) * 1,000

TOTPC94 **Table G.489** Expenditures of funds from all sources, per capita, 1994.
Calculated: (EXPTOT94 / POPEST94) * 1,000

STAPC95 **Table G.490** Expenditures of funds from state, per capita, 1995.
Calculated: (EXPSTA95 / POPEST95) * 1,000

FEDPC95 **Table G.491** Expenditures of funds from federal government, per capita, 1995.
Calculated: (EXPFED95 / POPEST95) * 1,000

TOTPC95 **Table G.492** Expenditures of funds from all sources, per capita, 1995.
Calculated: (EXPTOT95 / POPEST95) * 1,000

STAPC96 **Table G.493** Expenditures of funds from state, per capita, 1996.
Calculated: (EXPSTA96 / POPEST96) * 1,000

FEDPC96 **Table G.494** Expenditures of funds from federal government, per capita, 1996.
Calculated: (EXPFED96 / POPEST96) * 1,000

TOTPC96 **Table G.495** Expenditures of funds from all sources, per capita, 1996.
Calculated: (EXPTOT96 / POPEST96) * 1,000

STAPC97 Table G.496 Expenditures of funds from state, per capita, 1997.
Calculated: (EXPSTA97 / POPEST97) * 1,000

FEDPC97 Table G.497 Expenditures of funds from federal government, per capita, 1997.
Calculated: (EXPFED97 / POPEST97) * 1,000

TOTPC97 Table G.498 Expenditures of funds from all sources, per capita, 1997.
Calculated: (EXPTOT97 / POPEST97) * 1,000

STAPC98 Table G.499 Expenditures of funds from state, per capita, 1998.
Calculated: (EXPSTA98 / POPEST98)* 1,000

FEDPC98 Table G.500 Expenditures of funds from federal government, per capita, 1998.
Calculated: (EXPFED98 / POPEST98) * 1,000

TOTPC98 Table G.501 Expenditures of funds from all sources, per capita, 1998.
Calculated: (EXPTOT98 / POPEST98) * 1,000

STAPC99 Table G.502 Expenditures of funds from state, per capita, 1999.
Calculated: (EXPSTA99 / POPEST99) * 1,000

FEDPC99 Table G.503 Expenditures of funds from federal government, per capita, 1999.
Calculated: (EXPFED99 / POPEST99) * 1,000

TOTPC99 Table G.504 Expenditures of funds from all sources, per capita, 1999.
Calculated: (EXPTOT99 / POPEST99) * 1,000

STAPC00 Table G.505 Expenditures of funds from state, per capita, 2000.
Calculated: (EXPSTA00 / POPEST00) * 1,000

FEDPC00 Table G.506 Expenditures of funds from federal government, per capita, 2000.
Calculated: (EXPFED00 / POPEST00) * 1,000

TOTPC00 Table G.507 Expenditures of funds from all sources, per capita, 2000.
Calculated: (EXPTOT00 / POPEST00) * 1,000

ELESEC89 Table G.508 Percent of total state expenditures devoted to elementary and secondary education, fiscal year 1989. State Expenditure Report, 1989. National Association of State Budget Officers, 400 North Capitol Street, Washington, D.C. p. 14.

HIGHED89 Table G.509 Percent of total state expenditures devoted to higher education, fiscal year 1989. State Expenditure Report, 1989. National Association of State Budget Officers, 400 North Capitol Street, Washington, D.C. p. 14.

ASSIST89 Table G.510 Percent of total state expenditures devoted to cash assistance, fiscal year 1989. State Expenditure Report, 1989. National Association of State Budget Officers, 400 North Capitol Street, Washington, D.C. p. 14.

MEDIC89 Table G.511 Percent of total state expenditures devoted to medicaid, fiscal year 1989. State Expenditure Report, 1989. National Association of State Budget Officers, 400 North Capitol Street, Washington, D.C. p. 14.

CORREC89 Table G.512 Percent of total state expenditures devoted to corrections, fiscal year 1989. State Expenditure Report, 1989. National Association of State Budget Officers, 400 North Capitol Street, Washington, D.C. p. 14.

TRANS89 Table G.513 Percent of total state expenditures devoted to transportation, fiscal year 1989. State Expenditure Report, 1989. National Association of State Budget Officers, 400 North Capitol Street, Washington, D.C. p. 14.

OTHER89 Table G.514 Percent of total state expenditures devoted to all other areas, fiscal year 1989. State Expenditure Report, 1989. National Association of State Budget Officers, 400 North Capitol Street, Washington, D.C. p. 14.

ELESEC90 Table G.515 Percent of total state expenditures devoted to elementary and secondary education, fiscal year 1990. State Expenditure Report, 1990. National Association of State Budget Officers, 400 North Capitol Street, Washington, D.C. p. 15.

HIGHED90 Table G.516 Percent of total state expenditures devoted to higher education, fiscal year 1990. State Expenditure Report, 1990. National Association of State Budget Officers, 400 North Capitol Street, Washington, D.C. p. 15.

ASSIST90 Table G.517 Percent of total state expenditures devoted to cash assistance, fiscal year 1990. State Expenditure Report, 1990. National Association of State Budget Officers, 400 North Capitol Street, Washington, D.C. p. 15.

MEDIC90 Table G.518 Percent of total state expenditures devoted to medicaid, fiscal year 1990. State Expenditure Report, 1990. National Association of State Budget Officers, 400 North Capitol Street, Washington, D.C. p. 15.

CORREC90 Table G.519 Percent ot total state expenditures devoted to corrections, fiscal year 1990. State Expenditure Report, 1990. National Association of State Budget Officers, 400 North Capitol Street, Washington, D.C. p. 15.

TRANS90 Table G.520 Percent of total state expenditures devoted to transportation, fiscal year 1990. State Expenditure Report, 1990. National Association of State Budget Officers, 400 North Capitol Street, Washington, D.C. p. 15.

OTHER90 Table G.521 Percent of total state expenditures devoted to all other areas, fiscal year 1990. State Expenditure Report, 1990. National Association of State Budget Officers, 400 North Capitol Street, Washington, D.C. p. 15.

ELESEC91 Table G.522 Percent of total state expenditures devoted to elementary and secondary education, fiscal year 1991. State Expenditure Report, 1991. National Association of State Budget Officers, 400 North Capitol Street, Washington, D.C. p. 13.

HIGHED91 Table G.523 Percent of total state expenditures devoted to higher education, fiscal year 1991.

State Expenditure Report, 1991. National Association of State Budget Officers, 400 North Capitol Street, Washington, D.C. p. 13.

ASSIST91 Table G.524 Percent of total state expenditures devoted to cash assistance, fiscal year 1991. State Expenditure Report, 1991. National Association of State Budget Officers, 400 North Capitol Street, Washington, D.C. p. 13.

MEDIC91 Table G.525 Percent of total state expenditures devoted to medicaid, fiscal year 1991. State Expenditure Report, 1991. National Association of State Budget Officers, 400 North Capitol Street, Washington, D.C. p. 13.

CORREC91 Table G.526 Percent of total state expenditures devoted to corrections, fiscal year 1991. State Expenditure Report, 1991. National Association of State Budget Officers, 400 North Capitol Street, Washington, D.C. p. 13.

TRANS91 Table G.527 Percent of total state expenditures devoted to transportation, fiscal year 1991. State Expenditure Report, 1991. National Association of State Budget Officers, 400 North Capitol Street, Washington, D.C. p. 13.

OTHER91 Table G.528 Percent of total state expenditures devoted to all other areas, fiscal year 1991. State Expenditure Report, 1991. National Association of State Budget Officers, 400 North Capitol Street, Washington, D.C. p. 13.

ELESEC92 Table G.529 Percent of total state expenditures devoted to elementary and secondary education, fiscal year 1992. State Expenditure Report, 1992. National Association of State Budget Officers, 400 North Capitol Street, Washington, D.C. p. 17.

HIGHED92 Table G.530 Percent of total state expenditures devoted to higher education, fiscal year 1992. State Expenditure Report, 1992. National Association of State Budget Officers, 400 North Capitol Street, Washington, D.C. p. 17.

ASSIST92 Table G.531 Percent of total state expenditures devoted to cash assistance, fiscal year 1992. State Expenditure Report, 1992. National Association of State Budget Officers, 400 North Capitol Street, Washington, D.C. p. 17.

MEDIC92 Table G.532 Percent of total state expenditures devoted to medicaid, fiscal year 1992. State Expenditure Report, 1992. National Association of State Budget Officers, 400 North Capitol Street, Washington, D.C. p. 17.

CORREC92 Table G.533 Percent of total state expenditures devoted to corrections, fiscal year 1992. State Expenditure Report, 1992. National Association of State Budget Officers, 400 North Capitol Street, Washington, D.C. p. 17.

TRANS92 Table G.534 Percent of total state expenditures devoted to transportation, fiscal year 1992. State Expenditure Report, 1992. National Association of

State Budget Officers, 400 North Capitol Street, Washington, D.C. p. 17.

OTHER92 Table G.535 Percent of total state expenditures devoted to all other areas, fiscal year 1992. State Expenditure Report, 1992. National Association of State Budget Officers, 400 North Capitol Street, Washington, D.C. p. 17.

ELESEC93 Table G.536 Percent of total state expenditures devoted to elementary and secondary education, fiscal year 1993. State Expenditure Report, 1993. National Association of State Budget Officers, 400 North Capitol Street, Washington, D.C. p. 17.

HIGHED93 Table G.537 Percent ot total state expenditures devoted to higher education, fiscal year 1993. State Expenditure Report, 1993. National Association of State Budget Officers, 400 North Capitol Street, Washington, D.C. p. 17.

ASSIST93 Table G.538 Percent of total state expenditures devoted to cash assistance, fiscal year 1993. State Expenditure Report, 1993. National Association of State Budget Officers, 400 North Capitol Street, Washington, D.C. p. 17.

MEDIC93 Table G.539 Percent of total state expenditures devoted to medicaid, fiscal year 1993. State Expenditure Report, 1993. National Association of State Budget Officers, 400 North Capitol Street, Washington, D.C. p. 17.

CORREC93 Table G.540 Percent of total state expenditures devoted to corrections, fiscal year 1993. State Expenditure Report, 1993. National Association of State Budget Officers, 400 North Capitol Street, Washington, D.C. p. 17.

TRANS93 Table G.541 Percent of total state expenditures devoted to transportation, fiscal year 1993. State Expenditure Report, 1993. National Association of State Budget Officers, 400 North Capitol Street, Washington, D.C. p. 17.

OTHER93 Table G.542 Percent of total state expenditures devoted to all other areas, fiscal year 1993. State Expenditure Report, 1993. National Association of State Budget Officers, 400 North Capitol Street, Washington, D.C. p. 17.

ELESEC94 Table G.543 Percent of total state expenditures devoted to elementary and secondary education, fiscal year 1994. State Expenditure Report, 1994. National Association of State Budget Officers, 400 North Capitol Street, Washington, D.C. p. 18.

HIGHED94 Table G.544 Percent of total state expenditures devoted to higher education, fiscal year 1994. State Expenditure Report, 1994. National Association of State Budget Officers, 400 North Capitol Street, Washington, D.C. p. 18.

ASSIST94 Table G.545 Percent of total state expenditures devoted to cash assistance, fiscal year 1994. State Expenditure Report, 1994. National Association of State Budget Officers, 400 North Capitol Street, Washington, D.C. p. 18.

MEDIC94   Table G.546   Percent of total state expenditures devoted to medicaid, fiscal year 1994. State Expenditure Report, 1994. National Association of State Budget Officers, 400 North Capitol Street, Washington, D.C. p. 18.

CORREC94   Table G.547   Percent of total state expenditures devoted to corrections, fiscal year 1994. State Expenditure Report, 1994. National Association of State Budget Officers, 400 North Capitol Street, Washington, D.C. p. 18.

TRANS94   Table G.548   Percent of total state expenditures devoted to transportation, fiscal year 1994. State Expenditure Report, 1994. National Association of State Budget Officers, 400 North Capitol Street, Washington, D.C. p. 18.

OTHER94   Table G.549   Percent of total state expenditures devoted to all other areas, fiscal year 1994. State Expenditure Report, 1994. National Association of State Budget Officers, 400 North Capitol Street, Washington, D.C. p. 18.

ELESEC95   Table G.550   Percent of total state expenditures devoted to elementary and secondary education, fiscal year 1995. State Expenditure Report, 1995. National Association of State Budget Officers, 400 North Capitol Street, Washington, D.C. p. 18.

HIGHED95   Table G.551   Percent of total state expenditures devoted to higher education, fiscal year 1995. State Expenditure Report, 1995. National Association of State Budget Officers, 400 North Capitol Street, Washington, D.C. p. 18.

ASSIST95   Table G.552   Percent of total state expenditures devoted to cash assistance, fiscal year 1995. State Expenditure Report, 1995. National Association of State Budget Officers, 400 North Capitol Street, Washington, D.C. p. 18.

MEDIC95   Table G.553   Percent of total state expenditures devoted to medicaid, fiscal year 1995. State Expenditure Report, 1995. National Association of State Budget Officers, 400 North Capitol Street, Washington, D.C. p. 18.

CORREC95   Table G.554   Percent of total state expenditures devoted to corrections, fiscal year 1995. State Expenditure Report, 1995. National Association of State Budget Officers, 400 North Capitol Street, Washington, D.C. p. 18.

TRANS95   Table G.555   Percent of total state expenditures devoted to transportation, fiscal year 1995. State Expenditure Report, 1995. National Association of State Budget Officers, 400 North Capitol Street, Washington, D.C. p. 18.

OTHER95   Table G.556   Percent of total state expenditures devoted to all other areas, fiscal year 1995. State Expenditure Report, 1995. National Association of State Budget Officers, 400 North Capitol Street, Washington, D.C. p. 18.

ELESEC96   Table G.557   Percent of total state expenditures devoted to elementary and secondary education, fiscal year 1996. State Expenditure Report, 1996. National Association of State Budget Officers, 400 North Capitol Street, Washington, D.C. p. 15.

HIGHED96   Table G.558   Percent of total state expenditures devoted to higher education, fiscal year 1996. State Expenditure Report, 1996. National Association of State Budget Officers, 400 North Capitol Street, Washington, D.C. p. 15.

ASSIST96   Table G.559   Percent of total state expenditures devoted to cash assistance, fiscal year 1996. State Expenditure Report, 1996. National Association of State Budget Officers, 400 North Capitol Street, Washington, D.C. p. 15.

MEDIC96   Table G.560   Percent of total state expenditures devoted to medicaid, fiscal year 1996. State Expenditure Report, 1996. National Association of State Budget Officers, 400 North Capitol Street, Washington, D.C. p. 15.

CORREC96   Table G.561   Percent of total state expenditures devoted to corrections, fiscal year 1996. State Expenditure Report, 1996. National Association of State Budget Officers, 400 North Capitol Street, Washington, D.C. p. 15.

TRANS96   Table G.562   Percent of total state expenditures devoted to transportation, fiscal year 1996. State Expenditure Report, 1996. National Association of State Budget Officers, 400 North Capitol Street, Washington, D.C. p. 15.

OTHER96   Table G.563   Percent of total state expenditures devoted to all other areas, fiscal year 1996. State Expenditure Report, 1996. National Association of State Budget Officers, 400 North Capitol Street, Washington, D.C. p. 15.

ELESEC97   Table G.564   Percent of total state expenditures devoted to elementary and secondary education, fiscal year 1997. State Expenditure Report, 1997. National Association of State Budget Officers, 400 North Capitol Street, Washington, D.C. p. 15.

HIGHED97   Table G.565   Percent of total state expenditures devoted to hgher education, fiscal year 1997. State Expenditure Report, 1997. National Association of State Budget Officers, 400 North Capitol Street, Washington, D.C. p. 15.

ASSIST97   Table G.566   Percent of total state expenditures devoted to cash assistance, fiscal year 1997. State Expenditure Report, 1997. National Association of State Budget Officers, 400 North Capitol Street, Washington, D.C. p. 15.

MEDIC97   Table G.567   Percent of total state expenditures devoted to medicaid, fiscal year 1997. State Expenditure Report, 1997. National Association of State Budget Officers, 400 North Capitol Street, Washington, D.C. p. 15.

CORREC97   Table G.568   Percent ot total state expenditures devoted to corrections, fiscal year 1997. State Expenditure Report, 1997. National Association of State

Budget Officers, 400 North Capitol Street, Washington, D.C. p. 15.

TRANS97 Table G.569 Percent of total state expenditures devoted to transportation, fiscal year 1997. State Expenditure Report, 1997. National Association of State Budget Officers, 400 North Capitol Street, Washington, D.C. p. 15.

OTHER97 Table G.570 Percent of total state expenditures devoted to all other areas, fiscal year 1997. State Expenditure Report, 1997. National Association of State Budget Officers, 400 North Capitol Street, Washington, D.C. p. 15.

ELESEC98 Table G.571 Percent of total state expenditures devoted to elementary and secondary education, fiscal year 1998. State Expenditure Report, 1998. National Association of State Budget Officers, 400 North Capitol Street, Washington, D.C. p. 12.

HIGHED98 Table G.572 Percent of total state expenditures devoted to higher education, fiscal year 1998. State Expenditure Report, 1998. National Association of State Budget Officers, 400 North Capitol Street, Washington, D.C. p. 12.

ASSIST98 Table G.573 Percent of total state expenditures devoted to cash assistance, fiscal year 1998. State Expenditure Report, 1998. National Association of State Budget Officers, 400 North Capitol Street, Washington, D.C. p. 12.

MEDIC98 Table G.574 Percent of total state expenditures devoted to medicaid, fiscal year 1998. State Expenditure Report, 1998. National Association of State Budget Officers, 400 North Capitol Street, Washington, D.C. p. 12.

CORREC98 Table G.575 Percent of total state expenditures devoted to corrections, fiscal year 1998. State Expenditure Report, 1998. National Association of State Budget Officers, 400 North Capitol Street, Washington, D.C. p. 12.

TRANS98 Table G.576 Percent of total state expenditures devoted to transportation, fiscal year 1998. State Expenditure Report, 1998. National Association of State Budget Officers, 400 North Capitol Street, Washington, D.C. p. 12.

OTHER98 Table G.577 Percent of total state expenditures devoted to all other areas, fiscal year 1998. State Expenditure Report, 1998. National Association of State Budget Officers, 400 North Capitol Street, Washington, D.C. p. 12.

ELESEC99 Table G.578 Percent of total state expenditures devoted to elementary and secondary education, fiscal year 1999. State Expenditure Report, 1999. National Association of State Budget Officers, 400 North Capitol Street, Washington, D.C. p. 11.

HIGHED99 Table G.579 Percent of total state expenditures devoted to higher education, fiscal year 1999. State Expenditure Report, 1999. National Association of State Budget Officers, 400 North Capitol Street, Washington, D.C. p. 11.

ASSIST99 Table G.580 Percent of total state expenditures devoted to cash assistance, fiscal year 1999. State Expenditure Report, 1999. National Association of State Budget Officers, 400 North Capitol Street, Washington, D.C. p. 11.

MEDIC99 Table G.581 Percent of total state expenditures devoted to medicaid, fiscal year 1999. State Expenditure Report, 1999. National Association of State Budget Officers, 400 North Capitol Street, Washington, D.C. p. 11.

CORREC99 Table G.582 Percent of total state expenditures devoted to corrections, fiscal year 1999. State Expenditure Report, 1999. National Association of State Budget Officers, 400 North Capitol Street, Washington, D.C. p. 11.

TRANS99 Table G.583 Percent of total state expenditures devoted to transportation, fiscal year 1999. State Expenditure Report, 1999. National Association of State Budget Officers, 400 North Capitol Street, Washington, D.C. p. 11.

OTHER99 Table G.584 Percent of total state expenditures devoted to all other areas, fiscal year 1999. State Expenditure Report, 1999. National Association of State Budget Officers, 400 North Capitol Street, Washington, D.C. p. 11.

ELESEC00 Table G.585 Percent of total state expenditures devoted to elementary and secondary education, fiscal year 2000. State Expenditure Report, 2000. National Association of State Budget Officers, 400 North Capitol Street, Washington, D.C. p. 11.

HIGHED00 Table G.586 Percent of total state expenditures devoted to higher education, fiscal year 2000. State Expenditure Report, 2000. National Association of State Budget Officers, 400 North Capitol Street, Washington, D.C. p. 11.

ASSIST00 Table G.587 Percent of total state expenditures devoted to cash assistance, fiscal year 2000. State Expenditure Report, 2000. National Association of State Budget Officers, 400 North Capitol Street, Washington, D.C. p. 11.

MEDIC00 Table G.588 Percent of total state expenditures devoted to medicaid, fiscal year 2000. State Expenditure Report, 2000. National Association of State Budget Officers, 400 North Capitol Street, Washington, D.C. p. 11.

CORREC00 Table G.589 Percent of total state expenditures devoted to corrections, fiscal year 2000. State Expenditure Report, 2000. National Association of State Budget Officers, 400 North Capitol Street, Washington, D.C. p. 11.

TRANS00 Table G.590 Percent of total state expenditures devoted to transportation, fiscal year 2000. State Expenditure Report, 2000. National Association of State Budget Officers, 400 North Capitol Street, Washington, D.C. p. 11.

OTHER00 Table G.591 Percent of total state expenditures devoted to all other areas, fiscal year 2000. State Expenditure Report, 2000. National Association of

State Budget Officers, 400 North Capitol Street, Washington, D.C. p. 11.

SCHOOL89 Table G.592 Per capita expenditures of total funds (state and federal) for elementary and secondary schools, 1989.
Calculated: (TOTPC89 * ELESEC89) / 100

COLLEG89 Table G.593 Per capita expenditures of total funds (state and federal) for higher education, 1989.
Calculated: (TOTPC89 * HIGHED89) / 100

HELP89 Table G.594 Per capita expenditures of total funds (state and federal) for cash assistance, 1989.
Calculated: (TOTPC89 * ASSIST89) / 100

MEDICA89 Table G.595 Per capita expenditures of total funds (state and federal) for medicaid, 1989.
Calculated: (TOTPC89 * MEDIC89) / 100

PRISON89 Table G.596 Per capita expenditures of total funds (state and federal) for corrections, 1989.
Calculated: (TOTPC89 * CORREC89) / 100

HIWAY89 Table G.597 Per capita expenditures of total funds (state and federal) for transportation, 1989.
Calculated: (TOTPC89 * TRANS89) / 100

ELSE89 Table G.598 Per capita expenditures of total funds (state and federal) for all other expenditures, 1989.
Calculated: (TOTPC89 * OTHER89) / 100

SCHOOL90 Table G.599 Per capita expenditures of total funds (state and federal) for elementary and secondary schools, 1990.
Calculated: (TOTPC90 * ELESEC90) / 100

COLLEG90 Table G.600 Per capita expenditures of total funds (state and federal) for higher education, 1990.
Calculated: (TOTPC90 * HIGHED90) / 100

HELP90 Table G.601 Per capita expenditures of total funds (state and federal) for cash assistance, 1990.
Calculated: (TOTPC90 * ASSIST90) / 100

MEDICA90 Table G.602 Per capita expenditures of total funds (state and federal) for medicaid, 1990.
Calculated: (TOTPC90 * MEDIC90) / 100

PRISON90 Table G.603 Per capita expenditures of total funds (state and federal) for corrections, 1990.
Calculated: (TOTPC90 * CORREC90) / 100

HIWAY90 Table G.604 Per capita expenditures of total funds (state and federal) for transportation, 1990.
Calculated: (TOTPC90 * TRANS90) / 100

ELSE90 Table G.605 Per capita expenditures of total funds (state and federal) for all other expenditures, 1990.
Calculated: (TOTPC90 * OTHER90) / 100

SCHOOL91 Table G.606 Per capita expenditures of total funds (state and federal) for elementary and secondary schools, 1991.
Calculated: (TOTPC91 * ELESEC91) / 100

COLLEG91 Table G.607 Per capita expenditures of total funds (state and federal) for higher education, 1991.
Calculated: (TOTPC91 * HIGHED91) / 100

HELP91 Table G.608 Per capita expenditures of total funds (state and federal) for cash assistance, 1991.
Calculated: (TOTPC91 * ASSIST91) / 100

MEDICA91 Table G.609 Per capita expenditures of total funds (state and federal) for medicaid, 1991.
Calculated: (TOTPC91 * MEDIC91) / 100

PRISON91 Table G.610 Per capita expenditures of total funds (state and federal) for corrections, 1991.
Calculated: (TOTPC91 * CORREC91) / 100

HIWAY91 Table G.611 Per capita expenditures of total funds (state and federal) for transportation, 1991.
Calculated: (TOTPC91 * TRANS91) / 100

ELSE91 Table G.612 Per capita expenditures of total funds (state and federal) for all other expenditures, 1991.
Calculated: (TOTPC91 * OTHER91) / 100

SCHOOL92 Table G.613 Per capita expenditures of total funds (state and federal) for elementary and secondary schools, 1992.
Calculated: (TOTPC92 * ELESEC92) / 100

COLLEG92 Table G.614 Per capita expenditures of total funds (state and federal) for higher education, 1992.
Calculated: (TOTPC92 * HIGHED92) / 100

HELP92 Table G.615 Per capita expenditures of total funds (state and federal) for cash assistance, 1992.
Calculated: (TOTPC92 * ASSIST92) / 100

MEDICA92 Table G.616 Per capita expenditures of total funds (state and federal) for medicaid, 1992.
Calculated: (TOTPC92 * MEDIC92) / 100

PRISN92 Table G.617 Per capita expenditures of total funds (state and federal) for corrections, 1992.
Calculated: (TOTPC92 * CORREC92) / 100

HIWAY92 Table G.618 Per capita expenditures of total funds (state and federal) for transportation, 1992.
Calculated: (TOTPC92 * TRANS92) / 100

ELSE92 Table G.619 Per capita expenditures of total funds (state and federal) for all other expenditures, 1992.
Calculated: (TOTPC92 * OTHER92) / 100

SCHOOL93 Table G.620 Per capita expenditures of total funds (state and federal) for elementary and secondary schools, 1993.
Calculated: (TOTPC93 * ELESEC93) / 100

COLLEG93 Table G.621 Per capita expenditures of total funds (state and federal) for higher education, 1993.
Calculated: (TOTPC93 * HIGHED93) / 100

HELP93 Table G.622 Per capita expenditures of total funds (state and federal) for cash assistance, 1993.
Calculated: (TOTPC93 * ASSIST93) / 100

MEDICA93 Table G.623 Per capita expenditures of total funds (state and federal) for medicaid, 1993.
Calculated: (TOTPC93 * MEDIC93) / 100

PRISON93 Table G.624 Per capita expenditures of total funds (state and federal) for corrections, 1993.
Calculated: (TOTPC93 * CORREC93) / 100

HIWAY93 Table G.625 Per capita expenditures of total funds (state and federal) for transportation, 1993.
Calculated: (TOTPC93 * TRANS93) / 100

ELSE93 Table G.626 Per capita expenditures of total funds (state and federal) for all other expenditures, 1993.
Calculated: (TOTPC93 * OTHER93) / 100

SCHOOL94 Table G.627 Per capita expenditures of total funds (state and federal) for elementary and secondary schools, 1994.
Calculated: (TOTPC94 * ELESEC94) / 100

COLLEG94 Table G.628 Per capita expenditures of total funds (state and federal) for higher education, 1994.
Calculated: (TOTPC94 * HIGHED94) / 100

HELP94 Table G.629 Per capita expenditures of total funds (state and federal) for cash assistance, 1994.
Calculated: (TOTPC94 * ASSIST94) / 100

MEDICA94 Table G.630 Per capita expenditures of total funds (state and federal) for medicaid, 1994.
Calculated: (TOTPC94 * MEDIC94) / 100

PRISON94 Table G.631 Per capita expenditures of total funds (state and federal) for corrections, 1994.
Calculated: (TOTPC94 * CORREC94) / 100

HIWAY94 Table G.632 Per capita expenditures of total funds (state and federal) for transportation, 1994.
Calculated: (TOTPC94 * TRANS94) / 100

ELSE94 Table G.633 Per capita expenditures of total funds (state and federal) for all other expenditures, 1994.
Calculated: (TOTPC94 * OTHER94) / 100

SCHOOL95 Table G.634 Per capita expenditures of total funds (state and federal) for elementary and secondary schools, 1995.
Calculated: (TOTPC95 * ELESEC95) / 100

COLLEG95 Table G.635 Per capita expenditures of total funds (state and federal) for higher education, 1995.
Calculated: (TOTPC95 * HIGHED95) / 100

HELP95 Table G.636 Per capita expenditures of total funds (state and federal) for cash assistance, 1995.
Calculated: (TOTPC95 * ASSIST95) / 100

MEDICA95 Table G.637 Per capita expenditures of total funds (state and federal) for medicaid, 1995.
Calculated: (TOTPC95 * MEDIC95) / 100

PRISON95 Table G.638 Per capita expenditures of total funds (state and federal) for corrections, 1995.
Calculated: (TOTPC95* CORREC95) / 100

HIWAY95 Table G.639 Per capita expenditures of total funds (state and federal) for transportation, 1995.
Calculated: (TOTPC95 * TRANS95) / 100

ELSE95 Table G.640 Per capita expenditures of total funds (state and federal) for all other expenditures, 1995.
Calculated: (TOTPC95 * OTHER95) / 100

SCHOOL96 Table G.641 Per capita expenditures of total funds (state and federal) for elementary and secondary schools, 1996.
Calculated: (TOTPC96 * ELESEC96) / 100

COLLEG96 Table G.642 Per capita expenditures of total funds (state and federal) for higher education, 1996.
Calculated: (TOTPC96 * HIGHED96) / 100

HELP96 Table G.643 Per capita expenditures of total funds (state and federal) for cash assistance, 1996.
Calculated: (TOTPC96 * ASSIST96) / 100

MEDICA96 Table G.644 Per capita expenditures of total funds (state and federal) for medicaid, 1996.
Calculated: (TOTPC96 * MEDIC96) / 100

PRISN96 Table G.645 Per capita expenditures of total funds (state and federal) for corrections, 1996.
Calculated: (TOTPC96 * CORREC96) / 100

HIWAY96 Table G.646 Per capita expenditures of total funds (state and federal) for transportation, 1996.
Calculated: (TOTPC96 * TRANS96) / 100

ELSE96 Table G.647 Per capita expenditures of total funds (state and federal) for all other expenditures, 1996.
Calculated: (TOTPC96 * OTHER96) / 100

SCHOOL97 Table G.648 Per capita expenditures of total funds (state and federal) for elementary and secondary schools, 1997.
Calculated: (TOTPC97 * ELESEC97) / 100

COLLEG97 Table G.649 Per capita expenditures of total funds (state and federal) for higher education, 1997.
Calculated: (TOTPC97 * HIGHED97) / 100

HELP97 Table G.650 Per capita expenditures of total funds (state and federal) for cash assistance, 1997.
Calculated: (TOTPC97 * ASSIST97) / 100

MEDICA97 Table G.651 Per capita expenditures of total funds (state and federal) for medicaid, 1997.
Calculated: (TOTPC97 * MEDIC97) / 100

PRISON97 Table G.652 Per capita expenditures of total funds (state and federal) for corrections, 1997.
Calculated: (TOTPC97 * CORREC97) / 100

HIWAY97 Table G.653 Per capita expenditures of total funds (state and federal) for transportation, 1997.
Calculated: (TOTPC97 * TRANS97) / 100

ELSE97 Table G.654 Per capita expenditures of total funds (state and federal) for all other expenditures, 1997.
Calculated: (TOTPC97 * OTHER97) / 100

SCHOOL98 Table G.655 Per capita expenditures of total funds (state and federal) for elementary and secondary schools, 1998.
Calculated: (TOTPC98 * ELESEC98) / 100

COLLEG98 Table G.656 Per capita expenditures of total funds (state and federal) for higher education, 1998.
Calculated: (TOTPC98 * HIGHED98) / 100

HELP98 Table G.657 Per capita expenditures of total funds (state and federal) for cash assistance, 1998.
Calculated: (TOTPC98 * ASSIST98) / 100

MEDICA98 Table G.658 Per capita expenditures of total funds (state and federal) for medicaid, 1998.
Calculated: (TOTPC98 * MEDIC98) / 100

PRISON98 Table G.659 Per capita expenditures of total funds (state and federal) for corrections, 1998.
Calculated: (TOTPC98 * CORREC98) / 100

HIWAY98 Table G.660 Per capita expenditures of total funds (state and federal) for transportation, 1998.
Calculated: (TOTPC98 * TRANS98) / 100

ELSE98 Table G.661 Per capita expenditures of total funds (state and federal) for all other expenditures, 1998.
Calculated: (TOTPC98 * OTHER98) / 100

SCHOOL99 Table G.662 Per capita expenditures of total funds (state and federal) for elementary and secondary schools, 1999.
Calculated: (TOTPC99 * ELESEC99) / 100

COLLEG99 Table G.663 Per capita expenditures of total funds (state and federal) for higher education, 1999.
Calculated: (TOTPC99 * HIGHED99) / 100

HELP99 Table G.664 Per capita expenditures of total funds (state and federal) for cash assistance, 1999.
Calculated: (TOTPC99 * ASSIST99) / 100

MEDICA99 Table G.665 Per capita expenditures of total funds (state and federal) for medicaid, 1999.
Calculated: (TOTPC99 * MEDIC99) / 100

PRISON99 Table G.666 Per capita expenditures of total funds (state and federal) for corrections, 1999.
Calculated: (TOTPC99 * CORREC99) / 100

HIWAY99 Table G.667 Per capita expenditures of total funds (state and federal) for transportation, 1999.
Calculated: (TOTPC99 * TRANS99) / 100

ELSE99 Table G.668 Per capita expenditures of total funds (state and federal) for all other expenditures, 1999.
Calculated: (TOTPC99 * OTHER99) / 100

SCHOOL00 Table G.669 Per capita expenditures of total funds (state and federal) for elementary and secondary schools, 2000.
Calculated: (TOTP00 * ELESEC00) / 100

COLLEG00 Table G.670 Per capita expenditures of total funds (state and federal) for higher education, 2000.
Calculated: (TOTPC00 * HIGHED00) / 100

HELP00 Table G.671 Per capita expenditures of total funds (state and federal) for cash assistance, 2000.
Calculated: (TOTPC00 * ASSIST00) / 100

MEDICA00 Table G.672 Per capita expenditures of total funds (state and federal) for medicaid, 2000.
Calculated: (TOTPC00 * MEDIC00) / 100

PRISON00 Table G.673 Per capita expenditures of total funds (state and federal) for corrections, 2000.
Calculated: (TOTPC00 * CORREC00) / 100

HIWAY00 Table G.674 Per capita expenditures of total funds (state and federal) for transportation, 2000.
Calculated: (TOTPC00 * TRANS00) / 100

ELSE00 Table G.675 Per capita expenditures of total funds (state and federal) for all other expenditures, 2000.
Calculated: (TOTPC00 * OTHER00) / 100

SCHOOL Table G.676 Average per capita expenditure for elementary and secondary education over 12-year period (1989–2000).
Calculated: (SCHOOL89 + SCHOOL90 + SCHOOL91 + SCHOOL92 + SCHOOL93 + SCHOOL94 + SCHOOL95 + SCHOOL96 + SCHOOL97 + SCHOOL98 + SCHOOL99 + SCHOOL00) / 12

COLLEGE Table G.677 Average per capita expenditure for higher education over 12-year period (1989–2000).
Calculated: (COLLEG89 + COLLEG90 + COLLEG91 + COLLEG92 + COLLEG93 + COLLEG94 + COLLEG95 + COLLEG96 + COLLEG97 + COLLEG98 + COLLEG99 + COLLEG00) / 12

CASHHELP Table G.678 Average per capita expenditure for public assistance over 12-year period (1989–2000).
Calculated: (HELP89 + HELP90 + HELP91 + HELP92 + HELP93 + HELP94 + HELP95 + HELP96 + HELP97 + HELP98 + HELP99 + HELP00) / 12

MEDICAID Table G.679 Average per capita expenditure for medicaid over 12-year period (1989–2000).
Calculated: (MEDICA89 + MEDICA90 + MEDICA91 + MEDICA92 + MEDICA93 + MEDICA94 + MEDICA95 + MEDICA96 + MEDICA97 + MEDICA98 + MEDICA99 + MEDICA00) / 12

PRISONS Table G.680 Average per capita expenditure for corrections over 12-year period (1989–2000).
Calculated: (PRISON89 + PRISON90 + PRISON91 + PRISON92 + PRISON93 + PRISON94 + PRISON95 + PRISON96 + PRISON97 + PRISON98 + PRISON99 + PRISON00) / 12

HIGHWAYS Table G.681 Average per capita expenditure for transportation over 12-year period (1989–2000).
Calculated: (HIWAY89 + HIWAY90 + HIWAY91 + HIWAY92 + HIWAY93 + HIWAY94 + HIWAY95

+ HIWAY96 + HIWAY97 + HIWAY98 + HIWAY99 + HIWAY00) / 12

ALLOTHER Table G.682 Average per capita expenditure for all other expenditures over 12-year period (1989–2000).

Calculated: (ELSE89 + ELSE90 + ELSE91 + ELSE92 + ELSE93 + ELSE94 + ELSE95 + ELSE96 + ELSE97 + ELSE98 + ELSE99 + ELSE00) / 12

SALESTAX Table G.683 Sales tax collected, in millions. Fiscal 1996 revenue sources in the General Fund. State Expenditure Report, 1996. National Association of State Budget Officers, 400 North Capitol Street, Washington, D.C. Table A-34, p. 109.

PERINTAX Table G.684 Personal income tax collected, in millions. Fiscal 1996 revenue sources in the General Fund. State Expenditure Report, 1996. National Association of State Budget Officers, 400 North Capitol Street, Washington, D.C. Table A-34, p. 109.

CORPTAX Table G.685 Corporate income tax collected, in millions. Fiscal 1996 revenue sources in the General Fund. State Expenditure Report, 1996. National Association of State Budget Officers, 400 North Capitol Street, Washington, D.C. Table G.A-34, p. 109.

GAMETAX Table G.686 Gaming tax collected, in millions. Fiscal 1996 revenue sources in the General Fund. State Expenditure Report, 1996. National Association of State Budget Officers, 400 North Capitol Street, Washington, D.C. Table A-34, p. 109.

GOVERNMT Table G.687 General factor based on eight variables that relate directly to state government procurement of funds, generally in the form of taxes.

Calculated: (RTAXRATE + RPCSTALO + RPCLOCGO + RFEDFUNP + RPCTAXAL + RPCFEDTA + RPCLOCTA + RPCFSLTA) / 8.

EXPEND Table G.688 General factor based on average per capita expenditures on seven variables over a 12-year period by state governments.

Calculated: (RSCHOOL + RCOLLEGE + RCASHHEL + RMEDICAI + RPRISONS + RHIGHWAY + RALLOTHE) / 7.

CRIME Table G.689 General factor based on eight variables that relate directly to state government efforts to cope with crime in terms of 39-year average crime rates for murder, rape, assault, burglary, and the like.

Calculated: (RMURDER3 + RRAPE39 + RROBBER3 + RASSAUL3 + RBURGLA3 + RLARCEN3 + RMVT39 + RASLGUN) / 8

PROTECT Table G.690 General factor based on five variables that relate directly to state government efforts to cope with crime by providing funds for police protection.

Calculated: (RPOLIEMP + RPOLICE + RPOLICOS + RPOLTOTR + ROFFPPOP) / 5.

PUNISH Table G.691 General factor based on eleven variables that relate directly to state government efforts to punish persons found guilty of various crimes through incarceration.

Calculated: (RCORRATE + RPRRATE9 + RPRISCOS + RPRCH929 + REXPT506 + REXPT770 + RCORRECT + RCORRCOS + RCORREM + PRFOODPI + RPRISPI9) / 11

DEATH Table G.692 General factor based on six variables that relate to death rates from natural causes (e.g., heart disease, cancer, diabetes).

Calculated: (RINFMORT + RDEATHAR + RDEATHCA + RDEATHAL + RDEATHCE + RDEATHDI) / 6

HIWAYDEA Table G.693 General factor based on eleven variables that relate to death rates from highway fatalities (e.g., auto death fatalities, gasoline taxes, bridge repairs, alcohol).

Calculated: (RFATALCO + RTRAFATP + RPEDEATH + RCARINSU + RBRIDGDE + RBRIDGOB + RDEATHMV + RANYALCO + RPCFATCH + RNOBELT + RGASTAX) / 11

TRAUMA Table G.694 General factor based on two variables that relate to death rates from suicide and accidents.

Calculated: (RDEATHAC + RDEATHSU) / 2

HEALTH Table G.695 General factor based on eight variables that relate to health (e.g., obesity, smoking, birth weight, etc.)

Calculated: (ROBESITY + RMCIGARE + RFCIGARE + RAIDSPT + RTBPT + RNOIMMUN + RLOWBIRW + RSYPHILP) / 8

MEDICAL Table G.696 General factor based on eight variables that relate to costs for providing medical care (e.g., persons covered by insurance, availability of physicians).

Calculated: (RNOCOVER + RCHINOCO + RLACKINM + RLACKINF + RPAYENRO + RPAYRECI + RDOCTORS + RHOSPBED) / 8

TEENPROB Table G.697 General factor based on nine variables that relate to kinds of problems teenagers deal with (e.g., unwanted pregnancies, sexually transmitted diseases).

Calculated: (RTEENBRT + RUNMARRB + RGONTEEN + RPCTBRB9 + RNHWHBR + RTOTPCUN + RTOTPCIN + RBRYT96 + RPCTBAL9) / 9

EDUCACHI Table G.698 General factor based on four variables that relate to achievement in school (e.g., high school graduation rate, college graduation rate, patents issued).

Calculated: (RHSGRAD + RCOLLGRA + RCOLLEGP + RPATENTP) / 4

EDUCSUPP Table G.699 General factor based on nine variables that relate to providing support for public education (e.g., per capita expenditures for K–12 schools, per capita expenditures for colleges and universities, average teacher salary).

Calculated: (RSTALOCP + RCOLUNIP + RELESECP + RSUPSERV + RAVRSALR + RSTUMEDI + RCOMPUTE + RINTERNE + RRDUNIPC) / 9

WORK **Table G.700** General factor based on seventeen variables that relate to employment (e.g., percent persons employed in manufacturing, percent persons employed in service industries, average pay, unemployment compensation, percent in unions).

Calculated: (RCONSTRP + RMANUFAP + RTRANSPC + RTRADEPC + RFINANCP + RSERVICP + RPCUNION + RGOVFSLP + RUNEMPAV + RMALABOR + RFEMLABO + RINSUNEM + RAVRPAY + RRDINDPC + RFARMINP + RMINERLP + RMANPEMP) / 17

ECONOMIC **Table G.701** General factor based on seven variables that relate to economic opportunities in a state (e.g., percent below poverty, per capita income, unemployment rate).

Calculated: (RPERBELP + RCHBELPO + RUNEMRAT + RPCINCOM + RBUSFAIL + RMEDINC9 + RRETAIL) / 7

SUMMARY **Table G.702** SUMMARY factor based on fifteen general factor scores (e.g., state expenditures, crime rates, highway fatalities, educational achievement, health care, work).

Calculated: GOVERNMT + EXPEND + CRIME + PROTECT + PUNISH + DEATH + HIWAYDEA + TRAUMA + HEALTH + MEDICAL + TEENPROB + EDUCACHI + EDUCSUPP + WORK + ECONOMIC

Index of Rankings

About the Authors

Jack Frymier was born and raised in Indiana. He received his bachelor's and master's degrees from the University of Miami and his doctorate from the University of Florida. Frymier served in the U.S. Army during World War II and the Korean War. He has been a public school teacher, administrator, university professor, and researcher, and is currently professor emeritus at Ohio State University. His major areas of interest are motivation, values, risk factors, human development, program development, and public policy.

Arliss L. Roaden is a professional consultant on higher education and educational assessment following his retirement as executive director of the Tennessee Higher Education Commission. The commission designated him executive director emeritus following his ten years of service as the state's higher education executive officer. He is also president emeritus of Tennessee Technological University, following eleven years as president of the university. He served for twelve years at Ohio State University as professor of educational development and administration, where he taught and did research and held various administrative positions. During his last five years at Ohio State University, he was dean of the graduate school, vice provost for research, and was vice president of the research foundation.

Dr. Roaden is a graduate of Cumberland College in Kentucky and Carson Newman College in Tennessee, and he holds graduate degrees from the University of Tennessee, Knoxville. In addition, he has been awarded two honorary doctorates. Since retirement, he continues to be active professionally and in community service. He and his wife, Mary Etta, reside in Nashville, Tennessee.